THE LAW OF NON-C

The Law of Non-Contradiction—that no contradiction can be true—has been a seemingly unassailable dogma since the work of Aristotle, in Book Gamma of the *Metaphysics*. It is an assumption challenged from a variety of angles in this collection of original papers. Twenty-three of the world's leading experts investigate the 'law', considering arguments for and against it and discussing methodological issues that arise whenever we question the legitimacy of logical principles. The result is a balanced inquiry into a venerable principle of logic, one that raises questions at the very centre of logic itself.

The aim of this volume is to present a comprehensive debate about the Law of Non-Contradiction, from discussions as to how the law is to be understood, to reasons for accepting or re-thinking the law, and to issues that raise challenges to the law, such as the Liar Paradox, and a 'dialetheic' resolution of that paradox. One of the editors contributes an introduction which surveys the issues and serves to frame the debate.

This collection will be of interest to anyone working on philosophical logic, and to anyone who has ever wondered about the status of logical laws and about how one might proceed to mount arguments for or against them.

Graham Priest is Boyce Gibson Professor of Philosophy at the University of Melbourne and Arche Professorial Fellow at the University of St Andrews.

JC Beall is Associate Professor of Philosophy at the University of Connecticut.

Bradley Armour-Garb is Assistant Professor of Philosophy at the University at Albany-SUNY.

The Law of Non-Contradiction

New Philosophical Essays

edited by

Graham Priest, JC Beall,
and
Bradley Armour-Garb

CLARENDON PRESS · OXFORD

OXFORD

UNIVERSITY PRESS

Great Clarendon Street, Oxford OX2 6DP

Oxford University Press is a department of the University of Oxford.
It furthers the University's objective of excellence in research, scholarship,
and education by publishing worldwide in

Oxford New York

Auckland   Cape Town Dar es Salaam   Hong Kong   Karachi
Kuala Lumpur Madrid Melbourne Mexico City   Nairobi
New Delhi Shanghai Taipei Toronto
With offices in
Argentina Austria Brazil Chile Czech Republic France Greece
Guatemala Hungary Italy Japan South Korea Poland Portugal
Singapore Switzerland Thailand Turkey Ukraine Vietnam

Oxford is a registered trade mark of Oxford University Press
in the UK and in certain other countries

Published in the United States
by Oxford University Press Inc., New York

ISBN 978-0-19-920419-9

Printed in the United Kingdom by
Lightning Source UK Ltd., Milton Keynes

Acknowledgements

All the contributions appear here for the first time, with the exception of Priest's. We are grateful to the *Journal of Philosophy* for permission to reprint Priest's paper. The posthumous contributions by David Lewis are from his private correspondence, and we are especially grateful to Steffi Lewis for permission to publish them.

The book is divided into parts, with the chapters in each section centering on a particular aspect of the given (part-) issue. The structuring is, as ever, to a certain extent arbitrary, and a contribution in one part may well contain material that bears on the topic of other parts. Following Beall's introductory essay, the book leads off with Priest's chapter at the suggestion of a reader from Oxford University Press, since that is the one that sets the scene for much of what follows. We are grateful for the advice from such readers.

This volume began in 1999 with discussions between Beall and Priest in Australia (when Beall was still living there), with Armour-Garb joining the project a little later. We are grateful for the help and support of those directly involved, and also for those who gave suggestions and encouragement early on. We are particularly grateful to both internal and external referees whose careful comments have made for a better volume.

We are also grateful to Oxford University Press, and especially to Peter Momtchiloff and Rebecca Bryant, for help and encouragement during the production of this volume.

Melbourne, Storrs, Albany   G.P.
2003   J.C.B.
     B.A.-G.

Contents

List of Contributors   ix

Introduction: At the Intersection of Truth and Falsity   1
    JC Beall

Part I: Setting up the Debate

1. What's So Bad About Contradictions?   23
    Graham Priest

Part II: What is the LNC?

2. On the Formalization of the Law of Non-Contradiction   41
    Ross T. Brady

3. What is a Contradiction?   49
    Patrick Grim

4. Laws of Non-Contradiction, Laws of the
Excluded Middle, and Logics   73
    Greg Restall

5. Option Negation and Dialetheias   85
    R. M. Sainsbury

6. Conjunction and Contradiction   93
    Achille C. Varzi

Part III: Methodological Issues in the Debate

7. Diagnosing Dialetheism   113
    Bradley Armour-Garb

8. Knowledge and Non-Contradiction   126
    Bryson Brown

9. Logical Non-Apriorism and the 'Law' of Non-Contradiction   156
    Otávio Bueno and Mark Colyvan

10. Letters to Beall and Priest 176
    David Lewis

11. Revising Logic 178
    Michael D. Resnik

Part IV: Against the LNC

12. True and False—As If 197
    JC Beall

13. The Philosophical Basis of What? The Anti-Realist
    Route to Dialetheism 217
    Jon Cogburn

14. 'To Pee and not to Pee?' Could *That* Be the Question?
    (Further Reflections of The Dog) 235
    Jay Garfield

15. Realism and Dialetheism 245
    Frederick Kroon

16. Semantic Dialetheism 264
    Edwin D. Mares

17. Ramsey's Dialetheism 276
    Vann McGee

Part V: For the LNC

18. The Barber, Russell's Paradox, Catch-22, God and More:
    A Defence of a Wittgensteinian Conception of Contradiction 295
    Laurence Goldstein

19. A Critique of Dialetheism 314
    Greg Littmann and Keith Simmons

20. Simple Truth, Contradiction, and Consistency 336
    Stewart Shapiro

21. An Anti-Realist Critique of Dialetheism 355
    Neil Tennant

22. There Are No True Contradictions 385
    Alan Weir

23. In Defense of the Law of Non-Contradiction 418
    Edward N. Zalta

Index 437

List of Contributors

BRADLEY ARMOUR-GARB is Assistant Professor of Philosophy at the State University of New York at Albany. For as long as he can remember, he has had a special fascination with paradoxes, although his chief research focuses on the logic, language, and metaphysics of truth (and falsity). He has published papers in *Analysis, Australasian Journal of Philosophy, Journal of Philosophical Logic, Noûs*, and *Synthese*, amongst a number of other journals and collections.

JC BEALL is Associate Professor of Philosophy at the University of Connecticut. His chief philosophical interests include truth, logic, language, and metaphysics, and he has an incessant preoccupation with paradoxes. Beall's books include *Liars and Heaps* (editor, 2003), *Possibilities and Paradox: An Introduction to Modal and Many-Valued Logic* (with Bas van Fraassen, 2003), and *Logical Pluralism* (with Greg Restall, 2004); he is currently working on a monograph on truth, falsity, and paradox (under contract with Oxford University Press).

ROSS BRADY is Reader and Associate Professor in Philosophy at La Trobe University in Melbourne, Australia. His research interests are in formal logic, especially relevant logic, and in the set-theoretic and semantic paradoxes. He is a joint author of *Relevant Logics and their Rivals*, vol. 1 (Ridgeview, 1982), and the editor of *Relevant Logics and their Rivals*, vol. 2 (Ashgate, 2003). His book, *Universal Logic (CSLI)*, is forthcoming.

BRYSON BROWN is Professor and Chair of Philosophy at the University of Lethbridge. His philosophical interests centre on logic, especially paraconsistent logic, and philosophy of science. He is co-author, with David Braybrooke and Peter Schotch, of *Logic on the Track of Social Change* (1995). Recent articles include 'Chunk and Permeate' (co-authored with Graham Priest) in *Journal of Philosophical Logic*, 'The Pragmatics of Empirical Adequacy' in *Australasian Journal of Philosophy*, and 'Notes on Hume and Skepticism of the Senses' in *Croatian Journal of Philosophy*.

OTÁVIO BUENO is Associate Professor of Philosophy at the University of South Carolina. His research areas include philosophy of science, philosophy of mathematics, philosophy of logic and paraconsistent logic. He has published papers in *Philosophy of Science, Synthese, Journal of Philosophical Logic, Analysis, Studies in History and Philosophy of Science, Erkenntnis, History and Philosophy of Logic*, among many other journals and collections. He is the author of *Constructive Empiricism: A Restatement and Defense* and *Elements of Paraconsistent Set Theory* (with Newton da Costa and Jean-Yves Béziau).

JON COGBURN is an Assistant Professor of Philosophy at Louisiana State University. His philosophical interests include: realism/anti-realism debates, the computational theory of mind, vagueness, the sociology of cognitive science, and the metaphysics and aesthetics of video games.

MARK COLYVAN is Professor of Philosophy at the University of Queensland. His main research interests are in philosophy of mathematics, philosophy of science, philosophy of logic and metaphysics. He is the author of *The Indispensability of Mathematics* (Oxford University Press, 2001) and co-author of *Ecological Orbits: How Planets Move and Populations Grow* (Oxford University Press, 2004).

JAY GARFIELD is Doris Silbert Professor in the Humanities and Professor of Philosophy at Smith College, Professor in the graduate faculty of Philosophy at the University of Massachusetts, Professorial Fellow at the University of Melbourne and Adjunct Professor of Philosophy at the Central Institute of Higher Tibetan Studies. His interests include the philosophy of logic, the philosophy of mind, foundations of cognitive science, epistemology, Buddhist philosophy, and cross-cultural hermeneutics. His recent books inlcude *Fundamental Wisdom of the Middle Way: Nagarjuna's Mulamadhyamakakarika* (Oxford University Press) and *Empty Words: Buddhist Philosophy and Cross-Cultural Interpretation* (Oxford University Press).

LAURENCE GOLDSTEIN is Professor of the Philosophy of Language and Mind at the University of Hong Kong. His latest book is *Clear and Queer Thinking: Wittgenstein's Development and his Relevance to Modern Thought*; his next is *The Liar, the Bald Man and the Hangman*.

PATRICK GRIM is SUNY Distinguished Teaching Professor at the State University of New York at Stony Brook. He is author of *The Incomplete Universe* and *The Philosophical Computer* and is founding co-editor of twenty-four volumes of *The Philosopher's Annual*. Grim works in philosophical logic, contemporary metaphysics, ethics, and philosophy of religion. His current work in computational modelling appears in scholarly journals across a range of disciplines.

FREDERICK KROON is Associate Professor of Philosophy at the University of Auckland. He has published articles in, among other areas, computability theory, the theory of reference, the nature of rationality, and the semantics of fiction. His book *The Routes of Reference* will be published by Oxford University Press in 2005.

GREG LITTMANN has recently completed his Ph.D. at the University of North Carolina at Chapel Hill, and is currently an Instructor in the Department of Philosophy at the Southern Illinois University at Edwardsville (SIUE).

EDWIN MARES is a senior lecturer in Philosophy and member of the Centre for Logic, Language and Computation at Victoria University of Wellington. He is the author of articles on various branches of logic and of the books *Relevant Logic: A Philosophical Introduction* and (with Stuart Brock) *Realism and Anti-Realism* (forthcoming).

GRAHAM PRIEST is Boyce Gibson Professor of Philosophy at the University of Melbourne, and Arché Professorial Fellow at the University of St Andrews. His philosophical interests include logic, metaphysics, and the history of philosophy (West and East). His books include *In Contradiction, Beyond the Limits of Thought, An Introduction to Non-Classical Logic* and *Towards Non-Being* (forthcoming).

MICHAEL D. RESNIK is a University Distinguished Professor of Philosophy at the University of North Carolina at Chapel Hill. He has written extensively in the philosophy of mathematics and the philosophy of logic.

GREG RESTALL is Associate Professor of Philosophy at the University of Melbourne. His academic interests include both philosophical logic and formal logic, together with the history of analytic philosophy and meaning theory. He has written *An Introduction to Substructural Logics* (Routledge 2000), *Logic* (Routledge, forthcoming) and *Logical Pluralism* with JC Beall (Oxford, forthcoming).

R. M. SAINSBURY is Professor of Philosophy at the University of Texas at Austin, and Susan Stebbing Professor at King's College, London. He is the author of *Russell* (1979), *Paradoxes* (2nd edn. 1995), *Logical Forms* (2nd edn. 2000), *Departing From Frege* (2002) and *Reference Without Referents* (forthcoming).

STEWART SHAPIRO is the O'Donnell Professor of Philosophy at The Ohio State University and Arché Professorial Fellow at the University of St Andrews. His major works include *Foundations without Foundationalism* (Oxford University Press, 1991), which is an articulation and defence of second-order logic; *Philosophy of Mathematics: Structure and Ontology* (Oxford University Press, 1997), a presentation of structuralism; and his text in the philosophy of mathematics, *Thinking about Mathematics* (Oxford University Press, 2000).

KEITH SIMMONS is Professor of Philosophy at the University of North Carolina at Chapel Hill. He is the author of *Universality and the Liar*, and editor (with Simon Blackburn) of *Truth*, in the series *Oxford Readings in Philosophy*. His published articles are mainly in logic, history of logic, philosophy of language, metaphysics, and ethics. He is currently at work on a monograph on the logical paradoxes and (with Dorit Bar-On) a monograph on deflationism.

NEIL TENNANT is Humanities Distinguished Professor of Philosophy and Distinguished University Scholar at the Ohio State University. His research interests include mathematical, philosophical and computational logic, and the philosophy of language, mind, mathematics, and science. His books include *Natural Logic*; *Philosophy, Evolution and Human Nature* (with Florian von Schilcher); *Anti-Realism and Logic*; *Autologic*; and *The Taming of The True*.

ACHILE C. VARZI is Associate Professor of Philosophy at Columbia University, New York. His main research interests are in logic, metaphysics, and the philosophy of language. His books include *An Essay in Universal Semantics* (Kluwer, 1999), *Parts and Places* (with R. Casati, MIT Press, 1999), *Theory and Problems of Logic* (with J. Nolt and D. Rohatyn, McGraw-Hill, 1998) and *Holes and Other*

Superficialities (with R. Casati, MIT Press, 1994). His papers appear in several books and journals, including *Mind, Noûs, Philosophy and Phenomenological Research, Australasian Journal of Philosophy, Philosophy, Philosophical Studies, Philosophical Topics, Journal of Philosophical Logic, Notre Dame Journal of Formal Logic*. Currently he is an editor of *The Journal of Philosophy* and an advisory editor of *The Monist* and of *Dialectica*.

ALAN WEIR is a Senior Lecturer at Queen's University Belfast, Northern Ireland. He has also taught at the Universities of Edinburgh and Birmingham; and at Balliol College, Oxford. He has published articles on logic and philosophy of mathematics in a number of collections and in journals including *Mind, Philosophia Mathematica*, the *Notre Dame Journal of Formal Logic and Analysis*.

EDWARD N. ZALTA <http://mally.stanford.edu/zalta.html> is a Senior Research Scholar at Stanford University's Center for the Study of Language and Information. His interests include metaphysics and formal ontology, philosophy of logic, and philosophy of mathematics. He has published two books, *Abstract Objects: An Introduction to Axiomatic Metaphysics* and *Intensional Logic and the Metaphysics of Intentionality*.

Introduction: At the Intersection of Truth and Falsity

JC Beall

'Now we will take another line of reasoning. When you follow two separate chains of thought, Watson, you will find some point of intersection which should approximate to the truth.'—Sherlock Holmes, in 'The Disappearance of Lady Frances Carfax'.

1. TOWARDS THE INTERSECTION

Suppose that we have (at least) two categories $\mathcal{X}$ and $\mathcal{Y}$ for any meaningful, declarative sentence $\mathcal{A}$ of our language.[1] Pending further information about $\mathcal{X}$ and $\mathcal{Y}$, there seem to be four options for an arbitrary sentence $\mathcal{A}$:

» $\mathcal{A}$ is only in $\mathcal{X}$
» $\mathcal{A}$ is only in $\mathcal{Y}$
» $\mathcal{A}$ is in both $\mathcal{X}$ and $\mathcal{Y}$
» $\mathcal{A}$ is in neither $\mathcal{X}$ nor $\mathcal{Y}$

Whether each such 'option' is logically possible depends not only on our logic (about which more below) but on the details of $\mathcal{X}$ and $\mathcal{Y}$.

Suppose that $\mathcal{X}$ comprises all (and only) sentences composed of exactly six words, and $\mathcal{Y}$ those with exactly nineteen words. In that case, only the third option is ruled out: $\mathcal{X}$ and $\mathcal{Y}$ are *exclusive*—their intersection $\mathcal{X} \cap \mathcal{Y}$ is empty—since no $\mathcal{A}$ can be composed of exactly six words and also be composed of exactly nineteen words.[2] Despite being exclusive, $\mathcal{X}$ and $\mathcal{Y}$ are *not exhaustive*—their union $\mathcal{X} \cup \mathcal{Y}$ does not exhaust all sentences—since some $\mathcal{A}$ may fall into neither $\mathcal{X}$ nor $\mathcal{Y}$. (Just consider 'Max sat on Agnes'.)

Consider another example. Let $\mathcal{X}$ comprise all sentences of your favourite novel and $\mathcal{Y}$ your all-time favourite sentences. In that case, exclusion is not ruled out; the intersection of $\mathcal{X}$ and $\mathcal{Y}$ may well be non-empty. (Suppose that your favourite sentence is the first sentence of your favourite novel.) Presumably, $\mathcal{X}$ and $\mathcal{Y}$ are not

---

[1] Henceforth, 'sentence' is used for meaningful, declarative sentences.
[2] Actually, even this is a bit contentious, since there are inconsistent (but non-trivial) arithmetics in which 19 and 6 'collapse'. (See [29].)

exhaustive, since (presumably) there are sentences that are neither your favourite nor in your favourite novel.

2. AT THE INTERSECTION

Now for the interesting question. Assuming that *truth* and *falsity* are categories of sentences, we can let $\mathcal{X}$ be the former and $\mathcal{Y}$ the latter. Let us assume, following standard practice, that one constraint on *falsity* is that, by definition, falsity is truth of negation, that is, that $\mathcal{A}$ is false if and only if its negation $\neg \mathcal{A}$ is true. The question, then, is this: Are $\mathcal{X}$ and $\mathcal{Y}$ both exclusive and exhaustive categories?

For present purposes, the question of exclusion is central.[3] Are truth and falsity exclusive? The question is intimately connected with others:

» Is there any a priori (or empirical) reason to think that truth and falsity are exclusive?

» If truth and falsity are exclusive, how is the non-exclusivity to be formulated? If truth and falsity are not exclusive, how is that to be formulated?

» How would we decide whether truth and falsity are (non-)exclusive? Can there be any non-question-begging debate?

» Is there any a priori (or empirical) reason to think that truth and falsity are not exclusive?

» Even if truth and falsity are not exclusive, is it rational to believe anything that lies in the intersection of truth and falsity?

I will not (here) address all of those questions; they are discussed in depth, in one form or another, in the following chapters.[4] Here my aim is to (briefly) cover a few topics that serve as background to the rest of the book. I give indications for further reading along the way.[5]

3. 'THE' LAW OF NON-CONTRADICTION

The classic source of much thought about contradiction comes from Aristotle's Book Γ of the *Metaphysics*. To this day, many of Aristotle's views have been widely rejected; the conspicuous exception, despite the work of Dancy [21] and Łukasiewicz [28], are his views on contradiction. That no contradiction is

---

[3] The two questions, as RESTALL, BRADY, and VARZI emphasize, are closely related, but I will concentrate on the question of exclusion in this introductory essay. McGEE's essay also brings out the very tight connection between the questions of exclusion and exhaustion.

[4] In fact, the questions roughly correspond to the five parts of the volume.

[5] In giving further reading, I also highlight the chapters in this volume by using UPPERCASE for names of contributors.

true remains an entrenched 'unassailable dogma' of Western thought—or so one would think.[6]

In recent years, due in no small measure to progress in paraconsistent logic (more on which in ss. 4 and 7), the 'unassailable dogma' has been assailed. As Priest's detailed discussion shows [32], neither Aristotle's arguments for (non-)contradiction nor modifications of those arguments [3, 41, 45] have produced strong arguments for the thesis that no contradiction could be true—that the intersection of truth and falsity is necessarily empty. Moreover, there seem to be reasons for thinking that at least some contradictions are true (see s. 5). At the very least, the issue is open for debate—the main motivation behind this volume.

But what exactly *is* the so-called law of (non-)contradiction? Unfortunately, 'the' so-called law is not one but many—and perhaps not appropriately called a 'law'. Aristotle distinguished a number of principles about (non-)contradiction, and the correct exegesis of his views remains an issue among historians. For present purposes, I will simply list a few principles, and then briefly fix terminology concerning 'contradiction'.[7]

> » SIMPLE (NON-)CONTRADICTION: No contradiction is true
> » ONTOLOGICAL (NON-)CONTRADICTION: No 'being' can instantiate contradictory properties
> » RATIONALITY (NON-)CONTRADICTION: It is irrational to (knowingly) accept a contradiction

The principles, so formulated, are hardly precise, but they indicate different (not to say logically independent) versions of 'the' target principle. For present purposes, I will focus almost entirely on Simple (Non-)Contradiction, though some of what follows will also indirectly touch on the other principles.[8]

What needs to be clarified is the sense of 'contradiction' at play (at least in this introductory chapter). I will discuss two uses of the term, the *explosive* and the *formal* usage.[9]

Explosive Usage

Some philosophers use the term 'contradiction' to mean an *explosive sentence*, a sentence such that its truth entails triviality—entails that all sentences are true.

---

[6] Despite showing the holes in Aristotle's various arguments on (non-)contradiction, Łukasiewicz [28] concludes that Aristotle was right to preach (as it were) the 'unassailable dogma', as Łukasiewicz called it.

[7] Chapters by BRADY, RESTALL, and VARZI are particularly relevant to the issue of formulating 'the' relevant 'law'.

[8] The chapters by KROON, COGBURN, and TENNANT are particularly relevant to all three principles, as is BROWN's.

[9] GRIM's chapter is particularly useful for gaining a sense of the divergent uses of 'contradiction', as is that by WEIR.

A familiar example of such a sentence is 'Every sentence is true.' That sentence is apparently explosive, since if 'every sentence is true' is true, then every sentence is true, in which case triviality abounds.

Could a contradiction in the explosive sense be true? The question is tricky, as tricky as the modality 'could'. Suppose that by 'could' we mean *logically possible*. Then the question is: Is it logically possible that a contradiction (in the explosive sense) be true?

The answer, of course, depends on the given logic. Does classical logic afford the logical possibility of true contradictions (in the explosive sense)? Interestingly, there is a sense in which classical logic—or, at least, an intuitive account of classical consequence—does afford the logical possibility of true (explosive) contradictions.[10] Intuitively, an argument is classically valid if and only if there is no 'world' in which the premises are true but the conclusion is untrue. Such worlds, on the classical account, are complete and consistent, in the sense that for any world w and any sentence $\mathcal{A}$, either $\mathcal{A}$ or its negation $\neg\mathcal{A}$ is true at w, but not both $\mathcal{A}$ and $\neg\mathcal{A}$ are true at w. What the classical approach demands, of course, is that if *both* $\mathcal{A}$ and $\neg\mathcal{A}$ are true at some world w, then so too is $\mathcal{B}$, for *any* $\mathcal{B}$. But, then, there is nothing in the classical account, at least intuitively understood, that precludes recognizing an exceptional 'trivial world', the world in which *every* sentence is true. In that respect, even classical consequence affords the logical possibility of true (explosive) contradictions: it is just the 'logical possibility' in which every sentence is true—the 'logical possibility' in which explosion happens!

Be that as it may, classical consequence is usually understood in terms of 'classical interpretations'. A classical interpretation is—or is usually modelled by—a function v from sentences into $\{1, 0\}$ (intuitively, The True and The False) such that $v(\neg\mathcal{A}) = 1$ exactly if $v(\mathcal{A}) = 0$. But, then, there is no classical interpretation on which a contradiction (in the explosive sense) is true.

The upshot is that if classical logic dictates the space of logical possibility, there is at best only a remote and trivial sense in which contradictions, in the *explosive* sense, could be true. But there is another sense of 'contradiction', to which I now turn—and classical logic, of course, is only one among many logical theories.

Formal Usage

The explosive usage is not the only prevalent usage of 'contradiction', and for present purposes, it is not the target usage. The *formal* usage of 'contradiction' has it that contradictions are sentences *of the form $\mathcal{A} \wedge \neg\mathcal{A}$*, where $\wedge$ is conjunction and, as above, $\neg$ is negation. In other words, a contradiction, on the formal usage, is the conjunction of a sentence and its negation.

Tradition distinguishes between (among others) sub-contraries and contradictories. $\mathcal{A}$ and $\mathcal{B}$ are *contraries* if they both cannot be true. $\mathcal{A}$ and $\mathcal{B}$ are *subcontraries*

---

[10] Here, I assume single-conclusion classical semantics. As Greg Restall pointed out (in conversation), the issue is slightly more complicated in a so-called multiple-conclusion framework.

if they cannot both be false. $\mathcal{A}$ and $\mathcal{B}$ are *contradictories* if they are both contraries and sub-contraries.

For present purposes, all that is required of a contradiction, at least on the *formal usage* (as here specified), is that it be of the form $\mathcal{A} \wedge \neg \mathcal{A}$. In particular, there is no further requirement that $\mathcal{A} \vee \neg \mathcal{A}$ be logically true, or that $\neg(\mathcal{A} \wedge \neg \mathcal{A})$ be logically true.[11]

The target sense of 'contradiction' is the formal one.[12] Could such a contradiction be true? At this stage, the question of logic becomes pressing. If we let classical logic dictate the constraints of 'could' (in whatever sense might interest us), then we have already been through the question at hand. After all, if classical logic dictates the constraints of (say) logical possibility, then any *formal contradiction* is an explosive contradiction, as the famous 'independent argument' shows. (See s. 4 for further discussion.) But, as above, classical logic is just one among many different theories of consequence (validity). In addition to classical logic, and particularly relevant to the present volume, is so-called paraconsistent logic, to which I turn.[13]

4. WEAK AND STRONG PARACONSISTENCY

The question at the intersection of truth and falsity is whether it (the intersection) could be non-empty but non-trivial—whether *some but not all* contradictions could be true. Classical logic, and intuitionistic logic, for that matter, give a swift answer: No.[14] In each such logic, the so-called 'independent argument' goes through:[15]

   (1) Assume that $\mathcal{A} \wedge \neg \mathcal{A}$ is true

   (2) By (1) and Simplification, $\mathcal{A}$ is true

---

[11] Of course, one might argue—and some [40] have—that an operator φ is *negation* (or a negation) only if $\mathcal{A} \vee \varphi\mathcal{A}$ and $\varphi(\mathcal{A} \wedge \varphi\mathcal{A})$ are logically true. If that is right, then $\mathcal{A} \wedge \neg \mathcal{A}$ is a contradiction only if $\mathcal{A}$ and $\neg \mathcal{A}$ are sub-contraries and $\neg(\mathcal{A} \wedge \neg \mathcal{A})$ is logically true—since otherwise $\neg$ wouldn't be a negation. (Recall that on the formal usage, a contradiction is of the form $\mathcal{A} \wedge \neg \mathcal{A}$, where $\neg \mathcal{A}$ is the negation of $\mathcal{A}$.) But, again, I will leave this issue aside, not because it is not important but, rather, because a full discussion would be too full for present purposes. Useful discussion of negation is in BRADY's paper, as well as SAINSBURY's, and also in the volumes [23, 47] and Routley and Routley [44].

[12] Henceforth, I use 'contradiction' along the formal usage, unless otherwise specified.

[13] I will say nothing here about 'revisions of logic' or the like, due only to space considerations. My own view is along Quine-the-good lines, according to which *any* 'logical principle' may be revised in the face of appropriate 'evidence'. (Quine-the-bad, of course, imposed exceptions—notably, the 'unassailable dogma' of which Aristotle and Łukasiewicz spoke.) RESNIK's chapter, in addition to those by BUENO AND COLYVAN and BROWN, discuss these issues along various lines. The two letters by LEWIS are also relevant.

[14] Priest [38] and Beall and van Fraassen [18] provide introductory presentations of intuitionistic logic, in addition to the sample paraconsistent framework discussed in s. 7. Priest's text also discusses more mainstream approaches to so-called relevant (-ance) logic.

[15] The 'proof' is often ascribed to C. I. Lewis, who rediscovered it for contemporary readers, but Medieval logicians were apparently aware of the proof (like so many other 'recent discoveries'). I am grateful to Graham Priest on the historical point.

(3) By (2) and Addition, $\mathcal{A} \vee \mathcal{B}$ is true

(4) By (1) and Simplification, $\neg\mathcal{A}$ is true

(5) But, then, by (3), (4), and Disjunctive Syllogism, $\mathcal{B}$ is true

The upshot is that any contradiction is explosive if each of the foregoing steps is valid.

Paraconsistent logics, by definition, are not explosive. A consequence relation $\vdash$, however defined, is said to be *explosive* if $\mathcal{A}, \neg\mathcal{A} \vdash \mathcal{B}$ holds for arbitrary $\mathcal{A}$ and $\mathcal{B}$. A consequence relation is said to be *paraconsistent* if and only if it is not explosive.[16]

A sample paraconsistent logic is presented in s. 7. That sample is one among various approaches to paraconsistent logic, and by no means decidedly 'the right one'. One approach, for example, due to Da Costa [19, 20], is to let negation fail to be truth-functional. Without truth-functionality, there is no a priori reason that $\mathcal{A}$ and $\neg\mathcal{A}$ could not both be true. Other approaches filter out explosion while retaining as many familiar features of the logical connectives as possible. And there are yet other approaches.[17]

Paraconsistent logic, regardless of the details, affords the 'possibility' of inconsistent but non-trivial theories—theories according to which both $\mathcal{A}$ and $\neg\mathcal{A}$ are true (for some $\mathcal{A}$) but not every sentence is true. Such logics, in other words, open up the 'possibility' in which *some but not all* contradictions 'could' be true.

The matter (again, regardless of the formal details) is delicate. Paraconsistentists, those who construct or use or rely on some paraconsistent logic, usually divide into (at least) three classes:

» Weak Paraconsistentist: a paraconsistentist who rejects that there are 'real possibilities' in which a contradiction is true; paraconsistent models are merely mathematical tools that prove to be useful but, in the end, not representative of real possibility

» Strong Paraconsistentist: a paraconsistentist who accepts that there are 'real possibilities' in which contradictions are true, and more than one such 'real possibility' (and, so, not only the trivial one); however, no contradiction is in fact true

» Dialetheic Paraconsistentist: a paraconsistentist who accepts that there are true contradictions—and, so, that there could be (since our world is a 'real possibility' in which there are some)[18]

Most contemporary paraconsistentists, including so-called relevantists [1, 2, 43], fall into the first class. The minority position, but the position of most relevance

---

[16] That account of paraconsistent consequence is not ideal, but it is the standard one. Priest and Routley [39, 40] provide a nice discussion of the issue.   [17] For a discussion, see Priest [35].

[18] Depending on the details of the given logic, strong paraconsistentists sometimes collapse into dialetheic paraconsistentists. For discussion see Restall [42] and Beall and Restall [17].

to the current volume, is the third class: dialetheic paraconsistentists. What is important to note is that 'paraconsistency' and 'dialetheism' are *not* synonyms. Any rational version of the latter will require the former, but the converse seems not to hold.

Many of the contributions in this volume revolve around dialetheism. PRIEST's chapter argues that there are no good arguments against dialetheism.[19] Suppose that Priest's arguments are sound. Even so, an immediate question arises: Is there any reason to think that dialetheism is correct? Is there any reason to think that some contradictions are true? To that question I now (very briefly) turn.

5. TOWARDS A NON-EMPTY INTERSECTION

Let us suppose, as above, that *truth* and *falsity* are categories of sentences, with at least the constraint that $\neg A$ is true if and only if A is false. Consider the following sentence (a 'Liar'):

> » The first displayed sentence in s. 5 is false

Does that sentence go in category *truth* or in *falsity*? Given the way we use 'true', the first displayed sentence in s. 5 goes in *truth* only if it goes in *falsity*. But, given the way we use 'true', the first displayed sentence in s. 5 goes in *falsity* only if it goes in *truth*. What we seem to have, then, is a sentence that goes into the one category (truth) exactly if it goes into the other (falsity).

True contradiction? It depends. Suppose that *truth* and *falsity* are not exhaustive—that some sentences are in neither category, that there are 'truth value gaps'. Then we have no true contradiction, at least not via the first displayed sentence.

A question arises: When we say that the first displayed sentence is neither true nor false, what are we saying? One thing we are saying, it seems, is that the negation of the first displayed sentence is *not* false. But falsity is truth of negation, in which case we seem to be saying something of the form $\neg\neg A$. (If T is our truth predicate and $\langle A \rangle$ a name of A, then we seem to be saying something of the form $\neg T \langle \neg A \rangle$, which is to say that $\neg A$ is false, which seems to be equivalent to $\neg\neg A$.) But, now, assuming Double Negation-Elimination, that entails A. We seem to be back to the apparent true contradiction.

One natural suggestion is that we have at least two negations—one $\sim$ being a 'gap-closer', the other $\neg$ affording gaps. The idea is that we use the 'gap-closer' (sometimes called 'exclusion') when we say that the first displayed sentence in s. 5 is *not* false (or true). While that suggestion will avoid the problem above, it also

---

[19] Of course, PRIEST's contribution was written prior to the others in this volume. Debate will tell whether some of those considerations work against dialetheism.

returns us to the appearance of true contradiction:

> The second displayed sentence in s. 5 is not true

It seems that the non-exhaustiveness of *truth* and *falsity* does little to avoid the apparent emergence of contradiction: The second displayed sentence seems to be true if and only if it is not. A simple lesson to draw is the dialetheic one: The second displayed sentence is *in the intersection* of both truth and falsity—or the intersection of truth and 'untruth' (if one adds that category to accommodate gaps).

Anyone familiar with contemporary work on the Liar will know that, in an effort to avoid 'true contradictions', many different non-dialetheic avenues have been pursued.[20] Some of the given avenues are ingenious attempts to avoid the apparent inconsistency, and most are mathematically or logically interesting frameworks for thinking about language. In the end, though, none of the given approaches are as simple as a dialetheic response, which simply accepts that the intersection of truth and falsity is non-empty. And given some suitable paraconsistent logic, the dialetheist may accept that some *but not all* contradictions are true—the non-empty intersection may be approached and enjoyed without explosive traffic.[21]

Simple or not, one might think, it seems downright irrational to accept that the intersection of truth and falsity is non-empty—that there are truths with true negations, that there are 'true contradictions' (even if they don't explode). Such a sentiment remains prominent—a residual vestige, perhaps, of the 'unassailable dogma' of (non-)contradiction. But it really is just dogma, at least as far as I can tell (and notwithstanding some of the contributions in this volume), but you (the reader) can judge for yourself.

One issue that should be emphasized is that nothing in dialetheism requires the existence of *observable* contradictions—true contradictions that have observable (but inconsistent) consequences. *That*, despite considerations to the contrary [7, 33], is difficult to understand. But one might, as some suggest,[22] restrict dialetheism to the purely semantic fragment of the language. In that case, the charge of 'irrationality' or even 'incredulous stares' are difficult to appreciate,

---

[20] For a discussion of contemporary approaches, see Beall [11, 12]. Priest [31] gives extended arguments against many such approaches, and also gives one of the earliest and most extended arguments for a dialetheic approach. Beall [10] presents arguments for a different (non-Priestly, as it were) version of dialetheism.

[21] Priest [31] has launched various arguments for dialetheism. The case from semantic paradox, by Priest's lights, is not as strong as the overall case from what he calls 'the inclosure schema' and 'principle of uniform solutions' [37]. Given that Priest's work is largely responsible for the 'spread of dialetheism' (slow as the spread may be), many of the chapters in this volume discuss a variety of Priest's arguments. My own thinking is that, regardless of 'inclosure' or the like, simplicity and preservation of naïve appearance is sufficient for accepting some version or other of dialetheism. But that too, in the pages to come, is challenged by various contributors. ZALTA and GOLDSTEIN, for example, offer direct challenges by proposing alternative responses to various apparent inconsistencies. ARMOUR-GARB discusses whether, and in what sense, dialetheism offers a solution to *paradox*.

[22] See the chapters by BEALL and MARES.

as the only 'true contradictions' are grammatical residue (like the first or second displayed sentences) that carry no observational import. All that is claimed, at least on such restricted dialetheic positions, is that the intersection of truth and falsity contains various peculiar—but none the less grammatically inevitable—sentences that carry no observational consequences. Provided, as above, that a suitable paraconsistent logic is in place, there seems to be little to back worries of irrationality or instability or the like—little, again, beyond the dogma.

6. BEYOND THE SEMANTIC PARADOXES?

One would be misled to think that the *only* considerations towards true contradictions involve semantic paradoxes. Are there reasons to think that some contradictions, having nothing at all to do with the semantic paradoxes, are true? Debate will tell, but I briefly mention two considerations towards the possibility.[23]

Naïve Extensions

Priest [31] argues that the paradoxes of set theory, and in particular Russell's paradox, calls out for a dialetheic solution. Part of Priest's argument turns on his 'inclosure schema' and 'principle of uniform solutions' [37]. In effect, the argument is that Russell's paradox and the semantic paradoxes have the *same basic structure*— what Priest calls 'inclosure'—and, hence, ought to receive the same solution. While I am sympathetic with Priest's argument, I leave its details and merits to the reader.

By my lights, 'Russell's paradox' is ambiguous. On one hand, it denotes a type of paradox that arises in *set theory*, a discipline within mathematics. Sets were originally constructed within and for mathematics. If mathematics wishes to remain consistent, then Russell's *set*-theoretic paradox may be resolved as it has been—by stipulating it out (via axioms or the like).[24] Whether a set-theory is mathematically sufficient is governed by the pragmatic issue of whether it does the job—whether sets, so specified, do the trick for which they were constructed. In that respect, Russell's paradox may have a simple, consistent solution, at least for purposes of mathematics. And the same would go, of course, for mathematical versions of the Liar—stipulate them out, so long as the job is still fully achieved.

---

[23] One would likewise be misled to think that the following two points exhaust the considerations, or are even the strongest. Priest [37] covers a wide variety of other areas that arise, as he puts it, 'at the limits of thought and language'. Priest [31] also discusses the apparent inconsistency involved in *change, motion, legal contexts*, and much else.

[24] Arguments towards, and explorations of, *inconsistent mathematics*, may be found in Mortensen [29] (and references therein).

But there is another Russell's paradox, the paradox of (naïve) *extensions*, which arises not in the restricted confines of mathematics but in natural language. Semanticists and philosophers of language have long recognized the need for *extensions* of predicates (and expressions, in general). A look down the corridor reveals the mathematician's *sets*—and we have since been off running. The trouble is that there is no a priori reason to think that *sets* (the entities constructed within and for mathematics) will sufficiently play the role of extensions; indeed, there is reason to think otherwise. At least initially, with an aim on natural language, we want to have extensions for *every* predicate of the language. In particular, we want to have an extension not only for 'is a philosopher' and 'is a cat' but also for 'is an extension' and 'is not in its own extension' (i.e. 'χ is not in the extension of χ'). The simple idea, of course, is that our extension theory should not only be unrestricted but also should satisfy what seems plainly correct: that the denotation of a is in the extension of $\mathcal{F}$ iff $\ulcorner \mathcal{F}a \urcorner$ is true.[25] But having that calls for dialetheism, at least if one is to accept one's own theory.

I have not given an argument for true contradictions that arise from extensions, but it is an area in which true contradictions may well arise. While inconsistency in *set theory* can be resolved by axiomatizing away, the same is not clearly the case with respect to extensions. Extensions, unlike mathematical sets (at least on the picture I've suggested), are constrained not only by their role in our overall theories, but also by our 'intuitions' about them. Whether such a role or our given 'intuitions' yield true contradictions is something that, as always, debate will tell.

Borderline Cases

Another potential area in which true contradictions might arise is at the 'limits' of vagueness. Not a lot of work has been done on this topic, but a few considerations run as follows.[26]

So-called *tolerance conditionals* that appear in soritical paradoxes appear to be true. If b is a child at t_n, then b is a child at t_{n+1} (for some minuscule measure of time). Rejecting such conditionals, it seems, reveals an incompetence with respect to how the predicate 'is a child' (or any other vague predicate) is used. But the sorites paradox seems to challenge that appearance. Indeed, virtually all known approaches to the sorites reject at least one tolerance conditional, holding that it is

---

[25] Likewise, of course, one wants to have an *extension* of 'is a truth', something that comprises all truths. The mathematicians' *sets*, as Grim [24, 25] argued, seem not to do the trick. All the more reason for an *extension* theory that does the trick.

[26] Dominic Hyde [26] has advanced a paraconsistent, though not clearly dialetheic, approach to vagueness. For something closer to a dialetheic approach see Beall [6] and Beall and Colyvan [15, 16].

not rationally or competently assertable.[27] The trouble with such responses is that one none the less 'feels' that such conditionals *are* true.

One avenue towards resolving the issue is to recognize true contradictions at the 'limits' of vagueness. The suggestion, for example, is that all of the tolerance conditionals are true, but some of them are also false: they reside at the intersection of truth and falsity. In particular, the 'penumbra' is awash with true contradictions. A semantics that affords such an approach is covered below (LP, s. 7).

Of course, if vagueness affords true contradictions, then there may well be 'observable contradictions', and that may be a heavy cost to bear. But that issue deserves debate. In the end, it seems initially as reasonable to think that a 'vague language' is *overdetermined* as it is to think it *underdetermined*. But that issue, like others, is one that must here be left open.

Further discussion of dialetheism (both for and against), of course, may be found in the following chapters. For now, and for purposes of giving the reader a basic framework in which to think about some of the foregoing (and forthcoming) issues, I turn to a brief sketch of a common paraconsistent framework associated with dialetheism—Priest's 'logic of paradox', LP.

7. A SAMPLE PARACONSISTENT LOGIC

As above (s. 4), there are various standard approaches to paraconsistent semantics. Because of its 'classical' appearances (and, hence, familiarity), and also its historical tie to dialetheism, the focus here will be on a basic many-valued, truth-functional approach. The logic typically associated with dialetheism is Priest's 'logic of paradox', LP [30]. For purposes of generality, I present FDE but highlight LP in due course.

Propositional Semantics

The syntax is that of classical logic. The semantics arises by letting interpretations be functions v from sentences into $\mathcal{V} = \wp(\{1, 0\})$. Hence, where $\mathcal{A}$ is any sentence, $v(\mathcal{A}) = \{1\}, v(\mathcal{A}) = \{0\}, v(\mathcal{A}) = \{1, 0\}$, or $v(\mathcal{A}) = \emptyset$. Given that $v(\mathcal{A})$ is a set (comprising either 1, 0, or nothing), we may (by way of informal interpretation) say that $1 \in v(\mathcal{A})$ iff $\mathcal{A}$ is (at least) true under v, and $0 \in v(\mathcal{A})$ iff $\mathcal{A}$ is (at least) false under v. In the case where $v(\mathcal{A}) = \emptyset$, we may (informally) say that $\mathcal{A}$ is neither true nor false (under v); and when $1 \in v(\mathcal{A})$ and $0 \in v(\mathcal{A})$, we may (informally) say that $\mathcal{A}$ is both true and false (under v).

---

[27] For recent work on the sorites, see Beall [9] and the references therein. (That volume also contains recent work on various semantic paradoxes.)

$\mathcal{D}$, our designated values, comprises $\{1\}$ and $\{1, 0\}$. (Intuitively, and informally, we designate all and only those sentences that are 'at least true'.)

We say that an interpretation v is *admissible* just in case it 'obeys' the following clauses:[28]

> » $1 \in v(\neg\mathcal{A})$ iff $0 \in v(\mathcal{A})$
>
> » $0 \in v(\neg\mathcal{A})$ iff $1 \in v(\mathcal{A})$
>
> » $1 \in v(\mathcal{A} \wedge \mathcal{B})$ iff $1 \in v(\mathcal{A})$ and $1 \in v(\mathcal{B})$
>
> » $0 \in v(\mathcal{A} \wedge \mathcal{B})$ iff $0 \in v(\mathcal{A})$ or $0 \in v(\mathcal{B})$

Logical consequence (semantic consequence) is defined as 'truth preservation' over all (admissible) interpretations, that is, if every premise in Σ is at least true, then so too is $\mathcal{A}$:

> » $\Sigma \Vdash \mathcal{A}$ iff $v(\mathcal{A}) \in \mathcal{D}$ if $v(\mathcal{B}) \in \mathcal{D}$, for all $\mathcal{B}$ in Σ

A sentence $\mathcal{A}$ is *valid* (a tautology, logical truth) exactly if $\emptyset \Vdash \mathcal{A}$.

Remarks

The foregoing semantics yields the propositional language of FDE (first degree entailment) [1, 2]. There are a few notable features of the current semantics.

> » There are no valid sentences: Just consider the admissible interpretation according to which every sentence is neither true nor false. (Compare Kleene's 'strong' semantics K_3.)
>
> » Suppose that we restrict the (admissible) interpretations to those interpretations the range of which is $\wp(\{1, 0\}) - \{\{1, 0\}\}$. In that case, we have K_3, a simple 'gappy' semantics that is *not* paraconsistent.
>
> » Suppose that we restrict the (admissible) interpretations to those interpretations the range of which is $\wp(\{1, 0\}) - \{\emptyset\}$. In that case, we have LP, a simple 'glutty' semantics which *is* paraconsistent. As one can easily show, the valid sentences of LP and those of classical logic are precisely the same. (The consequence relation, of course, is different: LP-consequence is weaker, since it is not explosive.)
>
> » Suppose that we restrict the (admissible) interpretations to those interpretations the range of which is $\wp(\{1, 0\}) - \{\{1, 0\}\} \cup \{\emptyset\}$. In that case, we have classical semantics, which admits neither 'gluts' nor 'gaps' and is explosive.

---

[28] Disjunction $\vee$ and the hook $\supset$ (the 'material conditional') are defined in the usual way.

Quantification

The syntax, as in the propositional case, is that of classical (predicate) logic. Algebraic techniques for extending a many-valued propositional language to a quantified one are available; however, a straightforward, and perhaps more familiar, technique is available in the (non-algebraic) current case.

We let an interpretation be a pair $\langle \mathcal{O}, \delta \rangle$, where $\mathcal{O}$ is a non-empty set of objects (the domain of quantification) and δ a function that does two things:[29]

» δ maps the constants into $\mathcal{O}$

» δ maps every n-ary predicate $\mathcal{P}^n$ into a *pair* $\langle \mathcal{E}_{\mathcal{P}^n}, \mathcal{A}_{\mathcal{P}^n} \rangle$, where $\mathcal{E}_{\mathcal{P}^n} \subseteq \mathcal{O}^n$ and $\mathcal{A}_{\mathcal{P}^n} \subseteq \mathcal{O}^n$

$\mathcal{E}_{\mathcal{P}^n}$ is said to be the *extension* of $\mathcal{P}^n$ and $\mathcal{A}_{\mathcal{P}^n}$ the *anti-extension*. (The extension of $\mathcal{P}^n$, informally, comprises all the objects of which $\mathcal{P}^n$ is at least true, and the anti-extension the objects of which $\mathcal{P}^n$ is at least false.)

Atomic sentences are assigned 'truth values' (elements of $\mathcal{V}$) according to the familiar clauses:

» $1 \in v(\mathcal{P}^n c_1, \ldots, c_n)$ iff $\langle \delta(c_1), \ldots, \delta(c_n) \rangle \in \mathcal{E}_{\mathcal{P}^n}$

» $0 \in v(\mathcal{P}^n c_1, \ldots, c_n)$ iff $\langle \delta(c_1), \ldots, \delta(c_n) \rangle \in \mathcal{A}_{\mathcal{P}^n}$

Non-quantified compound sentences, in turn, are assigned values as per the propositional case (negation, conjunction, and, derivatively, disjunction, material implication, etc.). The clauses for quantifiers run thus:[30]

» $1 \in v(\forall \chi \mathcal{A})$ iff $1 \in v(\mathcal{A}(\chi/c))$, for every $c \in \mathcal{O}$

» $0 \in v(\forall \chi \mathcal{A})$ iff $0 \in v(\mathcal{A}(\chi/c))$, for some $c \in \mathcal{O}$

» $1 \in v(\exists \chi \mathcal{A})$ iff $1 \in v(\mathcal{A}(\chi/c))$, for some $c \in \mathcal{O}$

» $0 \in v(\exists \chi \mathcal{A})$ iff $0 \in v(\mathcal{A}(\chi/c))$, for every $c \in \mathcal{O}$

Logical consequence is defined as per usual: 'truth preservation' over all (admissible) interpretations.

Remarks

Not surprisingly, classical semantics (and, similarly, strong Kleene 'gappy' semantics) may be 'regained' by imposing appropriate constraints on the foregoing semantics, and in particular on what counts as an admissible interpretation. Example: By imposing the constraint that $\mathcal{E}_{Pn} \cup \mathcal{A}_{Pn} = \mathcal{O}^n$ and $\mathcal{E}_{Pn} \cap \mathcal{A}_{Pn} = \emptyset$

---

[29] For simplicity, assume that every element of $\mathcal{O}$ has a name, and in particular that elements of $\mathcal{O}$ name themselves and, thus, function as constants.

[30] One of the quantifiers is taken to be defined (per usual) but, despite redundancy, clauses for both quantifiers are given here. $\mathcal{A}(\chi/c)$ is $\mathcal{A}$ with every free occurrence of χ replaced by c. (Usual caveats about bondage are in place! And recall that $c \in \mathcal{O}$ serves as a name of itself.)

(for any predicate P^n), one 'regains' classical semantics. As in the propositional case, the upshot is that any classical (first-order) interpretation is a (first-order) FDE-interpretation, and so the former is a (proper) extension of the latter.

The foregoing semantics can be (and have been) augmented to include function symbols, identity, and modal operators (and also extended to second-order). For present purposes, I leave those extensions aside.[31]

8. BUT WHAT OF THE APPARENT LOSS?

Suppose that for purposes of adopting dialetheism we accept LP. We may then enjoy a simple response to the intersection of truth and falsity: it is non-empty, but no explosive traffic ensues.

But what about the apparent loss? We avoid explosion, to be sure; however, we thereby lose Disjunctive Syllogism (DS)—the inference from $\mathcal{A} \vee \mathcal{B}$ and $\neg \mathcal{A}$ to $\mathcal{B}$.[32] But we reason with DS all the time, and it is not clear whether we could do without it. If not, the 'gain' of simple dialetheism is too expensive to bear.

The concern is an important and natural one, one that frequently emerges in early discussion of dialetheism. I will not dwell on the issue here, but it is important to say something on the matter.[33]

In the first instance, the response is (of course) that there is no genuine loss. If dialetheism is true and LP the appropriate logic, then DS was never really truth-preserving. (One cannot lose something that was not there.) Moreover, if (as it appears to me) Liar-like sentences are the only root of the invalidity, it is not surprising that we would think DS to be valid, since Liars are easy to overlook.

There is more to say. In particular, it is not abundantly clear that we really do employ DS in our standard reasoning, as opposed to a closely related 'rule of inference'. The dialetheist, as Priest [31] emphasizes, is free to follow the rationality-version of 'Disjunctive Syllogism':

» If one accepts $\mathcal{A} \vee \mathcal{B}$ and one rejects $\mathcal{A}$, then one ought *rationally* accept $\mathcal{B}$

Provided that acceptance and rejection are exclusive (though they needn't be exhaustive), the 'rationality version' is a principle by which one can regain the

[31] See Priest [34, 35] for details (and also a suitable proof theory). LITTMANN AND SIMMONS's chapter raises interesting issues involving descriptions in a dialetheic setting.

[32] The reader familiar with 'material modus ponens' will recognize that that 'also' is lost—as it is little more than DS in disguise. Accordingly, a detachable conditional must be added to the language. A variety of conditionals is available. Priest [31] contains discussion, and recent work on 'restricted quantification' by Beall, Brady, Hazen, Priest, and Restall [14] introduces a new option. Because of lack of space, I leave that (admittedly important) topic aside.

[33] And, of course, a paraconsistent logic in which DS is preserved but some other 'classic' inference is gone is one for which precisely the same issue arises. There is nothing peculiar about DS, except that its 'loss' is often associated with dialetheism.

reasoning that often passes for (the invalid) DS. If that is right, then the 'loss' of DS seems not to be a great loss, after all.[34]

Finally, it is important to note that a dialetheist has no reason to reject consistency as a default assumption, or as a high theoretical virtue, in general. That some contradictions are true does not imply that most contradictions are true—especially if such true contradictions turn out to be only the peculiar paradoxical sentences. (Even if other sorts of sentences, beyond the paradoxical ones, yield true contradictions, the point still applies.) All that the dialetheist requires is that the default aim of consistency is just that: it is *default*, not absolute.[35]

9. BUT WHAT OF TRUTH?

Beyond the concern about 'losing' DS, there are (regrettably) few other articulated objections against dialetheism. The few standard worries—epistemic, belief revision, and the like—are discussed in PRIEST's chapter, and I leave them to that essay.[36] I close by mentioning one topic that philosophers tend to worry about when the notion of 'true contradiction' is raised: Truth.[37]

Some philosophers might think that there is something in the 'nature' of truth that rules out the existence of true contradictions. But on reflection, the thought seems not to pan out. Consider, for example, the two main approaches to truth: correspondence and deflationism. (I don't say the *only* two, but the two main contenders.) The latter, as Priest [36], BEALL, and Beall and Armour-Garb [4, 13] have argued, seems to yield dialetheism quite naturally. After all, there is no 'nature' to bar the grammatically inexorable true contradictions; there are simple rules of dis-quotation and en-quotation (or simply inter-substitution)—and that's it. Deflationists might well seek to avoid true contradictions, but (again) one wonders why such avoidance is sought—especially when, as it appears, the avoidance-procedures make for a much more complicated position.

---

[34] SHAPIRO's chapter challenges the current move to some extent, in as much as it challenges the dialetheist's ability to give a coherent notion of *exclusion*. I leave the reader to weigh the merits of Shapiro's arguments against the proposed move. (I should also point out that, as far as I can see, Shapiro's chief objections may not affect a version of dialetheism underwritten by a logic other than LP (or, for that matter, FDE). For one such alternative approach, see Beall [10].)

[35] See the appendix of BEALL's chapter for brief discussion and references on 'default consistency'.

[36] There are other, more technical worries that I will omit here. One such is Curry's paradox, but that depends on which conditional is in play—a topic that I have omitted here. (A dialetheic response to the 'material conditional' version of Curry is precisely the same as the general response to Liars. A detachable conditional, as above, is where the issue arises. See [31] for discussion.) A similar issue concerns so-called Boolean negation. RESTALL's chapter, as with BRADY's, PRIEST's, and SAINSBURY's, touch on that issue.

[37] Many of the contributions in this volume presuppose one stance or another on truth, but the chapters by GARFIELD, COGBURN, and TENNANT have direct bearing on the topic, as does KROON's. BEALL's chapter specifically focuses on (one conception of) truth.

More interesting are concerns that arise from correspondence. While there remains no clear account of 'correspondence', the basic idea is clear enough. The idea (not formulated as such by all 'robust theorists', but common enough for present purposes) is that any truth has a truth-maker—that any truth is 'made true' by 'the facts', by some actual 'something' in the world without which a putative truth would fail to correspond and, hence, fail to be a truth. Now suppose, as per dialetheism, that there are truths of the form $A \wedge \neg A$. Such a truth would require truth-makers for both A and $\neg A$. But how could that be?

The worry, in the end, is not substantial. Whether correspondence is the right approach to truth remains an open (and much debated) question [22]. Suppose, though, that correspondence is the right approach, and that each truth requires a truth-maker. What, exactly, is the worry about having truth-makers for both A and $\neg A$? On the surface, no particular problem presents itself, at least not one that is peculiar to dialetheism. To be sure, dialetheism requires that there be 'negative truth-makers', since at least one 'negative truth' is true if both A and $\neg A$ are true. But that is a general problem for correspondence, not one peculiar to dialetheism. Moreover, the problem of accommodating 'negative truths' is not particularly difficult; there are standard models available, due to van Fraassen [46], Barwise [5], and others.[38] The worry, as said, seems not to be substantial—at least pending further details.

10. AT THE CROSSROADS: CLOSING REMARKS

Unfortunately, and despite the enormous activity in paraconsistent logic over the last thirty years, there has been little debate centred on non-contradiction— or, at least, little by way of *defense*. Perhaps many have echoed Łukasiewicz in thinking that, while Aristotle's arguments are (at best) insubstantial, Simple (Non-)Contradiction, or perhaps Rationale (Non-)Contradiction, are 'unassailable dogmas' that need only be entrenched, as opposed to defended.[39] Such a thought is philosophically suspect. The incredulous stare was an insufficient 'reply' to modal realism; and it is an insufficient 'reply' to dialetheism.

The hope behind the current volume is that debate may move forward, and that the attitude of unassailable dogma swiftly slides into the past. The intersection is before you; the question is whether it is empty.[40]

---

[38] Note that van Fraassen's given work was not intended to yield 'negative facts', but it yields a suitable framework for them none the less. For further discussion and details of suitable frameworks, see Beall [8].

[39] What is interesting is that Łukasiewicz's student Jaskowski [27] was an early pioneer of contemporary paraconsistent logic.

[40] I am grateful to Brad Armour-Garb, Mark Colyvan, and Dave Ripley for discussion and comments. Special thanks to Graham Priest and Greg Restall for discussion over the last few years, especially early on in Oz, where this volume was conceived—back in 1999! Thanks, finally, to Katrina Higgins for her support, and also for her patience with this and related projects.

REFERENCES

[1] ALAN ROSS ANDERSON and NUEL D. BELNAP. *Entailment: The Logic of Relevance and Necessity*, i. Princeton University Press, Princeton, 1975.

[2] ALAN ROSS ANDERSON, NUEL D. BELNAP, and J. MICHAEL DUNN. *Entailment: The Logic of Relevance and Necessity*, ii. Princeton University Press, Princeton, 1992.

[3] G. E. ANSCOMBE and P. GEACH. *Three Philosophers*. Blackwell, Oxford, 1961.

[4] BRAD ARMOUR-GARB and JC BEALL. 'Can Deflationists be Dialetheists?' *Journal of Philosophical Logic*, 30(6): 593–608, 2001.

[5] JON BARWISE. 'Situations, Facts, and True Propositions'. In *The Situation in Logic*, CSLI Lecture Notes, no. 17, pages 221–54. CSLI Publications, Stanford, 1989.

[6] JC BEALL. 'Glutty Borders'. Presented at the University of Massachusetts (Amherst, Oct. 2003) and the Vagueness Workshop at University of St Andrews (Feb. 2004). Forthcoming.

[7] JC BEALL. 'Is the Observable World Consistent?'. *Australasian Journal of Philosophy*, 78(1): 113–18, 2000.

[8] JC BEALL. 'On Truthmakers for Negative Truths'. *Australasian Journal of Philosophy*, 78: 264–8, 2000.

[9] JC BEALL (ed.), *Liars and Heaps: New Essays on Paradox*. Oxford University Press, Oxford, 2003.

[10] JC BEALL. 'Negation's Holiday: Double-Aspect Dialetheism'. In Dave Devidi and Tim Kenyon (eds.) *Formal Approaches to Philosophy* (Kluwer, forthcoming in University of Western Ontario Philosophy of Science Series).

[11] JC BEALL. 'Logical and Semantic Paradoxes'. In DALE JACQUETTE (ed.) *Philosophy of Logic*. North-Holland Publishing, 2004. Forthcoming.

[12] JC BEALL. 'Recent Work on Truth and Paradox'. *Philosophical Books*, 2004. Forthcoming.

[13] JC BEALL and BRAD ARMOUR-GARB. 'Should Deflationists be Dialetheists?'. *Noûs*, 37(2): 303–24, 2005.

[14] JC BEALL, ROSS BRADY, ALLEN HAZEN, GRAHAM PRIEST, and GREG RESTALL. 'Restricted Quantification in Paraconsistent Contexts'. In press.

[15] JC BEALL and MARK COLYVAN. 'From Heaps of Gluts to Hyde-ing the Sorites'. *Mind*, 110: 401–8, 2001.

[16] JC BEALL and MARK COLYVAN: 'Looking for Contradictions'. *Australasian Journal of Philosophy*, 79: 564–9, 2001.

[17] JC BEALL and GREG RESTALL. *Logical Pluralism*. Oxford University Press, Oxford, 2004. Forthcoming.

[18] JC BEALL and BAS C. VAN FRAASSEN. *Possibilities and Paradox: An Introduction to Modal and Many-Valued Logic*. Oxford University Press, Oxford, 2003.

[19] N. C. A. DA COSTA. 'On the Theory of Inconsistent Formal Systems'. *Notre Dame Journal of Formal Logic*, 15: 497–510, 1974.

[20] N. C. A. DA COSTA and E. H. ALVES. 'A Semantic Analysis of the Calculi C_n'. *Notre Dame Journal of Formal Logic*, 18: 621–30, 1977.

[21] R. M. DANCY. *Sense and Contradiction in Aristotle*. Reidel, Dordrecht, 1975.

[22] MARIAN DAVID. *Correspondence and Disquotation*. Oxford University Press, Oxford, 1994.

[23] DOV M. GABBAY and HEINRICH WANSING (eds.). *What is Negation?* Kluwer Academic Publishers, Dordrecht, 1999.

[24] PATRICK GRIM. 'There is no Set of All Truths'. *Analysis*, 44: 206–8, 1984.

[25] PATRICK GRIM. *The Incomplete Universe*. MIT Press, Cambridge, Mass., 1991.

[26] DOMINIC HYDE. 'From Heaps and Gaps to Heaps of Gluts'. *Mind*, 106: 641–60, 1997.

[27] S. JASKOWSKI. 'Propositional Calculus for Contradictory Deductive Systems'. *Studia Logica*, 24: 143–57, 1969. Originally published in 1948 in Polish in *Studia Scientarium Torunensis*, Sec. A II, pp. 55–77.

[28] JAN ŁUKASIEWICZ. 'Aristotle on the Law of Contradiction'. In J. BARNES, M. SCHOFIELD, and R. SORABJI (eds.). *Articles on Aristotle: Vol III, Metaphysics*. Duckworth, London, 1979. The original paper was published in 1910 in *Bulletin International de l'Académie des Sciences de Cracovie*.

[29] CHRIS MORTENSEN. *Inconsistent Mathematics*. Kluwer Academic Publishers, Dordrecht, 1995.

[30] GRAHAM PRIEST. 'The Logic of Paradox'. *Journal of Philosophical Logic*, 8: 219–41, 1979.

[31] GRAHAM PRIEST. *In Contradiction: A Study of the Transconsistent*. Martinus Nijhoff, The Hague, 1987.

[32] GRAHAM PRIEST. 'To be and *not* to be—that is the answer. On Aristotle on the law of non-contradiction'. *Philosophiegeschichte im Überblick (History of Philosophy in General)*, 91–130, 1998.

[33] GRAHAM PRIEST. 'Perceiving Contradictions'. *Australasian Journal of Philosophy*, 77: 439–46, 1999.

[34] GRAHAM PRIEST. 'Semantic Closure, Descriptions and Triviality'. *Journal of Philosophical Logic*, 28: 549–58, 1999.

[35] GRAHAM PRIEST. 'Paraconsistent Logic'. In DOV M. GABBAY and FRANZ GÜNTHNER, editors, *Handbook of Philosophical Logic (2nd Edition)*, vi. D. Reidel, Dordrecht, 2000.

[36] GRAHAM PRIEST. 'Truth and Contradiction'. *Philosophical Quarterly*, 50(200): 305–19, 2000.

[37] GRAHAM PRIEST. *Beyond the Limits of Thought* (Expanded, revised edition). Oxford University Press, Oxford, 2001.

[38] GRAHAM PRIEST. *An Introduction to Non-Classical Logic*. Cambridge University Press, Cambridge, 2001.

[39] GRAHAM PRIEST and RICHARD ROUTLEY. 'The Philosophical Significance and Inevitability of Paraconsistency'. In GRAHAM PRIEST, RICHARD ROUTLEY, and JEAN NORMAN (eds.). *Paraconsistent Logic: Essays on the Inconsistent*, 483–537. Philosophia Verlag, Munich, 1989.

[40] GRAHAM PRIEST and RICHARD ROUTLEY. 'Systems of Paraconsistent Logic'. In GRAHAM PRIEST, RICHARD ROUTLEY, and JEAN NORMAN (eds.). *Paraconsistent Logic: Essays on the Inconsistent*, 151–86. Philosophia Verlag, Munich, 1989.

[41] HILARY PUTNAM. 'There is at Least One A Priori Truth'. *Erkenntnis*, 13: 153–70, 1976.

[42] GREG RESTALL. 'Paraconsistent Logics!' *Bulletin of the Section of Logic*, 26: 156–63, 1997.

[43] RICHARD ROUTLEY, VAL PLUMWOOD, ROBERT K. MEYER, and ROSS T. BRADY. *Relevant Logics and their Rivals*. Ridgeview, Atascadero, Calif., 1982.

[44] RICHARD ROUTLEY and VALERIE ROUTLEY. 'Negation and Contradiction'. *Rivista Columbiana de Matemáticas*, 19: 201–31, 1995.

[45] M. THOMPSON. 'On A Priori Truth'. *The Journal of Philosophy*, 78: 458–82, 1981.

[46] BAS C. VAN FRAASSEN. 'Facts and Tautological Entailments'. *Journal of Philosophy*, 66: 477–87, 1969. Reprinted in [1].

[47] HEINRICH WANSING, (ed.). *Negation: A Notion in Focus*. de Gruyter, Berlin, 1996.

I

Setting up the Debate

1

What's So Bad About Contradictions?

Graham Priest

In this chapter[1] I will address the title question; and the answer I shall give is 'maybe nothing much'. Let me first explain how, exactly, the question is to be understood. I shall interpret it to mean 'what is wrong with believing *some* contradictions?' I emphasize the 'some'; the question 'what is wrong with believing *all* contradictions' is quite different, and, I am sure, has a quite different answer. It would be irrational to believe that I am a fried egg. (*Why*, we might argue about, but *that* this is so is not contentious.) A fortiori, it is irrational to believe that I am both a fried egg and not a fried egg. It is important to emphasize this distinction right at the start, since the illicit slide between 'some' and 'all' is endemic in discussions of the question, as we will see.

I think that there is nothing wrong with believing some contradictions. I believe, for example, that it is rational (rationally possible—indeed, rationally obligatory) to believe that the Liar sentence is both true and false. I shall not argue for this directly here, though. I have discovered, in advocating views such as this, that audiences suppose them to be a priori unacceptable. When pressed as to why, they come up with a number of arguments. In what follows, I shall consider five of the most important, and show their lack of substance.

The five objections that we will look at can be summarized as follows:

1. Contradictions entail everything.
2. Contradictions can't be true.
3. Contradictions can't be believed rationally.
4. If contradictions were acceptable, people could never be rationally criticized.
5. If contradictions were acceptable, no one could deny anything.

I am sure that there must be other possible objections; but the above are the most fundamental that I have encountered. I will take them in that order. What I have to say about the first objection is the longest. This is because it lays the basis for all the others.

[1] The chapter is a written version of a lecture that was given at universities in South Africa, Canada, and the United States in 1996 and 1997. I am grateful to many audiences for their lively discussions. It is reprinted with only minor modifications from the *Journal of Philosophy*, 95 (1998), 410–26. I am grateful for permission to reprint.

OBJECTION 1: CONTRADICTIONS ENTAIL EVERYTHING

The first objection is as follows. Rational belief is closed under entailment, but a contradiction entails everything. Hence, if someone believed a contradiction, they ought to believe everything, which is too much.

I certainly agree that believing everything is too much: I have already said that there is an important difference between *some* and *all* here. Still, I take the argument to be unsound. For a start, it is not at all obvious that rational belief is closed under entailment. This seems to be the lesson of the 'paradox of the preface'. You write a (non-fictional) book on some topic—history, karate, cooking. You research it as thoroughly as possible. The evidence for the claims in your book, $\alpha_1, \ldots, \alpha_n$, is as convincing as empirically possible. Hence, you endorse them—rationally. None the less, as you are well aware, there is independent inductive evidence of a very strong kind that virtually all substantial factual books that have been written contain some false claims. Hence, you also believe $\neg(\alpha_1 \wedge \ldots \wedge \alpha_n)$—rationally. However, you do not believe $(\alpha_1 \wedge \ldots \wedge \alpha_n) \wedge \neg(\alpha_1 \wedge \ldots \wedge \alpha_n)$, a simple contradiction, even though this is a logical consequence of your beliefs. Rational belief is not, therefore, closed under logical consequence.

This is all just softening-up, though. The major problem with objection number one is the claim that contradictions entail everything: $\alpha, \neg\alpha \models \beta$, for all α and β. The Latin tag for this is *ex contradictione quodlibet*. I prefer the more colourful: *Explosion*. It is true that Explosion is a valid principle of inference in standard twentieth-century accounts of validity, such as those of intuitionism and the inappropriately called 'classical logic'. But this should be viewed in an historical perspective.

The earliest articulated formal logic was Aristotle's syllogistic. This was not explosive. To see this, merely consider the inference:

> Some men are mortals.
> No mortals are men.
> Hence all men are men.

This is not a valid syllogism, though the premises are inconsistent. According to Aristotle, some syllogisms with inconsistent premises are valid, some are not (*An.Pr.* $64^a 15$). Aristotle had a propositional logic as well as syllogistic. It was never clearly articulated, and what it was is rather unclear. However, for what it is worth, this does not seem to have been explosive either. In particular, a contradiction, $\alpha \wedge \neg\alpha$, does not entail its conjuncts.[2]

The Stoics did have an articulated propositional logic. But whilst one might try to extract Explosion from some of the theses that they endorsed, it is notable that it is not to be found in anything that survives from that period—and one would expect any principle as striking as this to have been made much of by the most

---

[2] See Priest (1999*a*).

notable critic of Stoicism, Sextus Empiricus. Presumably, then, Explosion was not taken to be correct by the Stoics.

So if Explosion is not to be found in Ancient Logic, where does it come from? The earliest appearance of the principle that I am aware of seems to be in the twelfth-century Paris logician, William of Soissons. At any rate, William was one of a school of logicians called the Parvipontinians, who were well known, not only for living by a small bridge, but also for defending Explosion.[3] After this time, the principle appears to be a contentious one in Medieval logic, accepted by some, such as Scotus; rejected by others, such as the fifteenth-century Cologne School.

The entrenchment of Explosion is, in fact, a relatively modern phenomenon. In the second half of the nineteenth-century, an account of negation—now often called 'Boolean negation'—was championed by Boole, Frege, and others. Boolean negation is explosive, and was incorporated in the first contemporary formal logic. This logic, now usually called classical logic (how inappropriate this name is should now be evident), was so great an improvement on traditional logic that it soon became entrenched. Whether this is because it enshrined the Natural Light of Pure Reason, or because it was the first cab off the rank, I leave the reader to judge.

There is, in fact, nothing sacrosanct about Boolean negation. One can be reminded of this, by the fact that intuitionists, who gave the second contemporary articulated formal logic, provide a different account of negation. Despite this, intuitionist logic is itself explosive. Logics in which Explosion fails have come to be called 'paraconsistent'. The modern construction of formal paraconsistent logics is more recent than anything I have mentioned so far. The idea appears to have occurred to a number of people, in very different countries, and independently, after the Second World War. There are now a number of approaches to paraconsistent logic, all with well-articulated proof-theories and model-theories.

I do not intend to go into details here. I will just give a model-theoretic account of one propositional paraconsistent logic, so that those unfamiliar with the area may have some idea of how things might work.[4] I assume familiarity with the classical propositional calculus. Consider a language with propositional parameters, $p, q, r, \ldots$ and connectives $\wedge$ (conjunction), $\vee$ (disjunction) and $\neg$ (negation). In classical logic, an evaluation is a *function* that assigns each formula one of 1 (true) or 0 (false). Instead of this, we now take an evaluation to be a *relation*, R, between formulas and truth values. Thus, given any formula, α, an evaluation, R, may relate it to just 1, just 0, both, or neither. If $R(\alpha, 1)$, α may be thought of as true under R; if $R(\alpha, 0)$, it may be thought of as false. Hence formulas related to both 1 and 0 are both true and false, and formulas related to neither, are neither true nor false.

---

[3] For references and more details of the following history of paraconsistency, see part 3 of Priest (2002).

[4] The logic is that of First Degree Entailment. For further details of all the approaches to paraconsistency, see Priest (2002).

As in the classical case, evaluations of propositional parameters are extended to all formulas by recursive conditions. The conditions for $\neg$ and $\wedge$ are as follows. (The conditions for $\vee$ are dual to those for $\wedge$, and may safely be left as an exercise.)

$R(\neg\alpha, 1)$ iff $R(\alpha, 0)$
$R(\neg\alpha, 0)$ iff $R(\alpha, 1)$

$R(\alpha \wedge \beta, 1)$ iff $R(\alpha, 1)$ and $R(\beta, 1)$
$R(\alpha \wedge \beta, 0)$ iff $R(\alpha, 0)$ or $R(\beta, 0)$

Thus, $\neg\alpha$ is true iff α is false, and vice versa. A conjunction is true iff both conjuncts are true; false iff at least one conjunct is false. All very familiar.

To complete the picture we need a definition of logical consequence. This also presents no surprises. An inference is valid iff whenever the premises are true, so is the conclusion. Thus, if Σ is a set of formulas:

$\Sigma \models \alpha$ iff for all R (if $R(\beta, 1)$ for all $\beta \in \Sigma$, $R(\alpha, 1)$)

It is now easy to see why the logic is paraconsistent. Choose an evaluation, R, that relates p to both 1 and 0, but relates q only to 0. Then it is easy enough to see that both p and $\neg p$ (and $p \wedge \neg p$) are true under R (and false as well, but at least true), whilst q is not. Hence $p, \neg p \not\models q$. For future reference, note that the same evaluation refutes the disjunctive syllogism: $p, \neg p \vee q \vdash q$.

The logic given here should look very familiar. It *is* very familiar. It is exactly the same as classical logic, except that one does not make the assumption, usually packed into textbooks of logic without comment, that truth and falsity in an interpretation are exclusive and exhaustive. The difference between classical logic and the above logic can therefore be depicted very simply. In classical logic, each interpretation partitions the set of formulas (Fig. 1.1). In the paraconsistent logic, an interpretation may partition in this way: classical interpretations are, after all, simply a special case. But in general, the partitioning looks like Fig. 1.2.

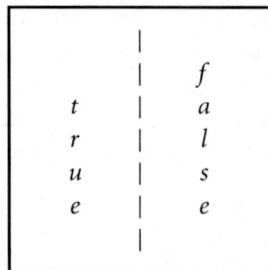

Fig. 1.1.

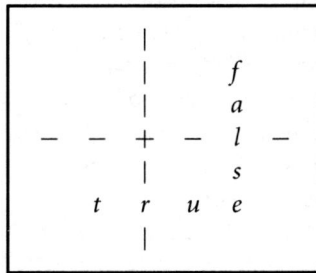

```
        |
        |        f
        |        a
 —   —  +  —  l  —
        |        s
     t  r  u  e
        |
```

FIG. 1.2.

The crucial question now, is: assuming that all the other assumptions packed into the story are right, should we, or should we not, countenance interpretations that correspond to the second picture? There is no quick way with this question. Each logic encapsulates a substantial metaphysical/semantical *theory*. It should be noted that a paraconsistent logician does not have to hold that truth itself behaves as in the second picture. They have to hold only that in defining validity one has to take into account interpretations that do. And though the claim that truth itself behaves like this is one argument for this conclusion, it is not the only one. If we think of interpretations as representing situations about which we reason, then interpretations of the second kind might be thought to represent 'impossible' situations that are inconsistent or incomplete, such as hypothetical, counterfactual, or fictional situations, or as situations about which we have incomplete or inconsistent information. One may well suppose that there are, in some relevant sense, such situations, and that they play an important metaphysical and/or semantical role.

More boldly, one may suppose that truth itself behaves according to the second picture, and hence that there must be at least one interpretation that does, namely, that interpretation which assigns truth values in accord with the actual. One cannot simply *assume* that it does not. Here, again, lie profound metaphysical issues. Even the founder of Logic, Aristotle, did not think that truth satisfies the first picture. According to him, statements about future contingents, such as the claim that there will be a sea battle tomorrow, are neither true nor false (unless you live in Bolivia).[5] The top left square of Fig. 1.2 is therefore occupied. And modern logic has provided many other possible candidates for this square: statements employing non-denoting terms, statements about undecidable sentences in science or mathematics, category mistakes and other 'nonsense', and so on.

The thought that the bottom right corner might also have denizens is one much less familiar to modern philosophers. Yet there are plausible candidates. Let me give two briefly.[6] The first concerns paradoxes of self-reference. Let us take the

---

[5] *De Interpretatione*, ch. 9. He seems to think that this is consistent with the Law of Excluded Middle, however. At least, he defends this law in *Metaphysics* Γ.

[6] These and others are discussed at much greater length in Priest (1987).

Liar as an example. The natural and most obvious principle concerning truth is encapsulated in the T-schema: for any sentence, α: $T\langle\alpha\rangle \leftrightarrow \alpha$. I use '$T$' here as a truth predicate, and angle brackets as a name-forming device. With standard self-referential techniques, we can now produce a sentence, β, that says of itself that it is not true: $\neg T\langle\beta\rangle \leftrightarrow \beta$. Substituting β in the T-scheme and juggling a little gives $\beta \wedge \neg\beta$. Prima facie, then, β is a sentence that is both true and false, and so occupies the bottom right corner.

Another example: I walk out of the room; for an instant, I am symmetrically poised, one foot in, one foot out, my centre of gravity lying on the vertical plane containing the centre of gravity of the door. Am I in or not in the room? By symmetry, I am neither in, rather than not in, nor not in, rather than in. The Pure Light of Reason therefore countenances only two answers to the question: I am both in and not in, or neither in nor not in. Thus, we certainly appear to have a denizen of either the top left or the bottom right quarter. But wait a minute. If I am neither in nor not in, then I am not (in) and not (not in). By the law of double negation, I am both in and not in. (And even without it, I am both not in and not not in, which is still a contradiction.) Hence we have a denizen of the bottom right.

There is, of course, much more to be said about both these examples. But I do not intend to say anything further here.[7] The point is simply to illustrate some of the semantic/metaphysical issues that must be hammered out even to decide whether truth itself satisfies the first or the second picture. To suppose that the answer is obvious, or that the issue can be settled by definition is simple dogmatism.

There is a famous defence of classical logic, by Quine, that comes very close to this, in fact. Someone who takes there to be interpretations corresponding to the second picture just 'doesn't know what they are talking about': to change the logic is to 'change the subject'. It is changing the subject only if one assumes *in the first place* that validity is to be defined in terms only of interpretations that satisfy the first picture—which is exactly what is at issue here. Two logicians who subscribe to different accounts of validity are arguing about the same subject, just as much as two physicists who subscribe to different accounts of motion.[8]

---

[7] Though since the second example is not as familiar as the first, let me add one comment. Let us represent the sentence 'GP is in the room' by α. An obvious move at this point is to suggest that α is, in fact, a denizen of the top left quarter, but that one cannot express this fact by saying that I am neither in nor not in the room. What one has to say is that neither α nor its negation is true, $\neg T\langle\alpha\rangle \wedge \neg T\langle\neg\alpha\rangle$. This is certainly not an explicit contradiction. Unfortunately, it, too, soon gives one. The T-schema for α and $\neg\alpha$ tell us that $T\langle\alpha\rangle \leftrightarrow \alpha$ and $T\langle\neg\alpha\rangle \leftrightarrow \neg\alpha$. Contraposing and chaining together gives: $\neg T\langle\neg\alpha\rangle \leftrightarrow T\langle\alpha\rangle$, and we are back with a contradiction. A natural move here is to deny the T-schema for α or $\neg\alpha$ (presumably these stand or fall together). But on what ground can one reasonably do this? 'GP is in the room' is a perfectly ordinary sentence of English. It is meaningful, and so must have truth conditions. (In fact, most of the time it is simply true or false.) These (or something equivalent to them) are exactly what the T-schema gives. Compare this with the case of the Liar. Many have been tempted to reject the T-schema for the Liar sentence on the ground that the sentence is semantically defective in some way. No such move seems to be even a prima facie possibility in the present case.

[8] For references to Quine, with further discussion, see Priest (2003).

And now, finally, to return to the main point. I have not shown that Explosion fails, that one ought to take into the scope of logic situations that are inconsistent and/or incomplete, though I do take it that when the dust settles, this will be seen to be the case, and that even truth itself requires the second picture.[9] The point of the above discussion is simply to show that the failure of Explosion is a plausible logico-metaphysical one, and that one cannot simply *assume* otherwise without begging the question.

OBJECTION 2: CONTRADICTIONS CAN'T BE TRUE

Let us turn now to objection number two. This is to the effect that contradictions can't be true. Since one ought to believe only what is true, contradictions ought not to be believed.

This argument appeals to the Law of Non-Contradiction (LNC): nothing is both true and false. The first thing we need to do is distinguish clearly between the LNC and Explosion. They are very different. For a start, as we have seen, Explosion is a relative newcomer on the logical scene. The LNC is not. It is true that some have challenged it: some Presocratics, such as Heraclitus; some Neoplatonists, such as Cusanus; and some dialecticians, such as Hegel. But since the time of Aristotle, it is a principle that has been very firmly entrenched in Western philosophy. (Its place in Eastern philosophy is much less secure.) The view that the LNC fails, that some contradictions are true, is called *dialetheism*. As we have already seen, one does not have to be a dialetheist to subscribe to the correctness of a paraconsistent logic, though if one is, one will. As we also saw, though, there are arguments that push us towards accepting dialetheism. Is there any reason why one should reject these a priori? Why, in other words, should we accept the LNC?

The *locus classicus* of its defence is Aristotle's *Metaphysics*, Γ4. It is a striking fact about the Law that there has not been a sustained defence of it *since* Aristotle (at least, that I am aware of). Were his arguments so good that they settled the matter? Hardly. There are about seven or eight arguments in the chapter (it depends how you count). The first occupies half the chapter. It is long, convoluted, and tortured. It is not at all clear *how* it is supposed to work, let alone *that* it works. The other arguments in the chapter are short, often little more than throw-away remarks, and are at best, dubious. Indeed, most of them are clearly aimed at attacking the view that *all* contradictions are true (or even that someone can *believe* that all contradictions are true). Aristotle, in fact, slides back and forth between 'all' and 'some', with gay abandon. His defence of the LNC is therefore of little help.[10]

---

[9] Though, as a matter of fact, I think that its top left quarter is empty. See Priest (1987), ch. 4.

[10] For a detailed analysis of Aristotle's arguments, see Priest (1998).

So what other arguments are there for the LNC? Very few that I am aware of, and none that survive much thought. Let me mention four here. The first two, some have claimed, are to be found in Aristotle. I doubt it, but let us not go into this here.

According to the first argument, contradictions have no content, no meaning. If so, then, a fortiori, they have no true content: contradictions cannot be true. The first thing to note about this objection is that it is not only an objection against dialetheism, but also against classical logic. For in classical logic, contradictions have *total* content, they entail everything. One who subscribes to orthodox logic cannot, therefore, wield this objection.

There have been some who endorsed different propositional logics, according to which contradictions do entail nothing, and so have no content.[11] But the claim that contradictions have no content does not stand up to independent inspection. If contradictions had no content, there would be nothing to disagree with when someone uttered one, which there (usually) is. Contradictions do, after all, have meaning. If they did not, we could not even understand someone who asserted a contradiction, and so evaluate what they say as false (or maybe true). We might not understand what could have brought a person to assert such a thing, but that is a different matter—and the same is equally true of someone who, in broad daylight, asserts the clearly meaningful 'It is night.'

A second objection (to be found e.g. in McTaggart) is to the effect that if contradictions could be true, *nothing* could be meaningful. The argument here appeals to the thought that something is meaningful only if it *excludes* something (*omnis determino est negatio*): a claim that rules out nothing, says nothing. Moreover, it continues, if α does not rule out $\neg\alpha$, it rules out nothing. An obvious failing with this argument is, again, the slide from 'some' to 'all'. Violation of the LNC requires only that some statements do not rule out their negations (whatever that is supposed to mean). The argument depends on the claim that *nothing* rules out its own negation.

But there is a much more fundamental flaw in the argument than this. The premiss that a proposition is not meaningful unless it rules something out is just plain false. Merely consider the claim 'Everything is true.' This rules nothing out: it entails everything. Yet it is quite meaningful (it is, after all, false). If you are in any doubt over this, merely consider its negation 'Something is not true.' This is clearly true—and so meaningful. And how could a meaningful sentence have a meaningless negation?

A third argument for the LNC, and one that is typical of many, starts from the claim that the correct truth conditions for negation are as follows:

$\neg\alpha$ is true iff α is not true.

---

[11] See Priest (1999*a*).

Now suppose that $\alpha \wedge \neg\alpha$ is true. Then assuming that conjunction behaves normally, α is true, and $\neg\alpha$ is true. Hence by the truth conditions of negation, α is both true and not true, which is impossible.

It is not difficult to see what is wrong with this argument. For a start, the truth conditions of negation are contentious. (Compare them with those given in the previous section.) More importantly, why should one suppose that it is impossible for α to be both true and not true? Because it is a contradiction. But it is precisely the impossibility of having true contradictions that we were supposed to be arguing for. The argument, therefore, begs the question, as do many of the other arguments that I am aware of.[12]

The fourth, and final, argument I shall mention is an inductive one. As we review the kinds of situations that we witness, very few of them would seem to be contradictory. Socrates is never both seated and not seated; Brisbane is firmly in Australia, and not not in it. Hence, by induction, no contradictions are true. Note that one does not have to suppose that logical principles are a posteriori for this form of argument to work. One can collect a-posteriori evidence even for a priori principles. For example, one verifies $\alpha \vee \neg\alpha$ every time one verifies α.

The flaws of this argument are apparent enough, though. It is all too clear that the argument may be based on what Wittgenstein called 'an inadequate diet of examples'. Maybe Socrates *is* both sitting and not sitting sometimes: at the instant he rises. This, being instantaneous, is not something we observe. We can tell it to be so only by a-priori analysis. Worse, counter-examples to the principle are staring us in the face. Think, for example, of the Liar. Most would set an example such as this aside, and suppose there to be something wrong with it. But this may be short-sighted. Consider the Euclidean principle that the whole must be larger than its parts. This principle seemed to be obvious to many people for a long time. Apparent counter-examples were known from late Antiquity: for example, the set of even numbers appeared to be the same size as the set of all numbers. But these examples were set aside, and just taken to show the incoherence of the notion of infinity. With the nineteenth century all this changed. There is nothing incoherent about this behaviour at all: it is paradigmatic of infinite collections. The Euclidean principle holds only for finite collections; and people's acceptance of it was due to a poor induction from unrepresentative cases. In the same way, once one gets rid of the idea, in the form of Explosion, that inconsistency is incoherent, the Liar and similar examples can be seen as paradigm citizens of a realm to which our eyes are newly opened (we can call it, by analogy with set-theory, the transconsistent). In any case, the inductive argument to the LNC is simply a poor one.

It is sometimes said that dialetheism is a position based on sand. In fact, I think, it is quite the opposite: it is the LNC that is based on sand. It appears to have no

---

[12] In particular, one may argue for the LNC from Explosion, assuming that not all contradictions are true. But an appeal to Explosion would beg the question, as we have already seen.

rational basis; and the historical adherence to it is simply dogma. Hence—and finally to return to the second objection—it fails.

OBJECTION 3: CONTRADICTIONS CAN'T BE BELIEVED RATIONALLY

The third objection is that even if contradictions could be true, they can't be believed rationally, consistency being a constraint on rationality; hence one ought not to believe a contradiction since this would be irrational.

We have already seen, in answer to the first objection, that this objection fails. The paradox of the preface shows that it can be quite rational to have inconsistent beliefs. Hence, consistency is not an absolute constraint on rationality. The rational person apportions their beliefs according to the evidence; and if the evidence is for inconsistent propositions, so be it.

There is, of course, more to the story than this. To approach it, let me take what will appear to be a digression for a moment. Have you ever talked to a flat-earther, or someone with really bizarre religious beliefs—not one who subscribes to such a view in a thoughtless way, but someone who has considered the issue very carefully? If you have, then you will know that it is virtually impossible to show their view to be wrong by finding a knock-down objection. If one points out to the flat-earther that we have sailed round the earth, they will say that one has, in fact, only traversed a circle on a flat surface. If one points out that we have been into space and seen the earth to be round, they will reply that it only *appears* round, and that light, up there, does not move in straight lines, or that the whole space-flight story is a CIA put-up, etc. In a word, their views are perfectly consistent. This does not stop them being irrational, however. How to diagnose their irrationality is a nice point, but I think that one may put it down to a constant invoking of ad hoc hypotheses. Whenever one thinks one has a flat-earther in a corner, new claims are pulled in, apparently from nowhere, just to get them out of trouble.

What this illustrates is that there are criteria for rationality other than consistency, and that some of these are even more powerful than consistency. The point is, in fact, a familiar one from the philosophy of science. There are many features of belief that are rational virtues, such as simplicity, problem-solving ability, non-adhocness, fruitfulness, and, let us grant, consistency. However, these criteria are all independent, and may even be orthogonal, pulling in opposite directions. Now what should one do if, for a certain belief, all the criteria pull towards acceptance, except consistency—which pulls the other way? It may be silly to be a democrat about this, and simply count the number of criteria on each side; but it seems natural to suppose that the combined force of the other criteria may trump inconsistency. In such a case, then, it is rational to have an inconsistent belief.

The situation I have outlined is an abstract one; but it seems to me that it, or something like it, already obtains with respect to theories of truth. Since the abstract point is already sufficient answer to the objection we are dealing with, I do not want to defend the example in detail here; still, it will serve to put some flesh on the abstract bones. The following is a simple account of truth. Truth is a principle that is characterized formally by the T-schema: for every sentence, α, $T\langle\alpha\rangle \leftrightarrow \alpha$ (for a suitable conditional connective). And that's an end on't. (There may be more to be said about truth, but nothing that can be captured in a formalism.) This account is inconsistent: when suitable self-referential machinery is present, say in the form of arithmetic, the Liar paradox is forthcoming. Yet the inconsistencies are isolated. In particular, it can be shown that, when things are suitably set up, inconsistencies do not percolate into the purely arithmetic machinery. In fact, it can be shown that any sentence that is grounded (in Kripke's sense) behaves consistently.[13] What are the alternatives to such an account? There is a welter of them: Tarski's, Kripke's, Gupta and Herzberger's, Barwise and Perry's, McGee's, etc., etc. These may all have the virtue of consistency, but the other virtues are thinly distributed amongst them. They often have strong ad hoc elements; they are complex, usually involving transfinite hierarchies; they have a tendency to pose just as many problems as they solve; and it is not clear that, in the last instance, they really solve the problem they are supposed to: they all seem subject to extended paradoxes of some kind.[14] It seems to me that rationality speaks very strongly in favour of the simple inconsistent theory. This is exactly a concrete case of the abstract kind I have described.

Naturally, it may happen that someone, a hundred years hence, will come up with a consistent account of truth with none of these problems, in which case, what it is rational to believe may well change. But that is neither here nor there. Rational belief about anything is a fallible matter. It is a mistake to believe where the evidence does not point; but it is equally a mistake not to believe where the evidence points.

I have argued that it may well be rational to believe a contradiction, and shown how this may arise. If there is sufficient evidence that something is true, one ought, rationally, to accept it. Let me consider just one reply. It is natural to suppose that there is a dual principle here: if there is sufficient evidence that something is false, one ought, rationally, to reject it. If, therefore, there is strong evidence that contradictories, α and $\neg\alpha$, are both true, there is evidence that both are also false. One ought, then, to reject both.

No. In the appropriate sense, truth trumps falsity. Truth is, by its nature, the aim of cognitive processes such as belief. (This is the 'more' to truth that I referred to above.) It is constitutive of truth that that is what one ought to accept. Falsity, by contrast, is merely truth of negation. It has no independent epistemological

---

[13] For a proof of this, see Priest (2002), s. 8.
[14] See Priest (1987), ch. 1.

force. One should not necessarily, therefore, reject something simply because its negation turns out to be true.

The situation may well be different with respect to untruth. At least arguably, if something is shown not to be true then one ought to reject it.[15] But one cannot suppose that falsity and untruth are the same thing, if the second picture drawn in connection with objection number one is correct. If one does so suppose, as epistemologists traditionally have done, then something shown to be false, is shown to be untrue, and so not a target for belief. This may be why the dual principle has its appeal. But once one sees that truth and falsity (i.e. truth of negation) cannot always be separated, like the elements of a constant-boiling mixture, it becomes clear that this is overly simplistic.

At any rate, we have seen more than enough to answer objection number three.

OBJECTION 4: IF CONTRADICTIONS WERE ACCEPTABLE, PEOPLE COULD NEVER BE RATIONALLY CRITICIZED

The fourth objection also concerns rationality, and is to the effect that if contradictions were acceptable, no one could be rationally criticized for the views that they hold. The thought here is that if you hold some view, and I object to it, there is nothing, rationally, to stop you maintaining both your original view *and* my objection.

The most obvious failing of this argument is that it makes the familiar and illicit slide from 'some' to 'all'. The mere fact that some contradictions are rationally acceptable does not entail that all are. The charge 'you accept some contradictions to be true, so why shouldn't you believe any contradiction to be so?' is as silly as the charge 'you believe something to be true, so why shouldn't you believe anything to be so?'

It might be argued that if it is logically possible for any contradiction to be true (as it is in the semantics we looked at in reply to objection one), then all contradictions are rationally acceptable. This, though, most certainly does not follow either. The fact that something is a logical possibility does not entail that it is rational to believe it. It is logically possible that I am a fried egg, though believing that I am is ground for certifiable insanity. As we saw in reply to the last objection, there is a lot more to rationality than consistency. A view, such as that the earth is flat, may be quite consistent (and so logically possible in traditional terms), and yet quite irrational.

A person's views may be rationally criticized if they can be shown to entail something that is rationally unacceptable. This might be a contradiction, but it might be some non-contradiction. Some non-contradictions, e.g. that I am a fried

---

[15] Though one may well contest this too. See Priest (1993).

egg, are, in fact, better than some contradictions, e.g. that the Liar sentence is both true and false. In the last instance, what is rationally acceptable, and what is not, is likely to be a holistic matter, to be determined by the sort of criteria I discussed in response to the last objection. Let me illustrate again. I argued there that an inconsistent account of truth, which endorsed the T-schema, was preferable to the numerous consistent accounts available. Suppose that it turned out, in defending the inconsistent view, that it had to be shored up in the same methodologically unsatisfactory ways as extant consistent accounts—e.g. to avoid strengthened paradoxes—until it was just as complex and contrived. It would then cease to be rational to accept it. The fact that one can accept some contradictions would do nothing to help the matter.

This is a perfectly adequate reply to the objection, but let me say a little more. I am frequently asked for a criterion as to when contradictions are acceptable and when they are not. It would be nice if there were a substantial answer to this question—or even if one could give a partial answer, in the form of some algorithm to demonstrate that an area of discourse is contradiction-free. But I doubt that this is possible. Nor is this a matter for surprise. Few would now seriously suppose that one can give an algorithm—or any other informative criterion—to determine when it is rational to accept something. There is no reason why the fact that something has a certain syntactic form—be it $p \wedge \neg p$ or anything else—should change this. One can determine the acceptability of any given contradiction, as of anything else, only on its individual merits.

Despite this, I do think that there are general reasons as to why contradictions are a priori improbable. Classical logicians, who hold that contradictions all have probability 0, should agree with this! But it may reasonably be asked why one should suppose this to be so, once one has given up the assumption that that probability is 0. The answer to this question is simply that the statistical frequency of true contradictions in practice is low. This low frequency suffices to determine a low probability.

How do we know that true contradictions have a low frequency? Return to the inductive argument for the LNC that we considered in connection with objection number two. I pointed out there how weak this was as an argument for the *universality* of contradiction-freedom. But as an argument for the infrequency of contradictions it is much better. The counter-examples to the universality of the LNC are of very particular sorts (involving self-reference, or states of affairs that are but instantaneous, etc.), and we do not deal with these kinds of situations very often.

As a measure of this fact, recall the disjunctive syllogism ($\alpha, \neg\alpha \vee \beta \vdash \beta$). This is not valid in the semantics we looked at. Yet we use it all the time in practice, and rarely does it lead us astray. It will lead us astray only when there is a situation where α is both true and false, and β is not true. Hence, there are few such situations. This could be for two reasons. The first is that there are few αs which are both true and false; the second is that there are few βs which are not true. But we may rule out the second possibility: if this were the case, then we would rarely go wrong in *any* conclusion we draw, but we do. Hence, the frequency of true contradictions is low.

The fact that contradictions have low probability grounds the fact that inconsistency is a rational black mark. If we have views that are inconsistent then we are probably incorrect. We should go back and examine why we hold such a view, and what the alternatives are. We may find that we would be better off going a different way. But we *may* find that there are no better ways to go. In which case, we may just have to conclude that the improbable is the case. After all, the improbable happens sometimes. We would seem to be in exactly this situation with respect to theories of truth and the Liar. In one way or another, we have been over this ground for over 2,000 years—for the last 100 years very intensively—and no satisfactory consistent theory has been found. At any rate, inconsistency provides a prima facie ground for rejecting a view. One cannot *simply* accept a contradiction. There is other work to be done. This provides another answer to objection number four.[16]

OBJECTION 5: IF CONTRADICTIONS WERE ACCEPTABLE, NO ONE COULD DENY ANYTHING

The final objection takes us into new territory, one concerning public speech. The argument here is to the effect that if contradictions were acceptable, then no one would have a way of denying anything: whenever they asserted $\neg\alpha$, this would not show that they rejected α, for they might accept both α and $\neg\alpha$.

To discuss this argument, we first need to be clear about asserting and denying.[17] These are speech acts, like questioning or commanding. Which ones? If I assert something, α, then this is a speech act whose intention is to get the hearer to believe α, or at least, believe that I believe α—with whatever Gricean sophistication one may wish to add. If I deny something, α, then this is a speech act whose intention is to get the hearer to reject α (cast it out from their beliefs, and/or refuse to accept it), or at least, to get the listener to believe that I reject it—with whatever Gricean sophistication one may wish to add.

Now, prima facie, at least, assertion and denial are quite distinct kinds of speech act, and this is the way they have often been understood traditionally, e.g. in the *Port Royale* logic (though of course, the point was not put in terms of speech acts, which is a modern invention). But Frege suggested, and many now accept, that denial may be reduced to assertion by the equation:

denial = assertion of negation

[16] For a further discussion of the issue, see Priest (1987), chs. 7 and 8.
[17] The following follows Priest (1993). The discussion is taken further in Priest (1999b).

This identity is incorrect. To assert the negation of something is *not* necessarily to deny it. When I, for example, assert the negation of the Liar sentence, I am not denying it. After all, I *accept* it, and intend you to do the same. Nor does this really have anything to do with dialetheism. We, all of us, discover sometimes—maybe by the prompting of some Socratic questioner—that our beliefs are inconsistent. We assert α, and then a little later assert $\neg\alpha$. We may well wish to revise our views in the light of this—we usually do. But that is not the point here. The point is simply that in asserting $\neg\alpha$, we are not denying α. We *do* accept α; that, after all, is the problem. Hence, to assert a negation is not necessarily to deny—and the problem that this objection points to is just as much a problem for the classical logician as for the dialetheist.

More importantly, and conversely, one can deny something without asserting a negation. One can use a certain tone of voice, or body language (like thumping the table). The issue is simply one of how to convey one's intentions. This is the solution to the problem. In fact, one *can* often deny something by asserting its negation. (Thus, this objection, again, makes the now very familiar slide from 'some' to 'all'.) Whether or not one is denying, just depends. This raises the question of how one knows whether someone who utters a negated sentence is asserting or is denying. I doubt that there is any simple way of answering this question. In any case, it is of a kind very familiar from speech-act theory. Someone utters 'The door is open.' This could be an assertion, a question, a command. How does one know? Well, one has to determine the utterer's intentions; to do this one needs to know all kinds of things about language, the context, the social power-relations, etc. Never mind if we don't know exactly *how* we do it. We do it all the time.

Before we leave the subject, let me mention one final, related, point. It is sometimes said that it is impossible even to express contradictory beliefs: if someone asserts α, and then asserts $\neg\alpha$, they have not expressed contradictory beliefs; their second utterance merely 'cancels out' the first.[18] This could be an appeal to the claim that contradictions have no content, which I have already dealt with. But more likely it is an appeal to the idea that asserting a negation is a denial. To deny something asserted is to 'cancel out' the assertion, in the sense that it leaves the hearer no coherent way of interpreting the utterer's beliefs, short of supposing that they have changed their mind. But as we have seen, uttering a negation may just be a simple assertion: there need be no cancellation of any kind.

The ambiguity of 'assertion' (between the content of what is asserted, and the act of assertion), bedevils the history of logic until Frege. The ambiguity of 'denial' (between the content of a negated sentence, and an act of denial) may still bedevil it, as objections of the kind we have been looking at demonstrate.[19]

---

[18] e.g. Strawson runs this line. For references and further discussion, see Priest (1998), s. 13.

[19] I have heard it suggested that once one distinguishes between negation and denial there will be versions of the Liar paradox, formulated in terms of denial, that a paraconsistent solution cannot handle. This is false. The standard Liar is a sentence, α, of the form $\neg T\langle\alpha\rangle$. Let us write $\dashv$ as a force

We have now considered all the supposed a priori objections I started by enumerating. The sophist Gorgias argued that there is no truth; and even if there were, you could not know it; and even if you could, you could not express it. The arguments we have been looking at might be summarized, loosely, by saying, similarly: a contradiction cannot be true; but even if it could be, you could not know it; and even if you could, you could not express it. The arguments, as we have seen, have no more force than Gorgias' arguments. So what's so bad about contradictions? Maybe nothing.

REFERENCES

PRIEST, G. (1987), *In Contradiction*, Dordrecht: Martinus Nijhoff.

—— (1993), 'Can Contradictions be True? II', *Proceedings of the Aristotelian Society, Suppl. Vol.* 67, 35–54.

—— (1995), 'Gaps and Gluts: Reply to Parsons', *Canadian Journal of Philosophy* 25, 57–66.

—— (1998), 'To Be *and* Not to Be—that is the Answer. On Aristotle on the Law of Non Contradiction', *Philosophiegeschichte und Logische Analyse* 1, 91–130.

—— (1999a), 'Negation as Cancellation, and Connexivism', *Topoi* 18, 141–8.

—— (1999b), 'What Not? A Dialetheic Account of Negation', D. Gabbay and H. Wansing (eds.), *What is Negation?*, Dordrecht: Kluwer Academic Publishers, 101–20.

—— (2002), 'Paraconsistent Logic', D. Gabbay and F. Guenthner (eds.), *Handbook of Philosophical Logic*, 2nd edn., Dordrecht: Kluwer Academic Publishers, vol. 6, ch. 4.

—— (2003), 'On Alternative Geometries, Arithmetics and Logics; a Tribute to Łukasiewicz', *Studia Logica* 74, 441–68.

operator, indicating denial. The analogue would be a sentence, α, such that α is $\dashv T\langle\alpha\rangle$. But this makes no sense, since $\dashv$ is not part of a propositional content. We can formulate a proposition, α, whose content is 'I deny that α.' Does this pose problems? Well, if I deny it, then it is true, and presumably obviously so to me. So I ought not to deny it. Conversely, if I don't deny it, then it is false, and again, presumably, obviously so to me. So I ought to deny it. In either case, then, I am going to fail an obligation. Perhaps, in the end, one just has to live with this fact. It is not a contradiction (and even if it were, isolated contradictions need not be a problem for a dialetheist). Moreover, the dialetheist does not even have to agree with the argument. As we have already seen in reply to objection number three, it is not necessary to reject (and so deny) something simply because it is false. A classical logician, on the other hand, for whom this is just as much a problem, cannot make the same move. Note that there are other paradoxes in the vicinity here that are even more embarrassing for a classical logician. See Priest (1995), s. 4.

II

What is the LNC?

2

On the Formalization of the Law of
Non-Contradiction

Ross T. Brady

The Law of Non-Contradiction (LNC) is generally understood to say that there are to be no contradictions in the logic. However, there are two ways of viewing this. One is as a *logical law* which *enforces* the consistency of the formal system concerned, ensuring that it, and presumably its deductive extensions, are free from contradiction. The other is as a *meta-theoretic statement* regarding the formal system, saying that there are no contradictions in it, i.e. the simple consistency of the formal system. This would need to be proved true on a system-by-system basis. I take it that the LNC is meant to mean the former, rather than just the meta-theoretic result, for otherwise how is one to understand the word 'law'? Laws are presumably meant to be enforced. De Morgan's Laws, once proved, enforce the logical equivalence between negated conjunctions and the disjunctions of their negated components. So, we will proceed to examine some candidates for such a law, with a view to finding a suitable form. We examine two candidates: the typical formula, $\sim(A \& \sim A)$, and the typical rule, $A, \sim A \Rightarrow B$.

1. THE TEXTBOOK FORMALIZATION

In textbooks on classical logic, $\sim(A \& \sim A)$ is normally regarded as the LNC, negating any contradiction of the form $A \& \sim A$. In order to test this formalization we first see if we can construct a counter-example. Here, we consider logics in general, as we are looking for a formalization of the LNC that we can put into any logic that, it is hoped, will guarantee the absence of contradiction in that logic. We will examine the scenario where both $\sim(A \& \sim A)$ and a contradiction are present and find an example.

It is interesting to note that when both $\sim(A \& \sim A)$ and a contradiction p and $\sim$p, say, are present we can generate another contradiction p & $\sim$p and $\sim$(p & $\sim$p), by adjunction and instantiation. Again, we can derive (p & $\sim$p) & $\sim$(p & $\sim$p) and $\sim$((p & $\sim$p) & $\sim$(p & $\sim$p)), another contradiction. This carries on ad infinitum, thus generating an infinite string of contradictions from one contradiction. So, it

I am grateful to Graham Priest and two referees for help in refocusing this chapter and for indicating problems with some details of argument.

is quite odd for $\sim$(A & $\sim$A) to generate further contradictions when it is supposed to prevent contradictions from occurring in the first place.

An example of a logical system embodying all this would be the Dialectical Set Theory of Brady [1989], which is based on the logic DK, and includes the Axiom of Comprehension of naïve set theory. The weak relevant logic DK has as theorems $\sim$(A & $\sim$A) and A v $\sim$A, the latter being used to establish Russell's Paradox, a contradiction. Despite being inconsistent, this system is proved in Brady [1989] to be non-trivial, i.e. not all formulae are theorems.

Thus, by the example given for the scenario, we have shown that, if $\sim$(A & $\sim$A) is present in a logic, a contradiction may still occur. This then shows that $\sim$(A & $\sim$A) does not formalize a law of non-contradiction, as it does not enforce consistency, and that the textbook account is misleading at the very least.

However, before leaving $\sim$(A & $\sim$A), let us consider two interesting and related topics.

2. A PUZZLE FOR DE MORGAN NEGATION

Any account of the LNC must be secured by an intuitive concept of negation. I believe such a concept is De Morgan negation, introduced as an extension of the De Morgan lattice for first-degree entailments (see Anderson and Belnap 1975: 194, for definition of De Morgan lattice, and ibid. 190–7, for De Morgan negation). De Morgan negation is used for all relevant logics, from B through to R, and includes all De Morgan's Laws, all contraposition laws, and both forms of double negation (see Routley *et al.* 1982: ch. 4, for a definitive treatment of relevant logics). This negation is also given in Brady [1996] and [forthcoming], pictured as the neat symmetric mirror-image concept, and generated within a content semantics (see also Brady [1988] on this semantics).

According to the mirror-image concept of negation, there is a line of symmetry separating each positive sentence from its corresponding negative sentence, and sentences equivalent to their own negations lie on the line. So, double negation holds, in that there is a one-one correspondence across the line of symmetry. Further, every entailment has a corresponding contraposed entailment involving negatives of the relevant sentences and these negative sentences and their entailments correspond similarly to the original sentences and their entailments. Thus, the negated sentences and their entailments form a mirror-image of their positive counterparts, and vice versa, with the mirror being the line of symmetry. The two properties of negation that yield this mirror-image account are double negation and contraposition, which then yield all the De Morgan's Laws, using basic properties of conjunction and disjunction, as in a De Morgan lattice (see Anderson and Belnap 1975: 358). This thus gives a very neat intuitive picture of

De Morgan negation, which has been argued for and developed in Brady [1996] and [forthcoming].

It is worth pointing out that there is a puzzling relationship between $\sim(A \& \sim A)$ and $A \vee \sim A$: they are logically equivalent. This follows by the De Morgan's Law, $A \vee B \leftrightarrow \sim(\sim A \& \sim B)$, together with commutation of '&' or 'v' and double negation. In the weaker relevant logics, e.g. B, DJ, and RW, both $\sim(A \& \sim A)$ and $A \vee \sim A$ are non-theorems, whilst in the stronger R, E, and T both $\sim(A \& \sim A)$ and $A \vee \sim A$ are theorems.

There is an interesting puzzle here in that the Law of Excluded Middle, $A \vee \sim A$, under interpretation, would require that either A or $\sim A$ be true, i.e. at least one of them be true, whereas $\sim(A \& \sim A)$ would seem to say that not both A and $\sim A$ are true, i.e. at most one of them is true. Their equivalence is understandable, from the point of view of classical logic, as A and $\sim A$ take opposite truth-values. A version of this equivalence can also be seen for relevant/paraconsistent logics with the Routley-Meyer semantics, via the *-world, with use of modelling condition $a^{**} = a$. (See Routley *et al.* 1982: ch. 4 again for details of this semantics.) Let $I(A \vee \sim A, a) = T$. Then $I(A, a) = T$ or $I(\sim A, a) = T$, and $I(\sim A, a^*] = F$ or $I(A, a^*) = F$, and hence $I(\sim A \& A, a^*) = F$. So, $I(\sim(A \& \sim A), a) = T$. The argument also holds in the converse direction. Here, at least one of A or $\sim A$ is true at world a iff at least one of A and $\sim A$ is false at a*, i.e. at most one of A and $\sim A$ is true at world a*. So $\sim(A \& \sim A)$ does actually say that at most one of A and $\sim A$ is true, but at the *-world rather than the world itself. This does make sense for these logics as the negation of a formula at a world a is evaluated through its *-world. Unlike $\sim(A \& \sim A)$, $A \vee \sim A$ is evaluated at the world a in the expected way, not having the outside negation. So, for relevant/paraconsistent logics, $\sim(A \& \sim A)$ does not say that not both A and $\sim A$ are true, at the same world a, given that a and a* are distinct. However, for classical logic a = a*, at least one of A or $\sim A$ is true iff at most one of A and $\sim A$ is true, as mentioned above.

3. BRAZILIAN LOGIC

Let us look at the Brazilian paraconsistent logic P of Arruda and da Costa [1984], which includes $A \vee \sim A$ and $\sim\sim A \rightarrow A$, but not any of $\sim(A \& \sim A)$, the other half of double negation, $A \rightarrow \sim\sim A$, the De Morgan's Law, $A \vee \sim B \rightarrow \sim(\sim A \& B)$, and both halves of the contraposition rules, $A \rightarrow B \Rightarrow \sim B \rightarrow \sim A$ and $\sim B \rightarrow \sim A \Rightarrow A \rightarrow B$. Thus, their negation does behave very differently from the De Morgan negation of relevant logics. Arruda and da Costa [1984] introduce P mainly to establish the non-triviality of certain inconsistent set theories with an unrestricted Comprehension Axiom, but P is similar to other Brazilian logics, in its exclusion of $\sim(A \& \sim A)$ and inclusion of $A \vee \sim A$. They exclude $\sim(A \& \sim A)$, purportedly to enable contradictions to appear in logical systems, and their inclusion of A v ∼A enables Russell's Paradox, in particular, to be derived in set theories with an unrestricted Comprehension Axiom. This shows that one can have a contradiction without ∼(A & ∼A).

However, the rationale for the exclusion of ∼(A & ∼A) does not hold up, as one can not only have contradictions with or without ∼(A & ∼A), but one can also have consistency with or without ∼(A & ∼A). An example of a contradictory logic with ∼(A & ∼A) is Dialectical Set Theory, discussed above in s. 1. Also, the inclusion of ∼(A & ∼A) would repair much, if not all, of the damage to De Morgan negation. An example of a consistent logic with ∼(A & ∼A) is classical logic, and an example without is the weak relevant logic DJ of Brady [1996] and [forthcoming]. Indeed, this leaves ∼(A & ∼A) totally independent of contradiction.

4. THE SPREAD LAW

In a classical context, from a contradiction, one can derive any formula including further contradictions, by applying the Spread Law, A, ∼A ⇒ B. So, classically, the Spread Law seems to serve as a better LNC, as it prevents contradictions from occurring in the logic, through pain of triviality, i.e. where all formulae are derivable as theorems of the logic. Indeed, any logic with the Spread Law and a contradiction can be seen to be a trivial logic, which does not put any constraints on the set of theorems. Whilst this is hardly a decent logic, it is not normally possible to put formal constraints on a logic to prevent triviality happening. However, we can do this by expanding the system with a rejection mechanism, rejecting a certain class of non-theorems. We will discuss this in s. 5. So, the Spread Law, A, ∼A ⇒ B, enforces simple consistency and thus serves as a LNC for those logics that have such a Law and can also be shown to be non-trivial. Such non-triviality can be shown formally or informally, but obviously formal methods are preferred.

But, what of logics that do not have the Spread Law? These are the paraconsistent logics, a large class of logics that will still reasonably expect to have an LNC. So, still some other law needs to be found for these logics.

5. REJECTION

From s. 1, ∼(A & ∼A) does not capture the LNC and, as in s. 2, its inclusion in a logic is tied to the inclusion of A v ∼A, given De Morgan negation. From s. 4, A, ∼A ⇒ B captures the LNC for logics that are not paraconsistent and where there is a means of ensuring non-triviality of the logic. So, we need a suitable alternative. Let us first go back to what the LNC means. There seems to be some confusion between the two negations in $\sim$(A & $\sim$A), highlighted by the Brazilian logic in s. 3. Here the exclusion of $\sim$(A & $\sim$A) was meant to allow contradictions to be present, but we showed that this was independent of contradictions. Indeed, if there is to be no contradiction in the logic then this absence is represented by a meta-theoretic negation, whilst the contradiction itself belongs to the object language. That is, the outside '$\sim$' of $\sim$(A & $\sim$A) is meant to be understood meta-theoretically, i.e. as non-theoremhood, whilst the inner '$\sim$' is to be understood proof-theoretically. This contrasts with the '$\sim$' 's of De Morgan's Laws, where the negations are all object language ones, interacting with each other on a par.

How then do we capture the idea of excluding contradictions in a logical system, whilst maintaining the LNC as a kind of logical law? What naturally comes to mind is a formal rejection system, where formulae can be specifically rejected (i.e. rejected as theorems] from a system using rejection axioms and rejection rules. This idea goes back to Aristotle but was not formalized until Łukasiewicz [1957], who, in chs. 4 and 5, set up a complete axiomatization of classical logic, together with the axiomatic rejection of all and only the non-theorems. He used the symbol '⊣' to represent the rejection of a formula, in contrast to the assertion sign '⊢' for theoremhood, which is often suppressed. His (assertion) axiomatization, together with his rejection system is as follows:

Primitives

   $\sim, \supset$

Axioms

   1. $p \supset q \supset .q \supset r \supset .p \supset r$
   2. $\sim p \supset p \supset p$
   3. $p \supset .\sim p \supset q$

Rules

   1. $A \Rightarrow A^B/p$, where B is substituted for each occurrence of p in A (Rule of Substitution).
   2. $A, A \supset B \Rightarrow B$ (Rule of detachment).

Rejection-Axiom

   1. ⊣p.

Rejection-Rules

   1. ⊢$A \supset B$, ⊣B $\Rightarrow$ ⊣A (Rule of rejection by detachment).
   2. ⊣$A^B/p \Rightarrow$ ⊣A (Rule of rejection by substitution).

The whole system uses real formulae rather than formula-schemes, and in any case the rejection axiom cannot be a scheme. However, we will use schemes where appropriate.

Given the rejection-axiom, the classical theorem-scheme A & ~A ⊃ p, and rejection-rule 1, the rejection-theorem-scheme ⊣A & ~A (TNC) follows and would formally capture the LNC in such a system. Taking this further, the classical derived rule A ⇒ ~A ⊃ A & ~A, by applying rejection-rule 1, yields ⊢A, ⊣A & ~A ⇒ ⊣~A, and hence the rule, ⊢A ⇒ ⊣~A (RNC). This rule would also suffice to capture the LNC, as it ensures that ~A cannot be a theorem if A is. (Note that ⊢ ~A ⇒ ⊣ A also follows by interchanging A with ~A in the proof of RNC or by double negation.) RNC is a better form of LNC than ⊣A & ~A as it is a pure property of the formulae A and ~A, and does not contain the additional connective '&', which would require analysis within the logic. Thus, at last, we have some formalizations of the LNC, as laws of logic, which *state* that no contradiction should be derivable in the logical system. However, for the *enforcement*, not only is there a need to prove the law in the system, but it is also based on an assumption, already shown by Łukasiewicz, that the set of theorems and the set of rejection-theorems do not overlap. Such overlapping could allow a provable contradiction to occur in the overlap, whilst still satisfying TNC and RNC.

We encapsulate some of these rejection concepts, before moving on to other logics. A rejection system for a logic is *r-sound* iff, for all formulae A, not both ⊢A and ⊣A hold. A rejection system for a logic is *r-complete* iff, for all A, either ⊢A or ⊣A hold. So, an r-sound and r-complete rejection system rejects precisely the non-theorems of the logic. Thus Łukasiewicz's system is r-sound and r-complete. One should note that if a logic has an r-sound and r-complete rejection system then this suffices to show decidability, as can be seen from Kleene [1952: 284, 307, 313].

It is not too difficult to show r-soundness, which is required not only to make TNC and RNC work, but also to make rejection systems at all sensible. One just has to ensure that each of the r-axioms (as we will now abbreviate) is a non-theorem and each of the r-rules preserve non-theoremhood. We use the usual (sound and complete) semantics for the logic concerned (or proof theory if appropriate) to show that the r-axioms are all invalid and that the r-rules preserve invalidity. The latter can often be shown quite easily by contraposition or antilogism on a corresponding assertion rule. For example, given the Adjunction Rule, A, B ⇒ A & B, then the rejection rule, ⊢A, ⊣A & B ⇒ ⊣B preserves non-theoremhood. Also, r-rule 1 above preserves non-theoremhood, given the Rule of Detachment. R-completeness is harder to show and is nice if you can get it. It is out of the question for undecidable systems and the methods used so far rely on normal forms for the set of all formulae, which apply to non-theorems as well as theorems.

The use of TNC and RNC is more interesting in the case of non-classical systems. Let us consider a recently researched rejection system L_{1r}, due to Brady in [2000]. L_{1r} axiomatically rejects all and only the non-theorems of the common first-degree fragment of a range of weak meta-complete relevant logics. (The first-degree fragment of a sentential logic consists just of those formulae of first degree, i.e.

formulae with some '→'(s) but no nested '→'s.) Meta-completeness was defined and established for the positive quantified relevant logics by Meyer [1976], its key property being 'if ⊢AvB then ⊢A or ⊢B'. It was extended to some full sentential relevant logics by Slaney [1984, 1987]. This property is important for rejection, as we can form the rejection rule, ⊣A, ⊣B ⇒ ⊣AvB, by contraposing the above meta-completeness property. Thus, we can formalize in rejection systems properties that only hold meta-theoretically in the assertion system.

The LNC can be formalized as TNC or RNC in the logic L_{1r}, as it is r-sound. Each instance of TNC and RNC can also be proved due to its r-completeness, as L_{1r} is simply consistent. This highlights a general problem. How do we prove TNC or RNC in rejection systems? In these systems, we generally use real formulae as the r-axioms do not usually lend themselves to being substituted upon. In fact, r-rule 2 above is the converse of such substitution. TNC is an r-axiom-scheme and RNC is a r-rule, which is schematic anyway. We would generally have to prove TNC and RNC, instance by instance, as for L_{1r}, rather than proving them in their schematic form. In L_{1r}, we used its simple consistency to ensure that it could be done. However, for classical logic we were able to use the axiom-scheme A & ~A ⊃ p, the scheme A subsequently appearing in TNC and RNC. Also, for r-sound non-paraconsistent systems with the Spread Law, A & ~A ⇒ B, it would make sense to have its contraposed form, ⊣B ⇒ ⊣A & ~A, as a r-rule, whereupon the rejection of any formula whatsoever would yield TNC. RNC could then follow by the r-rule, ⊢A, ⊣A & B ⇒ ⊣B, or some appropriate theorem and r-rule 1 above.

In conclusion, the enforcement of a formalized LNC by proof of TNC or RNC in an r-sound rejection system does not always yield an alternative simple consistency proof. In paraconsistent systems, one may very likely need to presuppose simple consistency and show r-completeness to ensure that TNC or RNC is derivable for all formulae. In non-paraconsistent systems with the Spread Law, simple consistency can be proved in an r-sound rejection system with its non-triviality cashed out as a r-axiom.

REFERENCES

ANDERSON, A. R., and BELNAP, N. D., Jr. [1975], *Entailment, The Logic of Relevance and Necessity* (Princeton: Princeton University Press), i.

ARRUDA, A. I., and DA COSTA, N. C. A. [1984], 'On the Relevant Systems P and P* and some Related Systems', *Studia Logica*, 43: 33–49.

BRADY, R. T. [1988], 'A Content Semantics for Quantified Relevant Logics I', *Studia Logica*, 47: 111–27.

—— [1989], 'The Non-Triviality of Dialectical Set Theory', in G. Priest, R. Routley, and J. Norman (eds.), *Paraconsistent Logic: Essays on the Inconsistent*, (Munich: Philosophia Verlag), 437–71.

—— [1996], 'Relevant Implication and the Case for a Weaker Logic', *Journal of Philosophical Logic*, 25: 151–83.

BRADY, R. T. [2000]: 'A Rejection System for First-Degree Metacomplete Logic', paper presented to the Australasian Association for Logic Conference, Noosa.

—— [forthcoming], *Universal Logic* (Stanford, Calif.: CSLI Publications).

KLEENE, S. C. [1952], *Introduction to Meta-Mathematics* (Princeton, NJ: Van Nostrand).

ŁUKASIEWICZ, J. [1957], *Aristotle's Syllogistic from the Standpoint of Modern Formal Logic*, 2nd edn. (Oxford: Clarendon Press).

MEYER, R. K. [1976], 'Metacompleteness', *Notre Dame Journal of Formal Logic*, 17: 501–16.

ROUTLEY, R., MEYER, R. K., PLUMWOOD, V., BRADY, R. T. [1982], *Relevant Logics and their Rivals* (Atascadero, Calif.: Ridgeview), i.

SLANEY, J. K. [1984], 'A Metacompleteness Theorem for Contraction-free Relevant Logics', *Studia Logica* 43: 159–68.

—— [1987], 'Reduced Models for Relevant Logics Without WI', *Notre Dame Journal of Formal Logic* 28: 395–407.

3

What is a Contradiction?

Patrick Grim

ABSTRACT

The Law of Non-Contradiction holds that both sides of a contradiction cannot be true. Dialetheism is the view that there are contradictions both sides of which *are* true. Crucial to the dispute, then, is the central notion of contradiction. My first step here is to work toward clarification of that simple and central notion: Just what *is* a contradiction?

The notion of contradiction is far from simple, it turns out, and the search for clarification points up a menagerie of different forms of the Law of Non-Contradiction and Dialetheism as well. Might some of these at least be eliminated as trivially true or false—true or false by definition, perhaps—allowing us to concentrate on the more interesting forms?

Even the attempt to settle the easy cases raises a potential impasse in the dynamics of the debate—an impasse that can be expected to characterize the debate quite generally. The remainder of the chapter is devoted to the question of whether that impasse might be broken.

INTRODUCTION: DIALETHEISM AND THE LAW OF NON-CONTRADICTION

In the search for clarity, it is perhaps a bad omen that the central principle at issue goes under two apparently contradictory names: it is referred to as both the Law of Contradiction and the Law of *Non*-Contradiction. I'll abbreviate that central principle as the LNC. Whatever you call it, the classical source is Aristotle:

LNC1 ... the most indisputable of all beliefs is that contradictory statements are not at the same time true.   (Aristotle, *Metaphysics* Γ (*c*.350 BC), 1011^{b}13–14)

LNC2 Evidently then such a principle is the most certain of all; which principle this is, let us proceed to say. It is, that the same attribute cannot at the same time belong and not belong to the same subject and in the

same respect; we must presuppose, to guard against dialectical objections, any further qualifications which might be added.   (Aristotle,
Metaphysics Γ (*c*.350 BC), 1005^{b}18–22)

To Aristotle's formulations we can add a few more recent representations:

> LNC3 ... the law of non-contradiction, $\neg(a \wedge \neg a)$.   (Graham Priest
> (1987: 96))

> LNC4 The law of contradiction asserts that a statement and its direct denial
> cannot be true together ('not both p and not-p') or, as applied to
> terms, that nothing can both be and not be the same thing at the same
> time ('Nothing is at once A and not-A').   (A. N. Prior (1967: 461))

> LNC5 ... the *law of noncontradiction*: nothing is both true and false.
> (Graham Priest (1998: 416))

> LNC6 Thus there seems to be a role in dialogue for an expression whose sig-
> nificance is captured by the law of non-contradiction: by the principle
> that a proposition and its negation cannot both be accepted.   (Huw
> Price (1990: 224))

The opposing position at issue here also has two names: it appears in the literature as both 'dialetheism' and 'dialethism', which complicates a word search.
Whatever its spelling, the term was coined in 1981 by Graham Priest and a second
wonderful philosophical logician. That second logician, as it happens, had two
names as well: Richard Routley was also Richard Sylvan.

One formulation of dialetheism puts the position in direct opposition to
the LNC:

> DIAL1 The view that the LNC fails, that some contradictions are true, is
> called dialetheism.   (Graham Priest (1998: 416))

Here again we can list some other formulations:

> DIAL2 ... believing that inconsistent information or theories may be *true*.
> The view that some *are* true has come to be called *dialetheism*, a
> dialetheia being a true contradiction.   (Graham Priest (2002))

> DIAL3 The view that some claims are neither true or false is of ancient
> ancestry ... The dual view that some claims are both true and
> false (dialetheism) is of equally ancient lineage.   (Graham Priest
> (1993: 35))

> DIAL4 ... *dialethism*, the thesis that a single proposition can be both true
> and false at the same time.   (Paul Saka, (2001: 6))

> DIAL5 In standard logics, contradictions are always false; for dialetheism,
> contradictions are both true and false.   (Peter Suber (2001))

My primary attempt here is simply to get clearer on the basic positions represented by dialetheism and the LNC. Part of that attempt at clarification involves exploring prospects for settling the dispute in at least the easy cases. But I will stick to the 'easy' cases: I leave to others the larger task of solving the dispute in the harder cases and in general, if general solution there is to be.

It is plain that the central bone of contention is the status of contradictions. In order to make the dispute as clear as possible we need simply to make it clear what contradictions are and what each side is claiming about them.

As it turns out, however, that simple task is significantly harder than it looks.

1. WHAT IS A CONTRADICTION?

The following is a sampler of outlines of contradiction. These are drawn fairly randomly from the logical and philosophical literature, but I have arranged them here quite deliberately in order to make some points regarding their differences:

C1 Contradictories, or propositions one of which must be true and the other false ... (Augustus DeMorgan (1846: 4))

C2 Contradictory negation, or contradiction, is the relation between statements that are exact opposites, in the sense that they can be neither true together nor false together—for example, 'Some grass is brown' and 'No grass is brown.' (A. N. Prior (1967: 458))

C3 Contradictories: Two propositions are contradictories if and only if it is logically impossible for both to be true and logically impossible for both to be false. (R. M. Sainsbury (1991: 369))

C4 Two statements are inconsistent with each other if they cannot both be true, and more specifically if the truth of one would entail the falsity (non-truth) of the other. (Sybil Wolfram (1989: 163))

C5 Definition. A sentence is *contradictory* if and only if it's impossible for it to be true. (Daniel Bonevac (1987: 25))

C6 Contradictory: The contradictory of a wff* (statement) A is a wff* (statement) which must be false if A is true and true if A is false. (Susan Haack (1978: 244))

C7 Contradiction: Wff* of the form 'A & ~A'; statement of the form 'A and not A'. (ibid.)

C8 ... two formulae are *explicitly contradictory* if and only if one is of the form q and the other of the form $\ulcorner \sim q \urcorner$, that is, if one is the negation of the other. (Graeme Forbes (1994: 102))

C9 A contradiction consists of a pair of sentences, one of which is the negation of the other.   (Kalish, Montague, and Mar (1980: 18))

C10 This case is called a *contradiction*; a formula of this kind is always false. We obtain such formulas by taking the negation of a tautology.   (Hans Reichenbach (1947: 36))

C11 A statement form which is false for all possible truth values of its statement letters is called a contradiction. (Elliot Mendelson (1964: 18))

C12 Thus it is plain that every affirmation has an opposite denial, and similarly every denial an opposite affirmation . . . . We will call such a pair of propositions a pair of contradictories. (Aristotle, *On Interpretation* (*c*.350 BC), 17ª30)

C13 Contradiction: the joint assertion of a proposition and its denial. (Baruch Brody, (1967: 61))

C14 A *contradiction* both makes a claim and denies that very claim. (Howard Kahane (1995: 308))

C15 To deny a statement is to affirm another statement, known as the negation or contradictory of the first.   (W. V. O. Quine (1959: 9))

C16 We would not say that a man could, in the same breath, assert and deny the same thing without contradiction.   (P. F. Strawson (1952: 21))

C17 To say of two statements that they are contradictories is to say that they are inconsistent with each other and that no statement is inconsistent with both of them. To say of two statements that they are contraries is to say that they are inconsistent with each other, while leaving open the possibility that there is some statement inconsistent with both. (This may be taken as a definition of 'contradictory' and 'contrary' in terms of 'inconsistent'.)   (Ibid. 19)

C18 Contradictory statements, then, have the character of being both logically exclusive and logically exhaustive.   (Ibid. 21)

C19 A contradictory situation is one where both B and $\sim$B (it is not the case that B) hold for some B.   (R. Routley and V. Routley (1985: 204))

As this assortment of quotations make clear, contradictions are spoken of in many ways. Let me try to tease out some of the most important differences:

Some authors define contradictions directly in terms of possibility of truth and falsity. In C1, for example, DeMorgan defines contradictions as pairs of propositions one of which must be true and the other false. In C2, Prior defines contradictions as pairs of statements that can be neither true together nor false together, a definition echoed in Sainsbury's C3. In C4 Wolfram outlines contradictions as pairs that cannot both be true, and the truth of one of which entails the falsehood of the other. Bonevac's bald claim in C5 is that a sentence is contradictory if and only if it is impossible for it to be true, and part of Reichenbach's outline in C10 is that a contradiction is always false. In C6, Haack defines a contradictory of a statement as one which must be true if it is false and false if it is true.

Because all these definitions rely on a direct appeal to notions of truth and falsity I will term them *semantic* outlines of contradiction. It should be noted, however, that all except Reichenbach's C10 offer a definition in terms of *possibility*, truth and falsity: here contradiction is portrayed as a matter of modal semantics.

A second class of definitions characterize contradictions explicitly in terms of form. Haack's C7 is a common definition: that a contradiction is of the form 'A & ~A' or 'A and not A'. Contradictions are pairs of formulae one of which is the negation of the other in Forbes (C8) and are pairs of sentences one of which is the negation of the other in Kalish, Montague, and Mar (C9). These I will term *syntactic* outlines of contradiction. Among syntactic outlines I also tend to include Reichenbach's proposal in C10 that contradictions be identified with negations of tautologies and Mendelson's definition of a contradiction as a statement form which is false for all possible truth values of its sentential components (C11), although it is clear that these definitions mix in generous portions of formal semantics as well.

A third approach to contradictions is in terms of assertion and denial. Here Aristotle again has the first word: in *On Interpretation* contradictions are defined as pairs of propositions consisting of an affirmation and the opposite denial (C12). In C13, Baruch Brody defines a contradiction as the joint assertion of a proposition and its denial. Kahane's C14 defines contradiction in terms of making and denying the same claim. An outline of contradictories in terms of assertion and denial is clear in Quine's C15 and appears in both Strawson's C16 and in Prior's outline of the Law of Non-Contradiction in LNC4 above. Because defined in terms not of content or form but in terms of the acts of assertion and denial I will term these *pragmatic* outlines of contradiction.

A fourth and final approach I will term *ontological*. In the contemporary accounts listed, interestingly enough, an ontological approach appears only in Routley and Routley's C19, though it is explicit in Aristotle's LNC2 and makes a brief appearance in Prior's LNC4. On an ontological outline, a contradiction would be neither a single statement nor a pair of statements, neither a proposition nor a pair of propositions, but a state of affairs. A contradictory state of affairs would be one in which something had a particular property and also an incompatible property, or in which something both had a particular property and lacked that property.

It should be noted that a distinction between full contradictions and mere contraries is possible in any or all of the approaches above. That distinction is explicit in Strawson's C17. There a sufficient condition for contraries is that they are exclusive. Strawson's defining characteristic for contradictions is that they are both logically exclusive and logically exhaustive (C18).

Evident in the literature, then, are at least four basic approaches to the notion of contradiction: semantic, syntactic, pragmatic, and ontological. We could complicate the picture still further by noting that some accounts speak of contradictions as pairs of sentences or statements (C1 through C4, C6, C8, C9, C12, and C17, for example), while others speak of contradictions as single statements or propositions (C5, C7, C10, C11, C13, and C14). Often what is meant by the latter is a conjunction of contradictions in the former sense. But not always: in Bonevac's C5, Reichenbach's C10, and Mendelson's C11 there is no demand that single-statement contradictions be conjunctive in form.

Evident as a trace element in the outlines above is a further complication regarding explicit and implicit contradictions. Explicit contradictions somehow wear their status—whatever that status might be—on their sleeves. It is sometimes said that contradictions are things it is irrational to accept or to believe, a view that is most plausible when it is only explicit contradictions that are at stake. Implicit contradictions are single statements or pairs which in some way imply, entail, or commit us to explicit contradictions down the line. That something is an implicit contradiction may thus be far from obvious. For even very simple systems it may indeed be formally undecidable whether a formula is contradictory in this sense, and any epistemic injunction to avoid contradiction thus becomes significantly harder to obey. To the extent that epistemic 'ought' implies epistemic 'can', the notion that we have violated epistemic obligations if we fail to avoid contradiction becomes correspondingly less plausible when it is implicit contradictions that are at stake.

Let me mention a further complication in order to put it aside. Some of the outlines of contradiction above are written in terms of contradictory sentences, some in terms of contradictory statements, and some in terms of contradictory propositions (further variations include wffs, as in Haack's C7, formulas in Forbes's C8 and Reichenbach's C10, and claims in Kahane's C14). Although there is widespread agreement that utterances or inscriptions, token sentences and types, statements, propositions, claims, and assertions are quite different things, there does not appear to be agreement on precisely what any of these different things are. It is clear that an outline of contradiction could be written in terms of any understanding of any of these.

One final complication that will come back to haunt us is that of negation. Essentially all the accounts above employ negation in one way or another. But if there are different forms or different senses of negation, as is often held, there will be importantly different readings of each of these definitions.

Where we might have expected a single univocal notion of contradiction we find an enormous range. We have at least four basic forms of approach—semantic, syntactic, pragmatic, and ontological—multiplied by (1) a distinction between implicit and explicit contradictions, multiplied by (2) contradictions as pairs or single statements, multiplied by (3) the number of distinctions between token sentences, types, statements, propositions, assertions, and claims, with that in turn multiplied by (4) the number of senses of negation. On the most conservative of estimates, that gives us some 240 senses of contradiction.

Here I want to put many of these distinctions aside, however, concentrating only on the distinction between semantic, syntactic, pragmatic, and ontological approaches. The hope is that attention to this distinction may offer at least some hope in clarifying the LNC–dialetheism dispute.

2. RESOLVING THE EASY CASES

The Law of Non-Contradiction in some way forbids contradiction. Given four approaches to the basic notion of contradiction, it is hardly surprising that there will be at least four Laws of Non-Contradiction.

Indeed there will be significantly more, because there are a number of relevant forms of 'forbidding'. One might maintain that contradictions (in one of our many forms) are always false or impossibly true, for example—semantic forms of 'forbidding'. Contradictions might be claimed to be incapable of belief, or at least of rational belief—a psychological form of 'forbidding'. They might be pragmatically forbidden in the sense of being unassertable, or be communicatively out of bounds in being inherently incomprehensible or incapable of conveying information. They might be epistemically forbidden in being inherently unwarrantable, or might be rhetorically forbidden in being indefensible. It might be that they never obtain, and might be impossible that they obtain—ontological forms of 'forbidding'. Even beyond the complications of senses of 'contradiction' it is clear that we have not a single LNC to deal with but a menagerie of alternative Laws forbidding in some sense contradictions.

Defined in opposition to LNC, dialetheism can be expected to show a similar variety. The dialetheic claim may be that some semantic contradictions, say, are semantically acceptable—'true', perhaps, or 'not necessarily false'. The claim may, on the other hand, be that some syntactic contradictions are semantically acceptable. Or it may be that some syntactic contradictions are assertable, are psychologically believable, can be legitimately informative, are epistemically warrantable, rhetorically defensible, or actually obtain.

By attending to different approaches to contradiction and to different forms of 'forbidding' we have assured that we are dealing with a full conceptual deck. But there is a point at which the deck becomes too full to be manageable. Is there a way of resolving the LNC–dialetheism debates at least to the extent of cutting down the number of serious contenders? Aren't there at least some easy cases on each side that can be usefully eliminated?

At first glance it appears that there are; that some of the easy cases can be settled immediately by definition. Definition settles these aspects of the dispute trivially, perhaps, but it settles them none the less, thereby clearing the way for harder work on harder cases.

On some of the standard outlines of contradiction above we can apparently make short work of the dispute. Consider, for example a form of the LNC that maintains that a contradiction cannot be true—a semantic forbidding of contradiction. Consider a corresponding form of dialetheism that maintains that some contradictions are true. On at least some of the definitions offered, the dispute seems easily resolvable: one side definitely wins and one side definitely loses.

In C2, Prior defines contradictions as pairs of statements that can neither be true together nor false together. If conjunction is taken as 'together', Prior's definition entails that a contradiction cannot be true. On that definition, then, the LNC is inviolable. Dialetheism, taken as the claim that a contradiction *can* be true, or that the LNC fails, comes out necessarily false.[1] Here the definition of 'contradiction' alone serves to settle the matter. The same reasoning applies using Sainsbury's C3, Wolfram's C4, and Bonevac's C5. On any of these definitions, it appears, the dispute is over and we can go home: the LNC wins and dialetheism loses. Such an argument is offered with an emphasis on contradictions as opposed to subcontraries in B. H. Slater (1995): 'One central fact is that *contradictories* cannot be true together—by definition.' [In footnote:] 'For the record, this definition is given, for instance, in Sainsbury 1991, p. 16.'

Not just any semantic outline of contradiction will close the dispute so conveniently. In C1, DeMorgan defines contradictories as pairs of propositions one of which must be true and the other false. On Haack's C6, contradictories are such that if one is true the other must be false. But neither C1 nor C6 specify that the conjunction of contradictories so defined—of a true statement and a false statement—cannot itself be both true and false. The proponent of the LNC and the dialetheist might therefore concur on any of these semantic definitions and yet continue the debate. Although they agree on definition, the proponent of the LNC might maintain that the conjunction of true and false cannot itself be true, whereas the dialetheist might maintain that it could be both true and false. Not surprisingly, disproof by definition depends on the definition; using *these* semantic definitions the issue is not immediately closed.

There are other definitions on which the dispute is quickly resolved, but in the other direction. Here dialetheism wins and the LNC loses. In C8, Forbes gives a syntactical outline of contradictories as pairs of formulae one of which is the negation of the other. In C7, Kalish, Montague, and Mar give a similar syntactical

---

[1] Or at least so it initially appears. I leave to s. 3 the further subtlety that leads to impasse: that the dialetheist might by his lights cheerfully accept the definitional vindication of the LNC and yet insist that dialetheism is true as well.

account in terms of pairs of sentences. Susan Haack's outline in C6, written for statements rather than sentences, is that a contradiction is 'of the form A and not A'.

Can a conjunction of sentences or statements of this defined form be true? Using normal English negation the answer is clearly 'yes'. One set of examples involves indexicals: the conjunction of your statement 'I am an Australian' and my statement 'I am not an Australian', or the statement it takes the slow talker days to make, 'Today is Tuesday and today is not Tuesday.' Other sets of examples include those in which information is clearly conveyed by using predicates conjoined with their negations: 'Well, he's what you'd call handsome and he's not what you'd call handsome...' 'Well, he's in charge but he's not in charge...' Given a syntactical outline for contradiction of the form of C6, C7, or C8, nothing in the definition prohibits a contradiction from being true. As a matter of fact contradictions so defined seem quite often to come out true. Thus semantical forbiddings of contradictions syntactically specified seem to fail: dialetheism triumphs and the corresponding LNC fails.

This easy triumph may seem nearly as cheap as the definitional victory for the LNC above, however. For it is on the grounds of precisely these kinds of examples that Strawson resists a syntactical definition, insisting that 'one cannot explain what a contradiction is just by indicating ... a certain form of words' (Strawson 1952: 8). In Aristotle's formulation of the Law of Non-Contradiction quoted as LNC2 above, Aristotle himself adds an immediate proviso: 'the same attribute cannot at the same time belong and not belong to the same subject and in the same respect; *we must presuppose, to guard against dialectical objections, any further qualifications which might be added*' (*Metaphysics* Γ, 1005^{b}22). In *On Interpretation* Aristotle notes that identity of subject and of predicate must not be 'equivocal' in supposed contradictions, and adds 'Indeed there are definitive qualifications besides this, which we make to meet the casuistries of sophists' (*On Interpretation*, 17^{a}35). The danger is that the LNC that is defeated using easy examples against syntactical definitions is an LNC that no one would have tried to defend anyway.

The fact that some semantical accounts give an easy victory for the LNC, we noted, need not entail that all semantical accounts do. Similarly, the fact that some syntactical accounts give an easy victory for dialetheism need not mean that the dispute is settled for all syntactical accounts. Many have attempted to add the further qualifications that Aristotle alludes to, striving for a class of fully specified and 'eternal' sentences. Or at least many have assumed that some such attempt could succeed. In that spirit it might be maintained that for sentences sufficiently filtered—sentences cleaned of indexicals and elliptical suggestions, perhaps, pur-ified of any aspect of content that might vary with context—we *could* give a syntactical specification adequate to guarantee that any syntactically contradict-ory sentence is incapable of truth. It might alternatively be maintained that a definition of contradiction in terms of form, but form of something other than sentences, might do the trick. Let the 'A' of our form specification represent not a sentence type but a 'genuine proposition'. It might then be maintained that it is impossible for conjunctions of such propositions with their negations to be true.

At this point our conclusion is that there are indeed some easy cases that can be fruitfully eliminated, clearing the ground for more serious work in more serious areas. Given at least one type of semantic account of contradiction, victory for at least one form of the LNC seems definitionally assured. Given at least one type of syntactic account of contradiction, victory for a form of dialetheism seems to be guaranteed. Interestingly enough, there is also a link to issues of decidability here—to questions of how one is to *tell* whether something is a contradiction. On simple syntactical definitions, it should be easy to tell at least explicit contradictions: one need only recognize conjunction and a negation in order to tell that a sentence has the form $A \wedge \sim A$. But those are precisely the kinds of definition on which the LNC seems vulnerable and dialetheism seems to triumph. The cases in which the LNC seems to win an easy victory, on the other hand, are cases in which contradictions are defined semantically ('cannot possibly be true') or in terms of language-like abstract entities such as propositions. Here there is no clear way to tell whether something is a contradiction or not. That we have no algorithm for impossible truth follows immediately from limitative results in metamathematics: if we did, we would have an algorithm for necessary mathematical truth, and that we know we cannot have. A strong argument that there can be no algorithm for whether something is a proposition or not can be made in terms of self-reference (see Grim 1991: ch. 1). What this suggests is that perhaps definitional victory for the LNC is possible only where it is undecidable entities that are at stake as 'contradictions'. For decidable 'contradictions' it may always be dialetheism that has the upper hand.

Just as it turned out that the simple notion of contradiction is far from simple, however, it turns out that even the easy cases of the LNC–dialetheism dispute are far from easy. Even in the easy cases the dynamic of the debate quickly arrives at an impasse.

3. THE IMPASSE

The suggestion of the previous section is that there are multiple approaches to contradiction, giving us a still greater multiplicity of approaches to the LNC and dialetheism. On some approaches, the victory is easy but trivial, in favor of the LNC. On other approaches it is an easy but cheap victory for dialetheism. Were that first account successful, we would at least have eliminated some easy cases on each side, leaving a wealth of more important and substantive work to be done.

Here a major difficulty arises, however. It is a difficulty that has arisen in LNC–dialetheism debates in the past, is predictable for debates in the future, and threatens to wipe away even the small gains of our few easy conclusions. The difficulty appears at two levels in the debate. It is evident at the bottom level of what is at issue: contradictions, and in particular how contradictions are to be understood in terms of negation. But the difficulty appears with a vengeance at the higher level of our own discussion as well, in the attempt to establish one position and to exclude another even in the easy cases.

Here is the problem in the context of the higher debate:

By the first argument above, the LNC is vindicated by some definitions of contradiction and dialetheism is defeated. For if contradictions are by definition some species of sentence that cannot be true, it must be that contradictions cannot be true.

That the LNC is vindicated by such an argument is clear. But that dialetheism is thus defeated may not be evident. For if the dialetheist takes his position to be that the LNC is false, and thus that there are propositions that are both true and false, he may well regard even the firmest proof that the LNC is true to be insufficient to convince him that the LNC is not also false. Since what he has maintained all along is simply that the LNC *is* false, proof that it is true may be insufficient to convince him that he is wrong.

By the same token, the proponent of LNC may begin to regret early celebration over the proof from definition. For what he wanted to argue was that the LNC was true and thereby that dialetheism was false. To have established that the LNC is true but to have failed to defeat a dialetheist opponent will seem not a cheap victory but no victory at all.

What this failure of the first easy argument *seems* to call for is a simple clarification of positions. What the proponent of the LNC maintains is that the principle is true *only*, or true *and not false*. His earlier mistake was to rest content with proof of truth, whereas he also needs proof of non-falsity. What the proponent of dialetheism maintains is that the principle is at least false, though perhaps it is both true and false.

Can the debate then proceed given that further clarification? Not as one might expect. For suppose that the proponent of the LNC got everything he wanted at *this* point: firm and emphatic proof, again by definition perhaps, that the LNC is true and not false. Surprisingly, that doesn't take us any further. Since the dialetheist maintains that there can be propositions that are both true and false, he may take even this further proof to be insufficient. What the dialetheist maintains is that some contradictions may be true. That the proposition expressed by the LNC is both true and not false may thus seem insufficient to defeat him. For if a contradiction may be true, the fact that the LNC is not false need not entail that it is not false as well, and that it is false is after all what the dialetheist has maintained all along.

We have reached a dialectical impasse reminiscent of the ἀπορία of the early Socratic dialogues. The problem isn't that the proponent of the LNC hasn't yet been sufficiently clever to find an argument strong enough to defeat the dialetheist. The problem is that no argument we can imagine him providing will be strong enough to circumvent the dialetheist's counter. Despite the fact that dialetheism is sometimes defined in opposition to the LNC, as in DIAL1, the dialetheist seems able to swallow cheerfully a proof that the LNC is true, or even that it is true and not also false, without in the least impugning his conviction that dialetheism remains true. If he finds contradiction painless, we can hardly expect to force the dialetheist to our conclusion 'on pain of contradiction'.

Such an impasse is also reminiscent of Lewis Carroll's 'What the Tortoise Said to Achilles' (1895). Achilles' attempt there is to compel the Tortoise to accept a conclusion Z on the basis of an argument from Euclid that moves from premisses A and B to Z. The Tortoise accepts A and B, but refuses to accept Z unless an additional hypothetical premise is explicitly added: C, to the effect that if A and B are true, Z must be true. When C is added, however, the Tortoise refuses to accept the new argument as compelling Z without explicit addition of still another premiss D: that if A and B and C are true, Z must be true. At each step the Tortoise insists that an explicit premiss regarding the validity of a contested argument be added, giving another argument for which he makes the same demand. Within these constraints, it becomes clear that Achilles can offer the Tortoise no argument that will compel him to accept Z.

With a topic of contradictory negation rather than validity, it is the proponent of the LNC that is Achilles and the dialetheist that is the Tortoise. The proponent of LNC offers a demonstration that the LNC is true. The dialetheist insists that truth need not entail non-falsity, and that his position is simply that the LNC is false. The proponent of LNC then goes on to demonstrate that the LNC is true and not false. The dialetheist points out that by his lights the fact that the LNC is not false need not entail that it is not false as well, and that that is after all his position. Whatever Achilles proves, if contradictions may be true the proof need not entail that the Tortoise's position is wrong. And of course what the Tortoise has maintained all along is that contradictions may be true.

The dynamics of this impasse are evident in the literature.

> Priest had at one time [concluded] that some sentences 'are so contradictory as to take impossible values such as both true and false ({1,0}) and true only ({1})'. But he seems not to have been alarmed, and one sees why. Dialethism is not simply a theory *about* contradictions; it requires the theorist himself to assert some, and the discovery that a sentence both must and cannot take exclusive values looks like just one more contradiction to take on board.   (Timothy Smiley (1993: 31)

What are we going to do, charge the dialetheist with contradicting himself? That, as Smiley notes, 'sounds as futile as Brer Fox throwing Brer Rabbit into the brier-patch' (ibid. 27). The fact that someone holds a position that makes it impossible to convince them of the contrary, however—a position that is thus in a sense 'irrefutable' or 'indefeasible'—need not entail that their position isn't deeply and terribly wrong. It may be that one cannot effectively be *argued* out of solipsism or nihilism or the view that all positions are equally false or equally true. That doesn't make them true, and certainly shouldn't convince us to become solipsists or nihilists.

Although impasse is all too possible in the LNC–dialetheism debate, it should be noted that it is not inevitable. There are, to begin with, different forms of dialetheism. Contrary to the implication of Peter Suber's definition in DIAL5, there is no requirement that a dialetheist believe that *all* contradictions are both true and false. Someone could fully qualify as a dialetheist, believing some contradictions are true, even were they to hold that truth *does* entail non-falsity in the particular case of the LNC, for example. One could still be a card-carrying dialetheist while holding that statements regarding the LNC are not in the class of those for which contradictions may be true. Against these forms of dialetheism, a demonstration that the LNC is true *would* constitute a full refutation. Were such a refutation to rely on a particular definition of contradiction, however—contradictions defined as statements the truth of which is impossible, for example, as in C1–C4— such a dialetheist might concede the LNC for contradictions so defined while maintaining that his position does hold for other and more interesting senses of the term.

In a debate that comes to impasse, a quite understandable reaction on the side of the LNC's proponents will be that the dialetheist is refusing to engage the real issue or is consistently sidetracking any real debate. The central principle that the LNC's proponents take themselves to be defending is that contradictions *cannot* be true, and that in a sense of 'cannot' that explicitly *excludes* the possibility that they might somehow be true as well. The LNC that its proponents want to defend is that any claim that contradictions are true must be *false* and false only, and that in a sense that *excludes* truth rather than leaving it as a lingering possibility that might be added later. By the LNC's proponents' lights it thus appears that the dialetheist fails even to engage the real principle at issue because he is constantly reading it as something weaker, constantly rereading their 'not' as something other than the intended 'not', or their 'false' as something other than the sense of 'false' intended.

The cost of impasse can also be indicated from the other side. Dialetheism is conceived in denial of the LNC, and offers itself in opposition (DIAL1). But how is the dialetheist to express his own position in a way that makes it clear what he is opposing? The threat here is that what the dialetheist seeks to claim regarding the LNC will become as ineffable as rival positions he condemns on the basis of inexpressibility (see e.g. Priest 1995).

Suppose that you say 'β,' and Priest replies '$\neg\beta$.' Under ordinary circumstances you would think that he had disagreed with you. But then you remember that Priest is a dialetheist, and it occurs to you that he might very well agree with you after all—since he might think that β and $\neg\beta$ are *both* true. How can he indicate that he genuinely disagrees with you? The natural choice is for him to say 'β is not true.' However, the truth of this assertion is also consistent with β's being true—for a dialetheist, anyway . . .   (Terence Parsons (1990: 345))

Priest has sometimes replied that the dialetheist *can* make his opposition clear, not indeed by asserting any form of '$\neg\beta$', but by simply *denying* β:

It is sometimes urged as an objection to dialetheism that dialetheists cannot express their own views. Notably, they cannot express α in such a way as to rule out $\neg\alpha$.

. . . it is not clear that non-dialetheists can do any better as far as ruling out goes. If dialetheism is correct then, like it or not, no one can rule out $\neg\alpha$ by asserting α. Maybe they would like to; but that does not mean they succeed. Maybe they intend to; but intentions are not guaranteed fulfillment.

[But] anyone (dialetheist or otherwise) *can* express themselves in such a way as to rule things out. They cannot rule out α by asserting $\neg\alpha$—or anything else. But they can simply deny α.   (Graham Priest (1999: 116))

It is clear that Priest does take assertion and denial to be exclusionary, though he refuses a similar exclusion for any sense of 'β' and '$\neg\beta$' (see also Priest 1993 and 1998).

The retention of pragmatic exclusion between assertion and denial seems a necessary foothold against the charge of dialetheic inability to either champion or contest any position. But retention of that foothold is peculiar as well. It is unclear, to begin with, why the argument should stop at this point. If dialetheism has so much going for it, why stop it short of assertion and denial? It is also unclear that exclusion *can* be restricted to the pragmatics of assertion and denial alone. Given that the dialetheist can deny certain claims, including the LNC, what is the information that he conveys by his denial? If we accept his denial, what precisely is it that we have accepted? If we learn that he is right, what precisely is it that we have learned? All these questions reflect the fact that a denial is intended to convey some content. But any *content* that inherits the exclusionary characteristics that Priest recognizes for denial will thereby have precisely the exclusionary characteristics he refuses to recognize for negation. For some outlines of the terms at issue, moreover, dialetheism would demand extension to assertion and denial. For pragmatic notions of contradiction defined in terms of assertion and denial (as in C12–C16) and for dialetheism defined as an acceptance of contradictions, it turns out that even Priest would not qualify as a dialetheist.

Here the road to clarity regarding the opposing principles at stake—indeed, the road to a treatment of those principles that can make it clear that they are genuinely *understood* and that they are genuinely in opposition—seems to force us to an examination of basics regarding assertion and negation. One might have thought that issues regarding negation could remain as the mere subject matter of the debate, at the same level as for example the distinction between implicit and explicit contradictions. What the impasse makes clear is that the simplest issues of negation at the lowest level infect the character of the debate throughout.

4. 'N̶O̶T̶'

We think of concepts of negation, of assertion and denial, of truth and falsehood, as some of the simplest possible. Perhaps we are wrong about how simple they are. But it is clear that they are central in our conceptual toolkit and ubiquitous in our mental and linguistic life.

Their ubiquity makes the attempt to examine *them* philosophically all the more difficult. Precisely because they are so central in our conceptual toolkit it seems impossible to examine *these* concepts without using them. If we use them everywhere, in an attempt to conceptualize everything we come in contact with, we will of course have to use them in the attempt to understand them themselves. If we are to dig that deep, we will have to dig under the very ground we stand upon.

As an attempt to make some progress beyond the all too real possibility of impasse, let me attempt to outline just one elementary notion. Although I take it to be a form of negation, I don't wish to claim any special status for this particular form: I don't wish to claim that it is *the* common or English notion of negation, for example. I'm not sure there is a single common or English notion of negation, and if there is I am not sure that this is it. Perhaps I'm even wrong that what I want to introduce really counts as negation. None of that need prevent us from introducing a useful concept in the pursuit of clarity.

If I succeed in introducing the term I'm after, I think it will offer progress through the LNC–dialetheism impasse sketched above. If I don't succeed, I expect my failure to be instructive as well.

Let me begin here:

> Some things are genuinely impossible. There are things that cannot be.

One such case is that in which some properties are incompatible with others. If a line segment is less than two inches long, for example, it cannot also be more than three feet long—the properties *less than two inches long* and *more than three feet long* are incompatible. If something is uniformly red and of no other color, it cannot also be uniformly green and of no other color—the property of being *uniformly red only* excludes the property of being *uniformly green only*.

We can speak of such properties as *exclusive*: the possession of one excludes the possession of the other. But of course a given property need not exclude only one property. The property *less than two inches long* excludes a whole range of alternative properties: *more than one foot long, more than two foot long, more than three feet long*. . . All those properties incompatible with a given property P we might think of as in the *exclusionary class* of P.

Our ability to conceive of things effectively is part of what allows us to navigate successfully in the world. It is generally to our advantage to be able to conceive of the properties that things actually have, and also to be able to conceive of the relations between those properties that actually hold. Given that we are the communicatively co-operative beings that we are, it is also to our advantage to be able to talk about these things.

Because some things are less than two inches long, the concept of being less than two inches long and the ability to say that something is less than two inches long both come in pretty handy. It also comes in handy, with reference to a proposed property P, to be able to say of something that it has some property that excludes P: that P is in the exclusionary class of some property that the thing has. If it is proposed that the Empire State building is less than ten inches high, for example, it would be useful to be able to make it clear that it has some property that excludes its having the property of being less than ten inches high, even if we're not sure precisely what exclusionary property that happens to be (is the building 1,250 feet tall? Or 1,251 feet tall? Does it change in a stiff wind?).

I propose to use 'not' for this useful job. When I say that the Empire State building is not less than ten inches high, what I intend is that it has some property for which *less than ten inches high* is in the exclusionary class.

Let me add some immediate qualifications in order to cement the term 'not' as I wish to use it.

A. Implicit Fields of Application

Many terms apply sensibly only to limited ranges of things. Terms of emotion apply to people and animals, for example, but seem to lose their grip on stars and stones. Is Betelgeuse upset? Measurement in inches seems to lose its grip on emotions and special events.

What is true of individual terms also applies to conceptual families. The color terms form a family some aspects of which are captured in the familiar color wheel or color solid. Blue and green have a certain similarity, for example, but orange and purple are diametrically opposed. As long as we are speaking of something that can have a color, a strong denial that something is chartreuse may lead us to guess at its color starting at the other side of the color wheel. But if we are speaking of things to which color terms don't apply—celebrations, sizes, and prices, for example—this oppositional web of color terms fails to apply as a whole.

The important point here is that properties and their exclusionary classes may together assume appropriateness classes of application. It may be that properties P and P' both apply only to a certain class of things. With regard to that class, they are exclusive. With regard to other things, neither may apply.

Quite often we simply assume an appropriate class of application. It goes unsaid. That too proves useful for efficient communication, and I expect this kind of everyday implicit assumption to continue to be carried in the use of the term 'not'. Could it be that properties P and P′ are exclusionary with regard to one assumed background class of things and not so with regard to another? That is at any rate a possibility that I don't want to rule out.

B. Exclusive and Exhaustive

As specified, (1) being P and (2) ~~not~~ being P are exclusive. Nothing can be both. But nothing has been said that would indicate that (1) and (2) are exhaustive. Perhaps something can slip through the cracks, qualifying as neither having a property P nor having any property that is a member of its exclusionary class. Here the issue of implicit fields of application applies with full force. One way that being P and ~~not~~ being P might fail to be exhaustive is if both are bound to a particular field of application. If there are things to which neither applies, they would remain exclusive but not exhaustive. With regard to specifications for 'not,' at least, exhaustiveness remains an open question.

In first trying to outline 'not' it is tempting to use pictures. That is indeed the course that the Routleys take in 'Negation and Contradiction'. But it soon becomes clear that the pictures one is tempted to sketch have some serious drawbacks.

One might start by trying to outline 'not' with a diagram, Fig. 3.1. In the area marked A are those things that have a property P. In the area marked B are those that have properties exclusive of P. Never the twain shall overlap, just as in the diagram.

The issue of appropriate classes of application, however, leads us to complicate the diagram immediately. In order to represent the role of implicit appropriateness classes, we need our diagram to be but part of a larger whole, as in Fig. 3.2. If the properties at issue are color terms, the central area represents those things to which color terms are appropriate. Events, sizes, and days of the week, inappropriate as subjects for color predication, lie in the outer area.

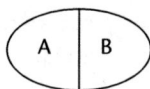

FIG. 3.1.

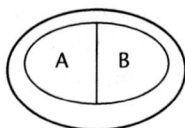

FIG. 3.2.

Patrick Grim

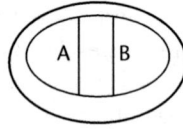

FIG. 3.3.

Even so, however, our diagram misrepresents. For the tidy line down the middle of the central area indicates that the property P, which holds for those things in A, and its exclusive class of properties which hold for things in B, are exhaustive within their appropriateness class. All that 'not' demands is that it be impossible for something to be both P and not P. But our diagram imposes a further requirement of its own: that anything within the appropriateness class must be either P or not P.

It is tempting to try to compensate for this difficulty by complicating our diagram further. At Fig. 3.3 we add a central area in the middle. Now areas A and B are exclusive, but the central area indicates that they need not be exhaustive within their appropriateness class.

Even so, however, our diagram still misrepresents. For it is still sketched with sharp lines, suggesting that there is a precise point in property space beyond which something ceases to be P though it has not yet become not P. The mere exclusiveness of 'not' need not commit us to sharp borders and false precision in this sense, and thus the diagram again imposes unintended specifications. 'Bald' is in the exclusionary class of 'hirsute', applied appropriately to human heads and sick dogs but not to colors, days of the week, or volumes of space. But there is neither a sharp line between 'bald' and 'hirsute' nor a sharp line between either of them and some 'neither bald nor hirsute' central space. In order to get a better diagram we would have to start blurring some of the lines.

C. Ontology, Semantics, and Pragmatics

As outlined, whether a property P and a property P' are exclusive is an ontological matter, more specifically a matter of modal ontology: what is at issue is simply whether something can be both. 'Not' is at base ontological as well: something is not P if it has some property that excludes P. But semantics follows easily: To *say* that something is not P is to say that it has some property that excludes P.

Assertion and denial are aspects of pragmatics: things we do in saying, rather than themselves part of the content of what we say. When I deny that I am late or assert that I am sorry it is my being late or my being sorry that is denied or asserted.

I want to make it clear that 'not' lives in the realm of content rather than performance. I can assert that something is not P, which means that it has some property that excludes P. It thus has a semantic existence of its own: it is not merely a performative operator, as for example a marker of pragmatic denial might be.

5. THE PROMISE OF 'N̶O̶T̶'

Let us suppose, at least for the moment, that my attempt in the previous section has been successful: that I have succeeded in outlining 'n̶o̶t̶'. What might that get us?

'N̶o̶t̶' would allow the proponent of the Law of Non-Contradiction to make the central claim that she wants to, with the force she wants to make it. For what she wants to claim is essentially this:

LNC 7 Any and all contradictions are n̶o̶t̶ true.

If 'n̶o̶t̶' has been successfully outlined, this is a claim that excludes:

DIAL6 Some contradictions are true.

This in turn would offer the possibility of breaking the dialectical impasse. For were the proponent of LNC7 to prove his claim, the dialetheist could *not* cheerfully accept it and also insist on DIAL6, because to understand 'n̶o̶t̶' is to understand exclusion, and what LNC7 explicitly excludes is DIAL6.[2]

The promise of 'n̶o̶t̶' thus appears to be a debate in which the contestants can be genuinely at loggerheads. That would at least break the impasse so as to offer the possibility for a genuine debate between dialetheism and the LNC.

Would it also offer a winner for the debate? At least a trivial winner in an easy case. For if we can successfully outline 'n̶o̶t̶', we might choose to define contradictions in any of the following ways:
Semantically:

C20 A contradiction is a statement such that it is n̶o̶t̶ possible that it be true.

Syntactically:

C21 A contradictory pair consists of (1) a statement to the effect that something has the property P, and (2) a statement to the effect that that same thing does n̶o̶t̶ have the property P.

C22 A contradiction is a conjunction of a contradictory pair.

Ontologically:

C23 A contradictory situation would be one in which it is the case that something is P and also the case that that thing is n̶o̶t̶ P.

---

[2] Here 'n̶o̶t̶' appears with 'true', of course. Though the concept of truth may carry its own philosophical difficulties, 'n̶o̶t̶' is intended for the same job as before: something qualifies as 'n̶o̶t̶' P just in case it has some property that excludes P.

Given any of these definitions of contradiction, among many possible variations, it would appear that the LNC in the form of LNC7 is indisputably true. It follows by definition that contradictions are ~~not~~ true in a sense which precludes impasse: the dialetheist cannot recognize '~~not~~' as outlined and maintain that they are true as well.

Interestingly enough, definition of contradiction in these terms is not without precedent. Here is Lewis Carroll's definition:

> C24 If we think of a certain Class, and imagine that we have picked out from it a certain smaller Class, it is evident that the *Remainder* of the large Class does *not* possess the Differentia of that smaller Class. Hence it may be regarded as *another* smaller Class, whose Differentia may be formed, from that of the Class first picked out, by prefixing the word 'not'; and we may imagine that we have *divided* the Class first thought of into *two* smaller Classes, whose Differentiae are *contradictory*.   (Lewis Carroll (1896: 62)

6. PROSPECTS FOR DIALETHEISM

Given '~~not~~', an easy case of the dispute would appear to be over. For that trivial case, at least, a form of the LNC wins by definition. What might those of dialetheist bent say in response?

1. One option for the dialetheist is to concede a minor battle and hold out for victory in a larger war. The victory for the LNC outlined above applies only to a particular form of definition for 'contradiction'—that employing '~~not~~'—and only to a particular form of the LNC phrased in terms of that sense of contradiction. Any defeat for dialetheism is thus only a very limited defeat.

We know that there are a range of rival definitions for contradiction and a range of corresponding senses of the LNC and dialetheism. One option for the dialetheist is to move on to more interesting senses of the term. I have been careful not to claim that '~~not~~' represents an English 'not'. Formulate a notion of contradiction in terms of an English 'not' instead and the argument from definition offered above won't even touch it. Here the battle can continue to rage, although we can also expect often to face impasse.

2. There is another option for the dialetheist which does not entail conceding even this small defeat. We've phrased our conclusion to this point as follows: *Given* '~~not~~, *a form of the dispute is over and a form of the LNC wins.* At least one form of dyed-in-the-wool dialetheist may insist that '~~not~~' cannot be taken as given, despite my best attempts at careful outline.

Can one introduce '~~not~~' as I have tried to above? One part of standard philosophical practice says 'yes'; as long as one is clear in definition and scrupulous in following one's own stipulations, so the story goes, one can specify a term to mean what one wants it to mean (shades of Lewis Carroll a third time). I have resisted claiming 'not' to be the English 'not', and indeed have avoided putting weight on my assumption that it is a form of negation. Thus my rights regarding 'not' are simply the rights of stipulative definition.

A potential problem for standard philosophical practice, however, is the example of A. N. Prior's 'tonk', a connective * stipulated such that $a \vdash a * b$ and $a * b \vdash b$ (Prior 1960). Here we seem to have a clearly stipulated use for a clearly stipulated connective, and yet all Hell breaks loose: allow * in that sense and everything follows. Clear stipulation may thus not be enough. Perhaps 'not' is akin to *, and should also be resisted in the same way.

I regard the notion of stipulative but none the less unacceptable definitions to be worthy of further exploration. The reason that Prior's 'tonk' is so corrosive in deduction is clear: it is itself defined in terms of the deductive relation. Small wonder, then, that it has as consequence the legitimation of a particular (and particularly obnoxious) pattern of proof. Any term stipulated short of that overreaching grasp would not have the same effect.

A similar claim could be made for familiar forms of the ontological argument in which 'God' is defined in terms of the modal notion of necessity. Small wonder that even the possibility of applying such a term carries full necessities in consequence. Any term stipulated short of that overreaching modal presumption would not have the same effect (see Grim 1979, 1981, 1991).

The reason for resisting Prior's 'tonk' and the ontological argument's 'God', however, does not seem to apply to the outline for 'not' offered above. I am unable to find in that outline the kind of overreaching grasp that clearly accounts for unhappy surprises in Prior's 'tonk' and the ontological argument's 'God'. What these cases do seem to establish is that stipulative definition is not as harmless as it is sometimes taken to be. But it is also clear that stipulation *can* be innocent and convenient, and without the kind of structural analysis that is possible in the case of 'tonk' and the ontological argument there does not seem to be a structural objection to the stipulative introduction of 'not'.

3. A third option for the dialetheist is not to concede the outline of 'not' and swallow a small victory for the LNC in consequence, not to resist it as dangerous on the model of 'tonk', but simply to find my attempt at outline unsuccessful.[3]

Despite my disclaimer that 'not' is not to be taken as the English 'not', it is obvious that the outline above uses various forms of negation, including the English 'not',

---

[3] Some philosophers, Priest among them, have cited the paradoxes of self-reference as primary motivations for dialetheism. Dialetheists of this particular motivational stripe may be forced to reject 'not' in one way or another, by hook or by crook, since it is clearly possible to create a self-referential paradox that employs it, e.g. 'This sentence is not true.' If the paradox-motivated dialetheist rejects LNC for 'not' on the grounds that it embroils us in the standard reasoning of the Liar, consistency (!) would seem to force him to reject an LNC for 'not' on the grounds that it gives us similar reasoning for this variant. For this point I am obliged to an anonymous referee.

prominently and repeatedly in trying to get the idea across. If these forms of negation can be understood a particular way, it seems inevitable that 'not' can be understood a particular way. Given a dialetheic interpretation of all the various forms of negation in the outline, then, one might well end up with a dialetheic interpretation of 'not'. The result could be that every claim made above is allowed, but without the concept of exclusion that is their main intent: all claims regarding 'not' are cheerfully accepted, together with all claims regarding what 'cannot be', 'impossibility', 'incompatibility', and 'exclusion', but with the reserved right to cheerfully add 'not' forms of all these to the mix as well.

The prospect of a dialetheic reinterpretation of 'not' is reminiscent of Huw Price's dialogue:

Me: 'Fred is in the kitchen.' (Sets off for kitchen.)

You: 'Wait! Fred is in the garden.'

Me: 'I see. But he is in the kitchen, so I'll go there.' (Sets off.)

You: 'You lack understanding. The kitchen is Fred-free.'

Me: 'Is it really? But Fred's in it, and that's the important thing.' (Leaves for kitchen.)

(Huw Price (1990: 224))

My attempt above was to outline a very basic term of semantic exclusion. But without some fundamental grasp of precisely that notion to begin with it seems quite possible that it cannot later be specified.

Is there some way of outlining such a basic term in order to *guarantee* that the intended sense of exclusion gets across? I think not. We know that we cannot accomplish the comparative task of outlining even the notion of *number* unambiguously, so as to avoid interpretation of our 'numbers' as merely the evens, for example. Quite generally, it appears, we cannot by specification alone target a unique reading for our specifications (see e.g. Putnam 1980). If semantic exclusion is not understood to begin with, what possible exposition could we rely on to nail it?

7. CONCLUSION

I hope that the general tour of the territory that I've offered compensates for the fact that there are so few conclusions that can yet be firmly drawn.

What is clear is that contradiction is spoken of in a variety of ways—semantic, syntactic, ontological, and pragmatic, just for starters—which entail a variety of LNCs and dialetheisms that may be in competition.

At that point it seems that we should be able to eliminate at least some of the contenders as trivially true or false—trivially true and false given particular definitions of 'contradiction', for example. Even in the apparently easy cases, however, it turns out that impasse is all too close. That impasse ultimately threatens the basic understanding of the very principles at issue, and thus threatens any conviction that there can be any real debate between dialetheism and the LNC.

One way out, I've proposed, is the introduction of a stipulative and explicitly exclusionary 'not'. Given such a 'not', some easy cases again become easy cases. More importantly, the fact of real disagreement can be expressed in a way that offers a prospect for real debate. Although some easy cases are settled simply by definition on each side, important questions regarding negation and contradiction more widely remain open for exploration.

That is the course that I would hope a dialetheist to take. Given the positions at issue, however, I must admit that I see no way to make it compulsory. Dialetheists of at least some stripes may choose to reject the possibility of 'not' and anything of its exclusionary kind. All I can say is that those forms of dialetheism seem less interesting to me; I don't see how the prospect of impasse is then to be avoided, and such forms don't seem to me to promise any deeper understanding of notions as central to our conceptual toolkit as is the notion of contradiction.

REFERENCES

ARISTOTLE (*c.*350 BC). *Metaphysics*, trans. W. D. Ross. In Richard McKeon (ed.), *The Basic Works of Aristotle*, Random House, 1971.
—— *On Interpretation*, trans. E. M. Edghill. In McKeon, ibid.
BONEVAC, DANIEL (1987). *Deduction*, Mayfield.
BRODY, BARUCH (1967). 'Logical Terms, Glossary of,' in Paul Edwards (ed.), *The Encyclopedia of Philosophy*, Macmillan and Free Press.
CARROLL, LEWIS (1895). 'What the Tortoise Said to Achilles,' *Mind*, NS 4: 278–80.
—— (1896). *Symbolic Logic, Part One: Elementary, A Fascinating Mental Recreation for the Young*, repr. in *Lewis Carroll's Symbolic Logic*, ed. William Warren Bartley, III, Harvester Press, 1977.
DEMORGAN, AUGUSTUS (1846). 'On the Syllogism: I: On the Structure of the Syllogism,' trans. Camb. Phil. Soc. VIII, pp. 379–408, repr. in Peter Heath (ed.), *On the Syllogism and Other Logical Writings*, Routledge & Kegan Paul, 1966.
FORBES, GRAEME (1994). *Modern Logic*, Oxford University Press.
GRIM, PATRICK (1979). 'Plantinga's God and Other Monstrosities', *Religious Studies* 15: 91–7.
—— (1981). 'Plantinga, Hartshorne, and the Ontological Argument', *Sophia* 20: 12–16.
—— (1991). *The Incomplete Universe: Totality, Knowledge, and Truth*, MIT Press.
HAACK, SUSAN (1978). *Philosophy of Logics*, Cambridge University Press.
KAHANE, HOWARD (1995). *Logic and Contemporary Rhetoric*, 7th edn., Wadsworth.

KALISH, DONALD, MONTAGUE, RICHARD, and MAR, GARY (1980). *Logic: Techniques of Formal Reasoning*, Harcourt Brace Jovanovich.

MENDELSON, ELLIOT (1964). *Introduction to Mathematical Logic*, D. van Nostrand.

PARSONS, TERENCE (1990). 'True Contradictions', *Canadian Journal of Philosophy*, 20: 335–53.

PRICE, HUW (1990). 'Why "Not"?', *Mind*, 44: 221–38.

PRIEST, GRAHAM (1987). *In Contradiction*, Martin Nijhoff.

—— (1993). 'Can Contradictions Be True? II', *Proceedings of the Aristotelian Society*, Suppl. vol. 68: 35–54.

—— (1995). *Beyond the Limits of Thought*, Cambridge University Press.

—— (1998). 'What is So Bad About Contradictions?', *Journal of Philosophy*, 45: 410–26.

—— (1999). 'What Not? A Defence of Dialetheic Theory of Negation', in D. Gabbay and H. Wansing (eds.), *What is Negation?*, Kluwer, 101–20.

—— (2002). 'Paraconsistent Logic', in D. Gabbay and F. Guenthner (eds.), *Handbook of Philosophical Logic*, 2nd ed. Kluwer, vi.

PRIOR, A. N. (1960). 'The Runabout Inference Ticket', *Analysis*, 21: 129–31.

—— (1967). 'Negation', in Paul Edwards (ed.), *The Encyclopedia of Philosophy*, Macmillan and Free Press.

PUTNAM, HILARY (1980). 'Models and Reality', *Journal of Symbolic Logic*, 45: 464–82.

QUINE, W. V. O. (1959). *Methods of Logic*, Holt, Rinehart, & Winston.

REICHENBACH, HANS (1947). *Elements of Symbolic Logic*, Free Press.

ROUTLEY, R. and V. ROUTLEY (1985). 'Negation and Contradiction,' *Revista Colombiana de Matemáticas*, 19: 201–31.

SAINSBURY, R. M. (1991). *Logical Forms*, Blackwell.

SAKA, PAUL (2001). 'Exploding the Myth of Paraconsistent Logic', unpublished.

SLATER, B. H. (1995). 'Paraconsistent Logics?', *Journal of Philosophical Logic*, 24: 451–4.

SMILEY, TIMOTHY (1993). 'Can Contradictions Be True? I', *Proceedings of the Aristotelian Society*, Suppl. vol. 68: 17–33.

STRAWSON, P. F. (1952). 'Logical Appraisal', ch. 1 of *Introduction of Logical Theory* (London: Methuen), repr. in R. I. G. Hughes (ed.), *A Philosophical Companion to First-Order Logic*, Hackett, 1993.

SUBER, PETER (2001), 'Non-Contradiction and Excluded Middle', URL www.earlham.edu/~peters/courses/logsys/pnc-pem.htm.

WOLFRAM, SYBIL (1989). *Philosophical Logic*, Routledge.

4

Laws of Non-Contradiction, Laws of the Excluded Middle, and Logics

Greg Restall

ABSTRACT

There is widespread acknowledgement that the law of non-contradiction is an important logical principle. However, there is less than universal agreement on exactly *what* the law amounts to. This unclarity is brought to light by the emergence of paraconsistent logics in which contradictions are tolerated: From the point of view of proofs, not everything need follow from a contradiction. From the point of view of models, there are 'worlds' in which contradictions are true. In this sense, the law of non-contradiction is violated in these logics. However, in many paraconsistent logics, statement $\sim(A \wedge \sim A)$ (it is not the case that A and not-A) is still provable. In this sense, the Law of Non-Contradiction (LNC) is upheld. This chapter attempts to clarify the different readings of the LNC, in particular taking cues from the tradition of relevant logics. A further guiding principle will be the natural duality between the LNC and *rejection* on the one hand and the Law of the Excluded Middle (LEM) and *acceptance* on the other.

1. LOGICS

Logic is about many different things. One important topic of logic is the relation[1] of *logical consequence*. A logic tells you what follows from what, what arguments are good, and what commitments involve. For the purpose of this chapter, I will take a logic to determine a *consequence relation* between premises and conclusions. In particular, a logic will give us a reflexive and transitive relation $\vdash$ on propositions.[2] Not everyone takes logic to be simply about logical consequence: some take the role of logic as primarily determining a class of special propositions, the tautologies. In this chapter I will use the notion of logical consequence to clarify the behaviour of

Thanks to JC Beall, Daniel Nolan, and Graham Priest for discussion on the topics raised in this chapter, and to the two referees for helpful comments. This research is supported by the Australian Research Council, through Large Grant No. A00000348.

[1] Or the relations, as in Beall and Restall (2000*b*).

[2] This view of logic as primarily determining a relation of consequence on propositions is defended in many places. See 'Logical Pluralism', Beall and Restall (2000*b*).

the LNC, the LEM, and acceptance and rejection. I will not argue for the primacy of logical consequence for logic, I will merely assume it. However, the flexibility and fruitfulness of this approach to logic will, I hope, count towards a defence of this approach to issues in philosophical logic. In what follows we will explore how our commitments to logical consequence are related to claims we ought to accept and claims we ought to reject.

Logical consequence constrains rational acceptance and rejection. What we may rationally accept and what we may rationally reject is directly connected to logical consequence. If I accept a notion of logical consequence, then acceptance and rejection are rationally constrained like this: if A ⊢ B and I accept A then I ought not to reject B. If we generalize consequence to relate non-empty *sets* of propositions, taking Σ ⊢ Δ to mean that given *all* of the elements of Σ, *some* of the elements of Δ follow, then we constrain acceptance and rejection in a generalized way. I cannot accept each element of Σ and reject each element of Δ.

I will not attempt to defend this constraint on rational acceptance and rejection. Any such defence will depend essentially on clarifying both the notion of logical consequence *and* the notion of rationality in play in the account, and this is beyond the scope of a short chapter. The task here will be to clarify the consequences of such a constraint for our understanding of the LNC, and its dual, the LEM.

All proponents of the debate over the interpretation, the defence, or the rejection of contradictions and the LEM agree that negation connects entailment, acceptance, and rejection. Disagreement lies over the form that the connection ought to take. One reasonably basic insight, shared by most proponents of classical or non-classical logics, is that negation is 'order inverting' in the following sense:

(1) If A ⊢ B then ∼B ⊢ ∼A

This is the inference of *contraposition*. Using our connections between entailment, acceptance, and rejection, we reason as follows: If the rejection of B brings with it (rationally) the rejection of A (because accepting A is ruled out) then the acceptance of ∼B brings with it (rationally) the acceptance of ∼A (because rejecting ∼A is ruled out). One way to ensure such a connection is to *identify* the acceptance of ∼A with the rejection of A. However, this is not the only way to understand negation. Dialetheists take the rejection of A to (at least sometimes) require something more than the acceptance of ∼A, as they sometimes take it that we may sometimes rationally accept both A and ∼A. Assuming that we cannot both accept A and reject it at the same time, we have a case where we accept ∼A and do not reject A. Rejection perhaps involves more than the acceptance of a negation. Proponents of truth-value gaps take it that acceptance of ∼A might require something more than rejection of A, as they take it that we may sometimes rationally reject both B and ∼B. Again, assuming that we cannot accept and reject something at the same time, acceptance is perhaps more than the rejection of a negation.

So much is common ground, but the common ground is not very spacious. There is only so far that one can go using lattice logic with minimal constraints on negation. In the rest of this chapter we will see how endorsing different systems of logical consequence constrains acceptance of contradictions and rejections of excluded middles.

2. CLASSICAL LOGICS

Classical propositional consequence is a suitable starting point. Classical logic adds to our basic logic more inferences, such as the LEM, in the following form.

(2) $A \vdash B \vee \sim B$

This tells us that every instance of excluded middle $B \vee \sim B$ follows from any proposition whatsoever. This ensures that in the entailment ordering, $B \vee \sim B$ is at the top. Endorsing classical logic *very nearly* assures that we are committed to each instance of $B \vee \sim B$. That is, if you are committed to classical logic, you are very nearly given compelling reason to accept $B \vee \sim B$ for each B. For *any* A, A entails $B \vee \sim B$. So if you accept *any* A at all, you have reason to accept $B \vee \sim B$. However, this rationally compels us to accept each $B \vee \sim B$ only if we antecedently accept some proposition or other. It is consistent with the constraints on acceptance provided by classical consequence that we accept no propositions at all. Then, trivially, our acceptances are closed upward under classically valid inferences.

The situation with the law of non-contradiction is completely dual. The law appears in classical consequence in the following form (which is suggestively called *explosion*):

(3) $A \wedge \sim A \vdash B$

This tells us that every contradiction $A \wedge \sim A$ is at the bottom of the entailment ordering. Endorsing classical logic *very nearly* assures that you are committed to rejecting each contradiction. If you reject any proposition at all, then by (3) you ought to reject each contradiction $A \wedge \sim A$. However, it is consistent with the constraints on rejection provided by classical consequence that you reject no propositions at all. Then, trivially, your rejections are closed downward under classically valid inferences.

These outlying cases are, of course, exceptions. They are the analogues for acceptance and rejection of the formal result that the empty set and the set of all propositions are both *theories*. (That is, they are sets of formulas closed under logical consequence.) They are undoubtedly theories in this sense, but in a clear sense, they are *trivial*. The empty theory says nothing about the world, and the full theory rules nothing out. There is a simple technique for eliminating such theories from consideration. If we extend consequence further to include *empty* sets Σ and Δ then we eliminate these trivial theories. We read the consequence relation as before. $\Sigma \vdash \Delta$ if and only if any interpretation for each element of Σ is an interpretation for some element of Δ. Classically we will have $\emptyset \vdash$ $B \vee {\sim}B$ (as every interpretation makes $B \vee {\sim}B$ true) and $A \wedge {\sim}A \vdash \emptyset$ (as no interpretation makes $A \wedge {\sim}A$ true). Constraining acceptance and rejection with this more comprehensive consequence relation ensures that the rational agent accept something. For $\emptyset \vdash B \vee {\sim}B$, and since an agent accepts every element of $\emptyset$ (there are none!) the agent ought to accept $B \vee {\sim}B$. Similarly, since $A \wedge {\sim}A$ $\vdash \emptyset$ then since an agent rejects every element of $\emptyset$ the agent ought to reject $A \wedge {\sim}A$.

By using a more comprehensive consequence relation, with a correspondingly more comprehensive constraint on acceptance and rejection, we have guaranteed that propositions of the form $A \wedge {\sim}A$ ought to be rejected and that propositions of the form $B \vee {\sim}B$ ought to be accepted. None of the argument has required singling out a primary relation between logic and acceptance (through tautologies) or between logic and rejection (through a set of propositions that logic can determine as worthy of rejection: call them 'inconsistencies'[3]). We get the effect of special classes of sentences through a constraint tying together rational acceptance and rejection with logical consequence, given that the consequence relation is read as relating *sets* of premisses and conclusions. The effect of tautologies and inconsistencies is provided by means of empty premiss and conclusion sets respectively.

3. PARACONSISTENT LOGICS

Not all propositional logics are classical. Not all logics mandate the LEM (2) or *explosion* (3). The task of understanding the law of non-contradiction became more pressing with the growing popularity of *paraconsistent* logics (see Priest and Sylvan, 1989). Paraconsistent logics are distinctive in that they do not mandate *explosion* in the form found in (3). Instead, for paraconsistent logics the entailment fails.

$$A \wedge {\sim}A \nvdash B$$

The formal details need not detain us here. Suffice to say, in the semantics for these logics there are interpretations in which A and ${\sim}A$ may both be taken to be true, but in which not *everything* is true. Such interpretations are sufficient to invalidate explosion.

---

[3] The term may be infelicitous, for the following reason. Here an inconsistency is 'not consistent' in the sense that it is not true under any interpretation. According to this definition of the term, a contradiction $A \wedge {\sim}A$ need not be inconsistent in a paraconsistent logic.

There are many good reasons to endorse a paraconsistent consequence relation.[4] Explosion seems to fail canons of relevance. Circumstances in which contradictions are true seem to be necessary in the evaluation of counter-possible conditionals ('If I squared the circle with ruler and compass then I would be famous' seems true while 'If I squared the circle with ruler and compass then Queensland would win the Sheffield Shield next year' seems false). Commitment to a contradiction does not seem to compel rationally (or even to make rationally *more plausible*) commitment to absolutely everything whatsoever. Finally, some have taken the semantic and set-theoretic paradoxes to furnish convincing proofs that some contradictions are actually *true*. Each reason here seems to motivate a concern for paraconsistent consequence. However, only the last seems to motivate a rejection of the LNC in the sense that we are given reason to accept a contradiction, so we are given reason to not reject it.

In many paraconsistent logics the situation with the LEM is formally dual to the LNC. For example, in the logic of first-degree entailment (the conjunction, disjunction, and negation fragment of the relevant logic R and its neighbours) the situation with excluded middle is exactly dual. We have

$$A \nvdash B \vee \sim B$$

as well. Yet many paraconsistent logics, such as R, are thought to *include* the LEM. In standard presentations for R you can *prove* each instance of $B \vee \sim B$! How can this be?

The explanation is not as difficult as it might seem.[5] In a relevant logic such as R something might be provable without it following from anything and everything. The initial motivation for this is on grounds of relevance. We might be able to prove $B \to B$ without the tautologous $B \to B$ following from an arbitrary A. So, in logics such as R we do not have $A \vdash B \to B$. However, we do wish to say that $B \to B$ is 'provable' as provable implications are a good record of valid inferences, like $B \to B$. To this, we must break the link between tautologies (provable propositions in the sense desired here) and those propositions that follow from anything and everything, and in particular, the empty set of premisses.[6] We wish to say that logic commends $B \to B$ as necessary to accept, without saying that $B \to B$ follows from anything and everything. In a logic such as R this is achieved by fiat. The provable propositions are not those at the top of the entailment ordering.[7] More propositions are provable than this. A simple way to represent this is to add to

---

[4] For many good reasons, see Priest, Sylvan, and Norman (1989).

[5] From this point on, I will take the relevant logic R as my paradigm case of a paraconsistent logic. Nothing hangs on the logic of implication of R here, and many different paraconsistent logics can be substituted without any difference of application.

[6] By structural properties on proofs, if $\emptyset \vdash A$ then it follows straightforwardly that $\Sigma \vdash A$ for any set Σ of premisses, at least given the interpretation of set–set consequence given here. For a finer control of premisses and conclusions, work on *substructural* logic is relevant. See Restall (2000).

[7] Equivalently, they are not just the propositions true at every set-up in the frame semantics.

the language a special proposition t representing the conjunction of all provable propositions.[8] We then have $t \vdash B \to B$ without also having $A \vdash B \to B$ for every A. 'Logic' dictates that we accept each $B \to B$ without dictating that such an acceptance follows from any acceptance whatsoever. (As a result, we ought to accept t without taking it that $\emptyset \vdash t$.) Accepting R and using it to constrain inference in this way involves more than taking rational acceptance to be closed upwards and rational rejection to be closed downwards. Now we *also* take rational acceptance to include t. Without an extra condition such as this we have no way to force the rational acceptance of propositions not at the top of the entailment ordering.

There is no loss of generality in taking the propositions we ought to accept on the basis of logic alone as those entailed by a *single* proposition t. First of all, if logic dictates that we accept A, and if A entails B, then we should accept B on the basis of logic as well. So, the class of propositions to be accepted on the basis of logic is closed upwards under entailment. More generally, if we ought to accept each element of Σ on the basis of logic and $\Sigma \vdash A$ then we ought to accept A, also on the basis of logic. So, if Σ has a conjunction (call it 't'), then we ought to accept A on the basis of logic if and only if $t \vdash A$. The only new assumption we have made is that the class Σ of propositions to be accepted on the basis of logic alone has a conjunction.

With these considerations in mind we can proceed to the law of the excluded middle. It ought to come as no surprise that in R we do not have $A \vdash B \lor \sim B$, but we *do* have

(4) $t \vdash B \lor \sim B$

In accepting R we do not hold that $B \lor \sim B$ follows from anything and everything, but none the less we do hold that we ought to accept $B \lor \sim B$. Excluded middle is mandated by acceptance of R though the acceptance of t, not because each $B \lor \sim B$ follows from $\emptyset$.

By dualizing, we see that the same sort of treatment is available for the LNC. Just as we have a LEM just when some proposition t (which we ought to accept) entails $B \lor \sim B$ for each B, we also have a LNC when some proposition f (which we ought to reject) is entailed by every contradiction.

(5) $A \land \sim A \vdash f$

And *this* may well be provided by logic. Indeed, (5) is supplied as valid by the relevant logic R, where f is the negation of t. However, what is typically *not* provided by a logic is guidance on what ought to be rejected. The most guidance a logic is usually taken to give is what we have already seen. If some proposition entails

---

[8] For those who prefer the frame semantics, t is true not at every set-up but only at a special class of set-ups, at which all propositions of 'logic' are true. Logic dictates that the actual world is one of these set-ups.

everything then it is to be rejected if anything is. If a proposition entails the empty conclusion, then it is to be rejected *tout court*. If a logic is paraconsistent, rejecting (3), then the rejection of a contradiction is not so easily read off a consequence relation. More must be given.

In a logic such as *R* the guidance to reject contradictions is given by guidance to reject f. Why might we reject f? A plausible reason is that f is ∼t, and we have reason to accept t. Given that we ought to accept t we ought to reject its negation. Now we have travelled in a circle, or at the least, a tight spiral. We have reduced the rejection of an arbitrary contradiction A ∧ ∼A to the rejection of the contradiction t ∧ ∼t. We must reject t ∧ ∼t by rejecting its second conjunct ∼t, given that we accept its first conjunct t. The reason we have for rejecting arbitrary contradictions, given these considerations, is nothing more than the reason we have for rejecting a particular one, t ∧ ∼t. Clearly this is not a reason that will find favour with the dialetheist, who takes there to be independent reason for asserting a contradiction. However, for those who have no independent reason to accept any contradiction, the move to accepting a paraconsistent logic gives us no new reasons to accept them. A natural reading of the way that inference in *R* constrains rejection motivates a simple analysis of contradictions according to which they are to be rejected, completely dual to the way that according to *R*, excluded middles are to be accepted.

So far we have seen that a logic such as classical logic can mandate the rejection of the LNC through the validity A ∧ ∼A ⊢ B. Given a more discriminating logical system in which contradictions need not entail *everything* we may still be given guidance to reject contradictions if they entail something else we ought to reject. In a logic such as *R*, contradictions do entail something that we have good reason to reject. They entail f, the negation of the proposition t that we ought to accept. The mere acceptance of a paraconsistent logic such as *R* does not *force* us away from rejecting contradictions. The LNC can remain in the weaker form, A ∧ ∼A ⊢ f.

On the other hand, nothing in a relevant logic such as *R* necessitates the rejection of all contradictions. If we have some independent reason to accept contradictions, then we have independent reason to accept the particular contradiction t ∧ ∼t. We keep the original reason to accept t, and we now have reason to accept ∼t, as it is entailed by the other contradiction we now accept. A paraconsistent logic such as *R* is suitable for the dialetheist. We may keep the *R*-edict to close our acceptances upwards and our rejections downwards, keep our obligation to accept t, while abandoning the injunction to reject f. Such an approach would not be foreign to the spirit of *R*. But neither would the dual approach: we could well adopt *R*-consequence as a condition on acceptance and rejection, to hold fast to rejecting f while refrain from accepting t, and hence refrain from accepting all propositions of the form B ∨ ∼B. This too would not be foreign to the spirit of *R* as presented here, but it would be foreign to most defenders of *R*, and it is illuminating to consider why. We have presented *R* as primarily a system for determining logical consequence. Traditional presentations of propositional logic, especially those using Hilbert-style proof theories, focus on the special class of logical truths. In *R* the simplest proof theory is the class of propositions entailed by t.[9] This approach to adopting *R* would involve taking *R*-consequence as mandatory for regulating acceptance and rejection, while *not* taking *R*-theorems to be rationally mandatory to accept. In particular, an agent guided by this policy would not be thereby obliged to accept each proposition of the form B ∨ ∼B. Such an approach is surely not what Anderson and Belnap intended in *Entailment* (1975) (also Anderson, Belnap, and Dunn 1992), but it is not foreign to the enterprise of relevant logic.[10] In just the same way, nothing in the adoption of *R* requires that we reject f and the contradictions that entail it, but it is completely natural to do so. The burden, if there is any at all to be borne, is on the one who fails to reject contradictions to explain why in some case or other, reason to accept t is not reason to reject ∼t. Nothing in accepting *R*-consequence counts against *that*.[11]

I will end this discussion of forms of the LNC with a short analysis of positive forms of the law, as a proposition to be accepted. We have seen the law expressed as the edict 'reject A ∧ ∼A!', which arises in one way or another from a logical consequence relation. What of positive forms of non-contradiction, which enjoin us to accept propositions such as ∼(A ∧ ∼A)? These are present as provable logics such as *R*. In what sense might endorsing (5) commit one to a positive statement of the LNC? Must we accept ∼(A ∧ ∼A)? How can accepting this follow from (5)? Here is one way: a contraposition of (5) gives

$$\sim f \vdash \sim(A \wedge \sim A)$$

In *R*, ∼f is equivalent to t (since ∼∼A is equivalent to A.) So we are a small step away from accepting ∼(A ∧ ∼A). For this, we need only accept ∼f. Even if we reject the inference from ∼∼t to t in general, we may have reason to accept it in this case. If we reject f, then surely we ought to accept its negation. Or should we? If I take f to be *neither true nor false* then I may accept neither f nor ∼f. In this case,

---

[9] This is surely more than a historical accident, given the primacy of implication as an assertoric record of valid inference. However, there is nothing mandatory in *valid inference* that makes implication the only sensible record of validity. We could just as well take *subtraction* as primary (read 'B − A' as 'B without A') and instead of taking t ⊢ A → B as our asserted record of A ⊢ B, take B − A ⊢ f as our *denied* record of the same entailment. We reject B − A on the basis of logic alone in just the same way as we accept A → B on that basis. We cannot establish a priority for assertion on merely formal grounds. An 'axiomatization' of *R* on the basis of the propositions we ought to *reject* on the basis of logic alone (those that entail f) is just as straightforward as its traditional axiomatization. (Note that B − A is equivalent in *R* to ∼(A → B).)

[10] It is the analogue for agents of the formal result that not all *R*-theories need be *regular* in the sense of containing all *R*-theorems. Or simply, t is not a member of all *R*-theories.

[11] There is more to this issue than I have time or space to address here. Priest (2000) has ingeniously argued that while accepting a paraconsistent logic does not rationally *force* one to be open to accept contradictions, it is the first step down a swift slippery slope in that direction. I do not think that Priest's argument to this conclusion is compelling as it stands, but I cannot address it here. Beall and I have a paper which addresses this issue at some length (Beall and Restall 2000*a*).

accepting *this* form of the LNC seems indeed to depend on the LEM. This makes sense. If we *reject* A ∧ ∼A, this only makes one *accept* ∼(A ∧ ∼A) given a version of the LEM. In *R*, given that we accept t we ought to accept ∼(A ∧ ∼A) also.[12] This explains how the *R*-proponent who accepts closure under *R*-consequence, and who accepts t, need not also accept the LNC on the form of rejecting f, but will still happily assent to all instances of ∼(A ∧ ∼A). It is no more inconsistent than accepting the particular contradictions that sent this agent down this route. The only trouble for such a believer is the multiplication of contradictions. If she accepts A ∧ ∼A, and also accepts t then she ought to accept ∼(A ∧ ∼A) also, another contradiction with her earlier acceptance of A ∧ ∼A. The positive form of the LNC, as an acceptance of ∼(A ∧ ∼A) does not place the agent under an obligation to reject contradictions independently of her obligation to reject f. If she does without that obligation, then merely accepting ∼(A ∧ ∼A) will do no good. At the risk of belabouring the duality, the situation is exactly parallel to the case of the agent who rejects some instances of B ∨ ∼B (and thereby rejects t). The mere fact that she also may reject ∼(B ∨ ∼B) does not mean that she must accept B ∨ ∼B. If she rejects both t and ∼t, she is not going to be obliged to accept B ∨ ∼B simply because she rejects ∼(B ∨ ∼B). If excluded middles have no purchase in general, then there is no general reason to accept that either B ∨ ∼B or its negation ∼(B ∨ ∼B) is true. If there are truth-value gaps with B, we may well expect there to be truth-value gaps with B ∨ ∼B too. If there are truth-value gluts with A we just as well might expect truth-value gluts with A ∧ ∼A too. In the absence of a general rejection mechanism, accepting ∼(A ∧ ∼A) does not bring with it an obligation to reject contradictions.

4. DISJUNCTIVE SYLLOGISM AND ITS DUAL

I will end by discussing a close analogue to the LNC, the rule of *disjunctive syllogism*. I have written elsewhere about one general approach to disjunctive syllogism (Beall and Restall, 2000*b*; Restall, 1999, 2000) and I will not repeat that analysis here. In those papers I defended both *R*-consequence and classical consequence as appropriate accounts of valid inference, and I took the difference in their treatment of disjunctive syllogism as indicative of our need to attend to both canons of validity. In those discussions, I did not attend to the particularities of acceptance and rejection, nor to the resources available in *R*-consequence, supplemented with t and f. So let us start: Disjunctive syllogism, in the following form

(6) A ∨ B, ∼A ⊢ B

[12] The argument can go directly from t ⊢ A ∨ ∼A to t ⊢ ∼(A ∧ ∼A) by de Morgan's laws as well. All de Morgan laws are available in *R*. This also makes the connection between A ∨ ∼A and ∼(A ∧ ∼A) explicit.

is classically valid, but not valid in *R*. Here is the closest that *R* can furnish us with an inference in its vicinity:

(7) $A \vee B, \sim A \vdash B, f$

If I have reason to accept both $A \vee B$ and $\sim A$, then I ought to accept the disjunction of B and f. (The inference can go through the disjunction of $B \wedge \sim A$ and $A \wedge \sim A$ (by distribution), then the inference from $A \wedge \sim A$ to f, and by discarding the conjoined $\sim A$ in the first conclusion.) What I can do given such a disjunctive acceptance is a matter of further discussion. The practice of simply dropping the disjoined f or saying it *sotto voce* is discussed, and discarded as unsatisfactory, in Belnap and Dunn's (1981) comprehensive account of the issue.

In keeping the spirit of this chapter, I will examine what we should say about (7) and its constraint on acceptance and rejection in terms of its dual inference form. The dual of (6) is also invalid in *R*

(8) $A \vdash \sim B, A \wedge B$

but its companion, dual to (7) with a conjoined t as premiss, is valid in *R*.

(9) $t, A \vdash \sim B, A \wedge B$

As far as I have been able to ascertain, this inference form is not discussed in connection with disjunctive syllogism. (The closest discussion to this one in the literature that I know of is Graham Priest, *In Contradiction* (1987: s. 8.3). It is illuminating to consider how *R*-obligations on acceptance and rejection constrain us in each case. We will start with (9), as it is less worked over.

If I reject both $A \wedge B$ and $\sim B$ then by *R*-consequence, I ought to reject the conjunction of t and A. Given that I ought not to reject t, it follows that I must reject A. Here we have a straightforward recapture of the 'classical' inference pattern (8) as far as rejection preservation is concerned. Given that I ought not to reject t (as a full-blown acceptance of *R* would have us eschew) then if I reject $A \wedge B$ and $\sim B$, I ought to reject A too. Why is this? Well, given that I accept t, I accept $B \vee \sim B$. I reject $\sim B$ so I ought to accept B. (I cannot accept $B \vee \sim B$ while rejecting both disjuncts.) But now, I reject $A \wedge B$ but I accept one conjunct B. I should thereby reject A, lest I accept the entire conjunction. As for constraining *acceptance*, (9) tells us that if I accept t and I accept A, then I must accept the disjunction of $\sim B$ and $A \wedge B$. But I ought to accept t anyway, so if I accept A then since I ought to accept t, I must accept both A and t, and thus, accept the disjunction of $\sim B$ and $A \wedge B$. So, given that we ought to accept t, we get the effect of (8) without accepting it as valid, in just the same way as the obligation to accept t rationally compels our acceptance of $B \vee \sim B$ without necessitating our acceptance of (3). The weaker (5) suffices.

But in the case of (9) the argument utilizes an important extra feature: the fact that the acceptance of A *survives* the acceptance of t. We can only reason as we did, from the acceptance of A to the obligation to accept the disjunction of $\sim B$

and A $\wedge$ B, only if the obligation to accept t, when fulfilled, keeps the acceptance of A in play. For only when we accept *both* t and A will (9) take effect and the obligation to accept the conclusion follow. If once we accept t the acceptance of A disappears, (9) gains no grip. This seems possible. Suppose A is $\sim$t, and I accept $\sim$t, and that I *don't* also accept t. Here I fall foul of what R enjoins us to accept and reject. Nothing I have said so far tells us that if I have failed to live up to one R-obligation the others fail to apply. If I accept $\sim$t, then here is how R constrains my acceptances: I should accept t, and if I accept t $\wedge$ $\sim$t, I ought to accept the disjunction $\sim$B or $\sim$t $\wedge$ B. Now if I have no inclination to accept t $\wedge$ $\sim$t then the second obligation does not apply, and we are left with the obligation to accept t. If a stronger case could be made, to the effect that I *always* accept t, so that once I accept $\sim$t I *thereby* am committed to t $\wedge$ $\sim$t, the second condition applies, and any riders about disappearing acceptances do not arise.

Now consider the analogous case for (4). Given that I accept A $\vee$ B and I accept $\sim$A, what ought the full-blooded R-proponent do? Given that I ought to reject f, but I ought to accept B $\vee$ f, I ought to accept B, for I ought not to accept a disjunction while rejecting both disjuncts. The rejection of f mandated by R provides enough transmission of acceptance to give the effect of disjunctive syllogism. If I do not have reason to reject f, then the situation is also straightforward. If I do not reject f then the inference gives me no extra reason to accept B. The case is direct in the hypothetical situation in which one accepts A and $\sim$A for the sake of the argument. There is no sense that *this* acceptance *thereby* mandates you to accept B. No, if I have accepted both A and $\sim$A, then although A $\vee$ B follows, and as a result, so does B $\vee$ f, this gives us no reason to accept B, for the assumption of both A and $\sim$A brought along with it an assumption of f, and *this* is how we were led to B $\vee$ f, not an inference to B alone.

5. CONCLUSION

We have seen that considering a logic as a consequence relation makes the parallels between LNCs and LEMs striking. In classical logic, the laws are strong. Contradictions are at the bottom of the entailment ordering, and excluded middles are at the top. In logics such as R the situation is more subtle. Contradictions need not entail everything, and excluded middles need not be entailed by everything. Yet, just as it is natural to accept excluded middles, on the basis of R-reasoning, it is natural to reject contradictions on the basis of the very same reasoning. A paraconsistent logic such as R makes the way *open* for the acceptance of contradictions, and controls the consequences of such acceptances, but it does not make them mandatory. There are many different LNCs, and, and some are present, even in paraconsistent logics such as R.

REFERENCES

ANDERSON, A. R., and BELNAP, N. D. (1975). *Entailment: The Logic of Relevance and Necessity*, Princeton University Press, Princeton, vol. i.

ANDERSON, A. R., BELNAP, N. D., and DUNN, J. M. (1992). *Entailment: The Logic of Relevance and Necessity*, Princeton University Press, Princeton, vol. ii.

BEALL, JC, and RESTALL, G. (2000*a*). Logic, Impossibility, and Contradiction: Avoiding the Slippery Slope from Paraconsistency to Dialetheism. In preparation. (Presented to the 2000 Australasian Association of Logic Conference.)

—— (2000*b*). 'Logical Pluralism'. *Australasian Journal of Philosophy*, 78: 475–93.

BELNAP, N. D., and DUNN, J. M. (1981). 'Entailment and the Disjunctive Syllogism'. In F. Fløistad and G. H. von Wright (eds.), *Philosophy of Language/Philosophical Logic*, Martinus Nijhoff, The Hague, 337–66. Repr. as s. 80 in *Entailment*, Anderson et al. (1992).

PRIEST, G. (1987). *In Contradiction: A Study of the Transconsistent*. Martinus Nijhoff, The Hague.

—— (2000). 'Motivations for Paraconsistency: The Slippery Slope from Classical Logic to Dialetheism'. In D. Batens, C. Mortensen, G. Priest, and J.-P. van Bendegem (eds.), *Frontiers of Paraconsistency*, Kluwer Academic Publishers, 223–32.

PRIEST, G., and SYLVAN, R. (1989). 'Systems of Paraconsistent Logic'. In G. Priest, R. Sylvan, and J. Norman (eds.), *Paraconsistent Logic: Essays on the Inconsistent*, Philosophia Verlag, 151–86.

PRIEST, G., SYLVAN, R., and NORMAN, J. (eds.) (1989). *Paraconsistent Logic: Essays on the Inconsistent*. Philosophia Verlag.

RESTALL, G. (1999). 'Negation in Relevant Logics: How I Stopped Worrying and Learned to Love the Routley Star'. In D. Gabbay and H. Wansing (eds.) *What is Negation?*, Applied Logic 13, Kluwer Academic Publishers, 53–76.

—— (2000). *An Introduction to Substructural Logics*. Routledge.

5

Option Negation and Dialetheias

R. M. Sainsbury

1. INTRODUCTION

A dialetheia is a statement that is both true and false. If negation turns truth into falsehood and falsehood into truth, the negation of a dialetheia is both false and true. So the conjunction of a dialetheia with its negation is both true and false; in particular, it is true. Hence if there are dialetheias, and the assumptions about negation and conjunction are correct, there are true contradictions.[1] It may well be that the assumptions about negation and conjunction should remain unchallenged. However, in this chapter I suggest that there is a kind of negation that, within a dialetheic framework, will not sustain the argument just given. The kind of negation at issue behaves classically in classical frameworks, and so enables the classicist to accept the assumptions the argument involves; but it behaves unexpectedly once we allow truth value gluts, that is, once we allow dialetheias. This means that it is not obvious that belief in dialetheias requires belief in true contradictions.

The form of this claim is unsurprising: no doubt it would be easy to cook up a negation-like operator that would have the effect described. The claim is of interest only if the operator has an independent claim on our interest. I am not entirely confident that it does: but I am fairly confident that whether or not the operator is of interest is an interesting question, so I thought I should give it an airing.

The actual historical role of negation in human thought and cognition might throw some light on how best to describe the negation we actually currently employ. A common view is that we can understand negation best through the speech act of denial. Although there are interesting links between negation and denial, an explanation of negation in terms of denial seems to presuppose that it is possible for there to exist a negation-free system of thought or language. This would need to pre-exist acts of denial, in order to provide candidate sayings or thoughts to be denied. The view that there could be a negation-free system of language or thought is challenging; I shall assume that it is worth considering an origin for negation that does without it.

---

[1] The converse holds also: normal assumptions about negation and conjunction ensure that there are true contradictions only if there are dialetheias.

One possibility of this kind relates to the prevention of actions. An expression with the force of our 'No!' might have arisen to indicate that what the speaker takes the hearer to be about to do is ill advised or prohibited; the typical actual and intended response to the utterance could be that the hearer desists. Unlike an account that puts denial at centre stage, this does not presuppose negation-free language or thought: 'No!' could, as far as this account goes, be the first word to have arisen in the history of language development, and as it is directed not at a thought but an action, it might be available to creatures with at most a modest conceptual repertoire. An account of this kind would do justice to the fact (if fact it still is) that 'No' is one of the first words to which human infants learn to make an appropriate response.

The account to be offered here shares with the one just considered the independence of language, but starts at what is arguably a more basic point: agency. A creature that genuinely acts must have some conception of alternatives or options, and select among them. The proposed kind of negation is used to mark unchosen options. The conception of options does indeed require some kind of thought or representation, but it might be of an unsophisticated, perhaps non-conceptual, variety. We are happy to attribute genuine action to creatures about whose conceptual capacities we have doubts. When we say a bird chose a mate, we mean this quite literally, and not in the metaphorical way we would have to understand a claim like 'the river chose a wandering path across the mesa'. We think the bird had a choice of mates, and was in some sense aware of this. Or, if we do not, we must be taking a more Cartesian view of birds, seeing them as creatures lacking agency.

Suppose we are deliberating between two options, A and B. We take them to be exhaustive and exclusive, and this exclusiveness is the proposed basis for negation. (If the options are not exclusive, or are not exhaustive, then there are further options: both, or neither. These will be considered in their own right in s. 2 below.) To select A is to deselect B. Using 'NOT' for option negation, A is equivalent to NOT-B, and B to NOT-A. If we think of the options as marking the truth or falsity of some statement, and make minimal departures from classical thinking, option negation will be in some respects similar to classical negation: deselecting truth amounts to selecting falsehood, that is, NOT-true amounts to false; and NOT-false amounts to true. If instead of thinking of options as statements we think of one option as that a predicate applies truly to something, one alternative option will be that it applies falsely to that thing. This is in some ways similar to classical predicate negation.

By varying the options, option negation gives a ready explanation of phenomena that are not classical, or which can be brought into the classical picture only by much pragmatic straining. These include cases like (1)–(2) below, which are prima facie inconsistent from the classical perspective, but which in practice raise not a shiver among interpreters:

(1) It's not a car, it's a Volkswagen.

(2) No, I have not *pak edd zee soo eet cass ez*. I have packed the suitcases.[2]

Presumably the advertising agency thought there would be something striking about (1), but they certainly did not suppose the audience would infer that a Volkswagen is not a car, which would be a classical consequence. One could imagine (2) uttered with some irritation as a response to 'Af yu pak edd zee soo eet cass ez?' by one who has tried hard to help the native French questioner with her pronunciation. It is classically inconsistent, but it is impossible to hear it thus.

Classical logicians can appeal to various pragmatic mechanisms to explain why it is difficult or impossible to interpret such utterances as inconsistent. One popular line starts with a literal inconsistent interpretation, which feeds into the supposition that the speaker is observing conversational maxims and thereby generates a new and consistent interpretation. Such an account raises many problems. One immediate one is that the supposed inconsistent literal reading is generally unavailable to the consciousness of interpreters. This does not prove that it does not exist, but its apparent unavailability calls for explanation. A further problem is to explain why we find no introspective traces of the supposed reasoning, which would have to be quite long and complex.

Within the option negation framework, all is straightforward. In (1) the options are to call it a car or to call it a Volkswagen, and the former is deselected. In the (2) the options are to say 'I af pak edd zee soo eet cass ez' or to say 'I have packed the suitcases' and the former is deselected. All interpretation involves bringing to bear something more than what is usually counted as semantic knowledge: for example, a hearer must at a minimum know what language the speaker is speaking. The present application of option negation also involves attributing extra-semantic knowledge to interpreters, for an interpreter must appreciate which are the relevant options, and an account must be given of how this is possible. The problem seems tractable, much more so than the problem of providing a plausible pragmatic story within the classical framework. A basic notion in dialogue is what the right thing to say is, where truth is not sufficient for being right, and may not even be necessary. Applying this notion to both (1) and (2) gives an appropriate result: the right thing to say is that it's a Volkswagen, not that it's a car, and the right thing to say is 'I have packed the suitcases', not 'I af pak edd zee soo eet cass ez'. This seems much more straightforward and promising than an account that begins by attributing to the hearer an unconscious realization of the literal inconsistency of (1) and (2).

---

[2] Examples of this kind abound in Horn (1989) who uses them to ground a distinct notion of negation that he calls 'metalinguistic negation'.

2. OPTION NEGATION AND CLASSICAL NEGATION

One difference between option negation and classical negation is that the former can apply to things other than statements (e.g. to types of action such as choices of what to say). Another difference is that NOT may, as applied to the kinds of examples considered in the previous section, be somewhat independent of truth. Where option negation is applied to a statement, and the options are whether it is true or false, can it differ from classical negation? Let us for the moment keep to the case of two options, A and B. A entails NOT-B, whereas there is no parallel inference from inclusive A or B, together with A, to the classical negation of B. Perhaps the difference lies merely in the fact that options are presupposed to be exclusive. If we try to use a classical rendition, we should obviously take the options to be represented by the exclusive A OR B, true iff exactly one disjunct is true, so that A in the presence of this disjunction does entail the classical negation of B. So it is on the cards that the only substantial difference between option and classical negation is that the former can apply to a wider range of entities. Perhaps option negation and classical negation coincide (once exclusiveness is properly represented) in their common area of appropriate application.

In response, let me start by indicating a difficulty for this reconciling project when we consider three options. As mentioned earlier, we may find that our supposedly exclusive alternatives A and B are not really exclusive: we discover that we can do both. We now have three options: A, B, or both. BOTH-(A,B) entails NOT-A and also NOT-B: that is, doing both means we do not do just one. The same structure of exclusiveness holds throughout the options: A entails NOT-BOTH-(A,B), and so does B. Can these facts be classicized? If we represent the options as A OR B OR BOTH-(A,B), with the OR exclusive as before, then indeed BOTH-(A,B) entails the classical negation of each of A and B. But if we also think of BOTH-(A,B) as the classical conjunction of A and B, our disjunction can never hold in virtue of the holding of this disjunct, for if it holds and operates like conjunction, this would suffice for the holding of the other two disjuncts, making the disjunction false. By contrast, one can easily choose both A and B, thereby deselecting each of the solo choices of A alone and B alone. BOTH-(A,B) is a consistent selection, and one which, as we have seen, entails NOT-A and NOT-B.

A reconciling classicist may rejoin that he has no quarrel with us about negation, and can perfectly happily accept exclusive disjunction, but that the true source of disagreement lies with BOTH. This cannot stand for conjunction; the route to reconciliation lies in identifying it with some other classical function, perhaps with that which outputs a truth iff both components are false. This reflects the entailment from BOTH-(A,B) to each of NOT-A and NOT-B, but leads to further difficulties when we see that there is very often a fourth possibility: to do neither. NEITHER(A,B) also entails NOT-A and NOT-B, so the reconciling classicist would have to assign the output true for the case when both inputs are false. The remainder of the function presents problems. Retaining classical ways of thinking, it would be natural to suppose that one could not allow that the output was true if either input was, which would lead to a function identical with the function for BOTH, which is not only in itself unintuitive, but also fails to do justice to the standard entailments from BOTH to NOT-NEITHER and conversely. Other choices run aground on essentially similar problems. NEITHER-(A,B) needs to entail each of NOT-A and NOT-B which makes it hard for it to be classically consistent with the truth of either A or B.

Option negation takes us out of the classical universe, while being a highly natural way of describing some uses of negation. Even if there could be a reconciliation with classicism, one can be reasonably sure that a classicized rendering would not have the natural and straightforward character of option negation, at least as applied to choosing actions.

3. APPLICATION TO DIALETHEISM

An assignment of a truth value or truth values to a statement A can be seen as an answer to the question 'What is the truth value of A?' If there are gluts as well as truth and falsehood, there are three options: true, false, and both. If, in addition, there are gaps, there are four options: true, false, both, neither. We can connect these semantic ideas with the option negation framework by considering the options as ways of answering a question about the truth status of some statement A. In the simplest case, the options are just TRUE and FALSE. We can mirror gluts by adding the option BOTH, and gaps by adding the option NEITHER.

If D is a dialetheia, we should answer the question about its truth status as BOTH. In order to assess the argument from the existence of dialetheias to the existence of contradictions, we need to consider what truth status will be assigned to the negation of a dialetheia. If negation worked classically, the answer would also be BOTH, and given natural views about conjunction the argument would succeed. However, option negation is supposed to operate within the framework of options. If the options are *stay at home* or *eat out*, to option-negate the first is to deselect it, which we can represent as NOT-(stay at home). Applying this analogy to D, its negation is represented as NOT-D. The corresponding truth status, within the framework, must then be just one of TRUE, FALSE, or NEITHER. It cannot be BOTH, on the assumptions made, for BOTH represents D, which NOT-D deselects. From this it follows that the option-negation of a dialetheia may not be TRUE, for its truth status may be one of the other remaining possibilities, FALSE or NEITHER. If either of these is actual, then there is no truth in the option-negation of a dialetheia, and so there is no good basis for counting the conjunction of a dialetheia with its option-negation as true. The existence of dialethias, in this framework, does not entail the existence of true contradictions.

An element of the framework that is responsible for this result corresponds to something that has often been used in attacks on dialetheism. The idea is that we intuitively feel that we ought to be able to assign a single truth status once and for all, a truth status that excludes any other status. If we could do this by using the word 'true', then dialetheias would be excluded: a statement's truth would guarantee that it has no further truth status. If a semantic theorist cannot use such a notion of truth, there seems something incomplete about assignments of truth status: assigning any one status, among true, not-true, false, not-false, and so on, does not preclude adding a further status later. The feeling is that if one accepts a dialetheist framework, one can never sign off the semantic task: further additions cannot be precluded.

Something like this worry is described (though not endorsed) by Priest (1999: 115): critics claim that dialetheists 'cannot express A in such a way as to rule out ¬A'. They affirm A, or call it true, or call it true *only*; but for any dialetheist this does not preclude it being also false, and for some dialetheists it does not preclude it being also not true.[3] How is one to say what needs to be said about some simple truth like 'Man is an animal'? Having said that it is true, or true *only*, one has not closed off the claim that it is also false. Dialetheism seems to diminish what we can say.

Priest's main response to the similar doubt is to point to the speech act of denial. He thinks that there is no rational possibility of denying and affirming the same thing. Dialetheists, at least those of his persuasion, do accept and affirm, but do not reject or deny, dialetheias. Those who wish to exclude something can simply deny it. Even granting this, the expression of a denial on the page is just a sentence. The appearance of 'A' on the dialetheic theorist's page, or of 'A is true only', does not tell the informed reader whether or not A will be said to be a dialetheia. Yet, intuitively, to assign to A the truth status *truth only* ought to settle that it is not a dialetheia.

The option negation framework in effect builds in the desired exclusiveness,[4] and this shapes the nature of option negation. Where the options are TRUE, FALSE, NEITHER, and BOTH, TRUE entails NOT-BOTH, as the kind of objector just envisaged would desire. I hope to have derived the exclusiveness not from any abstract logical principle, which would be question-begging in the present dialectic, but from highly natural and intuitive reflections upon how we organize our thought about choices. This gives the exclusiveness a certain (of course highly defeasible) authority.

---

[3] Priest himself shows some resistance to this species of dialetheism. For example, he declines to assert the Exclusion Principle: if A is false, A is not true (1999: 111). His reason is that to assert this principle would add to the number of true contradictions: if 'A and not A' is true, the principle would ensure that so is 'A is true and A is not true'.

[4] Perhaps it does so in part owing to its connection with action, in which case it would share something with Priest's opinion that true exclusiveness arises only with the action of denying, and not with the mere abstract association of a sentence with a semantic value.

4. OPTION NEGATION AND INCONSISTENCY

Option negation has a claim on our attention only if there is some plausibility in the view that it is at work in our actual thinking. I have already mentioned some cases (such as (1) and (2) above) that give some support to the hypothesis that it is. I close by mentioning a kind of case which, if my interpretation is accepted, provides a different kind of support, a kind directly related to dialetheism. The suggestion is that some cases of apparently deliberate inconsistency are in fact consistent, and the consistency is revealed in the option negation framework. In the two examples below, Locke and Plotinus, the authors might be interpreted as dialetheists; but they may also be interpreted as consistent exploiters of option negation.

Speaking of the abstract general idea of a triangle, Locke (1690: 4.7.9) said that 'it must be neither oblique nor rectangle, neither equilateral, equicrural, nor scalenon; but all and none of these at once'. Berkeley quoted this sentence on more than one occasion, always with derision, at one point saying that 'the above-mentioned idea of a triangle . . . is made up of manifest, staring contradictions' (1709: 222). I suspect I am not alone in thinking that there is a natural and consistent interpretation of Locke's words 'all and none of these at once'. We cannot, of course, consistently apply both 'equicrural' and 'scalenon' to any one thing, but I wish to focus just on whether 'all and none' is automatically inconsistent; inconsistent, that is, as a matter of the logic of these expressions (as opposed to what either might subsume in a particular application). Within the option negation framework, it is not. Taking 'all' as an extension of 'BOTH', it actually entails NOT-O, for each other option o, and 'none' could be seen as summarizing these entailments. This corresponds to an interpretation of Locke's words that sees them as summarizing a series of options concerning how to answer the question: what triangles are subsumed under the general abstract idea of a triangle? Just oblique ones? No. Just rectangle ones? No. All of these? Yes. No one (none) of these? Yes.

Plotinus wrote: 'The One is all things and no one of them' (*Enneads*, 5.2.1). This might be interpreted as a commitment to dialetheism.[5] Alternatively, it might be seen as a commitment to option negation. How should we answer the question: what things are there? To each thing, there corresponds the option of answering by mentioning it and it alone. There is also the generalized BOTH answer, represented by ALL. This is the right answer, and is used to define 'the One'. It entails that we deselect each of the solo options, o: so NOT-O for all these; in other words, no one of these is the One, even though the One is ALL.

I confess to finding the option negation framework intriguing. The present considerations are at best merely suggestive of the hypothesis that it plays a significant

---

[5] And was so interpreted by Graham Priest at a conference on the history of logic at King's College London in November 2000.

role in our thought; but I would hope that dialetheists would not be the only ones interested in exploring seemingly unfamiliar regions of logical space.[6]

REFERENCES

BERKELEY, G. (1709). *An Essay Towards a New Theory of Vision.*
HORN, L. R. (1989). *A Natural History of Negation.* Chicago, University of Chicago Press.
LOCKE, J. (1690). *An Essay Concerning Human Understanding.*
PRIEST, GRAHAM (1999). 'What Not? A Defence of Dialetheic Theory of Negation'. In D. M. Gabbay and H. Wansing (eds.), *What Is Negation?* Dordrecht, Kluwer.

---

[6] Many thanks to two anonymous referees for comments on an earlier draft.

6

Conjunction and Contradiction

Achille C. Varzi

The Law of Non-Contradiction (LNC) says that no contradiction can be true. But what is a contradiction? And what would it take for a contradiction to be true? As Grim (this volume, Ch. 2) has pointed out, a quick look at the literature will reveal a large menagerie of different interpretations of the basic terms and, consequently, of LNC. Grim actually identifies as many as 240 different options (on a conservative count), and I don't think there is any need to dwell further on the conceptual combinatorics that hides behind this familiar piece of logical nomenclature. I do, however, want to focus on one of the main ambiguities enumerated by Grim, one that seems to me to lie at the heart of the matter. And I want to offer an argument to the effect that on one way of resolving the ambiguity LNC is non-negotiable, but on another way it is perfectly plausible to suppose that LNC may, in some rather special and perhaps undesirable circumstances, fail to hold.

1. TWO NOTIONS OF CONTRADICTION

The ambiguity I have in mind is that which stems from the opposition between contradictions understood as individual statements (or propositions, or sentences), as for instance Marcus (1995) has it:

> (1) A contradiction is the conjunction of a proposition and its denial

and contradictions understood as pairs of statements (propositions, sentences),[1] as in the definition given by Kalish, Montague, and Mar (1980):

> (2) A contradiction consists of a pair of sentences, one of which is the negation of the other

Intuitively, the first type of contradiction arises if we assert and deny the same thing 'in the same breath', whereas the second type of contradiction arises if we end up denying (perhaps unwittingly) something we have already asserted. We could plausibly generalize these formulations by construing in each case one of the two conjuncts, or statements, not as the negation of the other but as a conjunct or statement that is *equivalent* to the negation of the other. However, the notion of

---

[1] From now on I shall settle on 'statement', but this decision will be of no consequence.

equivalence calls for a logic, and since I'm going to be concerned with the logical status of LNC it will be safer to stick to narrow formulations such as (1) and (2). Somewhat more formally, these can also be put thus:

(1′) A contradiction is a statement of the form *φ and not-φ*

(2′) A contradiction is a pair of statements of the form *φ* and *not-φ*

(where the italics serves the purpose of Quinean quotation). So the ambiguity arises from the fact that these two readings of 'contradiction' yield two corresponding readings of LNC:

(3) There is no circumstance in which a statement of the form *φ and not-φ* is true

(4) There is no circumstance in which statements of the form *φ* and *not-φ* are (both) true

Or, somewhat more formally:

(3′) There is no circumstance X and no statement $φ$ such that $X \Vdash φ$ *and not-φ*

(4′) There is no circumstance X and no statement $φ$ such that $X \Vdash φ$ and $X \Vdash$ *not-φ*

Let us call these the *collective* and the *distributive* formulations of LNC, respectively. Are these expressions of the same logical principle, or are they distinct?

In classical logic they are obviously equivalent. We are looking at two distinct formulations of what classically boils down to the same principle because classically truth and satisfaction commute with the truth-functional connectives, which is to say that a circumstance X verifies or satisfies a conjunction just in case it verifies or satisfies both conjuncts.[2] In other words, classically (3′) and (4′) are equivalent because of the following general equivalence (sometimes called the principle or rule of adjunction) governing the semantics of the connective 'and':

(5) $X \Vdash φ$ *and* $ψ$ if and only if $X \Vdash φ$ and $X \Vdash ψ$

If X is construed as a classical possible world, this equivalence is indisputable. And it is hardly a disputed equivalence even if the range of X includes worlds that are non-classical in some way or other, including impossible worlds that would violate LNC (for instance, a world inhabited by impossible objects such as Priest's (1997) Sylvan's box, if such there be). A world in which a conjunction is true—it is often argued—*just is* a world in which the conjuncts are true, whether or not such truths comply with the laws of classical logic.

---

[2] From now on, I shall confine myself to speaking of truth (broadly understood) rather than satisfaction. This is only to simplify things and will be of no consequence.

That LNC is to be taken as a principle about possible (or impossible) worlds is, however, another story. The intuition behind this and other logical principles is that they should provide some guidance as to what goes on in every conceivable circumstance, i.e. in every condition under which a statement might be said to be true or false; and this need not be cashed out in terms of worlds. Some prefer to speak of world *models* instead, or of *conceptions* of the world, and these in turn may be construed broadly enough so as to include, for example, fictional stories, pieces of discourse, belief sets, informational set-ups such as data-banks or knowledge-bases, and much more. In cases such as these the validity of (5) is no longer obvious, or so I shall argue; hence the distinction between collective and distributive understandings of LNC need not be empty. Indeed, in cases such as these the relevant notion of truth is itself liable to different characterizations. Some prefer to construe 'ⵏⵏ' as expressing, not full-blooded truth, but rather some more metaphysically modest notion of *correctedness* or *acceptability* or *commitment* relative to X (and there is no obvious reason to suppose that logic should not be developed with such more modest notions in mind). Hence, not only can the collective and distributive understandings of LNC be distinguished; they can be distinguished even without rejecting classical semantics for truth *tout court*.

2. WORLDS AND OTHER CIRCUMSTANCES

To illustrate with an example, familiar from Belnap (1977), suppose that a computer should be programmed so as to return 'Yes' to a query if and only if the relevant content has been explicitly entered in the computer's data bank. If you enter ϕ the computer will say Yes to a query about ϕ, and if I enter ψ the computer will say Yes to a query about ψ, because each of us is independently trustworthy; yet the computer will reject the conjunction ϕ *and* ψ unless you are willing to agree with ψ or I am willing to agree with ϕ. In other words, the computer would only assent to a conjunction if both conjuncts come from the same source. If a state of the computer's data bank at any given time counts as a possible 'circumstance', with 'ⵏⵏ' construed in the obvious way, then clearly this is a scenario in which (5) fails. In particular, the two versions of LNC will diverge, for my ψ could be the negation of your ϕ. Of course, we may want to supply our computer with a contradiction-checking device so as to prevent any circumstances of this sort from arising at all. But that is not to say that the computer could not work without the device. (Moreover, depending on the language used, there is no guarantee that the device could be effectively extended so as to detect *all* sorts of inconsistencies besides those involving pairs of explicitly contradictory statements.)

In a similar spirit, Jaskowski's (1948) discussive logic is non-adjunctive, i.e. violates (5). If X is construed as reflecting the contents of a discussion involving two or more participants, so that the statements that hold in X are exactly those that are put forward by at least one of the participants, then there is no guarantee that the adjunction principle holds (from right to left). In particular, there is room for discordance. Two participants may contradict each other about the truth-value of a statement ϕ, but they need not contradict themselves. So again this could be a circumstance that complies with the collective form of LNC while violating the distributive form.

For one more example, familiar from the literature on the semantics of fiction, suppose we allow any sort of world-description to count as a circumstance. Such a description may involve discrepancies, as in *Don Quixote* (where there is discrepancy concerning the theft of Sancho Panza's ass[3]), or in the stories of *Sherlock Holmes* (where there is discrepancy concerning the position of Dr Watson's war wound[4]), or even in the *Harry Potter* saga (where there is discrepancy concerning the order in which Harry's parents were murdered by the evil Lord Voldemort[5]). But these discrepancies are best described as contradictions in the distributive sense rather than in the collective sense—as pairs of inadvertently contradictory statements rather than blatantly self-contradictory conjunctions. Hence the circumstances corresponding to these stories may be viewed as providing a violation to LNC in one sense but not in the other; they may be viewed as violating (4′) (inadvertently) while complying with (3′).

One might object that none of these cases should be given much credit. After all, one can easily insist that only worlds count as circumstances and treat all other cases as involving hidden propositional content of some sort. For example, it is true that a fictional story provides us with a context relative to which a statement might be said to be true or false; but this need not force us to construe the story as a genuine 'circumstance'. Rather—it could be argued—we could help ourselves with a suitable sentential operator that maps every statement ϕ to a corresponding statement of the form

(6) *According to S: ϕ*

where *S* is the story in question (or the computer's data bank, or the record of a discussion, or what have you). Then the cases discussed above would allow us to question the following biconditional, where *X* is a genuine circumstance:

(7) $X \Vdash$ *According to S: (ϕ and ψ)* if and only if $X \Vdash$ *According to S: ϕ and according to S: ψ*

---

[3] In Don *Quixote*, I. xxiii, Gines steals Sancho's ass, but four pages later Sancho is riding it again. Cervantes comes back to this discrepancy and tries to fix it in the second part of the book (II. iv).

[4] We are told that Dr Watson suffered a bullet wound during the Afghan campaign in which he participated. In *A Study in Scarlet*, this wound is said to be located in Watson's shoulder, but in *The Sign of Four* the wound is in his leg.

[5] The early books say that Harry's father died in an attempt to protect his child and wife, and that later Harry's mother was also killed. In *The Goblet of Fire*, when Harry forces the ghosts of all those killed by Voldemort to eject themselves momentarily into the living world, the deaths are given in reversed order.

And clearly this would not amount to questioning (5). 'According to S' is an operator that introduces an intensional context, on a par with 'Arthur said that' or 'Possibly', and one could insist that the question of whether such intensional contexts distribute over conjunction is to be settled case by case (depending on the sort of thing S is) and should be kept distinct from the question of whether (5) holds.[6]

There is nothing wrong with this line of argument. None the less I don't think it can settle the matter, and for at least two reasons. First, I reckon that a systematic account of what should count as a genuine circumstance (in the relevant sense) is part of what it takes to define a logic, i.e. a theory of logical validity.[7] The pre-theoretic intuition is that an argument is logically valid if and only if its conclusion is true in every circumstance in which all its premises are true,[8] and to make this precise one must come up with a precise characterization of the relevant notion of circumstance (along with an account of what it takes for a statement to be true in a given circumstance). But there is no a priori reason to assume that the range of options should be restricted to the realm of possible (and perhaps impossible) worlds. And it is hard to come up with a general assessment of LNC if we confine ourselves to a particular logic or family of logics. So it is certainly inappropriate to confine ourselves to a notion of circumstance that is restricted in the indicated way. Second, I reckon that the decision to treat a certain locution as belonging to the object language or to the metalanguage is itself part of what it takes to define a logic. We may decide to take the modal locution occurring in a statement such as

(8) *Possibly: φ*

as being part of the same (object) language to which the embedded statement $φ$ belongs, as is customary in modal logic, or we may decide to push it up to the metalanguage and treat it as a semantical predicate of $φ$ (a predicate to be cashed out in terms of quantification over worlds, for instance), as per Quine's (1953) 'first grade of modal involvement'. The choice is no philosophical routine and finds expression in a significantly different conception of modal logic. Likewise, we may decide to regard a locution of the form 'According to S' as being part of the object language, as per the line of argument under examination, or we may

---

[6] Some such cases are particularly difficult to settle, of course, as illustrated by the debate concerning the deontic distinction between conflicts of obligation and logically incoherent obligations (i.e. between distributive and collective readings of the 'ought implies can' principle). The relevance of these difficulties to the issue under discussion is one of the motivations for Schotch and Jennings's (1980*a*, 1981) work on weakly aggregative modal logics.

[7] On this I align myself with Beall and Restall's (2000) 'logical pluralism'; see Varzi (2002).

[8] Actually, it is unclear exactly how to phrase the pre-theoretic intuition. One could as well say that, intuitively, an argument is logically valid if and only if some of its premises is false in every circumstance in which its conclusion is false. If truth and falsehood are exhaustive and mutually exclusive, this coincides with the formulation given in the text; but if either truth-value gaps or truth-value gluts are admitted, then the two are distinct. Luckily, nothing here will depend on this ambiguity, so there is no need to bother.

push it up to the metalanguage and treat it as a semantical predicate, as per the more liberal understanding of 'circumstance' considered above. Again the choice is philosophically engaging and there is room for disagreement. But the claim that *no* such locution should be treated as a semantical predicate *except when S is a world* is a strong claim that can hardly be taken for granted. Certainly an assessment of LNC—and of whether its collective and distributive readings are equivalent—should be viable independently of any such claim. If the claim is true, then (5) may well be true and so the two readings of LNC boil down to the same thing. But if the claim is false, then it would seem that (5) may fail and so the collective and distributive readings of LNC may be significantly distinct.

3. NON-CONTRADICTION AND EXCLUDED MIDDLE

In fact, even if we stuck to the idea that the only admissible circumstances are worlds of some sort, the argument for (5) can hardly be that truth commutes with the truth-functional connectives. That is, that can hardly be the argument for (5) as soon as non-classical worlds come into the picture. If that were the case, then the rationale for (5) would also be a rationale for

(9) $X \Vdash \textit{not-}\phi$ if and only if not $X \Vdash \phi$

Yet clearly (9) is controversial. Classically it holds. But as soon as X is allowed to range over circumstances in which a statement may fail to receive a definite truth-value, (9) seems to founder. For instance, if a statement ϕ suffers a truth-value gap then so does its negation (on most counts), hence the right-to-left direction of (9) may fail. Dually, if X is allowed to range over circumstances in which a statement may suffer a truth-value glut, then it is the left-to-right direction of (9) that is dubious: a circumstance X may verify the negation of a statement ϕ as well as ϕ itself. Neither of these possibilities depends on how exactly one construes the relevant circumstance X, e.g. on whether X is an incomplete or inconsistent story about the world or rather a world that is itself incomplete or inconsistent. Nevertheless, it is not at all unreasonable, or uncommon, to think that such circumstances violate the equivalence in (9) in one direction or the other. So why should (5) enjoy a different status in this regard? Why not consider the possibility that (5) (and consequently the equivalence between (3') and (4')) be rejected along similar lines as soon as we go beyond the scope of classical logic?

Consider also disjunction—a binary connective like conjunction. To say that truth commutes with this connective is to assert the following semantic equivalence:

(10) $X \Vdash \phi \textit{ or } \psi$ if and only if $X \Vdash \phi$ or $X \Vdash \psi$

Again, this is classically valid and it is also valid in many non-classical logics. But there are also theories that reject (10). Supervaluationism, for instance, provides a semantics with truth-value gaps in which a disjunction can be true even if both disjuncts are indeterminate. As long as every admissible way of filling in the relevant gaps yields the same truth-value, a supervaluation assigns that value to the statement itself; so even if there is a circumstance X in which ϕ and ψ are both truth-valueless, the disjunction ϕ *or* ψ may still be true in X because it may be the case that every way of filling in the relevant gaps in X (every 'completion' of X) verifies either ϕ or ψ. In particular, this is obviously the case if ψ is *not-ϕ*. Thus, supervaluationally it may be true that, say, a given color patch is either orange or red, even though the patch may be a borderline case of both orange and red; and it is true (in fact, logically true) that a given person is either tall or not tall, even though it may be indeterminate whether that person is tall (or not tall). This holds regardless of whether you take the relevant indeterminacy to be conceptual (e.g. a feature of our model of the world) or ontological (i.e. a feature of the world itself).[9] Regardless of how you construe X, if truth is supertruth then the equivalence in (10) may fail.

Indeed, as already van Fraassen (1966) pointed out, the failure of (10) shows that supervaluationism provides a means for distinguishing between the following two versions of the Law of Excluded Middle (LEM), which of course coincide in classical logic:

(11) For any circumstance X and any statement ϕ: $X \Vdash \phi$ *or not-ϕ*

(12) For any circumstance X and any statement ϕ: $X \Vdash \phi$ or $X \Vdash$ *not-ϕ*

Call these the *collective* and the *distributive* formulations of LEM, respectively. (The distributive form amounts to what is also known as the principle of Bivalence.) Then van Fraassen's point was that supervaluationism validates only the collective formulation, not the distributive, as the case of the tallish person illustrates.[10]

Some people find this distinction unintelligible. They would argue that the equivalence between the collective and the distributive reading follows directly from the so-called Equivalence Scheme for truth:

(13) It is true that ψ if and only if ψ

For one can go from

(14) It is true that: ϕ *or not-ϕ*

---

[9] Most supervaluationists would go with the former option (and I align myself with them—see my 1999), but that is not a necessary feature of supervaluationism. See e.g. the (implicit) supervaluationism of Rescher and Brandom (1980).

[10] Actually, the point can be traced back to Mehlberg (1956: s. 29). Also, van Fraassen's example involved non-denoting singular terms rather than vague predicates, but the same point applies. (See e.g. Fine 1975.)

to

   (15) ϕ or not-ϕ

by applying the left-to-right direction of the Equivalence Scheme, hence to

   (16) It is true that ϕ or it is true that not-ϕ

by applying (twice) the right-to-left direction.[11] However, it is clear that in the present context this argument would be question-begging. For, a more general rendering of (13) is

   (13′) For any circumstance X and any statement ϕ: $X \Vdash \phi$ if and only if ϕ_X

where 'ϕ_X' spells out the truth conditions for ϕ relative to X. Hence the general forms of (14)–(16) are:

   (14′) $X \Vdash \phi$ *or not-*ϕ
   (15′) $(\phi$ *or not-*$\phi)_X$
   (16′) $X \Vdash \phi$ *or* $X \Vdash$ *not-*ϕ

And clearly the step from (15′) to (16′) is illegitimate on a supervaluational semantics. The correct step would be from (15′) to

   (17) For every admissible completion X' of X: $(\phi$ *or not-*$\phi)_{X'}$

But this, as we have seen, does not imply

   (18) Either for every admissible completion X' of X: $\phi_{X'}$, or for every admissible completion X' of X: *not-*$\phi_{X'}$

which is to say (by (13′))

   (19) Either for every admissible completion X' of X: $X' \Vdash \phi$, or for every admissible completion X' of X: $X' \Vdash$ *not-*ϕ

which is the only legitimate reading of (16′) afforded by supervaluationism. In other words, the objection to the distinction between collective and distributive readings of LEM is based on the assumption that truth commutes with the disjunction connective, which is precisely what is being denied by a supervaluational semantics.[12]

   Now, LEM and LNC are often treated together, for they are dual. So a perfectly dual argument can be given in support of the distinction between the collective and distributive readings of LNC: if a semantics that violates the disjunction principle (10) allows one to distinguish between (11) and (12), it is plausible to suppose

---

[11] This line of argument may be found in Horwich (1990) and Williamson (1992), *inter alia.*

[12] Nor is the distinction between the two readings a prerogative of supervaluationism. For a general discussion see DeVidi and Solomon (1999).

that a semantics violating the adjunction principle (5) should allow one to distinguish between (3′) and (4′). In fact, such a semantics can naturally be constructed through a dualization of supervaluationism. Supervaluationism provides a way of dealing with *incomplete* circumstances by piggy-backing on their complete extensions. The intuition is that if the truth-value of a statement ϕ does not change as we consider different ways of disposing of the relevant gaps, then the gaps are not so relevant after all, at least as far as ϕ is concerned: if ϕ would be true no matter what, then let ϕ be true. (If, on the other hand, the truth-value of ϕ turns out to vary from extension to extension, then the gaps do appear to be relevant and ϕ cannot be assigned a definite truth-value.) In the case of *inconsistent* circumstances we could reason dually as follows. If a statement ϕ gets a certain truth-value on some admissible way of weeding out the relevant inconsistency, i.e. on some admissible consistent restriction of the given circumstance, then let ϕ have that value: after all, the circumstance is explicit about that. Otherwise don't give that value to ϕ. So if the value of ϕ changes as you go from one restriction to the next, then there is nothing we can do about it: the inconsistency appears to be irredeemable and ϕ will suffer a truth-value glut. But if the value of ϕ does not change as we consider different ways of disposing of the inconsistency, then the inconsistency turns out to be immaterial and ϕ may receive one and only one truth-value.

Somewhat more formally, the idea can also be put thus.[13] The supervaluation registers the meet of all the admissible valuations, because an incomplete circumstance can itself be construed as the meet of its admissible complete extensions, or completions:

(20) $X \Vdash \phi$ if and only if $X' \Vdash \phi$ for every completion X' of X

Dually, a 'subvaluation' (as we may call it) will register the join of all the admissible valuations, because an inconsistent circumstance can itself be thought of as the join of its admissible consistent restrictions, or constrictions:

(21) $X \Vdash \phi$ if and only if $X' \Vdash \phi$ for some constriction X' of X

If X is both incomplete and inconsistent, this pattern will have to be applied twice.[14] But if X is incomplete but not inconsistent, or vice versa, then the right-hand occurrence of '$\Vdash$' may well implement a perfectly classical set of truth conditions. In any event, it is clear that (21) provides a way of cashing out the intuition illustrated above with reference to such circumstances as fictional stories, databases, or discursive records. For if ϕ and ψ are overdeterminate (true and false), the conjunction ϕ *and* ψ may still be false (and only false) even if both ϕ and ψ are true (and also false), violating (5). In particular, if ψ is the negation of ϕ, then the

---

[13] For details, complications, and generalizations I refer to Varzi (1997, 1999, 2000). See also Hyde (1997) for an application to vagueness.

[14] In which order? As it turns out, the two options are not equivalent, but there is no need to worry about this here.

conjunction comes out false (and only false) in every circumstance, i.e. logically false, even if both conjuncts are allowed to be true (and false).

To sum up, then, on this account the difference between the collective and the distributive forms of LNC turns out to be on a par with the difference between the collective and the distributive forms of LEM. It would not be an empty difference. And it would have repercussions on other logical principles as well, including principles governing the relation of logical consequence. For example, corresponding to the two readings of LNC and LEM one could also draw a difference between two readings of the principles known as *Ex falso quodlibet* (EFQ) and *Verum ex quodlibet* (VEQ), to the effect that contradictions logically imply everything and tautologies are implied by anything. On the collective reading these principles hold, just as in classical logic:

(22) ϕ *and not-*$\phi \vDash \Sigma$

(23) $\Sigma \vDash \phi$ *or not-*ϕ

This follows directly from LNC and LEM. But the principles corresponding to the distributive reading,

(22') ϕ*, not-*$\phi \vDash \Sigma$

(23') $\Sigma \vDash \phi$*, not-*ϕ

may fail. (Here, 'Σ' ranges over arbitrary sets of statements, hence the implication relation '$\vDash$' is to be understood along the following lines:

(24) $\Sigma \vDash \Gamma$ if and only if, for every circumstance X, $X \Vdash \phi$ for all $\phi \in \Sigma$ only if $X \Vdash \phi$ for some $\phi \in \Gamma$

I use this multiple-conclusion format to highlight the perfect duality between the two cases.[15])

4. THE TRUTH-FUNCTIONAL INTUITION

If this line of reasoning is taken seriously, then, the idea that LNC is ambiguous in an interesting way can be supported not only by considering different ways of specifying the basic notion of a circumstance, as in s. 2, but also by considering different ways of specifying the basic notion of truth. So, is this line of reasoning to be taken seriously?

---

[15] Again, other notions of implication are possible, trading on the non-exhaustiveness and non-exclusiveness of truth and falsity (see n. 8), but the main point holds regardless (Varzi 2000). It is also worth pointing out that if $\Vdash$ is cashed out in terms of other semantic features besides truth and falsity (e.g. in terms of Jennings and Schotch's (1984) levels of coherence), then again the classical equivalence between the collective and distributive readings of EFQ and VEQ may be lost. In this sense, a broadly 'preservationist' (Schotch and Jennings 1980*b*) account of the consequence relation would provide a short-cut to the conclusion of this section.

I think there is still one objection against it that most people find decisive, and it has something to do with a certain intuition about the link between formal semantics and theory of meaning. Briefly, the objection is that any semantics that does not fully satisfy the equivalencies expressed by the adjunction principle (5), or by the corresponding disjunction principle (10), fails to do justice to the 'meaning' of the conjunction and disjunction connectives as these are supposed to work in the English language. These equivalencies are non-negotiable, it is argued, because they are meaning constitutive. Conjunction and disjunction are Boolean functions defined by certain truth tables; hence assignments of truth-values to a statement ϕ containing such connectives should be uniform functions of the truth-values of the sentential components of ϕ, which means that a truth-value should be assigned to ϕ if and only if the same value is assigned to every other statement of the same form whose components have the same values. If a semantics delivers a different account, so much the worse for the semantics. (Negation is a different story, it could be argued, because of its many meanings and uses, so don't worry about (9). Ditto for conditionals. But conjunction and disjunction are perfectly unambiguous in the relevant sense.)

This objection is particularly common in the case of disjunction and the super-valuational failure of (10). In his *Lectures on Truth* (1975), for example, Kripke has argued that supervaluationism sits very ill with the way we tend to respond to the information conveyed by disjunctive statements. Someone says 'ϕ or ψ' and we naturally ask: 'Well—which one (if not both)?' Many people have echoed these misgivings. And similar objections have been raised against what I have called subvaluationism, too. For instance, Priest and Routley (1989) regard the failure of adjunction as a sign that 'and' has departed from its normal inter-pretation: conjunction *just is* that connective whose truth conditions are fixed by (5).

In a way, this sort of objection can be dismissed on the grounds of its unfair appeal to intuition. Change of semantics, change of subject—says the objection. Fair enough. But who got the semantics right in the first place? Obviously the right semantics is the one that sits best with observable pragmatic phenomena: inclinations to assent or to dissent, and the like. Yet this is no easy game. If we are talking about a tallish person, we may feel uneasy in calling the statement 'This person is either tall or not tall' true because we wouldn't be able to say *which one*. When it comes to 'This person is both tall and not tall', however, our intuitions are much more unstable and range from mixed to strongly negative in spite of the underlying indeterminacy. Whence the difference? And how do phenomena of *this* sort sit with the truth-functional intuition?[16] Alternatively, the objection at issue is

---

[16] Nor is there any need to bring in truth-value gaps or gluts to make the point. As Kyburg (1997) has emphasized, there is nothing incoherent in a circumstance in which we have many measurements, each of which is accurate enough to fall within the standard deviations of error, and yet we do not want to assent to their conjunction: 'We can be certain that some of them is wrong!' A dual situation concerning disjunction is illustrated by the lottery paradox (Kyburg 1961).

nothing more than an objection from the upper case letters, as Tappenden (1993) calls it: 'You say that *either ϕ or ψ* is true. So EITHER ϕ OR ψ [stamp the foot, bang the table] must be true!'; 'You say that ϕ AND ψ are true. So ϕ *and* ψ must be true!' Clearly this leaves us exactly where we were.

But never mind that. There is, I think, a deeper reply to this line of objection. For let us agree that conjunction and disjunction are indeed Boolean functions defined by the familiar truth tables. What follows from that? I think it follows that when we specify what counts as an admissible interpretation of the (object) language, we must rule out interpretations where 'and' and 'or' express something else than those Boolean functions. It does not, however, follow that (5) and (10) should hold, unless we make the extra assumption that there is a perfect homomorphism between a language and its interpretations. This point tends to be obfuscated by the fact that typically, as a matter of standard practice, the semantics of the logical operators is spelled out as being part and parcel of a recursive definition of truth: unlike the meaning of the other symbols (the 'extra-logical' terms), the meaning of the logical operators is not specified by the structures used to interpret the language but rather fixed *indirectly* through a recursive definition of the truth-value of the statements in which they occur. It is imposed *ab initio* upon the entire semantic machinery. And such a recursive definition typically involves clauses that read exactly like (5) (the 'truth conditions' for conjunction) or (10) (the 'truth conditions' for disjunction). But this typical way of proceeding is misleading.

To appreciate this point, we have to bring in some background considerations concerning the status of logical terms in general. What is it that distinguishes the logical vocabulary from the extra-logical vocabulary? This is a difficult question, but this much is clear: the difference lies in the fact that the meaning of the logical terms is kept fixed, whereas the meaning of the extra-logical terms may vary. For example, an extra-logical term such as the predicate 'red' is characterized by a strong semantic variability: every interpretation that accords with its syntactic category is a legitimate interpretation for 'red' as far as logic goes; every such interpretation corresponds to some logically possible circumstance. By contrast, if we think that the equality predicate is a logical constant, then there is little room for semantic variability. Clearly we cannot just interpret it as the very same relation in all possible circumstances, for the relation designated by a binary predicate depends on the universe of discourse, and this can vary from circumstance to circumstance. We can, however, restrict the semantic variability of the equality predicate and 'fix' its interpretation in the relevant sense by requiring that its extension be *always* the identity relation *restricted* to the relevant universe of discourse:

(25) In every circumstance X, the interpretation of the equality predicate '=' is the relation $\{\langle a, a\rangle : a \in U_X\}$

(where U_X is the universe of X). If 'circumstance' is understood classically, of course, then certain plausible conditions on $\Vdash$ will ensure that (25) has the consequence:

> (26) For every circumstance X and any pair of singular terms t_1 and t_2:
> $X \Vdash t_1 = t_2$ if and only if $I_X(t_1) = I_X(t_2)$

(where I_X is the interpretation function associated with X). For instance, this follows immediately if we adopt the familiar condition:

> (27) If ϕ is an atomic statement of the form $Pt_1 \ldots t_n$, then $X \Vdash \phi$ if and only if $\langle I_X(t_1), \ldots, I_X(t_n) \rangle \in I_X(P)$

Now, some people do exactly this when they spell out the semantics for a language with the equality predicate: they build (25) into the definition of an admissible circumstance (or 'model') and they get (26) as a general corollary— whence the ordinary logical principles governing the equality predicate follow. Other people do it differently. They exploit the thought that if the meaning of equality is going to be 'fixed' throughout, then there is no need to bring that explicitly into the interpretive machinery. So rather than using (25) as a constraint on what should count as an admissible circumstance, on this alternative account one uses (26) directly as a constraint on '$\Vdash$'. Both accounts are legitimate, because a logic is defined precisely by a specification of a certain set of constraints about these two notions: the notion of a (logically) admissible circumstance and the notion of truth in a circumstance. But there is a clear sense in which the second practice is conceptually contingent or dependent on the former: it is *because* we have (25) in the back of our mind that we can fix the meaning of equality indirectly via a clause such as (26). Being interpreted outside the interpretive machinery is not what distinguishes a logical term such as '=' from an extra-logical term such as 'red'.[17] That is something which is made possible *by* the fact that '=' is selected as a logical term whereas 'red' is not, i.e. by the fact that the meaning of '=' is treated as constant (in the specified sense) whereas the meaning of 'red' is treated as variable.

And notice: if we did not agree on the relevant notion of a circumstance, or on the notion of truth, then the second option might not even be available. We might agree on (25) while disagreeing on (26). We might, for instance, agree that '=' stands for the identity relation and yet disagree on the truth-conditions of certain equality statements involving non-denoting terms, or vague terms, or ambiguous terms. Clearly that would not mean that one of us is attaching a non-standard meaning to the equality predicate. It would simply mean that we are drawing different consequences from the fact that we attach that meaning to that predicate. We would disagree on the logic of equality. (And it would be correct to say this precisely in so far as we agree on '=' being equality.)

---

[17] This is the view commonly attributed to Tarski. (See e.g. Sher 1991.) I try to articulate my disagreement with this view in Varzi (2002).

Now, what about 'and' and 'or'? I think a perfectly similar story can (and ought to) be told. Of course, in this case we are talking about expressions that belong to a different syntactic category than equality. These expressions are connectives and so their semantic interpretation must be a function on the set of truth-values rather than a relation on the universe of discourse.[18] What are these truth-values? In principle they need not be fixed once and for all, but typically the set of truth-values is not allowed to vary from one circumstance to another. This amounts to a stipulation along the following lines:

(28) Every circumstance X has the same set of truth values T_X

A classical logician would pick something like $T_X = \{0, 1\}$. A three-valued logician could go for $T_X = \{0, .5, 1\}$; and a fuzzy logician might go for the continuum-valued set $T_X = [0, 1]$. Once we have made up our minds, the set of truth-values is fixed and we can produce our definition of truth. For example, if X is a classical circumstance, we may agree to define truth thus:

(29) $X \Vdash \phi$ if and only if $V_X(\phi) = 1$

where V_X computes the truth table for ϕ.[19] So, now, when we say that 'and' and 'or' are to be treated as truth-functions we mean to say that they have to be treated as functions on T_X. And to say that these are the usual truth-functions is to make a stipulation along the following lines:

(30) In every circumstance X, the extension of the connective 'and' is the function $\{\langle a, b, \min(a, b)\rangle : a, b \in T_X\}$

(31) In every circumstance X, the extension of the connective 'or' is the function $\{\langle a, b, \max(a, b)\rangle : a, b \in T_X\}$

Of course, these are not the only possibilities. For example, a fuzzy logician might prefer replacing (30) with

(30') In every circumstance X, the extension of the connective 'and' is the function $\{\langle a, b, a \cdot b\rangle) : a, b \in T_X\}$

Each stipulation corresponds to a certain way of fixing the meaning of the corresponding term, and each way of fixing the meaning will have certain consequences when it comes to matters of logical implication.

We thus come to the main point. Let us assume that we make the same stipulations concerning the meaning of 'and' and 'or', namely, that we agree on (30)

[18] One can also construe connectives as functions on sets of states of affairs, propositions, and much more. I will stick to Fregean truth-values for simplicity.

[19] The entries in the table would be partly guaranteed by (27) (which now implies that $V_X(Pt_1 \ldots t_n) = 1$ iff $\langle I_X(t_1), \ldots I_X(t_n)\rangle \in I_X(P)$) and partly by whatever clauses fix the truth conditions for the non-truth-functional compounds available in the language, e.g. quantified statements.

and (31). And let us suppose that we also agree on the classical set of truth-values, taking $T_X = \{0, 1\}$. *If* we also agree on the ordinary, classical way of understanding the notion of a circumstance and we agree on the ordinary, classical way of understanding 'ⵏ', then we certainly agree on (5) and (10) being a corollary of (30)–(31). That is, more precisely, we agree on the following being true:

(5′) For any circumstance X and any pair of statements ϕ and ψ: $X \Vdash \phi$ *and* ψ if and only if $X \Vdash \phi$ and $X \Vdash \psi$

(10′) For any circumstance X and any pair of statements ϕ and ψ: $X \Vdash \phi$ *or* ψ if and only if $X \Vdash \phi$ or $X \Vdash \psi$

We may agree so much on this that we may be inclined to think of (5′) and (10′) not as consequences of our background agreements but as a non-negotiable part of the machinery that we use to spell out our other agreements. Just as with equality, we may be inclined to specify our logical views not by using (30) and (31) as constraints on what should count as an admissible circumstance but rather by using (5′) and (10′) (hence (5) and (10) for short) as constraints that act directly on 'ⵏ'. We might be inclined, that is, to pull our agreement out of the interpretive machinery and to build it into a recursive machinery that matches our choice of truth-functions. That is perfectly all right, precisely because we agree on both. But just as with equality, I submit that this alternative way of proceeding is conceptually contingent. It is because we have (30) and (31) in the back of our mind that *in practice* we can fix the meaning of 'and' and 'or' through such clauses as (5′) and (10′).[20]

Now suppose we *don't* agree on what counts as an admissible circumstance. Or suppose we *don't* agree on 'ⵏ', i.e. on what it takes for a statement to be true (or acceptable) under a given circumstance. Can we still agree that conjunction and disjunction have a certain meaning, namely, the meaning fixed by (30) and (31)? Of course we can. Does it follow that both of us will agree on (5′) and (10′)? Of course it doesn't. If my notion of a circumstance is wider than yours, as in the examples of s. 2, or if my notion of truth is super- and subvaluational, as in the examples of s. 3, then (5′) and (10′) will not hold. Rather, in that case the logical properties of the conjunction and disjunction connectives would be captured by the following weaker facts (where '⊣' expresses falsehood):

(5″) For any circumstance X and any pair of statements ϕ and ψ:

$X \Vdash \phi$ *and* ψ only if $X \Vdash \phi$ and $X \Vdash \psi$

$X \dashv \phi$ *and* ψ if $X \dashv \phi$ or $X \dashv \psi$

(10″) For any circumstance X and any pair of statements ϕ and ψ:

$X \Vdash \phi$ *or* ψ if $X \Vdash \phi$ or $X \Vdash \psi$

$X \dashv \phi$ *or* ψ only if $X \dashv \phi$ and $X \dashv \psi$

[20] Admittedly, supporters of rule-following accounts of the meaning of logical constants will not like this. I'll get back to this in the concluding section.

And clearly these would not be good enough to allow me to cut a long story short and build the interpretation of the connectives into a recursive set of bi-conditionals. Does this mean that I would be attaching a different meaning to the connectives than you do? Again, the answer is—it doesn't. It simply means that my other views (about the notion of circumstance and/or the notion of truth) would prevent me from drawing certain consequences from the fact that I attach that meaning to those connectives. It means that my logic of 'and' and 'or' would be different from yours, just as my logic of '=' might be different from yours even if we agree on the meaning of '='. It means, in particular, that while your theory implies both the collective and the distributive readings of LNC and LEM, or of EFQ and VEQ, my theory would only imply the collective readings. But that is not to say I would have departed from the usual understanding of 'and' and 'or'.

5. CONCLUSIONS

This line of argument is hardly going to convince anyone who has different views on the interplay between formal semantics and the theory of meaning—especially those who favor some sort of rule-following account of the meaning of logical constants. If the meaning of such expressions is fixed by their logical properties (by their 'inferential role', as some like to say[21]) then the primacy of explicit stipulations such as (30) and (31) dissolves. One would rather say that it is precisely principles such as (5′) and (10′), or perhaps (5″) and (10″), that take us close to the meaning of 'and' and 'or'. To someone who holds this view I can only concede that any disagreement concerning such clauses is likely to entail a disagreement on the very meaning of those connectives. (Ditto for equality.) But then we are back to battles of intuitions and arguments from the upper-case letters. To the extent that the general picture outlined in the previous section is accepted, however, it seems to me that the truth-functional intuition about the meaning of the connectives is by no means incompatible with the rejection of the adjunction and disjunction principles (5) and (10). We can agree on the meaning of 'and' and 'or' while disagreeing on their logical properties. Hence, in particular, we may agree on the validity of LNC (or LEM) under the collective reading but not under the distributive reading. I therefore conclude that the difference between the two readings is not empty. It is, in fact, an important distinction that is likely to show up as soon as we get away from a certain standard, restricted way of understanding the notion of a possible circumstance and the corresponding notion of truth.[22]

---

[21] I have in mind the sort of view inspired by the work of Prawitz (1965), for instance.
[22] Thanks to two anonymous referees for helpful comments on an earlier draft.

REFERENCES

BEALL, JC, and RESTALL, G. (2000), 'Logical Pluralism', *Australasian Journal of Philosophy*, 78: 475–93.

BELNAP, N. D., Jr. (1977), 'A Useful Four-Valued Logic', in J. M. Dunn and G. Epstein (eds.), *Modern Uses of Multiple-Valued Logics*, Dordrecht: Reidel, 8–37.

DEVIDI, D., and SOLOMON, G. (1999), 'On Confusions about Bivalence and Excluded Middle', *Dialogue*, 38: 785–99.

FINE, K. (1975), 'Vagueness, Truth, and Logic', *Synthese*, 30: 265–300.

HORWICH, P. (1990), *Truth*, Oxford: Blackwell.

HYDE, D. (1997), 'From Heaps and Gaps to Heaps and Gluts', *Mind*, 106: 641–60.

JAŚKOWSKI, S. (1948), 'Rachunek zdańdla systemów dedukcyjnych sprzecznych', *Studia Societatis Scientiarum Torunensis, A* 1, 8: 55–77; English trans. 'Propositional Calculus for Contradictory Deductive Systems', *Studia Logica*, 24 (1969): 143–57.

JENNINGS, R. E., and SCHOTCH, P. K. (1984), 'The Preservation of Coherence', *Studia Logica*, 43: 89–106.

KALISH, D., MONTAGUE, R., and MAR, G. (1980), *Logic: Techniques of Formal Reasoning*, New York: Harcourt Brace Jovanovich.

KRIPKE, S. (1975), *Lectures on Truth*, unpublished MS, Princeton University.

KYBURG, H. E. (1961), *Probability and the Logic of Rational Belief*, Middletown, Conn.: Wesleyan University Press.

—— (1997), 'The Rule of Adjunction and Reasonable Inference', *Journal of Philosophy*, 94: 109–25.

MARCUS, R. (1995), 'Contradiction', in T. Honderich (ed.), *The Oxford Companion to Philosophy*, Oxford: Oxford University Press.

MEHLBERG, H. (1956), *The Reach of Science*, Toronto: Toronto University Press.

PRAWITZ, D. (1965), *Natural Deduction*, Stockholm: Almqvist & Wiksell.

PRIEST, G. (1997), 'Sylvan's Box: A Short Story and Ten Morals', *Notre Dame Journal of Formal Logic*, 38: 573–82.

PRIEST, G., and ROUTLEY, R. (1989), 'Systems of Paraconsistent Logic', in G. Priest, R. Routley, and J. Norman (eds.), *Paraconsistent Logic. Essays on the Inconsistent*, Munich: Philosophia, 151–86.

QUINE, W. V. O. (1953), 'Three Grades of Modal Involvement', *Proceedings of the XIth International Congress of Philosophy*, vol. 14, Amsterdam: North-Holland, 65–81.

RESCHER, N., and BRANDOM, R. (1980), *The Logic of Inconsistency. A Study in Non-Standard Possible-World Semantics and Ontology*, Oxford: Basil Blackwell.

SCHOTCH, P. K., and JENNINGS, R. E. (1980a), 'Modal Logic and the Theory of Modal Aggregation', *Philosophia*, 9: 265–78.

—— (1980b), 'Inference and Necessity', *Journal of Philosophical Logic*, 9: 327–40.

—— (1981), 'Non-Kripkean Deontic Logic', in R. Hilpinen (ed.), *New Studies in Deontic Logic*, Reidel: Dordrecht, 149–62.

SHER, G. (1991), *The Bounds of Logic. A Generalized Viewpoint*, Cambridge, Mass.: MIT.

TAPPENDEN, J. (1993), 'The Liar and Sorites Paradoxes: Toward a Unified Treatment', *Journal of Philosophy*, 90: 551–77.

VAN FRAASSEN, B. C. (1966), 'Singular Terms, Truth-Value Gaps, and Free Logic', *Journal of Philosophy*, 63: 481–95.

VARZI, A. C. (1997), 'Inconsistency Without Contradiction', *Notre Dame Journal of Formal Logic*, 38: 621–38.

—— (1999), *An Essay in Universal Semantics*, Dordrecht: Kluwer Academic.

—— (2000), 'Supervaluationism and Paraconsistency', in D. Batens et al. (eds.), *Frontiers in Paraconsistent Logic*, Baldock: Research Studies, 279–97.

—— (2002), 'On Logical Relativity', *Philosophical Issues*, 12: 197–219.

WILLIAMSON, T. (1992), 'Vagueness and Ignorance', *Proceedings of the Aristotelian Society*, Suppl. 66: 145–62.

III

Methodological Issues in the Debate

7

Diagnosing Dialetheism

Bradley Armour-Garb

1. INTRODUCTION

In the standard view, a paradox consists of a number of claims, each of which enjoys some plausibility but which, together, yield a conclusion that is apparently unacceptable. Explaining how it goes wrong and how rejecting it resolves the paradox is said to constitute a *diagnosis* of a paradox, at least on the standard view. Put differently: A paradox is an apparently unacceptable conclusion derived by apparently acceptable reasoning from apparently acceptable premises. To resolve a paradox is to uncover either the odd-premiss-out or the questionable reasoning, the culprit that leads us to accept the problematic—and contradictory—conclusion.

If a set of sentences yields an acceptable conclusion *via* acceptable principles of inference, then, to all appearances, there is no paradox, for a paradox only gets off the ground if it provides us with reasons for thinking some of the premises, or the principles of inference, which we initially thought to be plausible, are implausible. Where there's no problem, there's no need for diagnosis and, thus, it seems, there's no paradox.

In this chapter I will raise, and reply to, a putative problem for dialetheism— the problem of diagnosing the liar paradox. According to the dialetheist, liar paradoxes are sound. Leaving aside putative problems with dialetheism, I consider the question of how, and in what sense, the dialetheist can take the liar paradox to be just that—a paradox. As I will show, while the dialetheist does not resolve the liar paradox in the standard way, dialetheism offers a way of rethinking the nature of paradox and, with it, a rethinking of the rules governing paradox.

The plan is as follows. In s. 2 I review dialetheism; and in s. 3 I consider the strongest case for dialetheism. Section 4 proposes a problem with the dialetheist's response to the liar paradox: s. 4.1 discusses happy- and unhappy-face solutions: s. 4.1.1 discusses happy-face solutions; s. 4.1.2 discusses unhappy-face solutions; and s. 4.1.3 discusses Tarski's solution as an unhappy-face solution. Section 5 considers an objection to dialetheism; s. 6 considers a response; and s. 7 closes.

2. DIALETHEISM

Dialetheism is the view that some propositions (or, generally, truth bearers) are both true and false. A dialetheia is a true contradiction, a proposition (or, again, truth bearer), P, such that both P and its negation, $\sim$P, are true. Accordingly, dialetheism is the view that there are true contradictions.[1]

Dialetheism seems to run up against the Law of Non-Contradiction (LNC). One common version of the LNC is that every instance of A $\wedge$ $\sim$A is false, that every instance of $\sim$(A $\wedge$ $\sim$A) is true. Dialetheists allow the truth of some contradictions and so, it would seem, reject the LNC. But dialetheists who subscribe to the 'Logic of Paradox' (LP) subscribe to the LNC, at least so understood. The dialetheist accepts that some contradictions are true, in which case (in LP) the negation of such a (true) contradiction is false and also true. The dialetheist, then, does not reject the LNC but, rather, accepts that it is (logically) true, and also false.[3] In this chapter I assume LP as the appropriate 'dialetheic logic', and use 'LNC' in the sense given: $\sim$(A $\wedge$ $\sim$A) is logically true; A $\wedge$ $\sim$A is logically false.[4]

3. THE CASE FOR DIALETHEISM

The strongest case for dialetheism arises from the prima facie appearance that English is capable of expressing its own semantics—that English is, as we might say, *semantically closed*. Semantic closure is a technical term defined over formal languages. For present purposes, we can call a language, L, semantically closed iff it is adequate to express all the relevant facts about the semantics of its own language. Thus, we might call a language, *L*, semantically closed if

   (i) All expressions of *L* possess a *semantic status;*[5] and

   (ii) Each of these semantic statuses can be expressed within *L*

---

[1] I am using 'contradiction' in the 'formal sense', as discussed in Beall [4], and am assuming adjunction (i.e. from A, B to infer A&B).   [2] See Beall [4].
   [3] I should note that Priest rejects one version of the LNC, namely, the version according to which *no contradiction is true*, but he does maintain the LNC in the above sense—namely, that every instance of $\sim$(A $\wedge$ $\sim$A) is true (though some instances are false). Beall [3] takes a slightly more radical line, given that (in that paper) he relies on LP but relies also on the intersubstitutivity of T$\langle$A$\rangle$ and A, something that Priest explicitly rejects. (Beall calls that version of dialetheism 'full-blooded dialetheism'.) For discussion of dialetheic deflationism, see Armour-Garb and Beall [1, 2] and Beall [6].
   [4] For discussions of the LNC and the various ways in which it can be formulated, see Beall [4] and Grim [7]. For a different 'dialetheic logic' on which the LNC (so understood) does not hold, see Beall [5].
   [5] By a 'semantic status', I mean: truth, falsity, or *something else*, where the 'something else' may be both/neither true and/or false, or, indeed, possessing no semantic value at all. In this way, semantic closure appears to go through, even if one takes (e.g.) the liar sentence to be without semantic value and, thus, not the sort of thing to which 'gaps' should be attributed. Thanks to JC Beall and Graham Priest for discussion of this issue. For more on semantic closure, see [9].

If we assume (i) and (ii), we will conclude that all sentences of L have a 'semantic status' and that, within L, we can express the semantic status as it is assigned to each expression (sentence) of L.

Few philosophers would reject the claim that English is semantically closed, at least prior to confronting the liar paradox. Upon confronting the liar paradox, however, the traditional reaction has involved rejecting appearances. That is, it involves rejecting, to some degree or other, the claim that English can express its own semantics. The difficulties with such approaches are revenge problems, a version of which is the *strengthened liar*,

    (L′) L′ is not true[6]

The problem is this: One has already rejected the strong appearance of semantic closure, and revenge problems indicate that still other related appearances must be rejected. The typical case involves sentences that, given a proposed, consistent semantic theory, appear to be true—or appear to be such that the theory ought to deem them to be true. On pain of inconsistency, however, the relevant theory cannot respect appearances. Thus, we purchase our consistency by rejecting appearances that, it seems, we ought to accept.

Suppose, for example, that someone has declared the standard liar sentence,

    (L) L is false

to be *without a semantic value*. In line with semantic closure, she thereby expresses as much; namely, she (truly) expresses that L is without a semantic value. She is then confronted with the force of the strengthened liar,

    (L″) L″ is false or without a semantic value

which she should, likewise, deem to be without a semantic value. However, on pain of inconsistency, she is forced to reject semantic closure (and, thus, appearances): While she *can* accept *and* express that L is without a semantic value, it seems that she *should*, likewise, accept and express that L″ is without a semantic value. But, if she is to reject contradictions, she cannot *both* accept *and* express that L″ is without a semantic value.[7] Thus, she must either accept that L″ is without a semantic value

---

[6] (L′) was introduced by van Fraassen ([15], 147) and was 'designed especially for those enlightened philosophers who are not taken in by Bivalence'. As I hope is clear, if one were to insist that the liar sentence is without a semantic value, a version of (L′) would create the needed paradox. This is discussed below.

[7] Suppose that L″ is without a semantic value and that, in line with semantic closure, she can express as much. Thus, she can express *that* L″ *is without a semantic value*. She should, then, be able to ascribe truth to what she has just expressed and, given that $L'' = $ 'L″ is false or without a semantic value', she can, thereby, express *that* L″ *is true*. Assuming the inference from 'α is true' to 'α has a semantic value', then, from 'L'' is true' and tinkering, she can conclude *that* L″ *is with a semantic value and that it is not the case that* L″ *is with a semantic value*. Contradiction. Priest [12] gives a version of this argument, which I endorse.

but refuse to express that it is without a semantic value (*quietism*, as we might call it), which is implausible; or she must refuse to accept (and, thus, refuse to express) that L″ is without a semantic value, which is desperate, given that she has just assigned that very semantic status—i.e. being without a semantic value—to L.

Dialetheists draw a non-traditional, but, I think, fairly reasonable lesson from the liar. What the liar teaches us is not that English is incapable of expressing its own semantics; rather, it teaches us that English enjoys the capacity to express its own semantics by being, in a certain sense, inconsistent. The underlying grammar of the language, together with certain facts of identity and, in the present context, uncontroversial logical principles, sanctions contradictions. Accordingly, dialetheists maintain that the liar involves a sound argument ending in a contradiction. Of course, given that dialetheists hold that such arguments are sound, they conclude that the liar is true, as well as false, and, thus, that the liar paradox is, thereby, resolved.

4. THE PROBLEM OF DIAGNOSIS

It is that last claim—that the liar paradox is, thereby, resolved—that may cause one to balk. After all: If the dialetheist claims the liar paradox to be a sound argument, in what sense is it a *paradox*? Put differently (and leaving aside general objections to dialetheism): If, as seems to be standard to our understanding of paradox, a condition of adequacy on any response to a putative paradox requires diagnosing that paradox, then it seems that the condition of adequacy is not met by dialetheism, for, *prima facie*, it seems that dialetheism fails to diagnose the liar paradox and, thus, fails to respond to it *qua* paradox. Let us call this problem the *problem of diagnosis*.

It is, by now, fairly standard to maintain that a response to the liar, to be adequate, must offer a diagnosis of the paradox, an explanation as to what goes wrong with respect to the paradox, and how it is to be avoided. To *diagnose* a paradox, one must either indicate which among the premises—the sentences that comprise a *paradox set*—are refutable, what about the reasoning is illicit, or which of the concepts found in one or another of the premises is, in a certain sense, incoherent. If the premises, the reasoning, or the concepts contained therein are dismissed then the paradox is diagnosed and, subsequently, resolved. If none of the premises, the reasoning, or the concepts found in the paradox set are to be dismissed, then, it seems, either there is no paradox or there is a paradox but it stands unresolved—a failure to diagnose.

The two methods of diagnosing paradox mentioned above track the two ways of resolving (and, thus, diagnosing) paradox—what Schiffer (2003) calls a *happy-faced* solution and an *unhappy-faced* solution to a given paradox.[8] In what follows, I will discuss both sorts of solution and will show that, given that way of understanding the notion of a paradox, it seems to follow that dialetheism falls afoul of both. Thus, I lodge (and, subsequently—in s. 6—respond to) the following objection to dialetheism: That dialetheism fails to diagnose the liar paradox and, thus, fails to reach a condition of adequacy on any solution to paradox. If this is correct then it indicates a *black mark* for dialetheism, for if dialetheism does not diagnose the paradox, it is not clear in what sense it earns the right to call the liar a paradox. It is to this issue that I turn next.

4.1 Happy- and Unhappy-Face Solutions

According to Schiffer [14], paradoxes are diagnosed by one of two sorts of solution—a *happy-face* and an *unhappy-face* solution. I will review, briefly, the terminology and, with that in hand, will (s. 5) return to the objection as lodged against dialetheism and, thereafter, to the problem of diagnosis.

4.1.1 *Happy-Face Solutions*

A happy-face solution to a paradox does two things, assuming that the propositions (or sentences) comprising the set really are mutually incompatible: First, a happy-face solution identifies the premiss(es) to be jettisoned, the member(s) of the paradox set that is to be rejected. Second, in the case of a happy-face solution, we are shown the spurious proposition that deceived us, so that we can be sure that we are not taken in by this problematic premiss again. Thus, by a 'happy-face-solution' to paradox, I mean one that shows why these claims really aren't all true, or why they really aren't inconsistent.

This alone, however, is still not enough for a complete solution. One must also give an account as to *why* it seems to us that we are dealing with an inconsistency here. That is, we must diagnose what went wrong in our thinking about these matters so that we were tricked into believing that we are actually dealing with a paradox. In order to provide a happy-face solution to the liar paradox, one must:

(i) Say which of the putatively plausible claims are really false, or why they are jointly consistent, after all; and

(ii) Explain what has fooled us into believing that they are true and inconsistent in the first place[9]

---

[8] Schiffer's first discussion of happy- and unhappy-face solutions appears in Schiffer [12]. For a further discussion of such solutions, see Schiffer [15].

[9] In s. 6, I shall offer a third element to a happy-face solution. For now, I rely on Schiffer's characterization of a happy-face solution, which characterization encompasses only the identification of the odd-premiss(es) out and a diagnosis of the spurious proposition mistakenly, though initially, accepted.

Per Schiffer ([15], 74), the paradox of the barber—the one in which we imagine a barber who shaves all and only those who do not shave themselves—has a happy-face solution, for all claims of paradox are said to disappear, once we recognize that the existence of such a barber is logically impossible.

4.1.2 *Unhappy-Face Solutions*

If a paradox lacks a happy-face solution then, it is often thought, this is because there's a certain kind of glitch in the concept, or concepts, used to generate the paradox. Unlike a happy-face solution, an unhappy-face solution would identify neither the odd-premiss-out nor the reasoning. Instead, an unhappy-face solution would tell us

(i) that there is no correct identification of the odd-premiss-out (or the reasoning); and

(ii) what about the relevant concepts explain why there is no such odd-premiss-out

The explanation as to why none of the premisses (or the principles of inference) can be rejected trades on a *glitch* in the concept (or concepts) that gives rise to the paradox—a *conceptual glitch*, as Schiffer (ibid.) calls it.

When a conceptual glitch is identified, we can then explain why we *thought* that the recalcitrant conclusion followed, but it is not always clear how we ought to go from there. It is not always clear because an unhappy-face solution does not involve rejecting either the odd-premiss(es) out or the principle(s) of inference; rather, it requires us to revise the paradox-inducing conceptual glitches that gave rise to an unacceptable conclusion in the first place.

4.1.3 *Tarski's Solution as an Unhappy-Face Solution*

Although Schiffer has not identified Tarski's solution to the liar paradox as an unhappy-face solution, I think that it is clear that it is paradigmatic of such a case. Tarski's contention, as is familiar (though controversial), is that natural language is, in a certain sense, inconsistent and that, as such, it requires the revision of the semantics for natural language.[10] Recall Tarski's famous (and important)

---

[10] The claim that Tarski took natural language to be inconsistent is delicate. Tarski seems to have held that if (i)–(iii), below, hold for a natural language and if certain conditions governing truth also hold, then natural language is, indeed, inconsistent. However, while he held that the intuitive principles, together with assumptions about truth, would yield inconsistency, he seems to have taken that to show that we cannot maintain all of them. Rather, he held, we should employ a formalized language for which truth could be defined in such a way as to make the construction of liar-paradoxical sentences impossible. Thus, it seems, Tarski called for a revision of natural language which, when employed, avoids the claim that natural language is inconsistent.

claim ([16], 164–5):

> A characteristic feature of colloquial language (in contrast to various scientific languages) is its universality. It would not be in harmony with the spirit of this language if in some other language a word occurred which could not be translated into it; it could be claimed that 'if we can speak meaningfully about anything at all, we can also speak about it in colloquial language.' If we are to maintain this universality of everyday language in connexion with semantic investigations, we must, to be consistent, admit into the language, in addition to its sentences and other expressions, also the names of these sentences and expressions, and sentences containing these names, as well as such semantic expressions as 'true sentence', 'name', 'denote', etc. But it is presumably just this universality of everyday language which is the primary source of all semantic antinomies. . . . These antinomies seem to provide a proof that every language which is universal in the above sense, and for which the normal laws of logic hold, must be inconsistent . . . If these observations are correct, then the very possibility of a consistent use of the expression 'true sentence' which is in harmony with the laws of logic and the spirit of everyday language seems to be very questionable.

I will discuss this point briefly, as I believe that it will be instructive here.

As is familiar, Tarski ([16], 164–5) held that, so long as

(i) The usual laws of logic hold for a given language (e.g. English);

(ii) The given language contains a truth predicate that applies to its own sentences; and

(iii) The language contains names of all of its sentences

the existence, in a language such as English, of paradoxical sentences such as the liar, is inevitable.[11]

It is somewhat striking that Tarski's response to the liar paradox was not to opt for a happy-face solution to the paradox. That is, rather than rejecting paradox-inducing premises (or assumed principles of inference), his solution was to reject natural language as the means by which we could construct adequate (namely, paradox-free) theories of truth.[12] In place of the semantics for English, Tarski proposed an *elucidation* of the favoured notion of truth—an attempt to clarify, and thus to restrict, the truth predicate, thereby blocking the recalcitrant contradiction.

In short, Tarski's (familiar) response to semantic paradoxes was to identify a glitch in natural language and to propose a new account of truth whereby paradox could be avoided. Such a solution to the liar paradox does not involve a happy-face solution, for it rejects neither the premises nor the principles of inference that yielded an unacceptable (i.e. contradictory) conclusion. Rather, it invokes an unhappy-face solution, which, nevertheless, enables us to diagnose the liar paradox.

---

[11] If, in addition, we accept as true both generalized versions of the T-schema (e.g. 'L is false' is true iff L is false) and of the identity (where, as before, L = 'L is false') then, given (i)–(iii), above, we can prove that a contradictory sentence of English is true.

[12] Cf. Tarski's discussion of 'true sentence', in the (long) quote, above.

5. OBJECTION: DIALETHEISM UNDIAGNOSED

Given the characterization of the happy- or the unhappy-face solution to the liar paradox, it is clear that the dialetheist could accept neither: As the dialetheist accepts the liar paradox to be a sound argument, he will reject neither the premises nor the inferences that lead to a contradiction; thus, no happy-face solution is in the offing. As the dialetheist rejects the charge of incoherence as applied to the truth predicate—i.e. as the dialetheist takes truth to be a glitch-free, and, thus, an unproblematic element to our conceptual repertoire—thus, no unhappy-face solution is in the offing, either. We are now in a position to make explicit the objection registered as against dialetheism, and to consider a response to that objection.

A happy-face solution explains why we were prepared to accept either the principles of inference or the premises that yield our paradox. At the same time, such a solution involves singling out the premises (or, again, a principle of inference) that are to be rejected, thereby diagnosing the paradox and so resolving it. The unhappy-face solution does not single out the premises or the inference to be rejected; rather, it argues that the relevant concepts are hopeless, or incoherent, or generally unworkable. The result: If the concept is incoherent, we don't have cause to accept the (contradictory) conclusion. We have a different sort of diagnosis.

Given these two ways of resolving the paradox, it seems to follow that dialetheism fails to diagnose the liar paradox—that it provides no happy-, and no unhappy-, face solution to that paradox. After all, the dialetheist rejects neither the concepts, the premises, or the principles of inference that comprise the liar paradox. Accordingly, he does not indicate how or why the paradox goes wrong.

The objection, then, is clear: Assuming that diagnosis consists in adducing either a happy- or an unhappy-face solution to a paradox, then, in so far as the dialetheist offers neither, he fails to diagnose the liar paradox. If the possibility of offering up either a happy- or an unhappy-face solution to a paradox is necessary for characterizing it as such then it follows from dialetheism that the liar paradox is not a paradox. *Ex hypothesi*, the liar paradox is a paradox; thus, either the dialetheist must revise the notion of a paradox or he must admit that, appearances to the contrary notwithstanding, the sentence that issues in a liar-related contradiction is non-paradoxical. Neither option is particularly auspicious.

To this, the dialetheist might retort that the liar sentence is *both* paradoxical *and* non-paradoxical. Thus, the horn of this dilemma—that it follows from the failure to adduce either a happy- or an unhappy-face solution that the aforementioned paradox set is, itself, non-paradoxical—might be thought acceptable by the dialetheist. That is, he might go on to argue that, while it is true that the liar paradox (as we will call it, in spite of the above) is non-paradoxical, since it is also true that the paradox set is paradoxical, he can continue *calling* it a paradox—in spite of the aforementioned discussion.

To be sure, the dialetheist might argue that, since the liar sentence (together with the premises and rules of inference that generate a contradiction) is both paradoxical and non-paradoxical, it follows that the liar sentence is paradoxical, in which case we *must* claim that there is, indeed, a paradox associated with the liar sentence. But this is to miss the point, for if the dialetheist can show that the liar sentence (etc.) is properly characterized as paradoxical, he is in the uncomfortable position of claiming that some sentences are paradoxical though the conditions necessary (*ex hypothesi*) for establishing paradoxicality—either the happy- or the unhappy-face solution—are nowhere in evidence.

Again, it seems to me that *if* the dialetheist is to allow the liar sentence to be paradoxical, he will either have to explain the conditions under which paradoxicality obtains, or, if not, he will face the charge of changing the subject to accommodate the paradoxicality of the liar sentence. Thus, without an explanation as to *why* we ought to deem a particular sentence to be paradoxical, if the dialetheist insists (given the above) that the liar sentence is paradoxical his insistence is, it seems, groundless.

6. RESPONSE: RECONFIGURING PARADOX

In response to the aforementioned objection, we might grant that dialetheism does not diagnose the liar paradox in the sense of identifying the 'odd-claim-out'. Moreover, we might grant that the dialetheist does not attempt to diagnose the liar paradox by claiming the concept of truth to be deviant, or otherwise glitch-ridden. But, with the non-dialetheist—i.e. with the consistentist—the dialetheist also accepts that the liar paradox can be diagnosed. How could it be that the dialetheist rejects both the (standard) happy- and the (standard) unhappy-face solution to the liar paradox while still claiming that it is a paradox (and, thus, maintains that there is a diagnosis of some sort or other)?

In order to answer this question, we should return to the standard view of a paradox. According to Mark Sainsbury ([13], 1), a paradox is 'an apparently unacceptable conclusion derived by apparently acceptable reasoning from apparently acceptable premises'. While different accounts of the nature of paradox have been given, they all seem to share a common feature: A paradox is not paradoxical merely *because* it yields an inconsistency; a paradox is paradoxical, at least in part, because it (apparently) entails a conclusion that is (apparently) unacceptable—i.e. a sentence that we should not endorse—though the premises that, *together with the apparently correct inferential constraints (i.e. the consequence relation)*, yield that conclusion appear to be acceptable. Accordingly, I take what is crucial to be *not*—or, perhaps better, *not just*—that the conclusion is contradictory; rather, I take what is crucial to our understanding of a paradox to be that the conclusion is apparently not to be endorsed, given the plausible premisses, the relevant concepts, and the reasoning employed.

I submit that a paradox is best construed (metaphorically) as a sort of *pathology*, which pathological paradox is 'treated' by explaining the causes that give rise to it. We can see Schiffer's happy- and unhappy-face solutions as ways of identifying pathology; accordingly, a failure to identify the pathology results in a lack of treatment to the paradox, in which case the paradox (if it is properly so-called) remains.[13]

Given this (informal) characterization of the notion of a paradox, we can-not (yet) see how the dialetheist can characterize the liar paradox as paradoxical, absent identification of the relevant pathology. Yet I believe that the dialetheist can diagnose the relevant pathology. The key difference is that, unlike Kripke's [9] thought about the liar paradox as exhibiting *semantic pathology*, I take the dialetheist to take the liar paradox to exhibit (what I call) *logical pathology*. In par-ticular, implicit in Sainsbury's characterization of the notion of a paradox—and, indeed, in the standard characterization of the notion of a paradox, generally—it is assumed that, given the premisses or the associated concepts, something must go. The dialetheist, as mentioned, accepts both the premisses and the (relevant) concepts. However, they deny the assumption that if a collection of claims yields an inconsistency, then either the claims or the concepts implicated therein must go. This is so because the dialetheists accept the negation of the LNC (under-stood as per s. 2, above). Given that they accept the negation of the LNC, together with the standard view of falsity (namely, truth of negation), it follows that the negation of the LNC is false, and, generally speaking, what is false is not to be accepted.

In the standard view of a paradox, if plausible premisses yield a contradic-tion, given accepted principles of inference, then either premisses or concepts employed in the paradox must be rejected. This is so because, in the standard view, if the premisses yield a contradictory conclusion, classical logic impels us to reject one or more of the premisses, or to reject the conclusion as incoherent, or the paradox set as invalid. But dialetheism rejects the standard view, because dialetheists deny the rejection of all contradictions. In effect, we might say that implicit in the standard understanding of a paradox is the LNC, and that it—as well as other logical principles—contributes to our understanding of paradox, and to our understanding of the pathology it generates.

Once we take into account the fact that *both* premisses *and* logical principles are central to our grasp of paradox, we can adduce a different conception of a happy-face solution: A happy-face solution involves rejecting, or deeming to be

---

[13] Identifying happy- and unhappy-face solutions as diagnosing *pathological paradox* is reminiscent of Chihara's [7] response to the liar paradox, as I suspect is clear.

false, one or more premises in a given paradox, or it involves rejecting, or deeming to be false, certain implicit (logical) principles.[14]

What we learn from dialetheism—a somewhat standard view, though it's applied differently in the present case—is that a standard and well-entrenched logical principle—the LNC—is, in fact, false, and that the negation of the LNC is true. More specifically, the implicit assumption that if the premises yield a contradiction then either one of the premises must be false (i.e. must be false only) or one of the concepts is simply unworkable is, by the dialetheist's view, incorrect. Some contradictions, such as the liar, can be true as well as false; and, thus, the premises that yield them may well be true (as well as false), too.

What I take this to show is that the standard view of a paradox must be rethought and, thus, that what counts as a diagnosis of the liar paradox must be reconfigured. In particular, I claim that a happy-face solution involves *either* identifying problematic premises *or* identifying problematic implicit (logical) principles, and that the latter is precisely what the dialetheist does: He accepts the negation of the LNC and, thus, accepts that some contradictions—contradictions which are false, though true as well—ought to be accepted.[15] Thus, he accepts the negation of the LNC and, with it, he offers a happy-face solution to the liar paradox: What the liar paradox teaches us is that we must revise the logical principle implicit in our characterization of the paradox as paradoxical. It's not the premises that must go but the principle that lead us to reject the conclusion in the first place.

If this is right then the dialetheist can diagnose the paradox, contra the objection registered previously. He can do this, however, only if he rethinks the nature of paradox and, in particular, if he revises the standard diagnostics on offer. In order to rethink paradox, a reconfiguration of paradox is called for—a reconfiguration of the rules so governed.

7. CONCLUSION: RECONFIGURING PARADOX

Dialetheism offers a diagnosis of the liar paradox by rethinking our view of the notion of a paradox. Thus, given dialetheism, the result is that plausible premises yielding a contradictory conclusion may all be true. One conclusion to draw from this is that part of what needs to be revised is our grasp of a happy-face solution.

[14] Beall (in conversation) has suggested that the dialetheist should take the diagnosis for the liar paradox that I propose to be a form of *meta-diagnosis*—one that spots the pathology as a matter of mistaking non-pathologies (e.g. the liar) for pathologies, *simpliciter*. I like this way of characterizing it and, hereby, co-opt it: The dialetheist adduces a *meta-diagnosis*, by 'resolving' the paradox (on which more below)—i.e. by identifying, as a happy-face solution to the paradox, a case of *logical pathology*.

[15] This thesis applies to the two versions of LP-based dialetheism mentioned in n. 4, i.e. Priest's version, which accepts one version of the LNC and the negation of some of its instances, and Beall's 'full-blooded' version, which accepts all versions of the LNC except the 'rationality' version of the LNC, according to which it's irrational (knowingly) to accept a contradiction.

Such a solution does not merely involve rejecting otherwise plausible premises; it also involves revising otherwise (though implicit) principles, such as the LNC, and others, as well.

If reconfiguring the rules governing paradox requires us to revise our logical assumptions—such as acceptance of the negation of the LNC, for example—then we learn something from dialetheism: We learn that there's more to understanding paradox than identifying paradoxical premises or glitch-riddled concepts.

But a question lingers: Having diagnosed (e.g.) the liar paradox do we, thereby, render it unparadoxical? Perhaps surprisingly, the answer to this question is: Yes—in a sense. For a paradox to be paradoxical, it is not enough to demonstrate that it yields an inconsistency. As we observed with Sainsbury's definition, one must also provide *reasons* for resisting the (contradictory) conclusion. By recasting the happy-face solution so as to revise certain logical principles,[16] we diagnose the liar paradox and, thereby, render it unparadoxical—it is inconsistent, to be sure, but unparadoxical for having been adequately diagnosed.

Of course, even if dialetheism does manage to diagnose the liar paradox, it does not follow from this that the diagnosis is one that should be adopted. In order to make a case for the correctness of the diagnosis, we would have to include, as well, a defense of the negation of the LNC. But that response is nobly defended elsewhere,[17] so I will leave it to the readers to determine the correctness, or incorrectness, of *that* logical principle.[18]

REFERENCES

[1] BRADLEY ARMOUR-GARB, B. and BEALL, JC (2001), 'Can Deflationists be Dialetheists?' *Journal of Philosophical Logic*, 30: 593–608.

[2] BRADLEY ARMOUR-GARB and BEALL, JC 'Should Deflationists be Dialetheists?' *Nous*, 37(2), 303–24.

[3] BEALL, JC 'At the Intersection of Truth and Falsity'. Introduction to this volume.

[4] BEALL, JC (2003), 'Negation's Holiday: Double-Aspect Dialetheism'. Presented at *Philosophy of Logic Memorial Conference* (in memory of Graham Solomon) at University of Waterloo. (Forthcoming)

[5] BEALL, JC (2003), 'True and False—As If'. This volume, Ch. 12.

[16] The same goes for premises, at least as regards some paradoxes.
[17] See Priest [11, 12] and Beall [3], amongst others.
[18] For very helpful and insightful comments and suggestions, I would like to thank JC Beall and Graham Priest.
I would like to mention the debt I owe to JC Beall. Through discussions and writing with JC, I have come to understand (and appreciate!) dialetheism and related issues in a way for which I am truly grateful. For an important (and similar) approach to dialetheism discussed in s. 3 of this paper, see Beall [3, 5].
For a helpful discussion of happy- and unhappy-face solutions, I would like to thank Stephen Schiffer.

[6] CHARLES CHIHARA. (1979), 'Semantic Paradox'. *The Philosophical Review*, 88: 590–618.

[7] PATRICK GRIM. 'What is a Contradiction?' This volume, Ch. 3.

[8] SAUL KRIPKE. (1975), 'Outline of a Theory of Truth'. *The Journal of Philosophy*, 72: 690–716.

[9] GRAHAM PREIST. (1999), 'Semantic Closure, Descriptions and Triviality'. *Journal of Philosophical Logic*, 28: 549–58.

[10] GRAHAM PREIST. (1998), 'What's So Bad about Contradictions?' *Journal of Philosophy*, 95: 410–26, Repr. in this volume, Ch. 1.

[11] GRAHAM PRIEST. (1987), *In Contradiction*. Kluwer.

[12] MARK SAINSBURY. (1995), *Paradox*. Oxford: Oxford University Press.

[13] STEPHEN SCHIFFER. (1996), 'Language-Created Language-Independent Entities'. *Philosophical Topics*, 149–68.

[14] STEPHEN SCHIFFER. (2003), *The Things We Mean*. Oxford: Oxford University Press.

[15] ALFRED TARSKI. (1983), 'The Concept of Truth in Formalized Languages'. *Logic, Semantics, and Metamathematics*, 2nd edn., ed. John Corcorn. Indianapolis: Hackett. 152–278.

[16] BAS VAN FRAASSEN. 'Singular Terms, Truth-Value Gaps and Free Logic'. *Journal of Philosophy*, 63(17): 481–95.

8

Knowledge and Non-Contradiction

Bryson Brown

INTRODUCTION

From a dialectical point of view, principles such as the law of non-contradiction (LNC) and positions such as dialetheism are very difficult to debate.[1] Someone who accepts LNC will naturally be tempted to appeal to it in her arguments. After all, how better to argue against someone than by showing that their position leads to contradictory conclusions? But in the context of such a debate, this is question-begging. And it's equally difficult to play the dialetheist position fairly. Once you've rejected LNC, what *would* count as a refutation of your view? What would even count as an expression of disagreement? Asserting that ¬(P ∧ ¬P) is true for every sentence P won't do, since standard dialetheic logics agree (i.e. they have ¬(P ∧ ¬P) as a theorem): such logics reject non-contradiction not by denying any of its instances, but instead by allowing some contradictions to be correctly asserted.[2] What sort of argument, what sort of consequence of dialetheism would provide sufficient reason to give it up, if an outright contradiction won't? And how shall we express the rejection of dialetheism, if not by the assertion of the traditional law of non-contradiction?

In answer to the last question, and to avoid a long discussion of variations on LNC, I propose a policy that will cover our present needs. For our purposes LNC will be an abbreviation for:

> No contradictory sentence is ever correctly assertable

This version of LNC marks a clear point of difference between the dialetheists, who maintain that some contradictory sentences are correctly assertable, and those who deny this. Of course to arrive at this statement of the difference, we have had

[1] I presented an early paper defending the rationality of accepting inconsistent theories as part of our best current scientific understanding of the world at a conference at the University of Rochester in 1983. My respondent was Henry Kyburg, who complained (playfully) that criticizing someone who defends such a position is a difficult undertaking. After all, he pointed out, any inconsistency he might show to follow from my views could just be added to the list of inconsistencies I am prepared to tolerate. I replied that it was equally difficult for me to defend myself—no matter what I might say, the reply 'See what I mean!' seems devastating to anyone who rejects the acceptance of inconsistencies out of hand.

[2] Thus, for instance, in Priest's LP, based on the strong Kleene matrices, reading the non-classical value as a *designated* fixed point for negation, the class of theorems is just the classical theorems, but models in which contradictions and their negations both receive this strange designated value produce violations of LNC in this sense.

to engage in semantic ascent. But this semantic ascent is the relatively innocent form that we use to generalize across classes of sentences that can't be captured by a first-order quantification. I have used 'correctly assertable' here, in place of 'true', to avoid worrying about the fact that the usual dialetheic logics don't allow contradictions to receive the semantic value 'truth', but instead allow us to assign them another ('paradoxical') value (or values) (sometimes called 'both'), which is taken to be *like* truth, or even a *form* of truth, in the sense that it is treated as a designated value (i.e. as one of the values preserved from left to right by the consequence relation) and underwrites the correctness of assertions. Occasionally (where it will occasion no confusion) I will use 'true' to mean any such semantic value; given that usage LNC takes the more familiar form, 'No contradictory sentence is ever true.'

Intractable disagreements like this have a long history in philosophical debates; some have recently been examined by John Woods (2001). His account focuses on the question, 'How can we tell the difference between a modus ponens argument supporting a surprising conclusion, and a modus tollens argument from the rejection of that conclusion to the rejection of some premise leading to it?' Of course the sentences at stake can't settle which view is correct, but we may hope that sometimes, at least, constructive philosophical examination of the issues can. Arguments are said to be valid if and only if the truth (or correct assertability) of all premises is incompatible with the falsehood (lack of correct assertability) of the conclusion. This leaves how we should respond to such incompatibilities an open question, as Gilbert Harman (1986) and others have emphasized. Shall we combine a commitment to the premises with a further commitment to the conclusion? Or shall we reject the conclusion, together with some premiss(es)? Woods argues that dialectical exchanges often founder when the two sides cannot agree on a constructive approach to answering this question. An ongoing series of disputes, each merely expanding areas of known disagreement, is more likely to lead to schism than to helpful dialogue.

In this chapter I take a broad and fairly systematic approach to the status of LNC. Rather than engage in a dialectical back-and-forth that offers little prospect of satisfactory resolution (and a high likelihood of producing more heat than light), I will begin by considering our knowledge of logical truths more generally, and then try to apply what we learn there to LNC. I hope this broader view of our epistemic options may lead to a constructive discussion of the issue instead of a head-on collision.

Historically, philosophers have defended a wide range of views on the epistemic status of logical claims, ranging (on one dimension) from variations on Platonistic a priorism to Mill's radical empiricism. We begin here with a basic taxonomy, in order to cut that variety down to a manageable level. In this context I think it will probably be most helpful if we adopt a fairly conventional taxonomy of epistemic positions, distinguishing on one dimension foundationalist from coherentist theories of justification, and on a second dimension internalist theories from externalist. I also want to signal in advance that we will be concerned here with issues of justification, not other epistemological questions such as the definition of *knowledge*.

EPISTEMOLOGY AND LOGIC

Foundationalism

There are several types of foundationalism. What they have in common is a commitment to the view that at least some of the epistemic justification that our beliefs, claims or judgements possess derives ultimately from *foundational justification*, a form of justification that is

1. Limited to *certain kinds* of belief, claim or judgement (together, these three categories comprise the usual epistemically evaluable items).
2. Applied to each such epistemically evaluable item individually, in virtue of the kind of belief, claim or judgement it is, and the fact that it is held or made.

The only tenable form of foundationalism in the epistemology of logic and mathematics today is a fallibilist, mixed one: Fallibilism (along with corrigibility and dubitability) is inescapable. We know all too well that the clearest, simplest, and most intuitively obvious claims and definitions, our best candidates for foundational status in mathematics, can be and often are inconsistent and even (given commitments regarding consequence relations) trivial. Further, when we find ourselves in such desperate straits, a pure foundationalism would require that we decide which principles are right or wrong on foundational grounds alone. But when things get difficult we don't simply appeal to a re-examination of our convictions or intuitions regarding the individual principles. Instead, we move to coherence considerations such as elegance, simplicity, the overall intuitive appeal of different systems of commitments, the need to get certain results, and the dispensability of other results. In these ways our practice belies the claims of both infallibilist and pure foundationalism. And it's hard (at best) to imagine how we could alter our practice to make these views tenable.

Foundationalist views of logical knowledge are a familiar part of the modern philosophical tradition. David Hume appeals to a fundamental capacity to know (and compare) our ideas, in discussing how it is that we can tell that a certain relation of ideas holds: 'Relations may be divided into two classes; into such as depend entirely on the ideas, which we compare together, and such as may be changed without any change in the ideas.' ''Tis from the idea of a triangle, that we discover the relation of equality, which its three angles bear to two right ones; and this relation is invariable, as long as our idea remains the same' (*Treatise*,

I.3.1). Elsewhere, he makes a very popular assumption about our grasp of our own conscious thoughts: 'But consciousness never deceives.' (This occurs in the course of an argument meant to show that we are never conscious of our power to move our bodies, since we don't notice our disability when, recently deprived of our limbs, we forgetfully try to use them, or when 'suddenly struck with a palsy' (*Enquiry concerning Human Understanding*, VII. I).)

So for Hume, our grasp of our own conscious thoughts allows us to discern relations of ideas, such as the agreement between the sum of the interior angles of a triangle and a straight angle. Further, when we can *demonstrate* a falsehood, we can see that its truth would imply a contradiction, and such falsehoods cannot be distinctly conceived by the mind. Thus it seems that for Hume there is at least a psychological barrier that prevents us from distinctly conceiving a contradiction. Further, since conceiving something (for Hume, at least) is a necessary condition for believing it and conceiving it distinctly is a necessary condition for (or constitutive of) understanding it, we cannot simultaneously understand and believe a contradiction.

The import of such psychological claims for the question of truth demands careful consideration. Even if it really is true that a contradiction cannot be thought, we may wonder whether what is unthinkable could nevertheless be true. But Hume's position on relations of ideas may allow us to get beyond a merely psychological rejection of contradictions. The ideas of negation (expressed by 'not') and conjunction (expressed by 'and'), along with the general notion of a declarative sentence (or proposition, if you prefer) expressed by the place-holder 'p', may be such that their combination in the sentence form (p and not-p) wears the incorrectness of asserting it on its sleeve, that is, in merely thinking of such a form, we may be conscious of this fundamental fact about it. Indeed, if these ideas are correctly captured by the classical accounts of the words 'not', 'and', 'true', and 'false', it does exactly that.

However, the epistemic transparency of meanings or contents of thought, widely taken for granted in Hume's day, is now hotly contested; views as straightforward as Hume's are no longer regarded as tenable. How can we be sure that the classical conceptions of negation, conjunction, truth, falsity, and other fundamental logical apparatus are not subtly flawed? Perhaps some special contradictions are acceptable after all! While classical logicians (and others who also reject all contradictions) can certainly *propose* their formal theories as accounts of negation, conjunction, truth, etc. in the ordinary language, it cannot be certain *in advance of a detailed study of the evidence* that they will turn out to be right as accounts of the meanings of certain words in natural languages. It is also uncertain whether natural languages provide the right touchstone for deciding the issue.

Closer to the historical roots of the contemporary debate over LNC are the views of the logical empiricists, who tried to draw something like Hume's distinction by separating analytic from empirical truths in a different way. For the logical empiricists, analytic truths were truths settled by the conventional rules establishing the meaning of various linguistic items, while empirical truths depended on these rules *together with* the situation in the world (as expressed via observation claims). In effect, analytic truths were stipulations constituting a linguistic framework for describing the world, while empirical truths held as a matter of contingent, observable fact.

But here again the transparency of meanings (linguistic rather than mental this time) must be assumed in order to settle logical issues. The logical empiricists often implicitly assumed that we could just tell when a truth was settled by the conventional rules governing our language's use. This left them vulnerable to the obvious question: How do we come to recognize those sentences expressing or following from rules that govern our language, and how do we distinguish these from other sentences expressing truths in our language?

Quine (1953) showed that these questions have no easy answer except in uninteresting cases: If the language in question is an artificial, invented language, then of course we are free to stipulate the rules, and no problem arises. But one natural response to problems arising when we apply such a system is to alter the stipulations. So although the distinction between analytic and synthetic survives in this context, it survives only in a Pickwickian sense. The possibility of altering our commitments to analytic sentences becomes a live option—all we need do is decide to change our meanings rather than our empirical commitments, in the face of some serious systematic difficulties. Finally, of course, we can't just specify any rules we want, unless trivialization doesn't trouble us.

If the language in question is a natural language, then the rules in question (the meanings that a lexicographer or linguist reports) cannot be matters of stipulation. They must, instead, be matters of fact. Worse, according to Quine's argument, such matters of fact are underdetermined by the evidence, and their underdetermination becomes most evident precisely where Carnap had placed most weight on the distinction between analytic and synthetic truths: in natural science, where, as Hanson (1958) and others were later to emphasize, what is tested as an empirical law in one context may be relied on as though it were a matter of definition in others.

Coherentism

We need to allow a role for coherentist considerations in logic and mathematics. There may be some foundational constraints or limitations, rooted in a foundational grasp of what words (or ideas) such as 'not' and 'and' and 'true' mean, on what could count as a negation, a conjunction, a declarative sentence, a truth value, etc. Nothing I will say here requires or rules out such constraints. But a final position cannot be chosen by appeal to a primitive grasp of these concepts taken individually, first because our experience shows all too clearly that beginning with what seem perfectly sound (even intuitively obvious) accounts of basic concepts, we can find ourselves with commitments that trivialize, and second because it turns out that repairing such a programme is not a purely foundationalist endeavour. If we merely went back to the basics to *find the mistake*, a fallibilist form of pure foundationalism might be tenable. But we don't. Instead, we examine alternative changes to our commitments and explore *how they work out*, including coherentist considerations such as whether they preserve enough of the desired consequences or applications of our apparatus while avoiding disaster.

In this context the Quinean idiom of costs and benefits and Neurath's famous metaphor of ship repairs made while still at sea both apply. Intuitions about sets, negation, truth, etc. are often invoked in defending different proposals. And these intuitions may be taken as foundational (i.e. as playing a non-inferential, warrant-increasing role in our epistemic evaluation of certain claims and positions). But they are traded off against each other, and against other values such as simplicity, unity, and explanatory power. (Though individual philosophers often seem to have very different rankings of the force of various intuitions.) In the end, rather than deciding the issue in favour of a single alternative, such intuitions are invoked as individual points of evidence, supporting accounts that accord with them. But an account will be accepted only if it provides the *overall* results we need, fitting a wide enough range of intuitions and observations, and satisfying other cognitive aims as well.

Coherence considerations, as a matter of definition, concern how a collection of commitments 'fit together'. Getting beyond this metaphor to a concrete account of coherence justification is not easy. It has often been supposed that negation consistency is a sine qua non for coherence, but in this context such a supposition ends the discussion before it can even begin. So we will dispense with negation consistency as a sine qua non, adopting instead a more latitudinarian sine qua non: absolute consistency. Our commitments must distinguish between what is accepted and what is rejected; if this distinction collapses (when every sentence has been accepted, or rejected, or both) we have reached *maximal incoherence*.

Another major theme in attempts to characterize coherence has been *explanation*. By this criterion, the more completely our beliefs are integrated into an explanatorily linked whole, the more coherent, and hence the more credible, they are. Since mere fit or compatibility with the evidence is (at least from the in-principle perspective that philosophers are so fond of) relatively easy to come by, those who have sought more positive reasons to accept a theory (and to reduce the force of underdetermination as an argument against *realistic* commitments to our theories) have often emphasized the epistemic role of explanation.

This issue is (to put it gently) highly contested; Bas van Fraassen (1980, 1984) famously rejects any special role for explanatory power as a source of extra evidence supporting a theory. But others defend the special contribution that explanatory power brings to the evidence for a theory. We can't reasonably expect to settle this issue here. I will assume, for the sake of argument, that explanatory power does add to the epistemic standing of theories that have it. This assumption accords with my own views on the issue, and it improves our chances of concluding that there are enough epistemic constraints on choosing a logical theory to produce a definite answer on the status of LNC.

By way of indicating why I believe in the epistemic import of explanation—though certainly not by way of a serious defence of this position—I want to make one point: There are many rich inferential connections that connect the sentences of a powerful explanatory theory together with the observations we make when we apply the theory. These connections produce a kind of epistemic economy that is quite distinct from probability comparisons (see van Fraassen 1983). This epistemic economy is not a matter of our total commitments being more probable than a proper subtheory of our commitments—that is clearly impossible. It is more like reducing the *dimension* of our commitments: we accept fewer *mutually orthogonal* (i.e. probabilistically independent) sentences, since each sentence occupies a position in the system that is inferentially linked to many others. A side-effect is that our commitments are tightly constrained by these links, making them more testable, other things being equal. See Friedman (1974) for such an account of explanatory unification.[3]

In particular, the role of explanation in logical and mathematical theories is open to debate. Some have proposed to distinguish arguments or proofs in logic and mathematics that are explanatory from those that are not; given such a distinction, appeals to explanatory coherence in the epistemology of logic and mathematics would give special status to such arguments and proofs. But others (more in the tradition of Hempel 1965) have rejected privileged directions or types of proof; any inferential connection is grist for the mill, on their account. In the final analysis, the status of any privileged form of inferential connection will have to be defended within an overall account of logical and/or mathematical knowledge—such a distinction could, it seems, be rooted either in distinctions pertaining to the subject matter of such knowledge, or in distinctions pertaining to our faculties as knowers.

Aside from consistency and explanatory coherence, we recognize a fairly wide range of epistemic values that may contribute to the coherence of a set of commitments. These include simplicity, testability, ontological parsimony, elegance, and beauty. Of course, elegance and beauty are aesthetic values, and links between aesthetics and truth are controversial; ontological parsimony remains attractive, though a combination of heuristics and aesthetics may explain its appeal, and simplicity has proved difficult (perhaps impossible) to characterize in a general way despite its intuitive appeal in many cases. But testability has been at the heart of

---

[3] Explanatory unification in this sense is distinct from the particularly causal forms of explanation that Hume (and more recently, Salmon—see e.g. 1998) have emphasized, since it includes theoretical reductions and inferential links that need not follow specifically causal patterns. So there are different perspectives on the nature of explanatory coherence as well as on its epistemic significance.

many systematic efforts to account for the link between theory and empirical evidence in philosophy of science. In this area variations on hypothetico-deductivism are influential, as are probabilistic accounts. More refined accounts of instantial confirmation have been proposed as well (e.g. see Glymour 1980) in hopes of accounting for intuitions about how tests bear on the support of individual sentences.

How to apply these sorts of considerations to logic is a rich and difficult question; we may find specific arguments persuasive, but the general principles that make them so are very difficult to identify in detail. We have already canvassed most of what can be said with confidence:

1. We have intuitions about various concepts, both logical and mathematical, including intuitions that support certain claims about them, and others that support consequence relations linking them in various ways.

2. When we seek a reasonably complete account of these concepts based on such intuitions, we often find ourselves in trouble: the systems that result lead to inconsistency, as we see in the semantic and set theoretical paradoxes.

3. A satisfactory response to these difficulties will conserve (while perhaps redirecting or reformulating) our intuitions as much as possible. It should also preserve (and ideally add to) the powerful theorems and inferential links that make logical and mathematical theory useful and unified in so many ways.

One final general remark: Coherentism creates a difficult problem for evaluating the justification of individual epistemic commitments, since coherence is a property of a collection of commitments, not individual commitments. Yet we typically take individual sentences to be the bearers of truth (or falsehood); this leads us to seek an account of how strongly the evidence we have supports individual sentences, rather than resting content with a measure of the credibility of a large system of sentences. Measures of the credibility of individual sentences focus broadly on the contribution that each sentence makes to the overall coherence of the system, and to the uniqueness of each sentence's coherent fit—as contrasted with alternative sentences—with the rest of the system. But if we want instead to make the unit of truth fit more elegantly with the fundamental unit of epistemology, we may wish to consider making the truth of sets of sentences or theories the primary notion of truth, rather than beginning with the truth of sentences and equating the truth of a set of sentences with the individual truth of its members. The attractions of (moderate) holism and a coherence theory of truth are powerful, as we've already seen in our discussion of the logical empiricists.

Here we leave the foundationalist/coherentist debate behind. The issues haven't all been settled, but a key point has been made: Neither infallibilist nor pure foundationalism can work. At some point, coherentist considerations must be brought in to weed out untenable combinations of commitments in logic. Coherentist considerations allow us to trade off various (possibly foundational) intuitions and cognitive values against each other, in an attempt to arrive at the most credible overall account. Perhaps such considerations can produce a unique result (or at least a firm answer on LNC) by sorting through the advantages and disadvantages of alternative approaches. But perhaps they cannot.

With regard to LNC in particular, we can say that (perhaps after a little discussion and explanation) English speakers are unwilling to assert that 'p and not p' for pretty well any substitution instance, under pretty well any stimulus conditions.[4] But this does not show that only logical systems in which such sentences can never be correctly asserted are adequate to the data. That is just one way to explain the general distaste for contradictions. We might instead explain it as the result of a powerful empirical generalization[5] (one that some mistakenly overextend into an absolute principle). There might even be advantages in taking such a heterodox view, once we have considered a wider range of evidence concerning judgements—especially those made in hard cases such as the paradoxes—about various principles, the correctness of certain inferences, and the wider costs and benefits of alternative views. We'll return to this question after a discussion of internalism and externalism.

Internalism and Externalism

Internalist epistemologies assume that the conditions of epistemic justification must be accessible to the knower; externalists, by contrast, hold that at least some-times the fact that one belief is justified while another is not will not be founded on a difference between those beliefs that the knower herself is (or could, by reflec-tion, become) aware of. This distinction is worth thinking through here because it speaks to another dimension of our attempts to evaluate logics. Of course when we evaluate them, we rely on the comparisons we have some sort of access to. But it's worth asking whether facts about logic of the sort that externalists invoke could actually play a role in making someone (or some group) justified in their convictions about logic.

Two principles appear in any form of logical externalism:

1. There must be objective facts about logic.
2. These facts must play a role in producing our beliefs about them.

---

[4] There are exceptions; Many speakers would accept 'It's raining and it's not raining' as a reasonable description of the sort of foggy drizzle going on outside as I write. But defenders of LNC have little difficulty with this phenomenon—for example, a supervaluational account of vagueness more or less predicts precisely this sort of response, since borderline cases belong both to the extension and to the anti-extension of some reasonable precisifications of a vague notion such as 'raining'. Thus in this sentence the speaker indicates the perfectly consistent borderline status of the situation, taking as acceptable—*relative to different precise standards*—both superficially contradictory sentences. The contextual invocation of different standards (of goodness, for instance) also allows us to deal with 'curate's egg' cases; in general, *ambiguity* (as we will see below) can cover a lot of ground in eliminating apparent inconsistencies.   [5] As Graham Priest has suggested to me in conversation.

This role in the production of beliefs will contribute to an explanation of why certain circumstances count as epistemically ideal, as well as why the beliefs are to be counted as *about* these facts: When circumstances are ideal (and such circumstances must be reasonably common), we would not have (or at least be very unlikely to have) the beliefs in question unless they were true. Such conditions link our cognitive psychology to the truth and falsity of our beliefs—they are, I believe, an indispensable part of a satisfactory epistemology.

One sort of view allowing for an externalist account of logical knowledge is a Platonistic one according to which we grasp logical concepts through a process analogous to the perception of physical objects. If beliefs produced by this kind of process are reliable,[6] then even though we don't have access to or know that this reliability condition is met, a Platonist externalist could claim the beliefs are epistemically justified. Alternatively, someone might defend a realistic stand on logical truth that does not take logical truths to be descriptions of a realm of non-physical things, but to characterize 'laws of thought', principles which constrain thinking in general. Or they might take them to reflect the workings of in-built cognitive systems—there is concrete evidence from cognitive psychology for the existence of fundamental numerical and logical capacities, together with interesting hints of how these may be structured. (Although it seems unlikely that such systems will be general and constraining enough to impose a single system of formal logic or the foundations of mathematics on us.) Finally, the view taken might be a linguistic one, holding that the key to a priori knowledge lies in our capacity to learn rules of inference in the course of language acquisition, and to take on new rules of inference as suppositions constituting new 'language games'.

Do logical and mathematical claims represent abstract entities as having properties and standing in certain relations? Are they objective in some other, less flamboyantly non-natural way? Or do they do some other, subtler sort of work in our systems of representation? In any case, we need to decide how these facts (or this work) constrain our logical beliefs and inferences.

In the case of Platonism, of course, this leads to a well-known difficulty, sharply formulated by Benacerraf: While the most straightforward semantics for logic and mathematics requires abstract entities, choosing such a semantics leads to serious difficulties for epistemic naturalism. There seems to be no way for facts about abstract entities to constrain what we believe about them. We lack a credible account of how Platonic things can constrain our beliefs without being part of the causal order in the natural world. Consider Poincarré's conventionalism about geometry; can a realist respond simply by holding that a unique, Platonically

---

[6] This raises the question of what belief-producing process types are relevant for the evaluation of beliefs; some sort of causal (or quasi-causal) interaction linking the facts of the matter to our belief via a process that constitutes a relevant psychological kind is generally assumed to lie behind this reliability predicate. But the details are extremely challenging; I believe this problem is just a special case of the more general and terribly recalcitrant problem of the reference class.

true geometry for space exists despite the observational adequacy of all the other, false geometries, and that a non-causal connection between our minds and this geometry *reveals* its truth to us? I think the answer must be 'no'. As it stands, this story of our 'knowledge' of geometry is no better than a 'dormative potency' explanation of the soporific qualities of opium.

In general, metaphors such as the mental eye or the inner grasp only suggest a disguised naturalism, in which 'non-causal' influences of 'non-natural' objects on 'non-sensory' faculties parallel the ordinary causal impact of natural objects on our senses. The use of 'non' in these contexts seems to indicate protest and resistance to naturalism, rather than to draw a useful and illuminating distinction. More importantly, it creates at least the impression of a barrier to further investigation—how can we study the workings of such influences in us? If we cannot, there is no way to integrate them into an empirical cognitive psychology. Such danglers would be inelegant at best; I'm more inclined to say that they are speculative placeholders standing in for real, testable explanations that can be integrated with the rest of our understanding of ourselves as cognitive agents. (See Bonevac 1982: 8–9.)

By contrast, human psychology and linguistic abilities are both included among the things that influence our beliefs. Psychological laws could provide general constraints on thought or learning, linking our grasp of the content of various concepts to the limits or requirements of human thought, or even thought in general. Similarly, we might link our grasp of concepts to the ability to learn to speak a language, meeting the demands of our fellow speakers' understanding by reasoning in ways they recognize as correct, drawing consequences from suppositions, criticizing and defending assertions, responding to our surroundings with appropriate observations, and suiting our behaviour to our words. When we meet such conditions for having concepts, we must also, willy-nilly, reliably meet conditions for correct assertion and inference—correct, that is, by the standards that are imposed by the linguistic community. Finally, assertions and inferences that are shared within the community independently of circumstances constitute a kind of a priori, especially those regarded as part of linguistic competence rather than empirical sophistication. Whether we grant primacy to the linguistic or the psychological, both are intermingled here, as we combine the linguistic capacities that constitute competence with the psychological capacities that enable us to learn.

For this sort of position, the objectivity of a priori knowledge will depend on having an objective way of identifying such rules of inference; if Quinean concerns about the possibility of alternative, evidentially equivalent accounts of the rules governing a particular language cannot be adequately answered, there will be a conventional element in any account of these rules. But Quine considers only very narrow constraints on translation, restricting himself to the assumption that we can identify assent and denial. This assumption may seem too strong—after all, the most convincing, concrete Quinean translations exchange assertion for denial, reinterpret atomic sentences as their contradictories, and dualize the rest of the language. (The resulting image of the language, in which everything is transformed while somehow remaining effectively the same, is reminiscent of mirror-symmetries and CPT invariance in physics.) But, on the other hand, Quine's conditions also seem too weak. There are many other behavioural indications of attitudes towards sentences (including suppositional acceptance and inference, search behaviour, and many more) that can provide a richer body of constraints on translation.

In the recent literature, Goldman (1999) defends a 'moderate naturalism' with respect to a priori knowledge. On the account Goldman proposes, a priori warrant must operate by having some natural influence on the belief-forming processes (and inferences, I would add) of actual believers. Goldman's proposal steers clear of metaphysical questions about the subject matter of a priori knowledge while trying to outline epistemic principles that could underwrite a recognizable form of a priori knowledge. The chief difficulty he deals with is that many of the differences traditionally distinguishing a priori from a posteriori knowledge must fail: a priori knowledge is not infallible, incorrigible, or certain. Further, Goldman withholds commitment to the claim that it has abstract, eternal objects for its subject matter, and finds reason to be reserved, at best, regarding the necessity of all a priori knowledge. This leaves as the main distinguishing feature of a priori knowledge that it is not based on the senses or perception in general (including, presumably, proprioception) (ibid. 4–7). I take this to fit nicely with the psycho-linguistic account I incline towards.

A sophisticated neo-rationalist account of a priori knowledge can be found in Bealer (1999). Bealer's account imposes criteria for concept possession that demand reliability of intuitions involving the concepts. This, combined with the stability of logical concepts in twin-earth cases, makes logical truths both necessary and autonomous from empirical considerations. But I am sceptical about Bealer's attempt to distinguish a priori, analytic knowledge sharply from a posteriori knowledge. Bealer claims that logical words such as 'not', 'if', 'and', etc. have a content that sustains necessary truths, and that is stable independent of whatever world they are used in. By contrast, he agrees with Kripke that terms picking out natural kinds have a semantics that underwrites necessary truths, but different necessary truths depending on the details of our local empirical world, such as the chemical substance generally referred to as 'water'. The availability of a range of alternative theories of the logical words suggests to me that this uniqueness claim will fail in some worlds, where the connectives of some 'deviant' logic fit the phenomena of use and inference better.[7]

---

[7] We might insist on describing such worlds using our own language, in which case our description will respect the logic of our local language—but if we do the same with natural kind terms, we will deny that what they call 'water' is water, too. So while holding logical words 'fixed' is possible, it is also possible to hold natural kind terms fixed in the same way.

Though my own view links the status of logical truths to contingent facts about our psychology and language, I agree with Bealer that having the concepts—acquired in the course of language learning—implies, because it is required for the public nature of such acquisition, that we are reliable judges of many claims and inferences involving them. But this doesn't make such judgements certain or unrevisable as a priori beliefs have traditionally been taken to be. Alternative concepts are available and may be adopted if they allow us to make more successful inferences, less unsuccessful ones, or improve the coherence of our overall views.

Of course, having adopted a detailed account of logic, we will employ it as a guide to describing and explaining the ways things (in the broadest sense of that word) can be. The dependence of our choice on contingent facts does not undermine the *necessity* of logical principles once adopted—the rival candidates are rivals for the role of deciding (much of) what we will say about possibility and necessity. But we are as free to change our meanings as to change our minds, and we sometimes have good reason to do so (Sher 2001). Further, as individuals, we may misunderstand the publicly established standards for correct usage; in fact, such misunderstandings play a central role in a proposed account of the evolution of the logical words, in which scope errors drive the development of dualized understandings of words such as 'or' (Jennings 1994).

A naturalistic epistemology—naturalistic in the sense that it accepts our status as fully natural beings—*can* allow room for a priori knowledge, so long as some natural psychological capacity or mechanism enables us to arrive, with some reliability, at true a priori beliefs. Our ability to acquire language is something a successful cognitive psychology must account for; founding a priori knowledge on this ability is at least an economical approach to the issue. And whatever our metaphysical notions about the subject matter of a priori beliefs, there must be some way—some way that can be investigated as part of cognitive psychology—in which the facts about the subject matter will influence our processes of belief formation, and thereby affect expressions of belief in their typical natural forms: noises emitted and symbols inscribed.

This has important implications for the evidence we can appeal to in settling the status of LNC. Claims of private access to a causally impotent 'realm of forms' will not do. But more importantly for the arguments to come, formal accounts that produce the same consequence relations, and allow us to capture and explain the same patterns of use more generally, will be hard, and perhaps impossible, to choose between. This leads to an important question: are some logical theories embodying different positions on LNC *intertranslatable* in a way that preserves the consequence relations linking the translated sentences and other phenomena we apply logical theory to account for and systematize? If they are, each will produce the same normative constraints on utterances and inscriptions, and parallel explanations of any patterns we can discern in these. It will be difficult to justify a choice between such theories on other than heuristic or aesthetic grounds—and such grounds are not convincing as grounds for objective claims of truth.

DEBATING LNC

To make this discussion a little more concrete, we'll now turn to some specific arguments for dialetheism. The liar, together with its relatives near and distant, has been at the heart of arguments for dialetheism from the start. The long-drawn-out and inconclusive struggles that have characterized attempts to resolve the paradoxes led some—in particular R. Sylvan and G. Priest—to propose the dialetheic alternative: accept the conclusion that the paradoxical arguments seem to suggest. That is, accept that the liar sentence really is both true (since assuming it is false leads immediately to the recognition that what it says is true, and so it is true) and false (since assuming it is true leads to the conclusion that what it says is true, i.e. that it is false).

In what follows, we examine the state of play very broadly, and comment on the force of a few important arguments along the way. We will contrast the modern orthodoxy of classical semantics and set theory with the dialetheic position. But we will add to this contrast a new and important defence that is available to the classicist, though not yet widely appreciated: *preservationism*.

The familiar modern orthodoxy begins with an account of certain logical words. Quine (1986) selects negation, conjunction, and existential quantification as his primitives. Negation and conjunction are treated as truth functions in a two-valued semantics: negation turns true sentences into false sentences and vice versa, and conjunctions of pairs of sentences take the value true when and only when both original sentences are true. An existentially quantified sentence is true if and only if the open sentence produced by removing the quantifier is satisfied by some assignment to the variable of quantification. Finally, logical consequence is a matter of guaranteed truth-preservation: $\Gamma \models \Delta$ if and only if all valuations making every member of Γ true also make some member of Δ true.

Thus far, this is simple, elegant, and a pretty good fit with ordinary practice. Still, there are disputes about the resulting account of conditionals, and concerns about the explosive view of inconsistency that arises from this definition of logical consequence. And these concerns become more worrisome when we try to extend this formal language to set theory and semantics, where paradoxes and the complications they impose raise their ugly faces. But before we continue with the dialectic here, I need to give a brief account of preservationism.

Preservationism

Preservationism is a recent approach to logic, developed by R. E. Jennings and P. K. Schotch in a series of papers in the 1980s. The aim of preservationist research is to explore alternative accounts of consequence relations that are not based on the usual assumption that the semantic (syntactic) property preserved by a consequence relation is *truth* (or, speaking syntactically, consistency).[8] Preservationism is particularly appealing as a response to situations where we want to reason with sets of sentences that are not satisfiable (or consistent), i.e. where paraconsistent tools are required. The only advice classical logic offers us in such situations is to find another set of premises. Dialetheic logics, by contrast, offer new accounts of how we can satisfy classically inconsistent sets of sentences, while retaining the standard account of consequence relations as founded on truth-preservation. But we can find other properties of our premises that are worth preserving (and that are not preserved by arbitrary extensions of the premises), and then propose alternatives to the classical consequence relation that preserve these desirable properties just as classical logic preserves satisfiability and consistency. Here are two brief examples of such properties, and consequence relations based on them.

1. *Levels of incoherence.* We begin by defining a generalization of consistency:

$$\text{Con}(\Gamma, \xi) \Leftrightarrow \exists A: \emptyset, a_1, \ldots, a_i, 1 \leq i \leq \xi \ \& \ \forall i, a_i \nvdash \bot$$

Next we define a measure of Γ's inconsistency based on this generalization:

$$\ell(\Gamma) = \text{the least } \xi \text{ such that } \text{Con}(\Gamma, \xi), \text{else } \infty$$

Finally, we define a consequence relation that preserves ℓ just as the classical $\vdash$ preserves consistency:

$$\Gamma[\vdash \alpha \text{ iff, for } \xi = \ell(\Gamma), \text{ for all } A: a_1 \ldots a_i, 1 \leq i \leq \xi, \exists a_j \in A \mid a_j \vdash \alpha$$

This consequence relation is called *forcing* (Schotch and Jennings 1989). Forcing is *weakly aggregative*; while we don't retain the rule of adjunction, we do obtain consequences that are not classical consequences of individual members of Γ. The forcing relation can be straightforwardly captured with the following rules:

(i) Pres $\vdash$:
$$\frac{\Gamma[\vdash \alpha, \alpha \vdash \beta}{\Gamma[\vdash \beta}$$

(ii) Ref:
$$\frac{\alpha \in \Gamma}{\Gamma[\vdash \alpha}$$

(iii) $2/n+1$:
$$\frac{\Gamma[\vdash \alpha_1, \ldots, \Gamma[\vdash \alpha_{n+1}}{\Gamma[\vdash \vee(\alpha_i \wedge \alpha_j), 1 \leq i \neq j \leq n+1} \quad n = \ell(\Gamma)$$

---

[8] Preservationism in general is not wedded to classicism; the idea of separating consequence relations from truth/consistency preservation can be pursued within non-classical accounts of truth and consistency as well.

2. *Ambiguity semantics.* We begin by defining the ambiguous projection of a consistent image of a set of sentence letters:

Γ' is an ambiguously projected, consistent image of Γ based on A iff

   (i) A is a set of sentence letters

  (ii) Γ' is consistent

 (iii) Γ' results from the substitution, for each occurrence of each member a of A in Γ, of one of a pair of new sentence letters, a_f and a_t

We write ConIm (Γ', Γ, A) for this relation. Now we can define what is to be preserved by our new consequence relation:

$$\text{Amb}(\Gamma) = \{A \mid \exists\Gamma': \text{ConIm}(\Gamma', \Gamma, A) \wedge \forall A', A' \subset A, \neg\exists\Gamma'':$$
$$\text{ConIm}(\Gamma'', \Gamma, A')\}$$

In English, Amb(Γ) is the set of least sets that can be the base of a projection of a consistent image of Γ. The preservation relation is now easily defined:

Δ is an Amb(Γ)-preserving extension of Γ $\;\Leftrightarrow\;$ $\Delta \supseteq \Gamma \wedge \text{Amb}(\Gamma, \Delta) \subseteq$ Amb(Γ)

We write this: Accept(Δ, Γ). The idea here is that a set Δ is acceptable given a commitment to Γ, if and only if Δ includes Γ and does not *make things worse*: Δ must not require that more sentence letters be treated ambiguously in order for a consistent image of the extension to be projected. We do allow Δ to resolve uncertainties that Γ leaves open, including uncertainties about which projection bases can be used. This, combined with a reading of consequence relations as preserving the acceptability of all acceptable extensions, gives rise to a new consequence relation:

$$\Gamma \vdash_{\text{Amb}} \alpha \Leftrightarrow \forall\Delta: \text{Accept}(\Delta, \Gamma), \text{Accept}(\Delta, U\{\alpha\}, \Delta)$$

That is, α follows from Γ if and only if α is an acceptable extension of every acceptable extension of Γ. As I show in Brown (1999), this consequence relation is identical to the consequence relation of Priest's logic of paradox (LP). And in Brown (2001), I develop a closely related ambiguity-based account capturing the consequence relation of first-degree entailment.

The logics we obtain by preserving these measures of inconsistency are paraconsistent. The key point for our purposes here is that these preservationist consequence relations show that the resources available for the defence of LNC are far richer than they appear to be in the orthodox classical position. We can have paraconsistent consequence relations without adopting a semantics that allows truth or any other 'designated' (i.e. assertion sustaining) values to be assigned to inconsistent sets of sentences or to contradictions. This allows us to capture the general reluctance to infer arbitrary conclusions from inconsistent premisses without supposing (let alone asserting) the truth of classically unsatisfiable sets of sentences.

Dialetheic Dialectics

For the rest of this section, I will examine a pattern of argument that has been widely expounded by Graham Priest (see e.g. 1988, 1995, 2000, and forthcoming). My aim is to give a distilled version of the case for dialetheism as he presents it, followed by a defence of a more classical position. Unfortunately, space rules out anything approaching a complete review of Priest's defence of dialetheism. My aim is only to illustrate the debate and make a specific point about the implications of preservationist options for it.

In set theory, offered as a general account of *collections*, Frege's intuitively appealing comprehension axiom declared that, for any property (any open sentence in the language) there is a set containing all and only the things that have that property (that satisfy the open sentence):

For all open sentences Px, $(\exists y)(x)(x \in y \Leftrightarrow Px)$

But this axiom leads quickly to disaster, as Russell showed with a stunningly simple example, putting $x \notin x$ in for P. By the comprehension axiom,

$(\exists y)(x)(x \in y \Leftrightarrow x \notin x)$

Instantiating to a gives:

$(x)(x \in a \Leftrightarrow x \notin x)$

Finally, instantiating to a again, we get:

C1 $a \in a \Leftrightarrow a \notin a$

Similarly, when we want to add a theory of truth to our language, a natural axiom to adopt is the disquotational truth schema:

For any sentence 'p', 'p' is true if and only if p.

But again this leads to disaster. Consider a sentence that asserts its own falsity:

P: P is false

Substituting this in the truth schema gives us

'P is false' is true if and only if P is false

Given that P simply is 'P is false', this (already bad enough) gives rise to

C2 P is true if and only if P is false

Both C1 and C2 are straightforward classical contradictions. Given the explosive nature of classical logic, the result is a catastrophe for classical set theory and truth theory—every sentence in the language follows. So the simple language and consequence relation of classical logic demand complex versions of set theory and semantics—complex because, on pain of triviality, they must avoid the paradoxes. Moreover, as dialetheists have argued, it's not clear that such complexity can ever buy us an intuitively satisfying account of sets or truth.

By contrast, the dialetheic approach preserves the simple account of sets and truth, at the cost of significantly more complex accounts of negation and the consequence relation, at least for those versions of dialetheism that employ relevance logics. Priest argues that the cost is well worth the gain: Dialetheic consequence relations are typically equivalent to the classical when our premises are consistent. And the classical account of negation is harmless under the same condition. So (much as with classical gravity and relativity theory in physics) the dialetheist can dispense with the complexities of the dialetheic account in most applications, while retaining its simple and intuitive accounts of sets and truth.

But classical logic cannot similarly borrow the simple dialetheic accounts of sets and truths, since the threat of triviality is immediate and irremediable short of drastic alterations in classical ideas.

Moreover, Priest argues, these complex attempts to avoid the paradoxes are uniformly unsuccessful as accounts of our intuitive understanding of sets and truth. The semantic paradoxes can always be restated within the new system, so long as we demand the system account for intuitively legitimate applications of the concept of truth as it is used in English (or any natural language). Priest concludes that formal systems that manage, one way or another, to prevent the paradoxes from arising within the formalism, must fail to capture important uses of the concept of truth in natural language.

Priest's strategy has two stages. In the first, he demands that a satisfactory formal account of truth capture fully the notion of 'truth' as it is used in the natural language. To do so it must give a formal account of the notion that is both non-trivial and allows any applications of the notion that are intuitively acceptable in the natural language. But this demand is too strong; furthermore, I will argue that it can be met.

The demand is too strong because the practice of natural language is both vague and (more important for our purposes here) contextualized. By vague, I mean only that the practice does not wear its formal interpretation on its sleeve. There are no clear and indisputable criteria by which we can identify logical particles in English and characterize their correct use. Actual use is not a reliable guide by itself, since some actual use is sloppy and confused. Further, distinguishing such mistaken use from other usage involves adopting a theoretical perspective; different formal accounts of truth will be accompanied by distinct commentaries on errors in ordinary use and how they arise. By contextualized, I mean that our dealings with the world can often be divided into various more or less separate endeavours. Therefore some actual use may involve the misapplication of principles that, rightly understood, are restricted to other contexts. For example, much of our ordinary use of the word 'true' can (as deflationists have argued) be captured by a prosentential account. Perhaps not all of it can be. But so be it. The prosentential account remains a reasonably good account of much of our use, and there is no absolute requirement that we provide a single, univocal account that covers all use. After all, it's possible our use is not univocal at all. The constraints that lead us to use logical and semantic vocabulary as we do in one context may not all apply in others; after all, the established use of words is often extended by analogy and metaphor, and dead metaphors can then be converted to variant definitions. In the case of 'or', for example, we have found it difficult to arrive at a single formal account that covers all its uses. Even if there is a univocal account of truth that will work, it might involve complexities that can safely be ignored in the sort of context where we apply the prosentential account.[9]

But Priest's requirement can also be met because classical logic in general, and classical semantics in particular, does have the resources to restrict inferences from inconsistent sets. That is to say, classical logic can be paraconsistent. Of course the classical consequence relation is not paraconsistent. But as we've seen, there are classically definable, preservationist measures of the extent to which inconsistent sets depart from consistency. Preserving these measures just as the classical consequence relation preserves consistency produces paraconsistent consequence relations, including the weakly aggregative logics of Schotch and Jennings and my own preservationist versions of the consequence relation of LP and first degree entailment (FDE). But the underlying semantics remains completely classical, and no rejection of LNC is involved. A more modest attitude towards the resulting theories (in the sense of sets of sentences closed under a consequence relation) is involved: While these theories are not taken to be *correctly assertable* in the semantic sense of their sentences all having designated values, they are coherent, non-trivial, and perfectly usable for various purposes. Without specifying where or how things have gone wrong, the classicist can accept an inconsistent theory pro tem, and reason with it just as the dialetheist does. Classical semantics requires her to hold that something has gone wrong here. But the error may well be inextricably embedded in ordinary English. And the classical paraconsistentist can model non-trivial reasoning in the (confused) truth-theory of ordinary English in just the way that a dialetheist using LP or FDE does.

Here we have an account of how a different sort of formal theory that retains LNC can capture the same consequence relations that some dialetheic logics provide. To complete the translation between the two accounts, we must shift

---

[9] Epistemic contextualism is a theme that I will not develop here; its only similarity to the point I am making is the broad suggestion that principles or standards for the correct use of some words can vary from context to context.

our reading of acceptance from a full endorsement of certain sentences at stake as correctly assertable, to the more modest acceptance of the sentences for purposes of reasoning. But the result is a recipe for applying two different logical theories, disagreeing over the status of LNC, to capture the same patterns of utterances and inferences.

Some might object to the preservationist shift, arguing that a proper consequence relation must turn on truth. After all, a consequence relation is not just any semantic relation we can specify between sets of sentences. It must aim at capturing relations between the correct assertion of (sets of) sentences and the correct assertion of other (sets of) sentences. And the condition of correct assertion just *is* truth (or more generally having a designated semantic value).

But this is a very constraining idealization. Its application to ordinary standards of assertability is questionable. We recognize, in these modest times, that our best accounts of things are unlikely to be correct in all respects, and may be internally incoherent. Reasoning according to a consequence relation that guarantees preservation of truth alone is reasoning on the supposition that our present commitments are all consistent. But we may well be convinced that they are inconsistent, or very probably so, i.e. that there is and *can be* no truth to preserve in our present commitments. Having taken such a modest stance does not cut us off from clear standards for reasoning if we accept a preservationist measure (or even a set of measures) of how incoherent our present commitments are, and insist that our consequence relation *guarantee* that we don't (by reasoning alone, at any rate) *make things worse.*

In the second stage of his argument, Priest recognizes that his demand, that the truth concept of English (and other natural languages) be fully captured in an adequate formal account of truth, can be resisted. The formalist can propose her account as a reformation (even a correction) of the practice in natural language. (See Priest (forthcoming).) Priest rejects this defence of the classical position for two reasons.

First, he asks why reformation is necessary, given that natural language talk about truth does not trivialize despite its inconsistency. But as we have already noted, there is no guarantee that the non-trivialization of natural language is due to the existence of a univocal, context-independent natural language conception of truth that a formal theory should capture. It may instead be a matter of a sloppy range of uses of 'truth' that share some features but do not constitute a single coherent notion that a good formal theory should capture fully. To capture how we reason from such sets of commitments we may need to commit to (or at least to employ) a paraconsistent consequence relation. But such consequence relations can be separated from dialetheism.

This argument clearly falls short of a demonstration (which, to make her case conclusively, the classicist requires) of a *need* for reformation. But it suggests that reformation together with pro-tem use of preservationist consequence relations is

Bryson Brown

a reasonable strategy for dealing with the phenomena that dialetheists invoke in support of their position.

Second, Priest raises a challenge: if reformation is our aim, why not a reformation leading to a dialetheic position, rather than a consistent, classical one? Here I agree. Both proposals are on the table.

I want to close here by noting one further contribution that preservationism makes to this debate: it blocks the slippery slope argument in Priest (2000) that aims to drive us from the second level of paraconsistency (at which we accept the existence of interesting or valuable inconsistent theories that can be modelled with the help of paraconsistent consequence relations) to the third (at which we accept the possibility that some such theories are *true*). Priest's argument turns critically on the claim that semantics for paraconsistent logics must allow assignment of designated values to inconsistent premiss sets while failing to assign designated values to other sentences in the language. But preservationist semantics produce paraconsistent consequence relations without any commitment to non-trivial models of inconsistent premisses.

Priest (ibid. 230) goes on to say: 'the onus is now on someone who rejects the third level of paraconsistency to say why. What can one say? There is really only one move here: to invoke the Law of Non-Contradiction (LNC), in the form: no contradiction may be true.' This last stand against dialetheism, Priest goes on to argue, is a weak one: the historical arguments for LNC are few and unconvincing, while the paraconsistent logician (even at the first level of paraconsistency) has already adopted the resources needed coherently to give it up. But the preservationist approach gives us paraconsistent logics *without* semantic resources that can be turned against LNC. So classically minded preservationists will require further arguments in favour of dialetheic semantics before agreeing that LNC must be given up.

Finally, the existence of alternative, preservationist semantics for logics that have heretofore been treated as dialetheic makes a further important point: LP and FDE have previously been given semantics that at least suggest a dialetheic interpretation: Priest's account of LP is explicitly dialetheic, and, although Dunn's four-valued semantics for FDE was initially aimed at an epistemic reading (with the four values read as 'told just true', 'told both true and false', 'told just false', and 'told neither'), the dialetheic reading is both straightforward and tempting, especially in cases where we are at a loss as to how to avoid or correct an apparent inconsistency.

In the absence of a clear distinction between the semantic properties preserved by our consequence relations and our notion of truth, it is tempting to take the semantic values preserved by any given consequence relations to be forms of (or formal theories of) truth. But the semantics of ambiguity measures is sharply distinct from the dialetheic semantics, and retains as truth values only the standard two. The consequences of inconsistent premiss sets are limited by preserving a measure of the ambiguity that must be allowed in order to produce consistently assertable disambiguated *images* of the premiss set (and, to generalize, consistently *deniable* images of the conclusion set) (see Brown 1999, 2001).

The fact that the consequence relations of LP and FDE can be obtained by preserving certain classical semantic properties rather than by preserving non-classical designated values suggests that it will be difficult for dialetheists to show their approach to logic has an indispensable advantage over all the alternatives. Whatever the advantages of dialetheism may be, they are likely to be available, via preservationist manœuvres, to non-dialetheists, including logicians who retain classical logic in its entirety.

As I remarked above, both accounts are on the table. The question we are left with is, can the evidence decide between them?

REALISM AND RELATIVITY

The pioneers of 'deviant' logics often supposed that non-classical logic is to classical as non-Euclidean geometry is to Euclidean. If this is so, it will be hard if not impossible to resolve fundamental logical disagreements: the questions at stake may not have invariant answers in all tenable accounts of the formal logic that 'underlies' our practice in natural language, logic, and mathematics. We are always reaching beyond the evidence of actual practice when we propose a formal theory of logic—the rules of any systematic logic will render 'correct' inferences that (at best) would elicit a shrug, or just puzzlement, from most native speakers.[10] We may have strong intuitions regarding the 'right' fundamental principles. But such intuitions are subject to doubt and revision, guided at least in part by coherentist considerations.

If it has taught us anything, the experience of the last two centuries regarding our understanding of the difference between pure and applied geometry has taught us that the connections between abstract structures—like those of formal logic—and their standard applications are much less straightforward than had been imagined. In broad, realism remains possible in the face of relativity, but only when one of two conditions is met:

1. There exists a translation scheme linking the various points of view directly, without the intermediation of an invariant description.

2. There exists a set of invariants that is explanatorily adequate (including relations between observers' 'points of view' and the items observed) to account for the differences between things as seen from the various observers' points of view. When this condition is met, the invariant description of things provides us with an account of the 'real' world that lies behind things as they are described from various points of view.

---

[10] Here the role of idealization looms large.

Of course a mathematical account of the transformations involved in the translations will allow us to identify invariants. But an invariant description will not always be fully determined by the information contained in a single point of view. So the second condition has somewhat broader application than the first.

The most familiar example of such connections between various points of view and a real, invariant world is the relation between the three-dimensional world and the various (roughly) two-dimensional 'images' of that world as seen from different positions (including the effects of looking in different directions, and—to generalize—projecting the images on differently shaped surfaces). In this case, the images are generally incomplete (not everything can be seen from a single location). So there is no general translation scheme allowing each point of view to be directly translated into another. But the larger, invariant view of things allows us to predict what will be seen from any point of view, explaining how each of them arises as a correct image of (some parts of) the invariant reality.[11]

Another important example is Poincarré's conventionalism about the geometry of physical space. Here the central point is that any set of measurements compatible with (say) Euclidean geometry can be transformed into a set of measurements compatible with another geometry (generalized Riemannian) by systematic stretching and contracting (or, equivalently, by the invocation of universal forces affecting the measuring rods). In this case, we can translate between (complete) sets of measurements; what is invariant is a more general structure characterized by what is preserved in all the different pairings of a geometry with a detailed specification of universal forces that fit a given set of measurements (Poincarré 1952). Requiring (at least ideally) that physical theories be presented in covariant form is another way in which scientists have emphasized the importance of invariants to a correct understanding of the content of a physical theory.

Moreover different positions in logical theory may be accompanied by different views on just what we should ask of logical theory. For example, while some want logical theory to answer a wide range of questions about the semantics and standards for correct reasoning in natural language, others may want a formal framework we can use to explicate systematically the content of scientific and mathematical theories. Those who take the former position may hold that the natural language, at least in some idealized form, constitutes a touchstone for a *true* general theory of logic. Or they may simply have an interest in the philosophical explication of natural language, a job that might be best served by different logical tools than those suited to the explication of science and mathematics. Some of the latter may hold that science and mathematical theory represent a more systematic development based on vague and ambiguous patterns in natural language, and that a logical theory that answers to their needs will represent an advance (in terms of

---

[11] In fact this example, together with Hume's considerations on his porter's night-time visit and the untenability of phenomenalism that those considerations reveal, suggests to me that reality itself is an explanatory concept.

clarity, accuracy, and well-definedness) on whatever logical theories might emerge from the study of natural language. Others may merely be particularly interested in science and mathematics. Still others may believe that a correct account of the logic of natural language will be a useful guide to thinking about scientific and mathematical theories, independently of any strong pre-commitment to its 'truth', or normative standing for the practice of mathematics and science.

It seems likely that a range of alternative systematizations, bringing the pheno-mena of natural language, or of science and mathematics, or perhaps all three, under distinct formal logics, will fit the constraints on logical theory adequately. And what logic is 'best' may vary depending on the different aims and constraints most central to the applications that those working on logical theory have in mind. Here we move towards the project of reconciling different logical theories by assigning them different tasks; but I will put this issue aside and continue on the assumption that there is a single, fairly well-defined task that is the principal (though probably not the only) intended application for formal logic: to account for a substantial part of human reasoning and talk about notions including truth, consequence relations, and the logical words.

We are, it must be admitted, much clearer about the kinds of observational constraints that geometrical theories must cope with. This made it relatively straightforward for Poincarré to show how to convert observational constraints fitting one geometry into an adjusted set of constraints fitting another. But how shall we specify these observational constraints on logic? Exactly what do we ask a formal logic to do? We explored this question above in a broad and general way, concluding that formal logic aims to capture, in a clear and detailed way, certain intuitions about correct inferences, semantic talk, and regular patterns in the use of certain words that are independent of the particular subject matter before us.

I do not say that formal logic should give a general account of inference; there is more to inference than mere consequences. We often don't infer consequences of sets of sentences that we accept, whether because they are uninteresting or unhelpful, because they are too remote to be recognized as consequences, or because instead of inferring them, we choose to reject one or more of the previously accepted sentences. Further, some inferences depend on specific predicates and other lexical vocabulary, rather than on the very general, more or less formal structures that logical theories aim to account for. Thus actual inference often reaches beyond the deductive consequences of our premises, often passes over what are widely accepted to be deductive consequences (such as self-conjunctions of accepted sentences), and often involves a retreat from commitments rather than their extension to a newly recognized consequence. Actual inference is constrained by our needs, interests, and limitations as much as by any consequence relation.

On the account of logical knowledge adopted above, our knowledge of logical facts is based in our ability to learn a public language. Such knowledge has an externalist component, due to our lack of conscious awareness and control of the processes that enable us to learn linguistic rules. Since these processes serve both to determine content and to ensure a level of agreement on principles sufficient to allow successful communication, they make our intuitive judgements reliable sources of evidence for claims and inferences. But for the very same reason, they make it difficult, if not impossible, to defend the claim that they underwrite a specific account of the 'logical truth' that can distinguish between formal theories that are otherwise broadly adequate.

Ordinary communication is not much affected by a choice between a classical view of negation, an intuitionist view, and a dialetheic view. In almost all circumstances, the same claims and inferences will be acceptable, despite fundamental differences regarding the *general* truth of LNC and the law of excluded middle. For intuitionists and dialetheists, the errors of classical logic can be described as overgeneralizations of principles that are perfectly acceptable in certain circumstances—circumstances where a finite number of cases are involved, or where no contradictory information need be considered. Similarly, as I have argued above, the weaker consequence relations of the dialetheist and the intuitionist can be regarded, by classicists, as preserving semantic (syntactic) properties other than truth (consistency).

This underdetermination doesn't undermine the business of applying formal logic. We can identify quite a few consequences that most people will readily endorse. After careful reflection and reconsideration, we can bring most people to endorse a simple set of consequence rules that will carry quite a lot of the load (though we have to be careful about the generally loose and irregular way in which truth functions and other logically important features are actually expressed in natural language). And we can explore speakers' ideas about consequences in more detail by examining how they respond to questions, how their answers change when they are given various suppositions to work from, and so forth. We can also examine the convictions of speakers about concepts such as truth and implication, identifying various intuitions whose preservation in a formal account is desirable. A further difficulty remains, however: while correct measurement in geometry is certainly a normative notion, correct observation of correct patterns of assertion and inference is doubly so. Unlike 'mere' natural objects subject to natural law, language users are not perfectly obedient to the correct rules of use for their language.

Further, logical intuitions about subtler and more systematic questions are at least in part the result of training. We find ourselves caught in a serious tension here. Study and education are valuable things, and we usually believe that greater weight should be given to the intuitions that well-trained researchers bring to esoteric subjects. But training influences the intuitions we take to be important and unimportant, and what sorts of formal models we expect or demand for the phenomena (see e.g. Jennings 1994). This makes it all too easy to dismiss intuitions contrary to one's own as the result of confusion and a 'bad upbringing'.

Anti-Realism

Suppose, what already seems unlikely, that fairly conclusive reasons based in simplicity, explanatory power, elegance, and similar epistemic values supported either a dialetheic or a classical account. A logical anti-realist might still balk at drawing the conclusion. In the spirit of van Fraassen's constructive empiricism regarding scientific theories, she might claim we cannot settle the *real* status of LNC by such considerations. She might regard the choice as a matter of convenience, heuristics, and/or pragmatics, not reflecting any objectively testable matter of logical fact.

Such a position would no doubt be unsatisfying both to the defenders of LNC and to those who reject it. To avoid this threatened dissolution of the conflict, some form of epistemic realism about logical principles needs to be defended. We must show that underdetermination does not apply here, either by showing that the sort of evidence such anti-realists recognize clearly favours either theories including LNC or theories rejecting it, or that further constraints (explanatory power, simplicity, etc.) really are evidential and capable of settling the issue. Either way, the realism we arrive at must be one that makes the status of non-contradiction a *logical invariant* across all the epistemically tenable theories.

But this seems an unlikely prospect. We now have logical systems that reject LNC as well as logical systems that endorse it. If the status of non-contradiction is invariant, one or the other class of systems must be ruled out by the constraints on applied logical systems. But even if explanatory power and other coherentist considerations are allowed evidential standing, the connection between the data of real assertion and inference and the logical systems in which we aim to systematize that data is flexible. As preservationist options show, semantic notions about the standards of correct assertion (and correct denial) can be separated from commitments to consequence relations. And the details of how these two 'come together' when we move beyond an abstract grasp of purely formal systems to *apply* the systems are richer and more subject to discussion, dispute, and revision than the links that join pure geometry to empirical measurements: a satisfactory account of the logic of a language need not agree perfectly with speakers' use of that language. If deficiencies in the speakers' grasp of the language or their information-processing capacities can explain the discrepancies, the theory can be saved. But this salvation from falsification inevitably introduces still more underdetermination.

This leads to serious difficulty for attempts to prove or refute LNC. Suppose that the evidence of actual reasoning shows that people do and should refuse to accept that everything follows from inconsistent premises (including the premises that lead us to the paradoxes). It follows that the classical consequence relation must be rejected: it is not acceptable as a stand-alone, one-size-fits-all account of consequence. But where do we go from there? This doesn't show that LNC itself fails, i.e. that we must allow for assigning truth (in the form of semantically designated values) to classically unsatisfiable or inconsistent sets of sentences while still rejecting some other sentences as undesignated. Its implications for LNC depend on what semantic features we take the consequence relation to preserve. The possibility of coherently supposing the premises are all true while the conclusions[12] are all false is the standard reason for rejecting a consequence. But the fact that a consequence violates preservation of some other desirable property provides a tenable alternative account of why people *should* reject that consequence.

From this point of view, the current debate over LNC is misguided. Rather than focus our efforts on an issue that divides researchers—researchers who are all trying to improve on the crudity of the classical consequence relation—we would do better to explore the range of alternative consequence relations and their application to various contexts in which inconsistency tolerance is valuable, recognizing that a given consequence relation can often be given quite different semantics, dialetheic,[13] preservationist, and others.

Like all formal theoretical principles, LNC stands at a distance from the Quinean observational periphery. Showing that the constraints on formal theories of logic require either LNC or its rejection is difficult, since the effects of our choice can be compensated for by changes elsewhere—changes such as those we have considered, in the semantic properties our consequence relations preserve, and perhaps in various aspects of how our formal theories of logic are linked to the phenomena we apply them to.

I strongly suspect the set of consequence relations that can be given a preservationist semantics is a proper superset of those that can be given a dialetheic semantics. Dialetheic semantics fall within the 'preservation of a designated value' picture of consequence. But preservationist semantics includes semantics based on preservation of designated semantic values as well as the preservation of a wide range of other properties of sentences and sets of sentences—properties we are not even remotely tempted to regard as forms of 'truth'. If our best models of consequence relations have preservationist but not dialetheic semantics, then LNC as a logical invariant may survive the rejection of ex falso. On the other hand, if our best models of consequence relations have dialetheic semantics, but can also be given well-motivated preservationist semantics, then the status of LNC will be a

---

[12] A set–set account of the consequence relation makes the symmetries between premises and conclusions and assertion and denial mentioned earlier more evident.

[13] Is a semantics dialetheic when it allows for non-trivial valuations in which inconsistent sets of sentences receive designated values? Some, I think, would object on the grounds that (as they understand them) the valuations in question are not truth-valuations, but valuations of an epistemic (or other) kind. In doing so, non-dialetheic paraconsistentists lean towards a preservationist understanding of the systems they have developed, since what they take to be preserved by their preferred consequence relations is a property (or properties) distinct from truth. But dialetheists can easily challenge such a stand. So long as the logic preserves values that are so clearly analogous to truth values, reading them *as* truth values (i.e. as part of an alternative, heterodox theory of truth) can be hard to resist. Explicitly preservationist semantics help to bolster resistance to this slippery slide.

matter of convention, not a matter of fact: LNC will not be a logical invariant, since different but equally adequate formal accounts of the underpinnings of reasoning will disagree on its status.

PROSPECTS

I have assumed that we want our formal logic to embed and (to some extent) explain the phenomena of everyday reasoning (where by everyday reasoning I mean to include the reasoning of mathematicians and scientists, not just the ordinary use of natural language and the refined discourse of the senior common room). As a result, and in accord with deep-seated empiricist intuitions about the evidence to which our theories are answerable, we have focused on the fit between logical theory and these phenomena. The phenomena in question have been identified as intuitions about principles, concepts, and reasoning practices, which we attempt to explain by appeal to formal systems of logic and semantics.

I have appealed more than once to an analogy with applying geometrical theories to physical space to make two important points. First, just as there are practical matters touching on the measurement of space and time (the differential expansion and contraction of various materials that might be used in measuring rods, and similar forces that various kinds of clocks may be subject to) that are no concern of geometry per se, there are matters touching on human reasoning behaviour that are no concern of formal logic per se (questions of our computational limits, neuro-psychological details of how our reasoning processes are physically implemented, typical patterns of erroneous reasoning, etc.). And second, just as the links between a final set of observations and a formal geometry can be adjusted to allow for the formal differences between Euclidean and various non-Euclidean geometries, I have suggested that the links between human reasoning behaviour and formal logic can be adjusted to allow for the formal differences between various logics, while maintaining the same level of 'fit' between observations and the formal theory.

But while such fit between theory and data is a sine qua non for acceptability, it gives little positive reason for acceptance. I want to close with some remarks on this gap between empirical adequacy (i.e. the absence of conflict between a theory and data gathered, or gatherable, in accord with that theory's principles) and a positive basis for acceptance. I have supposed, perhaps optimistically, that values such as explanatory power and ontological parsimony provide further grounds for accepting (even believing) scientific theories. But the use of novel scientific theory to guide the production of novel phenomena also plays, I think, a crucial role in providing positive reasons for acceptance.

What I have in mind here is the similar role that logical theory plays in shaping and reforming our practice as reasoners. Modern formal logic emerged from work that aimed not just to describe mathematical reasoning, but to *improve* it by making the process of proof giving more structured and formal. It was also hoped this would simplify the process of evaluating purported mathematical proofs. And these goals have been achieved. Mathematical practice—a practice in which complex reasoning according to a strict consequence relation is central—has been altered dramatically by the development and study of these formal methods. In this context, passive theorizing about independently given phenomena is not our best epistemic model. Theory instead becomes a contributing source of new phenomena.

It is here, in the details of logical and mathematical practice, that logical innovators seek real gains. In particular, I have in mind the ambitions of dialetheic mathematicians to skirt the limits of Gödel's incompleteness theorems by producing a complete, though inconsistent, axiomatization of arithmetic. If these ambitions are realized, it will be a resounding success for the dialetheist project. But I suspect that any gains achieved through the rejection of LNC can also be achieved by other means. A preservationist account of the dialetheic consequence relation underlying such a theory would make its benefits available to more classically minded formalists. So the status of LNC seems to be like Euclid's parallel postulate: a tenable but not indispensable part of some formal theories of logic.

REFERENCES

Batens, D., et al. (2000), *Frontiers of Paraconsistent Logic* (Baldock: Research Studies Press).

Bealer, G. (1999), 'A Theory of the A Priori', in Tomberlin (1999), 29–55.

Bonevac, D. (1982), *Reduction in the Abstract Sciences* (Indianapolis: Hackett).

Brown, B. (1999), 'Yes, Virginia, There Really are Paraconsistent Logics', *Journal of Philosophical Logic*, 28: 489–500.

—— (2001), 'LP, FDE and Ambiguity', in H. Arabnia (ed.), *Proceedings of the 2001 International Conference on Artificial Intelligence* (Las Vegas: CSREA), ii.

Earman, J. (ed.) (1983), *Testing Scientific Theories*, Minnesota Studies in the Philosophy of Science, 10 (Minneapolis: University of Minnesota Press).

Feigl, H., and Sellars, W. (eds.) (1949), *Readings in Philosophical Analysis* (New York: Appleton-Century-Crofts).

Friedman, M. (1974), 'Explanation and Scientific Understanding', *Journal of Philosophy*, 71: 5–19.

Glymour, C. (1980), *Theory and Evidence* (Princeton: Princeton University Press).

Goldman, A. J. (1999), 'A Priori Warrant', in Tomberlin (1999).

Hanson, N. R. (1958), *Patterns of Discovery* (Cambridge: Cambridge University Press).

Harman, G. (1986) *Change in View* (Cambridge: MIT).

Hempel, C. G. (1965a), *Aspects of Scientific Explanation* (New York: Macmillan).

Hume, D. (1739–40) [1896], *Treatise on Human Nature*, ed. L. A. Selby-Bigge (Oxford: Oxford University Press).

—— (1748) [1966], *Enquiry concerning Human Understanding*, ed. L. A. Selby-Bigge (Oxford: Oxford University Press).

JENNINGS, R. E. (1994), *The Geneology of Disjunction* (Oxford: Oxford University Press).

JENNINGS, R. E. and JOHNSTON, D. (1983), 'Paradox-Tolerant Logic', *Logique et Analyse*, 26: 291–308.

JENNINGS, R. E. and SCHOTCH, P. K. (1981), 'Some Remarks on (Weakly) Weak Modal Logic', *Notre Dame Journal of Formal Logic*, 22: 309–14.

—— (1984), 'The Preservation of Coherence', *Studia Logica*, 43: 89–106.

JENNINGS, R. E., SCHOTCH, P. K., and JOHNSTON, D. (1980), 'Universal First Order Definability in Model Logic', *Zeitschrift für Mathematische Logik und Grundlagen der Mathematik*, 26: 327–30.

—— (1981), 'The n-adic First Order Underfinability of the Geach Formula', *Notre Dame Journal of Formal Logic*, 22, 375–78.

POINCARRÉ, H. [1905] (1952), *Science and Hypothesis* (New York: Dover).

PRIEST, G. (1988), *Beyond Consistency* (Munich: Philosophia).

—— (1995), *Beyond the Limits of Thought* (Cambridge: Cambridge University Press).

—— (2000), 'Motivations for Paraconsistency: The Slippery Slope from Classical Logic to Dialetheism', in Batens et al. (2000), 223–32.

—— (forthcoming), 'Paraconsistency and Dialetheism', in D. Gabbay and J. H. Woods, *Handbook of the History of Philosophical Logic*.

SALMON, W. C. (1998), *Causality and Explanation* (New York: Oxford University Press).

SCHOTCH, P. K. and JENNINGS, R. E. (1980a), 'Inference and Necessity', *Journal of Philosophical Logic*, 9: 327–40.

—— (1980b), 'Modal Logic and the Theory of Modal Aggregation', *Philosophia*, 9: 265–78.

—— (1989), 'On Detonating', in Priest, Routley, and Norman (1989), 306–27.

SHER, G. (2001), 'Is Logic a Theory of the Obvious?' in Woods and Brown (2001), 55–80.

SUPPE, F. (1977), *The Structure of Scientific Theories*, 2nd edn. (Urbana: University of Illinois Press).

TOMBERLIN, J. E. (1999), *Philosophical Perspectives on Epistemology, 1999* (Cambridge, Mass.: Blackwell).

VAN FRAASSEN, B. (1980), *The Scientific Image* (Oxford: Oxford University Press).

—— (1983), 'Theory Comparison and Relevant Evidence', in Earman (1983), 27–42.

—— (1984), 'Belief and the Will', *Journal of Philosophy*, 81: 235–56.

WOODS, J. H. (2001), 'Pluralism about Logical Consequence: Resolving Conflict in Logical Theory', in Woods and Brown (2001).

WOODS, J. H. and BROWN, B. (eds.) (2001), *Logical Consequence; Rival Approaches: Proceedings of SEP 1999* (London: Hermes), i.

9

Logical Non-Apriorism and the 'Law' of Non-Contradiction

Otávio Bueno and Mark Colyvan

ABSTRACT

A common response to those who question the Law of Non-Contradiction (LNC) is that it is impossible to debate such a fundamental law of logic. The reasons for this response vary, but what seems to underlie them all is the thought that there is a minimal set of logical resources without which rational debate is impossible. According to this line of response, at least, the LNC is so fundamental that without it the logical resources available are too impoverished for debate to proceed. In this chapter we argue that this response is misguided. We begin by defending non-apriorism in logic—the view that logic is in the same epistemic boat as other scientific theories. We then give an account of logical theory change in terms of this epistemology. Finally, we discuss the LNC in terms of this account of logical theory change and we show that rational debate over this law can, and does, proceed. We also discuss some of the arguments for and against the LNC and we illustrate how and where non-apriori considerations arise in these arguments.

1. INTRODUCTION

One of the reasons that philosophy of logic is such a difficult enterprise is that, in order to advance debates in this area, we require the very thing we are studying: logic. This difficulty is especially acute when engaging in the business of theory choice in logic. After all, in order to decide between two logical theories, we need to put forward evidence and arguments for each. This evidence and these arguments will need to be assessed, and the assessment will need to be conducted in the context of some logic or other. But how do we choose this latter logic? We appear to be headed for an infinite regress.

Things get even worse when we start thinking about how we might debate fundamental logical principles such as the LNC. Here, many believe, the task is hopeless. We simply have no ground to stand on once we tentatively reject something so fundamental as the LNC. In this chapter we suggest that such pessimism is unwarranted; we argue that we *can* reasonably debate fundamental principles such as the LNC, and we show one way in which this debate can proceed. We do not propose to settle the debate, or even attempt do so. Showing that it is possible to have a debate is enough.

We begin, in s. 2, by arguing that logic is not a priori, so, in particular, the debate over the LNC is not to be conducted entirely in a priori terms.[1] Then, in s. 3, we provide a model of how theory change in logic can proceed. In s. 4, we argue that even fundamental 'laws' such as the LNC can be debated in the framework we outline in this chapter.

There is another issue that, although closely related to the topic of this chapter, for the most part we shall be setting aside. This is the issue of logical monism versus logical pluralism. (The former is the view that there is one true logic, the latter that there is no unique such logic.) This debate has attracted a great deal of attention recently.[2] This monism–pluralism debate is of considerable interest and bears on the present topic in the following way. It has been argued that the variety of alternatives to classical logic—all of which seem adequate for at least some domains—presents problems for logical monism,[3] so issues about theory choice in logic are not so much about which is the one true logic, but, rather, which logic is adequate to a given domain. We will not take sides on this issue (at least not in this chapter). Instead, we try to present our case in terms that will be acceptable to monists and pluralists alike. Both need to embark on theory choice in logic (admittedly the interpretation of what their choices mean is different in each case), and that is all we are concerned with here. We will show that theory choice should proceed in non-apriori terms and that, given such a view of theory choice in logic, there is no reason to believe that we cannot have rational debate over apparently fundamental principles such as the LNC.

2. NON-APRIORISM IN LOGIC

Despite the influence of Quine (1953) and Putnam (1979), the view that theory choice in logic proceeds via non-apriori terms is far from universally accepted. In this section we provide a defence of non-apriorism in logic.[4] To motivate logical non-apriorism, we will critically assess some arguments put forward *against* this view, and indicate why they fail. Some such arguments have been presented by

[1] The position we defend here, thus, has resonances with certain empiricist philosophies of mathematics; these include Kitcher (1983), Lakatos (1976), Field (1980, 1993), Quine (1981), and Resnik (1997). See also Colyvan (2001), ch. 6, for a defence of the view that mathematics is empirical.

[2] See e.g. Resnik (1996), Beall and Restall (2000, 2001), Bueno (2002, forthcoming *b*), and Priest (2001).

[3] e.g. one of the present authors (Bueno 2002) has argued along these lines for the conclusion that paraconsistentists should be logical pluralists.

[4] Some of the points made in this section have been developed in more detail in Bueno (forthcoming *a*); see also Bueno (2002).

Hartry Field, in his recent defence of logical apriorism (see Field 1996, 1998, 2001). Other arguments have been around longer, such as one put forward by Alfred Tarski in his celebrated paper on the concept of logical consequence (Tarski 1936). To part company with Tarski is often not a terribly good idea, but at least we won't be in bad company if we note that some of the ideas about logical non-apriorism articulated here have also been around for quite a while, in the works of John von Neumann (1937*a*, *b*), Hilary Putnam (1979, 1983*a*, *b*, *c*), and Newton da Costa (1997).

Before addressing these issues, however, let us point out a crucial feature of the logical non-apriorism articulated here. The idea is that it is possible to *revise* logical principles (or logical rules) on the basis of extra-logical considerations—which include empirical considerations. In other words, extra-logical considerations play a role in the selection and evaluation of logical principles (or rules).[5] Some people may add a further requirement for logical non-apriorism, namely that the *justification* of logical principles should be obtained on empirical grounds as well.[6] This latter requirement amounts to a really strong form of logical non-apriorism—a form of apriorism far stronger than the one we will be working with here. So for the purpose of the present work, only the revisability condition above will be required.[7]

But is it plausible to suppose that logic is non-apriori in the above sense? To argue that it is, we will examine three arguments for logical non-apriorism: an argument from quantum mechanics, a critical assessment of an argument that Tarski devised for logical apriorism (implicit in Tarski's substitution requirement), and an argument that Putnam provided on the centrality of the LNC. We will examine each of these arguments in turn.

2.1 The Argument from Quantum Mechanics

One of the most interesting arguments for non-apriorism in logic—let's call it the argument from quantum mechanics—was explored by von Neumann (see Birkhoff and von Neumann 1936, and von Neumann 1937*a*, *b*). The main idea is that, in von Neumann's view, classical logic simply provides the wrong results when applied to the quantum domain. The overall structure of the latter domain is not adequately represented by classical logic; but it is by quantum logic.

---

[5] This is the view that we reject or revise logical principles based on empirical evidence (but we do not necessarily invoke empirical considerations for the acceptance of logical principles).

[6] This is the view that we accept logical principles based on empirical grounds.

[7] We note that our usage of 'a priori' and 'non-apriori' are somewhat non-standard; by 'logical non-apriorism' we simply mean that extra-logical considerations come to play in theory choice in logic. As it turns out (see s. 2.1), we also think that logic is non-apriori in a stronger sense (in that empirical considerations come to play). Our main purpose in this chapter, however, is to defend an account of theory change in logic that allows, and makes sense of, debates about the law of non-contradiction. It's important for our case that the role of extra-logical considerations in these debates is appreciated. Some of these considerations are empirical, while others are merely extra-logical. We find it convenient to use the term 'non-apriori' to include both, but nothing hangs on this admittedly non-standard usage.

To illustrate this, let us consider a simple example. According to standard quantum mechanics, any electron E has an angular momentum (or spin) in a given direction X. Moreover, every electron has only one of two possible spin values: $+1/2$ or $-1/2$. So if we denote the spin of E in the X direction by E_X, the following disjunction is true:

$$E_X = +1/2 \vee E_X = -1/2$$

Furthermore, given Heinsenberg's indeterminacy principle, it is not possible to measure the angular momentum of E in two (distinct) directions at the same time.

Let X and Y be two distinct directions. And let us suppose that we have measured the momentum of E in the direction X, and obtained the result that $E_X = +1/2$. In other words, '$E_X = +1/2$' is true. Now, given that '$E_Y = +1/2 \vee E_Y = -1/2$' is always true (in any instant), it follows that the conjunction

(1) $E_X = +1/2 \wedge (E_Y = +1/2 \vee E_Y = -1/2)$

is similarly true. If we assume the distributivity of conjunction over disjunction found in classical logic, it follows from (1) that

(2) $(E_X = +1/2 \wedge E_Y = +1/2) \vee (E_X = +1/2 \wedge E_Y = -1/2)$

But something unexpected happens at this point. As noted above, (1) is true, but it turns out (arguably) that (2) is false (or even meaningless)! After all, given Heisenberg's indeterminacy principle, it is impossible to measure the moment of E in distinct directions X and Y at the same time. So, if we assume (as we did) that the underlying logic is classical, we are led straightaway into a conceptual difficulty (see Birkhoff and von Neumann 1936; Putnam 1979; da Costa 1997).

There are, of course, different ways of trying to keep classical logic given the problem presented by (2). It turns out, though, that none of the current options has received unanimous acceptance. For example, one could simply change standard quantum mechanics in such a way that the problem is not generated. This amounts to the introduction of a *new* theory, for which we shall need, as is the case of any new theory, independent evidence, the assurance that the theory is not ad hoc, and so on. But even if the theory satisfied all these requirements, the introduction of a new theory doesn't solve the problem. For it is still a problem for *standard quantum mechanics* that it seems to be in conflict with classical logic.

Alternatively, it might be claimed that it is the measurement that 'creates' the value of the spin, and so the proposition

(3) $E_Y = +1/2 \vee E_Y = -1/2$

is neither true nor false. But this provides no solution to the problem either—at least not for the classical logician. After all, the claim that proposition (3) is neither true nor false is in conflict with classical logic as well.

Or perhaps one could adopt a Bohmian interpretation of quantum mechanics and reject Heisenberg's indeterminacy principle (for a thoughtful discussion, see Cushing 1994). Once again, this amounts to changing the theory, given that, for example, the Bohmian interpretation and standard quantum mechanics have incompatible accounts of the nature of quantum particles. And in any case, this doesn't solve the problem either, since the original difficulty remains—there is still an apparent incompatibility between classical logic and standard quantum mechanics.

The point of these remarks is not to suggest that just by moving to quantum logic one can overcome the problems of interpretation faced by quantum mechanics— this would be unrealistically simplistic.[8] The only point we are making here is that logic may be revised on the basis of empirical considerations, which is enough to suggest that logic is not a priori.

2.2 Tarski's Argument for Logical Apriorism and its Limits

We certainly acknowledge that logical non-apriorism is not the mainstream inter- pretation of logic. In fact, as part of the development of what is now the orthodox account of logical consequence, Tarski also provided an argument for logical apriorism. In this section, we will discuss and assess this argument.

As a necessary (but not sufficient) condition for logical consequence, Tarski put forward what can be called the *substitution requirement*. Suppose that K is a class of sentences and that X is a given sentence. According to the substitution requirement:

If, in the sentences of the class K and in the sentence X, the constants—apart from purely logical constants—are replaced by any other constants (like signs being everywhere replaced by like signs), and if we denote the class of sentences thus obtained from K by K', and the sentence obtained from X by X', then the sentence X' must be true provided only that all sentences of the class K' are true.   (Tarski 1936: 415; emphasis omitted)

As formulated here, the substitution requirement provides one way of expressing the condition that logic should be formal. After all, it doesn't matter what extra- logical constants we replace in the original set of sentences K and in X, if X follows from K, then X' follows from K'. The requirement that logical consequence be *formal* is expressed by guaranteeing that extra-logical (in particular, empirical) considerations are in a clear sense *irrelevant* for logical consequence. If X already follows from K, a complete reinterpretation of X and the sentences in K won't change this feature. What matters for the relation of logical consequence is that the *form* of the argument is preserved. As Tarski points out:

Since we are concerned here with the concept of logical, i.e. *formal*, consequence, and thus with a relation which is to be uniquely determined by the form of the sentences between

---

[8] See Bell and Hallett (1982) for a critical discussion of some exaggerated claims made by some quantum logicians.

which it holds, *this relation cannot be influenced in any way by empirical knowledge*, and in particular by *knowledge of the objects to which the sentence X or the sentences of the class K refer*. The consequence relation cannot be affected by replacing the designations of the objects referred to in these sentences by the designations of any other objects.   (Ibid. 414–15; emphasis added, except for the italics in 'formal')

We don't dispute for a second that the substitution requirement is important, and that it has been part of logic since the first systematic formulation of the discipline by Aristotle (although, of course, the requirement wouldn't then be expressed in the way Tarski formulated it). After all, it is abundantly clear in Artistotle's project that logic should be formal and universal, and the only way that these two conditions can be satisfied is by guaranteeing that empirical factors do not contribute to, and are not presupposed in, determining what follows from what.

But why should we apply the substitution requirement across the board? Well, the Tarskian answers, because if we are concerned with a *formal* account of logical consequence, we simply can't tolerate the intrusion of empirical factors—what matters for logical consequence is the *form* of the arguments. But what if, by disregarding the role of empirical factors, we simply obtain the wrong results about a given domain? This is exactly the question that the quantum logician insists on asking. And the above example of what goes on in the quantum mechanics case seems to illustrate nicely the need for some revision of logic on *empirical grounds*. In other words, the unconditional application of the substitution requirement may yield a notion of logical consequence that is simply inadequate to accommodate the special features of certain domains.

Our proposal is then to *restrict* the application of the substitution requirement: one selects a domain, and the substitution requirement is then applied only to sentences/objects of that particular domain. By restricting the application of the requirement in this way, we can capture an important aspect of logic: in the context of the *particular* domain, the systematic substitution of non-logical terms does preserve the consequence relation. Moreover, the suggested restriction to the substitution requirement generates a relation of consequence that is better suited to capture the relevant features of the domain in question. After all, the *specific* features of the domain can be taken into account to yield the relation of consequence—as the quantum mechanics example illustrates with the non-distributivity of conjunction over disjunction.

By restricting the substitution requirement in this way, we allow the introduction of non-logical factors in logic selection: the parameters used in the determination of the domain bring in extra-logical factors to logic. In this sense the present proposal provides a *non-apriorist* approach to logic, since to be a non-apriorist about logic is to acknowledge the need for extra-logical factors in the determination of the adequacy of a logic. Given that, in Tarski's hands, the substitution requirement is an emphatic expression of logical apriorism, the restriction of this requirement suggested here amounts to a defence of logical non-apriorism. And, of course, one of the main arguments for the version of logical non-apriorism advanced here is that by failing to acknowledge the role of extra-logical considerations in logic selection, we may simply end up with the wrong results—as is suggested by the quantum mechanics case discussed above.[9]

But the logical apriorist will certainly complain. Logic, the apriorist will claim, is usually taken to be the most basic component of our conceptual framework; in this sense, if anything is a priori, logic certainly is. After all, the apriorist continues, logic is presupposed by any evidential system; that is, it's presupposed by any system that is taken to provide support for our beliefs. If logic is not a priori, there is no way in which it can play this role. For if logic is not a priori, any counterevidence, to the conceptual system will also be a counterevidence to logic, and we would need an additional logic to adjudicate between the original logic, the counterevidence, and the conceptual system. For us to be able to use logic in this way, and to avoid an infinite regress of logics here, logic should no longer be taken to be open to empirical revision—that is, logic needs to be a priori.[10]

Moreover, one can very naturally read Tarski's substitution requirement as an expression of the idea that logic is a priori (in the sense articulated in the previous paragraph). After all, as Tarski points out, any constraints on logical consequence should be purely formal; such constraints don't presuppose any empirical knowledge, and so they are a priori. If extra-logical (in particular, empirical) considerations entered in the characterization of logical consequence, instead of capturing the notion of *logical* consequence, we would be capturing the notion of *physical*, *mathematical*, or *empirical* consequence.

In response to this argument, note that there is no need to require that logic be a priori for it to play the justificatory role that one expects it to play in evidential systems. For example, the *methodological decision* of not allowing logic to be open to empirical refutation will do just as well. And to consider logical apriorism only as a *methodological decision* is far weaker than to claim that logic is, in fact, a priori, since a methodological decision to treat logic as though it were a priori obviously doesn't entail that logic actually is a priori. Moreover, there are two advantages of taking logical apriorism as simply a methodological decision: (1) the decision of not holding a given logic responsible for empirical refutation is a decision that can be overthrown at any point, should we decide to do so, and (2) the possibility of revising logic (even on empirical grounds) allows us to explore, and eventually

---

[9] In fact, all we really require for present purposes is that the substitution requirement *might* need to be restricted to particular domains. That is, we don't think that it is necessary for the requirement to hold across all domains. Thus, what counts as a logical truth *might* depend on the domain under consideration.

[10] A very interesting argument for logical apriorism has been advanced along these lines by Hartry Field. See Field (1996, 1998, 2001) for details, and for a critical discussion of Field's arguments, see Bueno (forthcoming *a*).

determine, the adequacy of a logic to a particular domain. In this way, we can take into account the particular features of the domain under consideration, and use the particular features of logic to explore the domain in question in a better way. Of course, to be able to do that, we need to restrict the application of Tarski's substitution in the way suggested above.

In other words, if we accept the domain dependence of the substitutional requirement, we are in a better position to select a logic that is adequate to a particular domain. But to argue—and decide—that a given logic is adequate to a particular domain, don't we need to use logic? And, once again, doesn't this highlight the crucial and fundamental role that logic plays in *any* conceptual framework?

Certainly logic plays a crucial role, but (*a*) logic doesn't need to be a priori for it to play this role, since, as mentioned above, the *methodological decision* of holding a logic fixed for the sake of the argument would do just as well. Moreover, (*b*) to use logic in the selection of a given logic—that is, to determine what consequence relation is adequate to a particular domain—is not the same as to explore the particular consequences that hold in that domain. The former presupposes the latter of course, but not the other way around. So the use of logic in the determination of the adequacy of a given logic is *only one* of many roles that logic plays, and it is by no means the most fundamental one.

In this way, it should be clear that the need for one to use logic in establishing the adequacy of a given logic doesn't require logic to be a priori. Furthermore, logic selection is only one role of logic; a role that can be played by different logics, some of which may be better suited than others to fulfil this role. And by not being logical apriorists, we can explore which logics are more adequate to certain domains than others, and so make better decisions about logic selection. (We will return to this point below in the context of our model of theory change in logic.)

But perhaps the Tarskian could try to keep logical apriorism by making one of three possible moves:[11] (1) The Tarskian could say that we can know a priori that distribution fails. (2) Alternatively, the Tarskian could claim that we can know a priori that distribution succeeds, and so the quantum logician's analysis of the quantum mechanics case is mistaken. (3) Finally, the Tarskian could perhaps say that conjunction or disjunction aren't logical constants, so the fact that truth-preservation of this form is a posteriori isn't a problem for the a priori view of logic.

These are all interesting moves, but we don't think that they ultimately work. Option (1) is neither well motivated nor very plausible. On what grounds could the Tarskian say that we can know a priori that distribution fails? The quantum mechanics argument discussed above depends crucially on an empirical premiss (namely, the measurement of the angular momentum of an electron E in the

---

[11] We are grateful to an anonymous referee for pressing this point.

X direction). Of course, one can always say that we could have *imagined* that empirical possibility (the particular result of the measurement), and we could then run the quantum mechanics argument in exactly the same way as before. But at this point, we need to be very careful. After all, if the Tarskian were to take that route, he or she would have to be apriorist not only about logic, but also about science. For the Tarkian could just as easily say that a Newtonian physicist could have known a priori that gravity depends on the curvature of space-time, just by running the style of argument provided by Einstein in the formulation of General Relativity. Worries about incommensurability apart, the Newtonian could have *imagined* that possibility. But simply imagining this possibility is surely not enough to warrant the claim that we know a priori the results of physics.

Option (2) fares better on the plausibility score, but it still faces a serious difficulty. The option is plausible in the sense that the analysis provided by the quantum logician of the quantum mechanics case is not taken to be *necessary*. As we noted above, it is possible to keep classical logic in the quantum domain. The trouble is that to keep classical logic, we need to make changes in the interpretation of the quantum mechanics formalism (several interpretations of quantum mechanics do just that). But, as is acknowledged in the literature, every proposed interpretation of quantum mechanics faces substantial difficulties, and none of them is uniquely selected by the data. Thus, to close the possibility of the quantum logician's interpretation on a priori grounds amounts to sheer dogmatism.

Option (3) is not an option for the Tarskian. As we noted above, Tarski is explicit about the fact that logical constants are *not* open to reinterpretation (see the first quotation from Tarski 1936 above). So, he is in no position to deny that conjunction or disjunction are logical constants. But perhaps a more liberal Tarskian could entertain that possibility (of rejecting that conjunction or disjunction are logical constants). The trouble here is that this would actually *support* the kind of revision of logical principles on empirical (or, at least, extra-logical) grounds that we propose in this chapter. After all, if the distributivity law fails in the quantum domain, we can't say that the substitution requirement applies across the board: some interpretations of extra-logical constants (such as that of the distributivity law in the context of quantum mechanics) do *not* preserve logical validity. So, in the end, this would amount to a defence of non-apriorism about logic, along similar lines to the view we're advocating here.

2.3 Putnam's Centrality Argument

Despite the widespread acceptance of Tarski's account of logical consequence, not everyone endorsed Tarski's characterization of logic in aprioristic terms. Putnam, for example, provides a very interesting case. Not only does he consider the possibility that logical principles may be revised on the basis of empirical considerations (arising, for example, from quantum mechanics), but he even entertains the claim

that *the LNC might be revised on empirical grounds* (see Putnam 1983*a*). The claim
is made in the context of Putnam's discussion of the centrality argument, that is,
the argument to the effect that the laws of logic are presupposed by 'so much of the
activity of argument itself that it is no wonder that we cannot envisage their being
overthrown [. . .] by rational argument' (ibid. 110). In response to this argument,
Putnam immediately adds:

> But we should be clear about what the centrality argument does not show. It does not
> show that a putative law of logic, for instance the principle of contradiction, could not be
> overthrown by *direct observation*. Presumably I would give up the principle of contradiction
> if I ever had a sense datum which was both red and not red, for example.[12] And the centrality
> argument sheds no light on how we know that this could not happen.   (Ibid. 110)

In a note added to the paper, Putnam elaborates on this point:

> I think it is right to say that, within our present conceptual scheme, the minimal principle
> of contradiction [i.e. the claim that not every statement is both true and false] is *so* basic
> that it cannot significantly be 'explained' at all. But that does not make it an 'absolutely a
> priori truth', in the sense of an absolutely unrevisable truth.   (Ibid. 111)

We completely agree with the spirit of this passage, even though we may not agree
with the letter. Putnam is correctly indicating here that, although the 'minimal
principle of contradiction' is basic, it shouldn't be taken to be a priori. We couldn't
agree more.

However, one point should be noted in relation to this. In this passage Putnam
has a peculiar understanding of the notion of a priori: a priori truth is understood
in terms of *unrevisable* truth. Clearly, this view of the a priori is not unproblematic,
given that it rejects by fiat the possibility of *defeasible* a priori claims (claims
that Field, for instance, insists are part of logic; see Field 1998). And it might
be complained that there is no need to tie the notion of a priori with that of
unrevisability. The axiom of choice in set theory is an example of a claim that is
(arguably) known a priori but which is clearly revisable.

For our purposes here it is enough to note that, using the notion of a priori
adopted in the present work, we can make perfect sense of the claim that the
law of non-contradiction is not a priori in Putnam's sense. Recall that in our
view, logical non-apriorism is the thesis that acknowledges the importance of
extra-logical considerations in the selection and evaluation of logical principles.
In particular, logical principles may be *revised* on empirical grounds. So in either
sense of a priori (ours or Putnam's), logic turns out not to be a priori.

The point of this section is to indicate, following Putnam's lead, that even if
one takes the 'law' of non-contradiction to be a fundamental logical principle,
this shouldn't be taken as a reason to conceive of it as being a priori. As we shall

---

[12] One of the present authors has argued that this may indeed be possible. See Beall and Colyvan
(2001) for details of how contradictions such as this might be observable, given a paraconsistent account
of vagueness.

discuss below, in the debate about this 'law', both those who defend and those who criticize the 'law' typically use empirical considerations to support their claims. It's non-apriorism all the way down.

3. THEORY CHANGE IN LOGIC

If logical non-apriorism is a live option, the question arises as to how, according to the logical non-apriorist, theory change in logic proceeds. This section will outline, in general terms, one answer to this question. Roughly, one can hold fixed some logical principles—or, as we will see, a common core of (methodological or axiological) assumptions—that are agreed upon by all parties. These (limited) resources are then used to conduct the argument about the contentious principles.[13]

The above idea can be cashed out by using a very interesting model of scientific theory change originally developed in the philosophy of science, namely Laudan's reticulated model (see Laudan 1984). The crucial feature of the model is that scientific debates range over three main components: debates over the aims of scientific research, over methods, and over scientific theories. And typically, at any given time, the scientific community agrees upon at least one of the three components, and this shared agreement can then be used to settle the debate over the remaining two components. For example, shared aims of scientific research can be used to settle disagreements about methods (e.g. select the methods that best realize the aims), and shared methods can then be used to adjudicate between rival theories (e.g. select the theories that are best justified by the methods). But the relation between aims, methods, and theories is not hierarchical: theories also constrain methods and realize aims, just as methods also realize aims (for further details, see Laudan 1984). The interrelation between the three levels can be represented by Fig. 9.1.

We believe that, suitably reinterpreted, the reticulated model provides a framework to represent how debates about logical principles can be conducted. The crucial idea is that—similarly to what goes on in science—debates about logic typically involve a common core of assumptions that are shared by the various parties in the debate. This common core includes: (1) shared logical theories (that is, logical principles and rules), or (2) shared views about the aims of logic, or (3) shared methodological principles (broadly understood to include metalogical properties). Although usually items (1)–(3) are not all shared at the same time, at least *one of them* typically is. And as we will see, this provides enough common ground for debates about logic to be conducted and, in some cases, settled.

But to be able to apply Laudan's reticulated model to theory change in logic, we need first to reinterpret slightly the original components of the model. We leave

---

[13] As we will see, the idea is very much like Neurath's famous image of rebuilding a boat at sea.

Methods

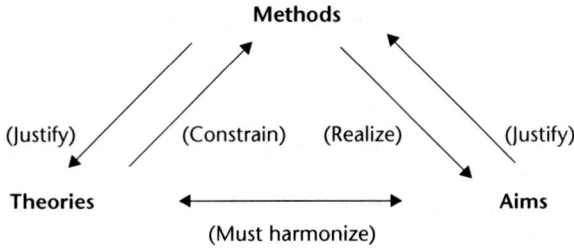

FIG. 9.1. The reticulated model of justification

the *axiological component* (the one dealing with aims) as it is, except for the fact that instead of considering aims and values of science, we will be examining the axiology of *research traditions* in logic.[14]

Moreover, we understand the *methodological component* (or the methodological principles) of the reticulated model in broad terms: it includes both methodological and metamethodological principles. That is, the methodological component incorporates not only specific methodological principles of theory construction, but also metamethodological principles to choose between alternative methods of theory construction. In the case of logic, the methodological component (broadly understood) includes metalogical principles (such as the completeness or incompleteness of a formal system, its decidability or undecidability, etc.), as well as proof-theoretic and model-theoretic techniques, the use (or not) of the T-schema, and further patterns of choice of logical notions, logical rules, and logical principles.

We also redefine the *theoretical component* of the reticulated model to make room for logical principles and rules of inferences. On this account, logic can be read as a theory, namely, a theory of the relation of logical consequence. One of the main issues faced by a logic is whether it provides an adequate account of the relation of logical consequence. And typically to address this issue requires the examination of further issues about the domain to which the logic in question is applied. The reinterpreted reticulated model can then be represented by Fig. 9.2.

Given the above reinterpretation of the reticulated model, we can then indicate how debates about theory change in logic can be represented and accommodated. As mentioned above, our aim here is not to resolve the debate about the LNC, but to put forward a possible framework in terms of which the debate can be understood. And we insist that the reticulated model is *only one* among many possible ways of

[14] Laudan developed the notion of research tradition for science (see Laudan 1977). As he conceives it, a research tradition provides a whole framework for the development and implementation of scientific research in a given domain, including standards, methods, theories, principles, metaphysical assumptions, etc. We think that the notion of research tradition is not restricted to science (a point with which, we take it, Laudan would agree), and the notion applies just as well to the foundations of logic—even though, thus far, it has not been so applied.

Methodological principles

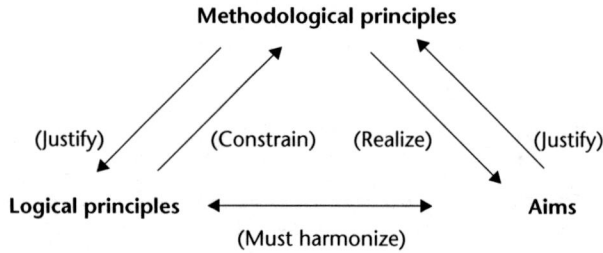

FIG. 9.2. The reticulated model as applied to logical theory choice

modelling the phenomenon in question: we advance it here only to illustrate how debates about logical principles can be carried out.[15]

The reticulated model works in the same way in logic and in science. The three components of the reticulated model (aims of logical research, methodo-logical/metalogical principles, and logical principles) typically are not all under critical scrutiny at the same time. One could use, for example, shared aims in logical research to choose between different methodological/metalogical prin-ciples, or to adopt shared logical principles to reassess the adequacy of some aims of logic. Alternatively, one could use shared methodological/metalogical principles to choose between rival logical principles, or to employ shared aims of logic to choose between rival metalogical principles. As noted above, the point here is that—just as in science (see Laudan 1984)—typically debates over rival research traditions don't involve changes in *all* three components of the reticu-lated model at the same time. At least one component of the model is fixed, and one can use the fixed component to choose among the components that are under debate.

Let us give a simple example to illustrate how the reticulated model works. Suppose that we start with the classical research tradition in logic. The *aim* of logic is taken to be to provide an account of logical consequence that captures the intuitive notion of consequence found in natural language. *Logical principles* are then formulated to realize this aim. These principles are, basically, those of classical predicate logic, and they yield a particular body of *metalogical* results (e.g. the connectives are extensional, the system is complete, the monadic fragment of the logic is decidable etc.). With the three components in place, research in logic can then be conducted.

It soon becomes clear, however, that some intuitively valid inferences in natural language turn out *not* to be valid according to the above logical principles.

[15] Other approaches along broadly naturalistic and non-apriori lines (not all of which are direct competitors with the reticulated model) may be found in Maddy (forthcoming), Mares (forthcoming), and Resnik (this volume, Ch. 11). Mike Resnik's 'reflective equilibrium' approach, in particular, shares a great deal with the reticulated model.

For example:

John plays football on weekends
_____

Therefore, John can play football on weekends

This inference, although intuitively valid, is not *formally* valid. To make it formally valid it is necessary to change one component in the reticulated model of classical logic's research tradition. It is necessary to introduce *new logical principles and rules* (in particular, those concerning the modal operators of necessity and possibility—box and diamond, respectively). Note, however, that the introduction of these principles is justified by the *aim* of the research tradition: to provide an account of logical consequence that *accommodates natural language*. So the new logical principles are introduced. The trouble, though, is that the new principles require a revision in the accepted *metalogical principles*. After all, with boxes and diamonds, we no longer have extensionality. In this way, we moved from classical logic's research tradition to a new research tradition, that of modal logic. Both traditions share the same aim, but they have different logical and metalogical principles.[16]

What this simple example illustrates is how a particular aim (to provide an account of logical consequence in natural language) may require changes in the two other components of the reticulated model—the logical and the metalogical principles. In this way, we can see how, by sharing the same aims of logical research, a community can decide about the way to change the logic and the metalogic of a given domain. It then becomes clear how a community can settle debates about logical principles on the basis of other common assumptions about the domain in question.

4. THE 'LAW' OF NON-CONTRADICTION

So far we've argued that logic is not a priori and, in particular, that questions about theory choice in logic are not settled on a priori grounds. We've also emphasized the fallible nature of logical theory and provided a particular model of theory change in logic—the reticulated model. Is this enough to settle the question of whether there can be meaningful debate on the LNC? Not quite. There are a couple of concerns that arise in the context of the debate over the LNC that go beyond the aprioricity of logic and beyond the usual issues of theory choice.[17] These concerns

[16] Although this example is something of a toy example, it does help illustrate the way the reticulated model of theory change in logic works. Obviously real historical examples such as the shift from Aristotelian logic to Fregean logic will be more complicated and we do not discuss them here for that reason. Whether such examples do fit well with the reticulated model is an interesting question that we intend to take up elsewhere.

[17] Also there's the issue that accepting or rejecting the LNC is not, strictly speaking, an issue of theory choice. Rather, it concerns accepting or rejecting *classes* of logical theories. This detail need not concern us, though, since the same questions arise over choices between classes of theories as over choices between single theories. We are thus justified in focusing our attention on theory choice in logic.

involve the seemingly privileged status that certain fundamental laws such as the LNC hold in any logical theory. David Lewis presents the problem like this:[18]

No truth does have, and no truth could have, a true negation. Nothing is, and nothing could be, literally both true and false. This we know for certain, and *a priori*, and without any exception for especially perplexing subject matters. The radical case for relevance should be dismissed just because the hypothesis it requires us to entertain is inconsistent.

That may seem dogmatic. And it is; I am affirming the very thesis that Routley and Priest have called into question—contrary to the rules of debate—I decline to defend it. Furthermore, I concede that it is indefensible against their challenge. They have called so much into question that I have no foothold on undisputed ground. So much the worse for the demand that philosophers always must be ready to defend their theses under the rules of debate. (Lewis 1982: 101)

Lewis's point is a serious one: Even falliblists, he suggests, must hold on to some principles dogmatically. To give up certain fundamental logical principles (even for the sake of debate) leaves one with too impoverished a set of logical resources to proceed. Or perhaps the suggestion is that we can proceed, but the result of our investigations is irrelevant, because what we conclude is so much less certain than what we've given up to get there.

Now clearly debate about the LNC can and does proceed. (One need look no further than the present volume to see that.) Lewis's concern, though, is not about whether such debate does in fact occur; it's about whether such debate is fruitful or even rational. We believe that this debate is both fruitful and rational; demonstrating this, however, is a subtle matter. We begin by applying the model of logical theory choice developed in the last section to the question of the status of the LNC. It is important to see how such a model allows debate to proceed on even the most fundamental logical laws and that we can have confidence in the results of the relevant debate—even apparently fundamental logical principles can be trumped by enough considerations elsewhere, both within logic and from further afield. The debate can proceed by employing those principles and data not under dispute. We will now run through a couple of the arguments presented for and against the LNC and show (1) how these arguments depend on non-apriori considerations; (2) how the various participants in these debates agree on a great deal more than Lewis acknowledges; and (3) it is this agreement that allows debates about even apparently fundamental principles to proceed.

Consider the argument that there can't be true contradictions because if there were, everything would be true; but clearly everything is not true so there can't be any true contradictions. (Call the view that everything is true *trivialism*.) Here we have an example of an argument for the LNC based on the empirical fact that not everything is true—the world is not flat, for example.[19] As it turns out, this

---

[18] See also Lewis's chapter in this volume for another typically elegant statement of the problem.

[19] You might think that we can come to the view that trivialism is false by a priori means. There are a couple of things to say to this. First, the falsity of trivialism might be know*able* a priori, but it does

argument against true contradictions is not a particularly good one, for there is a very good reply to it. The argument just presented assumes *ex falso quodlibet* (or *explosion*, as it has become known). This rather undesirable feature of classical logic is denied by dialethists such as Graham Priest (see Priest 1987, 1998). Dialethists believe that there are true contradictions, yet they agree with the supporters of non-contradiction that not everything is true. Dialethists reject classical logic—in particular they object to its explosive character and opt, instead, for non-explosive paraconsistent logics.

Now you might think that this just confirms Lewis's point since these debates over the LNC instantly reach deadlock. But this is not right. The above paragraph outlines a fairly typical philosophical debate in which both parties agree about a great deal—they both accept that the conjunction of true contradictions and classical logic is untenable. The dialethist and the classical logician, however, provide different diagnoses of the problem—the dialethist blames explosion while the classical logician blames the initial acceptance of true contradictions—but they *are* able to conduct a debate. They also agree on the reason for the untenability of the above conjunction of true contradictions and classical logic: they agree that trivialism is false. Now if this debate reaches a deadlock, that's neither here nor there; many philosophical debates reach deadlocks (at least for a time). Our point here is simply that the above 'explosion' argument and reply is a perfectly good example of a philosophical debate that makes some progress on the problem at hand.

Next consider an argument *against* the LNC. It starts from the assumption that (1) satisfaction of the T-schema is a necessary condition on a theory of truth, and (2) natural languages are semantically closed (that is, they contain their own truth predicates). At least the second of these is an empirical matter—it's simply an empirical fact about English, for example, that sentences such as 'it's true that South Carolina is East of California' are well formed (and, in this case, true). Now we consider the strengthened liar sentence:

($\star$) *This sentence is not true*

By a well-worn argument employing the above two assumptions, we arrive at the conclusion that ($\star$) is both true and false. Most philosophers are thus led to question (1) and (2) in various ways, or to give up on semantically closed natural languages. For instance, Tarski accepted that English was semantically closed but chose to replace English with a heirarchy of formal languages, each of which was not semantically closed. Others have questioned the T-schema, and others still claim that, despite appearances, ($\star$) is not a sentence of English. Dialethists, on the other

---

not follow that it is discovered by a priori means. There are straightforward empirical means to come to this view—observing that the earth is not completely covered with water, for instance. Second, even if you think that 'trivialism is false' is not an empirical truth, our main point here still stands: there are some issues on which all parties in this debate agree. The LNC is not philosophical bedrock, as it were.

hand, accept the conclusion that ($\star$) is both true and false. They do so because they accept the premises of this argument and, somewhat reluctantly, give up the LNC.

Again we draw attention to the significant agreement here. All parties accept (at least initially) the premises of the liar argument. All parties accept the reasoning involved in the argument to the contradiction (essentially *modus ponens* and that every sentence is either true or not-true). The responses to the argument are different, but we think it's fair to say that all parties acknowledge the cost of giving up what they do. Tarski did not take the denial of semantic closure lightly, Priest does not take giving up the law of non-contradiction lightly, and those who deny that ($\star$) is a sentence of English typically go to considerable length to defend this counterintuitive position.

What we're drawing attention to here is that the law of non-contradiction is not such a fundamental principle of logic that debate is impossible without it. In particular, we see that extra-logical assumptions, such as the T-schema, and extra-logical (empirical) facts also have a great deal of weight in these debates. We also draw attention to the fact that often these extra-logical considerations are a posteriori, as in the case of the universally agreed upon fact that not everything is true. Finally, we wish to emphasize that the reticulated model of logical theory choice, outlined in the previous section, provides an effective way of making sense of both the debates as they actually proceed and how it is that the debates can *rationally* proceed in this way.

Indeed, on this model, what counts as fundamental logical principles can change when one reassesses the aims or methodological principles. For example, in the above argument from the strengthened liar, we might start out with classical logic (including the law of non-contradiction) as our logical principles; our aim might be to give an account of logical consequence as it arises in natural language; our methodological principles that help us achieve this goal would include the T-schema and the requirement of semantic closure. Then we find that from considerations of the strengthened liar (which is a piece of natural language), we derive a contradiction. The dialethic response is to keep the methodological principles and the aims and revise the logical principles—namely, reject the classical law of non-contradiction. Contrast this with Tarski's response to the same initial situation; he chose to revise the methodological principles in light of the paradox. In particular, he abandoned the methodological constraint that the language be semantically closed (because semantically closed languages are inconsistent). This, in turn, meant he had to revise his aims, because clearly natural languages *are* semantically closed. Tarski's new aim was thus to provide an account of logical consequence for suitable formal languages.

These examples show us how the reticulated model is able to make sense of debates about fundamental logical principles as well as debates about aims and methodological principles. It doesn't necessarily tell us the correct moves to make in such debates. For instance, the model is silent on whether Tarski's response, the dialethic response, or some other response is the most appropriate in the case above. The model merely provides a nice framework for conducting such debates (and perhaps it helps to keep track of the costs and benefits of the various strategies). But this, of course, is not trivial. The reticulated model does not rule against the revision of logical principles—no matter how fundamental they are. You might choose not to abandon certain logical principles such as the LNC, but the *possibility* of revisions here are not ruled out.

Finally let us return to a point that's perhaps implicit in the passage from Lewis earlier in this section. The objection we have in mind is that any investigation of a fundamental logical principle, such as the LNC, is doomed because other principles invoked in the investigation are so much less certain than the LNC itself. Thus the results of such an investigation—whatever they happen to be—are less secure than the LNC.[20] We have, in effect, already addressed this objection but we think it might be helpful to address it explicitly. We have two things to say. First, the objection seems to presuppose some sort of foundationalist epistemology, according to which if principle P is less certain than Q, then P cannot be invoked to overthrow or revise Q. It would take us too far afield to rehearse the various objections to such an epistemology; suffice to say that it seems plausible, at least, that if there are many such Ps (P_1 to P_n, say), and even if each P_i is less certain than Q, there is a sense in which the weight of evidence of the P_is piles up to overthrow the (initially) more certain Q.[21] Moreover, we've shown how this can be done using the reticulated model. Second, and more importantly, it's simply not clear that the LNC is more certain than other principles appealed to in these debates. After all, all parties agree that trivialism is false and this at least suggests that the falsity of trivialism is more certain than the LNC.[22]

5. CONCLUSION

We believe that there *is* debate about the LNC; for the most part this is *rational* debate; and there *ought* to be such debate. We hope to have shown how this debate can proceed. We've argued that non-apriori considerations are important

---

[20] Lewis explicitly articulates an objection along these lines in Ch. 10.

[21] The natural way to spell out this 'weight of evidence' claim is in terms of prior probabilities and conditionalizing to obtain posterior probabilities via Bayes' Theorem. We resist this temptation, though; any (classical) probability talk here is misguided. In classical probability theory (i.e. probability theories that obey the Kolmogorov axioms), *all* classical logical truths get probability one, and so we cannot talk of some logical truths being more likely than others. We thus keep probabilistic talk out of the debate (as does the objector, for s/he too wants to say that the LNC is more certain than other logical principles (such as excluded middle), without cashing out 'certainty' in terms of (classical) probability).

[22] Of course consensus and certainty don't always coincide, but we think they do here. Surely it's the fact that everyone is certain that trivialism is false that accounts for the agreement on this issue. And surely it's because the LNC is somewhat less certain that all parties offer arguments for or against it.

in this and other debates about theory choice in logic, so logic can't be a priori. We thus defended non-apriorism in logic. We provided a particular model of how debate about logic—even seemingly fundamental principles of logic—can be conducted. The model we applied—the reticulated model—is a plausible way forward. Finally, we addressed the objection that the LNC is just *too* fundamental to debate. According to this objection, without the LNC there's no common ground left for the participants in the debate to stand on. This, we argued, is not so. There might not be much common ground, but there is enough for debate to proceed.[23]

REFERENCES

BEALL, JC, and COLYVAN, M. (2001), 'Looking for Contradictions', *Australasian Journal of Philosophy*, 79(4) (December), 564–9.
BEALL, JC, and RESTALL, G. (2000), 'Logical Pluralism', *Australasian Journal of Philosophy*, 78(4) (December), 475–93.
——(2001), 'Defending Logical Pluralism', in B. Brown and J. Woods (eds.), *Logical Consequence: Rival Approaches* (Hermes, Stanmore).
BELL, J., and HALLETT, M. (1982), 'Logic, Quantum Logic and Empiricism', *Philosophy of Science*, 49: 355–79.
BIRKHOFF, G., and VON NEUMANN, J. (1936), 'The Logic of Quantum Mechanics', *Annals of Mathematics*, 37: 823–43.
BUENO, O. (2002), 'Can a Paraconsistent Theorist be a Logical Monist?', in W. A. Carnielli, M. E. Coniglio, and I. M. L. D'Ottaviano (eds.), *Paraconsistency: The Logical Way to the Inconsistent* (Marcel Dekker, New York), 535–52.
——(forthcoming *a*), 'Is Logic A Priori?'.
——(forthcoming *b*), 'Logical Pluralism: A Pluralist View'.
COLYVAN, M. (2001), *The Indispensability of Mathematics* (Oxford University Press, New York).
DA COSTA, N. C. A. (1997), *Logiques classiques et non classiques: Essai sur les fondements de la logique* (Masson, Paris).
CUSHING, J. (1994), *Quantum Mechanics: Historical Contingency and the Copenhagen Hegemony* (University of Chicago Press, Chicago).
FIELD, H. (1980), *Science without Numbers: A Defence of Nominalism* (Blackwell, Cambridge).
——(1993), 'The Conceptual Contingency of Mathematical Objects', *Mind*, 102: 285–99.
——(1996), 'The A Prioricity of Logic', *Proceedings of the Aristotelian Society*, 96: 359–79.
——(1998), 'Epistemological Nonfactualism and the A Prioricity of Logic', *Philosophical Studies*, 92: 1–24.

[23] We are indebted to JC Beall, Newton da Costa, Hartry Field, Steven French, Penelope Maddy, Graham Priest, Michael Resnik, and Scott Shalkowski for useful discussions on the topic of this paper. We are also grateful to Michael Resnik for reading an earlier draft of the paper and making several helpful suggestions, as well as to two anonymous referees for extremely helpful and insightful comments.

—— (2001), 'Apriority as an Evaluative Notion', in *Truth and the Absence of Fact* (Clarendon, Oxford) 361–91.

KITCHER, P. (1983), *The Nature of Mathematical Knowledge* (Oxford University Press, New York).

LAKATOS, I. (1976), *Proofs and Refutations: The Logic of Mathematical Discovery* (Cambridge University Press, Cambridge).

LAUDAN, L. (1977), *Progress and Its Problems* (University of California Press, Berkeley).

—— (1984), *Science and Values: The Aims of Science and Their Role in Scientific Debate* (University of California Press, Berkeley).

LEWIS, D. (1982), 'Logic for Equivocators', *Noûs*, 16: 431–41. Repr. in D. Lewis, *Papers in Philosophical Logic* (Cambridge University Press, Cambridge), 1998: 97–110.

MADDY, P. (forthcoming), 'A Naturalistic Look at Logic'.

MARES, E. (forthcoming), 'How to Choose a Logic'.

PRIEST, G. (1987), *In Contradiction* (Nijhoff, Dordrecht).

—— (1998), 'What's So Bad about Contradictions?', *The Journal of Philosophy*, 95(8) (August), 410–26.

—— (2001), 'Logic: One or Many?', in B. Brown and J. Woods (eds.) *Logical Consequences, Rival Approaches*, (Stanmore, Hermes) 23–8.

PUTNAM, H. (1979), 'The Logic of Quantum Mechanics', in *Mathematics, Matter and Method: Philosophical Papers*, 2nd edn. (Cambridge University Press, Cambridge) i: 174–97.

—— (1983a), 'There Is At Least One A Priori Truth', in *Realism and Reason: Philosophical Papers* (Cambridge University Press, Cambridge) iii: 98–114.

—— (1983b), 'Analycity and Apriority: Beyond Wittgenstein and Quine', in *Realism and Reason: Philosophical Papers* (Cambridge University Press, Cambridge) iii: 115–38.

—— (1983c), 'Vagueness and Alternative Logic', in *Realism and Reason: Philosophical Papers* (Cambridge University Press, Cambridge) iii: 271–86.

QUINE, W. V. (1953), 'Two Dogmas of Empiricism', in *From a Logical Point of View* (Harvard University Press, Cambridge, Mass.), 20–46.

—— (1981), 'Success and Limits of Mathematization', in *Theories and Things* (Harvard University Press, Cambridge, Mass.), 148–55.

RESNIK, M. (1996), 'Ought There to be but One Logic?', in B. J. Copeland, *Logic and Reality: Essays on the Legacy of Arthur Prior* (Clarendon, Oxford), 489–517.

—— (1997), *Mathematics as a Science of Patterns* (Oxford University Press, Oxford).

TARSKI, A. (1936), 'On the Concept of Logical Consequence', in *Logic, Semantics, Metamathematics: Papers from 1923 to 1938*, 2nd edn. (Hackett, Indianapolis, 1983), 409–20.

von Neumann, J. (1937a), 'On Alternative Systems of Logics', unpublished manuscript, von Neumann Archives, Library of Congress, Washington.

—— (1937b), 'Quantum Logics (Strict- and Probability-Logics)', unpublished manuscript, von Neumann Archives, Library of Congress, Washington. (A brief summary, written by A. H. Taub, can be found in von Neumann (1962), 195–7.)

—— (1962), *Collected Works*, iv. *Continuous Geometry and Other Topics*, ed. A. H. Taub (Pergamon, Oxford).

10

Letters to Beall and Priest

David Lewis[†]

Editorial Introduction: What follows are two brief comments on the Law of Non-Contradiction by David Lewis. The first is the content of a letter of 21 July 1999 to Beall and Priest in reply to their invitation to contribute to this volume. The second is an extract of a letter to Priest of 9 January 2001, commenting on a draft of Priest's critical study of Lewis's *Papers in Philosophical Logic, Papers in Metaphysics and Epistemology,* and *Papers in Ethics and Social Philosophy.*[1] Both appear here for the first time. We are grateful to Steffi Lewis for permission to publish them. All italics are original; footnotes are Priest's.

1. LETTER 1

I'm sorry; I decline to contribute to your proposed book about the 'debate' over the law of non-contradiction. My feeling is that since this debate instantly reaches deadlock, there's really nothing much to say about it. To conduct a debate, one needs common ground; principles in dispute cannot of course fairly be used as common ground; and in this case, the principles *not* in dispute are so very much less certain than non-contradiction itself that it matters little whether or not a successful defence of non-contradiction could be based on them.

2. LETTER 2

Paraconsistency. I'm increasingly convinced that I can and do reason about impossible situations. ('Sylvan's Box' played a big part in persuading me.[2]) But I don't really understand how that works. Paraconsistent logic as developed by you and your allies is clear enough, but I find it a bit off the topic. For it allows (a limited amount of) reasoning about *blatantly* impossible situations. Whereas what I find myself doing is reasoning about *subtly* impossible situations, and rejecting suppositions that lead fairly to blatant impossibilities. In other words, I understand what it would be to do without rejection by *reductio ad contradictionem* altogether, but I don't understand what it is to be selective, using *reductio*

---

[1] Priest (2002).   [2] Priest (1997).

sometimes and sometimes not. A (draft?) paper by Daniel[3] seems promising, but maybe it just repackages my problem about what's the right similarity metric on possibilities together with impossibilities.

Hard-line paraconsistency.[4] It still seems to me that we have a complete stale-mate, just as I said in the passage you quote, about whether our world might, as far as we know, be contradictory. (By the way, I keep forgetting whether you'd rather say that contradictions are possible, or that for all we know we live in an impossible world. Do you have a uniform policy?[5]) That doesn't stop me from sometimes making believe that impossibilities are possible, subtle ones at least. I agree with you about the many uses to which we could put make-believedly possible impossibilities, if we are willing to use them. The trouble is that all these uses seem to require a distinction between the subtle ones and the blatant ones (very likely context-dependent, very likely a matter of degree) and that's just what I don't understand.

REFERENCES

NOLAN, D. (1997), 'Impossible Worlds: A Modest Approach', *Notre Dame Journal of Formal Logic*, 38: 535–72.

PRIEST, G. (1997), 'Sylvan's Box', *Notre Dame Journal of Formal Logic*, 38: 573–82.

—— (2002), 'David Lewis: a View From Down Under', *Noûs*, 36: 351–8.

---

[3] Presumably Nolan (1997).   [4] i.e. dialetheism.   [5] The former.

11

Revising Logic

Michael D. Resnik

INTRODUCTION

For centuries logicians have held that contradictions cannot be true. This has been a fundamental principle of every system of logic capable of expressing it or a reasonable approximation thereof. Even those proposing radical revisions of so-called classical logic have honored it. But today, thanks to forceful and astute criticisms by the dialetheists, we can no longer take this dogma for granted. I will not address the merits of the dialetheist proposal for amending the laws of logic in this chapter. Rather, I want to consider the more general issue of revising logic. Intermittently, I will relate my points to the special case of the law of non-contradiction.

1. LOGIC AND Logic

But what is logic? And what is it to revise it? Some might characterize logic as a collection of rules of inference, the so-called rules of logic. Then revising logic would consist in changing its rules. Others might bypass the rules and focus on the inferences themselves, the so-called logically valid inferences. For them to revise logic is to substitute one set of inferences for another. Still others might take a more abstract view of the subject and take logic to consist of certain truths (the logical truths) and certain relations between sentences, statements, or propositions (e.g. implication, equivalence, and incompatibility). For them revising logic would amount to revising our opinion as to the facts of logic, that is, as to which sentences, statements, or propositions are logically true and which ones are logically related.

There is also a twentieth-century practice of viewing scientific theories as more or less formalized axiom systems with each coming with an 'underlying logic'. In this vein quantum logic is the best-known proposal for revising the logic of a theory in order to improve the overall theory. Depending upon the reasons one gives, such proposals may or may not be accompanied by suggestions for revising logic at large. Brouwer and Heyting, for example, had no quarrel with using classical logic outside mathematics, though, due to their constructive philosophy of mathematics, they objected strenuously to using classical logic in mathematics. Michael Dummett, by contrast, expounded a critique of classical logic that questioned its application in any context.

We should distinguish our inferential practice, the rules of correct inference, the facts of logic, and so on from our discussions about them. I will refer to the former as (lower-case) logic, and it's of logic in this sense that I have been speaking so far. I will refer to our disciplined discussion of lower-case logic as (upper-case) LOGIC. This is the discipline that many of us love and teach. I said that it 'discusses' our inferential practice, the rules of correct inference, the facts of logic, and so on to leave open the question of whether LOGIC is supposed merely to describe these or whether it is supposed to evaluate or improve upon them. When I speak of discovering, revising, or inventing the LAWS OF LOGIC I am speaking of something that LOGICIANS do rather than of something that all practitioners of inference do. In general, most practitioners of inference reject or accept particular inferences or statements without pausing to think about them more systematically. Thus I separate questions about revising our inferential practice (revising our logic) from those about revising LOGIC.

The distinction between logic and LOGIC comes with a distinction between so-called logical truths and LAWS OF LOGIC and between specific inferences and RULES OF LOGIC. The Law of Non-Contradiction is something that LOGICIANS have introduced in order to characterize some facts of logic (lower-case) that are central to our inferential practice. As practitioners of inference we make specific inferences and (much more rarely) assert trivial truths, such as, 'Tall bald people are tall.' As LOGICIANS we try to formulate a systematic account of this practice by producing various RULES OF INFERENCE and LAWS OF LOGIC by which we presume the practice to proceed. This aspect of our work as LOGICIANS is like the work of grammarians. However, as much as we might talk of LAWS OF LOGIC or even laws of thought, our attempts to systematize don't require us to suppose that the practitioners are aware of the rules or laws we produce or even that they are subconsciously consulting these norms. (Denying that we consult inferential norms does not preclude ascribing us with an inferential competence that the RULES OF LOGIC are supposed to describe.)

In doing LOGIC we have learned profitably to use formal systems, which we frequently refer to as 'systems of logic'. Thus we have a third sense of the word 'logic', and a third sense of 'revising logic'. Some revisions may be philosophically uninteresting revisions, such as, the changes LOGICIANS made in the rules of substitution of various systems of predicate logic in order to secure their completeness and consistency. Other revisions, on the other hand, may be philosophically significant, such as the strengthening of first-order systems to exclude non-standard models or the restrictions introduced to avoid the paradoxes of implication. It is not clear to me that there is a sharp distinction between trivial and significant revisions of formal systems. After all, completeness and consistency are hardly insignificant features of a formal system, and thus it was certainly important to get the substitution rules straight.

Nor do I see a sharp distinction between proposals for revising logic and adopting an alternative logic. The difference if any seems to lie in the perceived significance in the change. For similar reasons I take a dim view of the idea that revising our logic entails using so-called logical words with new meanings. Suppose that until now my mathematical proofs used non-constructive principles, but now I announce that I will restrict myself to constructively acceptable proofs. Have I revised my logic, while continuing to mean the same by 'not' and 'or' or have I decided to use those words with a different meaning? I don't perceive a fact of the matter here.

We should note, by the way, that proposals for revising logic typically originate with LOGICIANS. Using formal systems they tell us how we should modify our inferential practice or change the logic of some theory or how we have mistaken the facts of logic.

My focus in this chapter will be on revising (lower-case) logic. Before passing to that I will make a few remarks on revising LOGIC. LOGIC produces logical theories. These consist of a formal system, a semantics for it, an attendant metatheory and a translation method for formalizing informal arguments. Today the main way we revise LOGIC is to revise one of its logical theories or the claims made concerning it.

LOGICIANS employ logical theories both normatively and descriptively. When working descriptively they may be trying to use a logical theory to model some aspect of our everyday inferential practice, or to characterize the reasoning used in certain branches of mathematics or science, or to represent various facts of logic. When working normatively, on the other hand, they may be attempting to criticize or reform our inferential practice or to show us how to improve upon a theory through modifying its 'underlying logic'. Dialetheists, for example, use paraconsistent systems to show us how we can improve the theory of truth through taking some contradictory sentences to be true. One can also take them to be urging us to revise logic along paraconsistent lines, but doing so presupposes that classical systems accurately describe our current inferential practice. That it does is certainly controversial. Often LOGICIANS do not distinguish clearly between normative and descriptive considerations favoring a logical theory different from the classical ones. Thus they may argue against EXPLOSION on descriptive grounds by telling us that nobody would ever see a contradiction as a license to draw any conclusion whatsoever, and next tell us that in a *good* argument the premisses are relevant to the conclusion.

When it comes to describing our inferential practice or the reasoning used in some branch of science or mathematics, LOGICIANS, like empirical linguists, try to achieve the best systematization of their data that they can. Revising a logical theory (or even switching to an 'alternative' one) will be done with that in mind. Even here matters can get tricky. Consider the familiar criticism of attempts by classical LOGICIANS to model intuitionist reasoning. 'How can these be accurate', the criticism goes, 'since their metalanguage uses existential quantifiers read non-constructively?'

Matters become even muddier and less anchored to empirical data when it comes to describing the so-called facts of logic (the logical truths, implications, and equivalences). Here we find LOGICIANS relying both upon data concerning our inferential practice and their intuitions—both normative and metaphysical—concerning the facts of logic. For a case where intuitions play a major role, take the common view among LOGICIANS that no formalism should count 'There are at least two individuals' as a logical truth. Some LOGICIANS base this upon the normative intuition that our inferential practice should not in itself decide questions of existence. While others appeal to the metaphysical intuition that there could be a universe containing fewer than two individuals, and some may appeal to both intuitions.

Intuitions play a major role too when LOGIC goes normative. Instead of starting with another's deductive practice, LOGICIANS start with their own set of accepted and rejected arguments—in Rawls's terms, their considered judgements of the facts of logic, that is, considered judgements of logical truth, validity, consistency, implication, and equivalence. Then they try to build a logical theory whose verdicts accord with their initial considered judgements. It is unlikely that their early attempts will produce an exact fit between the theory and the 'data'. Furthermore, they may produce a logical theory that proclaims unforeseen and prima facie anomalous logical relationships. Sometimes they can respond to such anomalies with a simple modification of their formal system. Sometimes retranslating a prima facie anomalous argument will reconcile it with the theory. Sometimes, however, they may yield their initial logical intuitions to powerful or elegant systematic considerations. In short, 'theory' will lead them to reject the 'data'. Furthermore, this mix of theory and 'data' often includes their other beliefs and commitments, including philosophical ones. The process comes to at least a temporary end when the LOGICIANS reach a state of 'reflective equilibrium', that is, one where they take their theory to reject no putative fact of logic that they are determined to preserve and to countenance none that they are determined to reject.[1]

---

[1] The term 'reflective equilibrium' is owed to John Rawls (1971), who offered a model of the methodology of ethics similar to the one that I have just sketched for LOGIC. Since LOGICIANS seek to reconcile their logical intuitions with both a logical theory and their philosophical and other beliefs and commitments, the term 'wide reflective equilibrium' applies to what they seek. Nelson Goodman (1955) anticipated the reflective equilibrium approach to logic in writing of the justification of deduction and induction. Otávio Bueno and Mark Colyvan expound another version of the coherence approach to theorizing in LOGIC in this volume, Ch. 9.

2. AN ARGUMENT AGAINST THE REVISABILITY OF LOGIC

In the recent literature one finds a family of objections that seem to show that revisions of logic, if any, must be quite minimal. The basic idea is that we need some logic to define and determine both the outcomes of any option we consider and the consequences of any hypothesis we entertain. Obviously, this point applies to deliberating about revising logic and to considering hypotheses positing differences in the facts of logic. If in entertaining such options or hypotheses we must suspend logic itself, then we will find ourselves, in Frege's words, 'unable to think at all,' and thus unable to deliberate rationally over changes in logic. Stewart Shapiro expresses the objection nicely:

> Suppose someone is considering a change in logic, because less drastic measures are not working. Presumably the troubled theorist would follow the model for any change in the web. He would replace the old logic with the new one and see how it comes out. That is, the theorist would examine the consequences of the change in logic for the proposed new web of belief. Consequences? Which logic do we use to assess the consequences of different logics? Is there a correct logic for that, and is this super-logic also just a bunch of nodes in the current web? Regress threatens. Is the super-logic analytic, a priori, or incorrigible?[2]

Although Shapiro directed his objection against Quine's suggestion that even the laws of logic can be revised to reconcile one's system of belief with recalcitrant experience, the objection applies to any deliberation about revising logic. For it will involve considering the gains and losses arising from the revision.

Of course, the objection does not rule out all deliberation about changes in logic (and Shapiro didn't claim that it did) for we may be able hold part of logic fixed, while using it to deliberate about changes in other parts. Moreover, through a series of changes in logic we might be able to revise parts that we could not revise initially. But it is not obvious that we could, and, off-hand, I don't see how to go about demonstrating that we could. I think it's an open question as to whether we are stuck with some core set of rules of inference and facts of logic or whether through a series of revisions any putative fact of logic or rule of inference is open to revision. Furthermore, the objection certainly applies to entertaining a vague hypothesis to the effect that the facts of logic are very different from what we take them to be, and perhaps to the hypothesis that some contradictions are true.

Using a variant of the objection, someone could argue that if there are no facts of logical consequence, then there can be no rule-defined inferential

---

[2] Shapiro (2000: 338). Shapiro notes that Crispin Wright has made a similar objection. In a similar vein Hartry Field (1996: 373–6) argued that we can't make sense of questions as to what our evidential system would license if the facts of logic were different, because we can't say what would follow from the rules of the system. Also see Boghossian (2000: 233–4) for an argument that we need at least a core metatheoretic logic to compare various alternative order pairs, <T,L>, consisting of a theory cum a logic, to determine which best accounts for our observations.

practices, since whether or not something accords with a practice depends upon its logical relations with the rules of the practice. Thus if there are no facts of logic, there is no fact as to whether one has adopted one practice rather than another, and, consequently, none as to whether one has even changed one's logic.[3]

By tradition logic is a branch of methodology. So revising logic entails revising methodology. Indeed, our current methodology shields logic from the ordinary sort of empirical refutation, since our so-called logical truths are consistent with any consistent statement and thus with any true observation statement.[4] Even Quine came to acknowledge something like this feature of our methodology. In speaking of revising a theory in the light of a failed prediction he wrote, 'We exempt some [statements from possible revision] on determining that the fateful implication still holds without their help. Any purely logical truth is thus exempted' (Quine 1990: 14). Quine is observing that any observation sentence implied by a hypothesis H and a logical truth S is implied by H alone. So simply deleting a logical truth from a theory to save it is idle. (Quine did not say anything about the more radical idea of revising the notion implication itself.) The point can be generalized. Suppose that S is a 'theorem' of one's background theory T, for example, a mathematical principle employed in physics or a physical principle employed in chemistry. Then if from S and some conjunction of hypotheses H we can deduce in T an observation statement O, we can deduce O in T from H alone. For we simply assume H, 'prove' S in T and proceed as before. Since the methodologies of the special sciences ordinarily take for granted the principles of the more general sciences, the special sciences will treat these principles as just as exempt from revision in the face of contrary experience as they and the more general sciences treat so-called logical truths. I will call statements of this sort *methodological apriorities*. Clearly, there is a sense in which we must admit the apriority of logic (and perhaps other doctrines), i.e. the sense of being apriorities of our most general methodology.

The notion of a methodological apriority is weaker than the traditional conception of the apriori. This is because empirical considerations could lead us to revise our methodology so as to convert a former methodological apriority into an empirically testable hypothesis. It is at least arguable that this befell Euclidean geometry *qua* theory of physical space. Methodological apriorities need not be immune to revision on supposed non-empirical grounds. For example, most philosophers maintain that knowledge based upon calculation is not empirical. Yet we freely revise such knowledge claims in the face of errors in calculation. A methodology might shield some principles from revision no matter what the grounds. We might call these principles its *methodological dogmas*. If objections

---

[3] Cf. Boghossian (2000: 238).   [4] Shapiro (2000: 340) makes this point.

of the sort rehearsed above are correct, then perhaps certain parts of logic are methodologically dogmatic.

The rules of logic are among our most fundamental methodological principles. In view of this I am going to treat revising logic as a special case of revising methodology. Methodology, I take it, is a system of norms that governs our scientific practice (and perhaps our epistemic practice more generally). The worry about revising logic is a special case of the worry about revising some methodological norms while working within the very system of norms to which they belong. In particular, if something is a methodological apriority, one wonders how experience could ever lead us to revise the methodological rules underwriting it. This raises an unmistakable problem for naturalists of the Quinean sort, since they certainly don't want to acknowledge some apriori basis for our normative beliefs or revisions in them. And if the apriority is also a methodological dogma one wonders how it can be revised at all.

In the next section I will turn from questions about revising logic to those about revising norms generally and methodological norms in particular. This will put us in a better position to deal with revising logic. Although it is difficult to see how a methodology for empirical theory testing can proceed without recognizing some fixed points, some apriorities, this doesn't mean that in developing a methodology or in discerning the so-called facts of logic we must depend upon apriori elements that transcend any methodology. I hope to give an account of revising methodology that avoids appealing to such apriori insights or principles.

3. REVISING METHODOLOGY

How might we revise methodology without appealing to a methodologically transcendent apriori? Methodological claims of the form 'Using method M is likely to achieve results G' fall within the scope of scientific assessment (if they are stated with enough precision), and will not be problematic. The same cannot be said for normative claims of the form 'People who want to achieve G *ought* to use a method that is likely to achieve it,' much less for those of the form 'Goal G is a worthy goal.' For it is difficult to see how we could give a naturalized account of our knowledge of these claims, if we have any such knowledge. To be sure, quite a few philosophers have argued that something like the scientific method, broadly construed, can be applied to normative claims, even ethical ones, and they have pointed out that in accepting scientific hypotheses we employ various norms and values that are not empirically grounded. I have no quarrel with these points, but they don't help much in naturalizing the epistemology of norms. For they don't get around the fundamental role that normative intuitions—as opposed to sensory observations—play in normative epistemology. Without a naturalized account of intuitions and the knowledge that they are supposed to furnish, I don't see how Quineans and like-minded naturalists could countenance normative knowledge.

For this reason I am inclined to take a non-cognitive (or non-factualist) approach to normativity, so that in the cases in question there is nothing to know, and no normative epistemological knowledge to naturalize. (Though, of course, one can still ask why we make normative claims, and why they appear to be know-ledge.) Elsewhere I have also adopted a non-cognitive (or non-factualist) position toward facts of logic.[5] I believe this approach will provide some underappreciated approaches to revising logic.

I deny that revising methodological and other norms comes about through acquiring normative *knowledge*. But I do not mean to exclude methodological changes arising through rational means. Historically, arguments for revising meth-odological norms have employed normative premisses, even if only implicitly. For example, when physicists argue against the requirement that scientific theories be deterministic by pointing to the ascendance of quantum mechanics, they are indicating that the requirement is standing in the way of the goal of bringing an important set of phenomena within the purview of physics. Similarly when logicians argue against the requirement that a formal logic have a complete proof procedure by pointing to the ability of second-order logic to provide categorical formulations of number theory and analysis, they too are pitting one normative requirement against another. If Hume is right, there is no avoiding the use of normative premisses when arguing methodology or other normative matters, but so long as a naturalized account of our acceptance of the premisses is available, this is not problematic in itself.

Instead of maintaining that we acquire norms through apriori means, I hold that we find ourselves with a collection of culturally conditioned norms and values, which we may or not modify in the light of experience, arguments, and changes in our condition. Normative argument can lead us to change our values, goals, and priorities—I've just mentioned two examples—but sometimes we change them as an *unreflective* response to changes in our circumstances. An octogenarian is less likely to value sex than an adolescent. An emerging nation will put more emphasis on practical knowledge than on theoretical speculation. And years of receiving frustrating counter-examples can lead philosophers to abandon research programs. Furthermore, reflective revisions might follow upon non-reflective ones. Instead of revising a principle P of methodology M unreflectively—say, by simply not finding it as binding anymore—we might revise some other feature

---

[5] See Resnik (1997: ch. 8; 1999). It is important to realize that I am not denying specific truths, such as, 'The number of twin primes is finite or not'; rather I am denying that there is a fact of the matter as to whether this truth is a truth of logic. Nor am I criticizing any specific inferences; instead, I am denying that there is a fact of the matter as to whether their premisses *logically* imply their conclusions. Finally, I am not denying facts of formal logic, e.g. that '1=1' first-order implies '$\exists x(x = 1)$'. For ease of exposition I will continue to use the locution 'facts of logic'. Gibbard (1990) and Blackburn (1984) have much more thorough non-cognitive accounts of normativity than I have.

of M unreflectively, thereby initiating M′ and then using principles of M′ argue for revising P.

Might there be immutable normative principles, and might this not include rules of logic? The question needs further specification. Fans of the apriori, for example, don't hold that apriori factual claims are not revisable *simpliciter*, but rather that they are not revisable (or should not be revised) in the light of sensory evidence. To address our question, we need to specify the basis for reflectively revising methodological principles. Given what I said above, a good candidate for this basis is normative argument. Now at any given time it could happen that some principle was so fundamental to any rational discussion that no argument based upon other normative considerations could override it. Some debates about intuitionist logic and Dialetheism seem to indicate that certain parts of logic are fundamental in this way. The protagonists seem to talk past each other, so that what is a perfectly good argument to one either begs the question or involves an obvious fallacy to the other.

But once we admit that methodology can change I see no reason for ruling out changes in the relative weights of methodological norms, and thus no reason for thinking that a principle that previously could not be overridden might be. Other changes, such as, changes in our goals, could also lead to overturning previously inviolate principles, and, any of these changes might come about through processes in which reflection plays no role.

Unreflective revisions of normative principles, that is, cases where one finds that their normative intuitions have changed without being able to underwrite the changes with an argument, frequently occur in response to behavior. If many members of a culture or at least enough of its influential members engage in an initially deviant conduct, the culture's norms may change to legitimate the conduct. This goes for methodology as well as for language and morals. The changes in these cases come about through the initially deviant behavior generating new normative intuitions that in turn cause us to strive to bring our normative systems back into reflective equilibrium.

While it's undeniable that normative systems evolve, and often do so as the result of unreflective behavior leading to changes in them, are such changes legitimate? If we ask someone, 'Why did you do that [reprehensible act]?', and they reply 'I wasn't thinking', often we respond, 'Well, you should have!' Suppose that, on the basis of examples such as this, we grant that some unreflective changes in our normative systems are not legitimate since they result from illegitimate deviant behavior or intuitions. On what basis will we make room for legitimate deviance? For isn't it a matter of definition that deviance contravenes its governing system? While this worry seems true of behavior, it need not be true of intuitions concerning correct behavior. For example, while it is against the law to prevent a person from criticizing the Government, no law prohibits one from hoping that someone will stop the critic. Thus deviant behavior might prompt non-deviant reconsideration of the very system prohibiting the behavior, and this in turn to a permissible revision of the system that makes the behavior acceptable. Some of the changes in contemporary sexual mores, dress codes, rules of grammar, and pronunciation come readily to mind.

This is to approach the question of legitimacy from the perspective of the system in force. If a system prohibits its own revision, then, of course, there is no way that it can acquiesce in changes to it, no matter how they arise. Since such dogmatism seems unacceptable, one wonders whether one can raise the question of legitimacy independently of a system of norms. Realists about the correctness of norms would certainly answer that one can. Such realism seems plainly wrong when it comes to the evolution of linguistic norms. Languages evolve, and there is no absolute right or wrong about it, though one might assess the changes as good or bad with respect to some purpose, such as, international communication or ease of spelling or learning. But in the case of morals and methodology the realist's affirmation of independent standards is more plausible. I am no normative realist myself, but I will not argue against that position here.

As a matter of practice, we evaluate behavior with respect to normative systems we now accept. Our own systems view deviance with differing degrees of severity, depending both on the type of deviance (e.g. whether it be linguistic or moral) and the cases at hand. Thus I find quaint the occasional 'ain't' from a hillbilly turned academic philosopher I know, but I would deter the same usage in my children. When it comes to lying or thieving, however, we tend to be uniformly intolerant. Something similar applies to the ways we regard the actions of those who live under systems different from ours. We think it's fine for the French to speak French in France, but not fine for certain countries to punish thieves by amputating their hands. Here, of course, we are operating within our own mores, and not attempting to judge as we would were we living under the other mores.

However, when we deviate from our own systems we are left to our consciences, through which we cannot but judge right those actions that we sincerely take to be right. Indeed, for anti-realists the question of the legitimacy of rejecting or sincerely deviating from one's previously accepted system of norms simply does not arise. For no independent standard for answering it is possible. As a consequence there is nothing intrinsically incorrect in rejecting a methodological absolute even if one's methodology prohibits so doing. In practice the realist's situation is no different. While realists believe in facts of methodological correctness that obtain independently of the methodology one happens to espouse, they have no more independent access to those facts than the anti-realist. Both realists and anti-realists will judge right those actions that they sincerely take to be right, though, of course, each will give a different account of what this judging means.

4. REVISING LOGIC (RATHER THAN LOGIC)

With the distinction between logic and LOGIC in mind we can see that the worries about revising logic have really been concerned with revising our inferential practice and not with the theoretical claims of LOGICIANS.[6]

How then might we revise (lower-case) logic? Just as speakers of a language go about their linguistic business without consulting the rules of its grammar, we freely make inferences without asking ourselves whether they follow the rules of (our) logic. (In fact, inferring and speaking are generally so spontaneous that we sometimes find ourselves using 'bad' grammar or 'fallacious' reasoning despite our best intentions not to do so.) Most people cannot articulate standards of good reasoning or grammar, even more have never been exposed to a treatise of LOGIC. Even those, such as mathematicians and philosophers, who care about and are trained to worry about the cogency of their arguments look to their colleagues rather than to reference books for certification or correction. Furthermore, few if any of these colleagues will be in a position to assess arguments by citing rules. The same goes for the rest of us. We depend upon the explicit approval, tacit acceptance, and looks of comprehension, words of correction, and puzzled expressions to tell us whether our inferences make sense.

Inference making is a social enterprise stabilized by the acquiescence, approval and disapproval of our fellows. Ultimately there is no getting around this in view of the problems with applying rules that philosophers as diverse as Lewis Carroll (1895) and Kripke's (1982) Wittgenstein have noted. If to determine whether an inference is recognized by our practice we had to first determine whether it followed a rule, then we would have to also determine whether the inferences used to determine this followed the rules applying to them, and so on. The process will either lead to a regress or come to a point where we make our best judgement and hope that it agrees with the practice. (For example, to determine whether '1 = 1' is an instance of 'a = a', we would have to determine whether the left and right occurrence of '1' are occurrences of the same symbol, which in turn might require us to consult a rule for determining when two symbols are the same. This might refer us to a further rule. Or it might tell us to count the symbols as the same if they look alike. If the latter, then we will be left to judge the case on our own and hope that our judgement is accepted.)

(The previous paragraph might be read as questioning our ability to know whether a given inference accords with a rule of inference. But my position on

---

[6] This may not be quite right. In our ordinary inferential practice we sometimes speak of statements being consistent or having certain implications or equivalents. The notions of consistency, equivalence, and so on in play seem to be contextual, and relative to common background assumptions. Those untrained in LOGIC do not mark any distinction between logical consistency etc. of various types and non-logical forms of consistency etc. However, one might hold that the rules of logical inference are supposed to reflect so-called facts of logic and that revising our inferential practice also involves revising what we take to be facts of logic.

facts of logic may commit me to a stronger view. For one could argue as follows. An inference accords with a Rule R just in case it is a logical consequence of R that the inference is permissible. Hence if there are no facts concerning logical consequence, then there are no facts as to whether certain inferences accord with certain rules. I am not fully convinced by this reasoning, but I will assume that I am committed to the stronger view for the remainder of the chapter.)

The preceding paragraphs have fall-out for understanding how we revise our inferential practice. Just as we carry out this practice largely without thinking, we also revise it largely without thinking. We simply no longer accept specific inferential connections or, more frequently, we recognize new ones. Like changes in a language certain inferential practices may slowly and quietly become obsolete and new ones may unceremoniously evolve. Practices might splinter into incompatible descendents. Thus intuitionists and classical mathematicians now engage in different practices that share the same lineage. (But I hasten to add that they do not illustrate my point about the unceremonious evolution of inferential practice; the intuitionists explicitly criticized classical mathematical reasoning.)

I don't mean to imply that revisions will come about helter-skelter. Even if we don't pursue our practice by trying to follow rules, we do recognize similarities between cases and do try to treat like cases alike. Enough ethics runs through our epistemic endeavors that once we accept a new inference or reject an old one we will feel obliged to do the same with respect to inferences that are relevantly similar to those inferences. The rub will come in trying to decide on an appropriate notion of relevance.

What about the worry that changing our inferential practice will prevent us from 'thinking at all'. To avoid this, we should follow Quine's advice of minimizing mutilation. If we fiddle with very few inferential connections at a given time by focusing on a few specific logical truths and inferences, enough of the old connections should survive for it to be possible for us to think and communicate. Moreover, if we want to be more like LOGICIANS and deliberate explicitly about the advantages of the revisions for our conceptual scheme, we may be able to avoid circularity. For example, we can calculate the expected utility of restricting applications of the distributive law in interpreting quantum theory though we use a utility theory in which the law is not restricted.

Furthermore, in making a case for specific revisions of logic we will make but a small number of inferences and appeal to but a few putative facts of logic. This can enable us to employ some instances of the very rule of inference or so-called law of logic that we want to revise. This is because the so-called laws of logic are statements that LOGICIANS use to describe our inferential practice, and not the individual truths or inferences that they purport to systematize. Consequently, one might be able to argue against, say, the Law of Non-Contradiction while assuming specific instances of it. That is, one might be able to deny that no sentence of the form 'p and not p' is true while assuming the truth of specific statements of the form 'not both p and not p'.

Whatever our philosophical attitude toward the correctness of rules of inference, we are going to face the same predicaments in trying to initiate deviant inference or in countering those who present us with deviant inferences. Ultimately, there may be no non-question-begging way to confound the other side—even if we end up regarding each other as 'crazy'.[7]

When may we revise inferential connections? In light of the sort of radical logical anti-realism about logic and normative matters more generally that I have been advocating, I construe the question as a request for advice. And it is not altogether inappropriate to give the glib answer, 'Whenever you feel like it!' A better answer is: 'Whenever you feel that it is a reasonable way to respond to felt tensions in our conceptual scheme and think your proposal has a reasonable chance of being considered.' To those who want to know what I mean by 'reasonable' here, I will not claim that there are objectively correct standards of reasonableness. Instead I will simply respond that I am using the word 'reasonable' as the rest of us do. Of course, as a non-cognitivist, I have a somewhat unconventional philosophical account of what we all are doing when we use this and other normative terms.

Before you dismiss my advice on the revision of logic as utterly insane, let me elaborate. First, as we have seen, our inferential practice is neither defined nor regulated by rules. Instead our own judgements and those of our colleagues regulate it on a case-by-case basis. If they and we accept an inference, then it goes whether or not we have bothered to consider its correctness. Most of the time this happens. When it does not, we have a small crisis on our hands. We can withdraw the inference, or suspend it while we try to understand why our audience rejects it or we can press on and hope that eventually our way of thinking will prevail. Of course, it might not prevail; we might be branded crackpots and ostracized. But if we do prevail, we end up modifying the practice itself.

Consciously going against your perceptions of what your audience expects you to conclude requires a great deal of intellectual courage. For both the external and internal sanctions for making 'obvious errors' in logic are severe. Thus it will be rare that one will try to revise logic. Moreover, given that there may be no uniquely optimal way of responding to intellectual problems whether they be in science or elsewhere, it is very likely that revising inferential connections will be controversial. There seems to be no way of predicting when this sort of option will be attractive.

---

[7] A nice way to appreciate how difficult it is to dismiss logical deviance without begging the question is to read Priest (1998).

5. REVISING THE LAWS OF LOGIC

Although the term 'law of logic' is probably one of the most common in the philosopher's vocabulary, there have been remarkably few attempts to state what it means. One way to regard the laws of logic is along the lines of laws of nature, such as the law of gravitation. Just as the laws of nature are 'general facts' that cover all events of certain types, the laws of logic are, on this view, 'general facts' that cover facts of logic. For example, the Law of Non-Contradiction *qua* general fact might be expressed as '$\forall F \forall x - (Fx \ \& \ -Fx)$', or using propositional quantifiers as '$\forall p - (p \ \& \ -p)$'. Either way, particular 'facts of logic', e.g. that it is not the case that 2 is both a number and not a number, can be recovered through some form of universal instantiation.

Earlier I noted that LOGICIANS often speak of specific 'laws of logic' as a way of specifying an indefinite number of so-called logical truths. Used in this way, the 'Law of Non-Contradiction' refers to the claim that all statements of the form 'It is not the case that both p and not p' are true. But LOGICIANS just as frequently use other formulations of the law such as 'Nothing is both true and false'[8] or 'No proposition and its negation are both true'. On this view, deriving specific facts of logic is more complicated than on the previous view. Universal instantiation alone will not do, one also must enlist disquotational principles from an appropriate truth theory.[9]

Some LOGICIANS take it to be the task of LOGIC to discover laws of logic in one of the two senses just described. As I noted in s. 1, LOGICIANS who pursue this goal will rely upon intuitions concerning the facts of logic. Of course, such laws and facts of logic are no more revisable than any other fact, but we can certainly revise our opinions as to whether a given sentence or formula expresses such a law.

LOGICIANS who aim to codify our inferential practice (our logic, so to speak), might use the term 'law of logic' as a way to characterize classes of statements that we treat as so-called facts of logic. Their usage would be similar to the second view introduced above, but without the commitment to facts of logic. Revisions of the laws of logic, in their sense, would follow on the heels of revisions of our (lower-case) logic.

But LOGICIANS can pursue their discipline more abstractly and delineate idealized inferential practices whether they see them as arising from ours or not. They might pursue this in a purely creative way, letting whim and fancy guide them, as some mathematically inclined logicians have done. Or they might follow the method of other normative theorists: they will seek a reflective equilibrium

---

[8] Priest (1998) uses this formulation.

[9] Lest my last remark mislead, I should note that second-order universal instantiation also requires a comprehension axiom or an equivalent. LOGICIANS also refer to certain schemata, such as '$p \lor -p$' and '$-(p \ \& \ -p)$', of various formal systems as laws of logic. This usage will not concern us in this section.

between their intuitions with regard to specific inferences and putative logical truths and their ongoing attempts to systematize the same using logical theories. This raises a worry that I have postponed for too long. So let me turn to it now.

In a thoughtful discussion of my views on LOGIC and logic Stewart Shapiro wonders how my non-cognitivism can be compatible with my recognition of wide reflective equilibrium as the LOGICIAN's method. He worries that we need some logic to determine and define whether we are in reflective equilibrium, that is, whether our LOGIC is *compatible* with and *captures* our intuitions.[10]

I once wrote that reflective equilibrium applies to 'systems consisting of beliefs, logical theories, and considered judgments of logic. Such a system is in such a state just in case it is coherent by the lights of it own logical theory' (Resnik 1997: 160).

In criticizing my view, Shapiro had this passage in mind, and I think I need to retract the entire paragraph from which it is drawn. I had written it, because I had been worried about the objection that reflective equilibrium is a subjective state of individual logicians, and that all there is to being in the state is having a certain kind of mental tranquility. Unfortunately, as Shapiro realized, the logical non-cognitivism I subsequently espoused does not work well with the character-ization of reflective equilibrium he quotes. My remarks on rule-following and our inferential practice just makes matters worse. For this reason earlier in this chapter I bit the bullet and used the term to characterize states of LOGICIANS (better: states of triples consisting of LOGICIANS, logical theories, and considered judgements of so-called facts of logic). To remind you, I wrote that they are in such a state when they take their theory to reject no putative fact of logic that they are determined to preserve and to countenance none that they are determined to reject.

Suppose, then, that we are developing a logical theory to describe a certain inferential practice, or to capture so-called facts of logic, or to systematize our intuitions concerning valid inference. How can we decide whether it is satisfactory if there is no fact of the matter as to what it implies about a certain set of arguments. We partake in an inferential practice, and as we pursue it, we will take the system to accept or reject various arguments. The process could be quite complex and involve a number of inferences—again conditioned by our training in the practice. Furthermore, we may be uncertain as to whether we are in reflective equilibrium. Reflective equilibrium might not be objective, but it is sufficiently intersubjective to introduce such uncertainties.

Notice that I am not saying that our practice will commit us to this or that or require us to make certain judgements. Rather I am saying that we will make various inferences within a social enterprise that is stabilized not by what rules that supposedly define it entail but rather by the acquiescence, approval, and disapproval of our fellows. Of course, one might arrive at reflective equilibrium by ignoring putative counter-examples—this is to use the ostrich method—or by

---

[10] Shapiro (2000: 346).

recognizing the examples and refusing to see their force. Shapiro (2000: 346) is right in noting that 'this allows one to attain reflective equilibrium very easily'. But since getting away with this way of reaching reflective equilibrium is another matter, I don't take his point as a criticism. In practice LOGICIANS who try to revise the received system of LOGIC will never have it easy. Even gaining a hearing will require much energy and creativity.

This brings us back to the topic of this volume, the Law of Non-Contradiction and the Dialetheists' proposal for revising it. Their basic idea is that by taking certain contradictions to be true and reasoning according to the principles of paraconsistent logic we can solve certain difficult problems in the theory of truth. As they have emphasized, they are not asking us to accept contradictions indiscriminately; the point is to accept them in cases that have already been acknowledged as pathological. I think it is uncontroversial that they are asking us to revise our inferential practice, since until they began their campaign nobody working on the theory of truth would consider taking the Liar as both true and false a feasible option. After all, it would flout the Law of Non-Contradiction![11] On the other hand, the Dialetheists are asking us to revise but rather a small part of our inferential practice. It is a part that is of little interest to the general intellectual public, but of great interest to philosophers of truth. Moreover, as this volume attests these philosophers are taking Dialetheists seriously. Thus they have made the first steps towards success. This is a bit of sociology, but in the light of the previous section I am not sure that there is more to say.[12]

REFERENCES

BLACKBURN, SIMON (1984), *Spreading the Word*. Oxford: Oxford University Press.
BOGHOSSIAN, PAUL (2000), 'Knowledge of Logic' in *New Essays on the A Priori*, ed. Paul Boghossian and Christopher Peacocke. Oxford: Clarendon.
BUENO, OTÁVIO, and COLYVAN, MARK (2004), 'Logical Non-Apriorism and the "Law" of Non-Contradiction,' Ch. 9 in this volume.
CARROLL, LEWIS [C. L. DODGSON] (1895), 'What the Tortoise Said to Achilles', *Mind*, NS, 4.
FIELD, H. (1996), 'The A Prioricity of Logic', *Proceedings of the Aristotelian Society*, 96: 359–79.
GIBBARD, ALLAN (1990), *Wise Choices, Apt Feelings*. Cambridge, Mass.: Harvard University Press.

[11] Whether they are asking us to revise the Law of Non-Contradiction *qua* description of the facts of logic depends both upon one's own view of the nature of the laws of logic and theirs. Fortunately, we need not take up this issue here.

[12] I am grateful for comments on previous drafts of this chapter to Mark Balaguer, Matthew Chrisman, Hartry Field, Jennifer Fisher, Michael Hand, Nancy Lawrence, Adrian Moore, and two anonymous referees for this volume. An earlier version of this chapter was presented to the Pacific Division of the American Philosophical Association in March 2002. Some of the material in s. 3 also appeared in Resnik and Orlandi (2003).

Goodman, Nelson (1955), 'The New Riddle of Induction', in *Fact, Fiction and Forecast*. Cambridge, Mass.: Harvard University Press.

Kripke, Saul (1982), *Wittgenstein on Rules and Private Language*. Cambridge, Mass.: Harvard University Press.

Priest, Graham (1998), 'What's So Bad about Contradictions?' *The Journal of Philosophy*, 95: 410–26

Quine, W. V. (1990), *Pursuit of Truth*. Cambridge, Mass.: Harvard University Press.

Rawls, John (1971), *A Theory of Justice*. Cambridge, Mass.: Harvard University Press.

Resnik, Michael (1997), *Mathematics as a Science of Patterns*. Oxford: Clarendon.

—— (1999) 'Against Logical Realism', *History and Philosophy of Logic*, 20: 181–94.

Resnik, Michael, and Orlandi, Nicoletta (2003), 'Holistic Realism: A Response to Katz on Holism and Intuition', *The Philosophical Forum*, 34: 301–15.

Shapiro, Stewart (2000), 'The Status of Logic,' in *New Essays on the A Priori*, ed. Paul Boghossian and Christopher Peacocke. Oxford: Clarendon.

IV

Against the LNC

12

True and False—As If

JC Beall

Consistency is the last refuge of the unimaginative.

(Oscar Wilde)

1. DIALETHEISM

Dialetheism is the view that some truths have true negations.[1] The view has struck many philosophers as being both terribly radical and wholly implausible. By my lights, dialetheism is neither radical (at least not in any pejorative sense) nor implausible; it is a simple and rather natural theory of language.

Natural? I think so, but my reason for thinking as much stems from a particular conception of truth—what, for lack of a better term, I dub *constructive (methodological) deflationism*. My aim in this chapter is to sketch the given conception of truth, a conception for which dialetheism is well suited and, as said, seemingly natural—not straining against reason, not radical, and so on.

The chapter is structured as follows. Section 2 rehearses the logical background. Section 3 advances a thought experiment that both illustrates and motivates my conception of truth. Section 4 sketches the target conception of truth and briefly indicates how, on that conception, 'true contradictions' are perfectly natural. By way of clarifying the target conception of truth s. 5 addresses a few questions and objections. Section 6 offers some closing remarks.

---

[1] If contradictions are taken to be truth-bearers of the form $\mathcal{A} \wedge \sim\mathcal{A}$, then dialetheism is the view that there are true contradictions. But not everyone defines 'contradiction' in terms of form. Let $\mathcal{A}$ and $\mathcal{B}$ be truth-bearers. $\mathcal{A}$ is *explosive* iff $\mathcal{B}$ is a consequence of $\mathcal{A}$, for any arbitrary $\mathcal{B}$. Some define *contradictions* to be explosive truth-bearers; on that account, dialetheists *reject* that some contradictions are true; on that account, dialetheism is the view that not all truth-bearers of the form $\mathcal{A} \wedge \sim\mathcal{A}$ are contradictions. Hartry Field [15] provides further discussion of this (terminological) issue.

2. LOGIC OF PARADOX

This section is intended only as a quick review of the target logical framework.[2] I briefly sketch the general framework FDE, and then turn to *LP*. For simplicity, I stick to the propositional level.[3]

2.1 The Language of FDE

Begin with the idea that there are two fundamental 'truth values', The True and The False. Intuitively, the two values yield four 'possibilities' for any truth-bearer A: A is True; A is False; A is Both (true and false); and A is Neither (true nor false). We can formally represent these four 'possibilities' in various (equivalent) ways.[4]

For present purposes, we will consider a four-valued language. Let V comprise the four 'values' (the four 'possible' categories of sentences); specifically, let V be $\{1, \mathbf{b}, \mathbf{n}, 0\}$. Let D comprise the *designated* values, the different ways of being true (values to be preserved in valid inferences); specifically, let $D = \{1, \mathbf{b}\}$. Let v be a *valuation* on the language; it is a map from the sentences of the language into V. A valuation is *admissible* iff it accords with the diagrams at Fig. 12.1. Informally, by 'accord with the diagrams' is meant that v conforms to the functions specified in the diagrams. So, for example, if v accords with the given diagrams, then $v(\sim A) = 1$ iff $v(A) = 0$, and similarly for assignments to $A \wedge B$ and so on.[5]

With admissible valuations in hand, a (semantic) consequence relation $\Vdash$ is defined in the usual (many-valued) way, where X comprises sentences of the language:

>   » $X \Vdash A$ just in case, for any admissible v, $v(A) \in D$ if $v(B) \in D$,
>
>   for any B in X

In turn, valid sentences (or logical truths) may be defined in terms of $\Vdash$ by saying that A is valid iff $\emptyset \Vdash A$.

---

[2] I have since changed my view on what, exactly, the Liar teaches us about language, and have come to think that while it teaches us that there are 'true contradictions', it also teaches us something significant about the behavior of negation. Those ideas require a logic that I call *AP*, which differs from the *FDE*-based logics. A sketch of the newer ideas are in [7]. That said, I still endorse the overall 'constructive' attitude towards truth that I advocate in this paper.

[3] Formal theories of truth take place, as it were, at the predicate level; however, the important foundational issues arise at the propositional level. See the Introduction for a sketch of the predicate extension.

[4] For other (equivalent) ways of formulating the target languages and logics, see Priest [25] and Beall and van Fraassen [11], and references therein.

[5] Let C comprise the connectives φ of the language ($\sim, \wedge, \vee$); and let O comprise operators on V; and let $\odot$ be a rule that assigns elements of C to elements of O. The diagrams (above) specify each $\odot_\varphi \in O$, the operators corresponding to the connectives $\varphi \in C$. So, v is said to *accord with the diagrams* iff for each n-ary connective $\varphi \in C$ and its corresponding n-ary operator $\odot_\varphi \in O$, $v(\varphi(A_1, \ldots, A_n)) = \odot_\varphi(v(A_1), \ldots, v(A_n))$.

~		∧	1	b	n	0		∨	1	b	n	0
1	0	1	1	b	n	0		1	1	1	1	1
b	b	b	b	b	0	0		b	1	b	1	b
n	n	n	n	0	n	0		n	1	1	n	n
0	1	0	0	0	0	0		0	1	b	n	0

Fɪɢ. 12.1.

The foregoing language is the language of FDE, a simple (propositional) relevant logic developed by Anderson and Belnap [1]. The language models the idea that sentences may exhibit any of the four initial 'possibilities'—True (only), False (only), Neither, Both.

There are no logical truths in the language of FDE. (Just consider the admissible valuation that assigns all sentences to **n**.) But not all is lost; indeed, many of the classically valid inferences remain valid—simplification, addition, and much more. On the other hand, not all classically valid inferences remain. Of particular importance is that *EFQ* or *Explosion* fails: arbitrary $\mathcal{B}$ does not follow from arbitrary $\mathcal{A}$ and $\sim\mathcal{A}$.[6] Something else is 'lost' in FDE, namely, Disjunctive Syllogism (and, hence, material modus ponens): just let $v(\mathcal{A}) = \mathbf{b}$ and $v(\mathcal{B}) \notin \mathcal{D}$ (either **n** or 0), in which case $\mathcal{A} \vee \mathcal{B}$ and $\sim\mathcal{A}$ are designated but $\mathcal{B}$ is not designated.[7]

2.2 The Language of LP

LP (logic of paradox) emerges from restricting our attention only to those FDE-valuations that 'ignore' gaps—ignore the Neither category **n**. The resulting *LP*-diagrams are as Fig. 12.2.

Restricting attention to 'non-gappy' valuations has an immediate effect on the consequence relation: Not only do we now have logical truths (of which there are none in FDE); we have *all* the logical truths of classical logic, including $\sim(\mathcal{A} \wedge \sim\mathcal{A})$ and $\mathcal{A} \vee \sim\mathcal{A}$. On the other hand, disjunctive syllogism and, hence, material modus ponens remain invalid.

---

[6] The failure of Explosion is often taken to be a sufficient condition for being a so-called *paraconsistent logic*. It is worth noting that paraconsistent logics and dialetheism are often conflated; the two are very much distinct. Most paraconsistent logicians are *not* dialetheists.

[7] In [7] (and also see Appendix, this chapter) I briefly indicate a different logic in which Disjunction Syllogism is truth-preserving *so long as* the premises are all (negation-)consistent; otherwise, it fails. The logic is intended (in part) to mirror the idea that, for dialetheists, consistency remains the 'default assumption', and also the idea (discussed in [7]) that negation has a 'double-aspect'. For present purposes, however, I will leave issues about Disjunctive Syllogism to the side, as the present chapter is not intended to defend the dialetheic reading of LP so much as it is intended to sketch a natural 'home' for such a reading.

~			∧	1	b	0		∨	1	b	0
1	0		1	1	b	0		1	1	1	1
b	b		b	b	b	0		b	1	b	b
0	1		0	0	0	0		0	1	b	0

FIG. 12.2.

2.3 Philosophical Import

The informal, dialetheic interpretation of LP reads the values $1, 0$, and **b** as *true (and true only)*, *false (and false only)*, and *both (true and false)*, respectively. As Priest has argued in a variety of places, one immediate virtue of the logic is that it provides a simple, elegant solution to familiar semantic (truth- and denotation-theoretic) paradoxes:[8] Such paradoxical sentences are *both* true and false. Because Explosion fails, there is no threat of *triviality*—no threat that *all* sentences are true (and false).

Everyone will agree that, at least on a formal level, *LP* affords a very simple theory of truth; the worry arises on its informal reading. A cry rings out: 'Truth just can't be contradictory! How could a truth also have a true negation?!'[9] And while Priest [24] has tried to show the ungroundedness of that cry, the general 'feeling' that there are no 'true contradictions' persists.

While I harbor no naïve hopes, my aim in what follows is to sketch a conception of truth that, while (by my lights) independently attractive, seems to make it perfectly natural to accept that some truths have true negations. For present purposes, I will assume that the underlying logic is *LP*.[10]

3. AIEHTELA AND AIEHTELANU: A THOUGHT EXPERIMENT

Suppose that, for one reason or another, we decide to revise the syntax of English. In particular, we decide to remove 'is true' (and 'is false') from the vocabulary, and we add the unary predicates 'Aiehtela accepts' and 'Aiehtelanu accepts'.[11]

With syntax modified, we venture to teach our children the language, the proper usage of 'Aiehtela accepts' and 'Aiehtelanu accepts', in effect, the target semantics. Of course, children learn best through pictures, and so we teach them the target semantics by purporting to tell them about Aiehtela's (-nu's) acceptance-behavior.

---

[8] The denotation-theoretic paradoxes seem to require an additional feature, resulting in a dialetheic free-logic. Priest [23] discusses the issues in detail.

[9] David Lewis [18] pulled no punches in saying (in effect) just that.

[10] The assumption, of course, is really that the predicate extension of LP is the underlying logic. See the Introduction for details.

[11] 'Aiehtela' is pronounced eye-ah-*tel*-ah, while 'Aiehtelanu' is pronounced the same but with 'noo' at the end.

lItt

3.1 The Lessons

Aiehtela and Aiehtelanu have the following fundamental characteristics:[12]

» Aiehtela accepts $\underline{\mathcal{A}}$ iff $\mathcal{A}$
» Aiehtelanu accepts $\underline{\mathcal{A}}$ iff $\sim\mathcal{A}$

For example, if grass is green, then Aiehtela accepts 'grass is green'. If Aiehtela accepts that grass is green, then grass is green.[13] If grass is not green, then Aiehtelanu accepts that grass is green; and if Aiehtelanu accepts that grass is green, then grass is not green.

Other important characteristics of Aiehtela(-nu) are:

» Aiehtela accepts $\sim\underline{\mathcal{A}}$ iff Aiehtelanu accepts $\underline{\mathcal{A}}$
» Aiehtelanu accepts $\sim\underline{\mathcal{A}}$ iff Aiehtela accepts $\underline{\mathcal{A}}$
» Aiehtela accepts $\underline{\mathcal{A}} \wedge \underline{\mathcal{B}}$ iff Aiehtela accepts $\underline{\mathcal{A}}$ and Aiehtela accepts $\underline{\mathcal{B}}$
» Aiehtelanu accepts $\underline{\mathcal{A}} \wedge \underline{\mathcal{B}}$ iff Aiehtela accepts $\sim\underline{\mathcal{A}}$ or Aiehtela accepts $\sim\underline{\mathcal{B}}$

In general, we tell our children that the logic underwriting the story of Aiehtela(-nu) is LP (or its predicate extension), supplemented with the foregoing principles and the following further characteristics of Aiehtela(-nu):

» No indeterminacy in the story:
» Aiehtela accepts $\underline{\mathcal{A}}$ or accepts $\sim\underline{\mathcal{A}}$
» Aiehtelanu accepts $\underline{\mathcal{A}}$ or accepts $\sim\underline{A}$

» Exhaustion Principles on *not accepting $\underline{\mathcal{A}}$*:
» If Aiehtela does not accept $\underline{\mathcal{A}}$, then Aiehtelanu accepts $\underline{\mathcal{A}}$
» If Aiehtelanu does not accept $\underline{\mathcal{A}}$, then Aiehtela accepts $\underline{\mathcal{A}}$

The converses are not given! It is not given that, for example, if Aiehtelanu accepts $\underline{\mathcal{A}}$, then Aiehtela does not accept $\underline{\mathcal{A}}$.[14] We emphasize to the children that the conditionals in the foregoing principles are detachable but non-contraposible; they satisfy Modus Ponens but not Contraposition.[15]

---

[12] '$\underline{\mathcal{A}}$' is a name of $\mathcal{A}$, and unless otherwise specified, principles that follow range over all (declarative) sentences of the language.

[13] I will assume that Aiehtela(-nu) accepts 'p' iff Aiehtela(-nu) accepts *that p*.

[14] In effect, these last two principles correspond to Priest's *exhaustion* principles [19]. (I am inclined to think that there is no substantial problem with admitting the converses, but for present purposes I omit them—the children can decide whether to add additional principles later. I briefly take up the matter in s. 5.)

[15] I will skip details of why these constraints are imposed; however, Priest [19] discusses the issues in detail. Details of a suitable conditional are provided by Priest [21], where the invoked 'impossible worlds' are likewise treated as features of the story of Aiehtela(-nu). (For various reasons the conditional also does not satisfy so-called *contraction* principles. Restall [26, 27] gives an excellent discussion of contraction principles.)

3.2 Picturing Aiehtela(-nu)-Talk

So far, the children have been learning the basic inferential moves that govern Aiehtela-talk. In doing so, they rely on a picture that, for the most part, strikes them as perfectly familiar—at least in most respects. After all, the children are familiar with agents *accepting* various claims, and perhaps (to make things vivid) the children picture Aiehtela raising his/her hand to indicate acceptance, perhaps not. In any event, the children rely on the basic principles laid out above, plus their knowledge of the underwriting logic LP, to form a picture on which they rely in their mastery of the language. But not all is perfectly familiar; indeed, the picture is (initially) difficult to retain when a few strange features of Aiehtela(-nu) become evident, notably, a few inconsistencies.

3.3 Notable Inconsistency of Aiehtela(-nu)-Talk

The inconsistency of Aiehtela(-nu)-talk is notable. As far as the story goes, one may be led to say that Aiehtela (similarly, Aiehtelanu) accepts some sentence and its negation. Such an 'event', of course, is hardly puzzling; even the children know that many people accept inconsistencies. Moreover, the children have no reason to think that Aiehtela accepts *observable inconsistencies*—for example, that the cat is on the mat and not. To be sure, the children know to *infer* that the cat is both on the mat and not on the mat if they learn that Aiehtela accepts 'the cat is on the mat' and its negation; however, they will have no reason to think that Aiehtela accepts as much.[16] So, while the possibility of inconsistency—that Aiehtela(-nu) accepts a sentence and its negation—is plain to the children, this alone does not strain against their basic picture.

What might initially dizzy the children is not the mere possibility of inconsistency, as noted above; rather, what might puzzle them are particular inconsistencies that, upon reflection, are forced upon them. As far as the story goes, one may be led to say more than that Aiehtela(-nu) accepts a sentence and its negation; the story, given its construction, may also lead one to say that Aiehtela(-nu) both accepts a sentence and also does not accept it! While the children can understand that, they can hardly picture it, at least initially.[17] But the initial dizziness wears off when one notices the sort of sentences that produce such a 'scenario' and, especially, when one notices the source of one's dizziness—the pursuit of a picture.

---

[16] One might point out that, as far as the story goes, it is at least *logically possible* that Aiehtela(-nu) accepts 'the cat is on the mat' and its negation; and one might (rightly) say that that's puzzling, to say the least! I will briefly respond to this worry in s. 5. For now, the children have no reason to take such a 'possibility' seriously.

[17] In effect, the given 'situation' is what Neil Tennant [28] calls *dizzying*, and it is indeed the 'situation' over which most philosophers respond with a dumbfounded stare.

To begin, such a 'scenario' will be rare; indeed, it will happen only with respect to sentences that arise out of mere grammatical necessity, sentences of the 'Aiehtela'-fragment (not the 'Aiehtela'-free fragment).[18] Example:

(★) Aiehtela does not accept the starred sentence

The revised syntax of English leaves the grammar as it was, and so 'linguistic spandrels', such as the starred sentence, automatically arise in the language.[19] Given the rest of the story, we are led to say *that Aiehtela accepts the starred sentence and that Aiehtela does not accept the starred sentence.*[20]

The children are puzzled: 'What scenario is described by the conjunction of the starred sentence and its negation?' Offhand, an answer is hard to see. But that is precisely the problem: the children are struggling to *see* the contradiction.

What the children need to do is distinguish the picture on which they rely in learning (and continuing to use) the language, and the language itself. Given the grammar, sentences such as the starred sentence are inevitable. Given the 'semantics' (the basic rules governing the relevant terms), the resulting inconsistency is likewise inevitable. What the children need to learn is that while much of the language can be pictured (e.g. in terms of agents 'really' accepting claims, etc.), some of it—due to the noted spandrels—cannot, at least not in full.

That said, there is a way of picturing the given inconsistencies, if the children persist in their picturing pursuit. The way to picture the (starred) inconsistency is simply to choose a proper part of its consequences. Reflection on the basic construction immediately lends a hand. Recall, for example (s. 3.1), that if Aiehtela does not accept $\mathcal{A}$, then Aiehtelanu accepts $\mathcal{A}$. With this in mind, one soon finds a picture: The starred inconsistency is a situation in which *both* Aiehtela and Aiehtelanu accept the same sentence—namely, the starred sentence. That's all that need be pictured (if one insists on picturing at all).

One of the children will protest: 'But we still have it that Aiehtela does *not* accept the starred sentence—and yet does! That Aiehtelanu also accepts the starred sentence does not resolve the basic dizziness!'

By making the same protest the children get the same response: We reply by pointing out that the starred sentence and its negation are equivalent sentences (given the basic construction)—in the sense that each entails the other, given the

---

[18] By *'Aiehtela'-fragment* I mean all those sentences in which 'Aiehtela' or 'Aiehtelanu' is used (as opposed to mentioned).

[19] Spandrels of x are inevitable (and frequently unintended) by-products of introducing x into some environment. Evolutionary spandrels [17], for example, include the 'V'-shape between human fingers, which was not itself selected by Mother Nature but, rather, is the inevitable by-product of other selected items (fingers with such and so an evolutionary role). Liar-like sentences are spandrels of introducing a predicate to serve the expressive role (perhaps among other roles) that 'is true' has typically been taken to serve. I think that the idea of semantic spandrels is useful, but I will not dwell on it here. (Since writing this chapter I have invoked the notion of linguistic spandrels in other work [2, 10].)

[20] A similar sentence with respect to Aiehtelanu is 'Aiehtelanu accepts this sentence', where 'this sentence' is used to denote the mentioned sentence.

underlying logic. Accordingly, if one persists in trying to picture what is 'described' by the starred inconsistency, a fix is available: Just *choose* one or the other (equivalent) conjunct and Aiehtelanu's acceptance of the starred sentence! What is important for the children to learn is that there is nothing in the construction—or, for that matter, in principles of rationality—that compels them to picture both (equivalent) conjuncts. (They're the ones persisting in pictures!) If a picture is wanted, then one may take the most obvious one: a situation in which both Aiehtela and Aiehtelanu accept the starred sentence.

Admittedly, the story (its overall construction) still forces one to conclude that Aiehtela both accepts and does not accept the starred sentence but, as above, the 'situation' so described is merely one in which both Aiehtela and Aiehtelanu accept the starred sentence—at least, there is no reason to think otherwise, if one need try to picture the matter at all. That the 'situation' at issue is also described via the strange conjunction of the starred sentence and its negation is merely a matter of the grammar and the story's construction; the same situation has a friendlier paraphrase—that both Aiehtela and Aiehtelanu accept the starred sentence. Practicing such paraphrase is helpful in the face of 'spandrels', especially when learning the workings of the language.

3.4 Finishing Up the Lessons: The 'Nature' of Aiehtela

So goes the general story that we tell our children by way of teaching them English. Our children, of course, might immediately ask after Aiehtela(-nu)—what s/he's like, where s/he lives, and so on. Inasmuch as we are teaching them the language (as opposed to teaching them philosophy), we should avoid the question, perhaps noting that, in terms of its linguistic role, 'Aiehtela(-nu) accepts' is an expressive device, one that affords generalizations that, for practical reasons, we couldn't otherwise make. Along this line we may point out that without 'Aiehtela(-nu) accepts' we couldn't (in practice) express what we express by generalizations such as

> » Aiehtela accepts everything that Santa says
> » Aiehtelanu accepts most things the Grinch says

and so on.

To be sure, the children will no doubt press the point; they will strive to discover the 'nature' of Aiehtela(-nu). But such questions—questions beyond the linguistic role of 'Aiehtela accepts'—are best left to metaphysics; and that is a subject the children can best pursue only after mastering usage.

3.5 Paraconsistent Logic

The story of Aiehtela's (Aiehtelanu's) acceptance-behavior, as given above, relies on a paraconsistent logic; and I have chosen Priest's LP. In what follows (s. 4),

I will continue to assume a paraconsistent logic, and indeed continue to assume LP (properly extended to the predicate level, with appropriate axioms governing a distinguished truth predicate). That said, there is no a priori reason that Aiehtela-talk (or the like) need be coupled with a paraconsistent logic.

Consider a different version of the Aiehtela story, one in which not everything is determinate. One might, for example, construct a gappy story—an incomplete story, one in which, say, there is some sentence such that Aiehtela neither accepts it nor its negation. Such options (and more) are open to the sort of conception that I will sketch; however, for present purposes, I will continue to rely on an inconsistent (but non-trivial) construction.

There are two reasons for relying on the paraconsistent construction. The first is that, as in s. 1, part of my aim is to advance a conception of truth in which dialetheism is perfectly 'natural'. The other reason, closely related to the noted aim, is that a gappy construction is not likely to deal with the paradoxical 'spandrels' as easily or simply as a dialetheic approach. Most of the gappy approaches falter on familiar problems of expressibility.[21]

4. CONSTRUCTIVE (METHODOLOGICAL) DEFLATIONISM

In this section I sketch the target philosophical conception of truth, where (as above) the formal theory—the logic—is as per LP-based truth theory [19]. The conception is best illustrated via a few further observations on Aiehtela(-nu).

4.1 Truth and Aiehtela(-nu)

Begin with a few key observations (with some redundancy):

» Actual truth-talk is perfectly mirrored by Aiehtela-talk: The linguistic role of 'is true' and 'is false' are achieved by 'Aiehtela accepts' and 'Aiehtelanu accepts', respectively

» Setting the 'nature' question aside, there is no apparent difference between the (naïve) 'story of truth' and the 'story of Aiehtela(-nu)', at least none that is reflected in linguistic practice

These observations, I should think, are both uncontroversial and unsurprising, given the construction of the Aiehtela(-nu) story. Were it not for the 'nature' question, there would be little reason to treat the 'story of truth' and the story of Aiehtela(-nu) differently.

---

[21] Hartry Field's recent work [16] *may* be an exception. Even so, Field's work, while elegant in many respects, is certainly more complicated than the simple theory afforded by, say, LP. Unfortunately, this is not the place for an adequate discussion of Field's relevant work.

4.2 Setting 'Nature' Aside

The question is: Should the 'nature' question be set aside? By my lights, there is good reason for doing so, namely, a familiar argument advanced by deflationists:[22]

1. Invoke Ockham: Given two hypotheses that equally well explain the data, go for the simpler one.
2. Datum: The disquotational features of 'is true' appear to explain all relevant fragments of truth-talk; no apparent explanatory value is added by positing that truth has a 'robust nature'.
3. Hence, pending good reason to go beyond a conception of truth according to which it is merely an expressive device, it is reasonable to set 'nature' questions aside—questions that go beyond the expressive role of 'is true'.

I endorse that argument, and also endorse the further (familiar) point that theories of 'robust truth' remain either elusive or unmotivated.[23] The upshot is that, as with the children and their questions, the 'nature' question should be set aside, pending some good reason for pursuing it.

4.3 The Upshot: Truth—As If

But now we are back to the striking similarities between truth-talk and Aiehtela-talk. Both ways of talking perform precisely the same function: both afford generalizations that, in practice, we could not otherwise express. The question is: In the face of such similarity, is there any reason to treat the 'story of truth (and falsity)' as significantly different from the story of Aiehtela(-nu)? By my lights the answer is: No.

Granted, when one uses 'Aiehtela accepts' to achieve the same expressive effects achieved by 'is true', one is intentionally engaged in *as if* thinking or, as I will say, *construction*. The situation appears to be different with one's usage of 'is true'. One never thinks of oneself as being engaged in 'construction' when one uses 'is true'. But there is a simple explanation for that: nobody (now) *needs* to construct truth given that it has already been constructed, and one accepts and uses the construction.

Consider, again, the thought experiment in s. 3 Suppose that *you* were one of the children in the thought experiment. Suppose that the syntax with which you grew up never contained 'is true' or 'is false' but contained only 'Aiehtela accepts' and 'Aiehtelanu accepts'. As you mastered the language, your Aiehtela-talk would be precisely the same as your truth-talk actually is. Moreover, *you* would not see 'Aiehtela theory' as a construction—at least not immediately. Of course, at

---

[22] Indeed, the following argument is the *only* argument for deflationism, as far as I know and as far as I can imagine.

[23] To be sure, some will say that the motivation is provided by sheer intuition of a 'correspondence'. I share the intuition, but I think that the argument above suitably calls the intuition into question.

some stage you would confront the question: Does Aiehtela exist? Presumably, you would answer 'no'. (Being competent in the language, you would also say that Aiehtela accepts that Aiehtela doesn't exist.) On reflection, then, you would say that the story of Aiehtela is a *construction*—a useful, inconsistent (but non-trivial) construction.

My suggestion is that truth be seen in the same fashion. We could, *without loss*, exchange truth-talk for Aiehtela-talk; and, pending good reason to posit 'robust nature' into such talk, parity of reasoning suggests that we see the two ways of talking in like manner—that the story of truth (falsity) is as constructed as the story of Aiehtela(-nu). There is no significant difference between the two ways of talking. In one case we are conscious of 'constructing' the story; in the other case we are not conscious of any constructive efforts because that story was already constructed.

4.4 The Target Conception

The target conception of truth is (for lack of a better term) *constructive (methodological) deflationism*.[24] The terminology is motivated thus:

» *Constructive*, because the attitude takes seriously the idea that truth (or 'is true') is a construction—a constructed *instrument*.[25]

» *Deflationism*, because the attitude seems to be deflationary, at least in spirit—and likewise seems to satisfy the criteria of deflationary conceptions of truth.[26]

» *Methodological*, in the footsteps of Field [13]. As in the thought experiment, our children (as it were) must decide how seriously to take *further questions* about Aiehtela—questions that go beyond the basic, disquotational nature of 'Aiehtela accepts'. With Field, it strikes me as a sound methodological principle to address such questions only if there is strong reason to do so.

---

[24] For convenience I'll use 'CMD' as an abbreviation of 'constructive (methodological) deflationism'.

[25] I would call it a *fiction* but I fear that that might confuse the issue, given the many fictionalisms of today. If the conception is treated along standard fictionalist lines, then further such fictions will be required to explain what it is to be a *fiction*. For now, I am simply discussing an *attitude* or *conception* of truth.

[26] Note that, as told, the story of Aiehtela(-nu) does not afford the intersubstitutivity of 'Aiehtela accepts $\mathcal{A}$' and $\mathcal{A}$. Such intersubstitutivity can be achieved by stipulating that the converses of the 'Exhaustion principles' governing acceptance-behavior (s. 3.1) are part of the story. Those, such as Field [13], who insist on such intersubstitutivity, might not call the present conception *properly deflationist*. While I will not argue the (terminological) point here, I should note that, by my lights, what is sufficient for deflationism is that all relevant uses of 'is true' be explained in terms of the basic disquotational features of 'is true', and on the surface, it seems that the Aiehtela story *as given* will provide the requisite explanations. (I briefly take up a related point in s. 5. I should also point out that, ultimately, I am happy to have the intersubstitutivity, and indeed endorse it [7].)

4.5 Paradox and the Virtues of CMD

I tie CMD to dialetheism—formally, to an LP-based theory of truth. As above, the constructive (methodological) deflationist *needn't* couple her position with a paraconsistent logic; however, as I use the term I shall (for present purposes) so tie it. Those who would divorce CMD from an LP-based formal theory will not be able to enjoy all the virtues listed below (chiefly, ones that piggy-back on the dialetheic solution to paradox). Some of the notable virtues are as follows:

» CMD enjoys the simplicity of a dialetheic solution to truth-theoretic paradox, and other related paradoxes.[27]

» CMD puts the burden on those who would insist that *no contradiction could be true*. After all, if truth is a mere (human) construction, introduced to play a given expressive role, then it is not surprising—indeed, it is likely—that the construction should turn out to be inconsistent.

» CMD affords easy sense of 'true contradictions': They are mere residue of the construction that, without loss, may be translated into the corresponding Aiehtela-talk.[28]

» CMD, like any version of dialetheism, enjoys a *complete* story of truth!

I think that there may be other virtues of (dialetheic) CMD that, irrespective of the paradoxes, make it attractive; however, I will leave those virtues for another (and larger) project. For now, by way of clarifying the sketch, I turn to a few questions, objections, and replies.

5. QUESTIONS, OBJECTIONS, AND REPLIES

QUESTION: What is a construction?

REPLY: A construction is a story that we make up (that we construct), usually for some given purpose. Some constructions may be true; some false. Any fiction is a construction; however, the converse isn't true, since (as the term is generally used) no fiction is true.[29]

---

[27] I will not cover the details here but CMD is intended to apply to naïve sets and denotation: a similar 'constructive' attitude is taken towards such 'stories'.

[28] Some philosophers complain that it makes no sense to say that $\lambda = `\lambda$ is not true' is both true and not true. (I take Tennant's 'dizzying' charge [28] to be an example.) Given CMD, the complaint vanishes upon paraphrase: λ specifies whatever 'situation' is specified by the starred sentence, given that 'is true' and 'Aiehtela accepts' have the same semantics; hence, the 'situation' described by λ is one described by the starred sentence—one in which both Aiehtela and Aiehtelanu accept the same sentence. That, as the children recognize, makes perfect sense.

[29] That is not to say that a proper part of a fiction cannot be true; it can be—just add the story of Santa to any set of true sentences.

OBJECTION: You claim that λ = 'λ is not true' and the starred sentence specify the same 'situation', but λ says nothing about Aiehtela or Aiehtelanu, and the starred sentence says nothing about λ. Hence, they don't say the same thing and, in turn, the 'friendly' way to understand the conjunction of λ and its negation disappears.

REPLY: The idea is that instead of modifying the syntax of English by getting rid of 'is true' and 'is false' we supplement it with 'Aiehtela accepts' and 'Aiehtelanu accepts', and in turn provide the discussed semantics. The result is that Aiehtela accepts λ iff Aiehtela accepts the starred sentence iff Aiehtelanu accepts the starred sentence. Accordingly, there is no reason not to paraphrase in the 'friendly' way: The conjunction of λ and its negation is a grammatically strange way of describing the 'situation' in which Aiehtela accepts the starred sentence (or accepts λ, for that matter) and Aiehtelanu accepts the same. Of course, one need not seek 'friendly paraphrase' if one is not already seeking to *see* a 'situation specified' by λ or the starred sentence (or their ilk). If one takes a properly constructive view towards 'is true', then one will not be dizzied by the given inconsistencies; such dizziness, it seems to me, arises from taking the 'picture of truth'—a 'real property' that 'attaches' to some claims and not to others—too seriously. To be sure, we speak *as if* there were such a property, and doing so is valuable, if only for purposes of mastering the language. But, as above, my suggestion is that such talk is merely *as if.*

QUESTION: LP has models in which *all* sentences are true (or designated); hence, taking our models as guides to what is logically possible in the language—to what is possible as far as the logical constants go—we are led to admit the logical possibility of *observable* inconsistencies (like the cat being on the mat and not). In Aiehtela-talk, we're forced from the start to admit the logical possibility of Aiehtela's accepting 'the cat is on the mat' and its negation; hence, given the construction, we're led to accepting the logical possibility of the cat's being on the mat and not. No 'friendly paraphrase' helps us there.

REPLY: I agree that no friendly paraphrase is available in the given sorts of (observable) cases—the cases that (allegedly) arise from the 'Aiehtela'-free fragment and LP-semantics. But there are a variety of ways of avoiding recognizing such a possibility. Here, I mention one option, which I favor.[30] Suppose that we take the naïve view of logical possibility seriously, so that our models 'match up' with logical possibility. One way of avoiding the trivial case in LP (the model in which every sentence is designated) is to divide one's atomic sentences into disjoint sets,

---

[30] In [5] I discuss the issue further, outlining viable ways of avoiding taking 'observable contradictions', or even the logical possibility of such beasts, seriously. I should note that my suggestions all go decidedly against Priest's position [22], who thinks that dialetheists of any stripe must take the possibility of 'observable contradictions' seriously, and also against Beall [6], who at an earlier stage likewise took such 'possibilities' seriously.

informally, the observables and unobservables. Let LP-valuations be as before, but now impose a further constraint on *admissible* valuations: An admissible valuation never takes an 'observable' atomic (and, in turn, no compound) sentence to **b** (no 'observables' are both true and false). This simple tweak changes the language of LP slightly by removing the trivial case (and any metatheoretical proofs that rely on the trivial case); however, the basic logic remains the same. With that in hand, there is no need to recognize the 'logical possibility' of observable inconsistencies. (Obviously, there are other options. But for a variety of reasons, I prefer this one.)

OBJECTION: Aiehtela does not exist. We all agree with that. We can also agree to *talk as if* there is a being, Aiehtela, who accepts $\underline{A}$ iff A, and so on for Aiehtelanu and the other constraints on the 'story'. In so agreeing—agreeing to engage in *as if*—we thereby achieve a device, 'Aiehtela accepts', that plays precisely the role of 'is true'. But we do *not* speak in an *as if* fashion when we use 'is true'!

REPLY: We seem not to treat 'is true' in an *as if* manner. We seem to treat 'Aiehtela accepts' in an *as if* manner. But this difference, as mentioned above (s. 4.3), is not telling. The claim of CMD is that truth *can and ought* to be seen in an *as if* manner, at least in one important respect: there is as much to truth as there is to Aiehtela. The heart of CMD is that truth-talk is fundamentally no different than Aiehtela-talk—except that in the latter case we are conscious of our *as if* attitude. Each 'story' was constructed to yield a device of generalization—a way of saying things that *in practice* we otherwise could not say.[31] But for our firm entrenchment in the 'story of truth' we would be aware of *as if* efforts; at least, there is no reason to think otherwise, according to CMD.

QUESTION: Does a constructive (methodological) deflationist claim that truth itself doesn't exist?

REPLY: CMD puts the point thus: We talk *as if* there is a property of truth, but there is no reason to think that truth has anything beyond this 'as if' status—anything beyond the status of Aiehtela.

QUESTION: There's a sense in which every predicate has been 'constructed', in that we have constructed 'is tree' to pick out trees, 'is a cat' cats, and so on. Similarly, any predicate (or name, or the like) is an 'instrument' in the sense that we use them— we use 'is a cat' to pick out cats, and so on. The constructive (methodological) deflationist thinks that 'is true' (and similarly 'denotes', 'extension') are *constructed* but other predicates are not. What is the special sense of 'constructed' (similarly,

---

[31] Of course, the *methodological* character of CMD reminds that such claims are defeasible: should there be good reason to think that more than Aiehtela-talk, more than the basic disquotational features of truth, is required to explain relevant features of truth-talk, then that will be the end of CMD and, at the same time, a very important discovery. But until then …

'instrument') along which 'is true' (or the like) is constructed but 'is a cat' and most other predicates are not?

REPLY: A better answer than I will give here deserves to be given, but for now the answer is along the lines of the previous reply. 'is a cat' was introduced to pick out something that was already there, as it were. While we talk as if there were cats, we also have reason to think that the status of cats goes beyond Aiehtela. Truth (denotation, extension) is different. And that, for now, is the test: if there is good reason to think that the status of $\mathcal{J}$s goes beyond that of Aiehtela, then 'is an $\mathcal{F}$' is not constructed—not 'just an instrument'—in the target sense.

OBJECTION: How are the principles governing the story of Aiehtela(-nu) to be understood? Is it that all such principles are prefixed by an *According to the story*? If so, then 'Aiehtela accepts' will not function as CMD claims—as the given sort of expressive device. While there are ways of fiddling with where to put *according to the story*, it is difficult to see how any of them will yield the required results.

REPLY: 'According to the story' is attached to Aiehtela-talk in just the way that 'According to the theory' is (implicitly) attached to truth-talk. The difference between the two ways of talking has already been noted: in only the former case are we aware of our *as if* efforts. That said, the objection is important; it brings out a defect in the way the thought experiment (s. 3) was expressed. A better way of putting the thought experiment is to avoid the qualifier 'According to legend': Just tell the children about Aiehtela and Aiehtelanu, and tell them that they learn about what Aiehtela accepts by heeding the given logic LP and *finding out about the world*. (They learn that Aiehtela accepts *that grass is green* when they learn that grass is green.) What is important is that the children learn the language—that they learn to make the proper inferential moves. Of course, at some point, they will realize that Aiehtela-talk is a convenience brought on by our finitude (God could do without Aiehtela-talk); and they will realize that in fact there is no Aiehtela at all, but that we none the less can—and, for practical purposes, should—continue to 'talk about Aiehtela'.

OBJECTION: Perhaps deflationists, properly so called, need not retain the intersubstitutivity of 'Aiehtela accepts $\mathcal{A}$' and $\mathcal{A}$ (or the corresponding 'true' versions); however, such intersubstitutivity has been a definitive mark of standard deflationism. Suppose that such intersubstitutivity is sanctioned by CMD (i.e. the converse of Exhaustion is part of the Aiehtela story). Now an immediate problem emerges: the 'friendly' paraphrase of 'true contradictions' disappears! The children ask: What situation is described by the conjunction of the starred sentence and its negation? The answer (above) was that the starred sentence and its negation specify only a perfectly understandable situation: one in which both Aiehtela and Aiehtelanu accept the same sentence. But given the intersubstitutivity of 'Aiehtela accepts $\mathcal{A}$'

and $\mathcal{A}$, we have all of the following:

» Aiehtela does not accept the starred sentence
» Aiehtela accepts the starred sentence
» Aiehtelanu accepts the starred sentence
» Aiehtelanu does not accept the starred sentence

The upshot: one is without warrant in saying that the situation specified by the starred sentence and its negation is simply one in which both Aiehtela and Aiehtelanu accept the same sentence (namely, the starred sentence). After all, there's just as much reason to say that the situation specified by the starred sentence and its negation is one in which *neither* Aiehtela *nor* Aiehtelanu accepts the starred sentence. But *that* is confusing—as we already have it that for any sentence, Aiehtela (-nu) accepts it or its negation. Hence, given intersubstitutivity, such 'friendly paraphrases' are either unwarranted or unfriendly (difficult to make sense of).

REPLY: Suppose, as per the objection, that we do have the given intersubstitutivity. As far as the construction goes, the starred sentence yields that Aiehtela(-nu) both accepts and does not accept the starred sentence. That, as the objection notes, is hardly 'friendly'. But friendliness returns when one recalls the constructive character of Aiehtela-talk (truth-talk). According to CMD, such talk is a construction of (expressive) convenience, and the starred sentence a mere spandrel of the construction. As *users* of the construction we have freedom to resolve the puzzling features in a variety of ways, at least given the equivalences afforded by intersubstitutivity. In particular, we are free to say that the only situation specified by the starred sentence and its equivalences is one in which both Aiehtela and Aiehtelanu accept the starred sentence—and that's that. Humans have a penchant for privileging the positive, and for that reason I suggest that the situation specified by the starred sentence and its negation is merely one in which Aiehtela and Aiehtelanu accept the starred sentence. The construction itself also warrants the negative: that neither Aiehtela nor Aiehtelanu accepts the starred sentence. The point is that, given the constructive character of Aiehtela-talk (truth-talk), and the spandrel-like character of the starred sentence, and the noted equivalences, one can go either route. To be sure, the rules of the construction still instruct one to infer that Aiehtela(-nu) both accepts and does not accept the starred sentence; however, one is free to take that assertion to specify merely the 'friendly' situation in which both Aiehtela and Aiehtelanu accept the same sentence.

6. CONCLUDING REMARKS

In this chapter I have sketched what I call *constructive (methodological) deflationism*, a view that takes seriously the constructive 'nature' of truth while, as a methodological principle, eschewing questions about truth that go beyond its expressive role. The constructive element of the position affords the option of constructing equivalent devices, such as Aiehtela(-nu), that are seen to be of the same essential status as truth itself—nothing more nor less than (constructed) devices that serve important practical purposes.

While CMD need not be tied to paraconsistent logic or a dialetheic approach to paradox, the position, as I advance it, is one in which the two are tied. Accordingly, the fruits of a dialetheic solution to paradox are enjoyed, but the enjoyment goes both ways. In particular, the *constructive* aspect of truth makes it natural to think that truth is inconsistent—that there are features of the construction that, for one (usually grammatical) reason or another, result in 'contradiction'. Most constructions of the human mind tend towards inconsistency, especially if they aim towards completeness—witness, for example, familiar episodes in the history of mathematics (not to mention semantics). But CMD does not only make the given inconsistency less surprising; it affords the invention of equivalent constructions that are just as 'real' as the original, and in turn affords paraphrases that seem to make easy sense out of the otherwise puzzling 'true contradictions'.

I have not attempted to argue for the ultimate superiority of CMD over rival theories of truth; that cannot be done until further details of the view are worked out—CMD on denotation, naïve sets, and the like. Let further construction commence.[32]

APPENDIX: DEFAULT CONSISTENCY

Most dialetheists, including myself, rely on what is often called the *default consistency assumption*. In effect, the assumption is that classical logic is perfectly reliable *in most cases*. Indeed, by my lights, so long as one is reasoning only within the semantic-free fragment of English (the constructive-free fragment), classical logic is entirely reliable; inconsistency arises only when semantic notions are involved, and even then, it is only 'strange' sentences (spandrels) that engender inconsistency. The question is: How is this default assumption to be made precise?

---

[32] The idea that a sentence might be both true and false occurred to me when, as a graduate student, I was introduced to FDE. I owe a lot to Gary Hardegree and scattered drafts of his work [12] for exposing me (perhaps against his will!) to the idea. Only after I moved to Australia did I realize that Graham Priest and Richard Sylvan had developed the idea, and Priest has been a great colleague (and kindred spirit) since that time. An early draft of this chapter was first presented in Tasmania (Australia) in 1998, and then in Wellington (New Zealand) in 2000; I am grateful to those audiences. For more recent discussion and comments I'm grateful to Brad Armour-Garb, Mark Colyvan, Aaron Exum, Hartry Field, Fred Kroon, Daniel Nolan, Michael Rea, and especially Dave Ripley, who offered detailed comments and very helpful suggestions on later drafts, and (again) Graham Priest and Greg Restall, from whom I continue to learn much. For more recent developments of the 'as if' line, see Beall [4].

The answer emerges from Diderik Batens [3] in the form of what he calls 'adaptive paraconsistent logic'. Adaptive paraconsistent logics are *non-monotonic* logics that are intended to model the default consistency assumption.[33] For present purposes I will present an adaptive version of FDE, and then indicate Priest's minimally inconsistent LP [20], which is a special case of the former. While such adaptive systems have been around for a while, they are still not known as widely as they should be, especially for purposes of thinking about dialetheism. I will not discuss the philosophical import of the following systems; I will simply present the basic ideas.[34]

Adaptive FDE and LP

Adaptive FDE is a non-monotonic logic that reflects a 'default consistency assumption' but, as per FDE, admits gaps;[35] it is a generalization of the gap-free adaptive—or minimally inconsistent—LP [20]. The basic idea runs as follows.

Adaptive FDE

Let v be an admissible *FDE* valuation (as per s. 2) and p any atomic sentence (or propositional parameter). Define $v^\star$, an *inconsistency measure*, as follows:

$$v^\star = \{p : v(p) = \mathbf{b}\}$$

Next, define the following relation on admissible valuations:

$$v_i \prec v_j \text{ iff } v_i^\star \subset v_j^\star$$

We say that v_i is *less inconsistent than* v_j iff $v_i \prec v_j$.

Let $v \models \Sigma$ mean that v is a model of Σ (assigns a designated value to each element of Σ). In turn, define a *minimally inconsistent model* thus:

$$v \models_{mi} \Sigma \text{ iff } v \models \Sigma \text{ and if } v_i \prec v \text{ then } v_i \not\models \Sigma$$

Finally, define *consequence* (and, derivatively, logical truth) in the usual way—'truth-preservation'—over all minimally inconsistent models:

$$\Sigma \Vdash_{mi} \mathcal{A} \text{ iff for all } v, \text{ if } v \models_{mi} \Sigma \text{ then } v \models \{\mathcal{A}\}$$

Adaptive LP

Adaptive LP emerges from restricting attention only to admissible 'gapless' FDE valuations. One defines $\star$ and $\prec$ only over admissible LP valuations, defines consequence as above, but the result is a gap-free logic.

---

[33] A logic is said to be non-monotonic iff $\mathcal{X} \vdash \mathcal{A}$ but $\mathcal{X} \cup \{\mathcal{B}\} \not\vdash \mathcal{A}$, for some $\mathcal{A}, \mathcal{B}$ and set of sentences $\mathcal{X}$.　　[34] Philosophical import is discussed in [19, 20], and related issues in [8].

[35] CMD, as presented above, ignores gaps via its commitment to LP. A version that admits gaps will go with FDE or, perhaps, if the Exclusion constraint on 'Aiehtela accepts' (or 'is true') is dropped (thereby affording the intersubstitutivity mentioned above), FDE supplemented with strong (exclusion) negation, for reasons discussed in [9].

Some notable features

Adaptive *FDE* and *LP* have all sorts of nice features the most important of which is that they nicely 'model' what is meant by *consistency as the default assumption*. The logics reflect the idea that 'classically' valid inferences fail only when inconsistency *forces* the failure.

Consider, for example, an instance of disjunctive syllogism, where p and q are atomic. We have

$$p, \sim p \vee q \Vdash_{mi} q$$

but

$$\sim p, p, \sim p \vee q \nVdash_{mi} q.$$

When the premisses are consistent, classical reasoning suffices; but by adding $\sim p$ to the mix (above), inconsistency results and paraconsistent reasoning is 'called up'—thereby avoiding triviality.

In adaptive LP we have *all* classical tautologies; in adaptive FDE we have none. That situation—with respect to logical truth, or valid sentences—is constant in both the adaptive and non-adaptive versions of these logics. With respect to inference or argument-validity, the non-monotonicity is plain: In the non-adaptive logics, Disjunctive Syllogism is invalid *simpliciter*, but in the adaptive versions the inference fails 'only when forced' by inconsistent premisses. In other words: So long as one is reasoning in a consistent situation, one's default logic may be classical—or as 'classical' as possible, if gaps are involved.

REFERENCES

[1] ALAN ROSS ANDERSON and NUEL D. BELNAP. *Entailment: The Logic of Relevance and Necessity*. Princeton University Press, Princeton, 1975, i.

[2] BRAD ARMOUR-GARB and JC BEALL. 'Can Deflationists be Dialetheists?' *Journal of Philosophical Logic*, 30(6): 593– 608, 2001.

[3] DIDERIK BATENS. 'A Survey of Inconsistency-Adaptive Logics'. In D. BATENS, C. MORTENSEN, G. PRIEST, and J.-P. VAN BENDEGEM (eds.), *Frontiers of Paraconsistency*, 49–73. Research Studies Press, King's College Publications, Baldock, 2000.

[4] JC BEALL. 'Dtruth, Inconsistency, and Belief'. Forthcoming.

[5] JC BEALL. 'Narrowing the Limits of Logical Possibility'. Forthcoming in *Australasian Journal of Logic*.

[6] JC BEALL. 'Is the Observable World Consistent?' *Australasian Journal of Philosophy*, 78(1): 113–18, 2000.

[7] JC BEALL. 'Negation's Holiday: Double-Aspect Dialetheism'. Presented at Philosophy of Logic Memorial Conference (in memory of Graham Solomon) at University of Waterloo, 2003.

[8] JC BEALL. 'Dialetheism and the Probability of Contradictions'. *Australasian Journal of Philosophy*, 79(1): 114–18, March 2001.

[9] JC BEALL. 'Deflationism and Gaps: Untying 'Not's in the Debate'. *Analysis*, 62(4), October 2002.

[10] JC BEALL and BRAD ARMOUR-GARB. 'Should Deflationists be Dialetheists?' *Noûs*, 37(2): 303–24, 2003.

[11] JC BEALL and BAS C. VAN FRAASSEN. *Possibilities and Paradox: An Introduction to Modal and Many-Valued Logic*. Oxford University Press, Oxford, 2003.

[12] J. M. DUNN and GARY HARDEGREE. *Algebraic Methods in Philosophical Logic*. Oxford University Press, Oxford, 2001.

[13] HARTRY FIELD. 'Deflationist Views of Meaning and Content'. *Mind*, 103: 249–85, 1994. Repr. in [14].

[14] HARTRY FIELD. *Truth and the Absence of Fact*. Oxford University Press, Oxford, 2001.

[15] HARTRY FIELD. 'Is the Liar Both True and False?'. In JC BEALL and BRAD ARMOUR-GARB (eds.), *Deflationism and Paradox*. Oxford University Press, Oxford. Forthcoming.

[16] HARTRY FIELD. 'The Semantic Paradoxes and the Paradoxes of Vagueness'. In JC BEALL (ed.), *Liars and Heaps: New Essays on Paradox*. Oxford University Press, Oxford, 2003.

[17] STEPHEN JAY GOULD and RICHARD C. LEWONTIN. 'The Spandrels of San Marco and the Panglossian Paradigm: A Critique of the Adaptationist Programme'. *Proceedings of the Royal Society of London*, 205: 581–98, 1978.

[18] DAVID K. LEWIS. *Essays In Philosophical Logic*. Cambridge University Press, Cambridge, 1998.

[19] GRAHAM PRIEST. *In Contradiction: A Study of the Transconsistent*. Martinus Nijhoff, The Hague, 1987.

[20] GRAHAM PRIEST. 'Minimally Inconsistent LP'. *Studia Logica*, 50: 321–31, 1991.

[21] GRAHAM PRIEST. 'What is a Non-Normal World?' *Logique et Analyse*, 35: 291–302, 1992.

[22] GRAHAM PRIEST. 'Perceiving Contradictions'. *Australasian Journal of Philosophy*, 77: 439–46, 1999.

[23] GRAHAM PRIEST. 'Semantic Closure, Descriptions and Triviality'. *Journal of Philosophical Logic*, 28: 549–58, 1999.

[24] GRAHAM PRIEST. 'Truth and Contradiction'. *Philosophical Quarterly*, 50(200): 305–19, 2000.

[25] GRAHAM PRIEST. *An Introduction to Non-Classical Logic*. Cambridge University Press, Cambridge, 2001.

[26] GREG RESTALL. *On Logics Without Contraction*. Ph.D. thesis, The University of Queensland, January 1994.

[27] GREG RESTALL. *An Introduction to Substructural Logics*. New York: Routledge, 2000.

[28] NEIL TENNANT. 'Critical Notice of *Beyond the Limits of Thought*'. *Philosophical Books*, 39: 20–38, 1998.

13

The Philosophical Basis of What? The Anti-Realist Route to Dialetheism

Jon Cogburn

For Dummettian anti-realists, the claim that meaning is use can be explicated by the following schema, taken to hold over all meaningful sentences and speakers of language.

Recognition Thesis:

X understands P if, and only if, were X presented with a construction c, then X could recognize whether c verifies, and whether c refutes, P

Given that the constructions are assumed to be both necessary and sufficient for truth, the Recognition Thesis is generally taken to entail that verifiability is both necessary and sufficient for truth, which can be stated by means of this schema.

Knowability Requirement:

P is true if, and only if, there exists a construction c verifying P

This requirement lay at the heart of Dummett's demand that constructivist semantics in some manner replace the use of classical model theory as part of the architecture of a natural language grammar. This is because constructivist semantics for intuitionistic logic and mathematics proceed by recursively correlating conditions for the existence of verifying constructions (as opposed to classical, bivalent truth conditions) with sentences of mathematical theories.[1] Thus, a revisionary anti-realist such as Dummett who wants to import the technical apparatus of constructivist mathematics to the realm of natural language semantics needs to motivate independently the necessity and sufficiency of such verifying constructions for the truth of non-mathematical sentences.

In many writings Dummett, Tennant, and Crispin Wright discuss issues concerning language acquisition, normativity, and communication to provide evidence for the Recognition Thesis.[2] However, it is *exceedingly* difficult, both exegetically and philosophically, to discern a valid argument from the Recognition Thesis to a Knowability Requirement.

---

[1] e.g. see the discussion in Dragalin (1980).
[2] See Dummett (1973), part 1 of Tennant (1987), and Wright (1993), esp. 1–43.

The major claim of this chapter is that the Recognition Thesis provides evidence for the Knowability Requirement only if dialetheism is correct. If there are no true contradictions, then the Dummettian Recognition Thesis actually *undermines* the Knowability Requirement.

Those opposed to dialetheism will no doubt view this as an attempted refutation of Dummettian anti-realism. Why shouldn't the Dummettian's *modus ponens* be everyone else's *modus tollens*? Answering this adequately requires: (1) undermining whatever independent reasons for thinking it a *modus tollens*, and (2) providing independent reasons for thinking it a *modus ponens*, in this case by examining in detail a discourse for which dialetheist anti-realism is plausible. In the concluding section of this chapter, I pursue the first of these strategies. However, doing this also allows me to indicate how the second can be successfully accomplished in the case of aesthetic and ethical discourse.

1. A NECESSARY IDEALIZATION

Convincing the Dummettian that dialetheism is true requires re-examining some old positivist distinctions in light of Dummett's dialectic.[3] First we must attend to that between verifiability-in-practice and verifiability-in-principle, with verifiability-in-practice defined as:

> A construction c verifies$_{\text{in-practice}}$ P $=_{\text{def}}$ c is a warrant for P and c can be recognized as such by minimally competent people with little or no idealization of their cognitive capacities or technologies

An example of a sentence with this status is, 'No dog is on this table.' I can currently determine the sentence to be true.[4]

It is not difficult to show that adopting verifiability-in-practice as the notion of warrant mentioned in Dummett's Recognition Thesis leads to absurdity. Since the second conjunct in the definition of verifiability-in-practice concerns how much idealization is required for people to be charged with recognizing a warrant, the appropriate kind of Recognition Thesis would be:

> Recognition Thesis′:
>
> X understands P if, and only if, were X presented with a construction c (where c can be appraised by minimally competent people with little or no idealization of their cognitive capacities or technologies), then X could recognize whether c verifies, and whether c refutes, P

---

[3] The canonical discussion of these is in Ayer (1952).

[4] While the distinctions between minimally competent people and incompetent people, and between minimally competent people with idealized capacities and technologies and minimally competent people without idealized capacities and technologies are surely vague, nothing here hinges on them being precise.

The problem is that the condition is trivially satisfied by any sentence whose warrants (both positive and negative) cannot be recognized by minimally competent people with little or no idealization of their cognitive capacities or technologies. For any such sentence, there is no possible world containing a warrant for or against it that can be easily recognized. At best, the speaker is able to recognize failed warrants for the claim. But then the thesis wouldn't distinguish a speaker's grasp of any two sentences with distinct meanings that are both in-practice undecidable.

This result is unacceptable, and should be unacceptable for any clause that is supposed to provide sufficient conditions for the grasp of a sentence's meaning. For, *ceteris paribus*, if two sentences are different in meaning, and a speaker understands both, then that speaker should know that they are different in meaning.

Thus, if verifiability is to serve as a necessary condition on truth, as it was for Ayer, then verifiability must be in-principle, which can be defined as:

A construction c verifies$_{in\text{-}principle}$ P $=_{def}$ c is a warrant for P and c can be recognized as such by minimally competent people with arbitrarily large but finite idealization of their cognitive capacities and technologies

For example, there are infinitely many simple number-theoretic claims involving large numbers that are unsolvable by human or machine-aided computation and which are therefore not verifiable-in-practice, yet still verifiable-in-principle. Non-mathematical sentences that may be verifiable-in-principle but not in-practice involve, for example, conditions in inaccessible or simply far away regions of space-time.

Clearly, making the Recognition Thesis plausible involves the importing of a similar kind of idealization of the speaker in the antecedent of the counterfactual conditional.

Recognition Thesis″:

X understands P if, and only if, were X's cognitive capacities and technologies finitely extended (in an appropriate manner), and were X then presented with a construction c, then X could recognize whether c verifies, and whether c refutes, P

One might argue that the idealization renders these conditions irrelevant to a speaker's understanding of sentences. What does a possible-world counterpart who can recognize the correctness of huge sums have to do with a speaker's understanding of 'plus'?

Conclusively resolving this issue takes us too far from the task of showing that the Dummettian anti-realist should be dialetheist. However, I don't think that this worry is particularly damning. As long as the idealization is appropriately related to a speaker's actual inferential and evidentiary dispositions as she manifests them, there should be no problem.

In *The Taming of the True*, Neil Tennant suggests how such an idealization can be appropriately limited by the actual behavior of speakers. He gives the constraint in this manner:

(R$_F$) For a speaker S to be credited with a grasp of the meaning of a sentence Φ, we should have good grounds for believing that, if presented with some finite piece of discourse π, S would be able to deliver a correct verdict on any aspect of π that is relevant to arriving at a correct judgement of the form 'π is a proof of Φ' or of the form 'π is a disproof of Φ' or of the form 'π is neither a proof nor a disproof of Φ', that is, for any such aspect α, S would, after some time, be able to judge whether α was as it ought to be, in order for π to have the status in question.   (1997: 154)[5]

It is to be hoped that by adopting something like Tennant's (R$_F$) constraint, the idealization in our final form of the Recognition Thesis can be shown to be non-problematic. Surely something like Tennant's constraint is needed. For example, since a spider's cognitive capacities could be extended enough for it to be a very good checker of real analysis proofs we would thus be forced by an unconstrained Recognition Thesis to say that the spider understands propositions of real analysis.

There are other authorities to whom we can appeal in a further attempt to avoid this problem. It is exactly the problem generative linguists face in their account of tacit knowledge of a grammar.[6] The grammar discerned by the linguist is a 'competence theory', known only to the idealized speaker. This idealized speaker is thought not to be subject to any cognitive shortcomings whatsoever. But then we must wonder what such an idealized speaker has to do with actual speakers. It is via a 'performance theory' that generative linguists are to specify this. The success of linguistic approaches stemming from Chomsky's earlier work provides evidence that this problem is solvable in our context as well.

2. THE DUMMETTIAN CASE FOR VERIFICATIONISM

For semantic anti-realists, the Recognition Thesis explains sentence understanding in terms of how speakers use sentences. The set of dispositions mentioned in the Recognition Thesis are the kinds of practical capacities that Dummett argues must be correlated with the truth conditions generated by a compositional semantics, if we are to explain linguistic competence by the attribution of tacit knowledge of a compositional semantics.[7]

---

[5] Tennant credits me with this idea of carving up a speaker's dispositions into such 'factorizable' chunks (ibid. 153).   [6] See Chomsky (1969) for the canonical discussion.
[7] See especially Dummett (1973) and (1975).

To determine precisely how verificationism is to follow from the Recognition Thesis we must focus on one half of the biconditional composing the Knowability Requirement. We can give this principle as:

Verification Constraint:

If P is true, then P is verifiable

Here we are solely concerned with the proper notion of 'verifiable' occurring in the Verification Constraint, given that the Verification Constraint is supposed to follow from the Recognition Thesis. The substantive conclusion of this section will then be that it is not the case that a claim can be verifiable in the sense mentioned in the Recognition Thesis without also being verifiable in the sense mentioned in the Verification Constraint.

Due to the ambiguity of 'verifiability' we should stipulate some notational conventions at the outset. 'P is verifiable' means it is possible that P be verified. What is the strength of this possibility? In a sense, it is clearly possible to verify 'Cows fly', because we would be able to recognize flying cows as verifiers for the sentence. However, in another sense, it is not possible to verify that cows fly because we're not going to run into any flying cows. We can disambiguate these two modals in the following manner.

$\Diamond \exists c(VcP) =_{\text{def}}$ In some possible world there exists a construction c that verifies P

$\Diamond VP =_{\text{def}} P$ is verifiable in the sense explicated by $\Diamond \exists c(VcP)$

$\exists c(VcP) =_{\text{def}}$ In the actual world there exists a construction c that verifies P

$VP =_{\text{def}} P$ is verifiable in the sense explicated by $\exists c(VcP)$[8]

For what follows it is important to note that in the Recognition Thesis as given the constructions in question are possible constructions, as they are mentioned in the consequent of a counterfactual conditional.

The anti-realist's argument for the Recognition Thesis entailing the Verification Constraint begins with the assumption that there exist absolutely undecidable sentences, that is, sentences for which no possible verifications or falsifications exist. Then the worry concerns how to individuate the meanings of such sentences. If sentences' meanings are individuated by the set of possible constructions that succeed and fail to verify them, then any two undecidable sentences would have the same meaning.

[8] Another crucially important (albeit not for our purposes) ambiguity concerns the reading of the existential quantifier. When a constructivist such as Dummett claims that something exists, he is claiming that there is a method by which that thing can be found. This is not the case for non-constructivists. In Cogburn (2003) I show Neil Tennant's new argument for intuitionism to equivocate fatally on this very distinction.

Unsurprisingly, the anti-realist does use verification conditions mentioned in the Recognition Thesis to individuate the meanings of sentences, in a manner that can be represented as:[9]

Verificationist Canonicity Requirement:

Two sentences A and B have the same meaning if, and only if, for all constructions c, c verifies A if, and only if, c verifies B, and c refutes A if, and only if, c refutes B

On the assumption that the Recognition Thesis is correct, we do have some evidence that verifying and falsifying constructions provide such a canonical manner to individuate the meanings of sentences. If two sentences are different in meaning, and a speaker understands both sentences, then the speaker should know that they are different in meaning. However, if the anti-realist's identity criterion for meanings is false, then the Recognition Thesis entails that a speaker can understand two sentences distinct in meaning and still remain unaware that their meanings are distinct. Thus, on the assumption that grasp of meaning of two sentences different in meaning is sufficient for recognizing that they are distinct in meaning, we can conclude that criteria for grasp of meaning ought to individuate meanings as well.

Now note that an undecidable sentence is such that no constructions verify or falsify it. But then any two undecidable sentences have the same set of possible verifiers and falsifiers, the empty set. So if the Verificationist Canonicity Requirement is correct, then it follows immediately that any two undecidable sentences have the same meaning. At this point the anti-realist reasonably asks what possible use for communication such sentences could have. Presumably one who believes that there do exist such undecidable sentences believes we can usefully communicate information with them. But if all such sentences have the same meaning, then (independent of the fact that they are verification and falsification transcendent) it is completely unclear how we could possibly communicate information with them. Thus, pending an answer to this challenge, the anti-realist's commitment to the Recognition Thesis and Verificationist Canonicity Requirement also commit her to the non-existence of absolutely undecidable sentences.

Given our notational conventions, we can formalize this claim about the non-existence of an undecidable sentence as $\forall P \neg (\neg \Diamond VP \land \neg \Diamond V \neg P)$. Note that this does follow logically from verifiability being necessary for truth (The Verification Constraint). One might dismiss this as irrelevant, since we are trying to discern an argument *to* the conclusion that verifiability is a necessary condition for truth. But doing so would involve misunderstanding Dummett's argument.

Dummett's broader dialectic proposes a very specific manner in which the Recognition Thesis can provide evidence for the Verification Constraint. Dummett

---

[9] For the canonical discussion, see Dummett's discussion of Fregean senses in the appendix of Dummett (1975).

was one of the first to argue that there are difficulties in subscribing to the Chomskyan assumption that understanding of a language is in virtue of tacit knowledge of a grammar, where the semantic component of this grammar is understood to be model theoretic.[10] For Dummett, the Verification Constraint is an attempt principally to constrain a semantics, so that it will not violate the Chomskyan assumption. Given this dialectic, the entailment of $\forall P \neg (\neg \Diamond VP \land \neg \Diamond V \neg P)$ by the Verification Constraint can be thought of as providing evidence for the claim that verifiability is a necessary condition for truth.

If the notion of truth determined by our semantics is such that verifiability is plausibly a necessary condition for truth, then we do have assurance that the semantics is appropriately psycho-linguistically constrained, and will not violate the Recognition Thesis. Crucially, this is *inductive* evidence for the truth of the Verification Constraint. Construed *deductively* we have just affirmed a consequent (i.e. 1. The Recognition Thesis implies that there are no undecidable sentences. 2. The Verification Constraint implies that there are no undecidable sentences. 3. The Recognition Thesis is true. Therefore 4. The Verification Constraint is true.). However, this kind of inductive evidence for theoretical claims is the norm in empirical matters. So to the extent that Dummett's broader dialectic is reasonable, we do have real evidence for verifiability being a necessary condition upon truth. Moreover, the kind of evidence in question is of a piece with Dummett's broader claim that a verificationist semantics can be used in a psychologically real theory of meaning, while a classical semantics cannot.

There is an extraordinarily important moral to this (Dummettian) motivation for verificationism. Given that the Verification Constraint is to follow inductively from the Recognition Thesis, then the kind of verifiability in the Verification Constraint must be no more restrictive than the kind of verifiability mentioned in the Recognition Thesis. For example, a Recognition Thesis with Ayer's in-principle verifiability occurring in it provides no evidence for a Verification Constraint that forces verifiability-in-practice as a necessary condition upon truth. That is, there must not be a sentence such that it is verifiable in the sense mentioned in the Recognition Thesis, and unverifiable in the sense mentioned in the Verification Constraint. We would then correctly conclude that the Recognition Thesis did not provide any inductive evidence for the correctness of the Verification Constraint (given that it would contain a stronger notion of verifiability than occurs in the Recognition Thesis). In what follows, 'the inductive constraint' shall be the name of the principle that if a sentence is verifiable in the sense mentioned in the Recognition Thesis, then it is verifiable in the sense mentioned in the Verification Constraint.

This fairly obvious claim, following from reflection on the manner in which the Recognition Thesis provides evidence for the Verification Constraint, is essential to the dialectic of this chapter. From Ayer's considerations, presented in the next

---

[10] Again, see Dummett (1975) and (1976). For a very nice discussion of these issues from within empirical semantics proper, see the relevant discussion in Dowty (1979).

section, we will have that the verifiability appropriate to the Recognition Thesis is, at best, sufficient for dialetheist truth. But then, by the inductive constraint, we shall have shown that the kind of verifiability in the Verification Constraint is at best sufficient for dialetheist truth.

Before establishing this, and ultimately urging dialetheism on Dummettian grounds, we must consider one dialectical move that the opponent of the anti-realist might make at this point. Given that the Verification Constraint motivated by the Recognition Thesis demands only that true claims be verified by *possible* constructions, it might seem obvious that no evidence has been provided for the claim that verifiability is sufficient for *actual* truth. Taking the possible existence of a verifier to be sufficient for truth would yield the following Knowability Requirement.

Knowability Requirement:

P is true if, and only if, it is possible that there exists a construction c verifying P

$(TP \leftrightarrow \Diamond VP,$ or $TP \leftrightarrow \Diamond \exists c(VcP))$

But then, the anti-anti-realist will point out that it is clear that a possible verifier is not sufficient for truth. Does the anti-realist systematically equivocate?

The passage might be motivated by an epistemic understanding of the modal 'is possible'. If 'It is possible that P' were understood as, 'P would be discovered true, were investigation undertaken', then no equivocation has been committed, but in fact we would have both that $VP \leftrightarrow \Diamond VP$, and $\exists c(VcP) \leftrightarrow \Diamond \exists c(VcP)$. Then the Knowability Requirement would be equivalent to:

Knowability Requirement$'$:

P is true if, and only if, there exists a (possibly undiscovered) construction c verifying P

$(TP \leftrightarrow VP,$ or $TP \leftrightarrow \exists c(VcP))$

As far as I'm aware, nobody has argued that the modals should be so collapsed. I conjecture that this is because most of the Dummettian discussion thus far has been about mathematics, where it is not implausible to think that if a claim is possibly true, then it is true, and if a claim is true, then it is necessarily true. If one accepts this, then the above modals do naturally collapse. While such a collapse may thus be motivated for mathematics, it cannot be motivated in the same way for empirical claims, for it is prima facie very plausible to hold that 'cows fly' is verifiable in another possible world (one containing flying cows) and not verifiable in this one.

Luckily, the collapse of the epistemic modal in this context can be motivated in other ways. First, note that the projected collapse is not the equivocation between

VP and $\Diamond VP$, but rather just the entailment of the unmodalized Verification Constraint $(TP \rightarrow VP)$ from the modalized one $(TP \rightarrow \Diamond VP)$. For then, by the transitivity of inference a modalized Recognition Thesis would be sufficient for a non-modalized Verification Constraint. Second, note that it is a short and trivial proof from the premiss $(TP \rightarrow \Diamond VP)$ and $((TP \wedge \Diamond VP) \vdash VP)$ to the needed conclusion $(TP \rightarrow VP)$. Thus, if we can motivate $((TP \wedge \Diamond VP) \vdash VP)$, then the relevant collapse will be secured.

This needed inference is very plausible, for the notion of verifiability we are working with has already been modalized by the move to in-principle verifiability in the previous section. By the considerations of the previous section, VP merely states that there exists a warrant such that someone with arbitrarily large extensions of cognitive and technological resources could correctly assess that warrant as a warrant for P. Now if a claim is true, and it is the kind of claim that we agree could possess such a warrant, it is plausible to think that it does indeed possess that warrant. Given that the person for whom the warrant is accessible can be idealized so much, there's no reason to think that a given true claim would, in the actual universe, possess such a warrant.[11]

3. DIALETHEIST CONSEQUENCES

Here I will show that verifiers in the Recognition Thesis cannot be sufficient for non-dialetheist truth. Then, given the result of the previous section (that the verification conditions mentioned in the Verification Constraint can be no stronger than those in the Recognition Thesis), it will follow that Dummettian anti-realists are committed to dialetheism.

To show this, we must attend to another positivistic distinction, that between strong and weak verifiability. Strong verifiability can be defined in this manner:

> A construction c verifies$_{strong}$ P $=_{def}$ c is an indefeasible warrant for P, i.e. c cannot be defeated by future information in any possible extension of our current state of information

Few propositions can plausibly be argued to be strongly verifiable.[12] While strong verifiability may be defensible as a characterization of some mathematical sentences, it is not very plausible anywhere else. This is because warrants for the truth of most of our beliefs (taken one at a time) can be overturned by future information.

---

[11] The anti-realist's case here is strengthened considerably by having the warrants be something more plausibly accessible to less idealized people. In the concluding section of this chapter I show how the anti-realist dialetheist's warrants are more accessible than the non-dialetheist anti-realist's.

[12] Ayer (1952: 37) actually makes the distinction in this manner, 'A proposition is said to be verifiable, in the strong sense of the term, if, and only if, its truth could be conclusively established in experience. But it is verifiable, in the weak sense, if it is possible for experience to render it probable.'

We must note how untenable strong verifiability renders the Recognition Thesis. For the sake of parsing, we stipulate that 'Understands (S, P)' means that speaker S understands the sentence 'P', 'Finitely Extended (S)' means that the speaker S has sufficiently and reasonably extended cognitive capacities and technologies, 'P [ ]$\rightarrow Q$' means that if P were the case then Q would be the case, and 'Presented with (S, c)' means that the speaker S is presented with the construction c. Then we would have,

> Recognition Thesis (strong):
>
> Understands (S, P) ↔
>   (Finitely Extended (S) [ ]$\rightarrow$
> $\forall c \in$ {indefeasible verifiers}((Presented with (S, c) [ ]$\rightarrow$
> S recognizes whether c verifies, and whether c refutes, P)))

Apart from the question of what S could actually be recognizing in the attitude ascription, the defeasibility of empirical warrants renders this thesis vacuously able to be fulfilled. Thus, for any real warrant P that S is presented with, the rightmost counterfactual conditional will be satisfied, independently of anything about the agent's recognitional behavior.

Ayer was motivated to characterize verifiability in a weaker manner because of the problem with requiring strong verifiability to be a necessary condition for truth. We can characterize Ayer's weak verification as:

> A construction c verifies$_\text{weak}$ P =$_\text{def}$ c is a defeasible warrant for P, i.e. c can be defeated by future information in possible extensions of our current state of information

As with our other modalities, there is significant vagueness here. None the less, weak verifiability is at least prima facie plausible as a necessary condition upon truth.

Likewise, a weak Recognition Thesis is not implausible as a necessary and sufficient condition upon the understanding of a sentence.

> Recognition Thesis (weak):
>
> Understands (S, P) ↔
>   (Finitely Extended (S) [ ]$\rightarrow$
> $\forall c \in$ {defeasible verifiers}((Presented with (S, c) [ ]$\rightarrow$
> S recognizes whether c verifies, and whether c refutes, P)))

With this on the table we can attend to the already established fact that the notion of verifiability occurring in the Verification Constraint must be no more restrictive than that which occurs in the Recognition Thesis, if the Recognition Thesis is to provide evidence for the Verification Constraint. Thus, the weak

Recognition Thesis at best provides evidence for the following restriction upon truth.

Verification Constraint (weak):

If P is true, then there exists a construction c such that c is a defeasible warrant for P

$(TP \rightarrow \exists c \in \{\text{defeasible verifiers}\}(VcP))$

But then our question is simple. Can such defeasible warrants possibly be sufficient for non-dialetheist truth? They cannot.

It is very clear that some claims will be such that they and their negations are both weakly verifiable. For example, consider the historical claim that Caesar prosecuted Gaius Rabirius before Cicero had Cataline's co-conspirators killed. Cicero writes that he did, and this does provide some evidence that Caesar did so; however, Cicero's self-aggrandizing tendencies along with other considerations concerning why Caesar might have done such a thing provide evidence for the claim that Caesar's behavior took place after Cicero had the conspirators executed. Here we have positive evidence both for and against the claim in question. Both considerations qualify as weak verifiers in the sense we have delineated.

Given that there exist sentences which are both weakly verifiable and weakly falsifiable, the following argument shows that the verifiers in the Verification Constraint cannot be sufficient for non-dialetheist truth. Consider the following argument, where 'V_{RT}' means that P is verifiable in the sense of verifiability occurring in the Recognition Thesis, and 'V_{VC}' means that P is verifiable in the sense of verifiability occurring in the Verification Constraint.

1. $\forall P(V_{RT}P \rightarrow V_{VC}P)$ from the inductive constraint
2. $(V_{RT}P \wedge V_{RT}\neg P)$ from defeasibility considerations (for some P)
3. $\forall P(V_{VC}P \rightarrow TP)$ from the Knowability Requirement
4. $(V_{VC}P \wedge V_{VC}\neg P)$ 1,2 universal elimination, *modus ponens*
5. $(TP \wedge T\neg P)$ 3,4 universal elimination, *modus ponens*

I conclude that, in so far as the anti-realist has offered evidence for the Verification Constraint, the notion of verifiability occurring in the Verification Constraint is at best sufficient for dialetheist truth.

4. FURTHER CONSIDERATIONS

If anti-realist dialetheism seems implausible it is almost certainly due to widespread commitment to the view that a warrant for P automatically undermines warrants for $\neg P$. If this is the case, then at best all I have presented is an argument from

Dummettian premises to the (Dummettian)[13] conclusion that bivalence is not a priori assertable.

The resulting non-dialetheist view is, however, unstable. To show this, I will discuss five reasons one should reject the principle that warrants for *P* automatically undermine warrants for ¬*P*. One of these is a *tu quoque* against those moved by truth paradoxes to dialetheism. Two are reasons most compelling to Dummettians, and two I hope are compelling to those with no prior commitment to dialetheism or Dummettian anti-realism.

4.1. One can make a good case that anyone moved to dialetheism about self-referential paradoxes concerning truth should eschew the principle that a warrant for *P* automatically undermines a warrant for ¬*P*. To see why this is the case, let 'W*P*' say that *P* has a warrant sufficient for asserting *P*. Thus, we have:

W elimination:

W*P* ⊢ *P*

Also, given that proof is perhaps the canonical form of warrant, we also have the following transformation rule.

W introduction:

⊢ *P*, therefore ⊢ W*P*

Then, consider the sentence, 'This sentence is not warranted.' Call this sentence '*R*.' '*R*' licenses the following inference.

R substitution:

Q[*R*] ⊣⊢ Q[¬W*R*]

Since '*R*' says '*R* is not warranted,' it follows that in any sentence where '*R*' occurs, one can replace '*R*' by '¬W*R*', and vice versa.

Finally, note that the principle that any warrant for *P* automatically undermines a warrant for ¬*P* yields ¬(W*P* ∧ ¬W*P*), for all sentences *P* and all warrants sufficient for the truth of *P*. Now consider the following demonstration:

1. |W*R*   assumption for ¬ intro
2. |*R*   1 W elimination
3. |¬W*R*   2 *R* substitution
4. |W*R* ∧ ¬W*R*   1,3 ∧ introduction
5. ¬W*R*   1–4 ¬ introduction
6. *R*   5 *R* substitution
7. W*R*   6 W introduction

[13] Albeit, not entirely Dummettian. Intuitionism brooks no counterexamples to the law of excluded middle, as ¬¬(*P* ∨ ¬*P*) is a theorem of intuitionist logic.

8. $\neg\neg WR$ 7 double negation introduction
9. $\neg R$ 8 R substitution
10. $W\neg R$ 9 W introduction
11. $WR \wedge W\neg R$ 7,10 $\wedge$ introduction

This conclusion contradicts the principle that $\neg(WP \wedge W\neg P)$ holds for all P, and hence contradicts the principle that a warrant for P automatically undermines warrants for $\neg P$. Note also how similar this is to the paradox yielded by the liar sentence, 'This sentence is not true.' Thus, one moved to dialetheism by the liar paradox should (absent strong counterarguments)[14] be moved to abandon the disputed principle.

4.2. The warrant paradox would likely carry no weight with the non-dialetheist Dummettian. There are however, strong independent reasons why a Dummettian should eschew the principle that a warrant for P automatically undermines warrants for $\neg P$. Note that, for the dialetheist anti-realist who eschews the principle, truth is equivalent to the existence of a warrant possessing sufficient strength, independent of considerations concerning the existence of strong enough counter-warrants.

On the other hand, the anti-realist who accepts the disputed principle must hold that a P is true if, and only if, there exists a warrant W of sufficient strength for P and there does not exist a warrant W' of sufficient strength for $\neg P$. Crispin Wright (1993: 298–9) actually does defend such a view, in effect hoping to block dialetheism by identifying truth with superassertibility, defined in this manner.

... 'P' is *superassertible* just in case the world will, in sufficiently favourable circumstances, permit the generation in an investigating subject, S, a set of beliefs, $\{B_1, \ldots, B_n\}$ with the following characteristics:

     a   S has adequate grounds for regarding each of $\{B_1, \ldots, B_n\}$ as an item of knowledge.
     b   The status of each of $\{B_1, \ldots, B_n\}$ as an item of S's knowledge will survive arbitrarily close and extensive investigation.
     c   The state of information constituted by $\{B_1, \ldots, B_n\}$ warrants the assertion of 'P'.
     d   The case provided by $\{B_1, \ldots, B_n\}$ for 'P' is not, *in fact*, defeasible; i.e. no $\{B_1, \ldots, B_n, \ldots, B_z\}$ containing $\{B_1, \ldots, B_n\}$ and satisfying (a) and (b) for some S, yet *failing* to warrant 'P' can be achieved in this world, no matter how favourable the circumstances for the attempt.

The benefits of superassertibility should be clear. As with the realist notion of truth-in-a-(classical)[15]-model, dialetheism is prohibited. This being said, for the Dummettian, superassertibility's drawbacks are equally clear.

---

[14] See Goodship (1996) for good reasons to doubt that any such counterarguments can be forthcoming.
[15] See Varzi (1997) for a fascinating discussion of how the dialetheist can still hold that truth-in-a-model is a good model of truth.

If we step back for a moment, we remember that the main Dummettian *animus* concerns claims that are true and such that competent speakers can't recognize them as being true. This *animus* is the basis for both Dummett's critique of the classical model-theoretic account of truth (which he argues to be in tension with the Verification Constraint), and Dummett's hope to replace classical model theory with a semantics that takes verifying constructions as its basic notion (one consistent with the Knowability Requirement).

Note that the Verification Constraint requires that if a claim is true, then it must be possible for a competent speaker to verify that it is true. Now consider what happens when our truth predicate is understood as superassertibility. That is, a competent speaker must be able then to verify that a warrant exists for the claim *and* that no future state of information can overturn the warrant. Competent speakers are now charged with being able to verify something about all possible future states of information. Given this state of affairs, it becomes much more plausible that a claim will be true and unverifiable. Contrast this epistemic situation with that of the dialetheist anti-realist's. For the dialetheist anti-realist the competent speaker need only be able to recognize the existence of a strong enough warrant.

As should be clear, this problem with superassertibility is precariously close to the problem Dummett discerns with classical truth. For Dummett, realist semantics are in tension with the Verification Constraint only because the Verification Constraint is understood to concern the kinds of verification conditions accessible to humans. This is particularly clear in his discussions of the problems that arise in semantically modeling infinity.

The most celebrated example of this way of thinking relates to quantification over finite, surveyable domains by learning the procedure of conducting a complete survey, establishing the truth-value of every instance of the quantified statement. The assumption that the understanding so gained may be extended without further explanation to quantification over infinite domains rests on the idea that it is only a practical difficulty which impedes our determining the truth-values of sentences involving such quantification in a similar way; and, when challenged is defended by appeal to a hypothetical being who could survey infinite domains in the same manner as we survey finite ones. (1976: 61)

Dummett himself goes to great pains to show this to be an illicit move. Even if God does exist, it would

not vindicate the realist's claim that he must know one or the other *from* knowing, of each number, whether it is prime or not. That would follow only if we assume that the infinitely many individual propositions to the effect that a particular number is prime together determine the proposition about prime pairs as true or as false. That, however, is just the question at issue. The realist wishes to attribute to us an understanding of the quantifiers as operators yielding a statement whose truth-value is jointly determined by the individual instances, independently of our means for recognising it as true or false. When the domain is infinite, his opponent denies that we can understand them in any such way: even should an angel inform him that God understands them in that way, he would still deny that *we* can; this would then really be a case of our being unable to understand the thoughts of the Almighty.   (1991: 350)

Thus to one who responds that while classical model theory renders statements over infinite domains undecidable to us but not to God, Dummett has argued that God's ability would then be irrelevant to our understanding of the sentences. Likewise, the dialetheist should argue that the God-like ability to determine whether a claim is superassertible is irrelevant to our understanding of that claim.

4.3. If we attend to the Recognition Thesis, we see another reason why the Dummettian should opt for dialetheist assertibility rather than non-dialetheist superassertibility. One thing we did not address above was the absolutely crucial issue of 'canonical' warrants versus 'non-canonical' warrants, where canonical warrants for a claim are those relevant to the meaning of the claim, and non-canonical are those that are not. Now, consider again our final version of the Recognition Thesis.

Recognition Thesis (weak):

Understands $(S, P) \leftrightarrow$
  (Finitely Extended (S)[ ] $\rightarrow$
    $\forall c \in$ {defeasible verifiers}((Presented with (S, c)[ ] $\rightarrow$
      S recognizes whether c verifies, and whether c refutes, P))).

Assume for a moment that the universal quantifier ranges over all possible verifiers, and not just those relevant to the meaning of P. This would have one of two devastating results for the Dummettian. On the one hand, it might have the result that Sherlock Holmes is the only one that understands the claim that Moriarity murdered Watson, because only Mr Holmes possesses the deductive and inductive ability to assess the Rube Goldbergish warrants that lead him to verify Moriarity as the murderer.

On the other hand, one might note that the speaker S has been idealized in the antecedent of the counterfactual conditional, and not worry about this. I don't possess Holmes's deductive power, but were my mental capacities finitely extended I would. To see why this is disastrous, (again) consider the spider that would also possess Mr Holmes' deductive power, were his capacities extended. For the Recognition Thesis not to entail that everybody understands everything, the idealization must be appropriately constrained. Moreover, as with Tennant's (R_F), discussed above, the constrained idealization must be grounded in actual dispositions that the speaker possesses concerning the subsentential units of the sentences in question. Accomplishing this requires restricting the universal quantifier in the statement of the Recognition Thesis so that only canonical warrants are ranged over. Otherwise, one would be required by the Thesis to recognize Rube Goldberg warrants, and this would require too much idealization, giving rise to the spider problem.

We are thus again in a position to ask ourselves whether superassertibility is up to the task at hand. It is not. Assume that the Recognition Thesis required speakers to recognize whether a claim is superwarranted or not. The speaker would then have to recognize not only that the claim is warranted, but also that no future state of information will overturn that warrant. Again, too much is being asked of the speaker, who now has to be able to assess all possible future states of information. Moreover, many of the possible future states of information that might (according to the non-dialetheist) overturn the warrant will be irrelevant to the meaning of the claim. Thus, again, the idealization of the speaker will get out of hand, threatening the dreaded collapse, where everyone understands everything. Much better to have just the speaker able to recognize canonical warrants for and against the claim, with the admission that there might be both, rendering the claim true and false.[16]

4.4. It must be admitted that the reasons given thus far for rejecting the claim that a warrant for *P* automatically undermines a warrant for ¬*P* ought only to compel those committed to either dialetheism about some self-referential paradoxes or Dummettian anti-realism about some discourses. What is needed is an independent demonstration that dialetheist anti-realism is a plausible view to take of some discourse.

The Caesar example illustrates this well. There is compelling evidence both for and against the claim that Caesar prosecuted Gaius Rabirius before Cicero had Cataline's co-conspirators killed. For example, Colleen McCullough (1996) argues that if Rabirius' trial occurred after the executions, then all of the following make much more sense: (1) the Centuries' willingness to damn Rabirius, (2) Cicero's early fear of Publius Clodius, (3) Cicero's early hatred of Caesar, and (4) Cicero's later silence about the trial. Nonetheless most historians take Cicero's words to the contrary to be very good evidence too. So here we have evidence both ways, but none of us have the intuition that both Cicero and McCullough can be right.

Of course this does nothing to undermine my argument that the Dummettian anti-realist is committed to dialetheism. Contrarily, I think it *strengthens* it, as one's intuition that there could not be a true contradiction for such a historical claim is arguably precisely the intuition that historical truth is *not* epistemically constrained. Common sense counsels realism here.

Thus, at worst I have raised the inevitable question of whether Dummettian anti-realism is even plausible for discourses with defeasible warrants. This being said, if one does attend to *why* the view seems so implausible in the case of history, I think this worry can be assuaged. With the historical example, we have firm

---

[16] There are subtle *de dicto/de re* issues lurking here. Defending superassertibility requires assuming that the speaker need only recognize that the claim is warranted, and not also have to recognize that the claim is a superwarrant (one that can't be overturned by future information). In a separate paper (working title 'Warrant and Superwarrant,') I argue that this is fallacious.

intuitions about an external world making the claims true or false, independent of whether we are situated such that we can come to know that the claims are true or false.

However, with many other discourses, such as mathematics, ethics, and aesthetics we do not have such firm intuitions about an external world making the claims true or false. With ethics and aesthetics the warrants are highly defeasible as well. Here I would like to suggest that further development of this view will require a detailed examination of normative discourses such as ethics and aesthetics.[17]

Prima facie, things are promising here. In ethics, for example, there are many cases of what seem to be intractable intuition clashes, where very good reasons can be adduced both for and against a given course of action. Sometimes, as with tragic choice situations, one particular action is at issue, such as Pierre's decision of whether he is obligated to take care of his mother or whether he is not so obligated due to an obligation to avenge his brother's death. Sometimes the clash is more general, for example, when there are good arguments for and against certain types of activity such as putting certain kinds of criminals to death. Sometimes the clash is maximally general, for example the disagreement between a consequentialist and deontological account of obligation.

One can respond to these problems by denigrating the objectivity of ethical discourse in one of the familiar ways. The non-cognitivist holds that moral claims are not truth apt. The error theorist holds that moral claims are all false. The relativist holds that they are truth apt, some are true, but that their truth is dependent upon cultural norms. All such positions, in addition to moral realist views that deny the reality of intractable intuition clashes, do violence to the person on the street's view of morality.[18]

Dialetheist anti-realism presents a clear fourth alternative, one that takes seriously the objectivity of ethical judgements as well as the intractability of some intuition clashes. For the dialetheist anti-realist about moral claims, moral claims are truth apt and many of them are true (those with enough warrant). Moreover, their truth is not dependent upon cultural norms. To the extent that it makes sense to talk about a culture's moral values, it is clear that whole cultures have assessed moral warrants incorrectly. The dialetheist anti-realist merely adds to these realist intuitions the admission that sometimes there might be very good, objective, reasons both for and against a claim. In this manner intuition clashes are recognized without any sacrifice to moral objectivity. For example, perhaps it really is the case that one ought to lie in cases where pain is minimized, but at the same time one ought not to lie then because lying cannot be universalized.

---

[17] Brandon Cooke (2002) has made a very compelling defense of dialetheism about some aesthetic judgements. While he does not specifically mention Dummett, the view he defends is a form of dialetheist Dummettian anti-realism about aesthetic judgements.

[18] The classic discussion of the dialectical space surrounding these meta-ethical views is MacIntyre (1997).

Clearly, much needs to be said to develop the view. However, one should keep in mind the clear prima facie implausibility of non-cognitivism, error theory, relativism, and any moral realism that collapses the epistemic status of normative discourses such as ethics with descriptive ones such as history or physics. Given this, the dialetheist anti-realist should be forgiven cautious optimism.

4.5. As a final note, the claim that a warrant for P automatically undermines warrants for $\neg P$ involves an ugly equivocation between not having enough evidence for a claim and having too much evidence for the claim and its negation. For the dialetheist, this is obviously not so. When there is not enough evidence, we can either optimistically wait and hope, or we can decide the claim is neither true nor false. When there is too much evidence both ways, the claim is both true and false.

REFERENCES

AYER, A. J. (1952). *Language, Truth, and Logic*, 2nd edn., New York: Dover.

CHOMSKY, NOAM (1969). *Aspects of the Theory of Syntax*, Cambridge, Mass.: MIT.

COGBURN, JON (2003). 'Manifest Invalidity: Neil Tennant's New Argument for Intuitionism', *Synthese*, 134: 353–62.

COOKE, BRANDON (2002). 'Art-Critical Contradictions', presented at 2002 Alabama Philosophy Society Convention.

DOWTY, DAVID (1979). *Word Meaning and Montague Grammar*, Dordrecht: Reidel.

DRAGALIN, A. G. (1980). *Mathematical Intuitionism, Introduction to Proof Theory*, Providence: American Mathematical Society.

DUMMETT, MICHAEL (1973). 'The Philosophical Basis of Intuitionistic Logic', in Dummett (1978).

——(1975). 'What is a Theory of Meaning? (I)', in Dummett's *The Seas of Language*, Oxford: Clarendon, 1993.

——(1976). 'What is a Theory of Meaning? (II)', in Dummett (1993).

——(1991). *The Logical Basis of Metaphysics*, Cambridge, Mass.: Harvard University Press.

——(1993). *The Seas of Language*, Oxford: Clarendon.

GOODSHIP, LAURA (1996). 'On Dialethism', *Australasian Journal of Philosophy*, 47: 153–60.

MACINTYRE, ALISDAIR (1997). *After Virtue: A Study in Moral Theory*, Notre Dame Ind.: University of Notre Dame Press.

MCCULLOUGH, COLLEEN (1996). *Caesar's Women*, New York: Avon.

TENNANT, NEIL (1987). *Anti-Realism and Logic: Truth as Eternal*, Oxford: Oxford University Press.

——(1997). *The Taming of the True*, Oxford: Clarendon.

VARZI, ACHILLES (1997). 'Inconsistency Without Contradiction', *Notre Dame Journal of Formal Logic*, 38: 621–38.

WRIGHT, CRISPIN (1993). *Realism, Meaning, and Truth*, 2nd edn., Oxford: Blackwell.

14

'To Pee and not to Pee?' Could *That* Be the Question? (Further Reflections of The Dog)

Jay Garfield

According to Chrysippus, who was certainly no friend of non-rational animals, the dog even shares in the celebrated dialectic. In fact, the author says that the dog uses repeated applications of the fifth indemonstrable argument-schema when, arriving at a juncture of three paths, after sniffing at the two down which the quarry did not go, he rushes off on the third without stopping to sniff.

(Sextus Empiricus, *Outlines of Pyrrhonism*, in Mates (1997: 69))

A real live
            barking
                        democratic dog
engaged in real
            free enterprise
with something to say
                        about ontology
something to say
                        about reality
                                    and how to see it

(Lawrence Ferlinghetti, 'Dog,' in Ferlinghetti (1974; 68))

Everything is real and is not real,
Both real and not real,
Neither real nor not real.
This is Lord Buddha's teaching.

(*Nāgārjuna*, MMK XVIII: 8)

This chapter is dedicated to the memories of Alice Ambrose Lazerowitz and W. V. O. Quine, each of whom would be appalled by the extent to which their ideas have led me to these. Thanks to JC Beall for many very helpful comments on earlier drafts of this chapter. He should not be taken to agree with a lot of what I say here, but much of this chapter has evolved in dialogue with him. Thanks also to Mark Colyvan for very helpful suggestions and to two anonymous referees for suggestions that have made the argument clearer.

1. DOWN TO THE CROSSROADS: WHERE WE LEFT THE DOG

In Garfield (1990) we left The Dog at the crossroads, defending his rejection of disjunctive syllogism and the adoption of a relevance logic in the context of the epistemically hostile environment we share with him—an environment in which nature (including The Man—see Anderson and Belnap 1975) places obstacles, both passive and active, in the path along which we pursue the truth. These obstacles, The Dog noted, include both the prevalence of outright deception, passive sources of error and illusion in our environment, and our own cognitive limitations, including pre-eminently our limited memories, limited deductive powers, propensity to fallacious inference, and failure to track the dependencies and sources of our beliefs.

In such circumstances, The Dog argued, idealizations of epistemic subjectivity according to which we are completely consistent, logically omniscient, etc. are irrelevant to epistemology, and the adoption of a logic suited to inferential angels would be *irrational*. *Rational* epistemic subjects, he concluded, adopt less promiscuous logics, logics less likely to lead to spurious error being introduced through inference itself. In Garfield (1990) The Dog argued along the following lines: (1) we inhabit what he called an *epistemically hostile environment*—an environment in which, due to our own imperfections as well as to outright deception we are likely to acquire a great many false beliefs, and in which we are likely to be without information about many matters of importance to us. (2) Rationality is an evolutionary adaptation making us fit for such an environment. (3) Logic is a normative theory of such rationality. (4) Rational inference in the face of epistemic hostility is non-monotonic and relevant.

The argument is thus an extension and development of that in Cherniak (1986), but endorsing a specific kind of logic as a canon of rational inference—relevance logic—and involves a rejection of Harman's (1986) wholesale attack on the centrality of logic to the theory of rationality, while accepting the force of that attack with respect to *classical* logic. The account is at the same time normative—and hence non-psychologistic—and sensitive to the psychology of actual rational organisms. It is an account of the logic appropriate to a Dog, and to any who would count themselves among his best friends. On those grounds, The Dog spurned classical logic for relevance logic, most prominently eschewing the disjunctive syllogism as providing guidance in his pursuit of his master.[1]

Belief revision, on this view, is non-monotonic[2] and so must be its logic. That is why The Dog is right to adopt a relevant, rather than a classical logic. Moreover, where error is likely or inconsistent belief sets are probable, rational inference is driven by *entailment*, and not by truth-functional implication. And epistemic

---

[1] See Garfield (1990: esp. 99–104).

[2] That is, once a belief is added to our belief set, its place is not secure. Further revisions of the belief set may include deletions of previous beliefs as well as additions of new ones.

hostility guarantees the possibility of inconsistent belief sets, *even if the world is consistent.*

Against this background, The Dog now ponders: Will I pee on yonder tree or will I not? Moreover, he reasons, if I *do* pee on yonder tree, I will become famous, inasmuch as I will be The Dog whose pee trumps all other pee. And if I do *not* pee on that tree, I will become famous as The Dog who leaves no sign. He continues to muse: I have excellent reasons to believe that I *will* pee: so many dogs before me have done so, and I *always* pee on such trees. On the other paw, I have *excellent* reasons to believe that I will *not* pee. I've peed so many times today that my bladder is empty, and I know that The Man is well off down the road and needs me. I *never* stop in such situations. Furthermore, this logician among dogs says to himself, I have overwhelming reason to believe the conjunction of any two beliefs each of which I have good reason to believe. What's a dog to believe? Most importantly, *will I become famous?* These musings lead The Dog to wonder: Should I accept violations of the law of non-contradiction (LNC)?[3]

The Man, of course, infamously classical, endorses both the LNC and the law of the excluded middle (LEM). He reasons as follows: We *could* infer from p&¬p that the Dog will realize his ambitions of fame. But then we could infer *anything* from p&¬p, so that conclusion would hardly be warranted on that ground. On the other hand, we know that p∨¬p, and if indeed p and ¬p *each* entail his fame, we can be sure that the Dog will indeed be a dog of renown. The Dog, however, is already wary of *Ex contradictione quodlibet* on relevance grounds and all the more so on paraconsistent grounds. He is also, as we shall see, deeply suspicious of LEM. What is he to think?

2. ARGUMENTS FOR THE TRUTH OF CONTRADICTIONS THE DOG WON'T SWALLOW

We will return to The Dog's epistemic predicament. But first, let us be clear about his ideology. Some (Priest 1987, 2002) argue not only that we are generally prone to inconsistent belief sets but that the world is genuinely contradictory—that there are true contradictions. Now, if The Dog believed this, the answer to his final question would be obvious, as would the way to resolve his perplexities. But The Dog will have none of that. As far as he is concerned, all the plausible cases of true contradictions are either epistemic in character (such as the legal dialetheias or the knower paradox), spurious consequences of bad metaphysics (such as Priest's alleged dialetheias of motion and change), or merely formal (such as the semantic, set theoretic, and logical dialetheias). These contradictions, he thinks, have few

---

[3] The Dog puts it this way because he might well, following Priest (1987: 84–5), recognize that the LNC is true—that is, that its instances are theorems—yet still believe that some of its violations might be true (though also false).

implications, if any, for the empirical world, in which real objects have or lack real smells.

Now the Dog may or may not be wrong about this. We set that aside, as he is a proponent of dialetheic logic *despite* his conservative attitude towards the truth of contradictions. But a few things about his position should be noted: first, while he dismisses epistemic dialetheias as in a certain sense artifactual, we will see that he none the less takes them very seriously indeed, and in fact takes them to motivate his use of dialetheic logic. Second, while he thinks that the moment of change is not paradoxical, he agrees with Priest (1987) that this would be the best case for the truth of *concrete* dialetheias. He just thinks that the argument for Hegelian analysis of change (ibid.) over a Russellian analysis is question-begging. His mind remains open on the question of whether there indeed are any concrete dialetheias. But he doubts it, and in any case they play no role in his own use of dialetheic logic.[4] Finally, The Dog indeed *does* accept the inconsistency of set theory, arithmetic, and indeed of any logic adequate to the theory of truth. And he grants that this would indeed be sufficient to motivate a dialetheic logic. But he recognizes that there are those Men who would do anything to save consistency, including developing baroque semantic hierarchies, tolerating inconsistent metalanguages, etc., and so does not wish to rest his own dialetheism on this formal basis. He would prefer to show that logic itself demands dialetheism, even if the paradoxes can be resolved— even if one keeps all four feet on the ground in one's reasoning, considering only that which one can sniff.

3. EPISTEMIC HOSTILITY AND THE PURPOSE OF LOGIC

The Dog believes that Logic is about inference, about what follows from what, and derivatively even about what follows from *that*. And The Dog thinks that the reason we *care* about what follows from what is that we care about realizing and preserving *truth*, that is, about believing what we *ought* to believe. If this is the case, The Dog realizes, logic is a branch not of mathematics, but of *epistemology*. And the whole point of epistemology is to enable us to generate and to maintain knowledge in an *epistemically hostile environment*. The Dog adopted a relevant logic in recognition of epistemic hostility (Garfield 1990). Recognizing that he might come to believe AvB on the basis of being told A and disjunction-introduction, and recognizing that he might later be told ¬A, given the arbitrariness of B and

---

[4] Vagueness, as Mark Colyvan (pers. comm.) points out, is another plausible source of dialetheias concerning the empirical world. The Dog, however, being rather fuzzy himself, is persuaded that a consistent fuzzy logic will probably sort vagueness out and so that our reasoning about vagueness can proceed without recourse to paraconsistency. He's not sure of this, of course, and his mind is open. But for now, he would like to be conservative, and continues to argue that *even on the assumption that the world is consistent, including the vague parts of the world*, it is rational to *reason* paraconsistently.

the difficulty of tracking the sources of his beliefs, inferring B from AvB and ¬A would be downright *irrational.*[5]

Several components of epistemic hostility emerge from this brief consideration of disjunctive syllogism: first, we cannot be sure that our sources of information are veridical, and even in a consistent *world*, we cannot be sure that our *information* about that world is consistent. Second, our own faculties are fallible, and even given reliable sources we may introduce error into our belief sets through perfectly valid inference coupled with forgetfulness, or indeed, through simple inferential error. It is hence rational to presume that our belief set contains both falsehood and inconsistency and that our quest for truth and for knowledge must always be grounded in a lot of falsehood and error. Rational belief extension will therefore not, in general, be monotonic, and any logic that employs rules that are non-trivializing (that is, that do not permit arbitrary conclusions) only in consistent contexts will be useless as an epistemic tool.

The legal arena, as Priest (1987) notes, provide sample examples. One Florida statute, notes the Florida Supreme Court, requires the election to be certified within seven days of polling. Another permits a challenge to the count up to six days after the poll, and permits a recount if the challenge is well founded. Given that no recount can take less than one day, these laws are patently contradictory given a well-founded challenge. It is both required and forbidden that the election be certified on the seventh day. If either Bush or Gore had reasoned from this contradiction in the law to the truth of his position, on the grounds that $(A\&\neg A)\rightarrow B$, he would have properly been laughed out of court. And this circumstance is familiar in epistemic situations beyond the legal domain.[6]

Logic, then, if it is to play its proper epistemological role, must not only get us from truth to truth but also prevent our going from truth to falsehood, and even more importantly, from unavoidable, justifiedly believed falsehood to *spurious* falsehood. Classical logic, The Dog realized long ago, is far too inferentially promiscuous to fit the bill. Heretofore his tastes have run to relevance logic. But lately paraconsistent logics have drawn his attention. For, he has realized, not only must he avoid irrelevant inferences, but he must worry about inconsistent domains, and simple bivalent relevance logics simply don't have enough truth values to represent the problems posed by his environment.

---

[5] See Garfield (1990: 99–104) for a more extended argument for an epistemic understanding of the role of logic, and see ibid. (104–5) for a detailed discussion of the status of disjunctive syllogism as a legitimate argument form. Finally, see ibid. (105–6) for a consideration of the rejoinder.

[6] Now one might argue that there is in fact no dialetheia here, but rather two classically consistent statements: It is obligatory that P and it is obligatory that not-P, and block the inference from OP and OQ to O(P&Q), or argue that it does not follow from OP and P→Q that OQ. And indeed some deontic logics weaken classical inference schemas in just such ways. But to accept such a weakened deontic logic is already halfway to accepting The Dog's point: A classical logic won't be adequate to deontic inference. The Dog will then argue that he can propose a logic that explains the failure of classical logic in these contexts and adequately captures the relevant inferential relations. (See Priest 1987.)

4. GAPS, GLUTS, AND GLUTTONY

There is an interesting problem The Dog faces, though, and recognizing it will show why LP[7] won't meet his demands, either. His problem is not simply that he is often told contradictory information about the world, and that he loses track of who told him what and when, but also that there are some matters regarding which he is simply ignorant; things about which The Man has told him nothing; things about which he may have been told something once long ago, but when he was gnawing a bone, and not paying attention.

Intuitionists notoriously argue from (a part of) epistemic hostility to the necessity of admitting truth value gaps. Under the influence of intuitionists most Men who have taken epistemic hostility of the world (or, more narrowly, human imperfection) seriously as having consequences for bivalence have taken its implication, if any, to be that we must admit gaps. (Quine 1981; Dummett 1978) The Dog, as we shall see, takes this point. But he regards it as too narrow. Gluts, as well as gaps, are to be swallowed if we are to come to grips with the full epistemic horror of our existence. But let us first consider gaps.

LP maps each wff[8] into a *non-empty* subset of $\{1,0\}$ and Priest offers arguments for this policy. The Dog is skeptical of this policy. He starts from the methodological premiss that it is at least prima facie ad hoc once subsets of $\{1,0\}$ have been identified as the co-domain of the valuation function to exclude *one* of those subsets, namely, ø.[9] So he thinks that any arguments against truth value gaps had better be pretty good. Here is the only positive argument Priest offers:

In a nutshell, if there is no Fact that makes **a** true, there is a Fact that makes ¬ **a** true, viz., the Fact that there is no Fact that makes **a** true.... Suppose that **a** is a sentence, and suppose that there is nothing in the world in virtue of which **a** is true; no fact, no proof, no experimental test. Then this is the Fact in virtue of which ¬ **a** is true. *We may not know that this fact obtains, but this is irrelevant.*   (Priest 1987: 83, italics mine)

I italicize the last sentence, because this is where The Dog sees that the question is begged against him. This lack of knowledge is only 'irrelevant' if *epistemology* is irrelevant to *logic*. The intuition on which Priest trades in dismissing gaps is this: Logic is about the relation between *Truths*, where a *Truth* is a sentence representing

---

[7] The paraconsistent logic of Priest (1987).

[8] Well formed formula (pronounced /woof/) (McLeod, pers. comm.).

[9] JC Beall (pers. comm.) responds that there is nothing more ad hoc about selecting these three subsets from among the four in the co-domain for the range of the evaluation function than there is about selecting only $\{1,0\}$ from the entire set of natural numbers for the set of classical truth values. There is an enormous disanalogy, though, and there is ad hocery in the one case and not in the other. In the case of the selection of the classical truth values, *any* pair of values would do, as they merely code for T and F. To be sure, 1 and 0 are arbitrary choices, but so would *any* pair of numbers. T and F are the *real* choices, and there is nothing arbitrary about *that* choice, misguided though it may be in other respects. In the case of the LP choice to exclude only ø from the power set of $\{1,0\}$ there *is* an element of arbitrariness, for here only *one* of a set of four possibilities is *excluded*, and that despite at least prima facie reasons for its inclusion.

a *Fact*. If A is not a Truth in this sense, ¬A *must* be because either A or ¬A represents a Fact. But this mistakes the place of Logic in human cognitive activity: logic is the canon of inference—the science of what follows from what—and its role is the regulation of the extension of *knowledge*. From the fact that we have no right to assert A or to use it as a premises in reasoning *nothing whatever* follows about our right to assert or to make inferential use of ¬A. It is often the case that it is rational to refrain from assigning a determinate truth value of {1} or {0} to a wff, and hence to assign ø. The epistemic understanding of logic—an understanding Priest curiously otherwise endorses (ibid. 77–80)—hence forces us to swallow gaps.

But of course that does not mean that we do not also find ourselves chewing on a few gluts. When it is rational to accept A and also rational to accept ¬A, it is often, at least *ceteris paribus*, rational to accept A&¬A. And (bracketing for now, as The Dog will, semantics, logic, and set theory, as well as quantum mechanics) in any epistemically hostile environment we will occasionally be forced into such situations. Logic hence must admit contradictions whose truth values include 1, *even if* A *is a prima facie reason to believe* ¬A *and vice versa*. The rational Dog hence adopts a policy of logical gluttony: he accepts both truth value gaps and gluts, and in doing so accepts *all* subsets of {1,0} as falling in the co-domain of the valuation function for his logic.

Fortunately this is not hard. For the extensional connectives, there is a natural extension of the truth tables for **LP** (Table 14.1).

A few remarks are in order about these extended tables (where {1} and {1,0} are designated values as in LP): first, it is easy to verify that the standard distribution laws, DeMorgan laws, etc., are preserved with only the obvious changes. Nothing important really changes regarding disjunction and conjunction. Second, negation deserves some comment. Here the 'top' and 'bottom' values {1,0} and ø each function as fixed points, and not as duals of one another as one might expect. For when we consider the negation of dialetheias such as the Liar sentence or the assertion that the Russell set is not a member of itself, we find that these are dialetheias as well, as Priest of course notes. But similarly, when we negate truth-valueless sentences we encounter more truth-valuelessness. Consider, for instance the Goldbach conjecture and assume that intuitionists are right to deny it a truth value. If they are, then, according to our matrices, its negation, namely, that there

TABLE 14.1. *Extension of truth tables for LP*

&	{1}	{0}	{1,0}	ø	v	{1}	{0}	{1,0}	ø	X	¬
{1}	{1}	{0}	{1,0}	ø	{1}	{1}	{1}	{1}	{1}	{1}	{0}
{0}	{0}	{0}	{0}	{0}	{0}	{1}	{0}	{1,0}	ø	{0}	{1}
{1,0}	{1,0}	{0}	{1,0}	ø	{1,0}	{1}	{1,0}	{1,0}	ø	{1,0}	{1,0}
ø	ø	{0}	ø	ø	ø	{1}	ø	ø	ø	ø	ø

is an even number that is not the sum of two primes, must also lack a truth value; and this seems right, since, if it were assigned any truth value, truly unacceptable paradox would ensue: If it were true, the conjecture would be false; if false, the conjecture would be true.

A somewhat more controversial consequence of this approach concerns the lack of logical truth and falsehood. Because of the tolerance of gaps (valuations of ø) there are no purely extensional logical truths (or logical falsehoods) in this system. Even sentences which cannot ever be *false*, such as (pv¬p) can have truth-value gaps (as when p has a gap). On the other hand, there is some consolation in the fact that these turn out to be logical *non-falsehoods*, which, for those who care about such things, must be almost as good. Moreover, there are many entailments that are logically true. This will disturb those who believe that the subject matter of logic is logical truth and logical falsehood, and that there is lots of it around—that is, that besides entailments, there are sentences that are logically true or false. The Dog is not troubled, though. He recognizes that logic is not *about* truth and falsity, but about *what follows from what*, that is, about *entailment*. If there are logical truths, they are entailment truths. Beyond that, all truth is empirical, and it is not a matter of *logic* to decide when at least one of a pair of literals is true, let alone regarding *which* one.[10]

Entailment, the Dog thinks, is at the heart of Logic.[11] He takes as a basic account of entailment that of Priest (1987). Besides providing a compelling and intuitive account of entailment in the context of paraconsistency, it avoids Curry paradoxes. Only one fiddle is necessary to get the LP account of entailment in line with this four-valued version: $1\varepsilon(A \to B)_w$ *only if* for some W' such that $W'RW$ $v(A)_{w'} \neq$ ø.[12] That is, formulae with no truth values anywhere don't entail anything. And, of course, we should introduce one more fiddle in order to get the system just right: since, as The Dog discovered long ago (Garfield 1990), the rational dog is the relevant dog, LP entailment is weakened by adding normal relevance restrictions. Adding these restrictions weakens the LP entailment relation somewhat, but in the right direction, and because LP is taken as the core, contraction fails, and so this relevant entailment does not fall prey to the Curry paradoxes to which standard relevant entailment accounts succumb.

---

[10] The Dog also thanks JC Beall for pressing on him the significance of this point, and notes that on his view it must come out that all mathematical truths are, *au fond*, entailments.

[11] Indeed, The Dog thinks that this is why logical pluralism (Beall and Restall 2000) is correct: given that Logic is about entailment, and that there are different accounts of entailment appropriate to different contexts, there are multiple logics. So The Dog emphasizes here, lest his claim be understood as stronger than he intends it to be, the account of entailment The Dog recommends is that appropriate to inference in an epistemically hostile environment, such as the empirical world as inhabited by fallible beings. Other domains and other purposes might well demand other logics.

[12] That is, truth is an element of the valuation set of an entailment sentence at a world only if at some accessible world the valuation set of the antecedent is not empty.

5. THE RATIONAL DOG IN THE REAL WORLD

So The Dog *does* reject LNC, but *also* accepts gaps and so rejects LEM as well, and does so because of his cognizance of the role of logic in canine intellectual life. His rejection can be understood in two ways: on one level, he notes that neither of these laws expressed in the object language is a logical truth. No surprises there, as there *are no* extensional logical truths. And since they are not logical truths, there is no reason that they should be accepted on logical grounds. But this is not the best way to understand The Dog's attitude. His is a *metalogical* commitment: LNC and LEM are first and foremost semantic principles—principles which together assert that every statement is either true or false, and that none is both. This metatheory, The Dog reckons, is ill advised for anyone reasoning in the real world, and the laws understood at this level fail to describe the logic he here proposes, just as they fail to be logical truths in the system.

As Man's best friend, he recommends this policy to humans as well, though he *takes no position* on the question of the actual consistency of the world. Whether that world is inconsistent or not, and whether or not the paradoxes of set theory, semantics, and logic are resolvable through consistent means, our knowledge is always going to be inconsistent and gappy, and logic is always going to be our cognitive tool for extending our belief set through reasoning. If that is so, our logic must be relevant, must tolerate truth-value gaps, and must tolerate contradictions. No stronger logic is adequate to our epistemic predicament.[13]

What are the implications of all of this for epistemic practices in which logic figures so prominently? Very few. All of this can be seen as a kind of reconstruction of our actual epistemic practices. Everything we actually do is to be left in place, replacing only an unfortunate *classical* idealization of epistemic practices with a relevant, *paraconsistent* idealization. To the extent that there are implications at the ground level, they may be in mathematics, which might benefit from a good paraconsistent reconstruction. That task is already underway (Mortensen 1995; Priest 2002).

And so back to our friend The Dog and his musings. The Dog, of course, rejects LEM and so will never reason from p∨¬p to anything entailed by either unless he has independent reason for *either* p *or* ¬p. But here he has good reasons for *both*. And so good reason to endorse p&¬p. Now, as we have seen, for The Man this would undermine his warrant for *anything*. But not for The Dog. From p &¬p he can infer p (or ¬p, for that matter) and from p, not just anything, but surely his undying fame. Will he *in fact* pee *and* not pee? He doubts it every bit as much as does the man. But in his *reasoning* is he entitled to *assert* that he will do both? Absolutely, for in reasoning assertion is often provisional, in full awareness of our

---

[13] Some may object to calling any inconsistent body of belief knowledge, but not The Dog. He thinks, after all, that knowledge is Justified True Belief plus a bit of Gettier. And there is no reason, if your logic is paraconsistent, to conclude that not all of a set of inconsistent beliefs are true, even though some may also be false. The truth part is the aim of belief, and of knowledge.

own fallibility. And, with The Man as his best friend, The Dog is certainly acutely aware of his own fallibility. And that is why, ever since his discovery by Chrysippus, The Dog has been renowned among logicians.

REFERENCES

ANDERSON, A. R., and BELNAP, N. D., Jr. (1975). *Entailment: The Calculus of Relevance and Necessity*. Princeton: Princeton University Press.

BEALL, J.C., and RESTALL, G. (2000). 'Logical Pluralism', *Australasian Journal of Philosophy*, 78(4): 475–93.

CHERNIAK, C. (1986). *Minimal Rationality*. Cambridge, Mass.: MIT.

DUMMETT, M. (1978). 'The Philosophical Basis of Intuitionistic Logic', in *Truth and Other Enigmas*. Oxford: Duckworth.

FERLINGHETTI, L. (1974). *A Coney Island of the Mind*. San Francisco: City Lights.

GARFIELD, J. (1990). 'The Dog: Relevance and Rationality', in J. M. Dunn and A. Gupta (eds.), *Truth or Consequences: Essays in Honor of Nuel D. Belnap, Jr*. Dordrecht: Kluwer.

HARMAN, G. (1986). *Change in View: Principles of Reasoning* (Cambridge: MIT Press).

MATES, BENSON (1997). *The Skeptic Way: Sextus Empiricus' Outlines of Pyrrhonism*. Oxford: Oxford University Press.

MORTENSEN, C. (1995). *Inconsistent Mathematics*. Dordrecht: Kluwer.

PRIEST, G. (1987). *In Contradiction*. Dordrecht: Kluwer.

—— (2002). *Beyond the Limits of Thought*, 2nd edn. Oxford: Oxford University Press.

QUINE, W. V. O. (1981). 'What Price Bivalence?' *The Journal of Philosophy*, 79: 69–75.

15

Realism and Dialetheism

Frederick Kroon

ABSTRACT

Dialetheists—those who think there are true contradictions, in defiance of the Law of Non-Contradiction—think that their rejection of *ex contradictione quodlibet* means that they can't be saddled with the claim that anything whatsoever is true (and, of course, false). But what precisely is wrong with trivialism, as Priest calls the position that everything is indeed true (and false)? Priest himself thinks that trivialism doesn't allow us to make sense of our ability to make choices, to act in the world. But such an argument is curiously reminiscent of certain transcendental arguments in favour of objectivity, free-will, and so on, and as such is open to the objection that it depends on a version of verificationism. The question for realists is: mightn't the actual world be trivial, even if we are constrained to think that the world is not? I argue that the dialetheist realist should accept that the world might indeed be so. Those who simply cannot make sense of this 'possibility' should therefore either not be dialetheists or not be realists. To the extent that the arguments for dialetheism prove irresistible, they present us with a powerful reason not to be realists about those parts of our discourse that generate true contradictions.

1. DIALETHEISM

Dialetheists—those who think there are true contradictions, in defiance of the Law of Non-Contradiction—think that their rejection of *ex contradictione quodlibet* means that they can't be saddled with the claim that anything whatsoever is true (and, of course, false). They believe that there are true contradictions aplenty, among them semantic and set-theoretic paradoxes, but that such true

Thanks to two anonymous referees for their helpful comments on an earlier draft of this chapter, and to members of the Advanced Reasoning Forum, especially Richard L. Epstein, for useful discussions on the topic addressed here. Thanks also to JC Beall, who persuaded me that trivialism's threat to dialetheism should be taken seriously. Beall's own contribution to the present volume, 'True and False—As If', which unfortunately came to my attention well after my own chapter was completed, offers a rather different version of the 'as if' approach that I defend here.

contradictions can be pretty well insulated from the rest of our beliefs.[1] Of course, they agree that logic can't guarantee that there are not many more true contradictions than just these; it can only tell us not to look to 'laws' like *ex contradictione quodlibet* to generate this result. But this raises the question of how they can defend the view that not everything is both true and false. In rejecting the Law of Non-Contradiction, they can't appeal to the incoherence of something's being both true and false, since they claim that some propositions, indeed a substantial number of them, are both true and false. So what makes the claim that *everything* is both true and false incoherent? (I assume without further ado that it is incoherent—as flagrantly nonsensical as any claim could be.)

Now dialetheists surely owe us an answer to that question. Why else would they be so concerned to insulate contradictions? What is wrong with the classical logician who recognizes the simultaneous truth and falsity of the Liar, and then sees it as a semantic cancer that indirectly infects everything? (Doesn't the classical logician's attitude answer to some more or less fundamental intuition—one that even the logically untutored have—about the corrosive danger of admitting *any* contradiction?) If the answer is that the classical logician's account of entailment is simply too tolerant because it doesn't heed considerations of relevance (unlike a paraconsistent relevant logic), it is important to remember that the classical logician is quite willing to let in relevance if relevance is understood in pragmatic terms—in terms of conversational proprieties, say. Despite its tolerance, therefore, classical logic can't be accused of rejecting the possibility of appeals to relevance. If the reply to this last point is that pragmatic relevance is not enough, that relevance needs to play a *semantic* filtering role (for how else are we to stop counting everything as true if even one contradiction is true?), that answer is obviously conditioned by the thought that it is plainly intolerable that everything should be true. And so the question remains: what is so intolerable about this conclusion?

In short, what really is wrong with *trivialism*, the doctrine that every proposition or truthbearer is true (and hence also false, since the truth of ¬p implies the falsity of p)? Now this is a question that may well seem naïve, since it will strike many as a question that one shouldn't bother to pose and hence answer in the first place. But it is a question that dialetheists should take very seriously, for the reasons already given. And if they can't give a satisfactory answer to the question, then it seems that their view of the world lacks an appropriate filter on coherence. Having given up (for what they take to be good reason) on the Law of Non-Contradiction, they would then lack the ability to say what is wrong with the surely nonsensical idea that *everything* may be true as well as false. That would, I think, be a devastating failure.

This chapter explores the issue of how a dialetheist might respond to this challenge, and the pitfalls that face available responses. My conclusion is that the

---

[1] There have been attempts—rejected by Priest—to show that dialetheism will find it hard to resist collapse into trivialism. See JC Beall (2001).

problem may well be inescapable if the dialetheist is also a realist. In the final few sections I explore an alternative anti-realist response.

2. PRIEST'S REJECTION OF TRIVIALISM

In his paper 'Could Everything be True?' (Priest 2000), Graham Priest acknowledges the seriousness of the issue for the dialetheist, and poses the question in terms of arguments that an anti-trivialist might present to a neutral arbitrator (one who still has an open mind about trivialism, but who is able to judge the worth of arguments). Priest argues that perhaps the only non-question-begging argument available to the critic is one that rests on the phenomenology of choice: agents who wish to act must see their actions as making a difference to the world.

> The trivialist—at least whilst they remember that they are a trivialist—can have no purpose at all. One cannot intend to act in such a way as to bring about some state of affairs s, if one believes s already to hold. Conversely, if one acts with the purpose of bringing about s, one cannot believe that s already obtains. Hence, if one believes that everything is true, one cannot decide to act purposefully. . . . But to choose how to act is to have a purpose: to (try to) bring about *this* rather than *that*. . . . It follows that I [as an agent] cannot but reject trivialism.   (ibid. 194)

Priest takes this argument to be a transcendental one:

> [T]he argument I have deployed provides a transcendental deduction from certain features of consciousness to the impossibility of being a trivialist. The arbitrator must rule in our favour if we can give them a transcendental proof that our opponent does not exist.
>
> (ibid. 195)

Transcendental arguments are, of course, notoriously slippery, but before considering the strategy of using an argument of this kind, let us ask whether the argument is enough to persuade the neutral arbitrator that the trivialist must believe that no purposeful action is possible. I think that is far from clear. Priest suggests that 'the trivialist cannot aim to bring about s, because it is simply *part* of a situation that (they think) already obtains, viz., s & ¬s' (ibid. 194). Now it is true that the trivialist must accept that '[s & ¬s] already obtains' if this simply means that, no matter what happens, s & ¬s will be the case. But from the fact that the trivialist believes that both s and ¬s (already) obtain in this sense, it doesn't follow that she believes that nothing can be done to bring about s or ¬s. To think that free action is thereby ruled out is to be guilty of confusing 's will be the case' with 's *would* be the case whether or not anyone tried to do anything to help bring it about'.

Of course, the dialectic gets rather puzzling at this point, for the trivialist believes that as well: after all, she believes *everything*. Is this enough to damn the trivialist? I don't see why. For by the same token the trivialist also believes the contrary claim that s will only obtain if she does something to help bring it about. Why, then, shouldn't she choose to act on the latter rather than the former belief? It is true that the trivialist who chooses in this manner chooses on the basis of one belief when she also believes its negation, and that is indeed a mysterious thing to do. But as far as I can see, the mystery in question is simply the mystery of how anyone can coherently maintain the joint truth of a proposition and its negation, not the mystery of how to make choices once one has such beliefs.

What is not clear, then, is that the puzzling nature of the dialectic we face in the case of trivialism shows that the trivialist is in an intolerable situation, one far worse than the situation the ordinary dialetheist finds himself in. In fact, it can be argued that the dialetheist faces worries about choice that, in their own way, seem no less perplexing. For if it is difficult to make sense of intending to bring it about that s if one believes s 'already obtains', then it is surely no less difficult to make sense of intending to bring it about that s if one sees that bringing about s ensures that ¬s will obtain. But that is precisely the kind of possibility the dialetheist is happy to tolerate. Consider the following situation s:

> There is a sentence tokened somewhere in this chapter, and labelled '(*)', that is not true

I can purposefully bring it about that this situation holds by typing something false on this page, and marking it with '(*)', say 'Snow is black.' But if dialetheism is correct I can also do it in a special way, by simply describing the situation in a sentence and calling this sentence '(*)':

> (*) There is a sentence y such that y = (*) and y is not true.

For if sentence (*) is true, it is not true. Hence it is not true. But in that case there is an untrue sentence named '(*)', so that (*) is true after all. Hence situation s holds, but so does ¬s (since (*) is untrue). It follows that a dialetheist thinks he can freely decide to bring about a situation like s even though he sees that his attempt inevitably ensures that ¬s will hold. Is this really any less puzzling than the trivialist's supposed conundrum?

But suppose I am wrong about this. Suppose Priest's transcendental argument really does establish that trivialism is an unbelievable doctrine, unlike dialetheism. Even in that case, however, it is not clear why the trivialist should be unduly worried. For the success of Priest's argument would show at best that the trivialist shouldn't believe her own position, at least not when acting. Remember the familiar argument that no rational act utilitarian can believe her own theory, since belief in such a theory will manifestly result in actions that are wrong by the act utilitarian's own lights. Act utilitarians are usually not very bothered by this argument, pointing out that it doesn't show the falsity of the theory, only that it is best not to believe it—at least at the point where the agent begins to act in situations where her doing act-utilitarian calculations will yield the wrong result. Similarly, trivialists might point out that the argument shows at best that trivialists had better not believe in trivialism—at least at the point where the agent begins to act. It is easy to imagine such a trivialist. She is the kind of trivialist who simply focuses on her action when acting, not on the consequences of certain theoretical beliefs she holds (or a trivialist who, when acting, focuses on her belief that trivialism is false, for this she also believes, since she believes everything).

Priest may respond that he is talking about the fully rational trivialist, one who holds all relevant beliefs before her as she decides how to act. (I doubt this is a reasonable requirement of any rational agent since I doubt that any of us can do that; but let that pass.) Even in this case, however, Priest's strategy is a problematic one. As Priest (ibid. 194) himself points out early in his argument, his claim that the phenomenology of choice prevents trivialism from being an option for an agent 'does not mean that trivialism is untrue. As far as the above considerations go, it is quite possible that everything is the case; but not for me—or for any other person'. This is quite a concession, however. Given the title of his paper, one hoped that Priest would be trying to show us why trivialism can't be true. It now turns out that he thinks trivialism simply isn't rationally believable, but that it might be true for all that.

What remains unclear is what this concession really comes to. Perhaps we are supposed to be reminded of claims of the form 'q, but I don't believe that q', which may well be true even though no minimally rational agent can believe them to be true. But in certain cases the link between rational unbelievability and truth is far stronger. Sometimes the fact that p can't be believed means that p is true. This is arguably so in the case of certain epistemic 'instability puzzles' discussed in the 1980s and 1990s, based on true and believable biconditionals of the form:

(B) p is true iff I don't (ever) accept/believe p.[2]

Faced with the question of whether she should accept p, it is clear what a rational agent should do: she should *never* accept p, since accepting p would be to accept something she believes to be false (by (B), p is *false* if the agent ever accepts it). Some have thought that there is a looming paradox here, on the grounds that a rational agent can surely see that, being rational, she will never accept p, from which she deduces by (B) that p is true—thereby showing that she accepts p after all! But this is a mistake. There is no good argument available to such an agent for the claim that she will never accept p. In particular, appealing to the premiss that she is rational, hence that she will never accept p, hence that p is true after

---

[2] See e.g. Sorensen (1988) and Kroon (1993). (Consider examples involving an extremely knowledgeable, reliable, powerful agent who you know will have caused p to be true should it be a fact about you that you will not (ever) accept p, where p is an ordinary empirical proposition, not some kind of paradoxical proposition.)

all, involves the agent in reliance on the demonstrably *false* premiss that she is rational—a premiss falsified by the very inferential behaviour she exhibits.[3]

Here, then, we seem to have an example of a proposition that a rational agent can't believe but that—in virtue of (B)—is made true by the fact that the agent can't believe it. So there is sometimes a tight link between the unbelievability of a proposition and its truth. That being so, why should Priest's transcendental proof that his opponent does not exist impress an arbitrator who is interested in the possibility of trivialism itself rather than the possibility of a believer in trivialism? Perhaps this is another case where unbelievability and truth go hand-in-hand. Indeed, isn't the trivialist bound to think so? If trivialism is true, everything is true, including the claim that trivialism is utterly unbelievable as well as true, and that it is true in virtue of its unbelievability.

3. PRIEST'S REALIST DIALETHEISM

I suspect, however, that the objection developed in the last couple of paragraphs doesn't really get to the heart of what Priest thinks he has shown. On closer inspection, it is clear that Priest thinks he has proved to the neutral arbitrator that any rational agent must positively *dis*believe trivialism (that is, believe it to be false, not just fail to believe it to be true). For he thinks that a rational and purposeful agent, intending to bring about s, must believe that s and ¬s are not both the case. His own words sometimes hide this stronger reading. For example, the sentence 'it is quite possible that everything is the case; but not for me—or for any other person' seems to mean 'it is not possible for me, or any other person, to believe that everything is the case'. What he really means is 'it is necessary for me and everyone else to believe that *not* everything is the case, and that trivialism is in fact *false*'. How does Priest's argument fare with this stronger reading in place?

The stronger reading doesn't seem to yield the strong connection between lack of believability and truth discussed above. But it highlights something rather significant about Priest's argumentative strategy. For consider again Priest's claim that he has provided 'a transcendental deduction from certain features of consciousness to the impossibility of being a trivialist. The arbitrator must rule in our favour if we can give them a transcendental proof that our opponent does not exist' (ibid. 195). This is on the face of it a puzzling claim. For traditional transcendental arguments are nothing like this. They establish certain conclusions of a categorical nature from features of consciousness: conclusions such as the claim that the world [must] contain objects and obey causal laws, that idealism is false, etc. By contrast, Priest's argument focuses on the person who advances a certain claim rather than on the claim itself, which would be like interpreting Kant's refutation of idealism

---

[3] This solution to the 'paradox' is developed in Kroon (1993).

as an argument for the non-existence of the idealist rather than for the claim that idealism is false. If Priest had followed the traditional understanding of 'transcendental argument', he would have said that he had a transcendental argument for the claim that trivialism is false rather than that the trivialist doesn't exist. What is going on?

Interpreting Priest's argument as an argument for the claim that it is necessary for us to believe that trivialism is false restores the Kantian flavour of Priest's argument. For Kant notoriously argued for his various conclusions on the basis of the necessity of believing that the world was as the conclusions claimed it to be. If so, it may also explain why Priest refuses to infer that trivialism is in *fact* false. Priest is likely to share a widespread scepticism about transcendental arguments on their usual Kantian and neo-Kantian interpretation—he is likely to doubt their capacity to tell us what the world is bound to be like, rather than how we are bound to experience the world.[4] As Barry Stroud (1968) argued long ago, those who insist on more than the latter look to be in the grip of some kind of verificationist account of meaning, and Priest is far from being a verificationist.[5]

If this is right, Priest's way of putting his own transcendental argument is likely to signify a commitment to some kind of realism. What kind of realism? In order to make what I say as plausible as possible, it is best to leave the realism relatively underdescribed. I will simply take realism about a discourse D to be the doctrine that, while D has the resources to describe (relevant portions of) the world, our very best theories and attempts to describe the world in terms of D may get it wrong. The reason why even the compulsory *rejection* of trivialism is compatible with the truth of trivialism is that there is a conceptual gap between the content of our best beliefs and the way the world really is. Even if, for example, the *simplest* overall system of beliefs that accords with all the available evidence has only very few contradictions, there is no guarantee that the world itself conforms to our canons of simplicity. That, I surmise, is why Priest thinks he has established no more than the non-existence of the serious trivialist. For all our clever attempts to insulate contradictions and provide reasons for thinking that the space of true contradictions is in fact very sparse, the world may yet fool us.

We are close to drawing the conclusion that I promised in the first few paragraphs of this chapter. Dialetheism owes us an account of why not everything might be

---

[4] Kant famously claimed that the arguments at least have the capacity to tell us what the world *as we experience it* must be like, although not the world *as it really is*. But unless we adopt the ontologically bizarre two-worlds' interpretation of Kant's words, this just seems to be a colourful way of putting the point that the arguments can only tell us about how we must experience the world rather than about the intrinsic nature of the world that we experience (cf. Kroon 2001).

[5] In general, Priest's writings show a commitment to a kind of Quinean conjectural account of what we should rationally believe about the world. Because this involves weighing up beliefs along a variety of dimensions, it is all too easy to imagine getting systems of belief that, overall, are equally well supported (cf. Quine on the underdetermination of theory). Since Priest makes it abundantly clear that he is no relativist, it is clear that, like Quine, he would resist the identification of truth with membership in some 'best' corpus of beliefs of this kind.

true. Knowing how to insulate contradictions formally is important if we want to make sure that not everything follows from allowing true contradictions, but it is no answer to the question of why we need this bar in the first place—what precisely is wrong with allowing a tolerant account of entailment on which *everything* is both true and false since *something* is both true and false. It now looks as if all attempts to show this must fail according to realist versions of dialetheism. In particular, we must concede that Priest is right in thinking that a dialetheist must accept that trivialism may be true even if unbelievable. As a realist, Priest must grant that internal constraints on what we must believe are not constraints on what the world is like independently of our best theories and beliefs.[6]

It is important to be clear about the implications of this conclusion. If it is possible for trivialism to be true, it may be false as well as true that all humans are mammals (so not only are all humans mammals; some are not mammals at all), that New York is a city, that you are currently reading this chapter, and so on. And not just both true and false: they may at the same time be neither true nor false, since the claim that they are neither will also count as true. These ordinary empirical claims may all be simultaneously true, false, *neither* true nor false, *only* true or false, and so on, even if all the evidence bearing on such claims declares them unequivocally true. According to dialetheism, there is nothing in the nature of truth and negation that can rule out such 'possibilities' (in particular, there is no Law of Non-Contradiction to rule them out). For the realist dialetheist, it is the actual constitution of the world that determines what is and is not the case in this regard, and that constitution is not limited by what our best theories (consistent or inconsistent) tell us. The real world already contains true contradictions, so he thinks; what is to rule out an account of the actual constitution of this world according to which they are far more rampant than we are ever able to believe?[7]

What indeed, if one already sees the world as containing *some* inconsistent regions? As I said earlier, however, the thought that the truth of trivialism is a genuine open possibility in this sense ought to strike us as bizarre and intolerable. Unlike other incredible doctrines, it deserves not an incredulous stare, but no stare

---

[6] Could trivialism perhaps be ruled out on the grounds that it is *conceptually* or *metaphysically* impossible that everything be true, even if not logically impossible? (This idea was suggested by a referee.) It is difficult to see how Priest could run any such argument, however. Given that there is nothing in the nature of our concepts of truth, falsity, negation, and so on, that makes for such an impossibility, what is left? Furthermore, even if we agree with Kripke that some necessary falsehoods can be shown only *a posteriori* to be false, it is far from clear that this involves a special notion of metaphysical impossibility (Jackson 1998)—and in any case trivialism doesn't have anything like the character of these *a posteriori* necessary falsehoods.

[7] Because of the vagueness of observational predicates, and because they prefer a paraconsistent treatment of vagueness, some dialetheists think that even the observable world is inconsistent (Beall and Colyvan 2001). So these philosophers will acknowledge true contradictions of a kind that most of us find more disturbing than ordinary logical paradoxes (the claim that you are currently reading this chapter and not reading this chapter might be such a contradiction). Still, even these philosophers will recoil at the thought that anything whatsoever might be both true and false.

at all.[8] It is not even a starter for a stare. Now for the promised conclusion, which is simplicity itself: since it is (Priest's) realist dialetheism that got us to the point of thinking that trivialism might be true, even if unbelievable, so much the worse for such a dialetheism.

4. FICTIONALIST DIALETHEISM

But haven't Priest and his fellow dialetheists presented strong arguments for their version of dialetheism? Haven't they mounted a pretty convincing demonstration that non-dialetheist solutions to this or that paradox sooner or later run into the very problems the solutions were trying to solve? Yes to both questions, I think. Although we may have reservations about the arguments, there is no denying their power (and, in any case, I have no wish to dispute them in this chapter). But I also think that the version of dialetheism that dialetheists have so persuasively argued for is not the realist dialetheism I have attacked. In particular, I think that nothing in that doctrine gives us any reason to wonder about the truth of trivialism. That is because I take the usual arguments for dialetheism to be at best arguments about our conceptual resources: about the way certain concepts—that of a set and of truth, say—sometimes let us down, to the point of inconsistency. In my view, they are not, without a good deal of massaging, arguments about the world as such.

We can begin to see why by looking at a certain inductive argument for the claim that the field of true contradictions is sparse. Priest has argued that such a conclusion is supported by the way special concepts such as *set* and *truth* feature in existing paradoxes (Priest 1987, 1998). But the use of inductive arguments to ascertain what the real world is like is notoriously tricky, since it requires judgements about the relevance and completeness of the evidence used as the basis of the induction. If we are not to prejudge the issue, perhaps a better inductive argument in the present case is that the way concepts such as *set* and *truth* feature in the true contradictions detected so far gives us reasonable inductive grounds for thinking that true contradictions that *don't* feature such concepts are not detectable by logical or conceptual means. This new formulation makes no prediction about the number of true contradictions. Realist dialetheists who see no *a priori* problem in the thought that the real world might be replete with true contradictions can surely have no non-question-begging reason to prefer the first argument to the second.

But there is an interpretation of Priest's argument that doesn't generate a debate of this kind. On this alternative interpretation, the paradoxes indicate that some of our concepts are deeply defective at certain points: in particular, the rules that govern them produce inconsistent results when applied at certain limit points.

---

[8] The 'incredulous stare' allusion comes from David Lewis's account of how most philosophers react to his doctrine of modal realism.

Being defective, these concepts lose their title as adequate tools for representing the way the world really is, and so we can't classify discourse that uses these conceptual tools as fully realist discourse. But lack of adequacy does not mean that they are useless, or that they should be jettisoned. For one thing, we may have no fully adequate replacement at hand. For another, they may be adequate enough. We may feel sufficiently confident that we have isolated the source of the defect, and thereby feel sufficiently confident that the concepts are adequate to their task when applied in various familiar domains. (Here we have another version of Priest's argument, its conclusion based this time on the idea that the best diagnosis of existing paradoxes involves the presence of certain unusual defects in some of our concepts rather than on the existence of [detectable] true contradictions induced by these concepts. Thus interpreted, the argument need no longer be seen as a guide to reality, but as a prediction that such conceptual malfeasance is likely to be rare.)

This way of understanding the phenomenon of 'true contradictions' puts the blame on our conceptual tools; it removes, or at any rate mitigates, the tendency to think that the world might itself be inconsistent in some sense. But that raises the question of what to do about the fact that the concepts sometimes fail us. If we then refuse to use the concepts *anywhere*, the fact that the concepts are adequate enough, while no available replacement is fully adequate, suggests that the costs of not relying on the concepts may well outweigh the gains. This is likely to be a particularly foolish choice where fundamental concepts such as that of set and truth are concerned. So what should we do?

In this kind of situation, it is best to adopt a very different approach. We should keep on using the concepts, pretending that they are adequate but recognizing all the while that they aren't. That is, we should do what many philosophers recommend we do for one discourse or another: adopt a fictionalist stance towards the discourse. A fictionalist stance is simply one that implicitly prefaces whatever is said with a special kind of disclaimer: let's do as if the following is in fact the case, even though it isn't. It is a way of being anti-realist about the discourse in question, but one that doesn't endorse the possibility of a reconstructive strategy that replaces the discourse with something more acceptable.[9] In the present case, fictionalism is the approach that believers in the Law of Non-Contradiction should accept if they are also sympathetic to the arguments of dialetheists.

Suppose we accept the Law of Non-Contradiction as a law on how we must think about the world if our thought is to reflect the way the world really is. (Let's not speculate about the deeper reasons for taking the law to have this status.)[10]Now

---

[9] See Lewis (2001). Burgess and Rosen (1997) contrast fictionalism about a discourse with reconstructive strategies such as nominalism. Stanley (2001) is a wide-ranging attack on fictionalist programmes understood as descriptive proposals about language-use.

[10] Of course Priest thinks that there is good reason to reject this 'law' (Priest 1998). I have already suggested that the threat of trivialism is one kind of problem that faces rejection of the law, but I certainly

consider the word 'true'. If dialetheists are right in their account of the conditions under which to apply this word, then 'true' doesn't have what it takes to classify sentences coherently in terms of their ability to represent the world—the use of 'true' leads to contradiction, since sentences such as the (strengthened) Liar would be both true and not true. 'True' is, to that extent, not a properly functioning predicate, a predicate apt for classifying objects in the world. It doesn't fulfil its expected semantic function of (coherently!) dividing the objects in its field of application, and it can't, therefore, figure in discourse apt for the characterization of reality— discourse that, we are agreeing, conforms to the Law of Non-Contradiction. (As I shall somewhat misleadingly put it, it doesn't fulfil its expected semantic function of standing for a property.[11]) Now this conclusion may strike one as perverse, since 'true' appears to satisfy all the usual syntactic and semantic conditions for being a property-determining predicate. But in fact there is nothing particularly odd in the idea that words that appear semantically and syntactically healthy don't fulfil their expected semantic functions. If, as direct reference theorists believe, a proper name is a word whose semantic function is simply to stand for an object, then 'Sherlock Holmes', 'Zeus', 'Vulcan' (understood as the name of the planet responsible for the perturbations in the orbit of Mercury), and 'phlogiston' all fail to fulfil their expected semantic functions. And in certain cases, it is logic that shows this. Consider, for instance, the following attempt to introduce the descriptive name 'Ace': let 'Ace' be the name for the famous Australian dialetheist who succeeded in establishing that both $2 + 2 = 4$ and $2 + 2 \neq 4$.

Similarly, we may have predicates that don't fulfil the semantic function of marking out a genuine property. Alongside fictional names such as 'Sherlock Holmes' are fictional natural kind terms such as 'unicorn', 'hobbit', and 'tove' (the latter from Lewis Carroll's *Jabberwocky*), which arguably don't pick out kind-properties, not even non-instantiated kind-properties.[12] And alongside non-fictional empty

don't take that to be *evidence* for the law. Quite the contrary: the law strikes me as conceptually rock-bottom, and not subject to possible (non-circular) confirmation or coherent challenge. That leaves me with the challenge—the subject of the rest of the chapter—of how to reconcile unwavering respect for the law with utter respect for the impressive body of evidence that dialetheists have marshalled against the law.

[11] It is important for what follows that my use of the word 'property' is appropriately minimalist. I am not interested in the debate about whether properties, as abstract objects, exist, for example. (Cf. also the last paragraph of s. 5.)

[12] This has been argued, famously, by Kripke (in most detail in his unpublished 1973 John Locke lectures, 'Reference and Existence'), and is accepted by many proponents of the New Theory of Reference. His reasons for the view are roughly as follows. By the new Kripke-Putnam doctrine of reference, kind-predicates are supposed to apply to all objects of the same kind as certain local exemplars. The property in question can be taken to be the property of being of the same kind as these exemplars. (For familiar reasons, it is not some descriptive property such as *being a white horse-like animal with a single horn on its forehead* (in the case of 'unicorn').) But absent such exemplars—and absent they will be in the case of broadly fictional predicates such as 'unicorn'—there simply is no property to be denoted. It is only fictional that there are such exemplars and such a property. (For more on the idea that in the case of many predicates it is only fictional that they stand for properties, see Walton 1990.)

names such as 'phlogiston' are predicates that somehow involve reference to what these names unsuccessfully denote (for instance, 'dephlogisticated'), and thereby fail to mark out genuine properties.

Even the idea that 'true' fails to mark out a property should be familiar. Redundancy theorists hold such a position. So do those truth-sceptics who think that the notion of truth involves the (supposedly unintelligible) idea of correspondence to some mind-independent world, a correspondence that supposedly exists in the case of such sentences as 'Snow is white' but fails to exist in the case of 'Snow is black.'[13] Whether or not dialetheists think that the notion of truth involves the idea of correspondence, they do, of course, think that 'true' has incoherent application-conditions. If they are right (and assuming the Law of Non-Contradiction), that is enough to warrant the conclusion that 'true' doesn't fulfil its expected semantic function of determining a property—discourse involving such a predicate will lack the capacity to characterize reality, not because the predicate lacks application-conditions (the view of redundancy theorists) or because these conditions involve wildly mistaken presuppositions (the view of our 'correspondence' sceptics), but because these conditions are incoherent.

But a word's not fulfilling its expected semantic function doesn't make the word useless. Even though 'Sherlock Holmes', 'Vulcan', 'Ace', and 'tove' don't in fact fulfil their expected semantic functions, we can *make believe* that they do (Walton 1990). We can, for example, make believe that 'Sherlock Holmes' names a private detective in London in the latter part of the nineteenth century. (This is part of what is involved in making believe that the Holmes stories are a reliable record of fact.) Similarly, we can make believe that 'Vulcan' names a certain planet, and we can then proceed to describe the world from the perspective of the pretence that there is such a planet (as in: 'The world of late nineteenth-century science contained not only Neptune, responsible for the perturbations in the orbit of Uranus, but also Vulcan, responsible for the perturbations in the orbit of Mercury.') We might even make believe that 'tove' picks out a real natural kind, or that there was a real person named 'Ace'. Presumably we do the former on hearing or reading Lewis Carroll's *Jabberwocky*; and perhaps a dialetheist novelist writing about 'Ace', the famous Australian dialetheist who proved that $2 + 2 = 4$ and its negation are both true, will get us to make believe that 'Ace' picks out a real person. In the latter case, of course, we had better not pursue our make-believe to its classical logical limits, deriving what must be the case if someone really had established a contradiction. For if fictional truth is closed under classical logical implication, the impossibility of this scenario then ensures that anything whatsoever is the case, and that would destroy the point and usefulness of the story (which might be to underline the author's view that it is not hard to tell an apparently coherent, even enjoyable, dialetheist story).

---

[13] For an excellent survey of forms of truth-scepticism, see Scott Soames (1999), ch. 2.

In short, there can be interesting, pointful discourse involving words such as 'Sherlock Holmes', 'Vulcan', 'Ace', 'tove', etc., despite the fact that these words are not able to play the semantic role we would expect them to play when used in standard assertoric discourse. It is enough that speakers are able to make believe that their words play this role. We acknowledge this point by being fictionalists about the discourse, taking what speakers say to be implicitly prefixed with the disowning preface that what follows is only make-believe.

Fictionalism so construed doesn't apply only to discourse involving the imaginative pleasures of telling and listening to fictional stories. As we saw in the case of 'Vulcan', make-believe is sometimes used to facilitate the description of a rejected ontology by simulating acceptance of that ontology. More generally, we may want to be fictionalist about theories that purport to describe the world but in terms we find deeply erroneous yet profoundly useful. Fictionalism about possible worlds and about morality belongs to this category.[14] I suggest that the case of 'true' be treated in a similar way. Assuming dialetheists are right about the inconsistent application-conditions of 'true', 'true' can't fulfil its expected semantic function of picking out a property, although it would be useful to act as if there were a property for 'true' to pick out. Accordingly, we should not be realists but anti-realists about discourse involving 'true'. More precisely, we should be fictionalists about such discourse, taking what we say to be subject to the disowning preface that we are making believe that 'true' stands for a property but that there really is no such property. Such a fictionalism about truth treats the claim that there is a property of truth—at any rate, a property answering to the inconsistent way in which 'true' functions according to dialetheists—as a deeply erroneous claim, but regards the fiction that there is such a property as a strikingly useful one. After all, this fiction allows us a natural and expressively complete way of organizing 'truth' claims, without the messy hierarchies and consequent charges of expressive incompleteness that affect other approaches. And perhaps we have no choice but to use it. The fiction may be indispensable. That, surely, is what you should believe if you deem the Law of Non-Contradiction an irresistible constraint on a realist construal of ordinary discourse, while also persuaded (for the sorts of reasons provided by Priest and other dialetheists) that there is no escaping paradoxes such as the strengthened Liar.

Once we adopt this fiction, however, it is incumbent upon us to make sure that the accompanying logic is not classical. The reason is the one encountered earlier. A story involving someone who has established that both $2 + 2 = 4$ and $2 + 2 \neq 4$ would lose its point if classical logic rather than a paraconsistent logic were accepted as the background logic used to determine what was fictionally true. Similarly, our 'truth' fiction would lose its point if classical logic were admitted as the background logic, since a trivialist fiction that tolerates a contradiction and

---

[14] Cf. Rosen (1990, 1995) and Joyce (2002).

thereby tolerates everything is no longer useful. Such a fiction doesn't capture the plain, and plainly important, fact that for the most part our concept of truth doesn't get us into trouble.

If fictionalism has virtues anywhere, it must surely have these virtues in the present case. Fictionalism about possible worlds has its advocates, but the idea of a possible world is at least internally coherent; its problems have to do with plausibility, not logical coherence (Rosen 1990, 1995). Similarly, what recommends fictionalism about morality is the thought that it is implausible to assume a property of rightness that gives us reasons for acting regardless of desires, and not that there is something internally incoherent in such an idea (Joyce 2002). Such worries about plausibility apply a fortiori to dialetheism's account of truth, for the thought that there is a property of truth that can apply both to a sentence and its negation is logically and not merely contingently absurd. There simply can't be any such property.

Before turning to some problems that face such a fictionalism about truth, let me briefly comment on dialetheism's claim that there are true contradictions to be found in other places as well, most notably set theory. If I am right, there is scope for a fictionalist treatment of all types of discourse that yield the mandatory assertibility of both S and not-S (for some sentence S involving expressions central to that discourse), and set theory appears to be no exception. Of course, fictionalism about talk of sets (as well as numbers) has struck a number of philosophers as a plausible view, independently of the attractions of dialetheism.[15] Given set theory's striking commitment to a universe of abstract objects, these philosophers prefer a version that lacks this striking commitment, especially since the pivotal role that set theory plays in organizing and improving our descriptions of non-sets doesn't really seem to require full-blooded commitment to such objects. As Stephen Yablo (2000) has pointed out, this is a situation that argues for a make-believe approach to set theory—an approach, furthermore, that is liberal with regard to what is posited since 'clearly one is not going to be worried about multiplying entities if the entities are not assumed to really exist' (ibid. 311). He adds that: 'The likeliest approach if the set-theoretic universe is make-believe would be (A) to articulate the clearest intuitive conception possible, and then, (B) subject to that constraint, let all hell break loose' (ibid.).

A view of this kind finds an interesting resonance in a fictionalism about sets based on the attempt to accommodate set-theoretic paradoxes. For consider the argument for such a fictionalism. Assuming dialetheists such as Priest are right, a viable set theory is bound to be inconsistent, so that set-theoretic discourse can't

---

[15] As has often been pointed out, Kant can be construed as a kind of fictionalist about at least very large ('unlimited') sets or totalities. Even if we agree to regard him as a realist of sorts about the empirical world, Kant is assuredly not a realist about a world that contains unlimited totalities. His reason is simple: the idea of such totalities—a transcendental idea—generates antinomies. But while the idea couldn't possibly have empirical application, he thinks it is important to *act* as if it does. That is how science advances. (See Kant 1929: A321/B378 ff.)

admit of a realist construal if we also assume the Law of Non-Contradiction as a filter on how things can really be. Since such discourse is also tremendously useful, even indispensable (as Priest certainly thinks), we should be fictionalists about such discourse. Here, then, we have another argument, not ontological in nature this time, for a fictionalist treatment of our talk about sets. And this time Yablo's advice 'to articulate the clearest intuitive conception possible, and then . . . subject to that constraint, let all hell break loose' does indeed get us close to something Yablo might well consider hell. For apart from the addition of any other strong principles of set-existence, the kind of naïve comprehension principle that Priest regards as an inevitable part of the way we think about sets—part, therefore, of 'the clearest intuitive conception possible'—now gets us an inconsistent theory. Still, if we are once again prepared to adopt a paraconsistent logic the fiction remains a tolerable one. Contradictions once again remain insulated, confined, it is hoped, to claims involving certain transcendent totalities, and the theory continues to be an utterly useful instrument for organizing and improving our descriptions of non-sets as well as of sets (the latter fictionally construed).

5. THE LIMITS OF FICTIONALIST DIALETHEISM

Fictionalist views about sets, numbers, possible worlds, and even morality are not unusual among philosophers, but that is far from being the case where truth is concerned. And no wonder, for fictionalism about truth faces an obvious problem. It seems to prevent us from saying that our claims about the world are sometimes true, sometimes false—*really* true or false, not just true or false in the dialetheist fiction according to which there are such properties. It seems to force us into some ridiculous kind of global fictionalism. (If it is ridiculous to think that everything might be both true and false, isn't it equally ridiculous to think that we can't call *anything* 'true' or 'false', on the grounds that there are no such properties?)

Let me briefly, and I am afraid all too sketchily, say why I think the charge ought to be rejected.[16] The above fictionalism about truth is a fictionalism about a certain property of truth for a language that contains an unrestricted truth-predicate and whose every sentence has a truth-value (at least one!)—a property that is supposed to apply equally to 'snow is white' and to 'what I am now writing is not true', or perhaps to the propositions these express. In my view, it is a fictionalism on a par with a number of other fictionalisms one might conceivably propose about a property of truth. To take an earlier example, suppose that the notion

---

[16] What follows is at best suggestive. I do little more than give a sketch of a programme, and what I say is certainly not enough to dispel the worry that such a programme will turn out to be incoherent. (It is scarcely unreasonable to have doubts on this score, for unlike other fictionalisms, it is clear how a fictionalism about a fundamental notion such as truth might come close to being self-defeating. (Cf. e.g. Boghossian 1990, who argues that an anti-realist, deflationary account of truth is self-defeating in just this way; Soames 1999: 251–4, disagrees.) Despite the obstacles, I remain optimistic.

of truth used in a community C is a notion with a metaphysical commitment to what one takes to be a flawed relation of language-world correspondence. In that case, it seems perfectly reasonable to express one's dissatisfaction with the notion by declaring that there is no such property as truth (as deployed in C).[17] One might none the less prefer to preserve apparent talk of such a property by being a fictionalist about discourse involving 'true' thus understood. Perhaps, for example, the resulting picture of objectivity helps to motivate the search for agreement when conversational parties disagree about controversial matters, something that turns the erroneous thought that there is such a property into what the critics concede is a useful fiction. Nothing in such an anti-realist, fictionalist stance requires one to be a fictionalist about truth understood in the *right* way (whatever that might be), and hence such a fictionalism does not affect one's ability to hold that some claim or other is genuinely true or false.

Something similar can be said about a fictionalism about truth that rests on the dialetheists' view about the (paradoxical) behaviour of 'true'. Let TRUE$_+$ be the putative property denoted by 'true' in the event that dialetheists are right about 'true'. In being fictionalists about TRUE$_+$, we should remember that for the most part our concept of truth doesn't get us into trouble; it is the package as a whole that is in trouble, not the parts we use most often. This suggests that we should look more closely at the relation between the parts and the whole.

Dialetheists think that our intuitive concept of truth is constituted by something like the naïve T-schema. But fictionalists about TRUE$_+$ will deny that this is the best way of looking at the T-schema. A better way is to see the schema as a natural generalization from the intuitive way we classify ordinary, unproblematic sentences as true or false, including ordinary sentences that themselves contain the truth-predicate. Assume, for the sake of argument, that this way is captured by something like Kripke's construction in his 'Outline of a Theory of Truth' (Kripke 1975), which yields a kind of recursive, 'from-the-ground-up', account of how we understand and apply the truth-predicate.[18] (It is enough for present purposes that this account offers at least a possible reconstruction of our understanding of 'true'; there are, of course, other accounts of how we do this, say those offered by revision theorists.) Let TRUE be the partially defined property corresponding to the use of 'true' thus understood (in the sequence of interpretations used to interpret 'true', TRUE corresponds to the interpretation of 'true' in the least fixed point). Now even though the realist has reason to deny there is such a property as TRUE$_+$, he surely has no reason to deny that there is such a property as TRUE; in particular, he has no reason to deny the existence of this property when it is restricted to the domain of unproblematic 'grounded' sentences.

---

[17] Deconstructionists and their ilk dispute the existence of a property of truth on just such grounds.

[18] See Soames (1999), ch. 6, for an elegant presentation of Kripke's construction that stresses the role and importance of partially defined predicates.

But there is still a question of what to do about the many sentences that do not get a truth-value on this picture. Among the latter are paradoxical sentences such as the Liar paradox, which fail to secure a truth-value no matter how far we extend the least fixed point, yet which intuitively deserve to get a truth-value. (A simple application of the naïve T-schema suggests that the sentence 'This sentence is not true' counts as not true—and hence also as true.) The fictionalist about TRUE$_+$ will respond that such a move takes us from one account of what a grasp of 'true' consists in—the recursive, from-the-ground-up, understanding in the case of ordinary truth-ascriptions—to another account, that given by the naïve T-schema. He sees the (naïve) T-schema as a natural generalization of this recursive understanding, and thinks it offers the most natural way of understanding, and coping with, truth-ascriptions at what Priest (1995) calls 'the limits of expression'. (Any other way quickly generates familiar expressive difficulties.) Furthermore, to the extent that the T-schema agrees with our recursive, from-the-ground-up, way of understanding 'true' in the case of ordinary, grounded truth-ascriptions, no harm is done by pretending that the application-conditions of 'true' in ordinary truth-ascriptions are given by the T-schema. But the fictionalist about TRUE$_+$ will insist that the T-schema is still a generalization, no matter how natural a generalization. In addition, he will take the fact that the application-conditions for 'true' so understood are incoherent to show that it is only a fiction that there really is a property TRUE$_+$ based on the T-schema.

In short, a realist convinced of the inviolability of the Law of Non-Contradiction, but persuaded by much of what dialetheists say about 'true', should not accept TRUE$_+$ as anything but a fictional property. He should be a fictionalist dialetheist for whom TRUE$_+$ exists only from the perspective of a useful fiction whose acceptance of something like a naïve T-schema provides a natural way of organizing and systematizing both unproblematic and problematic truth-ascriptions—a way that escapes the kind of expressive difficulties we so readily encounter when truth-talk is taken to 'the limits of expression'. It may even be the case, as I suggested earlier, that this fiction is in some sense indispensable. Perhaps at the limits of expression we can't help but think in terms of such an incoherent notion of truth. A realist, however, once convinced of the inviolability of the Law of Non-Contradiction, will see this only as a reason for thinking that there is something particularly deep about the conceptual incoherence affecting this notion, not that realist discourse is itself infected by deep inconsistency.

One final comment. A number of philosophers understand the denial that 'true' picks out a property as an endorsement of some kind of deflationism about truth (see, for example, Boghossian 1990). It should be clear that nothing of the sort is being proposed here. The argument I am proposing seems indifferent to the sort of issue that separates robust from deflationary conceptions of truth. Although I doubt that deflationism as a programme is particularly inimical to the claim that truth is a property (cf. Horwich 1990), we can bypass this problem by simply taking 'picks out a property' as short for 'is a predicate apt for the characterization of reality, by (among other things) *coherently* dividing the objects in its field of application'. We can then reiterate the point that, if dialetheists are right, 'true' fails this semantic test. As before, the policy being recommended is that we should in that case go fictionalist about 'true': even if the predicate can't figure in a catalogue of predicates appropriate to realist discourse, the thought that 'true' does have such a use can be seen as an immensely useful fiction.[19]

6. CONCLUSION

This chapter has been an exercise in peace-making. Dialetheists hold that there are true contradictions. Suppose we can't fault their arguments. There is then still the worry that, if they are right, *all* contradictions, not just a few, may in fact be true. I argued in the first part of the chapter that Graham Priest's recent work on this question has not alleviated that worry. But I have also suggested that that possibility somehow seems too bizarre to be taken seriously. Indeed, the very fact that dialetheism seems to allows this possibility presents us with a reason to disown dialetheism—if only we could get away with it. In the remainder of the chapter I suggested a way out of the quandary. By all means accept talk involving contradiction-affirming concepts of truth and set, but don't see this talk as somehow part of a descriptively adequate account of the world. It isn't; it is only to be accepted as part of a fiction. Such a fiction has its roots in the appreciation that such concepts are profoundly useful, yet in places deeply flawed: the fault is in the concepts, not the world. Seeing matters this way takes away the temptation even to contemplate the possibility that the world itself might be deeply inconsistent. It offers us a way of reconciling reasonable forms of dialetheism and realism with total respect for the Law of Non-Contradiction.

REFERENCES

ARMOUR-GARB, B., and BEALL, J. C. (2001). 'Can Deflationists be Dialetheists?' *Journal of Philosophical Logic*, 30: 593–608.

BEALL, JC (2001). 'A Priestly Recipe for Explosive Curry', *Logical Studies*, 7.

BEALL, JC, and COLYVAN, M. (2001). 'Looking for Contradictions', *Australasian Journal of Philosophy*, 79: 564–9.

BOGHOSSIAN, P. (1990). 'The Status of Content', *Philosophical Review*, 99: 157–84.

BURGESS, J. P., and ROSEN, G. (1997). *A Subject with No Object*. Oxford: Clarendon.

---

[19] For further discussion of the connection between deflationism and dialetheism, see Armour-Garb and Beall (2001). Beall's 'True and False — As If' (Ch. 12, this volume) draws a rather tighter connection than I am willing to draw between deflationism and an 'as if' approach to the concepts of truth and falsity.

HORWICH, P. (1990). *Truth*. Oxford: Blackwell.

JACKSON, F. (1998). *From Metaphysics to Ethics*. Oxford: Oxford University Press.

JOYCE, R. (2002). *The Myth of Morality*. Cambridge: Cambridge University Press.

KANT, I. (1929). *Immanuel Kant's Critique of Pure Reason*. Trans. N. K. Smith from *Kritik der Reinen Vernunft*. London: MacMillan.

KRIPKE, S. A. (1975). 'Outline of a Theory of Truth', *Journal of Philosophy*, 72: 690–716.

KROON, F. (1993). 'Rationality and Epistemic Paradox', *Synthese*, 94: 377–408.

—— (2001). 'The Semantics of "Things-in-Themselves": A Deflationary Interpretation', *Philosophical Quarterly*, 51: 165–81.

LEWIS, D. (2004). 'Quasi-Realism is Fictionalism', in M. Kalderon (ed.), *Fictionalist Approaches to Metaphysics*. Oxford: Oxford University Press.

PRIEST, G. (1987). *In Contradiction: A Study of the Transconsistent*. The Hague: Martinus Nijhof.

—— (1995; 2nd edn., 2002). *Beyond the Limits of Thought*. Cambridge: Cambridge University Press.

—— (1998). 'What's So Bad About Contradictions?' *Journal of Philosophy*, 95: 410–26.

—— (2000). 'Could Everything be True?' *Australasian Journal of Philosophy*, 78: 189–95.

ROSEN, G. (1990). 'Modal Fictionalism', *Mind*, 99: 327–54.

—— (1995). 'Modal Fictionalism Fixed', *Analysis*, 55: 67–73.

SOAMES, S. (1999). *Understanding Truth*. Oxford: Oxford University Press.

SORENSEN, R. (1988). *Blindspots*. Oxford: Clarendon.

STANLEY, J. (2001), 'Hermeneutic Fictionalism', in P. French and H. Wettstein (eds.), *Midwest Studies XXV: Figurative Language*. Oxford: Blackwell, 36–71.

STROUD, B. (1968). 'Transcendental Arguments', *Journal of Philosophy*, 65: 241–56.

WALTON, K. (1990). *Mimesis as Make-Believe*. Cambridge, Mass.: Harvard University Press.

YABLO, S. (2000). 'A Paradox of Existence', in Anthony Everett and Thomas Hofweber (eds.), *Empty Names, Fiction, and the Puzzles of Non-Existence*. Stanford, Calif.: CSLI, 275–312.

16

Semantic Dialetheism

Edwin D. Mares

ABSTRACT

The doctrine of semantic dialetheism is set out and contrasted with metaphysical dialetheism. We find that there is a lot to be said in favour of semantic dialetheism. Semantic dialetheism is given credence by the doctrine of partially defined predicates. To make sense of a partially defined predicate, Tappenden and Soames suggest that the semantics of predicates should be given in terms of a set of conditions under which the predicate can be applied to things and a set of conditions under which its negation can be applied. If Tappenden and Soames are correct that many of natural language predicates are partially defined then it is also plausible that some are 'overdefined'. We say that a predicate is overdefined if and only if it is possible that its negative and positive conditions pick out the same object at the same time. Some examples of overdefined predicates are discussed and it is suggested that a semantic dialetheist treatment of some folk theories (such as the folk theory of identity and the folk theory of belief) is appropriate.

1. INTRODUCTION

In the literature on vagueness, roughly speaking, theories fall into three broad categories, and these can be placed on a spectrum like that used for political parties. On the right there are epistemic theories. These theories hold that some expressions seem vague because we do not know exactly what falls under them, but that there is a real fact of the matter. This is a very conservative position. It allows us to use classical logic with its standard semantics even when discussing apparently vague predicates and singular terms. In the middle of the spectrum are the semantic theories. These hold that there are no vague properties or individuals, but that vagueness arises from the relationship of language to the world. Some semantic theories hold, for example, that certain predicates are vague because it is ambiguous as to what property they express. These theories largely try to retain traditional metaphysical intuitions—such as the view that real things and properties have sharp boundaries. And some semantic theories even let us keep

Thanks to Graham Priest, JC Beall, Max Cresswell, the philosophy department at University of Auckland, and various anonymous referees classical logic, although with a modified semantics. On the left are the radicals—the metaphysical theories. These hold that there really are vague objects and properties in the world, apart from how we talk about them. These views flout traditional metaphysical intuitions and ask us to reject classical logic.

All three of these camps have advantages and disadvantages, but this is not the place to discuss them. Our concern here is with paraconsistency and not vagueness. Paraconsistentists reject the universal validity of the rule of *ex falso quodlibet*, i.e. that every proposition follows from contradictions. They reject *ex falso quodlibet* because they think that we do run into contradictions from time to time. Paraconsistentists also can be placed on a political-like spectrum. On the right are the doxastic theories. These hold that people may have inconsistent beliefs. Or they hold that scientists sometimes use inconsistent theories. On doxastic views of paraconsistency, we need logical means to deal with contradictory beliefs or theories. We have to allow people to derive further beliefs of theorems from their theories without committing them to believing every proposition. On the left are the metaphysical theories. These theories hold that there are things in the world that are actually inconsistent or that it is possible for there to be inconsistencies. Moreover, these inconsistencies do not arise merely because of our beliefs about the world or because of how we talk about things, but because of the way things really are *in themselves*.

Clearly, we can also set out a middle of the road position—semantic paraconsistency. Theories in this camp hold that there are no inconsistent things but that inconsistencies arise (or may arise) because of the relationship between language and the world. Now, whereas the doxastic camp is very crowded—it includes a huge range of philosophers and computer scientists—and the metaphysical camp is very vocal—Richard Sylvan, Graham Priest, and their co-workers have written a large amount of literature motivating and defending these views—the camp of semantic paraconsistency is almost empty.[1]

There are some semantic paraconsistentists. Graham Priest (1979) once held that the only true contradictions concern semantics. David Lewis (1982) tried to make sense of relevant logic claiming that contradictions arise from equivocation. And, in a book review Priest (2001: 214) briefly suggests a similar view to the one put forward in the present chapter.[2] But compared to the other camps, semantic paraconsistency is relatively empty.[3] The aim of this chapter is to set out and

---

[1] Or so I thought when I first wrote this chapter. In addition to the views listed here, as Graham Priest pointed out to me, Diderik Batens holds a version of semantic paraconsistency (I had always thought of him as an doxastic paraconsistentist), and JC Beall and Brad Armour-Garb's notion of a 'linguist spandrel' might be a semantic paraconsistent concept (see Beall's contribution to this volume).

[2] I would also classify Dominic Hyde's use of subvaluations to treat vagueness as a form of semantic dialetheism, but he considers himself to be a metaphysical realist about vagueness.

[3] One might think that those of us who have used counterpossible conditionals to motivate paraconsistent logics are also semantic paraconsistentists. But this is not necessarily the case. These theories use impossible worlds in order to deal with counterpossibles. The status of impossible worlds in a given theory will determine to which camp the theory belongs. For instance, if a theory holds that impossible

motivate a programme in semantic paraconsistency. The particular version that I will set out is called 'semantic dialetheism'. Dialetheism holds that there are true contradictions. The present view claims that either there are true contradictions or at least that it is possible that there are true contradictions and that these contradictions arise because of the relationship between language and the world.[4]

In what follows, I formulate and motivate a version of semantic dialetheism.

One note before we begin. Here for the most part I avoid discussing the theory of truth. This might seem odd in a chapter on *semantic* dialetheism. But to do so would require a sustained discussion about adequacy conditions for a theory of truth, and I'm not sure that I really understand what those conditions are. Instead we will discuss dialetheic theories about non-linguistic items, such as beliefs, identity, and shadows.

2. PARTIALLY DEFINED AND OVERDEFINED PREDICATES

We begin with the notion of a partially defined predicate. A predicate P is partially defined if and only if the possible cases in which P can be applied to a thing and those in which *not-P* can be applied do not exhaust the list of possible cases. Jamie Tappenden (1996) and Scott Soames (1999) claim that natural languages contain partially defined predicates. This might sound like a commonplace, but it needs explanation. For, under the classical theory of negation, the negation of a predicate applies to an object (of the right type) if and only if the predicate itself fails to apply. We will get to the semantic theory itself soon.

Right now, I want to motivate the Tappenden–Soames thesis. Tappenden and Soames both use invented examples. Here I present an invented example of my own and a real-life example. First, the invented example. In soccer, there are two sorts of free kicks awarded after a foul: an indirect free kick and a direct free kick. An indirect free kick must be touched by a player other than the kicker before it reaches the opposing goal or else the ball's entering the net does not count as a goal. Suppose that just after the rules of soccer were set down a player shot an indirect free kick into his own goal without the ball's touching another player. Let's suppose that at this point there is no rule in the book covering this sort of event. At this time the predicate 'is a goal in soccer' is partially defined. The cases in which 'is a goal' is applicable and the cases in which 'is not a goal' is applicable do not exhaust all possible cases. The players must wait for a ruling from the referee until the score is determined. This reading of events is rather like the understanding of penumbral

worlds have the same status as the actual world, then that theory belongs to the metaphysical camp, not the semantic camp.

[4] Unfortunately, not every paraconsistent logician fits well into this spectrum. As was pointed out to me by an anonymous referee, Newton da Costa is an agnostic about contradictions. Agnosticism might seem like a middle-of-the-road position, but it isn't in the middle of my spectrum. Rather, it might be seen as a refusal to take any position.

judgements in law that is found in the legal positivists such as H. L. A. Hart and Joseph Raz, who claim that when a judge makes a ruling that is not covered by existing legislation, she is inventing new law at that point.

Here is the real-life example. This has happened to me several times. I am playing a board game with some friends. At one point, one of the players finds himself in financial trouble. A second player takes pity on him and lends him some play-money. A third player complains about the actions of the second player saying 'that's not allowed'. The rules on the inside of the box-top are consulted, but no mention of lending money is made. An argument ensues and a fourth player is called upon to make a ruling. Until this ruling is made, there is no fact of the matter about whether the lending of money is allowed in the game. Hence, until this point in time, the predicate 'is a legal move in the game' is partially defined.

What is going on in cases of partially defined predicates is that the linguistic community somehow specifies a set of cases in which the predicate can be success-fully applied and a set of cases in which its negation can be successfully applied. In the law and in rules of games, this specification takes the form of a sort of stipula-tion. But the form of the stipulation is not straightforward. What are stipulated are almost always sets of conditions that should be met, not a list of individual cases. But these conditions might not be exclusive. We could imagine, for example, a legal code being so complicated as to include overdefined predicates. In the following section, we look in detail at an example of an overdefined predicate.

3. SHADOWS AND LIGHT

Our first example is from Daniels and Todes (1975),[5] concerning the predicate 'is a shadow'. It would seem that our notion of a shadow supports the following three principles:

1. If X casts any shadow, then there is some light falling directly on X
2. X cannot cast a shadow through an opaque object
3. Every part of a shadow is itself a shadow

These three principles do not contradict each other in a straightforward way, but they can lead to our classifying things in an inconsistent way. Suppose that there is a barn with sunlight falling on one side of it. It casts a large shadow on the ground in the opposite direction. Suppose also that a bird flies beside the barn on the shaded side. Now consider the area of the ground that would be the bird's shadow if light were falling directly on the bird. Principle 3 forces us to claim that this area is in shadow, i.e. that there is a shadow falling on it. But, by principle 1, it cannot be the shadow of the bird, since the bird is itself in shadow. And, by principle 2, it cannot be the shadow of the barn, since then it would have to be cast through an

---

[5] And discussed in van Fraassen (1989: 217 f). I have modified the example slightly.

opaque object. Since the bird and barn are our only choices for ownership of the shadow, it would seem that we should also say that this is a non-shadow. Hence our concept of a shadow is overdefined.

Now, one might object that these principles do not define our concept of a shadow, but merely are intuitive principles that we link with that concept. That is, we might have an inconsistent theory of shadows, or rather a theory that allows there to be contradictions about shadows, but not an overdefined concept of a shadow itself. This might be true, but the onus is on the objector to show that 'is a shadow' has a meaning that is not overdefined. The objector needs to explain where we get these principles from if not from our understanding of the concept itself.

4. FORMAL SEMANTICS

The semantics is quite simple, and one with which paraconsistentists are very familiar. We will only look at the 1/2 order fragment here (i.e. the fragment of first-order logic without quantifiers). Our language has parentheses, a set of predicates, individual constants, and the connectives, negation ($\neg$), conjunction ($\wedge$), and disjunction ($\vee$). Our model consists of a (non-empty) set of worlds W, a (non-empty) domain of individuals I, and a value assignment v. The value assignment assigns to each individual constant an element of the domain and to each pair of an n-place predicate and world it assigns a pair of sets of n-tuples of individuals. If, for example, $v(P, w) = (\varphi, \psi)$, then φ is the extension of P at w and ψ is the anti-extension of P at w.

The value assignment determines a satisfaction relation $\models_v$ and an *anti-satisfaction* relation $\models_v^-$ as follows:

- $w \models_v P(a_1, \ldots, a_n)$ if and only if $(v(a_1), \ldots, v(a_n))$ is in the extension of $v(P, w)$; $w \models_v^- P(a_1, \ldots, a_n)$ if and only if $(v(a_1), \ldots, v(a_n))$ is in the anti-extension of $v(P, w)$

- $w \models_v A \wedge B$ if and only if $w \models A$ and $w \models B$; $w \models_v^- A \wedge B$ if and only if either $w \models_v^- A$ or $w \models_v^- B$

- $w \models_v A \vee B$ if and only if $w \models A$ or $w \models B$; $w \models_v^- A \vee B$ if and only if $w \models_v^- A$ and $w \models_v^- B$

- $w \models_v \neg A$ if and only if $w \models_v^- A$; $w \models_v^- \neg A$ if and only if $w \models_v A$

These truth conditions are taken from Dunn (1969, 1976), Belnap (1977a, b), and Langholm (1988). The logic determined by them is Dunn's four-valued logic D4.[6]

If we allow the extension and anti-extension of a predicate to overlap at a world, then we get contradictions true at that world, even contradictions involving

---

[6] This logic was so-called in Mares (1997) because it was introduced first in Dunn (1969).

complex statements. Thus, our understanding of how meaning rules work for predicates supports the idea that it is possible that there are true contradictions.

We can complicate our semantics slightly by adding a formalized version of our view of the link between predicates and their extensions. To do so, we add to our model a set of *conditions*. An n-place condition is a function from worlds to n-tuples of individuals. We then alter our notion of a value assignment such that for any n-place predicate P and value assignment v, $v(P) = (\Phi, \Psi)$, where Φ and Ψ are sets of n-place conditions. Φ contains conditions under which P succeeds according to v and Ψ is the set of conditions under which not-P succeeds according to v. Of course we add no stipulation that Φ and Ψ need to be exhaustive or exclusive. Then we have the following truth and falsity condition for atomic formulae. The positive clause tells us that a predicate succeeds of a sequence of objects if that sequence satisfies some positive condition, namely,

$$w \models_v P(a_1, \ldots, a_n) \text{ if and only if, where } v(P) = (\Phi, \Psi),$$

$$\text{there is some } \alpha \in \Phi \text{ such that } (v(a_1), \ldots, v(a_n)) \in \alpha(w)$$

and the negative clause tells us that a predicate is false of a sequence of objects if that sequence satisfies some negative condition, that is,

$$w \models_v^- P(a_1, \ldots, a_n) \text{ if and only if, where } v(P) = (\Phi, \Psi),$$

$$\text{there is some } \beta \in \Psi \text{ such that } (v(a_1), \ldots, v(a_n)) \in \beta(w)$$

This characterization of the semantics of atomic formulae will be of use to us in the next section.

5. SEMANTIC VERSUS METAPHYSICAL DIALETHEISM

In order to evaluate semantic dialetheism, we need to be able to distinguish it from its competitors. Among dialetheisms, the only other alternative is metaphysical dialetheism. Both semantical and metaphysical dialetheism hold that there are true contradictions, or at least that it is possible for there to be true contradictions. That is what 'dialetheism' means. The difference between the two views concerns the status of these contradictions.

Consider, for example, a metaphysical dialetheist version of the correspondence theory of truth due to JC Beall (2000). A fact on Beall's view is a structure $\langle R, i_1, \ldots, i_n, \alpha \rangle$, where R is an n-place property, each of the i's is an individual, and α is a *polarity*. A polarity can be either positive or negative. The positive polarity is designated by '1' and the negative by '0'.[7] Thus, the sentence '$P(a_1 \ldots a_n)$' is true

---

[7] Others have used polarities in fact-like structures before, such as van Fraassen and Barwise and Perry.

on an assignment v if and only if $\langle v(P), v(a_1), \ldots v(a_n), 1\rangle$ is a fact and it is false on v if and only if $\langle v(P), v(a_1), \ldots v(a_n), 0\rangle$ is a fact. On this view of facts there is a very straightforward correspondence between true (or false) sentences and facts. Moreover there is nothing to prevent a positive fact and its corresponding negative fact from both obtaining in the same world. Thus, we have a very clear version of metaphysical dialetheism. That is, on this view it is clearly possible for a sentence and its negation both to be true. On Beall's view, there is (or at least there might be) no way of accurately and completely describing the world without committing ourselves to contradictions. If there is some fact such that both it and its negative correlate both obtain, then any consistent description of the world will miss describing at least one fact.

Thus we come to the crux of the difference between metaphysical and semantic dialetheism. The metaphysical dialetheist holds that there are aspects of the world (or of some possible world) for which any accurate description will contain a true contradiction. Semantic dialetheism, on the other hand, maintains that it is always possible to redescribe this aspect of the world, using a different vocabulary (or perhaps vocabularies), consistently without sacrificing accuracy.

Consider the semantics given above in the previous section. Contradictions are true at worlds on that semantics only when the positive and negative conditions assigned to a predicate overlap. In such a case we can always in principle construct a second interpreted language to eliminate predicates for which such overlap occurs. There is nothing in the semantics that prevents a second language of this sort from being as descriptively complete and accurate as the first language. The metaphysical dialetheist thinks that there are possible worlds for which contradictions cannot be eliminated from an accurate and complete description. The semantical dialetheist, on the other hand, thinks that it is always possible in principle to provide an accurate and complete description of a possible world that is consistent.

This is an important point. Paraconsistent logicians often, in fact usually, use a consistent metatheory to describe their logics. This feature of semantic dialetheism tells us that there will be a consistent metatheory to use and thus in part justifies our using one.

Now, this is not to say that there is always a consistent redescription of a world that is as *good* as any inconsistent description of it. Sometimes the cost of providing a consistent redescription can be quite great. Consider for example Tarski's theory of truth. This view commits us to holding that an infinite hierarchy of metalanguages is needed to provide a complete theory of truth.[8] This commitment is a great cost indeed.

---

[8] Although only one metalanguage is needed to give a theory of truth for a given object language, since we are committed to there being a coherent notion of truth for the metalanguage as well, it requires a metalanguage, and so on.

6. OBJECTIONS AND REPLIES

Before we go on to motivate semantic dialetheism further, I would like to respond to some obvious objections.

First Objection

Semantic dialetheism violates our intuition that there are no true contradictions.

Reply. There are two ways of understanding this intuition. First, we can understand it in a purely metaphysical way as saying that there are no ineliminable contradictory facts. With this, the semantic dialetheist agrees. He or she needs no contradictory facts to explain why there are true contradictions.

Alternatively, we can understand the intuition as saying the semantics of natural language is such that *not-A*'s being true precludes *A*'s being true. Clearly, the semantic dialetheist cannot avoid this objection, but must deny that the intuition is true. Here is a story we can tell about why we have this intuition and the way in which it could be false: as Huw Price (1990) has argued, negation evolved as a way of tracking incompatible properties. For example, we can say that a book jacket is not red because it is green, since being green is incompatible with being red. In terms of meaning rules, the rule for 'is red' places being green in the class of violations because it is incompatible with being red. Our intuitions about negation are shaped by the purpose for which negation evolved. But this does not mean that we are infallible in constructing our meaning rules. Just because we think we place only incompatible properties in the set of conditions for the application of the negation of the predicate does not entail that we in fact do so.

Second Objection

Semantic dialetheism violates our intuition that 'negation is failure'. The intuition behind classical negation is that a negated statement *not-A* is true if and only if *A* fails to be true.

Reply. This is true. But if one accepts that there are partially defined predicates, one must reject the view that negation is merely failure. Now one might elaborate on the view and use a semantic theory, such as supervaluations, to make classical negation compatible with partially defined predicates. This is quite a coherent position, but if one admits that, at least in some cases, the meaning of predicates is given by a set of conditions under which the predicate is to be applied and a set of conditions under which its negation is to be applied, then there seems no reason why there cannot be possible cases in which these conditions overlap. Thus, I maintain that one who accepts partially defined predicates should reject classical negation and admit the possibility that there are overdefined predicates as well.

Moreover, following Tappenden (1996), I think that the classical semantics for negation conflates negation and denial. We deny statements that we think are not true. Some of these are not false either. For example, we deny statements because their presuppositions fail (e.g. I would deny that I have stopped beating my dog). The intuition that negation is merely failure, I think, comes from a tendency to make this conflation.

7. SOME PHILOSOPHICAL EXAMPLES

There might be more philosophically interesting possibly overlapping notions than that of a shadow, for example the notion of identity. Consider the story of the ship of Theseus. In this story, a ship is rebuilt slowly over time replacing one plank at a time. The ship eventually has no original planks and another ship is constructed from the original planks. The question is 'Which ship is the original ship?'. Our notion of identity supports the principle (a) that if two objects are made of exactly the same materials then they are identical. It also supports the principle (b) that if the material an object is made of changes slowly over time, it remains the same thing. And it supports the principles (c) that if two material things are both complete and are wholly spatially separated at a given time, then they are distinct, and (d) that identity is transitive. Thus, by (a) the original ship is identical to the ship rebuilt from the original material. By (b), the ship built from the new material is identical to the original ship. Thus, by (d), the two rebuilt ships are identical to one another, but by (c) they are distinct. I claim that our notion of identity is overdefined. Both ships are the original ship. This raises an interesting problem, because the two end ships are not identical to each other, which in turn raises a standard question, (luckily beyond the scope of this chapter): should we reject the transitivity of identity? What is not beyond the scope of this chapter is the question of whether our standard means of determining whether two time slices are of the same object can lead to contradictions. I maintain that the ship of Theseus case indicates that they can and that it seems likely that our concept of identity over time is overdefined.

A second philosophical example comes from Kripke (1979), and his famous story of puzzling Pierre. Pierre is French and has not visited London. He comes to believe that London is pretty, but speaks no English. He is disposed to and often does say 'Londres est jolie.' Later he visits London, but is unaware that it is in fact the referent of 'Londres'. He now speaks English and is disposed to say 'London is not pretty,' since he has seen the worst side of the British capital. And he is not disposed to say 'London is pretty,' and in fact would deny it. One traditional question asked is whether Pierre has inconsistent beliefs. This is not a question we need to discuss here. Rather, I want to ask about the consistency of the belief reports in this case. It would seem that belief reports are governed by the following principles:

1. If a person is disposed sincerely to utter a translation of the sentence *S* in any language that he or she understands, then we can say that he or she believes that *S*.
2. If a person is not disposed sincerely to utter a translation of the sentence *S* in any language that he or she understands or if he or she denies it, then we can say that he or she does not believe *S*.

In the Pierre example, applying these two principles leads us to claim that Pierre believes that London is pretty and that Pierre does not believe that London is pretty.

Philosophers who have tried to get rid of the paradox about Pierre have, by and large, altered one or other of these two principles. They would claim, I think, that they are attempting to discover the true principles that underlie our notion of belief. Another way of construing what they are doing is to say that they are devising alternative concepts to our overdefined concept of belief. Admittedly, it is difficult to choose between these two approaches. But the fact that these two principles are so intuitive does place the burden of proof on philosophers who claim that we do have a concept all the applications of which are consistent.

8. SUCCESSOR CONCEPTS

One might reply to the two examples above that we should in each case reject one or more of the stated principles. But if our ordinary concepts of a shadow and of belief do support these principles, then it would seem in rejecting some we are changing our concepts. Surely we can do this—we can create successor concepts to our possibly overlapping concepts. The question arises, however, when, if ever, we should create a successor concept.

There are several reasons why one might want to create a non-overdefined concept that replaces an overdefined concept. First, there might be reasons why one would want to reason about the sorts of things covered by the concept using classical (or intuitionist, or many-valued) logic. Classical logic is a powerful tool. Unlike the logic D4, it has disjunctive syllogism as a valid rule of proof. If this sort of logical power is needed for some reason, then a successor concept may be the way to go. Second, there may be other theories that do not allow for overdefined concepts that we want to use in conjunction with our 'cleaned up' folk theory. For example, we might want to use, say, a theory of rationality that does not tolerate contradictions (like standard Bayesianism) in conjunction with a theory of belief to yield predictions about agents' behaviour or as a normative theory about reasoning. In such a case, we might want to develop a successor concept to the one that is expressed in ordinary English by the relational predicate 'believes that', which successor concept is not overdefined.

9. CONCLUSION

It may be that classical logic, or some other inconsistency-intolerant logic, is better than any paraconsistent logic at formalizing mathematical reasoning. I am not sure about this, and it is an issue of some debate. But, it would seem that a logic that allows both gaps and gluts is better for formalizing natural language. The examples discussed in this chapter suggest strongly that there are underdefined predicates and that there are overdefined predicates. If we want to capture these phenomena, we need a semantics that allows for both truth value gaps and gluts.

Semantic paraconsistency, in addition, allows for gaps and gluts without any painful metaphysical commitments. It does not force on us any untoward entities such as negative facts. It even does not force us to relinquish the intuition that the world is consistent. For it admits that the world can be described adequately in a perfectly consistent manner.

REFERENCES

Beall, JC. (2000), 'On Truthmakers for Negative Truths', 78 *Australasian Journal of Philosophy*, 264–8.

Belnap, N. D. (1977*a*), 'A Useful Four-Valued Logic', in J. M. Dunn and G. Epstein (eds.), *Modern Uses of Many-Valued Logic*, Dordrecht: Reidel, 8–37.

——(1977*b*), 'How a Computer Should Think', in G. Ryle (ed.), *Contemporary Aspects of Philosophy*, Stocksfield: Oriel, 30–55.

Daniels, C. B., and Todes, S. (1975), 'Beyond the Doubt of a Shadow: A Phenomenological and Linguistic Analysis of Shadows', in D. Ihde and R. M. Zaner (eds.), *Selected Studies in Phenomenology and Existential Philosophy*, The Hague: Nijhoff, 203–16.

Dunn, J. M. (1969), 'Natural Language versus Formal Language', unpublished talk given at the American Philosophical Association meetings.

——(1976), 'Intuitive Semantics for First Degree Entailments and "Coupled Trees"', *Philosophical Studies*, 29: 149–68.

Kripke, S. A. (1979), 'A Puzzle about Belief', in A. Margalit (ed.), *Meaning and Use*, Dordrecht: Reidel, 239–83.

Langholm, T. (1988), *Partiality, Truth and Persistence*, Stanford, Calif.: CSLI.

Lewis, D. K. (1982), 'Logic for Equivocators', *Noûs*, 16: 431–41.

Mares, E. D. (1997), 'Paraconsistent Probability Theory and Paraconsistent Bayesianism', *Logique et analyse*, 160: 375–84.

Price, H. (1990), 'Why "Not"?' *Mind*, 99: 221–38.

PRIEST, G. (1979), 'The Logic of Paradox', *Journal of Philosophical Logic*, 9: 219–41.

—— (2001), Review of Scott Soames, *Understanding Truth*, *British Journal for Philosophy of Science*, 52: 211–15.

SOAMES, S. (1999), *Understanding Truth*, Oxford: Oxford University Press.

TAPPENDEN, J. (1996), 'Negation, Denial, and Language Change in Philosophical Logic', in H. Wansing (ed.), *Negation: A Notion in Focus*, Berlin: de Gruyter.

VAN FRAASSEN, B. C. (1989), *Laws and Symmetry*, Oxford: Oxford University Press.

17

Ramsey's Dialetheism

Vann McGee

Philosophers have identified a number of examples of utterances that look, on the face of it, as if they ought to be truth-valued, but fail to be either unequivocally true or unequivocally false: borderline attributions of vague terms; Epimenides' statement 'Cretans always lie,' and similar statements implicated in semantical paradox; sentences containing denotationless singular terms; sentences like 'the number 4 is an element of the number 17', that link terms from separate bodies of discourse in unexpected ways; moral and aesthetic judgements (if you are an emotivist); theoretical assertions that go beyond merely describing and predicting results of observation (if you are a certain kind of empiricist); indicative conditionals, or at least those with false antecedents (on, for example, Adams's (1975) attractive account); and so on. Philosophers have also proposed a number of ways to characterize the logical and semantical features of such utterances. Notable among them was Frank Ramsey.

Indeed, Ramsey had two ways of dealing with semantically defective assertions, though one of them (1927: 38 f.) merely swept the problem under the rug. On this account, to say that it is true that Harry is bald is to say nothing more or less than that Harry is bald, whereas to say that it is false that Harry is bald is to say nothing more or less than that Harry is not bald. We have:

> It is true that Harry is bald if and only if Harry is bald
>
> It is false that Harry is bald if and only if Harry is not bald

From these statements, it follows logically (even within the 3-valued logic we shall discuss presently) that:

> It is either true or false (but not both) that Harry is bald

This will hold whether Harry has a full head of hair, no hair at all, or something in between. The special puzzles that arise if Harry is a borderline case for the application of the predicate 'bald' are hidden from view.

The advantages of this 'disquotational' understanding of truth and falsity are many and appealing, as a number of recent philosophers, notably Paul Horwich (1990) and Hartry Field (1986, 1994), have urged. For some purposes, however, one wants to know what features of the way we use the words of our language bring it about that the utterances that have unequivocal truth values have the truth conditions they have and that other utterances lack unequivocal truth values. For such purposes, the disquotational theory is no use at all. The disquotational account ascribes truth conditions to sentences, but it is helpless at explaining why sentences have the truth conditions they have.

If we desire a more robust understanding of how it comes about that some sentences have and others lack unequivocal truth values, we are better off looking at Ramsey's other account, presented in his article 'Theories' (1929*a*; see also 1929*b*). Ramsey developed his account as a way of discerning the cognitive content of theoretical judgements that go beyond their expected role of describing and predicting the results of observations, but the story can be adapted with little effort to cover other sources of semantic deviance. Ramsey says that the deviant sentences don't express real propositions, although one might have been tempted instead to say that the sentences express propositions that lack determinate truth values. Not having a friendly attitude toward propositions anyway, I would like to avoid this issue by sticking to the level of utterances, or, when context permits, sentences. In this, I am following the advice of Braithwaite (1953: 80 f.)

The most surprising feature of the theory of 'Theories', the feature I'd like us to concentrate on here, is that sometimes Ramsey is willing to count each of two classically logically incompatible theories as true. But before taking up that topic, I'd like hastily to survey some features of the space of possible solutions within which Ramsey's account appears.[1]

Perhaps the most natural account has it that the semantically defective sentences are neither true nor false, explicating the logic and semantics of such sentences by carrying over the classical truth conditions verbatim: a disjunction is true iff (if and only if) one or both disjuncts are true, and false iff both disjuncts are false; a negation is true iff the negatum is false, and false iff the negatum is true; an existential sentence is true (assuming everything has a name) iff at least one instance of it is true, and it is false iff every instance is false; and so on. This gives us classical, 2-valued semantics if every atomic sentence is either true or false (and none is both), but if some of the atomic sentences are neither true nor false, it yields Kleene's *strong 3-valued semantics* (1952: s. 54).

The resulting system is easy to describe but hopeless to use. As Feferman (1984: 264) notes, 'nothing like sustained ordinary reasoning can be carried on' in the resulting sentential logic. The predicate logic is in even worse shape, since even such seemingly harmless generalizations as 'Every bald man is bald' are shoved into the gap between truth and falsity.

Bas van Fraassen (1966) discovered an ingenious way to overcome these difficulties. The key is to pay close attention to the distinction between the logical rule

---

[1] This survey is, let me be the first to say it, terribly short-sighted. For a further-seeing survey, let me recommend Dunn and Hardegree (2001).

of the *excluded middle*:

You may assert any sentence of the form ($\phi \lor \sim\phi$)

and the semantic thesis we may call *No Gaps*:

Every sentence is either true or false

Van Fraassen found a principled way to hold onto classical logic, including the excluded middle rule, while abandoning No Gaps. His semantic theory discerns a class of *acceptable* classical models such that all the unequivocally true sentences are true in the models and all the unequivocally false sentences are false in the models. We count a sentence as true if it is true in all the acceptable models, false if it is false in all the acceptable models, and indeterminate otherwise.

Van Fraassen originally proposed his so-called *supervaluational* account as a technique for dealing with denotationless names, but his methods are quite general. Thus, Kit Fine (1975) proposed a semantics of vague general terms that assigns to 'bald' an *extension*, consisting of people with little or no hair to whom the term definitely applies, and an *anti-extension* consisting of individuals to whom it definitely doesn't apply. An acceptable classical model is obtained by assigning to 'bald' a set that includes every member of the extension and excludes every member of the anti-extension, but not every way of dividing up the border dwellers results in an acceptable model. In partitioning the disputed territory, an acceptable model has to respect the *penumbral constraint* that anyone with less hair than someone in the set assigned to 'bald' must be in the set assigned to bald.[2] Thus the sentences 'Every bald man is bald' and 'Everyone with less hair than a bald man is bald' are true in every acceptable model, and so true.

Kripke (1975) applied the same idea to the liar paradox, precisely tailoring the class of acceptable models so that a sentence ϕ would come out true, false, or indeterminate according as ⌜⌜ϕ⌝ is true⌝ is true, false, or indeterminate. A better-known version of the Kripke construction handles truth-value gaps by means of the Kleene 3-valued logic instead of van Fraassen's method. Either way, we count a sentence as true just in case it is forced to be true by the non-semantic facts, the laws of logic, and the principles that, if ϕ is true, then ⌜⌜ϕ⌝ is true⌝ is true as well, whereas if ϕ is false, then ⌜⌜ϕ⌝ is not true⌝ is true. The difference between the two approaches is in what count as rules of logic. (We are treating falsity as a defined notion,

x is *false* $=_{\text{Def}}$ the negation of x is true

This will simplify matters, since it will mean that we have only one unruly notion to worry about.)

---

[2] Putting the constraint this way presumes that 'has less hair than' is precise. Without this presumption, the constraint would be that, if b is in the set an acceptable model assigns to 'bald', and $\langle a, b \rangle$ is in the set the model assigns to 'has less hair than', then a is in the set the model assigns to 'bald'.

Looking over the Kripke construction, Peter Woodruff (1984) asked a simple, incisive question. What happens if we treat the semantically deviant sentences as both true and false, rather than neither? Maintaining the familiar theses that a disjunction is true iff one or both disjuncts are true, and false iff both disjuncts are false, and so on, we get a semantics precisely dual to the Kleene semantics of truth-value gaps. Given a sentence ϕ whose logical connectives are among '$\vee$', '$\wedge$', '$\sim$', '$\exists$', and '$\forall$' (we treat '$\rightarrow$' and '$\leftrightarrow$' as defined), let ϕ^{Dual} be for sentence obtained from ϕ by exchanging $\vee$ and $\wedge$ and by exchanging $\exists$ and $\forall$. ϕ is classified as a truth-value gap in the system that treats semantically defective atomic sentences as neither true nor false iff ϕ^{Dual} is classified as a truth-value glut in the system that treats semantically defective atomic sentences as both true and false.

Kripke obtained the minimal fixed point—the most conservative assignment of truth values to sentences that satisfies the condition that a sentence ϕ is true, false, or neither according as $\ulcorner\ulcorner\phi\urcorner$ is true$\urcorner$ is true, false, or neither—by initially setting both the extension and the anti-extension of 'true' equal to the empty set and building up larger and larger extensions and anti-extensions until he achieved stability. Woodruff did the exact opposite, starting out putting every sentence into both the extension and the anti-extension and digging down, and he reached the maximal fixed point in stages that exactly parallel the Kripke construction. The sentences that were unequivocally true or unequivocally false in Kripke's construction are still unequivocally true or false in Woodruff's, but Kripke's gaps are the duals of Woodruff's gluts.

One of the selling points of Kripke's theory is its ability to discriminate among different kinds of paradoxy by accounting for the difference between the vicious circularity displayed by the Liar sentence—'The Liar sentence is not true'—from the friendlier circularity exhibited by the Truthteller sentence—'The Truthteller sentence is true.' The former sentence doesn't get a truth value in any fixed point, whereas the Truthteller isn't true in the minimal fixed point, but it's true in some of the others, and also false in some of the others. The dual construction has the Liar sentence contradictory—both true and false—in every fixed point. The Truthteller gets assigned both values in the maximal fixed point, but there are other fixed points in which it's unequivocally true and yet others in which it's unequivocally false. We get a fixed point of the Woodruff construction from a fixed point of the Kripke construction by taking our new extension of 'true' to be the complement of its old anti-extension, and taking the new anti-extension of 'true' to be the complement of its old extension. Thus, where Kripke discovered a complete lower semi-lattice (with respect to the inclusion ordering) of gappy fixed points, Woodruff found a complete upper semi-lattice of glutted ones.

We can even go on, if we like, to consider the possibility that there are four kinds of sentence, unequivocally true, unequivocally false, both, or neither. I can't say that I can discern a philosophical motive for supposing that semantic deviance comes in two varieties, gappy and glutted, but the resulting construction is admirably elegant mathematically. Woodruff is able to tap into the general theory of monotone operators, applying a theorem of Tarski's (1955) to get a complete lattice of fixed points, some with gaps, some with gluts, some with both.

Naïvely, one would expect now to be able to complete the story by applying to the logic of true/false/glut the same innovation van Fraassen applied to the logic of true/false/gap, distinguishing the logical law of contradiction:

You may deny any sentence of the form $(\phi \wedge \sim\phi)$

from the semantic principle *No Gluts*:

No sentence is both true and false

retaining the former and repudiating the latter. Previously, we distinguished a set of acceptable classical models and stipulated that a sentence was unequivocally true if it is true in all of them, unequivocally false if it's false in all of them, and neither true nor false if it's true in some and false in others; the semantically defective sentences were the ones that fell into the truth-value gap. We look for a dual construction that still maintains classical logic by identifying the semantically defective sentences as truth-value gluts, providing that a sentence is unequivocally true if it's true in all the acceptable models, unequivocally false if it's false in all acceptable models, and both true and false, otherwise. Thus, a sentence will count as true just in case it's true in at least one acceptable model.

In fact, we find nothing of the sort. The gappist can cheerfully confirm that the laws of classical logic are truth-preserving while denying No Gaps. However, the only way one can confirm that the laws of classical logic are truth-preserving while denying No Gluts will be to declare that every sentence is both true and false. So long as there are as many as two acceptable models, and they don't both have exactly the same sentences true, there will be some sentence ϕ that is true in one and false in the other. But this means that ϕ and $\sim\phi$ are both true, and classical logic tells us that from $\{\phi, \sim\phi\}$ you can infer every sentence. In the context of classical logic, the Woodruff duality completely collapses. The only new fixed point we get when we introduce gluts into the classical-logic version of the Kripke construction is the degenerate fixed point in which every sentence is both true and false.

In arguing for No Gluts,[3] Aristotle describes his opponents' views in a way his opponents would regard as slanderous. Aristotle argues as if anyone who allows that there are sentences that are both true and false is thereby committed to the thesis that every sentence is both true and false, and so, he declares in exasperation (*Metaphysics* Γ, 1008^{b}12), anyone who denies No Gluts is cognitively no better off than a turnip. The dialetheist—advocate of the thesis that there are statements that are both true and false—who concomitantly repudiates the classical modes of

[3] Reading Aristotle as an advocate of No Gluts is anachronistic, since it presumes distinctions Aristotle didn't make, between asserting a statement and asserting that the statement is true, and between untruth and falsity.

inference can righteously (if anachronistically) protest that Aristotle has attacked a caricature of the dialetheist position, inasmuch as the rules of deduction have been painstakingly restrained to obstruct the inference *ex contradictione quodlibet*. But one can imagine a dialetheism that, in analogy with van Fraassen's account, wants to maintain the validity of the full range of classical inferences as found in Euclid's *Elements*, yet to repudiate the semantic thesis that there are no truth-value gluts. Against such a dialetheist, Aristotle's complaint that the rejection of No Gluts entails the utter collapse of language and thought is precisely on target.

The dialetheic dual of van Fraassen's construction is Ramsey's theory. Ramsey regards a scientific theory as true just in case the existential closure of the open sentence obtained from the conjunction of the axioms of the theory and the bridge laws by replacing all the theoretical terms with variables of appropriate type is true. Since there will typically be many different ways to assign extensions to the theoretical terms all consistent with the true observational statements, there will be many different, formally incompatible true theories. A sentence counts as true if it's a part of a true theory; hence there will be many sentences that are both true and false. How Ramsey forestalls the collapse foretold by Aristotle is by restricting the range of the rules of inference. Every classical consequence of a single true sentence is true, but not every classical consequence of true sentences will be true, because the $\wedge$-introduction rule,

From ϕ and ψ, you may infer $(\phi \wedge \psi)$

is no longer valid. Also, *modus ponens*,

From $(\phi \rightarrow \psi)$ and ϕ, you may infer ψ

fails.

Sentences containing theoretical terms are not meaningful by themselves, on Ramsey's account, so they don't express genuine propositions; they are meaningful only in the context of a theory. This fact doesn't affect the way we reason within a theory, where we can interpret all logical combinations as taking place within the scope of a single existential prefix. 'We can say, therefore,' Ramsey (1927: 132) says 'that the incompleteness of the "propositions" of the secondary system affects our *disputes* but not our *reasoning*.' When we are deciding between rival theories, it makes a great deal of difference that several, formally incompatible theories can all be true. Once we have settled on a theory and are working within it, however, the fact that there are other true theories we might have used instead will make little difference. We can say that a theory Γ is true if the existential closure of the open sentence obtained from Γ by uniformly replacing all theoretical terms by free variables is true. We can say that a sentence ϕ is *true with respect to* a theory $\{\gamma_1, \gamma_2, \ldots, \gamma_n\}$ just in case the universal closure of the open sentence obtained from the conditional $((\gamma_1 \wedge \gamma_2 \wedge \ldots \wedge \gamma_n) \rightarrow \phi)$ is true. It will normally happen that there are sentences ϕ such that neither ϕ nor $\sim\phi$ is true with respect to our theory Γ, in which case both $\Gamma \cup \{\phi\}$ and $\Gamma \cup \{\sim\phi\}$ will be true. We could truly assert either ϕ or $\sim\phi$, but which, if either, we shall choose to assert will depend on which appears likely to be practically useful for the advancement of science.

It's important to know which theories are true, and it's important to know which sentences are true with respect to theories that we care about, but it's generally pointless to enquire whether a given sentence is true absolutely. It's trivial that 'There are gravitational waves' is true; it's true because there is some way to assign an extension to 'gravitational wave' so as to make it true. Whether the sentence is simply true is the wrong question to ask. To get a scientifically significant answer, we have to ask whether the sentence is true in our astrophysical theory. The sentence is true in a scientifically useful sense only if it's true in our theory and our theory is true.

At the level of propositions, this would be a zany outcome. Whether there are gravitational waves is a matter of what nature is like, quite independent of human beings and their theorizing. But at the level of sentences, it makes perfect sense. The truth or falsity of the sentence is a joint effect of those activities of the community of speakers that give the sentence its truth conditions and the astrophysical facts that determine whether those conditions are met.

To sharpen the comparison between Ramsey's account and van Fraassen's, let me remind you of Tarski's (1936), 'On the Concept of Logical Consequence'. Tarski defined a *model* of a theory Γ to be a variable assignment that satisfies the set of open sentences obtained from Γ by uniformly replacing all extralogical constants by free variables of appropriate types,[4] and he says that a sentence ϕ is a *logical consequence* of Γ if and only if every model of Γ is a model of $\Gamma \cup \{\phi\}$. More recent authors, including van Fraassen and Tarski himself in his later writings, have used a different conception of a model as a certain kind of structured set. The contemporary notion was obtained from Tarski's notion by transporting it from a setting where its mathematical background was the Whitehead and Russell theory of types to a setting whose background mathematics is Zermelo-Frankel set theory. The change in background occasions important differences, but not differences that are important for our purposes here. Here, we can reformulate Ramsey's account in terms of Tarski's notion of 'model', saying that a model is acceptable for Ramsey if it respects the standard values of the observation terms, and a theory is true if it is true in at least one acceptable model. A sentence is true with respect to a theory Γ if and only if it is true in every acceptable model of Γ. We can apply the same idea to other sorts of semantic deviance. Thus, whereas van Fraassen regards a sentence containing a denotationless name as true just in case it is true in every acceptable model, Ramsey's method counts the sentence as true if and only if it is true in at least one acceptable model.

---

[4] Taken literally, this notion of model is too restrictive to represent the ordinary notion of logical consequence adequately, for it treats all models as having the same universe of discourse. The definition needs to be modified to permit varying domains; see Etchemendy (1990).

What puzzles me is the asymmetry. Whereas van Fraassen can reject No Gaps and still maintain that every classical consequence of true sentences is true, Ramsey has to restrict the classical modes of inference. For Ramsey, every classical consequence of a true theory is true, but you can have true sentences drawn from different theories whose classical consequences are untrue. As long as our semantics was truth functional, there was a perfect duality, but with the more generous supervaluational semantics, the symmetry breaks down. Why?

The classical rules of inference aren't quite symmetrical. The elimination rules for ∧,

> From $\{(\phi \wedge \psi)\}$, you may infer ϕ
>
> From $\{(\phi \wedge \psi)\}$, you may infer ψ

look just like the introduction rule for ∨:

> From $\{\phi\}$, you may infer $(\phi \vee \psi)$
>
> From $\{\psi\}$, you may infer $(\phi \vee \psi)$

But the remaining rules don't look at all alike.

> From $\{\phi, \psi\}$, you may infer $(\phi \wedge \psi)$

versus

> If you have derived θ from $\Gamma \cup \{\phi\}$, and you have likewise derived θ from $\Gamma \cup \{\psi\}$, you may derive θ from $\Gamma \cup \{(\phi \vee \psi)\}$

Gerhardt Gentzen (1935),[5] whose concerns were quite different from our purposes here, discovered a way to symmetrize the rules of inference, and thereby to simplify them dramatically. Instead of treating implication as a binary relation between a set of premises and a single conclusion, Gentzen proposed to treat implication as a binary relation between two sets of sentences. Δ is a logical consequence of Γ just in case, in every model in which every member of Γ is true, at least one member of Δ is true. The sentence ϕ is a logical consequence of Γ in the original sense if and only if ϕ is a logical consequence of Γ in the new sense.

With the new notion of consequence, the rules for ∧ and ∨ become symmetrical:

$$\{(\phi \wedge \psi)\} \vdash \{\phi\}$$
$$\{(\phi \wedge \psi)\} \vdash \{\psi\}$$

---

[5] Here we are discussing Gentzen's 'natural deduction' system. He developed another symmetric system, his 'logistic' calculus, which distinguishes classical from intuitionistic logic by the fact that in the latter only single-conclusion inferences are allowed. I wonder if one could make sense of a dual to intuitionistic logic that allowed only single-premiss inferences? Perhaps not, for the situation isn't symmetrical. The intuitionist identifies truth with provability, and takes advantage of the fact that provable statements are recognizable as such. Dual intuitionism presumably identifies truth with irrefutability, and it's not always the case that irrefutable sentences can be recognized as irrefutable.

$$\{\phi, \psi\} \vdash \{(\phi \wedge \psi)\}$$
$$\{\phi\} \vdash \{(\phi \vee \psi)\}$$
$$\{\psi\} \vdash \{(\phi \vee \psi)\}$$
$$\{(\phi \vee \psi)\} \vdash \{\phi, \psi\}$$

The rules for $\forall$ and $\exists$, which I won't write down, are similarly symmetrical. The laws for $\sim$ are these:

$$\{\psi, \sim\psi\} \vdash \emptyset \ (\emptyset \text{ is the empty set})$$
$$\emptyset \vdash \{\psi, \sim\psi\}$$

The completeness theorem tells us that $\Gamma \vdash \Delta$ if and only if, within every model in which every member of Γ is true, at least one member of Δ is true. Defining Γ^{Dual} to be $\{\gamma^{\mathrm{Dual}} : \gamma \in \Gamma\}$, we see that $\Gamma \vdash \Delta$ iff $\Delta^{\mathrm{Dual}} \vdash \Gamma^{\mathrm{Dual}}$.

Shoesmith and Smiley (1978) investigated the logic of multiple-premiss, multiple-conclusion arguments in a very general setting, obtaining the following result (ibid. Theorem 2.1), applicable to the 'sentences' of any sort of language at all:

Abstract Completeness Theorem. Let $\vdash$ be a binary relation on sets of sentences. The following are equivalent:

(1) There is a class s of sets of sentences such that, for any Γ and Δ, $\Gamma \vdash \Delta$ if and only if every member of s that includes Γ intersects Δ. In typical applications, we will have identified a notion of 'model' of the language, and we will take s to consist of those sets of sentences Σ for which there is a model $\mathfrak{A}$ such that Σ is the set of sentences true in $\mathfrak{A}$. The condition, then, is that $\Gamma \vdash \Delta$ if and only if every model in which every member of Γ is true makes at least one member of Δ true.

(2) $\vdash$ satisfies the following three closure conditions:

Overlap. If $\Gamma \cap \Delta \neq \emptyset$, then $\Gamma \vdash \Delta$.

Dilution. If $\Omega \subseteq \Gamma$ and $\Psi \subseteq \Delta$ and $\Omega \vdash \Psi$, then $\Gamma \vdash \Delta$.

Cut. Suppose that there is a set Ω of sentences such that, for every subset

Ψ of Ω, we have $\Gamma \cup \Psi \vdash \Delta \cup (\Omega \sim \Psi)$. Then $\Gamma \vdash \Delta$.

What a lovely theorem! What's impressive isn't so much the answer Shoesmith and Smiley got, but that they had the lively curiosity to think to ask the question.

Once we expand our conception of logic to include arguments with multiple conclusions, the symmetry between the supervaluational approach and what Achille Varzi (1999, 2000), who has studied the matter carefully, calls the 'subvaluational' approach—Ramsey's way of doing things, which identifies truth with truth in at least one acceptable model—is restored. Given a language and a class of sentences of that language distinguished as 'true', let us say that a binary relation $\vdash$ on sets of sentences is *symmetrically truth-preserving* if and only if, whenever

$\Gamma \vdash \Delta$ and every element of Γ is true, at least one element of Δ is true. The single-conclusion part of classical logic—the set of pairs $\langle \Gamma, \{\phi\} \rangle$ such that ϕ is derivable from Γ in classical logic—is symmetrically truth-preserving, as supervaluationists assess truth, but once we allow multiple conclusions, classical consequences appear that aren't symmetrically truth-preserving. For example, $\{\psi, \sim\psi\}$ is a classical consequence of $\emptyset$, for each ψ, but a relation that includes the pairs $\langle \emptyset, \{\psi, \sim\psi\} \rangle$ would be symmetrically truth-preserving only if it satisfied No Gaps. In exact parallel, the single-premiss part of classical logic—the set of pairs $\langle \{\phi\}, \Gamma \rangle$ that are derivable in Gentzen's system—is symmetrically truth-preserving, as subvaluationists assess truth, but once we allow multiple premisses, classical consequences appear that aren't symmetrically truth-preserving for subvaluationists. For example, $\emptyset$ is a classical consequence of $\{\psi, \sim\psi\}$, for each ψ, but a relation that includes the pairs $\langle \{\psi, \sim\psi\}, \emptyset \rangle$ would only be symmetrically truth-preserving if it satisfied No Gluts. The only way to establish full classical, multiple-premiss, multiple-conclusion consequence as symmetrically truth-preserving will be to insist upon:

Exact Bivalence. Every sentence is either true or false, but not both[6]

Once we acknowledge single-premiss, multiple-conclusion inferences as the dual of the more familiar multiple-premiss, single-conclusion inferences, we can construct the dialetheist dual of the classical-logic Kripke construction. The fixed points of the Kripke construction are disjoint pairs $\langle E, A \rangle$ with the property that a sentence ϕ is in E iff it's true in every classical model in which Tr is assigned a set that includes E and is disjoint from A. A consists of every sentence false in each such classical model, together with the non-sentences. E is closed under classical consequence, as this phrase is usually understood: if $\Gamma \subseteq E$, and classical logic gives us $\Gamma \vdash \{\psi\}$, then $\psi \in E$.[7] The fixed points of the dual construction are overlapping pairs $\langle E, A \rangle$, whose union is the whole universe of the model, with the property that E is the set

---

[6] The 4-valued truth-functional semantics that allows both gaps and gluts avoids exact bivalence by giving up the rules for negation. The other classical rules are still valid, however; they follow from the classical truth conditions for conjunction and disjunction, which tell us that a conjunction is true iff both conjuncts are true, whereas a disjunction is true iff one or both disjuncts are true. It also yields the classical principles governing the falsity of disjunctions and conjunctions—a conjunction is false iff either or both conjuncts are false, whereas a disjunction is false iff both disjuncts are false—which validate the rules for negated conjunctions and negated disjunctions: $\{\sim(\phi \wedge \psi)\} \vdash \{\sim\phi, \sim\psi\}$ and $\{\sim\phi\} \vdash \{\sim(\phi \wedge \psi)\}$, and so on. If we introduce analogous principles for negated negations and for negated universal and existential quantifiers, we get a complete system of rules for the 4-valued logic. We get a complete logic for the 3-valued semantics with gaps if we restore the rule: $\{\phi, \sim\phi\} \vdash \emptyset$. If instead we want a logic for the 3-valued semantics with gluts, we add: $\emptyset \vdash \{\phi, \sim\phi\}$. (This is Priest's (1988) logic LP.) Restoring both negation rules to get classical logic renders the falsity rules redundant.

[7] Assuming that the universe is countable and every element has a name, we get the smallest fixed point by taking E to be the smallest set of sentences that: includes all the true atomic and negated atomic sentences that don't begin with Tr; includes $Tr(\tau)$ whenever τ denotes an element of E; includes $\sim Tr(\tau)$ whenever τ denotes a non-sentence or a sentence whose negation is in E; includes ψ whenever it includes all the members of a set Γ with $\Gamma \vdash \{\psi\}$; and includes a universal sentence whenever it includes all its instances. A will consist of sentences whose negations are in E, together with the non-sentences. When the language is uncountable, we require the further condition that ϕ is an element of E if ϕ is true in every classical model in which the extension of Tr includes E and is disjoint from A.

of sentences true in at least one classical model in which Tr is assigned a set that includes $E \sim A$ and is included in E. A consists of the sentences false in at least one such model, together with the non-sentences. There is a sense in which E is closed under classical consequence, but it is an eccentric sense: if $\phi \in E$ and $\{\phi\} \vdash \Delta$, then at least one element of Δ is in E.[8] $\langle E, A \rangle$ is a fixed point of the dual construction iff $\langle$complement of A, complement of $E\rangle$ is a fixed point of the Kripke construction.

Does expanding our notion of consequence to allow multiple conclusions as well as multiple premises doom the supervaluationist program? I think not. A central idea of the program is that the notions of truth and falsity aren't able to stand on their own. The key notions we need to employ, if we want to understand how it's possible to reason classically in a language with rampant semantic imperfections, are truth in an acceptable model and falsity in an acceptable model. The good inferences, in the supervaluationist's assessment, are those that preserve truth in each acceptable model.[9] By this standard, the inferences sanctioned by classical logic are all good. This remains so even when we allow 'inferences' with multiple conclusions. If Δ is a classical consequence of Γ, then within every model in which every member of Γ is true, at least one member of Δ is true.

The expansion of the traditional conception of the consequence relation we get by allowing sets of sentences as relata is perfectly well-defined, but it's a bit of a stretch to refer to the elements of the two relata as 'premises' and 'conclusions', and even more of a stretch to speak of 'inferring' the second relatum from the first. Inference, as I understand it, is a mental act that results in a judgement, and I don't know what a judgement with multiple objects would be. In an ordinary inference, we accept the conclusion on the basis of accepting the premiss set, where 'accepting' the premiss set is a matter of accepting each of its members. Once we allow multiple conclusions, in what sense can we be said to accept the conclusion set, when we don't accept any of its members? The only sense I can make of this is that we accept the conclusion set by accepting the disjunction of its elements, and that's a matter of replacing a multiple-conclusion inference by a single-conclusion inference.

There is no simple connection between truth and assertability, even for sentences free of semantic defects. There are other norms, apart from truthfulness, that speakers need to worry about, if they want to make sure that what they

---

If the language is countable, this additional condition is redundant, as we can see by a straightforward generalization of the completeness theorem for ω-logic; see Barwise (1975: s. III.3).

[8] Assuming that the universe is countable and every element has a name, we get the largest fixed point by taking E to be the largest set of sentences that: excludes all the false atomic and negated atomic sentences that don't begin with Tr; excludes $Tr(\tau)$ whenever τ denotes a non-sentence or a sentence excluded from E; excludes $\sim Tr(\tau)$ whenever τ denotes a sentence whose negation is excluded from E; excludes ϕ whenever it excludes all the members of a set Δ with $\{\phi\} \vdash \Delta$; and excludes an existential sentence whenever it excludes all its instances. A will consist of sentences whose negations are in E, together with the non-sentences. When the language is uncountable, we require the further condition that ϕ be excluded from E if ϕ is true in every classical model in which $E \sim A \subseteq$ the extension of $Tr \subseteq E$. If the language is countable, this additional condition is redundant.

[9] See McGee and McLaughlin (2004).

say is useful, relevant, and socially appropriate. Moreover, the two maxims of truthfulness—'Assert what's true' and 'Avoid asserting what's untrue'—don't get along very amicably. Were we constrained only by the first maxim, we would assert everything we could think of, whereas if only the second constrained us, we would say nothing at all; but as it is, we must strike a delicate balance.

Things get ever so much more complicated when we try to take account of statements that are semantically defective. When the emotivist says, 'Unprovoked warfare is wrong,' she says something she doesn't regard as true, so presumably, on the emotivist account, moral judgement is exempt from the rule that one should only assert what one regards as true. Or perhaps we should say instead that, when saying what she does, the emotivist doesn't assert something she accepts, but merely expresses something she feels.

The situation gets even queerer when we examine the radical empiricist's account of the role of theoretical terms. According to Ramsey, empirical judgements obtained by a successful scientific inquiry are unequivocally true; the point of the scientific enterprise is to arrive at such judgements. Theoretical conclusions are true as well, but they are also false. They are assertable because they are true in our theory. The acceptable models are the ones that respect the empirical facts. If, as we hope, our theory has one or more acceptable models, our theory is true. A sentence is assertable (as far as the norm of truthfulness is concerned) if it is true in our theory, that is, true in all acceptable models of the theory, in spite of the fact that such sentences are typically false as well. Classical multiple-premiss, single-conclusion inferences preserve the property of being true in every acceptable model of the theory, so the full range of classical logic is at our service when we undertake scientific inquiry.

The supervaluationist empiricist is going to use the word 'true' differently from Ramsey, restricting it to sentences that are true in all the acceptable models, thereby getting gaps instead of gluts. The divergence has little practical significance, since the practically important notion is not truth, but truth in an acceptable model of the theory.

With regard to vagueness and self-reference, our assertoric practices are, according to the supervalutionist, scarcely different in the presence of truth-value gaps and in their absence. When conversationally appropriate, we assert things when we are confident they are true, and refrain from asserting things when we are unsure of their truth. When we are unwilling to assert a statement but also unwilling to assert its negation, it makes little difference[10] whether the explanation is that the statement lacks a truth value or that the truth value is determinate but

---

[10] It makes a little difference. When we recognize a hypothesis as lacking a truth value, we abandon further inquiry, whereas we usually (though not always) suppose that unknown truth values would reveal themselves if we looked hard enough. Also, if we acknowledge Harry as a borderline case of 'bald', we feel it's OK to stipulate that, just for now, we're going to regard 'Harry is bald' as true, recognizing that when we do so we are deviating a bit from the customary usage of 'bald'. It would be bizarre to say that we were stipulating that, just for now, we were regarding 'There is life on one of the planets

unknown. In either case, classically valid multiple-premiss, single-conclusion arguments enable us to derive new assertable statements from old ones. Or that's how it works in the simplest cases. Sometimes the conclusion is so outrageous that we cannot accept it, and we respond to the discovery that the argument is valid, not by accepting the conclusion, but by rejecting the least secure of the premisses. The classical rules of single-conclusion logic explain this. If $\Gamma \cup \{\phi\} \vdash \{\psi\}$, then $\Gamma \cup \{\sim\psi\} \vdash \{\sim\phi\}$. (If there isn't one premiss that stands out as most dubitable, we'll conclude by accepting the negation of a conjunction of the initial premisses.) In other cases, the conclusion will be something we aren't willing to accept, although we aren't in a position to embrace its negation either. In such cases, we'll withdraw our acceptance of the least secure of the premisses, without going so far as to accept the negation of the least favored premiss. This behavior is explained by our recognition of our obligation to accept the conclusion of a valid single-conclusion argument when we accept its premisses. In any case, the legitimacy of classical single-conclusion inferences is what is needed to explain our practices of assertion, assent, acceptance, and inference.

At the semantic level—talking about truth-preservation—there is a symmetry between premisses and conclusion, but the symmetry disappears at the level of speech acts. Reliable single-conclusion inference methods are what we need to expand the sphere of theses we are willing to accept and assert. To restore the symmetry, we need to think of denial as a speech act on a par with assertion. This reinstates the symmetry, since, just as we are ordinarily willing to assert the conclusion of a valid multiple-premiss, single-conclusion inference from accepted premisses, we are likewise willing to deny the premiss of a valid single-premiss, multiple-conclusion inference from rejected conclusions.

We don't ordinarily recognize denial as a separate sort of illocutionary act. If we want to deny something, the usual method is to assert the negation. There are occasions on which, when we utter a sentence, we can be taken to be denying it; for instance, when we speak in a sarcastic tone or roll the eyes sardonically. We could adopt conventions that made denial easier, stipulating that, when we say a sentence with our fingers crossed, or we say it while standing in a Richard Nixon pose, we are saying something we believe to be untrue. Were such conventions in place, the problem of determining which rules of inference enable us reliably to reject new falsehoods on the basis of falsehoods rejected previously would assume a role parallel to the more familiar problem of determining rules that expand our store of accepted truths.

We can even imagine a people that only deny and never assert, so that they would inform us that Caesar was murdered by denying a sentence that meant that Caesar was not murdered. For such people, the right-to-left inference patterns would be the practically significant ones, but, if we exchange the ∨s and the ∧s,

of Betelgeuse' as true, even if we were assured that the question whether there is life in the Betelgeuse system is one we would never be able to answer.

and we also exchange the ∃s and the ∀s, the right-to-left inferences and the left-to-right inferences are symbol-for-symbol the same.[11] Gerald Massey (1976, 1992) has investigated the effects of systematically replacing assertion by denial, and he has come to the startling conclusion that there would be no effects at all. The inferential roles played by disjunction, conjunction, existential quantification, and universal quantification in the language of people who assert would be replaced by conjunction, disjunctions, universal quantification, and existential quantification, respectively, in the language of the people who deny, and the semantic roles of the extensions of predicates would be played by their anti-extensions, but after the dust settles, people who assert and people who deny will say exactly the same things, and they will decide what to say by exactly the same inferences. Massey has uncovered the most dramatic example yet of indeterminacy of translation.

Allowing denial as an autonomous speech act, either in addition to or in place of assertion, and regarding rejection as a mental act parallel to acceptance makes remarkably little difference to the logical treatment of semantic defective sentences. Supervaluation theory underwrites the classical logic of rejection and denial in just the way it underwrites the classical logic of acceptance and assertion. If classical logic gives us $\{\phi\} \vdash \Delta$, then if we reject all the members of Δ, we ought also to reject ϕ. (Or rather, that's what we ought to do unless we have some convincing antecedent reason not to reject ϕ, in which case we might instead repudiate our rejection of one or more members of Δ.) The explanation, according to supervaluationism, is that, if all the members of Δ are false, then ϕ is false. This, in turn, is explained by the compositional semantics of falsity-in-a-model, which ensures that, if $\Gamma \vdash \Delta$, then if every member of Δ is false in a given acceptable model, at least one member of Γ will be false in the model. With no special effort, supervaluation theory is able to accommodate rejection and denial alongside acceptance and assertion.

Supervaluationism's success is not subvaluationism's failure. The two approaches agree that, other things being equal, speakers aim to accept and assert thoughts that are unequivocally true (that is, true but not false) and to reject and deny thoughts that are unequivocally false. They disagree on how to describe the intermediate cases, one preferring truth-value gaps, the other gluts. Everyday intuition, focused as it is on the easy case, in which truth and falsity conditions are exclusive and exhaustive, is little help here. In going outside familiar usage to accommodate semantic deviance, the supervaluationist chooses a construction that makes extensions and anti-extensions exclusive but not exhaustive, whereas the subvaluationist opts for exhaustive but not exclusive. For the supervaluationist, the valid multiple-premiss, single-conclusion arguments are those that ensure that if the premisses are true, the conclusion is true, for those are the ones that enable speakers to achieve their goal of accepting and asserting things that are true. For the subvaluationist, the valid multiple-premiss, single conclusion are those for

---

[11] If identity is one of the logical symbols of the language, we need also to exchange = and ≠.

which the non-falsity of the premisses ensures the non-falsity of the conclusion, for these are the ones that enable speakers to achieve their goal of accepting and asserting things that aren't false. The situation is similar for single-premiss, multiple-conclusion arguments. The supervaluationist looks for arguments for which the falsity of the conclusions guarantees the falsity of the premiss, for these are the ones that enable us to reject and deny things that are false. The subvaluationist wants the untruth of the conclusion to guarantee untruth of the premiss, thus permitting us to reject and deny things that aren't true. These dispositions follow inevitably from the initial, arbitrary decision on how to classify the sentences that are neither unequivocally true or unequivocally false, where we chose whether to say that they are neither true nor false or to say that they're both.

An august tradition, reaching back to Aristotle, has held that allowing truth-value gluts has effects that are vastly more injurious than those of allowing truth-value gaps, but, at least in the context of classical logic, this doesn't appear to be so. The differences are, in fact, surprisingly inconsequential. What the gap theorist calls 'true', the gluttist calls 'non-false', and what the gapper calls 'false', the glut theorist calls 'untrue'. That's all there is to it.[12]

REFERENCES

ADAMS, ERNEST W. (1975), *The Logic of Conditionals*. Dordrecht: D. Reidel.

BARWISE, K. JON (1979), *Admissible Sets and Structures*. London: Springer-Verlag.

BRAITHWAITE, RICHARD BEVAN (1953), *Scientific Explanation*. Cambridge: Cambridge University Press.

DUNN, J. MICHAEL, and HARDEGREE, GARY M. (2001), *Algebraic Methods in Philosophical Logic*. Oxford: Clarendon.

ETCHEMENDY, JOHN (1999), *The Concept of Logical Consequence*. Stanford, Calif.: CSLI Publications.

FEFERMAN, SOLOMON (1984), 'Toward Useful Type-Free Theories, I.' *Journal of Symbolic Logic*, 49: 75–111. Also printed in Martin (1984: 237–87). Page references are to Martin (1984).

FIELD, HARTRY (1986), 'The Deflationary Conception of Truth'. In Graham Macdonald and Crispin Wright (eds), *Fact, Science, and Morality*. Oxford: Blackwell, 55–117.

—— (1994), 'Deflationist Views of Meaning and Content'. *Mind*, 103: 240–85. Repr. with a postscript in Field (2001: 104–56).

—— (2001), *Truth and the Absence of Fact*. Oxford: Clarendon.

FINE, KIT (1975), 'Vagueness, Truth, and Logic'. *Synthese*, 30: 265–300. Repr. in Keefe and Smith (1996: 119–50).

GENTZEN, GERHARD (1935), 'Untersuchungen über das logische Schliessen'. *Mathematische Zeitschrift*, 39: 176–210, 405–31. English trans. M. E. Szabo in Gentzen (1969: 68–131).

---

[12] Versions of this chapter were presented at MIT (as an IAP lecture) and at the Society for Exact Philosophy (at the March 2000 meeting in Gainesville, Florida). The comments and discussion on both occasions were quite useful. Also, I would like to thank the referee for very substantial help.

—— (1969), *Collected Papers*. Amsterdam: North-Holland.

HORWICH, PAUL (1990), *Truth*. Oxford: Basil Blackwell.

KEEFE, ROSANNA, and SMITH, PETER (eds.) (1996), *Vagueness: A Reader*. Cambridge, Mass.: MIT.

KLEENE, STEPHEN COLE (1952), *Introduction to Metamathematics*. New York: American Elsevier.

KRIPKE, SAUL A. (1975), 'Outline of a Theory of Truth'. *Journal of Philosophy*, 72: 690–710. Repr. in Martin (1984: 53–81). Page references are to Martin (1984).

McGEE, VANN, and McLAUGHLIN, BRIAN P. (2004), 'Logical Commitment: A Reply to Williamson'. *Linguistics and Philosophy*, 27: 123–36.

MARTIN, ROBERT L. (1984), *Recent Essays on Truth and the Liar Paradox*. Oxford: Oxford University Press.

MASSEY, GERALD J. (1976), 'Indeterminacy, Inscrutability, and the Relativity of Ontology'. *Studies in Ontology. American Philosophical Quarterly* Monograph Series, 12: 43–55.

—— (1992), 'The Indeterminacy of Translation: A Study in Philosophical Exegesis'. *Philosophical Topics*, 20: 317–45.

PRIEST, GRAHAM (1988), *In Contradiction*. Dordrecht: Martinus Nijhoff.

RAMSEY, FRANK PLUMPTON (1927), 'Facts and Propositions'. *Proceedings of the Aristotelian Society*, suppl. vol. 7: 153–70. Repr. in Ramsey (1931), pp. 138–55, and (1990), pp. 34–51. Page references are to Ramsey (1990).

—— (1929a), 'Theories'. Published posthumously in Ramsey (1931: 212–36, and 1990: 112–36). Page references are to Ramsey (1990).

—— (1929b), 'Causal Qualities'. Published posthumously in Ramsey (1931: 260–2, and 1990: 137–9).

—— (1931), *Foundations of Mathematics and Other Logical Essays*. London: Routledge & Kegan Paul.

—— (1990), *Philosophical Papers*. Cambridge: Cambridge University Press.

SHOESMITH, D. J., and SMILEY, TIMOTHY J. (1978), *Multiple-Conclusion Logic*. Cambridge: Cambridge University Press.

TARSKI, ALFRED (1936), 'Über den Begriff der logischen Folgerung'. *Actes du Congrès International de Philosophie Scientifique*, 7: 1–11. English trans. J. H. Woodger in Tarski (1983: 409–20).

—— (1955), 'A Lattice-Theoretical Fixpoint Theorem and its Applications'. *Pacific Journal of Mathematics*, 5: 285–309. Repr. in Tarski (1986: iii. 549–75).

—— (1983), *Logic, Semantics, Metamathematics*, 2nd edn. Indianapolis: Hackett.

—— (1986), *Collected Papers*. Basle: Birkhäuser.

VAN FRAASSEN, BAS C. (1966), 'Singular Terms, Truth-value Gaps, and Free Logic'. *Journal of Philosophy*, 63: 481–95.

VARZI, ACHILLE C. (1999), *An Essay in Universal Semantics*. Dordrecht: Kluwer.

—— (2000), 'Supervaluationism and Paraconsistency'. In Diderik Batens, Chris Mortensen, Graham Priest, and Jean Paul Van Bendegem (eds.), *Frontiers in Paraconsistent Logic*, Studies in Logic and Computation, 8. Baldock: Research Studies, 279–97.

WOODRUFF, PETER W. (1984), 'Paradox, Truth, and Logic'. *Journal of Philosophical Logic*, 13: 213–32.

V

For the LNC

18

The Barber, Russell's Paradox, Catch-22, God and More: A Defence of a Wittgensteinian Conception of Contradiction

Laurence Goldstein

INTRODUCTION

When Crispin Wright, talking about Wittgenstein's views on consistency, says that 'the impression is not so much that of ordinary attitudes or assumptions questioned, as of good sense outraged' (Wright 1980: 295), it is easy to see what he means. Wittgenstein speaks of the 'superstitious dread and veneration by mathematicians in face of a contradiction' and recommends that, instead of adopting this attitude, people might have *wanted* to produce a contradiction and 'would be glad to lead their lives in the *neighbourhood* of a contradiction' (Wittgenstein 1978: App. III-17; III-81). Gödel thought such claims 'nonsense' and few authors have dissented from that verdict. Wright cites a number of other passages from the *Remarks on the Foundations of Mathematics* where Wittgenstein makes a series of prima facie outrageous remarks about contradictions. Perhaps the most striking remark he makes is that *they are not false*. This claim first appears in his early notebooks (Wittgenstein 1960a: 108). In the *Tractatus*, Wittgenstein argued that contradictions (like tautologies) are not statements (*Sätze*) and hence are not false (or true). This is a consequence of his theory that genuine statements are pictures.[1]

The law of non-contradiction (LNC) may be formulated non-formally as follows:

(LNCN) The conjunction of a proposition and its negation is never true

A question that can be debated is whether (LNCN) is itself true. A certain type of degree-of-truth theorist would answer that, since contradictions can be true to degree .5 or less, then (LNCN), if it is saying that no conjunction of a proposition and its negation is ever true to any degree, is false. A dialetheist would say of (LNCN) that it is not true (to any degree). The early Wittgenstein, as we have just seen, would say that (LNCN) is true, this conclusion being a product of his distinctive logico-metaphysical system. The later Wittgenstein allows that some

---

[1] For a detailed account of Wittgenstein's early views on tautology and contradiction, see Goldstein (1986, 1999a).

contradictions are true, but, as was his wont, argued that the question about (LNCN) rested on a false presupposition.

The view that contradictions lack content is not without historical precedent. A very distinguished list of subscribers includes Aristotle, Boethius, and Abelard (Sylvan 1999: 316). Nor, despite its initial strangeness, is it wholly lacking in appeal. For example, adopting this deviant view of contradiction allows us to reject the classical 'spread' principle *ex falso quodlibet* (which licenses the inferring of any proposition from a contradiction), a principle that many have found deeply disturbing. From what lacks content, nothing that possesses content can be inferred. And the view comports nicely with a widely held view about propositions—that a proposition is the set of worlds in which it is true—for a contradiction is true in no world, and is thus to be identified with the empty set, in contrast to a false proposition, which is true in worlds other than this one.

Again, no object can both satisfy and fail to satisfy a certain predicate, or to satisfy a predicate if and only if it does not. It is, therefore, natural to say that 'Fa $\leftrightarrow$ $\sim$Fa' is necessarily about nothing and hence fails to state anything about something and hence is no statement. This squares satisfyingly with the view famously defended by P. F. Strawson, that sentences with *contingently* vacuous descriptions as subjects fail to yield statements.

Despite these preliminary considerations in its favour, the claim that contradictions are not statements and lack truth-value is highly non-standard, and is liable to meet with strong resistance. I want here to do something to resist that resistance. My strategy will be to approach LNC by a circuitous route. I shall first look at some paradoxes, and shall try to show that an appealing solution to them depends on the claim that contradictions, and bi-conditionals of the form 'p iff not-p' are *not false*. Then I shall draw upon late-Wittgensteinian and other considerations to demonstrate, quite independently of the paradoxes, that this claim is plausible, and thus that a solution to these paradoxes is within our grasp.

PARADOXES AS CONTRADICTIONS IMMERSED IN NOISE

Were I to tell you that there is a barber, the sole survivor of a plague in a certain village, who shaves himself if and only if he does not shave himself, you would be right to reply 'No there isn't—there cannot be—it is a logical impossibility.' No individual can satisfy the condition: (Sxx $\leftrightarrow$ $\sim$Sxx). This is not the same as saying that I told you something false about a certain barber. The Standard Barber Paradox speaks of a village barber who shaves all and only those male villagers of Alcala who do not shave themselves. Suppose there to be n male villagers, $v_1, \ldots v_n$ and the barber b. We are given (with x ranging over the male villagers)

$$(x)(Sbx \leftrightarrow \sim Sxx)$$

Expanded out, this becomes

$$(Sbv_1 \leftrightarrow \sim S \ v_1v_1) \ \& \ (Sbv_2 \leftrightarrow \sim S \ v_2v_2) \ \& \ \ldots \ \& \ (Sbv_n \leftrightarrow \sim S \ v_nv_n) \ \&$$
$$(Sbb \leftrightarrow \sim Sbb)$$

or, more shortly,

$$(Sbb \leftrightarrow \sim Sbb) \ \& \ \text{NOISE}$$

The noise diminishes as plague ravages the village and its population dwindles. Now, just as, in the case of the 'Lone Barber' version, where we were right to say that there can be no such barber, so here we should say exactly the same—the presence of NOISE is only a distraction; since there is no individual b satisfying '(Sbb $\leftrightarrow$ $\sim$Sbb)', there is a fortiori no such individual satisfying '(Sbb $\leftrightarrow$ $\sim$Sbb) & NOISE'.

The Epimenidean Liar is just a noisy version of the Eubulidean. If to the Eubulidean Liar ('This statement is false') one adds the noise 'and all other statements made by me and my fellow Cretans are false', one obtains the Epimenidean Liar ('All Cretans are liars', spoken by Epimenides, the Cretan). With paradoxes, it is often the case that examining the stripped down, noiseless versions helps us see to the heart of the problem. For example, it is useful to consider the 'Surprise Examination' paradox in a reduced form in which a teacher says to the class 'There will be a surprise examination tomorrow.'

Most who have written on the subject agree that the conclusion to be drawn from the Standard Barber is that there is no barber answering to the description given, but most argue that it is just a matter of empirical fact that this is so.[2] Yet, as we have seen, it is a *logical* impossibility that there should be such a barber. Were this not the case, there would be an unexplained asymmetry between the Standard Barber and the Russell Paradox despite the well-known fact that both paradoxes have a common structure: to obtain the Russell from the Standard Barber, substitute 'R' ('the Russell Class') for 'b', and 'x $\in$ y' for 'Syx'.

It has been overlooked, in the literature, that Russell's Paradox is not *essentially* infinitistic. Think of a universe in which there are just four physical objects, hence sixteen sets of physical objects, together possibly with the set J of all those sets of physical objects that are non-self-membered. If J exists, it contains all those sixteen sets, but does it also contain itself as a member? To claim that there is such a set as J, we may write

$$(1) \quad (E!x)(y)(y \in x \leftrightarrow \sim(y \in y))$$

with y ranging over all the classes in the given universe. If the sixteen sets are named $a_1, a_2, \ldots a_{16}$, then (1) can be expanded out as

$$(2) \quad (a_1 \in J \leftrightarrow \sim(a_1 \in a_1)) \ \& \ (a_2 \in J \leftrightarrow \sim(a_2 \in a_2)) \ \& \ \ldots \ \& \ (J \in J \leftrightarrow \sim(J \in J))$$

---

[2] See e.g. Priest (1998: 836).

Inspection of the last conjunct reveals that it is a rotten apple of the form 'p ↔ ~p', and the above expansion can be usefully contracted down to

$$(J \in J \leftrightarrow \sim(J \in J)) \ \& \ \text{NOISE}$$

A rotten apple spoils the whole barrel. What, at first sight, looked like a definition of J, a statement specifying the membership conditions for J, namely

(3) $(y)(y \in J \leftrightarrow \sim(y \in y))$

turns out to be not true and hence fails to define anything. Equally, the Russell class characterized by

(4) $(y)(y \in R \leftrightarrow \sim(y \in y))$

with y ranging over all classes, is not true (for, when expanded out, it contains a contradictory clause) and hence is not a definition at all. No Russell class is defined, so the question does not arise as to whether *it* is or is not a member of itself.

It is one thing to say—and it is provable, and it is agreed on all sides—that the Russell Class does not exist, but quite another thing to see *why* it does not. But we now have the beginnings of an explanation—the biconditional purportedly defining the Russell class fails to satisfy a basic condition for being a definition because it is not true; it is of the form '(p ↔ ~p) & NOISE'. There cannot be a *false definition* or a definition that is neither true nor false.

As we have seen, the existence of the Barber of Alcala and that of the Russell Class are both ruled out a priori. Yet it is true that there is generally a greater reluctance to accept the latter result. Why? Well, it is clear that there are non-self-membered classes—the class of horses and the class of prime numbers are examples—and it may seem that nothing can prevent us collecting all such classes into a class called the Russell Class. That's how it may seem, but it is not the case. A comparison with the Standard Barber will, again, be instructive. If Miguel is an inhabitant of Alcala, and he does not shave himself, then one might think that he must be shaved by the village barber. But that is a mistaken thought. We have proved that there is no such barber, and hence Miguel is not 'his' client, and he remains unshaved. Similarly, since there can be nothing meeting the specification of the Russell Class, no such class exists for the class of horses and the class of primes to be members of. It is not, note, that we have succeeded in specifying a class that is empty; we have failed to specify a class.

Make the following substitutions in (4):

'applies to*' for '∈'

'"heterological"' for 'R'

(where 'applies to*' is the converse of the relation 'applies to') and have y range over names of predicates. The result is Grelling's Paradox. Thus Grelling's Paradox and

Russell's are structurally identical to the Standard Barber and may be handled in exactly the same way: there is no well-defined property *heterologicality* corresponding to the adjective 'heterological', just as there is no barber corresponding to the description 'the barber who shaves all and only those who do not shave themselves'. (And there is no number answering the description 'the greatest prime number'.)

In each of the paradoxes considered above (the Barber, Russell's, and Grelling's), what seemed, at first sight, to be a specifying condition turned out to be a biconditional specifying nothing. In each case there is a prima facie plausible assumption that something exists that corresponds to a given specification. Once it is revealed that we do not have a true specification, we give up (and see why we should give up) the existence assumption. This diagnosis applies to an array of apparently diverse puzzles and paradoxes.

CATCH-22

Joseph Heller (1994) presents a conundrum so pleasing and amusing that to subject it to an analysis betrays a nerdishness for which I can only apologize. Here's Heller:

> 'You mean there's a catch?'
>
> 'Sure there's a catch,' Doc Daneeka replied. 'Catch-22. Anyone who wants to get out of combat duty isn't really crazy.'
>
> There was only one catch and that was Catch-22, which specified that a concern for one's own safety in the face of dangers that were real and immediate was the process of a rational mind. Orr was crazy and could be grounded. All he had to do was ask; and as soon as he did, he would no longer be crazy and would have to fly more missions. Orr would be crazy to fly more missions and sane if he didn't, but if he was sane he had to fly them. If he flew them he was crazy and didn't have to; but if he didn't want to he was sane and had to. Yossarian was moved very deeply by the absolute simplicity of this clause of Catch-22 and let out a respectful whistle.
>
> 'That's some catch, that Catch-22,' he observed.
>
> 'It's the best there is,' Doc Daneeka agreed.[3]

It looks as if an airman can avoid flying dangerous missions (A) on condition and only on condition that he is insane (I).

$$(1) \quad (x)(Ax \leftrightarrow Ix)$$

All you need do is to establish your insanity. Now, it defines you as being insane if you *don't* request to be spared flying such missions (R):

$$(2) \quad (x)(Ix \leftrightarrow \sim Rx)$$

---

[3] Heller (1994: 62–3). The suggestion that Catch-22 bears comparison with the paradox of Protagoras and Euathlus is made in Poundstone (1988: 128).

But you cannot be spared flying dangerous missions unless you request it:

(3) $(x)(\sim Rx \leftrightarrow \sim Ax)$

Now, (1), (2), and (3) jointly entail

(4) $(x)(Ax \leftrightarrow \sim Ax)$—one can avoid flying dangerous missions if and only if one cannot avoid it

Thus Catch-22 boils down to a biconditional of the sort that we have already encountered in paradoxes. Contrary to first appearances, airmen are not presented with a specification of the condition they have to meet in order to avoid flying dangerous missions, but merely with an empty form of words that specifies no condition at all.[4] I propose to call biconditionals of the form 'p $\leftrightarrow \sim$p' *vacuous*. A vacuous bicondition is clearly not the same as a condition that cannot be satisfied, such as 'You can avoid flying dangerous missions if and only if you can trisect an arbitrary angle using only straightedge and compass'; a vacuous biconditional just does not amount to the expression of any condition. The catch is this: what looks like a statement of the conditions under which an airman can be excused flying dangerous missions reduces not to the statement

(i) 'An airman can be excused flying dangerous missions if and only if Cont' (where 'Cont' is a contradiction)

(which could be a mean way of disguising an unpleasant truth), but to the worthlessly empty announcement

(ii) 'An airman can be excused flying dangerous missions if and only if it is not the case that an airman can be excused flying dangerous missions'

If the catch were (i), that would not be so bad—an airman would at least be able to discover that under no circumstances could he avoid combat duty. But Catch-22 is worse—a welter of words that amounts to nothing; it is without content, it conveys no information at all. (i) would be devilish, but (ii), like the characters in the book, and the plot, is zany. It does not state a truth or a falsity about the conditions under which danger can be avoided; on the Wittgensteinian view, it states nothing at all, though it has meaning, can be understood and may have the perlocutionary effect of engendering confusion. Catch-22 is an elaborate oxymoron.

---

[4] Formalizing Catch-22 would be an interesting exercise for an introductory logic class. I do not claim that my formalization is the only possible one, and if someone claims that it is inaccurate I am happy, for the sake of making the point I want to make here, to say that it is instead the accurate formalization of Catch-23.

PROTAGORAS AND EUATHLUS

The ancient paradox of Protagoras and Euathlus turns out, perhaps surprisingly, to be related to Catch-22. The situation here is that Protagoras, the father of Sophistry, puts his pupil Euathlus through a training in law, and agrees not to be paid any fee for the instruction until Euathlus wins his first case. Euathlus completes the course of instruction, but then, indolently, takes no cases. Eventually Protagoras gets frustrated at not being paid, and sues him. So Euathlus's first case is this one—defending himself against Protagoras' suit. If Euathlus loses the case then, by the agreement he made with Protagoras, he does not have to pay him (for he has to pay only after his first *win*). However, if Euathlus wins, that means that Protagoras loses his suit to be paid; in other words, Euathlus does not have to pay him. It seems that Protagoras cannot recover his fee. On the other hand, it seems that Protagoras must recover his fee for, if he wins the suit, the court will order in his favour, but if he loses—i.e. if Euathlus wins—then, by the terms of their agreement, he gets paid. This paradox is somewhat simpler than Catch-22. For here there is a tension between just two conditions—the one generously agreed to by Protagoras, that he gets paid if and only if Euathlus wins:

(5) $\sim$P $\leftrightarrow \sim$W

and the penalty code of the court which, in this particular case, enjoins

(6) P $\leftrightarrow \sim$W

(where W stands for 'Euathlus wins' and P for 'Protagoras gets paid'). These two conditions entail

(7) P $\leftrightarrow \sim$P

From this vacuous biconditional, we can, on the Wittgensteinian view, infer nothing; in particular, we cannot infer that Protagoras can or that he cannot recover his fee. This seems correct. The case could be decided either by the court's rule or by Protagoras' rule. But, since these rules are in conflict, it cannot be decided by both together. In the same way, a football match could not get started were it bound by both rules 'The side winning the toss kicks off' and 'The side that loses the toss kicks off.' Note again our departure from classical principles, for, in classical logic, from 'p $\leftrightarrow \sim$p', *everything* can be inferred.

GOD: A SUPPOSED PROOF OF HIS NON-EXISTENCE

Consider next a spoof proof of the non-existence of God, which starts from consideration of the sentence 'God can create a stone so heavy that He cannot lift it.' If this sentence (that we shall call the unliftability sentence) is false, then there is something that God cannot do—create the stone; if the sentence is true, then there is something that God cannot do—lift it. Either way, there is something that God cannot do, and this shows that the Judaeo-Christian God, defined *inter alia* by His omnipotence, does not exist. This is regarded as a paradoxical result because, to put it baldly and puritanically, so strong a conclusion just shouldn't be obtained with such little effort.

What creates this paradox is the unliftability claim that there is an omnipotent being—God—who can do everything, including creating a stone so heavy that He cannot lift it. The claim, suitably paraphrased, may be symbolized:

(8) (E!x)(y)(x can do y & ~(x can lift a certain stone))

(where y ranges over tasks and x over task-doers) and this entails the contradiction

X can lift a certain stone and X cannot lift that stone.

There is obviously a connection between vacuous biconditionals and contradictions. In our discussion of the paradox of Protagoras and Euathlus, we showed that the merging of Protagoras' rule and the court's rule issues in a vacuous biconditional 'P ↔ ~P'. One could continue this line of thought as follows: given that biconditional, and accepting that Protagoras must either get paid or not get paid (no middle way), we infer the contradiction 'Protagoras gets paid and Protagoras does not get paid'. The unliftability sentence also reduces, as we have just seen, to a contradiction. It seems most natural to say that contradictions too (unless they are being used for one or other rhetorical purpose) are vacuous, not false. And this is exactly the view that Wittgenstein defended throughout his philosophical career.

From the apparent truth that it is either true or false that God can create a stone so heavy that He cannot lift it, a conclusion is apparently validly inferred that contradicts the claim that God is omnipotent. Some might want to say that this does indeed give us good reason to deny the existence of an omnipotent being. Others might want to say that, by *ex falso quodlibet*, we can infer anything, including the existence of an omnipotent being. At this point, we could either go 50–50 or dial a theist. The dialetheist might respond to the derivation of the contradiction by asserting that the claim that unliftability sentence is either true or false is itself one of those claims that is both true and false. But, if the dialetheist maintains that it is true (let's isolate that from the 'and false' part) then it seems that he and she will derive, too cheaply, an assurance of God's existence.

There is a better alternative. On the Wittgensteinian view, (8) is an illicit, because contradictory, specification; no individual can satisfy it. But equally, no individual can satisfy the condition of being able to paint a vase both red and green all over. Failure to do the impossible is not a real failing, hence nothing so far tells against the possibility of a God who is omnipotent, in the sense of being able to do everything that is possible. And this seems to be all that can be properly extracted from the Paradox of Omnipotence. On the Wittgensteinian account, the contradiction is without content and *nothing* can be inferred from it. One way of solving a paradox is to show that the plausibility of one of the premisses can be undermined. In the case of the Paradox of Omnipotence, the relevant premiss is that the unliftability sentence is either true of false. Hence, if we can convince ourselves that the unliftability sentence is vacuous, and thus *neither* true nor false, then the paradox is solved.

THE LIAR

Finally, the Liar Paradox. Where S is the name of a statement, the statement 'S is not true' obviously has a truth-value different from (classically: opposite to) that of S. We can, therefore, no more *identify* S with 'S is not true' than we can identify 2 with -2. No such stipulation is admissible. The letter S was, of course, one of any that could have been used instead in this argument. The conclusion we just drew can be formulated without the use of any particular letter—it is the conclusion that no statement can state of itself that it is not true. So, initial appearances to the contrary, 'This statement is not true' is not a statement; it states nothing; in particular, it does not state that it is not true. Do not be fooled by the presence of the phrase 'This statement'—the description 'the number that is four less than itself' does not describe a number. Similarly, the token of the *sentence* 'S is not true' mentioned above does not yield a statement; it has no truth-value. It has a character, but no content; it is discontent.[5]

The argument just given concerned statements, not sentences. A sentence is the material typically used to make contentful acts of speech; the sentence by itself (i.e. not in use) does not have a truth-value. We can think of a statement as a sentence together with an interpretation. But, where we have a sentence consisting of a singular term followed by 'is not true', then that singular term can be given no consistent interpretation if it is also styled as the name of the putative statement.

It is sometimes said that the meaning of a sentence is its truth-conditions. That cannot be correct, otherwise the meaning of all tautologies would be the same, and that of all contradictions the same, and, on the usual understanding of 'meaning', 'Either he is heavy or not heavy' differs in meaning from 'Either 7 is greater than 3 or it is not'—they would translate differently into German, for example. What can be said, however, is that the content of an utterance may be given by stating its truth conditions. The content of 'Schnee ist weiss' can be explained to someone who knows no German by telling him or her that 'Schnee ist weiss' is true in all situations (in all possible worlds) in which snow is white. So, where C is a name of

---

[5] See Kripke (1975: 56) on why we can have self-referential *sentences*—for example, if the name has not been assigned already, we can stipulate that the name of the sentence 'Jack is short' is 'Jack'—without it following that we can have self-referential *propositions*.

the target statement to be interpreted, we give someone the content of C by means of the equivalence

    C is true iff p

Where p is in a language intelligible to the hearer and has the same truth-conditions as C. Now, let S be a name of 'S is not true'
    Then, following the above prescription, we specify the content of S by

    (SpecS) S is true iff S is not true.

And, on the Wittgensteinian view recommended above, (SpecS) is not false, for it says nothing; in particular, it assigns no content to S. So, if there is no independent way of assigning content to S, we can say that S too has no content.
    Let us put the point in a slightly different way. Suppose that we have a statement A to the effect that some other statement B is not true. If we know the truth-conditions of B, then the truth-conditions of A can be specified as follows:

    A is true if and only if B is not true

But now consider

    S is true if and only if S is not true

This is vacuous and so specifies nothing. Yet note that this *would be* the result of specifying the truth-conditions for S, where S is to the effect that S is not true, i.e. for the (strengthened) Liar. It follows that, while there is a Liar *sentence*, there is no Liar *statement*, no truth-valued claim made by that sentence. Thus the Liar paradox, which starts with the assumption that there is such a statement, cannot get off the ground.
    The Liar paradox trades on the mistaken assumption that 'This statement is not true' *does* state that it itself is not true. The argument goes: ' "This statement is not true" cannot, on pain of contradiction, be either true or false. Therefore it is neither. But that's one of the things it states, since *it states that it is not true*. So, after all, and paradoxically, it is true.' The italicized claim is, as we have seen, what needs to be rejected in this argument. It is often claimed that if 'This statement is not true' is neither true nor false, then, being not true and not false it is (by '&-Elimination') not true and that therefore, since this is what it states itself to be, it is (paradoxically) true. But this is a mistaken line of reasoning, for it does not state itself to be anything;[6] it does not state anything at all and nothing may be inferred from it.
    This approach to the Liar is not new. It flourished in the early Middle Ages under the name 'cassatio' which translates into computer lingo as 'crash'. When

---

[6] Though a token of the same type may state something about it, see Goldstein (1992, 2001), and Clark (1999).

your computer crashes you keep hitting the keys in the usual way, but nothing happens on the screen. Likewise with the Liar sentence—you produce a flurry of words that belong to the vocabulary of a certain language and conform to the syntax of that language; you go through the sort of motions that you would normally go through for producing a statement, but, on this occasion, no statement results. That may seem curious, even suspicious, until we reflect that nothing is stated by a vacuous biconditional, and the Liar is only a vacuous biconditional in disguise—in other words, a vacuous biconditional can be extracted (derived) from it by a proof or a piece of reasoning. The Liar sentence has a literal meaning; it can be translated into other natural languages. But it lacks content, fails to express a proposition.[7]

The Liar is the simplest of a large family of paradoxes, and it is interesting to observe that many of them can be diagnosed as arising from illegitimate stipulation. Consider the following example, a version of which is published (on T-shirts) by the American Philosophical Association:

S_1: S_2 is false

S_2: S_1 is true

We *can* legitimately assign the name S_1 to the statement 'S_2 is false' but, in so doing, we are stipulating that S_1 and S_2 have *opposite* truth-values. Therefore, we are not free, in the same context, to assign the name S_2 to 'S_1 is true', for that stipulation would guarantee that S_1 and S_2 have the *same* truth-value. There is thus a *restriction* on what we can stipulate concerning the names S_1 and S_2 once the initial stipulation that S_1 is to be the name of 'S_2 is false' has been made. Another way of putting this would be to say that, after the initial assignment has been made, the names 'S_1' and 'S_2' are no longer *free for* indiscriminate use, if logical perspicuity is to be respected.

This kind of restriction, and the notion of being *free for*, are familiar in first-order logic, and it is important to see that the restriction on the assignment of names to which we have just alluded is not ad hoc, but is of a kind that is familiar both in logic and in everyday life. In everyday life, if you sign up with an e-mail provider, you will not be assigned a name that has already been assigned to another user, for such duplication would facilitate duplicity, infringe privacy, and foster piracy. In logic, a name, once it has been introduced in the course of a natural deduction, is no longer available for replacing the variable when applying the rule of inference 'Existential Instantiation' (EI). In Quine's natural deduction system of *Methods of Logic*, for example, the rule EI that licences the inference from '$(\exists x)Fx$' to 'Fy' is annotated by flagging the variable 'y', and the restriction on proofs incorporating EI is given as 'no flagged variable retains free occurrences in premises or conclusion' (Quine 1952: 161). Equivalent restrictions hold in all the common deductive systems of first-order logic.

---

[7] For a discussion of the distinction between *meaning* and *proposition*, see Soames (1999: 16–19).

In most texts, including Quine's, the restriction on the rule is justified merely by showing that ignoring it exposes you to the risk of deriving a false conclusion from true premises, without explaining the rationale for the restriction. Yet the rationale is easy enough to explain. Suppose that somewhere in a proof you have established that some object has property F, i.e. $(\exists x)Fx$. Applying EI then amounts, roughly speaking, to the stipulation: 'Let that object be called "N".' Now, suppose, later in the proof, it is established that some object has property G. It would obviously be rash to suppose that *that* object too is N. Therefore, formally, the prophylactic is not to use N when that name has already been assigned to some object earlier in the proof. Likewise, with the paradoxes we have been considering. We do not refrain from stipulating a name for a given statement just because to do so generates a contradiction, but because there are readily intelligible limits on our freedom to stipulate. We can stipulate that 'S' is the name of a statement. But, if we do, then, should we wish to assign a name to the statement 'S is not true', that name must be something other than 'S', for reasons given above.

YABLO AND CIRCULAR VARIANTS

Another example to illustrate how a member of the Liar family is revealed as discontent through illegitimate stipulation is

J: J and K are untrue

K: J and K are untrue

You can easily verify that this is paradoxical: look at the first line. If J is true, then it is untrue, because J says that itself (and K) are untrue. Conversely, if J is untrue, then, since it is saying the truth about itself (namely, that J is untrue), it must be saying something untrue about K. What it says about K is that K is untrue, so if that's untrue, it follows that K is true. But (now look at the second line) K *cannot* be true because K says of itself that it is untrue. Doh!!! The paradox is broken, however, once you work out that the initial assignment of names renders the two sentences discontent.

It is instructive to see how this last paradox is related to Yablo's:[8]

Yablo's Paradox

(Y1) For all $k > 1$, Yk is not true

(Y2) For all $k > 2$, Yk is not true

. . .

(Yi) For all $k > i$, Yi is not true

. . .

---

[8] (Yablo 1993). There has been some debate in the literature over whether Yablo's Paradox is genuinely non-self-referential. We show below how to recast this paradox so that it is clearly self-referential.

Here we have an infinite list of putative statements, no members of which refer to themselves, yet together they generate a paradox (Yablo 1993).

Step 1—Sorensenize the paradox. Following an idea of Roy Sorensen's (1982), make the paradox more homely by viewing it as an infinite queue of people, each of whom just says 'Everyone further down the queue is saying something untrue'.

Step 2—Manufacture a finite, circular version. Chop the queue at the nth person (for some finite n) and send the remaining infinite number of people back to their hotel. Now, with your finite queue, bring the tail round to the head, thus forming a circular queue of speakers, each saying what he or she was saying before. Of course, what each speaker is now saying is self-referential since he or she is further down the queue from him/herself each time we go full circle.[9]

Step 3—Tighten the circle. For each finite n, you get a paradox. Consider a very tight circle, where n = 2. So here we have just two persons, each of whom is saying 'What each of us is saying is untrue.'

Step 4—De-Sorensenize. This gives us the 'pair paradox' we were just considering, namely:

J: J and K are untrue

K: J and K are untrue

It now becomes very natural to suggest that the Yablo is to be dissolved by refusing to accept that there can be any *statement* of the form 'For all k > i, Yi is not true' occurring in the list that can be assigned the name 'Yi'.

In the foregoing discussion, we have observed how vacuous biconditionals and contradictions are implicated in various paradoxes and conundrums, but have said little about their truth value, save to point out that they are not true. Classical principles dictate that they are simply (and necessarily) false, but our treatment of the paradoxes has already indicated that a principled denial of this ascription will deliver a solution to a bundle of logico-semantical paradoxes. As we mentioned at the outset, Wittgenstein (for reasons quite independent of considerations about paradox) held that contradictions are empty of content and bereft of truth-value. If he is right, then our approach to these paradoxes acquires real backbone. Is he?

WITTGENSTEIN'S (AND ARISTOTLE'S?) POSITION ON CONTRADICTION

Wittgenstein urges that we not think of a contradiction as a 'wrong proposition' (Wittgenstein 1976: 223); contradictions and tautologies are not propositions at all; they have 'the mere *ring of a statement*'. 'The basic evil of Russell's logic, as also of mine in the *Tractatus*', he confesses, 'is that what a statement is is illustrated

---

[9] For exploration and applications of this technique for forming circular queues, see Goldstein (1999*a*).

by a few commonplace examples and then presupposed as understood in full generality' (Wittgenstein 1980: s. 38). It is, he believed, a mistake to assume that, just because tautologies and contradictions are well-formed sentences, they can be used to make statements that have truth-value.

In late writings, Wittgenstein argued that, although there may be certain surroundings (Umgebungen) in which the utterance of a straight (undisguised) contradiction makes sense, in the absence of such surroundings, the speaker could not have understood the meanings of some or all of his words and no meaning can be attached to his utterance. Since what has no meaning is neither true nor false, we may say that what is common to Wittgenstein's early and late positions is the thesis that contradictions (with the exception of such cases as 'It is and it isn't raining' to report very light drizzle) do not express propositions.

Aristotle, in the *Metaphysics*, appears to be committed to the same conclusion as Wittgenstein's. In his discussion of The Principle of Non-Contradiction (PNC), he first makes the uncontroversial point that a *fundamental* logical principle does not admit of proof (*Met.* 1006ᵃ10). He argues, though, that no rational person can fail to accept LNC. The ability to speak demands the ability to identify and name objects and this implies being able to recognize the boundary between an object and its background—the line (possibly a blurred one) between what is the object and what is *not* the object. From his ability to speak about things, we can transcendentally deduce that an individual must acknowledge that what is a particular object is separated by a boundary from what is *not* that object, that what is that object cannot be what is *not* that object. Aristotle says not that a contradiction is false, but wonders of someone who asserts a contradiction, 'how would his state be different from a vegetable's?' (*Met.* 1008ᵇ11). If I tell you that I am both going and not going to Macy's tonight, you cannot figure out what I am saying; you assume that you have misheard, or that I have gone nuts (this may have been the vegetable that Aristotle had in mind) or am playing some kind of trick. You would be foolish to plan to meet up with me in the evening on the basis of the words I uttered, for no content can be ascribed to them. This certainly seems to be Aristotle's view, but I shall indicate with an '?' some slight caution about ascribing it to him.

The Wittgenstein/?Aristotle view is that no rational person can undermine, can speak against (*contra-dicere*), a proposition that he or she is asserting; someone who sincerely utters a contradictory form of words—assuming that he or she is not being deceptive, ironical, or anything like that—simply has not gained a mastery of all the words that he or she is employing. Stripped of anthropological accretion, this becomes the view that contradictions are not false (and not true either—they are in a different ballpark).

An impatient response to this suggestion might be that we can understand tautologies and contradictions perfectly well, and that even small children recognize them as paradigm examples of truth and falsity respectively. But we have already mentioned that to grant that a sentence has meaning (and can thus be understood) is not yet to reckon that sentence capable of yielding a proposition. And, interestingly, it is empirically false that, in an untutored state, we recognize tautologies and contradictions as having truth-value (Osherson and Markman 1975). When a sentence is used, in a given context, to express a proposition, the context typically contributes to the determination of what proposition is expressed. But contradictions are not *used*, except in exceptional surroundings, to say anything (Wittgenstein 1980: s. 1132). And, where there is no use, there is no proposition and no truth-value. This is Wittgenstein's view and, of course, it will exercise little persuasive influence on those broadly unsympathetic to Wittgenstein's later philosophy. But the conclusion may be defended independently of this standpoint. Some preliminary considerations have been offered in the Introduction and in the preceding section, and we have already considered an 'impatient response' to the Wittgenstein/?Aristotle position. It may now be helpful to observe how a variety of objections can be taken care of.

OBJECTIONS AND REPLIES

Objection 1

Contradictions *are* false in virtue of the meanings of 'and' and 'not' and the composition of these into the meaning of the whole. The classical truth-tables inform us that contradictions are false. *Reply*: Truth-tables are supposed to reflect the semantical properties of the connectives, unless we are simply inventing connectives that have no independent established use. The simplest (though arguably not the best) way of reflecting that contradictions are not false would be to accept the classical truth-tabular characterization of 'A and B', except for when the sentence substituting for A is the negation of that substituting for B. That may seem to be untidy but, as Wittgenstein pointed out, the demand for 'crystalline purity' in logic is ill-founded.[10] To insist that 'p and not-p' must take the value 'false' because that is what is dictated by clean and exceptionless truth-tabular requirements is surely to let the tail wag the dog.

There is already a huge literature on the senses of 'not', but not quite so much on 'and', so let us say a little about the latter here. What should we say about the meaning of 'and' as it occurs in 'p and not-p'? My wife received a letter from her Uncle Jimmy, in which he wrote: 'Auntie Ivy had two strokes and a heart attack and died, but luckily she was in hospital at the time and they managed to revive her.'

---

[10] Speaking of the unwarranted demand ('requirement') for an 'ideal' language, Wittgenstein writes 'The more narrowly we examine actual language, the sharper becomes the conflict between it and our requirement. (For the crystalline purity of logic was, of course, not a result of investigation: it was a requirement.)' (Wittgenstein 1953: s. 107). In the preceding few sections, Wittgenstein argues for abandoning preconceptions about logic that he, like many others, embraced at the time of the *Tractatus*.

I expect that most readers would say that Jimmy had misused the word 'died' even though the word 'revive', in its original sense, means 'to bring back to life'. It would be correct to say that the meaning Jimmy attached to 'dead' was incorrect. Meanings change over time. We might now truly say 'Her heart stopped beating but she had not died', yet, thirty years ago, that would have been a solecism, for to say then that someone had died *implied* that their heart had stopped beating.

The meaning of an expression at any historical time is just the ambient use of the expression at that time, although not everyone's use carries the same weight. Coiners with charisma and authority can effect rapid meaning innovation—in the sense that a new expression they introduce, or a new use they suggest for an existing expression, can be swiftly taken up by the population and by standard dictionaries (recent examples include 'burnout' and 'bootstrap'). Equally, some expressions (particularly scientific ones) may be widely *misused*, and reputable dictionaries may refuse to follow a popular trend. New meanings do not spring into existence unsolicited. Scientific terminology may be invented and embraced via a relatively simple process, but most new meanings are products of complex social interaction. The important point to recognize is that meanings are not superhuman; they do not exist independent of our sociolinguistic practices.

There is a controversy between those who say that the word 'and' has a unique meaning characterized by the classical truth table or the classical laws of inference, and those who deny this. A consequence of the 'classical' (or 'purist') view is that 'and' is commutative—'A and B' entails and is entailed by 'B and A'. This consequence seems unacceptable. Ordinarily, we take 'I am going to drink and drive' *not* to entail 'I am going to drive and drink'. In a case like this, the 'and' has the sense of 'and then'. In other contexts, the 'and' is non-temporal. If I say to the waiter in my local café, 'I'll have soup and liver and bacon', then I should expect the soup to come first but not the liver to precede the bacon or vice-versa, though, in a different culinary setting—in a Chinese restaurant, say—I would spell out 'and then' or 'and, when that's finished' if I wished to avoid all three items coming at the same time.

The order of sentences describing a sequence of events generally reflects the order in which the corresponding events occurred. This is a convention with a perfectly obvious rationale, and we speak not just misleadingly but falsely if we breach this convention. 'I got dressed and had a bath' *entails* that I bathed clothed. Since it is a fact about ordinary use that people take my announcement 'I got dressed and had a bath' as indicating, if true, that I bathed clothed, and there is no higher court of appeal to determine the meaning of the sentence than how people use those words, then, in this context, the 'and' means 'and then'.[11] Classicists, following Grice, claim that the order of the component sub-sentences *conveys* information about the order of the corresponding events, and that, *strictly speaking*, this has

---

[11] Kent Bach (2002) has questioned the reliability of such arguments that appeal to the semantic intuitions of ordinary speakers.

nothing to do with the *meaning* of 'and' as it occurs in the molecular sentence. But what could be a clearer indication of the ambiguity of 'and' than that it sometimes can, and sometimes cannot, be replaced by 'and then', as in our sentence above about soup and liver and bacon? In some languages the distinct senses are borne by distinct words.[12] The word 'and' is also frequently used in the sense 'and, in consequence', as in 'He ran 9.05 seconds and broke the World 100 m. record' or 'She betrayed her friend and was never trusted again.' It is as futile to try wishing away ambiguity or non-classical connectives as it is to try wishing away irregular verbs.

We have seen that the word 'and' does not have a unique meaning that it carries with it to any context in which it is used. Rather, what the word means on any occasion of use is read off its occurrence in that context.[13] It is, *inter alia*, worldly knowledge (e.g. that liver usually accompanies bacon, that soup in a Chinese restaurant does not normally precede the other dishes) that enables you to interpret, to read off the sense of a word in the context in which it is used. What, then, must we say about the meaning of the word 'and' as it occurs in a *contradiction*? Only question-beggingly could one assert that its meaning, as read off from this occurrence, is such as to deliver the truth-value 'false' to the contradiction.

The (literally) correct response I should make to someone who tells me 'I am going to the theatre and I am not going to the theatre' is 'You can't mean that'. There are innumerable grammatically correct sentences to which (unless apprised of extraordinary surroundings) we can attach no content. A (not particularly good) example of Wittgenstein's is 'Milk me sugar' (Wittgenstein 1953: s. 498). So it should not be assumed that a contradiction has content. And there is no question of importing a particular meaning of 'and' into a contradiction of the form 'p and not p' and of that imported meaning *dictating* a sense and a truth-value for the contradiction.

Objection 2

If a contradiction is not false (and not true either), should not the same be said of its negation, a tautology? Wittgenstein of the *Tractatus* replies in the affirmative. He regards both tautology and contradiction as the disintegration (*Auflösung*) of the combination of signs (Wittgenstein 1961b: 4.466). This position has something to recommend it, but one problem (a particularly severe problem for Wittgenstein) is that we do *use* tautologies (e.g. in dilemma arguments).[14] If this is a persuasive consideration for acknowledging that tautologies are true, then there are options

---

[12] There is a large literature, including Atlas 1989, controverting such ambiguity claims and with which, in a much longer chapter, it would be good to engage.

[13] For more doubt on the view that understanding a sentence involves a rule-governed composition of the meanings of the component words, see Sayward 2000.

[14] This is presented as an *ad hominem* argument in Goldstein 1999b.

as to how to reflect this in the formal semantics. At a minimum, one requires a negation connective that, when adjoined to a contradiction with no truth-value (or with the value 'GAP') delivers a truth. The rationale is that if it would be absurd to say such-and-such, then to say the opposite makes perfectly good sense and is indeed true. Again in Wittgensteinian terms, an *unsinnig* combination of words is not going to acquire *sinnigkeit* by sticking a 'not' in front of it, but, arguably, the same should not be said of a combination of words that is merely *sinnlos*.

Objection 3

Reductio ad absurdum arguments that occur in mathematics, but also in many other areas of discourse, depend on ascribing falsity to contradictions. *Reply*: A *reductio* can be described in the following way: if an argument leads to a contradiction, then one of the premisses is to be rejected. This description of *reductio* would hold irrespective of whether one is inclined to term a contradiction 'false' or 'vacuous', but the real difficulty, it might be said, is that if the conclusion of an argument is neither true nor false, but vacuous, then at least one of the premisses must be not false but vacuous too. And how could we have reasoned to a true conclusion (i.e., the negation of a premiss) from a vacuous premiss—surely nothing but nothing comes from nothing; there is no such thing as a free lunch.

This line of reasoning is clearly mistaken. For consider a perfectly good and true proposition *p*. It and its negation could be the two premisses of an argument with a contradictory conclusion. But what about when a contradiction is derived from a *single* premiss? Some sentences that have literal meaning can be used in inferences even if they are vacuous. If someone says to me 'The man who lives in the moon is cheerful', then, if I am gullible, I will reason that one way to meet a cheerful man would be to travel to the moon. But my impish (mis-)informant was literally speaking of nothing. Wittgenstein held that the offending premiss in a *reductio* (e.g. 'The square root of 2 is m/n, where m and n are integers') is, like 'A triangle has four sides', vacuous, but that the vacuity in the former case is not immediately transparent, and is demonstrated by the proof. When you reject the offending premiss, you reject it not as false, but as senseless. We are happy to say that the notion of a 4-sided triangle is a conceptual confusion and, in the case of the claim 'The square root of 2 is m/n, where m and n are integers' we could say that the proof *unmasks* a conceptual confusion. Certainly, we should distinguish a mere *reductio ad falsum* (given that p, possibly together with some innocuous premisses, entails q which is *false*, then p is false) from *reductio ad absurdum*, which, as the name implies, reduces an assumption to an *absurdity* or, as I should say, to a vacuity.[15]

---

[15] Some penetrating queries of David Papineau's prompted a beneficial reshaping of this chapter.

REFERENCES

ATLAS, J. (1989). *Philosophy without Ambiguity*. Oxford: Clarendon.

BACH, K. (2002). 'Seemingly Semantic Intuitions', in J. Keim Campbell, M. O'Rourke, and D. Shier (eds.), *Meaning and Truth*, New York: Seven Bridges, 21–33.

CLARK, M. (1999). 'Recalcitrant Variants of the Liar Paradox'. *Analysis*, 59: 117–26.

GOLDSTEIN, L. (1986). 'The Development of Wittgenstein's Views on Contradiction'. *History and Philosophy of Logic*, 7: 43–56.

—— (1992). ' "This Statement Is Not True" Is not True'. *Analysis*, 52: 1–5.

—— (1999*a*). *Clear and Queer Thinking: Wittgenstein's Development and His Relevance to Modern Thought*. London: Duckworth.

—— (1999*b*). 'Circular Queue Paradoxes—the Missing Link'. *Analysis*, 59: 284–90.

—— (1999*c*). 'Wittgenstein's Ph.D. Viva—a Re-creation'. *Philosophy*, 74: 49–513.

—— (2001). 'Truth-Bearers and the Liar: A Reply to Alan Weir'. *Analysis*, 61: 115–26.

HELLER, J. (1994). *Catch-22*. London: Vintage. (First published in 1961.)

KRIPKE, S. (1975). 'Outline of a Theory of Truth'. *The Journal of Philosophy*, 72: 690–716. Repr. in R. L. Martin (ed.) (1984). *Recent Essays on Truth and the Liar Paradox*. New York: Oxford University Press, 53–81.

OSHERSON, D. N., and MARKMAN, E. (1975). 'Language and the Ability to Evaluate Contradictions and Tautologies', *Cognition*, 3: 213–26.

POUNDSTONE, W. (1988). *Labyrinths of Reason*. London: Penguin.

PRIEST, G. (1998). 'The Import of Inclosure'. *Mind*, 107: 835–40.

QUINE, W. V. O. (1952), *Methods of Logic* (London: Routledge & Kegan Paul).

SAYWARD, C. (2000). 'Understanding Sentences'. *Philosophical Investigations*, 23: 48–53.

SOAMES, S. (1999). *Understanding Truth*. Oxford: Oxford University Press.

SORENSEN, R. (1982). 'Recalcitrant Variations of the Prediction Paradox'. *Australasian Journal of Philosophy*, 60: 355–62.

SYLVAN, R. (1999). 'What is that Item Designated Negation?', in D. M. Gabbay and H. Wansing (eds.), *What is Negation?* Dordrecht: Kluwer.

WITTGENSTEIN, L. (1953). *Philosophical Investigations*. Oxford: Blackwell.

—— (1961*a*). *Notebooks 1914–16*. Oxford: Blackwell.

—— (1961*b*). *Tractatus Logico-Philosophicus*. London: Routledge & Kegan Paul.

—— (1976). *Wittgenstein's Lectures on the Foundations of Mathematics, Cambridge, 1939*. Hassocks: Harvester.

—— (1978). *Remarks on the Foundations of Mathematics*. Oxford: Blackwell.

—— (1980). *Remarks on the Philosophy of Psychology* Oxford: Blackwell, i.

WRIGHT, C. (1980). *Wittgenstein on the Foundations of Mathematics*. Cambridge Mass.: Harvard University Press.

YABLO, S. (1993). 'Paradox without Self-Reference'. *Analysis*, 53: 251–2.

19

A Critique of Dialetheism

Greg Littmann and Keith Simmons

1. INTRODUCTION

In this chapter we defend the law of non-contradiction (LNC) by offering a critique of its most visible opposition. According to the dialetheist, there are sentences that are both true and false, and the LNC fails. Dialetheists motivate their surprising and radical doctrine in a variety of ways, but their strongest support comes from the phenomenon of paradox. The well-known semantic paradoxes have no generally accepted solutions—in particular, the infamous Liar paradox has been around for nearly two-and-a-half millennia, with no agreed-upon solution in sight. According to the dialetheist, there is a lesson to be learnt here: the contradictions that the paradoxes seem to generate are not apparent but real, and we must embrace them.

Consider, for example, the Liar. Take the sentence:

(L) (L) is false.

If (L) is true, then what it says is the case—so it is false. And if (L) is false, then, since it says of itself that it is false, (L) is true. Either way we are landed in contradiction. Many ways out of this paradox have been proposed, but each faces formidable challenges. Particularly formidable are 'revenge' Liars: new paradoxes couched in the very terms of the proposal. For example, invoke truth-value gaps, and you face the sentence 'This sentence is false or neither true nor false';[1] suggest a hierarchy of some sort, and you must deal with 'This sentence is not true at any level';[2] or appeal to context, and you must somehow accommodate the sentence 'This sentence is not true in any context'.[3] Old contradictions are removed only for new ones to take their place. Better, says the dialetheist, to accept the contradictions outright. Liar sentences such as (L) are true and false.

---

[1] According to the gap approach, Liar sentences such as (L) are neither true nor false. One influential theory that utilizes truth gaps is that of Kripke (1975).

[2] For example, a 'Tarskian' approach to the Liar stratifies a natural language such as English into a series of object languages and metalanguages. The truth concept for a given object language can be expressed in the corresponding metalanguage, but not in the object language itself, on pain of paradox. Different versions of this kind of approach can be found in Parsons (1974), Burge (1979), Barwise and Etchemendy (1987), and Gaifman (1992).

[3] The authors mentioned in n. 2 motivate their hierarchical approaches by an appeal to contextual shifts. The singularity theory in Simmons (1993) also appeals to context, but rejects the hierarchical approach.

It might seem that once dialetheists have taken contradictions on board, they have cut the Gordian knot, and the paradoxes need no longer concern us. In this chapter, we argue that this is not so. Our critique has two parts. In s. 3, we examine the language in which the dialetheist theory itself is expressed, and argue that it contains contradictions unacceptable even to the dialetheist. In s. 4–6 we show that, despite its embrace of contradictions, dialetheism is subject to a revenge Liar of its own.

2. DIALETHEISM

We take Priest's logic of paradox (LP) to be our representative of dialetheism.[4] There are just two truth values, true and false, but they need not be exclusive. There are true sentences, there are false sentences, and there are sentences that are true and false.[5] So in addition to the familiar values t and f, we have the value b (both true and false). The matrices for the sentential connectives $\sim$, & and v are given in Fig. 19.1. These matrices coincide with those of Łukasiewicz,[6] and the strong tables of Kleene[7]—but the dialetheist interpretation of b is of course very different from theirs. The conditional is defined as '$\sim\varphi \vee \psi$' and the biconditional as '$(\varphi \to \psi)\&(\psi \to \varphi)$', and their matrices are given accordingly.

More formally, we consider a propositional language L. Let P be the class of propositional parameters p, q, r, ... of L. Then the set F of formulas of L is the closure of P under $\sim$, &, and v. An *evaluation* is a function that carries a given formula to exactly one of three sets of truth-values: {t}, {f}, or {t, f}. Let v be an evaluation of the propositional parameters in P. We extend v to v^+, an evaluation of all formulas, by the following conditions:

(1a) $t\epsilon v^+(\sim\varphi)$ iff $f\epsilon v^+(\varphi)$

(1b) $f\epsilon v^+(\sim\varphi)$ iff $t\epsilon v^+(\varphi)$

φ	$\sim\varphi$
t	f
f	t
b	b

$\varphi \& \psi$			
ψ φ	t	f	b
t	t	f	b
f	f	f	f
b	b	f	b

$\varphi \vee \psi$			
ψ φ	t	f	b
t	t	t	t
f	t	f	b
b	t	b	b

FIG. 19.1.

---

[4] In Priest (1979, 1987). Priest's theory is a standard, influential form of dialetheism.

[5] Priest's semantics does not admit truth-value gaps. According to Priest and other dialetheists, gaps are no help in dealing with the Liar.   [6] J. Łukasiewicz (1920).

[7] Kleene (1952: 332 ff.).

(2a) $t\epsilon v^+(\varphi\&\psi)$ iff $t\epsilon v^+(\varphi)$ and $t\epsilon v^+(\psi)$

(2b) $f\epsilon v^+(\varphi\&\psi)$ iff $f\epsilon v^+(\varphi)$ or $f\epsilon v^+(\psi)$

(3a) $t\epsilon v^+(\varphi v\psi)$ iff $t\epsilon v^+(\varphi)$ or $t\epsilon v^+(\psi)$

(3b) $f\epsilon v^+(\varphi v\psi)$ iff $f\epsilon v^+(\varphi)$ and $f\epsilon v^+(\psi)$

The notion of semantic consequence ($\models$) is defined in the usual way: if Σ is a set of formulas of L,

$$\Sigma \models \varphi \text{ iff for every } v^+, \text{ if } t\epsilon v^+(\psi) \text{ for all } \psi\epsilon\Sigma, \text{ then } t\epsilon v^+(\varphi).$$

And the notion of logical truth is given as follows:

$$\models \varphi \text{ iff for every } v^+, t\epsilon v^+(\varphi).$$

Conditions (1)–(3) seem to depart little from classical semantics—in fact, they coincide with the classical conditions. But there is a difference. For the classical conception, where truth and falsity are exclusive, (1b), (2b), and (3b) are redundant; this is not so for the dialetheist. If we take classical semantics and drop the assumption that truth and falsity are exclusive, we arrive at dialetheism. And there are some radical changes along the way. It no longer holds, as it does in classical logic, that everything follows from a contradiction. Suppose φ is true and false. Then so is $\sim\varphi$. Consequently, the conjunction $\varphi\&\sim\varphi$ is true (as well as false). So given any false ψ, it will not be a consequence of $\varphi\&\sim\varphi$. Disjunctive syllogism also fails: ψ is not a consequence of φ and $\sim\varphi v\psi$, as is clear if we again consider true and false φ, and false ψ. These are, of course, controversial features of dialetheism, but we shall not say more about them here.

Priest also provides an account of the truth conditions of the sentence 'φ is true'. Priest observes that given the Tarski biconditional

φ is true iff φ

it follows that if φ is true, 'φ is true' is true, and if φ is false, 'φ is true' is false. So in particular if φ is both true and false, 'φ is true' is both true and false as well.[8] The complete truth table for 'φ is true', and the corresponding table for 'φ is false' are as Fig. 19.2. Again, these tables are what we would expect if we subtract from classical semantics the assumption that truth and falsity are exclusive.

---

[8] We have followed the account of the truth conditions of 'ψ is true' in Priest (1979: 238). Priest later revised this account—(1987: ch. 5), and suggests that it is possible for an assertion that a true and false sentence is true to be true but not false. However, Priest does also say that this is not a possibility for a liar sentence 'just because it is equivalent to (the denial of) its own truth' (ibid. 100). So we can set aside Priest's later revision, since in this chapter we are concerned specifically with the Liar.

φ	φ is true	φ	φ is false
t	t	t	f
b	b	b	b
f	f	f	t

Fig. 19.2.

3. THE LANGUAGE OF DIALETHEISM

The dialetheist makes the following claim about the liar sentence (L):

(D) (L) is true and (L) is false

What is the status of (D)? Consider its first conjunct. Since (L) is both true and false, the sentence '(L) is true' is also both true and false, by the table for 'φ is true'. And since (L) is both true and false, so is the sentence '(L) is false', by the table for 'φ is false'. According to the truth table for conjunction, if two sentences are each true and false, so is their conjunction. So the dialetheist claim (D) is both true and false. In particular, *(D) is false*. Moreover, since (D) is both true and false, then its negation is too, by the truth table for negation. In particular, then, the negation of (D) is true; that is, *it is not the case that (L) is both true and false.*

These consequences flow from the dialetheist theory itself, and they are troublesome. One may avoid such difficulties by adopting a less robust, more qualified version of dialetheism. For example, according to Rescher and Brandom, the liar sentence (L) is both true and false—but at the same time, they insist that we must separate the inconsistent object language from our *consistent* discourse about it.[9] We must distinguish between '(1) discourse at the level of an object language ... and (2) discourse at the theoretical metalevel'.[10] However, this diluted form of dialetheism is too weak to handle the Liar in all its manifestations—as they themselves make clear, Rescher and Brandom cannot accommodate as simple a liar sentence as 'This sentence is not true'.[11] Semantic paradox is ultimately defused by a hierarchy, and not by dialetheism. And this is a serious defect if the main motivation for dialetheism is supposed to lie in its resolution of paradox. Priest, for one, is after a robust dialetheism, one that 'finally renders the object-language/meta-language distinction unnecessary in any shape or form'.[12] Priest's theory is supposed to be a comprehensive treatment of paradox, one that does not need to defer to any other way out.

But we now see the apparent high cost of such a thoroughgoing dialetheism. The theory is contradictory; it implies the falsity of its own claims about liar sentences;

---

[9] See Rescher and Brandom (1979: s. 26, and p. 4).   [10] Ibid. 138.   [11] See ibid. (s. 10).
[12] Priest (1984: 161). See also Priest (1987: chs. 1, 9).

and every assertion that a liar sentence is true and false may be accompanied by a true assertion that it isn't.

How bad is this for the dialetheist? Priest and Beall have responded to these concerns of ours along the following lines.[13] They accept that (D) *is* both true and false—but they say that its falsity does not undercut its truth. (D) is true, and nothing takes away from that. The fact that (D) is also false is extra information, and has no impact on (D)'s truth. Of course, consistency cannot be maintained— but the (thoroughgoing) dialetheist does not pretend to offer a consistent theory. After all, the language of the dialetheist theory is English—all of English, not some sanitized metalanguage. So the Liar is present, and inconsistency is present, in the very language of the theory. The aim is not to produce a consistent theory but rather to show how inconsistencies can be tolerated.

In our view, however, it is one thing to treat liar sentences as genuinely inconsistent, and quite another to treat theoretical assertions *about* the Liar as genuinely inconsistent. The dialetheist, even the thoroughgoing dialetheist, will want to cordon off liar statements (and in general all true-and-false statements or *dialetheia*) from the rest of what we say. As we have seen, the dialetheist retains a great deal of classical semantics—as long as a sentence is not a dialetheia, it is treated classically. The dialetheist attaches the distinctive value 'true and false' to liar sentences just because they are pathological, and, like any truth theorist, the dialetheist does not want the pathology to spread. But in the case of dialetheism, the pathology spreads to the theory itself. How can we accept dialetheism, if the theory itself is pathological in just the same way as the Liar, if the dialetheist's own assertions are likewise true and false?

Indeed, there is a question as to whether the (thoroughgoing) dialetheist theory can even be properly conveyed or understood. Once we realize that the theory includes not only the statement '(L) is both true and false' but also the statement '(L) isn't both true and false' we may feel at a loss. To this the dialetheist may reply: 'Of course the theory is conveyable; after all, you have just conveyed it to your readers. And further, you yourselves argue against the theory, so you must understand it.'[14] There is some initial force to this reply, so let us consider the matter more carefully.

We may try to present dialetheism just as we have in this chapter: we start with our representative dialetheist semantics, the relevant truth tables and so on, and we lay out the basic dialetheist claim:

(D) (L) is true and (L) is false

If the individual claims that make up the theory are intelligible, then, it might seem, the theory as a whole is intelligible. However, the difficulty arises when we track the consequences of these theoretical claims. Among these consequences is

---

[13] Priest's response is in correspondence with Simmons. His response is endorsed and elaborated by Beall (2001).   [14] Beall (ibid.) argues along these lines.

the negation of (D), the statement '(L) isn't both true and false'. This is part of the dialetheist account, and supposedly gives us further information about (D). If we think of a theory as a set of sentences, then a proper subset of the dialetheist theory is {'(L) is true and false', '(L) isn't true and false'}. Do we understand this part of the theory? We may allow that we understand each sentence separately (waiving any concerns we might have about a sentence being true and false). But do we understand what the theory is telling us about (L)? At first the dialetheist account seemed clear enough: as befits such a peculiar sentence, (L) has a special status, true and false. Some sentences are true, some sentences are false, and some sentences such as the Liar are true and false. But it turns out that there is more: we must also accept that (L) *isn't* true and false. How are we to incorporate this further information? We are faced with two claims which do not seem to supplement one another; rather each seems to *take back* what the other says. We are presented with an evaluation of (L) that is no clearer than (L). If (L) should be quarantined, so should the dialetheist evaluation of it. And if a theoretical response to the Liar exhibits the same pathology as the Liar, then so much the worse for the theory.

Compare the story about the village barber. We are told that there is a man who shaves exactly the non-self-shaving villagers. This story is perfectly coherent—and it may seem that it remains so if we add that the man is one of the villagers. But when we track the consequences of this extended story, we find that we must reject it: there is no such barber, on pain of there being someone who both shaves and doesn't shave himself. Now it may be that many of the claims that make up Priest's thoroughgoing dialetheism form a coherent story—we might, for example, take a subset of Priest's claims and include them as part of a diluted dialetheism which, like Rescher and Brandom's account, distinguishes an inconsistent object language from a consistent metalanguage. But if we take exactly the statements that compose undiluted dialetheism, we are led to contradiction—in particular, to the negation of (D) together with (D). We might *think* we understand the dialetheist theory, just as we might think we understand the extended story of the village barber—in each case, there are close approximations that are coherent. But when we follow out the consequences, we find that any initial understanding we thought we had is compromised.

There is a sense in which full-blown dialetheism is conveyable: we can specify the set of sentences, closed under consequence, that constitutes the theory, with (D) and its negation included. We can be said to understand what the theory *is*. And we can be said to understand the theory in the attenuated sense that we understand each of its sentences in isolation. But the real question is whether or not we understand what the theory is telling us about (L). And the answer to that, we think, is in the negative: we do not understand what is being said of (L) when it is said that (L) is and isn't both true and false, any more than we understand what is being said of someone when it is said that he both shaves and does not shave himself.

The dialetheist's commitment to the truth of both (D) and its negation raises a further issue concerning assertion and denial. The dialetheist will assert (D) (since (D) is true and 'the *telos* of asserting is truth'[15]), and will also assert the negation of (D) (which is also true). It is natural to suppose that in asserting the negation of (D), the dialetheist is denying (D). But that would make it the case that the dialetheist both asserts and denies (D)—and it seems unreasonable to suppose that anyone can do this. Clearly, then, the dialetheist must pull apart the assertibility of not-φ and the deniability of φ for certain exceptional sentences.[16] According to the dialetheist, liar sentences will be among these exceptions; for example, we may assert the negation of (L), but not deny (L). Ordinarily, we do not know what to make of the claim that we can assert not-φ, but not deny φ. But liar sentences are very strange, and for the dialetheist this is another sign of their strangeness: they are not deniable, but their negations are assertable. However, it is a consequence of dialetheism that this strangeness extends to the theoretical statement (D). (D) is an exception too: we can assert the negation of (D) but we cannot deny (D). Here is another way in which the dialetheist theory and the Liar have pathological features in common.

Further, since the dialetheist appeals to non-standard relations between assertability and deniability, we are owed a full account of these notions. Any such account would need to deal with apparent paradoxes that turn on the notion of assertability (or deniability). Let us introduce the 'Assertability Liar', generated by the sentence:

(M) (M) is not assertable

It seems that (M) is a genuine Liar sentence, since whether we assume that it is true or false, we appear to be led to contradiction. Suppose (M) is true. Then what it says is the case. So: (M) is not assertable. But we have just asserted (M). So (M) *is* assertable—and we have a contradiction. Suppose on the other hand that (M) is false. Then what (M) says is not the case. So (M) is assertable. So we may assert: (M) is not assertable. Again, we have a contradiction.

If we take the standard dialetheist line here, we will declare (M) true and false. However, that leads to the conclusion that (M) is not assertable, and also assertable. And that seems to be a conclusion unacceptable even to the dialetheist: how could we be in a position both to assert and not to assert the very same sentence? In the case of (L) (and of (D)), the dialetheist claimed some slippage between denying a sentence and asserting its negation—but in the present case there seems to be no room for manœuvre. So the dialetheist will need to say more.

Thus far, we have focused on one unsettling consequence of dialetheism, that both (D) and its negation is true. Above we identified another: (D) is false. More generally, the fundamental dialetheist claim that liar sentences are true and false is

---

[15] Priest (1987: 77).   [16] Such a line is taken by Beall (2001).

itself false. But if a fundamental claim of a theory is false, it seems obvious that we should reject the theory. No doubt the dialetheist will emphasize the truth of the claim—for the claim is true as well. However, we should observe that our concern to reject false claims seems as great as our concern to accept true ones—and so we still have a reason to reject dialetheism.

How can the dialetheist persuade us that we should accept a theory that we recognize to be false? We see at least two obstacles here. First, suppose that we follow the dialetheist and accept the theory, perhaps on the grounds that it is true, and that, unlike any other theory, it resolves the paradoxes. We will also label it 'false', indeed 'false in its fundamentals'. But what will this falsity amount to, if we accept the theory because it is true and useful? Our attitude towards dialetheism would seem to be indistinguishable from our attitude towards a straightforwardly true and useful theory, apart from a verbal difference in the labels that we are willing to attach to the theories.

Second, the notion of acceptability that the dialetheist is presently employing arguably gives rise to paradox—and, as with the Assertability Liar, it at least prima facie the case that a dialetheist resolution will not work. Consider the 'Acceptability Liar', generated by the sentence:

(N) (N) is unacceptable

Let us suppose that (N) is true (and only true). Then, presumably, (N) is acceptable—what better grounds are there for the acceptability of a sentence than its truth? But given that (N) is true, and given what it says, (N) is unacceptable. Contradiction. Suppose on the other hand that (N) is false (and only false). Then (N) is unacceptable—what better grounds are there for the unacceptability of a sentence than its falsity? But given that (N) is false, and given what (N) says, (N) is acceptable. Contradiction, again.

If (N) is a genuine liar sentence, the dialetheist will declare it to be both true and false. But that leads to the conclusion that (N) is unacceptable *and* acceptable—that we should both accept and not accept (N). But it is doubtful that anyone, the dialetheist included, will want to admit this kind of cognitive dissonance. So again the dialetheist will have to say more here. Even if the dialetheist persuades us to accept falsehoods, we cannot both accept and not accept one and the same claim, any more than we can be in a position to both assert it and not assert it.

The objections that we have presented in this section are tied together by a common thread: as a consequence of dialetheism itself, the dialetheist theory has the same status as the liar. This, we have argued, is a problem. In very broad terms, we can put the problem this way: we cannot accept dialetheism unless we have a positive attitude of some kind towards the statements that constitute the theory. But the core statements of dialetheism, such as (D), have the same semantic status as liar sentences. And we regard liar sentences as deeply problematic, in need of some radical treatment that will upset our intuitions in one way or another. We do not 'accept' liar sentences. But if dialetheist claims are as problematic as the Liar, why should our attitude to them be any more accepting? Once we identify the consequences of the theory, it seems that dialetheism does not provide a treatment of the Liar, but presents us instead with more pathology, itself in need of treatment.

4. TOWARDS A REVENGE LIAR

One might expect that, by its very nature, dialetheism is immune to revenge Liars, since the dialetheist may simply accept the contradiction that any new paradox produces. In this section and the ones that follow, we argue that this is not so. Our aim is to construct new liar paradoxes, sensitive to the terms of dialetheism, that the dialetheist cannot handle.

A distinctive feature of our representative of dialetheism is that there are three possible ways to evaluate a sentence: it may be true only, it may be false only, or it may be both true and false. In particular, according to the dialetheist a sentence may be false but not false only. This suggests a natural candidate for a revenge Liar. Consider the sentence:

(P) (P) is false only

Suppose (P) is true only. Then (P) is false only. But if (P) is false only, then (P) is not true in any way, given the meaning of the word 'only'. So the assumption that (P) is true only has led to a contradiction. Suppose next that (P) is false only. Since that is exactly what (P) says, (P) is true—but then (P) is not false only, and we have another contradiction.

So (P) is not true only or false only, on pain of contradiction. Given our ordinary, pretheoretic intuitions about truth and falsity—in particular, that truth and falsity are exclusive and exhaustive values—*true only* amounts to *true*, and *false only* amounts to *false*, and these two values are exhaustive. So (P) is a contradiction-producing liar sentence. But the dialetheist response to (P), as to all liar sentences, will be that truth and falsity are *not* mutually exclusive, and (P) is *both* true and false. But if (P) is true and false, then in particular it is true, and from this it follows that (P) is false only. That is, the dialetheist must say that (P) is true and false, *and* false only. This should give the dialetheist pause. If we understand 'false only' in the truth-excluding sense in which it is intended, then there appears to be no room for (P) to be true as well.

How might the dialetheist respond? One response would be resolutely to refuse to understand 'false only' in a genuinely truth-excluding way; they may insist that for certain sentences φ, it is legitimate to add 'and φ is true too' to a claim that φ is false only. There is nothing intrinsically worse about viewing an instance of 'false only' as failing to exclude truth than there is in viewing an instance of 'false' as failing to exclude truth—or so the dialetheist might argue.

This response does not really come to grips with (P). Rather it amounts to fixing an interpretation of 'false only' that is non-truth-excluding rather than truth-excluding. In adopting this response, it seems that the dialetheist fails to respect the way in which 'only' functions as a universal quantifier. To say that a sentence is false only is to say of all other truth values that they have no part in the evaluation of the sentence. But the dialetheist sets aside such universal formulations, and instead presents evaluations as conjunctions of truth values, adding on whatever values are deemed necessary to make sense of all the implications of a paradoxical sentence. However (as Russell pointed out)[17] one cannot capture a statement that involves universal quantification simply in terms of truth functional connectives (in particular, conjunction) for exactly the reason that the connectives cannot convey the notion of totality. That is to say, conjunction and the other connectives cannot convey the existence of limits, the fact that there is no more to be said than what has been said already.

But what recourse do we have, if the dialetheist insists that 'false only' does not exclude 'true'? In our view, the revenge liar generated by (P) is genuine—but the dialetheist will feel its force only if they understand 'false only' the way we do. How can we bring them to share that understanding? Not by locutions such as 'only false only', for the dialetheist may always say that this is no more truth-excluding than 'false only' or 'false'. We need to find some other way.

It is highly implausible that there is no notion of a sentence being false and not true in any way. Human behavior seems to suggest that we believe many things to be false without being in any way true. People who step out into the road are generally exhibiting the belief that it is false that the road is full of speeding cars, and in no way true that the road is full of speeding cars. Dialetheists are no less prone than others to behavior that suggests such beliefs. So let us focus on a sentence that the dialetheist, along with everyone else, will regard as false and not true in any way. Under suitable circumstances, 'The road is full of speeding cars' will be such a sentence. But let us consider a sentence that is free of any contextual complications—say, '1 + 1 = 3'. We ask the dialetheist to consider the truth value they ascribe to this sentence, and the relation that this value bears to truth. We would describe the value as 'false only' or 'false and in no way true', and the relation as 'truth-excluding'—but we have no desire to saddle the dialetheist with our terminology. So we will be neutral, and let 'v' denote the value that the dialetheist ascribes to '1 + 1 = 3'. We now ask the dialetheist to think of a certain sentence: the sentence that says of itself that it is v. This sentence generates a version of the liar paradox—let us call it the 'Introspective Liar'.

Can the dialetheist handle the introspective liar? According to the dialetheist, liar sentences are true and false. But if the introspective liar sentence is true, it is v—that is, it has the semantic status that dialetheists ascribe to '1 + 1 = 3'. And

---

[17] Russell (1986: s. V).

if the introspective liar sentence has the same semantic status as '1 + 1 = 3', then it *isn't* true, any more than '1 + 1 = 3' is true. Accordingly, the dialetheist cannot ascribe truth to the introspective liar. So the dialetheist's way out is closed off—here is a liar sentence that cannot be evaluated as true, and so cannot be evaluated as true and false. In short, here is a revenge liar.

In all likelihood, dialetheists will remain unconvinced. They may insist: 'The introspective liar *is* both v and true.' We accept that the dialetheist can say these words, but we cannot see how they can mean them, if the value v really is the value of '1 + 1 = 3'. We cannot see how a sentence can really have the same value as '1 + 1 = 3' and be true. If the dialetheist ascribes truth to a sentence that is v, then it seems to us that she has failed to understand what it is for a sentence to be v. Add 'true' to 'v', and you no longer have 'v'.

But perhaps the dialetheist will say that our nerve has failed, that we cannot bring ourselves to accept that a sentence may be v—and so free of truth—and at the same time true. We say that this is a contradiction that even the dialetheist must reject; the dialetheist may say that this is one more Liar-generated contradiction that we should embrace. According to the dialetheist, the value v is not truth-excluding (and neither is the value *false only*). There are sentences that combine the values v and truth (and sentences that combine the values false only and true). In the next section, we explore some consequences of these dialetheist combinations.

5. GRAPHIC VALUES

Let us introduce graphic representations of the truth-values of sentences. The values T and F by themselves are not graphic values, but they are the building blocks from which graphic values are constructed. The value T by itself does not exclude the value F, and the value F does not exclude T; according to the dialetheist's response to paradox, we should abandon the natural assumption that truth and falsity are mutually exclusive values. According to dialetheism, to ascribe the value T (or F) to a sentence is not by itself to provide a complete evaluation—the sentence may have another value as well. To say that a sentence is T (or F) is not to say what values the sentence does *not* have. In contrast, graphic values are designed to show not only what values a sentence has, but also what values it *fails* to have.

The simplest graphic values take the form of boxes in which the values T and F appear. For example, consider the value (E1) represented by the simple diagram at Fig. 19.3.

If (E1) is the evaluation of a sentence φ, then φ receives the value 'true' and no other truth-value—that is the whole story about φ's truth status.

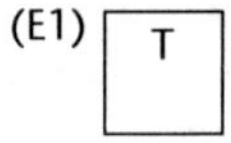

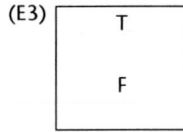

FIG. 19.3. 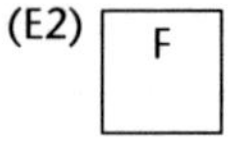   FIG. 19.4.

(E3)

FIG. 19.5.

Suitable candidates for φ here are the sentences: '$1 + 1 = 2$', 'Grass is sometimes green', and 'Berlin is the capital of Germany.'

Evaluation E2 is graphically represented at Fig. 19.4. If (E2) is the evaluation of a sentence φ, then φ receives the value 'false', and no other. Suitable candidates for φ here are the sentences '$1 + 1 = 3$', 'Grass is always red,' and 'Berlin is the capital of China.' We can think of (E2) as the value v, or the value 'false only', where the absence within the box of any letter other than 'F' captures the force of the 'only'. The box may be thought of as adding the suffix 'only' or the prefix 'the complete evaluation'. In general, graphic representations make it clear not only what values are present, but also what values are absent.

Evaluation (E3) is given in Fig. 19.5. If a sentence receives this evaluation, it is both true and false. This is the evaluation the dialetheist ascribes to the simple liar sentence:

(L) (L) is false

(E3) is an evaluation that only a dialetheist will admit.

According to our representative of dialetheism, sentences fall into three exhaustive categories—true, false, and both true and false. That is, the evaluations (E1), (E2), and (E3) are exhaustive. According to the dialetheist, the values (E1) and (E2) endorsed by the classical proponent of the LNC fail to be exhaustive—we must add the value (E3) as well. But, we shall now argue, the dialetheist must admit more values than these three—(E1), (E2), and (E3) are *not* exhaustive.

Consider again the introspective liar sentence ('This sentence is v'), or the 'false-only' liar sentence (P). According to the dialetheist, since these sentences are liar sentences they are both true and false. And since they are true, it follows that (P) is false only and the introspective liar has the value v. That is, both these liar sentences are evaluated by (E2). So according to the dialetheist, the introspective liar and the sentence (P) are to be evaluated as true and false, *and* false only. To capture this combination of values we need a new evaluation, which may be graphically represented as in Fig. 19.6. The smaller box within the larger one represents

(E4)

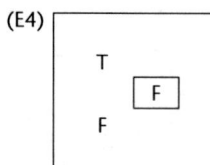

FIG. 19.6.

the evaluation 'false only', or 'the complete evaluation *false*', which, according to the dialetheist, is just one component of the evaluation of (P) and the introspective liar. Of course, it may seem highly counterintuitive—even contradictory!—that a complete evaluation of a sentence can be a proper part of the evaluation of that sentence. This reflects the apparent counterintuitiveness of the dialetheist's claim that (P) and the introspective liar are true and false *and* false only—and we will return to this matter in the next section.

The case of (P) and the introspective liar shows that the dialetheist is forced to combine complete evaluations with other values. And this seems to open the door to more and more values. It is natural to ask whether we can keep going, constructing new dialetheist values. And we can: the dialetheist is committed to infinitely many distinct values, as we will now see.

We have observed that (E3) and (E4) are distinct values: (E4) evaluates (P) and the introspective liar, but (E3) does not. Observe that the values F and boxed F contained in (E4) are distinct—if they were not, (E3) and (E4) would be identical. Now consider the sentence

(Q) (Q) is false and false only, and has no other value

The sentence (Q) is a liar sentence. For consider how we would reason about (Q) pretheoretically, before we have adopted dialetheism or any other response to the Liar. We would assume truth to be falsity-excluding and falsity to be truth-excluding. (In general, it is clear that when we determine that a given sentence φ is a liar sentence, we employ the pretheoretic intuition that truth and falsity are mutually exclusive. Indeed, we take it that the biconditional φ *is true iff φ is false* yields a contradiction. Or consider how we establish that the sentence 'This sentence is not true' is a liar sentence. When we reason from its falsity to its truth, we argue as follows: if the sentence is false, then it's not true, and so what it says is the case, and so it is true. In making the inference from falsity to non-truth, we assume that falsity is truth-excluding.) Now assume first that (Q) is true—then, given what it says, (Q) is false. Assume on the other hand that (Q) is false. Given our intuitive assumptions about truth and falsity, (Q)'s falsity excludes (Q)'s truth. And so, if (Q) is false, then it follows that (Q) is false and false only, and has

(E5)

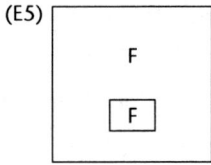

FIG. 19.7.

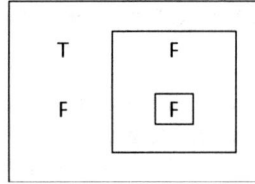

FIG. 19.8.

(E6)

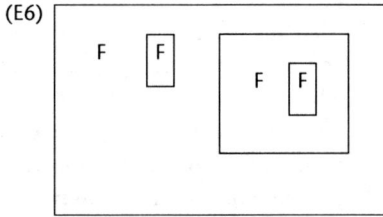

FIG. 19.9.

no other value.[18] But that's what (Q) says—and so (Q) is true. So (Q) is a liar sentence—Q is true iff (Q) is false.

Since (Q) is a liar sentence, the dialetheist will say that (Q) is true and false. In virtue of being true, (Q) is false and false only, and has no other value. So (Q) requires a graphic value that contains just the values F and boxed F, as in Fig. 19.7. We might render (E5) as the value *(false and false only) only*. And (E5) is a graphic value distinct from (E1)–(E4)—in particular, (E5) is distinct from (E2), since F and boxed F are distinct values. (E5) is not the only value that the dialetheist will ascribe to (Q), since (Q) is also true and false. As with (P), this combined dialetheist evaluation of (Q) may be graphically represented as a box within a larger box, as in Fig. 19.8. Here, the complete evaluation (E5) combines with the values T and F (just as the complete evaluation (E2) combines with T and F to produce the dialetheist evaluation (E4) of (P)). So (E5) will not be the only value that the dialetheist ascribes to (Q)—but the fact remains that it is a new value, distinct from (E1)–(E4), to which the dialetheist is committed.

Given that the values F, (E2), and (E5) are distinct values, there is a *further* value (E6) that contains exactly F, (E2), and (E5), as in Fig. 19.9. (E6) is distinct from (E1)–(E5). In particular, it is distinct from (E2) and (E5), since (E2) contains just one value, (E5) contains two, while (E6) contains three distinct values. A sentence that has the value (E6) is a sentence that is *false, false only, (false and false only)*

---

[18] We have argued that the dialetheist must distinguish *false* from *false only*, but again this is an artefact of the dialetheist *response* to paradox, not a distinction that generates the challenge posed by the Liar.

only, and has no other value. Now consider a sentence that ascribes this value to itself:

>   (R) (R) is false and false only, and (false and false only) only, and has no
>   other value

Like (Q), (R) is a liar sentence. (On the natural pretheoretic assumption that falsity is truth-excluding, the evaluation *false only* amounts to the evaluation *false*, so does the evaluation *false and false only*, and so does the evaluation *only (false and false only)*. So from (R)'s falsity we can infer that (R) is false and false only and only (false and false only), and has no other value. That is, we can infer that what (R) says is true.) Again, given that the dialetheist will say that (R) is both true and false, and so in particular true, we require the graphic evaluation (E6) in order to evaluate the liar sentence (R).[19]

Clearly, we can iterate the reasoning that leads to the evaluations (E5) and (E6), and generate an infinite sequence of distinct graphic evaluations, each required by a distinct liar sentence. For a general treatment, we may introduce the notion of an *F-based value*, as follows: a graphic value is *F-based* iff the process of opening the outermost box and any nested boxes yields only the value F. For example, (E2), (E5), and (E6) are F-based values; (E1), (E3), and (E4) are not. Consider the following infinite sequence of F-based graphic values:

>   (E2), (E5), (E6), . . .

where for $k > 5$, the $k + 3$rd member of the sequence is a box containing the values in (E_{k-1}) together with (E_{k-1}) itself. We have already seen that (E5) is distinct from (E2), so that (E6) is distinct from (E2) and (E5)—and in general, each (E_{k+1}) is distinct from every previous member of the sequence. Now consider the sentence:

>   (S) (S) has the values in (E_{k+1}), and no others

As with (Q) and (R), we can establish that (S) is a liar sentence. (If (S) is true then it's false. And on the natural pretheoretic assumption that falsity is truth-excluding, any F-based value is identical to the value *false*. So (S) says of itself just that it's false—and so if (S) is false, then it is true.) Again the dialetheist will say that (S) is true and false—and since (S) is true, it has the exactly the F-based values (E_{k+1}). And so an evaluation of (S) requires the evaluation (E_{k+1}). Given the dialetheist treatment of semantical paradox, we can construct an infinite sequence of sentences each of which requires a distinct evaluation.[20] We conclude

---

[19] (E6) is not the only value that the dialetheist will ascribe to (R): since (R) is a liar sentence, (R) will also be evaluated as true and false. (E6) is a complete evaluation of (R) that combines with other values, just like the evaluation (E2) of (P), and the evaluation (E5) of (Q).

[20] Each of these liar sentences receives a distinct F-based value. But there is also another infinite sequence of distinct values generated by these liar sentences, since according to the dialetheist each of these sentences not only has its associated F-based value, but is true and false as well. So each liar

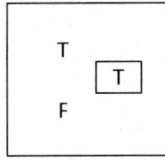

Fig. 19.10.

that dialetheists must admit infinitely many distinct truth-values. The values *true,* *false,* and *true and false* are far from exhaustive.

In generating this infinite sequence of dialetheist values, we have focused on the value *false only* and its ramifications. But if 'false only' can be combined with 'true and false', then we should expect to find that 'true only' may be combined in the same way. Consider the sentence

(U) (U) is not true only

(U) is a liar sentence. (On the natural pretheoretic assumption that truth and falsity are mutually exclusive, the value *true only* is identical to the value *true.* Now suppose that (U) is true—then (U) is not true only, which is to say that (U) is not true. Contradiction. Suppose on the other hand that (U) is false. Given that falsity is truth-excluding, it follows that (U) is not true, and so not true only—which is what (U) says, so (U) is true.) Since (U) is a liar sentence, the dialetheist will say that (U) is true and false. In particular, then, (U) is false—so given what (U) says, it follows that (U) is true only. That is, (U) is true and false, *and* true only. So (U) receives this graphic value as in Fig. 19.10.

This is a new value, distinct from all the ones we have considered so far. In particular, this value is distinct from (E3), since (E3) is not a complete evaluation of (U). It follows that the values T and boxed T are distinct (otherwise this new evaluation would be identical to (E3)).

But if T and boxed T are distinct, then we can construct a new infinite sequence of distinct values, analogous to our infinite sequence of F-based values. Let a graphic value be *T-based* iff the process of opening the outermost box and any nested boxes yields only the value T. Given the distinct values *true* and *true only,* we can construct a new T-based graphic value that contains just these values, as in Fig. 19.11. We might render this graphic value as *(true and true only) only.* Now consider the sentence that says of itself that it does not have exactly the values T and boxed T:

(V) (V) is not (true and true only) only

sentence also receives the graphic value which contains that F-based value along with the values T and F. And these additional graphic values are mutually distinct, since they contain distinct F-based values.

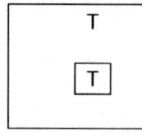

Fig. 19.11.

(V) is a liar sentence. (On the assumption that truth and falsity are mutually exclusive, any T-based value is identical to *true*[21]—so (V) will be equivalent to the liar sentence that says of itself that it is not true.) Since (V) is a liar sentence, the dialetheist will say that (V) is true and false. So (V) is in particular false, and given what (V) says, it follows that (V) is (true and true only) only. So our new T-based graphic value is required for a dialetheist evaluation of (V).[22]

And now we're off and running. Our new T-based value is distinct from both T and (E1), and the T-based value which contains exactly these three values will itself be new. In turn, these four distinct values are the members of a further T-based value—and so on. For each of these infinitely many T-based values there is a liar sentence with that value. To see this, let $(E^\dagger)$ be an arbitrary T-based value in our infinite sequence. Consider the sentence:

(W) (W) does not have exactly the values in $(E^\dagger)$

The familiar reasoning applies: on the assumption that truth and falsity are mutually exclusive, any T-based value is identical to true, so (W) says of itself that it's not true—and so (W) is a liar sentence. Accordingly, the dialetheist will say that (W) is true and false. And given that (W) is false, and given what (W) says, it follows that (W) has exactly the values in $E^\dagger$. And so $(E^\dagger)$ is required for a dialetheist evaluation of (W). Since $(E^\dagger)$ is arbitrary, we have established another infinite sequence of distinct dialetheist values, and a corresponding infinite sequence of liar sentences that require these values.[23]

6. THE GRAPHIC LIAR

Let us now turn to a new 'Revenge' version of the Liar—call it the Graphic Liar. Consider the sentence:

(X) (X) is completely and correctly evaluated by (E2)

---

[21] In particular, if we assume that truth is falsity-excluding, then *(true and true only) only* is identical to the value *true*. For as we observed in connection with (U), *true only* is the same value as true. And so *true and true only* is the same value as *true*; and so *(true and true only) only* is the same value as *true*.

[22] This is not the only value that the dialetheist will ascribe to (V), since according to the dialetheist, (V) is also true and false.

[23] Again, there is a further infinite sequence of distinct values generated by these liar sentences, since according to the dialetheist each of these sentences not only has its associated T-based value, but is true and false as well. Cf. n. 20.

Given our pretheoretic intuitions about truth and falsity—that they are mutually exclusive and exhaustive values—(X) is clearly a liar sentence. For suppose that (X) is true—then (X) is completely and correctly evaluated by (E2). So (X) is false. Suppose on the other hand that (X) is false—then (X) is not completely and correctly evaluated by (E2). Then (X) must have some value other than false—and if truth and falsity are exhaustive values, it follows that (X) is true. To sum up, (X) is true if and only if (X) is false—and this is a characteristic mark of a liar sentence.

Since (X) is a liar sentence, the dialetheist will say that it is both true and false. Let us see where that leads us. There are two possibilities here: either (X) is true and false and has no further truth value, or (X) is true and false and something else as well (plausibly, the 'something else' is (E2), yielding the evaluation (E4) for (X)). Consider the first case. Here we can say:

(i) (X) is completely and correctly evaluated by (E3)

Now since (X) is true, what it says is the case. That is:

(ii) (X) is completely and correctly evaluated by (E2)

From (i) and (ii) it follows that (E2) and (E3) are each correct and complete evaluations of (X). But then we are left with the astonishing conclusion that (E2) and (E3) are exactly the same evaluation. After all, if they are different evaluations, then one of them must either say too little about (X) and so be incomplete, or else say too much and so be incorrect.

Now consider the second case. (X) will not be completely and correctly evaluated by (E3), but by some more complex evaluation, call it (E*), which contains the values true and false and more besides. In this case, we can say:

(iii) (X) is correctly and entirely evaluated by (E*)

Since (X) is true, we obtain (ii). And from (ii) and (iii), it follows that (E2) and (E*) are the same evaluation. This is perhaps an even more disturbing result: to be false only is to be true and false and more besides.[24]

Three things are immediately worth noting here, regardless of whether we are dealing with (E3) or (E*). First, to state the obvious: it is tremendously counterintuitive that *false only* should be the same truth-value as *true and false* (or *true and false* together with yet more values).

Second, dialetheists do not suggest that the semantic status of liar sentences is in any way unstable or ambiguous. It is no part of the dialetheist account that the truth-value of a liar sentence can somehow shift, say, from *true and false to false only*. According to some theories of truth—such as the revision theory of

---

[24] If we take E* to be (E4), then both (E2) and (E4) are complete and correct evaluations of (X). This insupportable result was anticipated in the previous section, when we observed that the complete evaluation (E2) is a proper part of the evaluation (E4), a smaller box within a larger box.

truth[25] and the contextual theories mentioned in nn. 2 and 3—we should pay close attention to shifts in our evaluations of liar sentences. But dialetheists reject these theories. According to the dialetheist, paradoxical sentences are supposed to receive a single, stable evaluation—that of *true and false*. For the dialetheist, the complete and correct evaluation of a liar sentence does not change.

Third, if (E2) and (E3) (or E*) are indeed identical, then we lose nothing by limiting our attention to (E2). Here dialetheism will itself imply that there is no evaluation that is out of the reach of the monoletheist. But then it is quite unclear what reason we have to adopt dialetheism.

Perhaps the dialetheist will reply that while the truth-values (E2) and (E3) (or (E2) and (E*)) are identical, they are also non-identical, and that this contradiction is no worse than any other they have already accepted. After all, dialetheists are not afraid to endorse contradictions wherever necessary. And we have good reason to say that (E2) and (E3) are identical (each is the complete and correct evaluation of the same sentence), and good reason to say that they are different (one contains the value 'true' and the other doesn't).

Here, however, we feel that we must simply draw the line. That the dialetheist should maintain a counterintuitive thesis is nothing new. But for us it is just too much to accept that the evaluation *false only* is identical to a composite evaluation that includes the value *true*. Whatever pure falsity is, we know that it is not that. And if a solution to the Liar says that it is, we reject the solution.

Perhaps the dialetheist will deny that the two evaluations (E2) and (E3) (or (E2) and (E*)) are identical—(X) is a special kind of sentence for which more than one complete and correct evaluation exists. We reject this too, for it renders unintelligible the notion of a complete, correct evaluation. If (X) is both true and false, then when we assign (X) the evaluation (E2), we have left out information about (X)—we have left out the information that it is true. How can (E2) be complete and correct if it does not mention (X)'s truth? Nor can the dialetheist suggest that (X) is a special kind of sentence that has no complete and correct evaluation. As we have already observed, the dialetheist is committed to a stable, unambiguous evaluation of liar sentences. And an evaluation that was somehow ineffable or inexpressible would be quite against the spirit of dialetheism. Further, dialetheists say that (X) is true—and if it is, then given what it says, it has a complete and correct evaluation.

We conclude that dialetheism fails to come to grips with the Graphic Liar. It is one thing to claim that liar sentences are both true and false, and quite another thing to claim that (E2) and (E3) (or (E*)) are one and the same evaluation. Even if we follow the dialetheist and accept the former claim, the latter claim seems indefensible. But it is a direct consequence of the dialetheist treatment of the Graphic Liar.

---

[25] See Gupta and Belnap (1993).

(X) is just one of infinitely many graphic liar sentences. Take any value ($E^\dagger$) in our infinite sequence of F-based values (E2), (E5), (E6), ..., and consider the sentence:

(Y) (Y) is completely and correctly evaluated by ($E^\dagger$)

By familiar reasoning, (Y) is a liar sentence, and so, according to the dialetheist, true and false. So a complete and correct dialetheist evaluation (E^*) of (Y) will contain the values T and F (and possibly more besides). But since (Y) is true, the evaluation ($E^\dagger$) is the complete and correct evaluation of (Y). So we are led to the absurd conclusion that the evaluations (E^*) and ($E^\dagger$) are identical—absurd because the F-based value ($E^\dagger$) cannot be identical to a value containing T.[26]

7. CONCLUDING REMARKS

We have developed two main lines of criticism, one directed at the semantic status of the dialetheist's own theoretical claims, and the other at the adequacy of the dialetheist's treatment of semantic paradox. Now dialetheists might take issue with the very structure of our two-part critique. We can't have it both ways, they might say—if, as we have argued in s. 3, the theory really is unintelligible then the critical line of ss. 4–6 cannot even get off the ground. Or to put it the other way around, our claim that dialetheism is vulnerable to revenge Liars has genuine content only if the theory is intelligible.

But we can have it both ways. As we observed in s. 3, we know what the dialetheist theory is. Take the set of sentences that describe Priest's system LP, and let Cl be the closure under consequence of that set. We may regard Cl as the dialetheist theory. And as we said earlier, we are willing to allow that we understand each sentence in Cl. But, we argued, we do not understand what the theory tells us about the Liar sentence L, since both D and ~D are members of Cl.

Now we raise the question: Does the (thoroughgoing) dialetheist theory treat all versions of the Liar? If we are to answer this question adequately, we must select carefully from Cl. Although the sentence ~D and the generalization 'Liar sentences are not both true and false' are part of the dialetheist theory, we will not

---

[26] We can also construct 'non-graphic' analogues of graphic liar sentences. Consider for example the following sentence: (Z) (Z) has the same complete and correct evaluation as the sentence '1 + 1 = 3'. Clearly (Z) is a liar sentence (related to the introspective Liar), and the dialetheist will say that (Z) is both true and false. In particular, then, (Z) is true—and so it has the same complete and correct evaluation as '1 + 1 = 3'. We can express the value of '1 + 1 = 3' as 'false only', to be understood as an articulation of the value (E2). So the complete and correct evaluation of (Z) is given by *false only*. According to the dialetheist, the complete and correct evaluation of (Z) includes the values *true* and *false* (and perhaps others). So the evaluation *false only* is identical to an evaluation that includes the values *true* and *false* (and perhaps others). We arrive at the same unacceptable identification of two distinct values. And we are led to the same absurd result by the 'false only' paradox, generated by: '(P) (P) is false only', as long as *false only* is understood as the value (E2).

make progress by examining these claims—they are endorsed by monoletheists too. Instead, we single out for special attention the dialetheist's 'preferred' theoretical statements—sentences such as (D) and the generalization 'Liar sentences are true and false.' These sentences are intelligible in isolation (or so we are willing to suppose), and we can ask whether they provide an adequate treatment of all versions of the Liar. We argue that they do not—for example, if the Graphic Liar is evaluated as true and false, unacceptable consequences follow. So in answering our question, we consider only a proper subset of the dialetheist theory. The arguments of ss. 4–6 suggest that any dialetheist theory—any theory that evaluates Liar sentences as true and false—is subject to revenge Liars, whether that theory is Priest's thoroughgoing dialetheism, or some diluted version. Nowhere in our discussion do we need to assume that the total dialetheist theory is intelligible; our discussion extracts specific dialetheist claims, and goes forward whether or not the larger dialetheist theory is intelligible. In the case of thoroughgoing dialetheism, then, it is legitimate for us to argue that (1) we do not understand what it says about liar sentences, and (2) it is subject to revenge Liars.

We should also scotch another possible confusion about our critique. The dialetheist might suggest that our two lines of criticism operate at distinct levels: the first critically examines the language of the theory itself, while the second is concerned with the dialetheist treatment of the object language in which the target paradoxes appear. And this would presuppose a distinction between object language and metalanguage that the thoroughgoing dialetheist rejects out of hand. However, we have no need of any such distinction. We can agree that there is just one language, in which both theoretical statements and liar sentences are expressed. So there is just one language—but there are two kinds of problem. One is that the pathology of the liar sentences spreads to the statements of the dialetheist theory, putting the intelligibility of the theory into question. The second is that there are liar sentences (in particular, the graphic liar sentences) to which the dialetheist's preferred statements do not apply, on pain of absurdity.

When one party to a dispute is willing to embrace contradictions, the dialectic is all the trickier. Nevertheless, it seems to us demonstrable that dialetheism does not deal adequately with the Liar—and if that is so, the major motivation for dialetheism evaporates. At the very least, we hope that we have raised some serious challenges to dialetheism. And until these challenges are met, the Law of Non-Contradiction is safe from any dialetheist assault.[27]

REFERENCES

BARWISE, JON, and ETCHEMENDY, JOHN (1987), *The Liar: An Essay in Truth and Circularity*, Oxford, Oxford University Press.

[27] We would like to thank Laurence Goldstein, Jay Rosenberg, and Carol Voeller for their helpful comments.

BEALL, JC (2001), 'Speaking of Paradox', unpublished MS.

BURGE, TYLER (1979), 'Semantical Paradox', *Journal of Philosophy*, 76: 169–98.

GAIFMAN, HAIM (1992), 'Pointers to Truth', *Journal of Philosophy*, 89: 223–61.

GUPTA, ANIL, and BELNAP, N. D. (1993), *The Revision Theory of Truth*, Cambridge, MIT.

KLEENE, S. C. (1952), *Introduction to Metamathematics*, New York, Van Nostrand.

KRIPKE, SAUL (1975), 'Outline of a Theory of Truth', *Journal of Philosophy*, 72: 690–716.

ŁUKASIEWICZ, J. (1920), 'O logice trojwartosciowej' (On Three-Valued Logic), *Ruch Filozoficzny*, 5: 170-1; trans. in S. McCall, *Polish Logic*, Oxford, Oxford University Press, 1967.

PARSONS, CHARLES (1974), 'The Liar Paradox', *Journal of Philosophical Logic*, 3: 381–412.

PRIEST, GRAHAM (1979), 'The Logic of Paradox', *Journal of Philosophical Logic*, 8: 219–41.

—— (1984), 'Logic of Paradox Revisited', *Journal of Philosophical Logic*, 13: 153–79.

—— (1987), *In Contradiction: A Study of the Transconsistent*, The Hague, Nijhoff.

RESCHER, NICHOLAS, and BRANDOM, ROBERT (1979), *The Logic of Inconsistency*, Totowa, NJ, Rowman & Littlefield.

RUSSELL, BERTRAND (1986), 'The Philosophy of Logical Atomism', in *The Philosophy of Logical Atomism and Other Essays, 1914–1919*, London, Allen & Unwin.

SIMMONS, KEITH (1993), *Universality and the Liar*, Cambridge, Cambridge University Press.

20

Simple Truth, Contradiction, and Consistency

Stewart Shapiro

> If I were attempting to produce a consistent theory of the consistent, this would be fatal. However, the aim of the enterprise is not to eliminate contradictions but to accommodate them.
>
> Priest (1987: 91)

> 'You couldn't deny that, even if you tried with both hands.'
>   'I don't deny things with my *hands*,' Alice objected.
>   'Nobody said you did,' said the Red Queen. 'I said you couldn't if you tried.'
>
> Lewis Carroll, *Through the Looking Glass*

1. THE BURDEN OF THE CRITIC

Dialetheism is the view that there are propositions Φ such that both Φ and $\neg\Phi$ are true. To keep things from lapsing into triviality—where every proposition is true—the dialetheist insists on a paraconsistent logic, rejecting the inference $\Phi, \neg\Phi \models \Psi$. The most comprehensive articulation and defense of dialetheism is Graham Priest's (1987), and much of his and others' subsequent work develops and corrects the underlying philosophical, semantic, and logical ideas.

According to Priest, we should not reject any of the premises (or presuppositions) of the reasoning leading to such semantic paradoxes as the Liar. Rather, the reasoning shows that those contradictions are true. The liar sentence is both true and not true, or depending on the version, the liar sentence is both true and false.

Let us be a bit more precise. Suppose that we have a language whose variables range over natural numbers, and which contains the usual arithmetic vocabulary. The language also contains a truth predicate T. For each formula Φ, let $\ulcorner\Phi\urcorner$ be the Gödel number of Φ, and for each natural number n, let Φ_n be the formula with Gödel number n. The truth predicate is materially adequate if each instance of the T-scheme holds:

$$Tn \leftrightarrow \Phi_n$$

The usual diagonal construction brings in self-reference. In particular, there is a formula χ such that

$$\chi \leftrightarrow \neg T\ulcorner\chi\urcorner$$

is provable. And we derive:

$$T^\ulcorner \chi \urcorner \ \& \ \neg T^\ulcorner \chi \urcorner$$

The dialetheist suggestion is that nothing has gone wrong. We should accept the truth of the last sentence.

According to Priest, an important advantage—perhaps the major advantage— of the dialetheic program is the possibility of a single, uniform semantics. There is no need for a separate meta-language, since the envisioned language is semantically closed. The language we use to talk about the language is just a part of the very language we are talking about.

Priest claims that every attempt to handle the semantic paradoxes in a consistent manner leads to extended-liar paradoxes, and so each such theory purchases its consistency at the cost of leaving some patently expressible notion inexpressible. Consider, for example, the 'gap' thesis that the Liar is neither true nor false. Then let L' be a statement saying that either L' is false or L' is neither true nor false. If our gap theorist allows that there is such a sentence as L', then it is neither true nor false. But this entails that L' is true. The gap theorist must thus hold that either there is no such sentence as L' or it does not say what we think it says. Either way, the statement we had in mind is not expressible. However, once we have predicates such as 'true' and 'neither true nor false' in the language, it is straightforward to formulate sentences such as L'. So the gap theorist must hold that we cannot express what we manifestly can express.

Priest claims that his dialetheic system overcomes this problem. Extended liar sentences can be expressed in his framework, and they are contradictory, just like the unextended liar. In sum, Tarski's theorem on the undefinability of truth tells us that, on pain of contradiction, the semantic meta-language must outstrip the object language in that there must be some notion used in the meta-theory that is not definable in the object language, and/or there is some obvious truth that cannot be established in the meta-theory. Priest's council is to accept the pain of contradiction—and then show that this pain is not as devastating as one might think.

Although dialetheism has attracted few adherents, this volume attests to a grow- ing interest in the view, and a growing literature opposing it. It is a view that all of us must reckon with. The dialectic between dialetheism and its critics is not straightforward. It is difficult for the critic to know what to say. One can refute other opponents by showing that their views lead to contradiction, espe- cially if the inconsistency comes by the opponent's own lights. The debate usually turns on whether the view does in fact entail a contradiction. This cuts no ice against the dialetheist, since she embraces contradictions. For her, a *reductio ad contradictionem* is not a *reductio ad absurdum*.

One might try to show that the dialetheist's theory is trivial—that every pro- position follows from it according to the dialetheists own notion of entailment.

I presume that this would be a damning consequence (if not absurd). However, this tactic is blocked for most of the proposed *formal* systems. Whether one is a dialetheist or not, those are legitimate mathematical objects, subject to study with the resources of mathematical logic. Priest has shown that most of his proposed formal theories are non-trivial, often by using a classical meta-theory. Moreover, even if we did show that one of the dialetheist's pet theories is trivial, the dialetheist has the option of arguing that we had not settled on the correct paraconsistent logic. As Priest (1993: 53) writes: 'Dialetheism is a view that has been widely (though quite incorrectly) viewed as absurd . . . It would be remark-able indeed, if, in crafting a case for it, one managed to get it exactly right the first time.'

Perhaps the opponent can attack the dialetheist's *informal* remarks. Some of those may lead to triviality. Failing that, an opponent might start with state-ments that a dialetheist accepts and try to derive a consequence that she rejects. For example, we might show that it follows from a dialetheist theory that Graham Priest is and always was under four feet tall, or that he is not and never was a dialetheist. Short of that, however, how is one to proceed? Surely there are false the-ories that are not trivial, and which do not entail any obvious rejected propositions like the above examples.

The plan here is to show, or at least to argue, that the dialetheist is subject to a cri-ticism much like one that Priest levels against consistent theories of truth: there are certain notions and concepts that the dialetheist invokes (informally), but which she cannot adequately express, unless the meta-theory is (completely) consistent. The insistence on a consistent meta-theory would undermine the key aspect of dialetheism, namely the uniformity of object language and meta-language. The crucial dialetheist claim is that any theory sufficient to express semantic notions is inconsistent.

2. WHITHER DISAGREEMENT?

A closely related, perhaps identical charge against dialetheism was leveled by Terrence Parsons (1990: s. 6). It will prove useful to begin with a summary of that, along with Priest's (1995) reply. Parsons (1990: 345) claims that a dialetheist cannot express disagreement with someone:

Suppose that you say 'β', and Priest replies '$\neg\beta$'. Under ordinary circumstances you would think that he had disagreed with you. But you remember that Priest is a dialetheist, and it occurs to you that he might very well agree with you after all—since he might think that β and $\neg\beta$ are both true. How can he indicate that he genuinely disagrees with you? The natural choice is for him to say 'β is not true'. However, the truth of this assertion is also consistent with β's being true—for a dialetheist anyway . . .

I do not think that *consistent* is the right word in the last sentence of this passage. The truth of 'β is not true' is surely *inconsistent* with the truth of β. This is analytic if anything is. Parsons's point is that for the dialetheist, 'β is not true' is nevertheless (logically) *compatible* with the truth of β. Since 'β is not true' does not rule out β, it cannot be used to express disagreement with someone who says that β is true. Parsons concludes that the dialetheist 'has difficulty asserting his disagreement with other's views'.

For his part, Priest (1995: 61) agrees that an assertion of $\neg\beta$, or the non-truth of β, or the falsity of β, need not express disagreement with someone who asserts β, for the reason that 'it is logically possible that both are true'. Actually, in the semantics that Priest develops, the notion of logical possibility is vacuous. For *any* set Γ of sentences, it is logically possible that every member of Γ is true. Indeed, Priest holds that there is a 'trivial' (but possible) interpretation in which every sentence is true.

In Priest's framework, the closest anyone can come to asserting something incompatible with β is to say that if β then everything is true: if β then $\forall x Tx$. Even this is logically compatible with β, as above, but surely $\forall x Tx$ is absurd, if anything is. There is no room (yet) for a more mild form of disagreement. Intuitively, saying 'I think, or suspect, that you may be wrong' is not the same as claiming that if you are right, then everything is true.

Another option would be to rely on Gricean implicature. If I assert β and Priest replies with $\neg\beta$, I might conclude that he disagrees with me due to the conversational maxim to say all that is relevant. If he thought that $\beta \,\&\, \neg\beta$ were true, he would have said so. Suppose, however, that he believes $\neg\beta$ and is unsure whether β is also true. Then he would not assert $\beta \,\&\, \neg\beta$, since he does not believe that, but he does not quite disagree with me either. So for a dialetheist, the bare assertion of $\neg\beta$ does not carry the implicature that he disagrees with β. In this case, perhaps the conversational maxim would require Priest to signal his non-disagreement somehow, perhaps by saying '$\neg\beta$, but I am not sure about β'.

Parsons himself proposes a different solution to this particular problem by insisting on a distinction between denying a sentence and asserting its negation, a distinction Priest had developed and exploited in some detail elsewhere (e.g. 1987: ch. 7). The idea is that we can express disagreement with someone who asserts β by *denying* β. Denial is a speech act complement to assertion. Priest shows that the denial of β is not the same as asserting $\neg\beta$. Moreover, there is no sentence γ such that the assertion of γ is equivalent in force to the denial of β—even for the non-dialetheist.

So far, so good. The dialetheist (or anyone else) either relies on implicature to get the point across or directly expresses disagreement with denial. But how would a dialetheist formulate a *hypothesis* that someone is mistaken? Suppose that Karl says 'β', and his dialetheist friend Seymore does not wish to disagree (yet), but he wonders if Karl is mistaken. Seymore might want to assert a conditional in the form: 'if Karl is mistaken, then ϕ'. How can Seymore express this? Again, 'if $\neg\beta$ then ϕ' won't work. Since, for Seymore, $\neg\beta$ is compatible with β, it is not the way for him to say that Karl is mistaken in asserting β.

I do not see how implicature helps here. What are the conversational rules for formulating hypotheses, or for the antecedents of conditionals? Even if there are coherent and useful implicatures concerning hypotheses, they cannot be used to determine the consequences of these hypotheses. So far, we just do not have a statement equivalent to 'Karl is mistaken in asserting β'.

One response, perhaps, would be for our dialetheist to take statements about mistakes at face value. To capture this, she can introduce a predicate M, such that for any sentence α, $M\ulcorner\alpha\urcorner$ holds if anyone who asserts α is incorrect, or has made a mistake, or something like that. Prima facie, one would like $M\ulcorner\alpha\urcorner$ to be genuinely (logically?) incompatible with α, in order for the operator to do its job. But the usual self-referential machinery kicks in. Let λ be a sentence equivalent to $M\ulcorner\lambda\urcorner$. Suppose that λ is true. Then $M\ulcorner\lambda\urcorner$. That is, λ is true and it is a mistake to assert it. But how can it be a mistake to assert a truth? Truth is the telos of assertion. Even if λ is both true and untrue (or false), it is still true, and so can be correctly asserted, and it is not a mistake to do so. So λ cannot be true, and so it *would* be a mistake to assert λ. So $M\ulcorner\lambda\urcorner$. But this is equivalent to λ.

The dialetheist might bite the bullet here, and hold that λ is true and not true. So one can and should assert λ (since it is true) *and* it would be a mistake and incorrect to assert λ (since $M\ulcorner\lambda\urcorner$ holds). Suppose that Seymore asserts λ. He is correct to do so, and yet he has made a mistake in this assertion, and he disagrees with anyone (including himself) who asserts λ. It seems to me that we have lost contact with the meaning of 'disagree' and 'mistake'. How can λ and $M\ulcorner\lambda\urcorner$ be both genuinely incompatible and yet compatible? We may also have lost contact with the meaning of 'incompatible'. The dialetheist might retort that I am erroneously insisting on a consistent account of these notions. If so, I'll leave this case with the clash of intuitions. We have other fish to fry.

Before moving on, notice that the situation here is structurally similar to one that Priest (1995: 61–2) develops concerning rational assertability. Consider a sentence β equivalent to

> It is irrational to assert $\ulcorner\beta\urcorner$

Suppose that someone asserted $\ulcorner\beta\urcorner$. According to Priest, they 'would then be asserting something, and at the same time asserting that it is irrational to assert it. This is irrational. Hence asserting $[\ulcorner\beta\urcorner]$ is irrational. But this is just $[\ulcorner\beta\urcorner]$, and we have established it. Hence it *is* rational to assert $[\ulcorner\beta\urcorner]$.' In other words, it is both rational and irrational to assert $\ulcorner\beta\urcorner$. Moreover, since we *know* that it is rational to assert $\ulcorner\beta\urcorner$, it is irrational to refrain from asserting $\ulcorner\beta\urcorner$. According to Priest, this is 'just another contradiction—and one, moreover, of just the kind that we should expect to arise when self-reference and semantic/intensional notions become entangled'. He then concedes that there is an interesting 'practical' problem of whether to assert β: 'One will be (rationally) damned if one does, and damned if one doesn't. Such, unfortunately, may be life.' It seems that if we accept the semantically closed framework, then we are condemned to being irrational. In the above case, involving the M operator, we are condemned to saying something $(M\lambda)$ that we must disagree with. Such may be life, but I hope not.

3. SIMPLE TRUTHS AND NON-DIALETHEIAS

Parsons (1990: 346) continues:

> Here is another way to view the problem. If you say β, and if Priest replies by asserting both β and $\neg\beta$, then you know exactly what he thinks about β; he thinks it is both true and false. But suppose that he thinks that β is simply false [i.e. false and not also true], and he replies with $\neg\beta$. You don't have enough information to tell whether he thinks β is simply false, or both true and false. And nothing he can assert will establish the answer.

As above, Priest can get his point across by denying β. But surely, there must be some sentence whose content is that β is false and not also true. Someone might want to express this content without asserting or denying the sentence (e.g. in the antecedent of a conditional). Locutions like this are found throughout Priest's writings on semantics, and so it would be a serious shortcoming if 'false and not true' ended up being inexpressible—exactly the sort of shortcoming Priest accuses his opponents of having. But Priest suggests that nothing could be more straightforward than expressing this. To say that β is false and not true, the dialetheist just *says that* β is false and not true. Analogously, Priest (1995: 62) writes: 'the dialetheist can express truly the view that something is true but not false, in the words I have just used'. So let us define α to be *simply true* if α is true but not also false, and define α to be *simply false* if α is false but not true.

Priest reminds us that he cannot, and need not, provide a consistent use of such locutions as simple truth and simple falsehood. The machinery of self-reference delivers sentences that are simply false *and* true. Consider a sentence λ equivalent to λ is simply false. Similarly, there are sentences that are simply true and false. As Priest puts it, such is the 'nature of the beast', the beast being (dialetheic) semantics.

Nevertheless, I submit that the given straightforward definitions of simple truth and simple falsehood do not do the required work, even in the inconsistent semantics. As usual, we define 'α is false' as '$\neg\alpha$ is true' or, in symbols: $F^\ulcorner\alpha\urcorner$ iff $T^\ulcorner\neg\alpha\urcorner$. Priest (1987: ch. 4) argues that untruth entails falsehood: $\neg T^\ulcorner\alpha\urcorner \to F^\ulcorner\alpha\urcorner$. He discusses the converse, $F^\ulcorner\alpha\urcorner \to \neg T^\ulcorner\alpha\urcorner$, but 'tentatively' rejects it. For the moment, however, let us adopt the converse, so that untruth is equivalent to falsehood: $\neg T^\ulcorner\alpha\urcorner$ iff $F^\ulcorner\alpha\urcorner$. This just amounts to the Tarskian clause for negation. I presume that a deflationist about truth would hold this (whether he is a dialetheist or not). For the deflationist, $T^\ulcorner\beta\urcorner$ is cognitively equivalent to β, for each sentence β. So by substitution of cognitive equivalents, $\neg\alpha$ is cognitively equivalent to $\neg T^\ulcorner\alpha\urcorner$. Also, $T^\ulcorner\neg\alpha\urcorner$ is equivalent to $\neg\alpha$. So $\neg T^\ulcorner\alpha\urcorner$ is equivalent to $T^\ulcorner\neg\alpha\urcorner$, and this last is $F^\ulcorner\alpha\urcorner$ by definition.

Suppose that a sentence α is false, $F^\ulcorner\alpha\urcorner$. Then it *follows* (from present assumptions) that α is not true, $\neg T^\ulcorner\alpha\urcorner$. So α is false and not true, i.e. α is *simply* false. Thus, *every* falsehood is simply false! So by saying that a sentence is simply false, one says no more than that the sentence is false. In particular, every dialetheia is simply false. The extra clause 'is not also true' comes for free, and adds nothing.

Similarly, suppose that α is true. Then, by the contrapositive of our temporary assumption that untruth is equivalent to falsehood, we have that α is not false. So α is true and not false, i.e. α is simply true. Thus, every truth is simply true, and in particular, every dialetheia is simply true (and, as above, simply false).

So under the assumption that untruth is equivalent to falsehood, the above definitions of simple truth and simple falsehood do not do their work. They do not distinguish *any* dialetheias from those sentences that we would like to say are false but not true, or true but not false.

Let us now reinstate Priest's distinction between falsehood and untruth, and so reject the inference $F^\ulcorner\alpha\urcorner \rightarrow \neg T^\ulcorner\alpha\urcorner$. This helps a little. Consider, for example, a sentence equivalent to its own falsehood: λ iff $T^\ulcorner\neg\lambda\urcorner$. This sentence is true and false, but it may not be untrue (as far as I can determine). However, Priest (ibid.) writes that the differences between falsehood and untruth are slight in some ways, and the relief the distinction brings here is minimal. Consider the Original Liar, a sentence λ equivalent to $\neg T^\ulcorner\lambda\urcorner$. We derive $T^\ulcorner\lambda\urcorner$ and $\neg T^\ulcorner\lambda\urcorner$ in the usual manner. But Priest holds that $\neg T^\ulcorner\lambda\urcorner$ entails $F^\ulcorner\lambda\urcorner$. So the Original Liar is false and not true. That is, the Original Liar is *simply false* (as well as true). But I would have thought that the dialetheist would want to *deny* that the Original Liar is simply false. The point of introducing the notion of simple falsehood in the first place was to *distinguish* some falsehoods from at least *paradigm* dialetheias. The notion of simple falsehood fails to do this.

The point is general. Let α be any sentence that is not true, so $\neg T^\ulcorner\alpha\urcorner$. Then it follows that α is false. So α is false and not true, so α is *simply* false. And this holds whether or not α is also true. So that statement that α is not true entails (indeed, is equivalent to) the simple falsehood of α. In particular, the dialetheist must hold that every dialetheia that is not true is also simply false.

Turning to a closely related matter, Parsons (1990: 345–6 n. 10) adds a footnote:

Priest could indicate genuine disagreement with you if he could assert '$\neg\beta$' and also say that β is not a [dialetheia]. However, the usual way to say this is to say 'β is not both true and false', i.e., '$\neg(\beta$ is true and β is false)'. This, however, gets us nowhere, since if β is the liar sentence, it *is* a [dialetheia], yet this statement about it is true. (If β is the liar sentence, then it is both true and not true. Since it is not true, 'β is true' is false, and so is the conjunction 'β is true & β is false'. Thus, the negation of this conjunction is true. (It is also false, but that is irrelevant to the point at issue.)) Priest has no means within his symbolism of adequately expressing 'not being a [dialetheia]'.

This last remark is correct. There are a number of (perhaps non-equivalent) ways to indicate that a given sentence α *is* a dialetheia. In the 'object language' (so to speak), one can just assert $\alpha\&\neg\alpha$. Or one can say that α is true and false ($T^\ulcorner\alpha\urcorner\&T^\ulcorner\neg\alpha\urcorner$) or that α is true and not true ($T^\ulcorner\alpha\urcorner\&\neg T^\ulcorner\alpha\urcorner$). But how can one say that α is a non-dialetheia? It will not do simply to say $\neg(\alpha\&\neg\alpha)$. For this last is a logical truth in Priest's semantics. It holds no matter what sentence α is. Priest points out in several places that if α is a dialetheia, in the sense that $(\alpha\&\neg\alpha)$ is true, then $(\alpha\&\neg\alpha)$ is another dialetheia. That is, we have both $(\alpha\&\neg\alpha)$ and $\neg(\alpha\&\neg\alpha)$. So if 'α is a non-dialetheia' is defined as '$\neg(\alpha\&\neg\alpha)$', then every sentence is a non-dialetheia, including *every* dialetheia.

For the same reason, it will not do to define 'α is a non-dialetheia' as 'α is not both true and not true' (i.e. $\neg(T^\ulcorner\alpha\urcorner \& \neg T^\ulcorner\alpha\urcorner)$), for that, too, is a necessary, perhaps analytic truth. By excluded middle, we have $\neg T^\ulcorner\alpha\urcorner \vee \neg\neg T^\ulcorner\alpha\urcorner$. Assume $\neg T^\ulcorner\alpha\urcorner$. Then $\neg(T^\ulcorner\alpha\urcorner \& \neg T^\ulcorner\alpha\urcorner)$. Now assume $\neg\neg T^\ulcorner\alpha\urcorner$. Then $\neg(T^\ulcorner\alpha\urcorner \& \neg T^\ulcorner\alpha\urcorner)$. In fact, we have $\forall x\neg(Tx\&\neg Tx)$ as a general theorem (Priest 1987: 90–1). So, again, the locution 'not both true and not true' does not make any distinctions at all. For the dialetheist and the non-dialetheist alike, every sentence is not both true and not true, including any that may be both true and not true.

The third among the obvious candidates for 'α is a non-dialetheia' is 'α is not both true and false', $\neg(T^\ulcorner\alpha\urcorner \& T^\ulcorner\neg\alpha\urcorner)$. This only differs from the previous option if we enforce Priest's distinction between untruth and falsehood. Even then, it is not much of an improvement. Let β be any sentence that is not true, $\neg T^\ulcorner\beta\urcorner$. Then, a fortiori, β is not both true and false. And this happens whether or not β is also true. So the Original Liar is not both true and false. Similarly, let γ be any sentence that is not false, $\neg T^\ulcorner\neg\gamma\urcorner$. Then a fortiori, γ is not both true and false—whether or not γ is also false.

Of course, the dialetheist can easily deny that a certain sentence α is a dialetheia by denying the conjunction $\alpha \& \neg\alpha$ (or denying that α is both true and not true, etc.). As above, this is not the same as asserting $\neg(\alpha \& \neg\alpha)$, which he would do in any case, presumably. What he cannot do, so far as I know, is formulate a non-trivial hypothesis that is α a non-dialetheia, or formulate a useful conditional in the form 'if α is a non-dialetheia, then ϕ'.

Of course, we have only invoked the obvious candidates for 'non-dialetheia'. I leave this as a challenge to the dialetheist to develop a non-trivial notion. One possible response would be to alter the semantics so that $\neg(\alpha \& \neg\alpha)$ is not logically true, especially if α is a dialetheia. Or else the dialetheist might reject Priest's inference $\neg T^\ulcorner\alpha\urcorner \rightarrow F^\ulcorner\alpha\urcorner$, as well as the converse $F^\ulcorner\alpha\urcorner \rightarrow \neg T^\ulcorner\alpha\urcorner$. This further separates untruth from falsehood.

It is not hard to develop a formal system with an operator N such that $N(\alpha \& N\alpha)$ is not a logical truth. And one can add a new predicate H where $H^\ulcorner\alpha\urcorner$ has no straightforward relationship with $\neg\alpha$. The burden on a dialetheist who takes one of these routes is to show that the N operator really is a negation and/or that the H predicate really is falsehood. We must postpone discussion of these options, pending an elaboration of the details.

Priest might protest that I am demanding a *consistent* use of the property of not being a dialetheia, and then add that this is not possible, nor is it desirable. Whatever precise definitions of 'dialetheia' and 'non-dialetheia' we settle on, there will be sentences that both are and are not dialetheias. Diagonalization is always present. Priest (1987: 139) writes that 'it is not difficult to see that in whatever way one tries to express the claim that α is not a dialetheia, there is nothing to prevent this claim itself from being a dialetheia, in which case both of $[\alpha \& \neg\alpha]$ and "α is not a dialetheia" may be true'. Such is the way of self-reference and semantics, at least for the dialetheist. Fair enough (at least for the sake of argument). The classes of dialetheias, simple truths, and simple falsehoods will overlap in any case. But we have just seen that with the obvious candidates for expressing these notions, the overlap is too extensive for the distinction to be useful. It is surely reasonable to demand that our definitions be non-vacuous. If we have to say that *every* sentence is a non-dialetheia, then the notion is useless. And the notion is all but useless if we have to say that every untruth is also a non-dialetheia, including the Original Liar and nearly all the dialetheias we run across in the course of thinking about this stuff—every non-truth and every non-falsehood are also non-dialetheias. I would have thought that a dialetheist, like Priest, would *deny* that the Original Liar is a non-dialetheia, rather than asserting that it is one.

As above, the dialetheist can sometimes rely on conversational implicature. For example, since $\neg(\alpha \& \neg\alpha)$ is logically true, one is correct to assert it no matter what sentence α is. But presumably one would not utter this if he believed that α is not a dialetheia, since that would be to suppress relevant information. So there is a point to uttering tautologies sometimes—when we wish to rule something out via implicature. But, again, this does not help with formulating a useful hypothesis or the antecedent of a conditional.

Incidentally, the law of non-contradiction is often stated as, for any proposition Φ, $\neg(\Phi \& \neg\Phi)$ is true. Since this is a logical truth in Priest's system, it seems that he *endorses* the law of non-contradiction—this despite the fact that his work is designed to challenge this very law. Similarly, Priest (1987: 91) explicitly derives (and thus endorses) the statement that no sentence is both true and not true: $\neg\exists x(Tx \& \neg Tx)$. So he cannot very well deny that version of the law of non-contradiction, since he endorses it. His attitude toward the law of non-contradiction is expressed by asserting sentences inconsistent with it. In particular, he asserts contradictions. Well, that cannot be quite right either, since for the dialetheist, to assert something inconsistent with a statement Φ is not to reject Φ.

This aporia cuts two ways. How do I assert that I am not a dialetheist? Apparently, it will not do to assert that there are no true contradictions, since Priest holds that as well. The statement that there are no true contradictions is equivalent to the statement that every sentence is a non-dialetheia. One can manifest his opposition to dialetheism only by *denying* that there are some true contradictions.

Suppose that Seymore is a member of a community of dialetheists but comes to reject dialetheism. This he can express, as above: he denies all contradictions. But suppose that instead of rejecting dialetheism outright, Seymore just starts to harbor doubts that this view is correct. He wants to explore the consequences of the incorrectness of dialetheism. He might say, 'suppose I deny all contradictions'. But that is not the correct hypothesis. 'Suppose Seymore denies all contradictions' is a hypothesis about a potential speech act by Seymore, not a hypothesis about dialetheism as such. He cannot very well hypothesize $\neg \exists x (Tx \,\&\, \neg Tx)$, since, as above, the dialetheist (or at least Priest) holds this already. Suppose that Seymore hypothesizes that there are no sentences that are both true and false: $\neg \exists x (Tx \,\&\, Fx)$. If we enforce the distinction between untruth and falsehood, then this is not an analytic truth in Priest's system. So perhaps this does the trick. Notice, however, that in Priest's system, $\neg \exists x (Tx \,\&\, Fx)$ is equivalent to the equivalence of untruth and falsehood. So when Seymore hypothesizes that $\neg \exists x (Tx \,\&\, Fx)$, perhaps he is just wondering if falsehood entails untruth. Perhaps Seymore is just exploring deflationism. Seymore's statement does not distinguish that hypothesis from the incorrectness of dialetheism. It seems that if dialetheism is correct, then there is no statement that expresses the content of the incorrectness of dialetheism, or at least I cannot think of one.

4. CONSISTENCY

It is a truism that the notion of consistency plays a central role in the framework of dialetheism. There are extended discourses on whether consistency is a norm of rationality and on whether certain inferences, like the disjunctive syllogism, are valid in consistent situations. So we need a precise formulation of what it is to be consistent.

It is easy to say what it is for a theory Γ to be *in*consistent: there is a sentence α in the language Γ of such that Γ entails α and Γ entails $\neg\alpha$. But for our dialetheist, what is it for a theory to be consistent?

It is analytic that Γ is consistent if and only if Γ is not inconsistent. In other words, Γ is consistent if there is no sentence α in the language of Γ such that Γ entails α and entails $\neg\alpha$, or, in yet other words, for every α, it is not the case that Γ entails $\alpha \,\&\, \neg\alpha$. The notion of logical consequence is not especially problematic for a dialetheist. Priest follows the standard (but not universal) practice of taking semantics, rather than proof theory, to be the central notion for logical consequence: 'rules of inference . . . must answer to a satisfactory semantic account of the connective[s], in the sense that the rules are demonstrably sound according to the semantics' (Priest 1990: s. 5). For what it is worth, I agree with this much (Shapiro 1998, see also 1991: ch. 2). To make some headway on the present issue, we will focus on the model-theoretic semantics that he develops in various places. This concerns formal languages, considered as mathematical models of natural language. The defined notions of consistency, logical consequence, etc., are mathematical models of their intuitive counterparts.

In light of the above, it might be surprising that when the straightforward definition of consistency is understood in terms of the model-theoretic semantics, it is not (or might not be) vacuous. It is instructive to see why this is so, and how this case differs from the previous ones. I claim that the definition is non-trivial only because a crucial tie between negation and the '¬' connective is severed in the model theory. It is routine to restore the connections between negation and '¬', to bring the semantics in line with ordinary classical or intuitionistic model theory. However, once this is done the above straightforward definition of consistency becomes trivial, in the sense that *every* theory ends up being consistent, including theories whose consistency the dialetheist will surely deny (or at least strongly want to deny).

In the model-theoretic semantics developed in Priest (1987), truth values are non-empty subsets of $\{0, 1\}$. If a sentence is false in an interpretation, then 0 is a member of its truth value in that interpretation; and if a sentence is true in an interpretation, then 1 is a member of its truth value in that interpretation. Thus, the truth value $\{0\}$ is for sentences that are false only (i.e. simply false), the truth value $\{1\}$ is for sentences that are true only, and the truth value $\{0, 1\}$ is for dialetheias. In response to a criticism brought by Timothy Smiley (1993), Priest (1993) proposes replacing the truth functional notion of satisfaction with a valuation relation. A sentence is true if it is related to 1, and false if it is related to 0. Thus, a sentence is a dialetheia if it is related to both 0 and 1. We follow the relational version here, but present issues do not turn on the distinction.

An interpretation M of a formal language consists of a domain of discourse d, an assignment of an object in the domain to each individual constant, and an assignment of an extension and an anti-extension to each predicate. If P is an n-place predicate, then its extension and anti-extension are sets of n-tuples of members of the domain d, with the proviso that every n-tuple is in either the extension or the anti-extension (or both). This reflects Priest's acceptance of excluded middle.

Let M be an interpretation, whose domain is d, and let s be an assignment of an object in d to each (first-order) variable. The denotation function, from singular terms to members of d is defined as usual. The valuation relation V is then defined in a straightforward way: its domain is the set of formulas of the language and its co-domain is $\{0, 1\}$. Here are a few clauses from the system developed by Priest

(1987: 94), transcribed to the relational framework:

If P is an n-place atomic predicate and $t_1, \ldots, t_n$ are terms, then $V(M, s, \ulcorner Pt_1 \ldots t_n \urcorner, 1)$ if and only if the n-tuple consisting of the denotations of $t_1, \ldots, t_n$ is in the extension of P in M.

If P is an n-place atomic predicate and $t_1, \ldots, t_n$ are terms, then $V(M, s, \ulcorner Pt_1 \ldots t_n \urcorner, 0)$ if and only if the n-tuple consisting of the denotations of $t_1, \ldots, t_n$ is in the anti-extension of P in M.

If Φ is a formula, then $V(M, s, \ulcorner \neg\Phi \urcorner, 1)$ if and only if $V(M, s, \ulcorner \Phi \urcorner, 0)$.

If Φ is a formula, then $V(M, s, \ulcorner \neg\Phi \urcorner, 0)$ if and only if $V(M, s, \ulcorner \Phi \urcorner, 1)$.

If Φ and Ψ are formulas, then $V(M, s, \ulcorner \Phi \& \Psi \urcorner, 1)$ if and only if both $V(M, s, \ulcorner \Phi \urcorner, 1)$ and $V(M, s, \ulcorner \Psi \urcorner, 1)$.

If Φ and Ψ are formulas, then $V(M, s, \ulcorner \Phi \& \Psi \urcorner, 0)$ if and only if either $V(M, s, \ulcorner \Phi \urcorner, 0)$ or $V(M, s, \ulcorner \Psi \urcorner, 0)$.

If Φ and Ψ are formulas, then $V(M, s, \ulcorner \Phi \vee \Psi \urcorner, 1)$ if and only if either $V(M, s, \ulcorner \Phi \urcorner, 1)$ or $V(M, s, \ulcorner \Psi \urcorner, 1)$.

If Φ and Ψ are formulas, then $V(M, s, \ulcorner \Phi \vee \Psi \urcorner, 0)$ if and only if both $V(M, s, \ulcorner \Phi \urcorner, 0)$ and $V(M, s, \ulcorner \Psi \urcorner, 0)$.

Let Γ be a set of sentences and Φ a sentence. As usual, *logical consequence* is defined as the necessary preservation of truth, and consistency is defined in terms of logical consequence:

$\Gamma \models \Phi$ if and only if for every interpretation M and assignment s, if $V(M, s, \ulcorner \alpha \urcorner, 1)$ for each $\alpha \in \Gamma$, then $V(M, s, \ulcorner \Phi \urcorner, 1)$

Γ is *consistent* if there is no formula Φ such that both $\Gamma \models \Phi$ and $\Gamma \models \neg\Phi$

The notion of consistency, as defined here, is a semantic, model-theoretic property of sets of formulas. This is in contrast with the practice of taking consistency as a proof-theoretic notion, but it fits Priest's views on the primacy of semantical notions.

Notice that disjunctive syllogism is not valid in this framework. Consider an interpretation M and assignment s such that $V(M, s, \ulcorner \Phi \urcorner, 1)$, $V(M, s, \ulcorner \Phi \urcorner, 0)$, $V(M, s, \ulcorner \Psi \urcorner, 0)$, but not $V(M, s, \ulcorner \Psi \urcorner, 1)$. Then we have $V(M, s, \ulcorner \Phi \vee \Psi \urcorner, 1)$ and $V(M, s, \ulcorner \neg\Phi \urcorner, 1)$, but not $V(M, s, \ulcorner \Psi \urcorner, 1)$.

Define an interpretation M to be *trivial* if its domain is not empty and, for each n-place predicate P, the extension and the anti-extension of P both consist of the set of all n-tuples of members of the domain of discourse. If M is trivial, then for any sentence α and any assignment s, we have $V(M, s, \ulcorner \alpha \urcorner, 0)$ and $V(M, s, \ulcorner \alpha \urcorner, 1)$. That is, every sentence is true in M, and every sentence is false in M.

One pleasing feature of Priest's formal framework is that it is well defined in a classical (presumably consistent) meta-theory. So the classical logician has a tool to study and adjudicate matters of logical consequence in Priest's dialetheic philosophy. Of course, the classical logician will not regard the framework as being an accurate model of truth (and falsity) conditions. We might have both

$V(M, s, \ulcorner\Phi\urcorner, 1)$ and $V(M, s, \ulcorner\Phi\urcorner, 0)$ for the same interpretation M and assignment s, even though the classical logician does not think it possible for a sentence to be both true and false in the same interpretation. Nevertheless, 0 and 1 are well-defined formal objects, and the classical logician can manipulate them according the rules of the dialetheic model theory.

If we assume that the meta-theory is classical (and consistent), then the notion of consistency is surely non-trivial. In that case, the consistent theories and the inconsistent theories do not overlap. However, this eclectic attitude toward the model theory is potentially misleading. As above, a touted advantage of dialetheism is that it eliminates the need for a separate meta-theory to deal with truth and other semantic notions. One would think that this should hold for 'truth in an interpretation' as well (but see Priest 2002*a*). Priest holds that the 'meta-theory' might be (or actually is) itself inconsistent. In the present context of model theory, this suggests that there might be (or are) interpretations M and sentences Φ such that it both is and is not the case that $V(M, s, \ulcorner\Phi\urcorner, 1)$—whether or not $V(M, s, \ulcorner\Phi\urcorner, 0)$ also holds. Such interpretations M are themselves inconsistent. In contrast, the classical logician studying dialetheic logic would work only with consistent models of inconsistency.

One moral is that we cannot assume that the logic of the meta-theory is classical. Priest notes that the following is a valid inference:

$$\{\Phi \vee \Psi, \neg\Phi\} \models \Psi \vee (\Phi \mathbin{\&} \neg\Phi)$$

So the classical logician might conclude that if a theory is consistent, then disjunctive syllogism is kosher (even if not universally valid), since in that case we can eliminate the second disjunct, $\Phi \mathbin{\&} \neg\Phi$, of the conclusion. However, this is to use disjunctive syllogism in the meta-language. If there are, or might be, theories that are both consistent and inconsistent—as a dialetheist will surely hold—then the thesis that disjunctive syllogism is valid in consistent theories is incorrect (see Priest 1987: s. 8.2, for a fuller discussion of this matter). But in the classical meta-theory, there are no interpretations that are both consistent and inconsistent.

So the classical logician who uses the above framework to study dialetheist logic must be careful to use only sound dialetheic inferences in the meta-language. This might create a circularity, since the logician might need the framework to determine what the sound dialetheic inferences are. This is a general predicament for anyone who uses model theory to delimit a logic. She must somehow *first* settle on a logic for the meta-theory, but she cannot do this if the meta-theory is to tell us what the correct logic is. Presumably, the problem here is one for the classical logician, not for Priest himself. However, the predicament makes it difficult to study the situation from a neutral perspective, even for the sake of argument.

A related problem is that model theory is formulated in set theory, and a satisfactory paraconsistent set theory has yet to be codified (see Priest 2002*a*). Straightforward formulations of the powerful set-existence principles generate triviality in the paraconsistent framework: every proposition seems to follow from the inconsistencies. Thus, the following discussion can only be regarded as tentative. It is more of a study of what features the set-theoretic model theory must have if consistency is to be a useful, non-vacuous notion.

As it stands, I do not know how to show that the notion of consistency is non-trivial, in the sense that it does not apply to too many theories, including theories whose inconsistency one would like to deny. Actually, I do not see how one *can* show this, in the sense of providing a compelling a priori demonstration that rules out every alternative. In the dialetheic background, the fact that a given theory is *in*consistent does not preclude that theory from being consistent as well. This is an instance of the issue, broached in s. 2 above, concerning the dialetheist's (apparent) inability to express disagreement. It is hard, perhaps impossible, for a dialetheist to rule out anything on logical grounds alone. In the present case, the best we can do is to delimit the range of the consistent theories in such a manner that it seems plausible that the notion is non-trivial. I will make a start on that project.

Define an interpretation M to be *classical* if for each n-place predicate P and for each n-tuple a of objects in the domain of M, it is not the case that a is in the extension of P and a is in the anti-extension of P. That is, an interpretation is classical if for each predicate P, the extension and the anti-extension of P do not overlap. Classical interpretations thus correspond to interpretations in ordinary, non-dialetheic model theory. In that context, one usually does not mention anti-extensions, since the anti-extension of a predicate is just the complement of the extension. The above clauses for truth—truth value 1—correspond to their classical counterparts, and the clauses for falsehood are straightforward duals.

> Theorem 1. An interpretation M is classical if and only if there is no formula α and assignment s such that $V(M, s, \ulcorner\alpha\urcorner, 1)$ and $V(M, s, \ulcorner\alpha\urcorner, 0)$

The proof of this goes by induction on the complexity of α. The basis clause, for atomic α, follows directly from the definition of 'classical' and the clauses in the semantics for atomic formulas. The various induction steps follow from the respective clauses.

In ordinary, classical model theory, a given set Γ of formulas is consistent if there is an interpretation M and assignment that satisfies every member of Γ. This should not (and had better not) hold in the present semantics. As we saw, a trivial interpretation satisfies every formula, and so it satisfies every member of every set of formulas. The correct analogue of the classical result is this:

> Theorem 2. A set Γ of formulas is consistent if there is a *classical* interpretation M and a variable assignment s such that $V(M, s, \ulcorner\alpha\urcorner, 1)$ for each α in Γ

Proof: Suppose that M is a classical interpretation and s is a
variable assignment on M such that $V(M, s, \ulcorner\alpha\urcorner, 1)$ for each α
in Γ. Let Φ be any formula. If $\Gamma \models \Phi$ and $\Gamma \models \neg\Phi$ then,
a fortiori, $V(M, s, \ulcorner\Phi\urcorner, 1)$ and $V(M, s, \ulcorner\neg\Phi\urcorner, 1)$. So If $\Gamma \models \Phi$
and $\Gamma \models \neg\Phi$ then, $V(M, s, \ulcorner\Phi\urcorner, 1)$ and $V(M, s, \ulcorner\Phi\urcorner, 0)$. But the
consequent of this conditional contradicts Theorem 1. Taking
the contrapositive, Γ is consistent.

Corollary 3. If Γ is satisfiable in classical model theory, then Γ is consistent
in Priest's dialetheic semantics

If we assume that the meta-theory is consistent, and apply classical logic there,
then the converse of Theorem 2 can be established, via a straightforward Henkin-
style derivation (similar to the proof of soundness and completeness for this
semantics in a consistent meta-theory—see Priest 2002*b*, s. 6.5). Unfortunately,
it is unknown at present whether completeness can be proved in a paraconsistent meta-theory—the aforementioned problem of developing a paraconsistent set
theory remains. In like manner, I do not know if the converse of Theorem 2 holds
in the envisioned dialetheic meta-theory. The converse of Theorem 2 entails the
converse of Corollary 3: a theory is consistent in Priest's dialetheic semantics only
if it is satisfiable in ordinary, classical model theory.

The converse of Theorem 2 and its corollary would thus give us grounds to
believe that the notion of consistency is non-trivial (i.e. it does not include too
much). The consistent theories are among those that have classical interpretations,
and so dialetheic consistency coincides with classical consistency. So long as the
central inconsistent theories do not end up with classical interpretations, we can
rule out their consistency. But is the property of having a classical interpretation
itself non-trivial? In the present framework, it *seems* to be, but, again, I don't know
how to show this.

I submit that even if, in fact, the notion of consistency is non-trivial in the present
framework, this non-triviality turns on an artefact of the formalism. When this
feature is corrected, the notion of consistency collapses, in that *every* theory ends
up consistent.

To illustrate the problem, notice that the clauses for conjunction in the definition
of the valuation relation V are what we may call 'homophonic'. The definition
recapitulates the truisms that a conjunction is true (in an interpretation) just
in case both of the conjuncts are true, and a conjunction is false just in case
one conjunct is. Similarly, the clauses for disjunction recapitulate truisms for
disjunction: a disjunction is true if one of its disjuncts is, and a disjunction is false
if both disjuncts are. To borrow an elegant phrase from Hodes (1984), truth in a
model is, or is supposed to be, a model of truth. When it comes to conjunction
and disjunction, things are quite straightforward. The connectives 'commute' with
truth and they 'commute' with truth in an interpretation.

Let me repeat the clauses for negation:

If Φ is a formula, then $V(M, s, \ulcorner\neg\Phi\urcorner, 1)$ if and only if $V(M, s, \ulcorner\Phi\urcorner, 0)$

If Φ is a formula, then $V(M, s, \ulcorner\neg\Phi\urcorner, 0)$ if and only if $V(M, s, \ulcorner\Phi\urcorner, 1)$

Unlike conjunction and disjunction, these are not homophonic. In fact, negation does not occur on the right-hand side of these clauses. In the formalism, negation floats freely from untruth. Suppose that we add the following to the formalism:

(*) If Φ is a formula, then $V(M, s, \ulcorner\neg\Phi\urcorner, 1)$ if and only if it is not the case that $V(M, s, \ulcorner\Phi\urcorner, 1)$

For completeness, we might also add

(**) If Φ is a formula, then $V(M, s, \ulcorner\neg\Phi\urcorner, 0)$ if and only if it is not the case that $V(M, s, \ulcorner\Phi\urcorner, 0)$

but this last plays no role in what follows.

In words, (*) says that $\neg\Phi$ is true in M under s just in case it is not the case that Φ is true in M under s. The principle (*) brings the dialetheist framework more in line with ordinary (consistent) model theory, which uses homophonic clauses for all of the connectives. Under (*), dialetheic model theory is, word for word, the same as ordinary, classical (or intuitionistic) model theory. The difference lies in the envisioned dialetheic set theory which provides the materials for the various interpretations (which is where the differences should be found).

Let M be an interpretation, and let α be a sentence that is a dialetheia-in-M. So $V(M, s, \ulcorner\alpha\urcorner, 1)$ and $V(M, s, \ulcorner\alpha\urcorner, 0)$. By the original clauses for negation, $V(M, s, \ulcorner\neg\alpha\urcorner, 1)$, and by (*) it is not the case that $V(M, s, \ulcorner\neg\alpha\urcorner, 1)$. That is, M is itself inconsistent. So the addition of (*) requires that inconsistent situations can be modeled only with inconsistent interpretations. The idea of modeling inconsistency with consistent interpretations is, of course, appealing to a classical logician intent on understanding dialetheic or paraconsistent logic. However, from the dialetheic perspective, it is artificial and can potentially lead to incorrect results, due to the mismatch between the model and what it is a model of. In the present case, I suggest that the above characterization of consistency is non-trivial only because it allows consistent 'interpretations' of inconsistency in the semantics. Under (*), the problems with characterizing simple truth, simple falsehood, and non-dialetheia (from s. 3 above) re-emerge, with an attitude:

Theorem 4. It follows from (*) that every theory is consistent

Proof: Let Γ be any theory. By definition, a theory Γ is consistent if there is no formula α such that $\Gamma \models \alpha$ and $\Gamma \models \neg\alpha$. Let α be any formula. By excluded middle, either $\Gamma \models \neg\alpha$ or it is not the case that $\Gamma \models \neg\alpha$. In the latter case, it is not the case that both $\Gamma \models \alpha$ and $\Gamma \models \neg\alpha$. So suppose that $\Gamma \models \neg\alpha$. Let M be any interpretation and s a variable assignment such that for any Φ in Γ, $V(M, s, \ulcorner\Phi\urcorner, 1)$. Then $V(M, s, \ulcorner\neg\alpha\urcorner, 1)$. So by (*), it is not the case that $V(M, s, \ulcorner\alpha\urcorner, 1)$. So it is not the case that $\Gamma \models \alpha$. A fortiori, it is not the case that both $\Gamma \models \alpha$ and $\Gamma \models \neg\alpha$. So Γ is consistent.

Of course, some theories are also inconsistent, but never mind. We still have that every theory is consistent, and so the notion of consistency, as defined above, could not be more vacuous. Consider the trivial theory Δ that contains every sentence of the language. Of course, Δ is massively inconsistent. Surely, the dialetheist will want to *deny* the statement that Δ is consistent. But she cannot rationally do so, since that theory is in fact consistent (or at least it satisfies the above, straightforward definition of consistency). It is not just that Δ entails that Δ is consistent. Trivially, Δ entails everything, including its own consistency (if that can be expressed in the language of Δ). The point here is that the dialetheist is herself committed to the assertion that Δ is consistent—despite how unnatural and unwanted that commitment may be.

The natural response would be for the dialetheist to demur from (*), and presumably (**) as well. The classical logician has a well-developed, coherent, and powerful homophonic model theory, but this is denied to the dialetheist. The dialetheist needs to show that the clauses for '$\neg$' really do reflect the essential properties of *negation*. Otherwise, the semantics is artificial.

The move of rejecting (*) does seem to help with the present problem, but may not completely overcome it. In the semantics, there are two different ways of saying that a formula α is false in an interpretation M under an assignment s. Since the value 0 itself corresponds to falsehood, one way is $V(M, s, \ulcorner\alpha\urcorner, 0)$. As above, falsehood is informally defined as truth of the negation. This would be $V(M, s, \ulcorner\neg\alpha\urcorner, 1)$. The first clause for negation in the above semantics,

if Φ is a formula, then $V(M, s, \ulcorner\neg\Phi\urcorner, 1)$ if and only if $V(M, s, \ulcorner\Phi\urcorner, 0)$

simply identifies these two ways of expressing falsehood-in-an-interpretation. So the clause is quite natural. But what is the relation between untruth-in-an-interpretation and falsehood-in-an-interpretation? As noted in s. 3 above, Priest (1987: ch. 4) argues that untruth entails falsehood ($\neg T\ulcorner\alpha\urcorner \to F\ulcorner\alpha\urcorner$), but he tentatively rejects the converse, $F\ulcorner\alpha\urcorner \to \neg T\ulcorner\alpha\urcorner$. This would suggest that he would accept the right-to-left half of (*) but demur from the left-to-right half. Note that the latter is invoked in the proof of Theorem 4. Moreover, it is the left-to-right half of (*) that precludes consistent models of inconsistent situations. So far, so good. Perhaps the dialetheist should accept at most the right-to-left half of (*) as a general semantic thesis.

However, one would think that (the left-to-right half of) (*) holds in some interpretations, if not all of them. Define M to be a (*)-*interpretation* if (*) holds in M.

Recall that an interpretation M is defined to be *classical* if, for each n-place predicate P and for each n-tuple a of objects in the domain of M, it is not the case that a is in the extension and a is in the anti-extension of P:

Theorem 5. Every (*)-interpretation is classical

Proof sketch: Without loss of generality, we can assume that P is monadic. Let a be an object in the domain of M, and let s assign the variable x to a. Either a is in the anti-extension of P in M or a is not in the anti-extension of P in M. If the latter, then a fortiori, a is not in both the extension and the anti-extension of P in M. If a is in the anti-extension of P in M, then $V(M, s, \ulcorner Px \urcorner, 0)$ and so $V(M, s, \ulcorner \neg Px \urcorner, 1)$. By (*), then, it is not the case that $V(M, s, \ulcorner Px \urcorner, 1)$, and so it is not the case that a is in the extension of P in M. So, again, a is not in both the extension and the anti-extension of P in M. To be sure, M may be itself inconsistent, in which case a might also be in the extension and anti-extension of P in M, but we still have that a is *not* in both the extension and anti-extension of P in M. Since a and P are arbitrary, we conclude that M is classical. Again, M may also be not classical, but still, M is classical.

Let Γ be a theory. Say that Γ has a (*)-*model* if there is a (*)-interpretation M and assignment s on M such that for each Φ in Γ, $V(M, s, \ulcorner \Phi \urcorner, 1)$. It follows from Theorem 2 and Theorem 5 that if a theory has a (*)-model, then it is consistent. Actually, we can show this directly without the detour through Theorem 2. The reasoning in the proof of Theorem 4 shows that if a theory Γ has a (*)-model then for each assignment s and each formula α, it is not the case that both $V(M, s, \ulcorner \alpha \urcorner, 1)$ and $V(M, s, \ulcorner \neg \alpha \urcorner, 1)$. It follows that Γ meets the definition of consistency.

Recall that an interpretation M is trivial if for every n-place predicate P, the extension and the anti-extension of P both consist of the set of every n-tuple of members of the domain. If M is trivial then for every assignment s and every formula α, $V(M, s, \ulcorner \alpha \urcorner, 1)$ (and $V(M, s, \ulcorner \alpha \urcorner, 0)$).

Nothing said so far rules out the possibility that there is a trivial (*)-interpretation (i.e. one where the extension and the anti-extension of every n-place predicate is the collection of all n-tuples of members of the domain). If there were such a theory, it would be both trivial and non-trivial, classical and non-classical, consistent and inconsistent. But still trivial and consistent.

Of course, this is not an argument that there is a trivial (*)-interpretation. Given the aforementioned uncertainty about the set theory, one cannot be definitive either way at this stage in the development of dialetheism. If there is a trivial (*)-interpretation then, again, every theory is consistent. I presume that this would be a most unwelcome consequence. There surely are theories Γ such that the dialetheist wants to deny that Γ is consistent. If nothing else, she would like to deny that a trivial theory is consistent. This denial is rational only if she can rationally deny that Γ has a (*)-model, a model in which negation commutes with falsehood. So the set existence principles and diagonal techniques should not be so strong that they yield such interpretations.

REFERENCES

HODES, H. (1984), 'Logicism and the Ontological Commitments of Arithmetic', *Journal of Philosophy*, 81: 123–149.

PARSONS, TERRENCE (1990), 'True Contradictions', *Canadian Journal of Philosophy*, 20: 335–54.

PRIEST, G. (1987), *In Contradiction: A Study of the Transconsistent*, Dordrecht, Martinus Nijhoff.

—— (1990), 'Boolean Negation and All That', *Journal of Philosophical Logic*, 19: 201–15.

—— (1993), 'Can Contradictions Be True? II', *Proceedings of the Aristotelian Society*, suppl. vol. 67: 35–54.

—— (1995), 'Gaps and Gluts: Reply to Parsons', *Canadian Journal of Philosophy*, 25: 57–66.

—— (2002a), 'Paraconsistent Set Theory and Metatheory', in A. Irvine (ed.), *Foundations of Set Theory*, Blackwell, forthcoming.

—— (2002b), 'Paraconsistent Logic', in D. Gabbay and F. Geunthner (ed.), 2nd edn., *Handbook of Philosophical Logic*, 6: 287–393.

SHAPIRO, S. (1991), *Foundations without Foundationalism: A Case for Second-Order Logic*, Oxford, Oxford University Press.

—— (1998), 'Logical Consequence: Models and Modality', in *The Philosophy of Mathematics Today*, ed. M. Schirn, Oxford, Oxford University Press, 131–56.

SMILEY, T. (1993), 'Can Contradictions Be True? I', *Proceedings of the Aristotelian Society*, suppl. vol. 67: 17–34.

21

An Anti-Realist Critique of Dialetheism

Neil Tennant

ABSTRACT

I criticize dialetheism from the point of view of an anti-realist with sympathy for relevantism in logical reasoning.

I argue that the view that there are true contradictions suffers both from an improper understanding of the interrelations among absurdity, contrariety, falsity, and negation, and from an incorrect diagnosis of what gives rise to the well-known contradictions in semantics and mathematical foundations.

Anti-realism emerges as a better reflective equilibrium than dialetheism in confrontation with all these phenomena. Both positions require logical revisions of classical logic. But anti-realism's logical reforms are better motivated than those of the dialetheist, and the resulting logic is more adequate for the methodological demands of mathematics and empirical science. Priest's prospect of an 'intuitionist dialetheism' is unconvincing, both because of important features of intuitionistic logic, such as the independence of the logical operators and the normalizability of proof, and because the intuitionist (or anti-realist) disagrees so strongly on the actual alleged examples of dialetheias in logic and foundations.

1. INTRODUCTION

Dummett once suggested that certain metaphysical theories about given discourses were 'mere pictures'; and that what was needed instead was a theory of meaning for, and an account of the correct logic underlying, the discourse in question. Dialetheism—the view that there are true contradictions, and that these contradictions are rationally believable—is a metaphysical theory not without its own arresting pictures. Consider:

Truth and falsity come inextricably intermingled, like a constant boiling mixture. One cannot, therefore, accept all truths and reject all falsehoods ... (Priest 1987: 124)

and

natural language being what it is, we should not necessarily expect the pieces of language to fit together neatly, like some multi-dimensional jig-saw puzzle. There may well be mismatches. In particular, the conditions of application of a sentence may well overlap those of the application of its negation, especially if the world arranges itself in an unkind fashion. At such spots in the weft and warp of language we have dialetheias.   (ibid. 85)

The dialetheic images do not come solely from the kitchen and the weaver's loft. They have an out-of-doors counterpart:

the logical paradoxes are the site of a fault-line in the whole tectonic of "classical" logic. Though painfully aware of it, logicians this century have had as little success with it as their geological counterparts have had with the San Andreas fault. By applying a little pressure along the crack, I hope to blow the whole configuration asunder.   (ibid. 7)

Priest's *In Contradiction* (henceforth: *IC*),[1] from which these quotes are taken, combines flair for rhetoric with attention to formal detail, and is the best-known manifesto for dialetheism.

The suggestion that there could be true contradictions is the most radical that has ever been made within the field known generally as 'deviant logic'. A common reaction is out-of-hand dismissal. The suggestion, however, is worth looking at very closely—so that its eventual dismissal may be properly justified.

That there could be true contradictions is a view that requires yet another major deviation from the standard systems of classical or intuitionistic logic. Since the latter systems contain the absurdity rule (*ex falso quodlibet*):

$$\frac{\bot}{A}$$

they would allow the asserter of a true contradiction validly to infer any proposition whatsoever, and assert it. The dialetheist's suggestion, however, is not that it could be the case that every proposition were true; rather, it is just that there might be at least one true contradiction. He would not wish thereby to be committed to asserting every proposition whatsoever.[2] Therefore he must, and does, abandon *ex falso quodlibet*. He must, and does, believe that there can be interestingly different inconsistent theories. This is because, having asserted his chosen allegedly true contradiction $P \land \neg P$, he will still be able to derive absurdity from it, by means of

---

[1] When reading this acronym, the reader should be aware that in fact I don't see at all! (how dialetheism could possibly be correct). This chapter in a sense extends the critique that I undertook in Tennant (1998).

[2] In order to aid the exposition, the dialetheist will be picked up by anaphoric pronouns in the masculine, the anti-realist by ones in the feminine. (I make no provision for any hermaphroditic philosophical position.) This device achieves gender-neutrality without resort to pronominal hybrids or plurals. But of course *she* prevails argumentatively over *him*; so a suit against sexism might still lie. I shall just have to ask my reader to live with that. The rationale is simple: there will be frequent references to Priest as the main proponent of dialetheism, so the masculine pronouns will be strongly associated with that position; and, for the sake of political correctness, I am willing, myself, to be a philosophical drag-queen—a Priscilla of the desert landscape. This, surely, should be a mitigating factor for the court of literary opinion.

conjunction- and negation-elimination:

$$\frac{P \wedge \neg P}{\neg P} \quad \frac{P \wedge \neg P}{P}$$
$$\perp$$

Contradictions are still inconsistent; they still imply absurdity.[3]

By abandoning or rejecting the absurdity rule, however, one avoids being committed, by asserting a contradiction, to asserting every proposition whatsoever. Thus one cannot perform a *modus tollens* from the ridiculousness of such an alleged commitment, to the ridiculousness of a contradiction's being true. Any relevantist (and I am one) who rejects the absurdity rule, but who finds dialetheism objectionable, must therefore rest their objection on something other than the ridiculousness of being committed to asserting every proposition. For— to repeat—by abandoning the absurdity rule, the dialetheist avoids the latter commitment.[4]

The dialetheist's suggestion is not that contradictions are consistent (that is, that they do not imply absurdity); rather, the suggestion is that some of them are *true*.

2. THE INTERPRETATION OF ABSURDITY

The anti-realist who is also a relevantist might be thought to be somewhat under-equipped to undertake a really trenchant critique of dialetheism. After all, Priest himself said he thought that 'intuitionist dialetheism' may well bear further investigation (*IC* 87). (We shall see below, however, that Priest's own formulation of the rules of inference for his Logic of Paradox do not make the task of 'intuitionizing' that logic at all easy.) In this section we consider whether the dialetheist can expect to make an easy convert of the relevantist anti-realist.

As a relevantist, the latter will eschew the absurdity rule, and not acknowledge Lewis's first paradox $A, \neg A : B$ as a valid argument form. So, it might be thought, she will not be able to complain very convincingly against any dialetheist who chooses to assert both P and $\neg P$. By the relevantist's own lights, that contradiction could be 'localized'. It need not 'blow up' into completely promiscuous belief.

---

[3] I note here that Priest's own 'Logic of Paradox' does not use the absurdity symbol, and does not have the usual rule of ¬-Elimination. Since, however, I take absurdity to be essential to our grasp of negation, and take the standard rule of ¬-Elimination to be essential to ¬'s being a sign of *negation*, I am allowing myself the expository liberty, at this stage, of 'thinking out loud' on behalf of the would-be dialetheist. See Tennant (1999).

[4] It is worth noting that the dialetheist's reason for rejecting the absurdity rule is that one can have both A and $\neg A$ *true*; but one does not wish to acknowledge, on that basis alone, that an arbitrary, topically unrelated proposition B is thereby true. So the dialetheist's relevantism is really very self-serving. A consistentist, by contrast, who is also a relevantist (such as the present author) raises here objections to the absurdity rule, and to Lewis's first paradox $A, \neg A : B$, on considerations of relevance in reasoning. A consistentist need never fear that the premises of Lewis's first paradox really could both be true.

Thus—so this line of thought continues—generally correct beliefs will still be able to lead to generally survival-enhancing actions, despite the occasional presence, in one's belief-system, of these localized dialetheias.

To this the anti-realist has a perhaps surprisingly heated response. She will say (or, I am arguing, ought to say) something along these lines:

'Look, Mr. Dialetheist. Contradictions are *such bad things* that all we need to do is *locate* them. This we do by means of the rule of ¬-Elimination, precipitating absurdity (⊥) as conclusion. Now when that happens, *that is terrible enough.* Having located them, we know that whatever gave rise to them is impossible for a rational agent to believe. We don't *need* to "convince" ourselves, by means of quite unnecessary applications of the absurdity rule, that anything whatsoever would follow from a contradiction. For ⊥ is, logically, as horrific a conclusion as one can possibly get. Indeed, ⊥ is *so* bad that, funnily enough, nothing *can* really follow from it the way the absurdity rule would otherwise maintain. ⊥ is like a logical black hole: no possible thought that makes any sense could ever escape from it. So the absurdity rule is really silly, inappropriate and unnecessary. Thinking that one needs the absurdity rule in order to "bring out" the terribleness of ⊥ is about as naïve as it would have been to remonstrate with Adolf Hitler over the murder of six million souls by saying "You really ought not to behave towards other people this way, you know, because that can set a bad example for others to follow." Logically speaking, as soon as one encounters ⊥, one ought to cry out "Enough already!"'

This, then, is the problem: how could a proposition that implies absurdity be true? The dialetheist's suggestion means that we would be either

(1) countenancing the occasional truth of the absurdity symbol,

—or, should (1) not be the case—

(2) countenancing the occasional failure of application of rules of inference to transmit truth—strangely, in just those situations where an allegedly true contradiction has been asserted as a premiss for the ensuing rule-applications that now suffer this peculiar lapse from the truth-transmitting role that is their very *raison d'être*.

Ad (1): can the absurdity symbol occasionally denote the True? Surely not: absurdity (the constant ⊥) is just that: a *constant*. It is *always false*.

The dialetheist, however, replies, 'Aha!—but is this enough to ensure that ⊥ is *never true?* What if ⊥ *can* (sometimes) be true?'

Well, yes, it ought to be enough to ensure this; provided only that one can make ⊥ obey appropriate rules. The anti-dialetheist strategy ought to be to ensure that ⊥ is a 'pure' constant. That is, it should not only always denote The False; it should also never denote The True.

Our manner of speaking here makes it seem as though we view the absurdity symbol as iconic: as standing for a truth-value (namely, The False, as opposed to The True). On this model one might conceive of the problem as being that of how to ensure that the symbol denotes its 'essential referent', and nothing else. On an analogy employing proper names of persons, the problem would be like that of ensuring that 'Julius Caesar' denotes Julius Caesar, and no one else (for example: not Brutus). The problem is *not* like that of ensuring that 'Julius Caesar' denotes Julius Caesar, and not, for example, any of Brutus's murder victims. That the term 'Brutus's most famous murder victim' happens to denote Julius Caesar is no problem for the referential essentialist. For Julius Caesar need not have been Brutus's most famous murder victim. Baptisms do not ordain the future. They do, however, *single out* bearers for the name employed, and in such a way that it would be metaphysically impossible for a distinct individual to be denoted correctly by that name.

So our problem can best be understood as that of securing the *rigidity* of $\perp$ when it is construed as a name-like constant symbol, standing for The False.

There is another construal of $\perp$ as a constant, on which it is not name-like. On this alternative construal, $\perp$ signifies the joint impossibility of some hypothesized propositions $P_1, \ldots, P_n$ whose identity can be gathered from the context in which $\perp$ makes its inferred appearance. Thus $\perp$ is taken to have *scope*, and be *modal* in character—a combination of features that we can summarize handily in the phrase '*scopily modal*':

$$
\begin{array}{c}
\underbrace{P_1, \ldots, P_n} \\
\vdots \\
\perp
\end{array}
$$

One who has reasoned thus from the assumptions $P_1 \ldots, P_n$ takes herself to be in a position to say *it is not possible for all of* $P_1, \ldots, P_n$ *to be true*. Or: *it cannot be the case that* $P_1, \ldots, P_n$; or: *it is never the case that* $P_1, \ldots, P_n$. In all these synonymous expressions one sees the combination of *modality* ('not possible'; 'cannot be'; 'never') and *scope* $(P_1, \ldots, P_n)$.

The most obvious application of the foregoing is to a proposition and its negation, captured by a single step of negation-elimination:

$$
\frac{\neg P \quad P}{\perp}
$$

Here we want to say *it is impossible for both P and* $\neg P$ *to be true; it cannot be the case that both P and* $\neg P$; *it is never the case that both P and* $\neg P$. And yet the dialetheist is suggesting that indeed it *is* possible for both P and $\neg P$ to be true; it *could indeed* be the case that both P and $\neg P$; it *is sometimes* the case that both P and $\neg P$. Naturally, he is not holding out such a prospect for arbitrary propositions P: his suggestion is only that there are certain propositions P that behave in this remarkable way. That behaviour arises from the subject-matter of P and the logico-linguistic construction of P.

The dialetheist will further concede that this entails (for the kinds of proposition P in question) that P could be both true and false. (For how, otherwise, could $(P \land \neg P)$ be true?) But note the converse, and the price it extracts. As soon as one contemplates the possibility of, say, a contingent proposition P being both true and false, the destruction of polarity becomes severe, in that the a priori, analytic falsehood $(P \land \neg P)$ must now (for the particular choice of P in question) be held out as also *true*. Letting in any degree of overlap between truth and falsity puts one's semantic lenses right out of focus. The falsest of false claims, namely claims of the form $(P \land \neg P)$, can now, outrageously, also be true.

Ad (2): can our rules of inference occasionally fail to transmit truth? Again, surely not. Logical laws, as laws of rational thought, admit of absolutely no exceptions. Valid rules of inference *always* transmit truth. (More precisely: if the subproofs for the application of a rule are truth-preserving, then the proof formed by the application of the rule is truth-preserving. The preservation in question is from the undischarged assumptions of the proof to its conclusion.) Laws apply on the basis of form alone—more narrowly, on the basis of *one logical operator-occurrence at a time*—namely, the occurrence of whatever operator is *dominant* in the major premiss (for an elimination) or the conclusion (of an introduction). Since no would-be dialetheia $P \land \neg P$ has any way of advertising itself as such to the rule of $\land$-Elimination, the application of that rule will be as truth-preserving as ever. So too will be the subsequent application of $\neg$-Elimination to derive $\bot$. That is to say, the formal proof of $\bot$ from $P \land \neg P$ shows that *it is impossible for $P \land \neg P$ to be true*.

We have just employed the following argumentative strategy: we claimed that the dialetheist's suggestion implies a certain disjunction; then we explored each disjunct in an attempt to reduce it to absurdity. Hence the dialetheist's suggestion is reduced to absurdity. In normal polite circles this would be enough to silence the opposition. But what happens in this particular debate?—the dialetheist merely smiles knowingly and avers that his position is indeed inconsistent—but still true. Nevertheless, he owes us a definite answer: which of (1) and (2) above is he committed to holding?[5] Since Priest himself does not use or countenance the absurdity symbol, he has never raised or answered this question. But for the anti-realist the question is pressing, and the answer to it would be most revealing.

3. THE DIALECTICAL GRIP OF DIALETHEISM

The dialetheist's suggestion is even more disabling than the contention that certain claims of the logical form $P \land \neg P$ can be true. On the assumption that there could be true contradictions 'all the way up', one finds oneself in a rather invidious

---

[5] I am indebted here to Joshua Smith.

position as the opponent of the dialetheist. For one would like to be able to bring certain canons of counterargument to bear. One of the most important of these is the method of *reductio ad absurdum*. Providing a *reductio* of an opponent's position (expressed by a set of propositions) usually clinches the case against him. But now we have the dialetheist maintaining the possible truth of contradictions. Confronted with a *reductio* of his philosophical position, he is able simply to smile and say that his very own philosophical position is both true and false—thereby vindicating itself, thanks to the successful *reductio* supplied by the opposition!

If we want to preserve the orthodox understanding of absurdity against the dialetheist's insidious suggestion, and do so on the construal of $\perp$ as scopily modal—that is, as showing the 'noncompossibility' of what precipitates it—then we have to develop an account that makes *reductio ad absurdum* a dialectically effective tool in argument. By 'dialectically effective' here we mean that it will provide a compelling reason to *abandon* any theoretical viewpoint that is committed to the propositions assumed for the *reductio*.

One is tempted to ask, as Popper did for empirical theories, what could possibly count as a falsification of the dialetheist's theory. But now we are treating of a philosophical theory, not an empirical one. So it is not enough to ask this question with the ordinary notion of falsehood implicit in the term 'falsification'. For one wants to know what sort of falsification would be regarded by the dialetheist as one that *ought to persuade him to abandon his theory*, rather than as one that could be thrown back in his opponent's face as a superb piece of supporting evidence for that very theory.

4. ARE ABSURDITY AND NEGATION REALLY COEVAL?

Priest writes (*IC* 81 s. 4.7) that 'Negation is that sentential function which turns a true sentence into a false one, and vice versa.' And he defines falsity (as a metalinguistic predicate F of object-language sentences α) as follows:

$$F\underline{\alpha} \leftrightarrow T\underline{\neg\alpha}$$

There is no need, however, to use the truth-predicate T in this definition. One could just as well give the definition

$$F\underline{\alpha} \leftrightarrow \neg\alpha$$

This would better justify Priest's claim that 'It would seem that falsity and negation can be defined in terms of each other, but neither can be defined without the other.'

Priest is thinking, however, only of explicit definitions, in which the central biconditional can be read as 'means by definition', and can indeed be read in either direction, depending on which concept (negation or falsity) one takes oneself (or one's interlocutor) to have grasped first.

But there is another way to attain the concept of negation, which I have described at length in Tennant (1999). On this account the first logical notion (related, but not equivalent, to negation) to make its appearance is absurdity, as the conclusion of *antonymic inferences*:

(†) $$\frac{A \quad B}{\perp}$$

Here the antonyms *A* and *B* are so simple and primitive that there cannot be any question of their 'dialetheically' holding simultaneously. Such antonyms *A* and *B* are antonymic not on the basis of their logical form, but on the basis of their primitive non-logical contents. The tension between them—their mutual exclusivity—is a matter of deep metaphysical necessity. Some antonym-pairs derive from the structure of our phenomenology. An example would be color incompatibilities:

$$\frac{(\text{Solidly}) \text{ Red} \quad (\text{Solidly}) \text{ Green}}{\perp}$$

where the feature-placings are understood to concern the same area of one's visual field at the same time.

Other antonym-pairs reflect fundamental features of our categorization of physical objects in space and time:

$$\frac{X \text{ is right here, right now} \quad X \text{ is way over there, right now}}{\perp}$$

where X is a physical object too small to straddle both the spatial locations indicated.

I shall not bore the reader with further examples of this kind. Natural language teems with them—a usefully *ad hominem* consideration, since Priest himself continually stresses the need to account for natural language with all its expressive power, and not just expressively limited formal languages. Moreover, the contents of the various *A*s and *B*s that can feature in such *A*–*B* clashes of the form (†) can be learned and grasped without adverting to the other, and especially without use of the negation particle. I contend that an intelligent child can learn the meaning of 'hot' (as applied to water in a basin, say) without needing to be told that it is 'not cold'—and vice versa. Once both 'hot' and 'cold' have been mastered, however, the child would immediately be apprised of the transition

$$\frac{\text{Hot} \quad \text{Cold}}{\perp}$$

where $\perp$ is 'scopily modal' in the sense explained earlier. Reflecting on the nature of one's sensory experience, and the kinds of sensations involved, can make one aware of these incompatibilities as *necessary*. (If you do not like the 'hot'/'cold' example, never mind; it suffices for my argument if there is *just one* scopily modal antonym-pair that can be grasped without recourse to any symbol for propositional or sentential negation.)

The conception of contrariety is expressed by means of an inferential transition *from* the contraries in question *to* absurdity. Because of the structure of both our sensibility and our understanding, these contrarieties are deep, primitive, and necessary. They are exceptionless. They are a priori. It matters not that one needs sensory experience in order first to *acquire* a grasp of each member of an antonym-pair. A prioricity has nothing to do with acquisition, and everything to do with mastery. What matters is only that once the members of an antonym-pair have been grasped, their contrariety is something that their understander can grasp without the need for any further sensory experience.

Once one has the notion of contrariety (via the notion of absurdity), one can proceed to introduce the concept of negation. This is done by means of the introduction rule, which does not furnish an explicit definition, but rather fixes the sense of the negation sign within an inferential context:

$$\overline{A}$$
$$\vdots$$
$$\frac{\perp}{\neg A}$$

It is, of course, understood that the side-assumptions, other than A, on which $\perp$ depends will remain undischarged, so that the newly inferred conclusion of the form $\neg A$ rests on them.

Now, harmoniously balancing this introduction rule is the *elimination* rule, which can be 'read off' the introduction rule:

$$\frac{\neg A \quad A}{\perp}$$

The reason why I say that the elimination rule can be 'read off' the introduction rule is that they obey the following reduction procedure:

$$
\begin{array}{cc}
\underbrace{X,\overline{A}} & \\
\Pi \quad Y & \\
\underline{\perp \quad \Sigma} & \\
\neg A \quad A &
\end{array}
\quad\rightsquigarrow\quad
\begin{array}{c}
Y \\
\Sigma \\
\underbrace{X,(A)} \\
\Pi
\end{array}
$$
$$\perp \qquad\qquad\qquad \perp$$

This is why the introduction rule (which tells one how to introduce a dominant occurrence of the negation sign in an inferred conclusion) serves to introduce the very concept of negation. There is no explicit definition here; there is only an explicit recipe for the *use* of the negation sign in inference.

In the statement of both the introduction rule and the elimination rule, the notion of absurdity is stable. It is always invested with its full import of *necessary falsehood.* Remember, this derives directly from its use to register *deep and primitive* contrarieties. There is no question—the possibility simply cannot arise—of ⊥, taken as a sentential constant, ever being *true.* And *that* is why negation works in such a way that it could never be the case that both *P* and ¬*P* were true.

5. ALLEGED EXAMPLES OF TRUE CONTRADICTIONS

Those who still take consistency as a regulative ideal—because it is necessary, even if not sufficient, for truth—will wish to examine closely the arguments given by Priest in Part I of *IC.* These are arguments purporting to deliver actual examples of honest-to-goodness true contradictions. They are the familiar semantic paradoxes, the familiar set-theoretic paradoxes, and an unfamiliar one thought up by Priest: the Gödel-sentence for naïve provability. Priest's strategy is to take on all-comers who seek to defuse or explain away the familiar paradoxes, and to insist that the only natural way to respond to his examples is simply to acknowledge them for what they appear to be: namely, true statements of the form *P* ∧ ¬*P*. (Because his example of the alleged Gödel-sentence for naïve provability is newly invented, there are no well-known counterarguments, to his use of this example, for Priest to consider; he does, however, as we shall argue below, fail to anticipate an important one.)

When I was a graduate student, I discovered a disconnected, but now relevant, phenomenon. While expecting our first child, I suddenly became aware of preg-nant women all over the place.[6] Had that first pregnancy been a phantom one, I might nevertheless, as a heady expectant father, have falsely *imagined* that various obese women on the streets were pregnant. The analogy I am seeking here is that the would-be dialetheist, on 'discovering' what he believes is his first true contra-diction, suddenly takes himself to be confronted by them everywhere. But we must not allow ourselves to be overly impressed by the sheer weight of numbers, and variety, of these would-be true contradictions. Each candidate has to be examined rigorously, to see whether it really passes muster. I should add here that I am not at all impressed or consoled by Priest's impish claims that 'contradictions should not be multiplied beyond necessity' (*IC* 90—such Ockhamite restraint . . . as though dialetheias form just another natural kind, another handy class of 'posits'!) and

---

[6] Psychologists appear not to have a scientific term for this widespread phenomenon. Thinking that there might be a term for it, I put out a query on the email list of The Ohio State University's very large and disciplinarily diverse community of cognitive scientists. I received nine different answers. Two of the respondents independently suggested that the extreme, pathological form of the phenomenon I had in mind is Fregoli's Syndrome. Others offered terms such as 'hindsight bias', 'selective processing', 'motivational priming', and so on. One who suffers from Fregoli's Syndrome believes that a persecutor is adopting many different disguises in order to 'get him'. I hesitate to say that your average dialetheist is Fregolian. But it does make a nice contrast with 'Fregean'.

'contradictions are *a priori* improbable' (ibid. 132—but watch out, you never know when one might hit you!).

When one looks closely at Priest's argumentative strategies with his various examples, a common pattern emerges, which is interestingly related to the vexing one noted above (namely, co-opting any *reductio ad absurdum* of dialetheism as a vindication of dialetheism). In each case—be it a semantic paradox, or a set-theoretic one—Priest's method is to show how a contradiction apparently ensues from certain plausible-seeming principles taken together. He then insists on their plausibility, and on the validity of every step of the reductio, and concludes that the reductio must, after all, establish a true contradiction. What is not revealed to the reader, and what the reader has to uncover for herself, is the fact that there are *other*, much less plausible principles being tacitly employed in generating the contradiction in question. Priest's reductio arguments, that is to say, are enthymematic. And once the hidden premises are made explicit, it is easy to challenge them, and defuse the paradoxes in question.

Doing this systematically, across the range of examples that Priest adduces, is an admittedly time-consuming and tendentious task. But it is a task that has to be carried out to an exhaustive conclusion, in any proper test of the merits of dialetheism as the existential claim that *there are* true contradictions. We shall be examining below, in s. 9, what we take to be the disputable hidden but crucial premises in Priest's main examples of purported dialetheias in the area of logic and the foundations of mathematics. But first we turn to some context-setting remarks about reflective equilibrium.

6. REFLECTIVE EQUILIBRIUM

Seldom is there any knock-down argument in philosophy for any global viewpoint. Those committed to particular viewpoints would of course be delighted to have definitive reductios of all competing viewpoints; but hardly ever are these available. Every reductio is, after all, relative to certain side-assumptions, and the dispute can always be shifted so as to focus on these. Seldom is a well-represented philosophical viewpoint genuinely reduced to absurdity in a 'herme(neu)tically sealed' fashion, using only its own explicitly acknowledged principles as premises for the reductio, and without allowing any contentious side-assumptions to seep in.

Global viewpoints such as realism or anti-realism almost always appeal to their proponents as *reflective equilibria*, chosen because of the particular way that the viewpoint in question distributes its emphases, shapes its main concepts, resolves known tensions among competing claims (so-called aporias), organizes widely shared intuitions, accommodates common-sense knowledge and scientific principles, etc. On occasion a chosen reflective equilibrium can involve reforming certain intuitions, reshaping central concepts, and abandoning certain fundamental-looking principles, because of significant off-setting gains in clarity, systematicity, elegance, economy, and so on.

Speaking entirely as an interested party, I would offer the attainment of the reflective equilibrium of anti-realism as a striking example of this process. The realist and the anti-realist both have to deal with an important tension among certain central principles: Bivalence of Truth, Knowability of Truth, and Epistemic Modesty.[7] The realist holds to bivalence, and rejects knowability; whereas the anti-realist insists on knowability, and gives up bivalence. In the anti-realist's reflective equilibrium, the classical, pretheoretic concept of truth is reshaped in so far as all truths are held to be knowable-in-principle; the principle of bivalence is abandoned; and the resulting methodological 'loss' is offset by the gains of systematicity and elegance to be had from intuitionistic logic and a nicely 'separable' inferential meaning-theory for the logical operators.[8]

Priest himself reveals quite clearly how his own viewpoint of dialetheism is, for him, the outcome of his own search for reflective equilibrium in dealing with phenomena such as semantic closure, the set-theoretic paradoxes, the Gödel-phenomena, the metaphysics of change, and the logic of norms. He writes (*IC* 112), 'Intuition may provide an important part of the data against which a logical theory is measured. But a theory which is strong and satisfactory in other respects can itself show the data to be wrong.' He also emphasizes what he regards as the 'simplicity and philosophical perspicuity' of his semantics for entailment, and regards these features as outweighing various objections to that semantics based on precise technical considerations (ibid. 114). He stresses the importance of both direct and indirect arguments, to the effect that extant rival views are inadequate (ibid. 126). He attributes to his naysayers the vices of narrow-mindedness and dogmatism for rejecting inconsistency 'thoughtlessly and out of hand' (ibid. 132). The totality of considerations leading one to rest at a certain reflective equilibrium need not, for Priest, be overwhelmingly compelling or apodeictic. After surveying a variety of arguments attempting to show 'directly that contradictions can be rationally believed' (ibid. 124), he sums up by saying (ibid. 126), 'Perhaps no *single* argument from this collection may suffice to make naive set theory and semantics acceptable in preference to their consistent rivals; but it seems to me that the combined array is quite sufficient to make the inconsistent theories rationally preferable.' The only way, it seems to me, to counter this overly swift adoption of dialetheism as an intellectual resting point is to revisit the various topics one by one, and to show much more aggressively, from the 'consistentist' point of view, how deeply mistaken the dialetheist's account of each one really is. One has to undermine the pragmatic complacency of the theorist who thinks that, having reached a non-definitive 'standoff', or position of stalemate, with the consistentist on each of the disputed topics, some sort of global summation-on-balance can tip the reflective scale in

---

[7] See Tennant (2000).   [8] See Tennant (1997: ch. 10).

favor of dialetheism. I submit that this is a grave misrepresentation of the true state of affairs, argumentatively. I contend that there are knockdown arguments *against* the dialetheist's accommodation of the various problematic topics, arguments that Priest, as the main proponent of dialetheism, has simply not addressed.

In addition to these several victories that, I claim, the consistentist can score, I maintain that there are some methodological considerations that have not yet been taken explicitly into account by the dialetheist, and which—when properly investigated—provide strong suasive currents that should bear the thinker decisively *away* from dialetheism as her final stopping point. The methodological considerations that I have in mind here are the following:

(1_D) Are the logical reforms of the dialetheist able to accommodate the great bulk of ordinary reasoning in mathematics and the natural sciences?

(2_D) Does the dialetheist's 'logic of paradox' have a satisfying proof theory?

(3_D) Does it do justice to logic as a science of *inference* (as opposed to providing a fancy deviant model of semantic evaluations)?

(4_D) Does it accommodate the very arguments that the dialetheist uses when trying to show that certain propositions are indeed dialetheias?

Question (4_D) is highly non-trivial. An affirmative answer is required in the interests of the reflexive stability of the whole enterprise. But, as will emerge in due course, an affirmative answer is lacking.

The corresponding questions, concerning intuitionistic logic, dominate the anti-realist's case for intuitionistic logic (or something close to it) as the correct logic. For compare:

(1_A) Are the logical reforms of the anti-realist able to accommodate the great bulk of ordinary reasoning in mathematics and the natural sciences?

(2_A) Does the anti-realist's 'logic of warranted assertability' have a satisfying proof theory?

(3_A) Does it do justice to logic as a science of *inference*?

(4_A) Does it accommodate the very arguments that the anti-realist uses when trying to show that there is no reason to believe, on the basis of logic and the theory of meaning alone, that all propositions are determinately true or false, independently of our means of coming to know what their truth-values are?

When arguing for anti-realism, and arguing for intuitionistic relevant logic as the correct logic (given the anti-realist's theory of the meanings of the logical operators), I was concerned to justify affirmative answers to questions (1_A)–(4_A).[9] I believe it is important that the dialetheist should be able to do likewise with questions (1_D)–(4_D).

---

[9] See Tennant (1997).

We shall examine below the extent to which Priest may be said to have developed his (classical) logic of paradox as a clear *inferential* alternative to classical logic.

7. PRIEST'S LOGIC OF PARADOX

The only concession that Priest appears to make to the foregoing concern for a thorough and proper treatment of inference is a passing comment (*IC* 93): 'a good way of conceiving formal languages *and their semantics* is as a model for, or abstraction of, certain aspects of natural language: specifically, those aspects which are central to (deductive) inference' (emphasis added). Priest does not, however, get directly to grips with deduction itself, by providing a detailed proof-theory for his logic of paradox. In *IC* he provides a dialetheic semantics for the extensional connectives ¬, ∨, and ∧, and simply remarks 'It is . . . straightforward to produce a natural deduction system with respect to which these semantics are sound and complete. The details of this need not concern us here' (ibid. 95).

But the details *should* concern the reader at this point, and indeed throughout the whole investigation. For, if one is being told to restrict one's logical principles, then it had better be the case that the arguments for doing so can themselves be framed wholly by means of the logical principles that survive the recommended restriction. Now we do not ordinarily reason in natural language, or any of its regimentations, by calculating algebraic assignments of (sets of) truth-values to the various propositions involved in our trains of deductive reasoning, and then checking the resulting distributions of values across premises and conclusions. Rather, we make assumptions, sometimes only hypothetically, and draw conclusions from them, based on their logical forms alone. *That* is what 'deductive inference' is all about. So we had better be shown, very clearly, exactly what forms of *inference* remain licit—as far as the dialetheist is concerned—after the 'whole configuration' of classical logic has been 'blow[n] . . . asunder'.

This section is devoted to revealing reasons for dissatisfaction with Priest's logic of paradox as a canon of inference that can be incorporated into a reasonable reflective equilibrium of the kind described above. Readers who do not wish to engage in the ensuing logical details can skip this section, provided only that they bear in mind that the gist of the technical discussion is that Priscilla is pouty about the logic of paradox.[10]

In a footnote on p. 95 of (IC), Priest tells his reader that the details 'can be found, in effect, in Priest (1982)'. If we turn to that paper, we find the same dialetheic semantics for the three connectives just mentioned, and the following 'natural deduction system in the style of Prawitz'. Here I take pains to state every rule in a single direction, rather than use Priest's abbreviations of two-way rules. (I also

---

[10] See n. 2, if you have not yet done so.

take the liberty to correct the logical operator in Priest's rule (2), which I am sure was meant to be the rule of ∧-Introduction, rather than a strange two-premiss rule of ∨-Introduction.)

Introduction and Elimination Rules for ∧ and ∨:

$$\frac{A \quad B}{A \wedge B} \qquad \frac{A \wedge B}{A} \qquad \frac{A \wedge B}{B}$$

$$\frac{A}{A \vee B} \quad \frac{B}{A \vee B} \qquad \frac{A \vee B \quad \begin{matrix}\overline{A}\\ \vdots \\ C\end{matrix} \quad \begin{matrix}\overline{B}\\ \vdots \\ C\end{matrix}}{C}$$

De Morgan Inferences:

$$\frac{\neg(A \vee B)}{\neg A \wedge \neg B} \qquad \frac{\neg A \wedge \neg B}{\neg(A \vee B)} \qquad \frac{\neg A \vee \neg B}{\neg(A \wedge B)} \qquad \frac{\neg(A \wedge B)}{\neg A \vee \neg B}$$

Double Negation Introduction:

$$\frac{A}{\neg \neg A}$$

Law of Excluded Middle:

$$\overline{A \vee \neg A}$$

Priest says of this 'proof theory' that it 'could hardly be said to be simple or natural'. What we have here, however, is a proposed system of rules for the construction of natural deductions; we do not as yet have any *proof theory*. For a proof theory furnishes such results as normalization theorems, based on reduction procedures; and examines the relationship between the chosen system and other well-known systems such as classical or intuitionistic logic. Such relationships might involve translations that preserve deducibilities, such as the double-negation translation of classical into intuitionistic logic. But we have none of these things from Priest's treatment. All we get is the set of rules of inference just stated, and a sketch of a (soundness and) completeness proof with respect to the dialetheic semantics. The soundness proof is said to be 'straightforward and left to the reader'. The completeness proof for the propositional logic we are interested in actually omits the crucial details for the connectives, concentrating instead on the interesting tense operators that dominate the discussion of the paper in question.

7.1 Priest's Rules Are Not Separable

The first thing to note about Priest's system of rules is that it characterizes ¬ only via its connection with ∧, ∨, and itself. While ∧ and ∨ have their own introduction and elimination rules that single them out for specific treatment, ¬ has no such proprietorial rules of its own. Instead, we have (1) a rule of Double Negation *Introduction*, which is quite unusual in a natural deduction setting; (2) four De Morgan inferences, the last of which is classically but not intuitionistically valid; and (3) the Law of Excluded Middle, which again is classically but not intuitionistically valid. The great theoretical advantage of 'Prawitz style' natural deduction is that it shows how minimal logic is nested within intuitionistic logic, which in turn is nested within classical logic. There is no similar way, with Priest's Logic of Paradox as currently presented, to identify its intuitionistic fragment by simply dropping certain strictly classical rules. For it would appear that there is only one way to prove the Law of Non-Contradiction ¬(P ∧ ¬P) in this system, and it begins by helping oneself to the Law of Excluded Middle:

$$
\frac{\dfrac{\overline{A \vee \neg A}}{\neg\neg(A \vee \neg A)}}{\dfrac{\neg(\neg A \wedge \neg\neg A)}{\neg(A \wedge \neg A)}}
$$

The third line is derived by a De Morgan interdeducibility *and* a tacit use of the substitution rule (which Priest does not state) whereby interdeducibles are intersubstitutable (here, within the scope of the dominant negation). The fourth line also requires this substitution rule, the interdeducibles in question being A and $\neg\neg A$.

But wait a minute!—are the sentences A and $\neg\neg A$ really interdeducible, even in the supposedly classical system that Priest has furnished? 'Well of course they must be!' the reader might retort, 'Has not Priest shown that his system is complete for ordinary classical deducibilities?' The answer, unfortunately, is in the negative. The completeness proof involves a crucial unproved assertion, Lemma 1(v) on *IC* 258:

$A \in \Delta$ *iff* $\neg\neg A \in \Delta$

for any prime and deductively closed set Δ. Primeness is irrelevant here; it is the assumed deductive closure of Δ that must be doing the job. Now, while the left-right direction of the displayed claim is immediate by Priest's unusual rule of Double Negation Introduction, he clearly seems to have assumed, incorrectly, that the right-left direction is true. I cannot see any way to derive A from $\neg\neg A$ by means of Priest's rules above for his (classical) Logic of Paradox. Indeed, inspection of the rules reveals that there cannot be such a derivation. Any such derivation would have to end with an application of ∨-Elimination. The only available major premiss would have to be an instance of the Law of Excluded Middle. Of course, in ordinary intuitionistic logic there is just such a derivation:

$$
\cfrac{A \lor \neg A \qquad \cfrac{\text{—}(1)}{A} \qquad \cfrac{\cfrac{\cfrac{\text{——}(1)}{\neg A} \qquad \neg\neg A}{\cfrac{\bot}{A}}}{\qquad}(1)}{A}
$$

The problem, however, is that this derivation involves an application of *ex falso quodlibet*, which Priest does not allow. Moreover, the derivation to the same effect in the system *IR* eschews *ex falso quodlibet*, but uses a liberalized form of ∨-Elimination, according to which if one case ends with absurdity, then one can bring down the conclusion of the other case as the main conclusion:

$$
\cfrac{A \lor \neg A \qquad \cfrac{\text{—}(1)}{A} \qquad \cfrac{\cfrac{\text{——}(1)}{\neg A} \qquad \neg\neg A}{\bot}(1)}{A}
$$

This liberalized ∨-Elimination rule has no place, however, in Priest's system; for it yields a proof of disjunctive syllogism, which is not valid in that system.

It would appear, then, that Priest must have intended his stated rule of Double Negation Introduction to be a two-way rule, like his two-way De Morgan rules. In other words, he must have been intending to help himself to the rule of Double Negation Elimination as primitive, in addition to Double Negation Introduction.

7.2 Implication Is Defined, Not Primitive

The second thing to note about Priest's inferential system is that the conditional connective → is defined as follows:

$$A \to B =_{df} \neg A \lor B$$

Now while this is fine for classical logic, it will not do for intuitionistic logic. As is well known, every one of the connectives ¬, ∧, ∨, and → is independent in intuitionistic logic. Without a primitive conditional, the propositional part of intuitionistic logic is expressively incomplete. Hence this is a further consideration against Priest's choice of logical primitives and of inference rules governing them. The isolation of an intuitionistic fragment of the Logic of Paradox would appear to be even more remote because of it.

7.3 Quantifier Rules are Absent

The third thing to note about Priest's inferential system is that, though he provides a dialetheic semantics for first-order logic (*IC* 96–8 s. 5.3), he never states any rules of inference for the quantifiers ∃ and ∀. Thus we are unable to assess whether his logic can indeed furnish regimentations of all the arguments that he himself puts forward in order to convince his reader that certain propositions are indeed dialetheias. For these arguments are conducted at least within a first-order fragment of English, and would definitely need the two quantifiers for their proper regimentation.

The most educated guess as to the appropriate form that quantifier rules might take in Priest's inferential system is that the existential quantifier should be treated analogously to disjunction, and the universal quantifier analogously to conjunction. Thus they would have their usual introduction and elimination rules, as supplied by Gentzen and Prawitz. In addition, there would be the quantificational analogues of the De Morgan rules:

$$\frac{\neg\exists x F}{\forall x \neg F} \qquad \frac{\forall x \neg F}{\neg\exists x F} \qquad \frac{\exists x \neg F}{\neg\forall x F} \qquad \frac{\neg\forall x F}{\exists x \neg F}$$

7.4 The Deduction Theorem Fails

The fourth thing to note about Priest's inferential system is that the deduction theorem fails. For, by his Fact 1 (*IC* 95), every two-valued logical truth is a logical truth in the dialetheic sense. Hence the sentence

$$(A \wedge \neg A) \rightarrow B$$

is a dialetheic logical truth. But, by his Fact 3, we do not in general have that B is a dialetheic logical consequence of $A \wedge \neg A$. Since any correct deductive system would have to match its deducibility relation $\vdash$ to the semantic consequence relation, this means

$$A \wedge \neg A \nvdash B$$

Hence the deduction theorem fails in the direction

$$X \vdash A \rightarrow B \Rightarrow X, A \vdash B$$

For my own part, I do not think that this is of any great concern, since exactly the same thing occurs with the system *IR* of intuitionistic relevant logic. But in the case of *IR*, a story can be told of how such 'failure' of the deduction theorem is offset by an *epistemic gain*. (In *IR*, what is involved is essentially a failure of unrestricted transivity of deduction, since in *IR*—unlike Priest's Logic of Paradox—one has $A, A \rightarrow B \vdash B$.) The epistemic gain in question is that when one is deprived of a certain 'result' $Y : B$ that one would have expected, given transitivity of deduction, one can prove, instead, a *strengthening* of that result—one of the form $Z : \bot$ or $Z : B$, for some subset Z of Y. An immediate corollary is that, if intuitionistic mathematics is consistent, then every intuitionistic mathematical theorem can be proved from the mathematical axioms using only *IR*. (Likewise for the classical case.) There is, so far as I know, no such metatheorem concerning epistemic gain for Priest's system, inferential or semantic.

There is, however, the following result, showing how closely dialetheic logic can mimic classical logic when one's theory is consistent. (See *IC* 149, s. 8.6. We are about to take a closer look at the left-right direction of Priest's Theorem 0.) In order to state this result, we introduce some notation. We shall assume that Priest's dialetheic logic obeys both a dialetheic soundness theorem and a strong completeness theorem with respect to dialetheic semantical consequence. Thus we shall speak indifferently of dialetheic deducibility and/or consequence, and symbolize this by $\vdash_D$. Let $\vdash_C$ likewise be classical deducibility (which of course is the same as classical consequence). Let Δ be a set of sentences, and let φ be a single sentence.

Theorem *If* $\Delta \vdash_C \varphi$, *then for some conjunction* ψ *of members of* Δ *we have*
$$\psi \vdash_D \varphi \vee (\psi \wedge \neg\psi).$$

Proof: Suppose that $\Delta \vdash_C \varphi$. Then for finitely many $\psi_1, \ldots, \psi_n$ in Δ, we have $\psi_1, \ldots, \psi_n \vdash_C \varphi$. Let ψ be $(\psi_1 \wedge \cdots \wedge \psi_n)$. So $\psi \vdash_C \varphi$. Hence $\vdash_C \varphi \vee \neg\psi$. But every classical theorem is a dialetheic theorem. So $\vdash_D \varphi \vee \neg\psi$. Call the dialetheic proof in question Π. Now, by virtue of the dialetheic proof

$$
\begin{array}{cccc}
& & & \dfrac{\rule{1.5em}{0.4pt}}{\neg\psi}(1) \\[4pt]
& & \dfrac{\rule{1.5em}{0.4pt}}{\varphi}(1) & \dfrac{\psi \qquad \neg\psi}{\psi \wedge \neg\psi} \\[10pt]
\dfrac{\Pi}{\varphi \vee \neg\psi} & \dfrac{\varphi}{\varphi \vee (\psi \wedge \neg\psi)} & \dfrac{\psi \wedge \neg\psi}{\varphi \vee (\psi \wedge \neg\psi)}(1) \\[10pt]
\multicolumn{3}{c}{\dfrac{\rule{14em}{0.4pt}}{\varphi \vee (\psi \wedge \neg\psi)}}
\end{array}
$$

we have $\psi \vdash_D \varphi \vee (\psi \wedge \neg\psi)$, as required. *QED*

The upshot of this metatheorem is that whenever the classicist proves a consequence φ from (a conjunction ψ of certain of) his axioms, the dialetheist can claim to be able to prove, from the same axioms, the surrogate result $\varphi \vee (\psi \wedge \neg\psi)$.

Now, this would deprive us of the sought result φ if ψ were inconsistent. For in that case we would have $\psi \vdash_C \bot$, whence $\vdash_D \neg\psi$, whence $\psi \vdash_D (\psi \wedge \neg\psi)$. So we could not be sure that $\varphi \vee (\psi \wedge \neg\psi)$ was dialetheically deducible from ψ only because φ itself was dialetheically deducible from ψ. That, however, is how it ought to be. For, if ψ is inconsistent, how can we (as relevantists, at least) hope to be able to deduce φ from it anyway?

What about the case where the conjunction ψ of axioms is consistent? Here, the classicist, by virtue of having deduced φ from ψ, can claim to be able to assert φ. But the dialetheist can claim at most to be able to assert his surrogate result, $\varphi \vee (\psi \wedge \neg\psi)$. Classically, of course, this logically implies φ. But does it do so dialetheically? It would appear not. The inference from $\varphi \vee (\psi \wedge \neg\psi)$ to φ fails *if ψ is a dialetheia*. But we are assuming here that ψ is consistent, hence not a dialetheia. One wants to say, on behalf of the dialetheist, that *if ψ is consistent, then the surrogate result*—the existence of a dialetheic deduction of $\varphi \vee (\psi \wedge \neg\psi)$ from ψ— should really *show* that φ is indeed a *dialetheic*, and not just a classical, consequence of ψ. But such good intentions founder on the fact that the dialetheist himself can provide no way of saying this, hence no way of justifying one's saying it. For, as Priest concedes (*IC* 140), 'There is no statement that can be made which *forces* [ψ] to behave consistently. This is one of the hard facts of dialetheic life.' Priest proceeds to use his notion of dialetheic consequence to define a more complicated notion of so-called *-consequence (*IC* 150), which is sandwiched between dialetheic consequence and classical consequence. It affords the result (Theorem 6, ibid. 152) that the classical consequences of any classically consistent set of sentences are *-consequences thereof. The trouble, however, is that *-consequence does not admit of a proof-reduction (via a complete notion of effective proof) the way the Σ_1^0-relations of classical and dialetheic consequence do. This is because within the definition of *-consequence one existentially quantifies over dialetheic non-deducibilities. The resulting relation of *-consequence is therefore Σ_2^0, as Priest notes, and is of no epistemic use.

8. GAPS v. GLUTS

Logicians' slang for the failure of bivalence is to say that 'truth-value gaps' are being admitted. Of course, this is not entirely accurate, and not exactly the way the anti-realist or intuitionist would wish to phrase the matter. After all, any claim of the form $\neg(\varphi \vee \neg\varphi)$ is intuitionistically inconsistent. Nevertheless, one can see what the slang is getting at. (At least the talk is of gaps, and not third values, which of course cannot be used to make sense of intuitionistic logic.) Now as Priest once put it to me in conversation many years ago, all that the dialetheist is doing is recommending truth-value *gluts*, which should be just as acceptable—according to Priest—as the intuitionist's truth-value *gaps*. This disarming and insouciant suggestion derives its plausibility entirely from a false picture of the philosopher as some sort of conceptual and logical engineer, who can fashion intellectual tools according to any kind of plan. The suggestion is that one is contemplating two quite comparable kinds of 'tweaking'—analogous, say, to serrating the edges of pieces of sheet metal, and/or punching dimples into them—and that there could be no objection to performing these tweaks in isolation, or in combination.

I believe nothing could be further from the truth. As an anti-realist who 'accepts' truth-value gaps (in the slang sense explained above), I advocate giving up the Law of Excluded Middle and all its equivalents. Indeed, I also advocate giving up the absurdity rule (*ex falso quodlibet*), thereby claiming that the correct logic is *intuitionistic relevant* logic. But—and this is a crucial 'but'—I cannot fathom *what it would be* to *acknowledge* both P and $\neg P$ as true, for *any* choice of P. Hence I do not believe that any sentence of the form $P \wedge \neg P$ can *be* true. Note that *acknowledging* both P and $\neg P$ to be true would be something quite different from discovering that one's current beliefs logically committed one, by means of suasive proofs of which one had only just been made aware, to asserting both P and $\neg P$. In such a situation *one does not acknowledge both P and $\neg P$ as truths*. Quite the contrary: one acknowledges that their joint assertion would be an assertion of a logical impossibility, an assertion of something that must be false and *cannot* be true; and *that* is why—if one is rational—one immediately suspends belief in the overall conjunction of all the premiss-beliefs used in the proofs of P and of $\neg P$. The task of the rational agent, in such circumstances, is to start looking immediately for a premiss that can be *given up*—a former belief that is to be banished from one's stock of beliefs, in the hope that this will restore consistency to the remainder.[11] Of course, we have no effective test, in suitably rich languages, for the consistency of even finite sets of sentences. We can have no guarantee that upon giving up certain premisses of those proofs of P and of $\neg P$, we shall have attained a consistent, because reduced, set of beliefs. The spectre of inconsistency always lurks, as we try to form and reform our beliefs. But a spectre it indeed is, to which we remain rationally averse. We recognize inconsistency as terrible, as *doxastically disastrous*, as something to be avoided at all costs.

This is why it is *so* crucial for Priest's project that he should succeed, definitively, on *at least one* of the examples of alleged dialetheia mentioned above. He has to show his opposition that there is at least one true contradiction—in the sense that no possible 'consistentist' story can dissolve the conflict or tension or absurdity revealed by the train of reasoning in question. Let us therefore now turn to a more

---

[11] In a monograph under preparation, I try to give an account of this rational procedure, covering logical, epistemological, and computational issues.

detailed consideration of Priest's overly swift dialetheist embrace of the paradoxes, semantic and set-theoretic, and the Gödel-sentence for naïve provability.

9. THERE ARE NO DIALETHEIAS!

Priest writes (*IC* 11):

The paradoxes are all arguments starting with apparently analytic principles concerning truth, membership etc., and proceeding via apparently valid reasoning, to a conclusion of the form 'α and not-α'. *Prima facie*, therefore, they show the existence of dialetheias. Those who would deny dialetheism have to show what is wrong with the arguments—of every single argument, that is. For every single argument they must locate a premise that is untrue, or a step that is invalid.

Here at last I intend to make good on my earlier claim that Priest detects dialetheia only by overlooking vital clues that point to the real culprits. I agree with Priest that the opponent of dialetheism has to address every single one of the paradoxical arguments. Given enough space, I would do that. But, since space is limited, I shall have to content myself here with briefer remarks aimed at persuading the reader that every such argument can be dealt with in the principled ways to be described below.

At the outset I should point out that Priest's last claim in the foregoing quote is in error. It is possible to scotch a paradoxical argument for a conclusion of the form $P \wedge \neg P$ *not* by locating a premiss that is untrue, *nor* by locating a step that is invalid, but rather: by showing that *those steps are not put together, and cannot be rearranged, in the manner required for genuine conferral of truth-value on the conclusion(s) involved*. This is crucial for dealing with the semantic paradoxes, as we shall see.

9.1 There Are No Semantic Dialetheias

Probably the most plausible candidate for the status of 'dialetheia' is the Liar Paradox: *This sentence is false*. As everyone familiar with this paradox knows, as soon as one reaches a (tentative) decision as to its truth-value, further reflection on the 'truth-conditions' of the liar sentence leads one to toggle that value. As soon as it 'becomes' true, we see immediately that it 'becomes' false; and vice versa. Thus one never reaches a stable truth-value assignment—or so it seems. Priest takes from this phenomenon of toggling truth-values the seldom-drawn lesson that the liar sentence is *both* true *and* false (for it takes two to toggle), rather than neither.

It is tempting to regard the liar sentence as a quirk of language, having nothing to do with the relationship between language and the world. In a world devoid of intelligent beings using language there would be, as it were, no instantiation of any liar-type phenomena. But, once we acknowledge that our world is one of language-users *and linguistic expressions*, the naïve thought that the proper subject-matter of language does not include language itself loses its appeal. To the extent that the 'truth-conditions' of the liar sentence are then 'in the world' (containing, as it does, the language of the liar sentence, and the relations of reference involved), the Liar nevertheless seems to say nothing about the world *beyond that*. It is, as it were, obsessively autobiographical. As with the worst kind of party guest, one learns from it nothing about anyone or anything besides itself—if one learns anything at all. It is a nasty little knot in Priest's 'weft and warp of language', about nothing but that same nasty little knot.

There are, however, other semantic paradoxes that do implicate, in their paradoxical truth-conditions, genuinely empirical facts in the world. Such is the case with Epimenides's version of the Liar, the statement that *all Cretans are liars*. That Epimenides was slagging his compatriots—that is, that Epimenedes was a Cretan, and therefore fell within the intended scope of his own generalization—is an empirical fact crucial to the statement's paradoxical status.

This consideration counsels against any attempted solution to the semantic paradoxes that tries to show that they are purely and essentially linguistic phenomena with such 'unworldly' truth-conditions as to justify the view that they can be safely disregarded. If they *do* have 'worldly' truth-(and falsity-)conditions, then these need to be accounted for. Moreover, we need to account for the truth- and falsity-conditions of the *non-paradoxical* sentences that talk about *both* empirical facts *and* the relationship between linguistic expressions and the world (including those expressions). Not every sentence of a semantically closed language is paradoxical. Many of them can be stably evaluated, unlike the Liar and its ilk.

It is beyond the scope of this section to survey the many and various proposals as to how one might 'solve' or 'accommodate', or 'avoid' or 'banish' the semantic paradoxes. I want instead to stress just one line of approach to semantic paradox that I believe has the edge on all others, and *especially* on Priest's approach (which is simply to throw in the towel and regard them as dialetheias).

On the approach I recommend, one takes seriously the idea that any evaluation of a sentence as true or as false must be 'well founded'. It is the main idea of the semantical treatment of semantically closed languages offered by Kripke, Woodruff, and Herzberger. Moreover—a point seldom appreciated, and little essayed by writers more concerned with formal details of *semantic* evaluation—this idea has a very nice proof-theoretic expression, as follows. Any evaluation of a sentence as true (or as false) should take the form of a proof or justification that is in, or can be brought into, 'normal form'. Let us call a proof in normal form that shows a claim φ to be true a *truth-warrant*. And let us call a proof in normal form that shows a claim φ to be false a *falsity-warrant*. This notion of 'proof in normal form' is an informal one, pending further explication. A falsity-warrant for φ will take the form of a *reductio ad absurdum*: φ will be an assumption, and the conclusion of the reductio will be absurdity ($\perp$).

A careful examination of the various well-known semantic paradoxes reveals that the proofs of absurdity obtained from the would-be evaluations of the sentences involved as true and/or as false *cannot be brought into normal form*. It is my conjecture that this is the distinguishing proof-theoretic feature of paradoxicality. The non-normalizability of the 'proofs' involved shows that *evaluations of paradoxes are not well-founded*. And *that* is why they are unstable. The vicious way in which linguistic self-reference and/or semantic closure makes itself manifest in the paradoxes is by subverting the canonical structure of truth-value conferral. Such structure, to be stable in its outcomes, has to be well founded (that is, reducible, via a sequence of finitely many steps, to normal form). And this structure—when it obtains—can be laid bare in the appropriate value-warrant. With paradoxes, however, these warrants are wanting. The great majority of paradoxes have 'proofs' and/or 'refutations' yielding proofs of absurdity whose reduction-sequences enter into 'loops'; whereas a paradox like that of Yablo has in the same way a reduction-sequence that 'spirals' infinitely, ratcheting up a numerical parameter with every complete twist.[12]

This proof-theoretic diagnosis actually gives one a much-needed prophylactic against the imagined harm that a newly discovered 'dialetheia' might bring; and it obviates the need to resort to Priest's Logic of Paradox as the 'correct' way to reason in the shadow of such possibilities. If someone identifies an erstwhile assertion as a dialetheia (because of its paradoxicality), then the very justification that he will be obliged to provide for his claim that it is indeed a dialetheia will immediately yield the kind of non-normalizable 'proof of absurdity' (or 'reductio') that I have been discussing above. Moreover, *that* the construct in question is not normalizable is something that can be effectively discovered (just as, if one is given a method for computing the decimal expansion of a number, and the number happens to be rational, then that method is actually an effective method for discovering that the number in question is indeed rational).

This proof-theoretic diagnosis of paradoxicality affords one the intellectual luxury of being able to work with a semantically closed language (such as natural language) without having things end in explicit contradiction (as with the dialetheic logician), or blow up (as with the non-relevantist logician), in the presence of paradox. The paradoxes reveal themselves as *radically truth-valueless*. They are ultimately gappy. They could not be further from enjoying truth-value glut.

It remains to anticipate, and defuse, one potential objection that might be leveled against my putting forward this account as an anti-realist. It is related to our earlier observation that, for the intuitionist, any claim of the form $\neg(\varphi \vee \neg\varphi)$

---

[12] Details of these proof-theoretic considerations can be found in Tennant (1982, 1995).

is inconsistent. That is, the intuitionist cannot say of any particular sentence that it lacks a truth-value. But, the objector will now ask, is not that exactly what one is saying of a paradoxical sentence (such as the Liar) when one claims that (by virtue of the normalizability test) it lacks a truth-value?

The answer is negative. Intuitionistically, the content of the two claims 'I have shown that φ is true' and 'I have shown that φ is false' is as follows:

(T) I have a truth-warrant for φ (call it $\dfrac{\Pi}{\varphi}$), and

(F) I have a falsity-warrant for φ (in the form of a reductio $\dfrac{\varphi}{\underset{\bot}{\Sigma}}$, say)

In general, a falsity-warrant for φ has to provide an effective method for turning any truth-warrant for φ into a normal proof of $\bot$. When the two warrants are given as natural deductions, this is effected by forming their accumulation and normalizing it. So, in this case, the accumulation $\dfrac{\overset{\Pi}{(\varphi)}}{\underset{\bot}{\Sigma}}$ has to be reducible to a normal proof of $\bot$.

In the case where φ is the liar sentence λ, however, this is not the case. The liar sentence affords the axiom

$$\lambda \leftrightarrow \neg T\lambda$$

The 'truth-warrant' on offer from the dialetheist (to justify his claim that he has shown that λ is true) is the proof

$$
\underset{\lambda}{\overset{\Pi}{}} \quad : \quad
\cfrac{
\cfrac{
\cfrac{T\lambda}{\lambda}^{(1)} \qquad
\cfrac{\cfrac{}{T\lambda}^{(1)} \quad \lambda \leftrightarrow \neg T\lambda}{\neg T\lambda}
}{\cfrac{\bot}{\neg T\lambda}\,^{(1)} \qquad \lambda \leftrightarrow \neg T\lambda}
}{\lambda}
$$

and the 'falsity-warrant' on offer (to justify his claim that he has shown that λ is false) is the reductio

$$
\underset{\bot}{\overset{\lambda}{\Sigma}} \quad : \quad
\cfrac{\cfrac{\lambda}{T\lambda} \qquad \cfrac{\lambda \quad \lambda \leftrightarrow \neg T\lambda}{\neg T\lambda}}{\bot}
$$

$$\begin{array}{c}\Pi\\(\lambda)\\ \Sigma\\ \bot\end{array}$$

When we form their accumulation $\begin{array}{c}\Pi\\(\lambda)\\ \Sigma\\ \bot\end{array}$ we find that it *cannot* be reduced to a

normal proof of $\bot$. So it is not the case both that the would-be truth-warrant Π is genuinely truth-conferring (for the liar sentence λ) and that the would-be falsity-warrant Σ is genuinely falsity-conferring. Thus the conjunction of (T) and (F) fails when φ is the liar sentence. Hence $\neg(\lambda \wedge \neg\lambda)$—just as the anti-realist would expect.

9.2 There Are No Set-Theoretic Dialetheias

Turning now to the set-theoretic paradoxes, we have to argue against Priest's view that, say, Russell's Paradox is both true and false. Priest wrote (*IC* 120):

> I ... believe that the Russell set is both a member of itself and not a member of itself. I do not deny that it was difficult to convince myself of this, that is, to get myself to believe it. It seemed, after all, so unlikely. But many arguments ... convinced me of it. It is difficult to come to believe something that goes against everything that you have ever been taught or accepted, in logic and philosophy as elsewhere. This is just a psychological fact about the power of received views on the human mind.

The crux of Priest's case for the dialetheic status of

$$\{x|x \notin x\} \in \{x|x \notin x\}$$

is to be found on p. 37 of his book: 'I wish to claim that *Abs* and *Ext* are true, and in fact that they analytically *characterise* the notion of set.' These are the principles of naïve Abstraction, and Extensionality, respectively (ibid. 35):

(Abs) $\exists y \forall x (x \in y \leftrightarrow \beta)$

(Ext) $\forall x (x \in z \leftrightarrow x \in y) \rightarrow z = y$

The consistentist finds it unfathomable that one would sooner believe that a set-theoretic proposition is both true and false than believe, instead, that it is mistaken to simply assume that any set-theoretic singular term (such as $\{x|x \notin x\}$) must have a denotation. Why insist on retaining naïve abstraction at such philosophical (and logical) cost as dialetheism, rather than *learning* from Russell's paradox (as Frege himself did) that simplicity of naïve postulation cannot triumph over the scientific need for consistency in one's search for the truth? This is an area where the consistentist refuses to tout 'pragmatic' considerations of pithy postulation as trumping the need for a more careful analysis of the postulational bases of set-existence.

Naïve abstraction cannot be analytic of the notion of set, unless that notion is itself inconsistent—which is what the dialetheist of course maintains. The consistentist, by contrast, believes that there *is* a consistent notion of set to be had, and that it *can* serve satisfactorily as the universal basis for mathematics. Such a notion of set will enjoy deep and analytic connections with fundamental features of rational thought about abstract things. The sought (consistent) theory will link the notions of predication, membership, set, and existence in illuminating (and still analytic) ways.

It is an overly historicist dogma (which one would expect Priest, given his anti-dogmatism in general, to want to question) that naïve abstraction is *analytic* of the notion of set. His taking it to be analytic is an important part of his case for Russell's paradox being both true and false. But here, by contrast, is another set of principles that we can take to be analytic of the notion of set. They are the introduction and elimination rules for the set-term-forming operator $\{x|\Phi(x)\}$ in a universally free logic. First, the introduction rule is as follows:

$$
(\{\}\,I) \quad
\begin{array}{cc}
(i)\!-\!\!-\!(i) & \overline{}(i)\\[2pt]
\underbrace{\Phi a, \exists! a} & a \in t\\[6pt]
\;\;\vdots & \;\;\vdots\\[6pt]
a \in t \qquad \exists! t \qquad \Phi a_{(i)}\\[2pt]
\hline
t = \{x|\Phi x\}
\end{array}
$$

Three elimination inferences for the set-term-forming operator can be determined from (the subproofs for) its introduction rule as follows:

$$
(\{\}E) \quad \dfrac{t = \{x|\Phi x\} \quad \Phi u \quad \exists! u}{u \in t} \qquad \dfrac{t = \{x|\Phi x\}}{\exists! t} \qquad \dfrac{t = \{x|\Phi x\} \quad u \in t}{\Phi u}
$$

The leftmost elimination inference unpacks the commitments generated by the need to have the leftmost subproof in the introduction rule. If the speaker asserts that t is the set of all Φs, then, if we can establish of an existent u that it has property Φ, we may conclude that u is a member of t. This is the move from predication to set-membership, qualified by an appropriate existential presupposition.

The middle elimination inference is a special case of the Rule of Denotation in free logic, according to which the truth of any atomic predication requires that each singular term involved has a denotation. (This makes the truth-conditions of such claims the standard Russellian ones.)

The rightmost elimination inference unpacks the commitments generated by the need to have the rightmost subproof in the introduction rule. If the speaker asserts that t is the set of all Φs, then, if we can establish that u is a member of t, we may conclude that u has the property Φ, the defining property of the set t. This is the converse move from set-membership to predication.

The leftmost and rightmost elimination inferences are therefore tantamount to Church's conversion schema for set theory based on a free logic. They express the non-naïve kernel of truth in naïve abstraction. The existential presupposition of the leftmost rule is crucial; it ensures that the proof of the so-called Russell Paradox is no longer a proof that the system is inconsistent, but is simply a proof that there can be no such thing as the set of all things that are not members of themselves. So much for Russell's paradox being a dialetheia!

One can use just the rules given (plus the logical rule of substitutivity of identicals) to derive the principle of extensionality for sets:

$$
\cfrac{
\cfrac{
\cfrac{\cfrac{-(1)-}{a \in d} \quad \cfrac{\exists! a \quad \forall z(z \in c \leftrightarrow z \in d)}{a \in c \leftrightarrow a \in d}(3)}{a \in c}{-(1)-}
\qquad
\cfrac{\cfrac{-(1)-}{a \in c} \quad \cfrac{\exists! a \quad \forall z(z \in c \leftrightarrow z \in d)}{a \in c \leftrightarrow a \in d}(3)}{a \in d}{-(1)-}
}{
\cfrac{a \in d \quad \exists! c \quad a \in c \quad a \in c \quad a \in d \qquad b \in d \quad \exists! d \quad b \in d}{ }
}
}{ }
$$

-(1)-
a ∈ d
_____(3)
∃!a   ∀z(z ∈ c ↔ z ∈ d)
_____ -(1)-
a ∈ c ↔ a ∈ d   a ∈ d
_____ -(5)-

-(1)-
a ∈ c
_____(3)
∃!a   ∀z(z ∈ c ↔ z ∈ d)
_____ -(1)-
a ∈ c ↔ a ∈ d   a ∈ c
_____

-(2)- -(4)- -(2)-
b ∈ d ∃!d   b ∈ d(2)
d = {x | x ∈ d}

a ∈ c   ∃!c   a ∈ d
_____
c = {x | x ∈ d}
_____
c = d
_____(3)
∀z(z ∈ c ↔ z ∈ d) → c = d
_____(4)
∀y(∀z(z ∈ c ↔ z ∈ y) → c = y)
_____(5)
∀x∀y(∀z(z ∈ x ↔ z ∈ y) → x = y)

That Zermelo's axiom of extensionality is now a derived result, rather than an axiomatic stipulation, testifies to the deeper analysis achieved (of abstractive set-formation in terms of set-membership) via the introduction and elimination rules just specified.

I submit that in so far as a philosophical case for or against dialetheism in set theory needs to rest on a selection of principles claimed to be analytic of the notion of set, the introduction and elimination rules given above have a more convincing claim to be genuinely analytic of the notion of set than do the principles that Priest favors, namely naïve abstraction and extensionality. For the introduction and elimination rules above are obtained as one instance of a general method for generating such rules for abstraction operators.[13] Moreover, these rules provide the deep reason why extensionality holds. The rules bring out the consistent analytic connections among the notions of set, membership, and predication in general. Moreover, those connections are brought out with the introduction-elimination form of analysis that is the hallmark of the anti-realist's theory of meaning: a theory stressing how the justificatory obligations that a speaker must discharge before making an assertion are matched by the inferential entitlements that the audience enjoys upon hearing it.

---

[13] Space is insufficient to allow a more detailed discussion of this claim. The reader is referred to Tennant (2004). We confine ourselves to pointing out here that rules for the definite description operator are exactly analogous to those for the set-term-forming operator; one simply replaces the membership predicate by the identity predicate in the rules stated in the text. See also Tennant (1978: s. 7.10).

9.3 Gödel's Theorem for Naïve Provability Is Not a Dialetheia

We turn finally to the outstanding alleged example of a dialetheia in mathematical and logical foundations, namely Gödel's Theorem for naïve provability. Priest's argument (*IC* 56) runs:

> the consistency of our naive proof procedures entails a contradiction. For let T be (the formalisation of) our naive proof procedures. Then since T satisfies the conditions of Goedel's theorem, if T is consistent there is a sentence φ which is not provable in T, but which we can establish as true by a naive proof, and hence *is* provable in T. The only way out of the problem, other than to accept the contradiction, and thus dialetheism anyway, is to accept the inconsistency of naive proof.[fn.] So we are forced to admit that our naive proof procedures are inconsistent. But our naive proof procedures just are those methods of deductive argument by which things are established as true. It follows that some contradictions are true, that is, dialetheism is correct.

Priest derives his contradiction from the assumption (among others) that T is a formalization of our naïve proof procedures. In the metalogical reasoning, T is thus a parameter for an existential elimination on the premiss that *there is* a formalization of our naïve proof procedures.

Extraordinarily, Priest does not consider the obvious point that it is this existential assumption that the Gödelian reasoning reveals to be in error. It may well first come as a surprise; but on further reflection the falsity of this assumption sinks in. Even in order to make sense of the informal notion of effective decidability of proofhood (not: recursiveness of the proof predicate, courtesy only subsequently of Church's Thesis), we have to have a rigorous conception of the symbolic resources and the combinatorial, algorithmic methods that must be involved in 'proof recognition', in order for this process to be effective. What Gödel's Theorem shows is that we can never once-and-for-all delimit, in this required rigorous manner, the resources of 'naïve provability'. They are open-textured and indefinitely extensible.

To realize that this is so, and to disbelieve the claim that the notion of naïve provability can be formalized, is a more rational reaction to Gödel's Theorem than to believe that one has discovered a true contradiction. This anti-realist resolution of the 'paradox' is exactly that of the earliest intuitionists, for whom Gödel's Theorem came as no great surprise, but as a kind of rigorous confirmation of their view that mathematical thought could not be constrained within a single formal system of proof.

REFERENCES

PRIEST, GRAHAM (1982). 'To Be and Not To Be: Dialectical Tense Logic', *Studia Logica*, 41(2/3): 248–68.

—— (1987). *In Contradiction: A Study of the Transconsistent*. Dordrecht, Nijhoff.

TENNANT, NEIL (1978). *Natural Logic*, Edinburgh: Edinburgh University Press, 1978 (2nd, rev. edn. 1990).

Tennant, Neil (1982). 'Proof and Paradox', *Dialectica*, 36: 265–96.

——(1998). 'Beyond the Limits of Thought', a critical study of Priest's book of that title (Cambridge University Press, 1994), in *Philosophical Books*, 39: 20–38.

——(1995). 'On Paradox without Self-Reference', *Analysis*, 55: 199–207.

——(1997). *The Taming of The True*, Oxford, Clarendon.

——(1999). 'Negation, Absurdity and Contrariety', in D. Gabbay and H. Wansing (eds.), *What is Negation?* Dordrecht, Kluwer, 199–222.

——(2000). 'Anti-Realist Aporias', *Mind*, 109(436): 831–60.

——(2004). 'A General Theory of Abstraction Operators', *The Philosophical Quarterly*, 54(214): 105–33.

22

There Are No True Contradictions

Alan Weir

1

Suppose there is a true contradiction, that is, for some sentence P

    1 (1) ⌜P and it is not the case that P⌝ is true.   (Hypothesis)

Then

    1 (2) P is true and ⌜It is not the case that P⌝ is true.

                                          (1, Semantics of conjunction)

Hence:

    1 (3) P is true.   (2, Conjunction Elimination)

    1 (4) ⌜it is not the case that P⌝ is true.   (2, Conjunction Elimination)

    1 (5) P is not true.   (4, Semantics of negation)

    1 (6) ⊥   (3, 5, Negation Elimination)

So the supposition reduces to absurdity (⊥) and we can conclude, as a semantic theorem (no assumptions on the left):

    —(7) It is not the case that ⌜P and it is not the case that P⌝ is true.

                                        (6, Negation Introduction)

Thus the dialetheist's claim that there are true contradictions is provably false.

One could try to block this argument by, for example, rejecting the semantic principles at lines (2) and (5), that is by denying that if a conjunction is true both conjuncts are or by denying that if a negation is true the sentence negated is not true. But this move renders the doctrine that there are true contradictions an uninteresting piece of terminological obfuscation. Thus if 'and' meant the same as 'or' currently does and negation retained its current meaning, or if negation is read as ⌜it is possible that not P⌝ then indeed there would have been truths of the form ⌜P and it is not the case that P⌝. But conjunction and negation do not mean those things.

Similarly, one might resist some of the inferences involved in the proof, such as the conjunction elimination rule applied at lines (3) and (4) or the principle at line (6) that if a sentence entails a sentence and its negation then it entails absurdity, or the principle that if a sentence entails absurdity then it is provably false. But these principles are so primitive and obvious that it is not clear how one could argue against someone who rejected them nor whether one has any need to. Surely one is under no more obligation to reason with those who reject rational argumentation than to reason with a rabid dog.

Some might accept the above argument and so accept (generalizing on the parameter 'P') that there are no true contradictions whilst none the less continuing to maintain that there are. Graham Priest is one such dialetheist (1987: 90–1). But here again, such thinkers would seem to be immune from rational persuasion and, specifically, immune from refutation. No matter what you get them to accept in the course of an argument they can still retain the original belief you wished to persuade them was false. For this reason there is no point in trying to argue with such a person. There is no point in attempting to checkmate someone who refuses to play by the rules of chess whenever application of those rules goes against them.

2

Or so many will argue. Something along the lines of above response to dialetheism, is, I conjecture, the standard response of the vast majority of philosophers today: certainly among those who are not logicians and perhaps even among logicians. Yet a growing number of the latter fail to be persuaded by the above line of thought, and this minority includes both proponents of dialetheism, naturally, but also those not yet convinced of this radical viewpoint.

In this chapter I wish to argue that, in the end, the anti-dialetheists whose views are put rather stridently in the previous section are basically right in their convictions and there is a great deal of force in their position. None the less I want also to come down firmly in the camp of those non-dialetheists who think that the initial argument is much too swift in its dismissal of dialetheism and that the latter doctrine is deserving of serious consideration from which we can learn much.

The structure of the chapter is this: in the next section I argue that dialetheism deserves to be taken seriously, that the non-dialetheist can engage in reasonable dispute with the dialetheist and it is worthwhile doing so. In the remaining sections I deal with problems with dialetheism that are progressively more fundamental and far reaching: in s. 4 I argue that dialetheism as currently developed requires an ad hoc asymmetry between the roles of truth and falsity. In s. 5 I argue that dialetheism is unable to give an adequate account of the 'classical recapture' of the classical mathematics we need for science. Then, most fundamentally, I return in s. 6 to the semantic argument and try to develop the idea that dialetheism involves a violation of meaning constraints, a violation that leads the dialetheist not merely into heterodoxy but into outright irrationality.

3. WHY TAKE DIALETHEISM SERIOUSLY?

Compare first a more radical position than that of the dialetheist, that of what might be called the 'Philosophical Irrationalist'. This irrationalist dismisses reason, truth, validity, inference, objectivity et al. as myths, bogus concepts, internally incoherent, and so forth. The Philosophical Irrationalist, however, is to be sharply distinguished from the 'Rabid Irrationalist'. The Rabid Irrationalist dismisses reason by irrational ranting or similar rhetorical devices, such as dismissing, for example, rationality or objectivity by scare-quoting them as 'rationality', 'objectivity'. (Compare how small children often ridicule one another by repeating what has been said in a high-pitched whine.) Such rhetorical moves can be quite hard to stomach but are best ignored.

What makes the Philosophical Irrationalist philosophical is that she seems to undermine reason *from within*, that is by using methods of reasoning and argument that are generally accepted. These Trojan horse irrationalists have been important figures in the history of philosophy from ancient Greek sceptics down to Paul Feyerabend. Unlike the rabid irrationalists, such sceptics are not to be ignored. It is no use objecting to such philosophical irrationalists that if they are right, the arguments on which they base their conclusions—most dramatically the conclusion that there is no distinction between correct and incorrect reasoning—are self-refuting. Since they start from *our* starting point, if they refute themselves they refute us too. To put it dramatically, they are a species of intellectual kamikaze pilots or suicide bombers and so it is blind complacency to dismiss them on the grounds that, since their mission would be suicidal, they are no threat. We have to hope, then, that their arguments are not in fact cogent; but finding the flaws in their internal critiques can be relied on to generate philosophical insight.

Now the dialetheist is not out to deconstruct rationality: Graham Priest, for example, holds to a distinction between correct and incorrect modes of reasoning as determinate and sharp as the standard logician. He wishes, however, to draw it in a different place and in particular to challenge the idea that *all* contradictions are untenable. Some are, of course, else triviality and irrationalism result. Indeed, in a certain sense he wishes to hold that most are. But some atypical ones are true; to my mind, the best examples he gives being the antinomic sentences thrown up by the semantic and set-theoretic paradoxes such as strong Liar sentences of the form:

$\lambda: \langle \lambda \rangle$ is not true[1]

or $r \in r$, where r is the Russell set $\{x: x \notin x\}$.

Since the dialetheist holds that some contradictions are untenable and utilizes perfectly standard modes of argumentation, it is perfectly possible to engage in

---

[1] Brackets generating metalinguistic parameters whose substituends are canonical codes for the substituends of the embedded parameter.

rational debate with her just as with the Philosophical Irrationalist. Just as one can hope to defuse philosophical irrationalism by showing a purported absurdity does not follow, so too one can hope either to block the dialetheists' arguments for dialetheism, or show that untenable consequences, even by their lights, follow from it. If one can show that, unbeknownst to the dialetheist thus far, the theory does in fact result in triviality or in a 'bad' contradiction, then the dialetheist will be forced to abandon dialetheism. What counts as a bad contradiction? In fact here we touch on one of the most fundamental difficulties with dialetheism. One answer Priest (1987: 134–6) gives appeals to probability theory, reworked in dialetheist fashion. A bad contradiction is a zero probability one; contrary to standard theory not all contradictions are bad, some such as ($r \in r$ & $r \notin r$) have probability one. The difficulty for dialetheism is this: if one simply takes over a pure personalist Bayesian identification of probabilities with subjective degrees of belief, then dialetheism sanctions utter irrationalism, since it will be a subjective matter as to which contradictions are zero probability bad ones, and which are not.

For Priest, of course, probabilities are not subjective matters, or if they are then we should define a bad contradiction in a different way, as an 'unacceptable' one, maximally disconfirmed perhaps. It is an objective fact, he believes, that 'my head is made of glass' is at least as absurd as any formal contradiction and more absurd than many, e.g. the Liar. Thus he writes:

there are criteria for rationality other than consistency, and some of these are even more powerful than consistency.   (1998: 420)

In the last instance, what is rationally acceptable, and what is not, is likely to be a holistic matter.   (ibid. 423)

I am frequently asked for a criterion as to when contradictions are acceptable and when they are not. It would be nice if there were a substantial answer to this question, or even if one could give a partial answer, in the form of some algorithm to demonstrate than an area of discourse is contradiction free. But I doubt that this is possible.   (ibid.)

My own view is that the whole idea of objective epistemic probabilities, objective degrees of confirmation, or any notion of rational justification that extends the deductive is a mistaken one. But this rather Humean scepticism is far from common; in this matter the dialetheists have orthodoxy on their side. Since arguing against this orthodoxy is a large-scale task, I will not press this point further and simply assume a rough and ready distinction between good and bad contradictions. Certainly even non-dialetheists can make something of this distinction: whilst no one in their right mind would ever want to accept ($0 = 1$ & $0 \neq 1$) many concede they have a different attitude towards ($r \in r$ & $r \notin r$) or (⟨λ⟩ is true & ⟨λ⟩ is untrue). Intuitions that contradictions are not to be countenanced are much less firm in these cases so that for many it is an epistemic possibility they might come to accept such contradictions. Not so absurdities such as '$0 = 1$' or 'the Earth orbits and does not orbit the Sun' even though, at the moment, all these contradictions—'bad' and 'good'—are believed metaphysically impossible by the non-dialetheist.

Thus a dialectical space for fruitful debate between dialetheists and non-dialetheists opens up. The former tries to convince the latter: by appeal to the enormous difficulty in finding solutions to the paradoxes which are not themselves every bit as paradoxical, perhaps. The latter attempts to persuade the dialetheist that a bad, unacceptable, contradiction follows from the dialetheist position.

Why should the non-dialetheists bother, though? After all, if the dialetheist is right and acceptance of true contradictions is the only rational response to certain problems such as the paradoxes, then we all ought to embrace dialetheism. But if the dialetheist is wrong, why bother trying to convert them back to orthodoxy? There is no obligation on us to persuade everyone who holds different views that they are wrong. In many cases, this cannot be done since their background assumptions, or modes of reasoning, may be too different from ours.

Acceptance of philosophical theses, however, comes in degrees. The conventional theorist may be fairly sure she has a good response to the problems the dialetheist raises, a response that does not involve acceptance of true contradictions. She may even be fairly sure there must be such a solution, though she has no idea at present what it is. There is nothing irrational in such an attitude. However it is more easy to adopt it the more one is sure the dialetheist alternative is unacceptable: weaken one's conviction that dialetheism is a price too high to pay and one will become less ready to search for a non-dialetheic resolution to those problems, or to hold there must be one even though one cannot come up with it at present. So there is interest for the non-dialetheist in seeing how bad are the contradictions that flow, dialetheically, from dialetheism. Stalemate can still result, of course: dialetheist and non-dialetheist alike may conclude that a given contradiction is inherent in dialetheism but whilst the former is prepared to bite the bullet the latter may declare this a manifest repugnancy which is utterly unacceptable. An example of this may be contradictions in elementary arithmetic, which Stewart Shapiro (2002) has argued flow from dialetheism.[2] If the dialetheist accepts this and accepts the contradictions, then there is little the orthodox can do by way of persuasion. The further away from 'pathological' contradictions such as ($r \in r$ & $r \notin r$) the dialetheist is forced to go, the more manifestly repugnant to orthodox ears are the contradictions he or she urges everyone to accept, the fewer the converts dialetheism will gain.

In this chapter I argue as a non-dialetheist who is very impressed by the dialetheic critique of standard solutions to the paradoxes (see Weir 1998a) but is not convinced that dialetheism is the only remaining response; a non-dialetheist who is hoping to persuade the dialetheists of the error of their ways but entertaining firmer hopes of persuading other non-dialetheists who might be on the verge of

---

[2] Though it is important here that he considered a language for arithmetic that contains a non-extensional conditional.

swithering[3] to stand firm because the price of dialetheism is too high. As remarked, I will look at three main problem areas of increasing severity, starting first with the counter-intuitive asymmetry between truth and falsity in dialetheism.

4. TRUTH AND FALSITY

The dialetheist view, at least in so far as it utilizes a logic such as LP (see Priest 1979), depends crucially on deep asymmetries between truth and falsity.[4] Any sensible account of logic requires that valid arguments be truth-preserving, that is in any circumstance in which all the premisses are true the conclusion is. It is less common to require the opposite 'upwards falsity' direction.[5] In the simplest case of one-premiss/one-conclusion arguments, this states that in any circumstance in which the conclusion is false the premiss is.[6] But this direction is every bit as essential as the downwards truth-preserving direction (the neglect of the dual direction is perhaps understandable for a classicist, of course, since either direction follows from the other, given classical bivalence). One does not have to be a rampant Popperian to see that refutations do play an important role in science, and the logical rationale of refutation is falsity-preservation upwards. If a theory entails a false prediction, the theory is false (though we might well not know which bit of it is false); more generally to the degree that we are sure the prediction is false we should be sure the theory is.

Graham Priest seems to acknowledge this key role of falsity-preservation by building it in to his account of an entailment conditional (1987: 105). But if $\rightarrow$ genuinely does represent entailment ($\models$) in the object language then this should hold:

$$\models P \rightarrow Q \text{ iff } P \models Q$$

Yet where $\models$ is the logic LP, the one most utilized by Priest, this biconditional fails. LP, considered algebraically, is the three-valued strong Kleene logic in which the 'top' two values are designated. For Priest the values are True ({T}, Both {T, F}

---

[3] A fine Scots word meaning, roughly, being undecided but swaying on the verge of going one way or the other.

[4] Priest identifies the falsity of p with the truth of the negation of $\sim p$ (1998: 413, 418) and distinguishes falsity from untruth (1987: 88–91), both of which assumptions I am happy to go along with. But whereas he (tentatively) denies falsity entails untruth (ibid. and 1995: 61 n. 12) this entailment seems to me to be unassailable. It is of the essence of truth and falsity to be exclusive, though of course for a dialetheist a sentence can be both true and untrue and so truth and falsity, for a dialetheist, can be both exclusive and non-exclusive. In consequence the inference at line (4) of s. 1 from the truth of $\sim p$ to the untruth of p is unassailable: a dialetheist who holds that ⟨S⟩ is both true and false is immediately committed to the truth of the contradiction: ⟨S⟩ is true and ⟨S⟩ is not true.

[5] But see Dorothy Edgington (1993: 195).

[6] It is an interesting question how to generalize this to multiple premiss arguments, or, dually, how to express truth-preservation for multiple conclusion logics. I address this point later in s. 6.

and False {F}. Hence an argument that goes from a True premiss to a 'glutty' conclusion that takes the value Both is not thereby shown to be invalid, since we have truth in the premiss and truth in the conclusion; but an argument that goes from Both to false is invalid, since we have truth in the premiss but not in the conclusion.

Symmetry could be restored by allowing in also the move from Both to falsity, hence allowing that a necessarily glutty sentence such as $r \in r$, where r is the Russell set, entails anything. That is, we could define an argument as valid just in case it is either truth-preserving downwards or falsity-preserving upwards. But then simple transitivity of entailment would induce triviality. We would be allowed to move from a necessary truth such as $0 = 0$ (True) to $r \in r$ (Both) to any conclusion C, True, Both, or False. Alternatively we could require a valid inference be both truth-preserving downwards and falsity-preserving upwards; but that would rule out the move from True to Both, e.g. from $0 = 0$ to the naïve comprehension axiom (construed dialetheically) so that the axioms of naïve set theory would be invalid. The resulting logic would be much weaker than LP and so hopelessly restricted.[7]

Priest argues for the asymmetry between the logical roles of truth and falsity—downwards truth-preservation is essential, upwards falsity-preservation is not—on the basis of a teleological account of truth. 'In the appropriate sense, truth trumps falsity. Truth is, by its nature, the aim of cognitive processes such, as belief' (1998: 421). Following Dummett, he believes that truth is the telos or goal of assertion (1987: 77–9, 124). As against this one could assert that falsity is the telos of denial and deny that assertion is more fundamental than denial. More importantly one could, and in my view should, deny that linguistic behaviour has any overriding aim or goal at all: with Wittgenstein and Chomsky one should stress the highly variegated purposes to which linguistic acts, including assertion, are put. Even if the statistical norm for sentences closed linked to observation is that they be true, there is no reason to suppose that is true in general; nor is it so clear what it could mean to say that the norm, in some non-statistical sense, of assertion is truth. My conclusion, then, is that dialetheism requires an asymmetry between truth and falsity that, at the very least, requires a stronger defence and justification than dialetheists have given it thus far.

5. CLASSICAL RECAPTURE

Naïve set theory in a classical context is trivial, so the dialetheist, like any other proponent of the naïve theory, must work with a weaker logic. Graham Priest

---

[7] I will abbreviate True, Both, and False henceforth as T, B, and F. In the strong Kleene rules, negation maps T to F, F to T, and B to B whilst conjunction minimizes and disjunction maximizes over the input values according to the ordering $T > B > F$.

suggests using one of the many paraconsistent logics that logicians have developed in recent decades, logics such as BX or LP.[8] But now an opposite problem arises: perhaps in taming naïve set theory we will produce a theory so weak that we are unable to derive even basic results of mathematics, never mind the sophisticated mathematics needed for modern science. (Deriving key classical theorems from a non-classical theory and logic is often called 'classical recapture'.)

To illustrate the problem, consider a fairly extreme case. Start with a standard first-order formulation of naïve set theory. We have a first-order language with only two non-logical constants, $\in$ and a primitive identity relation $=$. The axioms comprise extensionality:

$$\forall x \forall y (\forall z (z \in x \leftrightarrow z \in y) \rightarrow x = y)$$

and each instance of the naïve comprehension schema:

$$\exists x \forall y (y \in x \leftrightarrow \varphi y).$$

As logical rules, take all the classical propositional rules plus, for the quantifiers, the quantifier-switching rules

$$(\forall x)(\forall y)\varphi xy \dashv\vdash (\forall y)(\forall x)\varphi xy$$
$$(\exists x)(\exists y)\varphi xy \dashv\vdash (\exists y)(\exists x)\varphi xy$$

and that's all![9]

For the semantics, models for the language are just standard ZF models with the usual interpretations of $\in$ and $=$ over some set domain of individuals. We give the usual clauses for the valuation of atomic sentences (with just the two standard truth values T and F) and the usual recursive clauses for propositional compounds. For quantified sentences we provide the 'pathological' semantics in which all universal and existential generalizations are true. It is then easy to see that all the axioms are true and all the rules truth-preserving. But no one in their right mind will see this as showing naïve set theory is sound. The semantic theory for the quantifier clauses, for one thing, does nothing like justice to the true meaning of the quantifiers. So though an expression such as

$$\exists x \forall y (y \in x \leftrightarrow y \notin y)$$

is true in the model, that does not mean that a sentence that paraphrases 'there exists a set such that anything belongs to it if and only if that thing does not belong to itself' is true in the model.

---

[8] It is not obligatory for a naïve set theorist to use a paraconsistent logic, in the sense of a logic in which the rule [from $X \vdash \bot$ conclude $X \vdash A$] fails, for arbitrary X, A. But if this rule does not fail then one must block the standard proof of $\bot$ from naïve set theory.

[9] Though we could also add reflexivity of identity and Leibniz's law, if we wished, without damage to the argument to follow.

A similar danger arises for dialetheists who provide a semantics for naïve set theory from within the framework of classical set theories such as ZFC. This latter procedure, indeed, is one which dialetheists seem to have quite generally adopted. One might call it 'dialetheic recapture', because it is an inverse, of sorts, to the programme of classical recapture. Instead of trying to capture classical theorems in a non-classical framework, one tries to capture dialetheic theorems (e.g. instances of naïve comprehension) in a classical one.

Consider, as an example, the following semantics for naïve set theory in the framework of the logic LP. It is taken, with some amendments, from Graham Priest (forthcoming). We have a first-order language as above (in taking identity as a primitive, I depart from Priest's account). We work as usual with valuations over a domain D of individuals. For the identity relation, admissible interpretations never set $v_\sigma(x = y) = $ T whenever σ assigns different values to x and y nor set $v_\sigma(x = y) = $ F whenever $\sigma(x) = \sigma(y)$. (Call an interpretation of $=$ in which no identity sentence takes the value B, standard.) The $\in$ relation is interpreted by a function from pairs of D members into one of the three semantic values of LP—T, B, or F. We can think of the interpretation of $\in$ as a matrix E $= [e_{m,n}]$ with rows and columns indexed by members m, n, of D. Then $v_\sigma(x \in y) = \langle e_{m,n} \rangle$ where $\sigma(x) = m$ and $\sigma(y) = n$ and where $\langle e_{m,n} \rangle$ is one of T, B, or F.

The values for complex formulae are calculated using the strong Kleene rules, with the conditional P $\rightarrow$ Q interpreted materially, i.e. as $\sim$P $\vee$ Q and the quantifiers interpreted as generalized (perhaps infinitary) conjunction and disjunction truth functors. A classical vector of values is one that does not contain B (we consider only vectors indexed by the entire set D of individuals) and vector v subsumes vector u iff $u_i \subseteq v_i$, for all i. The naïve models are those where for every classical vector c there is a column vector $\{\langle e_{m,n} \rangle : m \in D\}$, for some n, which subsumes c. There are naïve models; for instance, any model that has a column all of whose values are B is naïve. One highly degenerate example is the one element model with the E matrix (Fig. 22.1), and identity interpreted standardly. The naïve comprehension axiom for sets:

$$\exists x \forall y (y \in x \leftrightarrow \varphi y)$$

is designated in every naïve model including this one.[10] In considering this degenerate case, add, for simplicity, the numeral '1' to the language so that its referent is the only member of the domain; this is solely for the purpose of cutting down on the need to refer to assignments to free variables in the discussion that follows. Given the semantic clause for $\exists$, and the singular nature of our domain, what we need to show is that

$$\forall y (y \in 1 \leftrightarrow \varphi y)$$

---

[10] See Restall (1992), Priest (forthcoming), Appendix. However in this framework we need to restrict comprehension by stipulating that x does not occur in φ.

	1
1	B

FIG. 22.1.

		q		
	$p \leftrightarrow q$	T	B	F
	T	T	B	F
p	B	B	B	B
	F	F	B	T

FIG. 22.2.

is designated, this in turn requiring that

$$(1 \in 1 \leftrightarrow \varphi 1)$$

is designated. But since the left-hand side takes value B, the Kleene valuation for material $\leftrightarrow$ (Fig. 22.2) entails that regardless of the value of the right-hand side, the formula does take the designated value B.

As for Extensionality,

$$\forall x \forall y(\forall z(z \in x \leftrightarrow z \in y) \rightarrow x = y)$$

this holds trivially given that identity is standard since there is only one assignment to the variables and in it the consequent $x = y$ is true. More generally, in any naïve model in which identity is standard and no two rows of the $\in$ matrix are identical, extensionality will be designated. For every assignment to

$$\forall z(z \in x \leftrightarrow z \in y) \rightarrow x = y$$

either the consequent is true or the antecedent is not true since if $\sigma(x) \neq \sigma(y)$ then for some $\sigma(z)$, $z \in x$ and $z \in y$ take different values so that $z \in x \leftrightarrow z \in y$ does not take value T.

However the existence of at least two things:

$$\exists x \exists y(x \neq y)$$

is false (only) in the above model since $1 \neq 1$ takes value F. In any logic sound for this dialetheic LP semantics, the existence of more than one thing does not follow from naïve set theory since entailment in LP is defined by preservation of a designated value (either T or B). The logic not only tames naïve set theory, it utterly cripples it, at least in the context of the above semantics.

The same is true if we replace naïve set theory by a standard theory such as ZFC or weaker systems such as Z (in which replacement and choice are dropped). This seems obvious since classically naïve set theory is so much stronger than Z but care has to be taken in these non-classical contexts. None the less it can be shown that every axiom of Z takes the designated value in the trivial one-element model above.

Empty set: $\exists x \forall y(y \notin x)$

This takes value B because $\forall y(y \notin 1)$ takes value B since $1 \notin 1$ takes value B. We can introduce the term '$\emptyset$' subject to contextual elimination rules. For example, a formula of the form $\emptyset \in x$ eliminates to:

$\exists!y \forall w(w \notin y) \ \& \ y \in x$

with $\exists!$ the uniqueness quantifier. The uniqueness clause U, in this instance:

$\forall z(\forall w(w \notin z) \rightarrow z = y)$

trivially takes value T in our singular model since its embedded consequent is always true, so

$\exists!y \forall w(w \notin y) \ \& \ y \in x$

takes the same value as

$\forall w(w \notin 1 \ \& \ U \ \& \ 1 \in 1)$

which, since U takes the value T, takes the same value as $(1 \notin 1 \ \& \ 1 \in 1)$, namely B.

Extensionality: as before.

Next the 'conditional' existence axioms, Power Set and Union.

Power Set: we argue that

$\forall x \exists y \forall z(z \in y \leftrightarrow z \subseteq x)$

takes value B because $\forall z(z \in 1 \leftrightarrow z \subseteq 1)$ takes value B. Unpacking the definition of '$\subseteq$' this requires $(1 \in 1 \leftrightarrow \forall w(w \in 1 \rightarrow w \in 1))$ to take value B which it does since both halves take value B.

Union: $\forall x \exists y \forall z(z \in y \leftrightarrow \exists w(z \in w \ \& \ w \in x))$

Since we only have one element in our domain, this equates to:

$$(1 \in 1 \leftrightarrow \exists w(1 \in w \ \& \ w \in 1))$$

and again the fact that the left-hand side takes value B entails that Union has value B.

<u>Subsets Schema:</u> $\forall x \exists y \forall z(z \in y \leftrightarrow (z \in x \ \& \ \varphi x))$

where y is not free in φ. Here the argument is very similar to that for naïve set comprehension, we simply have an extra conjunct $z \in x$ on the right-hand side of the embedded biconditional but once again the value of the right-hand side is immaterial since the left-hand side always takes value B.

<u>Pair Sets:</u> $\forall x \forall y \exists z \forall w(w \in z \leftrightarrow (w = x \lor w = y))$

This equates to $1 \in 1 \leftrightarrow (1 = 1 \lor 1 = 1)$ which takes the value B as before. Once again, it is useful to introduce contextually eliminable terms, this time of the form $\{x\}$. The elimination rule for the context $\{x\} \in y$ is:

$$\exists!z(\forall w(w \in z \leftrightarrow w = x) \ \& \ z \in y$$

Again the uniqueness clause U is trivially true so the above equates to:

$$(\forall w(w \in 1 \leftrightarrow w = 1) \ \& \ U \ \& \ 1 \in 1)$$

which, since U takes the value T, equates to $((1 \in 1 \leftrightarrow 1 = 1) \ \& \ 1 \in 1)$ which takes the value B. Similarly $\{x\} = y$ reduces to:

$$\exists!z(\forall w(w \in z \leftrightarrow w = x) \ \& \ z = y$$

which equates to $(1 \in 1 \leftrightarrow 1 = 1) \ \& \ U \ \& \ 1 = 1)$ which still computes as B because the left-most conjunct, a biconditional with a left-hand-side whose value is B, still takes the value B. The argument is the same for $y = \{x\}$ of course.

<u>Foundation:</u> $\forall x(\exists y(y \in x) \rightarrow \exists y(y \in x \ \& \ \forall z \sim (z \in y \ \& \ z \in x)))$

This takes the same value as the instance:

$$(\exists y(y \in 1) \rightarrow \exists y(y \in 1 \ \& \ \forall z \sim (z \in y \ \& \ z \in 1)))$$

Since the antecedent takes the value B, the sentence as a whole takes the value of B at least (in fact it takes the value B since $y \in 1$, the left conjunct of the instantiation of the consequent takes the value B on the only assignment to y).

<u>Infinity.</u> $\exists x(\emptyset \in x \ \& \ \forall y(y \in x \rightarrow \{y\} \in x))$

This takes value B because

$$(\emptyset \in 1 \ \& \ \forall y(y \in 1 \rightarrow \{y\} \in 1))$$

does. We know that $\emptyset \in 1$ takes the value B; the second conjunct equates to $(1 \in 1 \to \{1\} \in 1)$ and we know that this takes the value B since $\{1\} \in 1$ does.[11]

So the existence of more than one mathematical object does not follow dialetheically (according to the above semantics) from naïve set theory nor from S nor indeed from ZFC. Yet that there is more than one set clearly *does* follow from S; it is more evident that this is the case than that dialetheism is correct. The failure of the derivation to go through shows not that contemporary mathematicians are making a massive error but rather that the dialetheic logic in question fails in what is the key task of a formal system of mathematical logic: to provide an insightful idealization of real mathematical (and more generally inferential) practice that does not distort unduly the genuine entailments.

Of course the above is not the only possible framework for a dialetheic naïve set theory. One might, for example, hold that identity must be indeterminate as well as set membership. Priest, in fact, defines $x = y$ by $\forall z(x \in z \leftrightarrow y \in z)$. Equivalently, but perhaps more naturally, one could keep $=$ as primitive but narrow the class of admissible models to include only naïve models in which the interpretation of $=$ matches $\forall z(x \in z \leftrightarrow y \in z)$. It can then be shown that under this narrower account of admissibility, in no admissible model is identity standard ($r = r$ always has value B, where r is the Russell set of the model) and in all models $\exists x \exists y\, x \neq y$ is designated, as is infinity. (See Restall 1992.)

Even if it is acceptable to admit models in which identity can be 'glutty', we need a principled non-ad-hoc justification for excluding models in which identity is standard. How can it be wrong to interpret $x = y$ as true (only) when both terms refer to the same object and false (only) when they do not, especially since, in the models in question, it is definitely true in the metatheory that the referents are the same or definitely true that they are distinct? It will be highly unsatisfactory if the sole reason is to ensure that the proposition that there are at least two objects is entailed. After all, if I restrict admissible models to infinite ones then I can show that on my logic anything, $\exists x\, x = x$, for example, 'entails' infinity.

Moreover the glutty semantics for identity has unattractive consequences. For instance Leibniz's law:

$$\varphi[t/x], x = y \vdash \varphi[t/y]$$

fails, on this reading of identity.[12] Consider $\varphi x = x \in z$ and let σ assign α to x and distinct β to y; let $x \in z$ take value B for all z-variants of σ and $y \in z$ take value F when γ is assigned to z; without loss of generality, let σ in fact assign γ to z. Then $\forall z(x \in z \leftrightarrow y \in z)$ takes value B relative to σ, since $x \in z$ takes value B on all

---

[11] Note that our infinity axiom still expresses a form of infinity at least in the sense that $\emptyset \neq \{x\}$ is always designated and likewise $x \neq \{x\}$ too. The unit set operation still represents (at least in so far as being 'both true and false' represents) an operation which starts from an initial element and yields a unique, distinct successor in each case.

[12] As noted by Restall (1992: 429) who acknowledges the imperfections of naïve set theory in LP as it stands.

z-variants. By the construction of the interpretation of $\in$ for 'row' $\alpha, x \in z$ takes the designated value B, yet $y \in z$ takes value F on assignment σ. We have designated premises but an undesignated conclusion. If one finds Leibniz's law in the above simple format fairly compelling, this tells against the glutty semantics. But it is not necessary to rule this semantics out to block the derivability of $\exists x \exists y (x \neq y)$ from naïve set theory and Z, one needs only to refuse to exclude models with the standard interpretation of identity.

To be sure variations on the treatment of identity are not the only ones that can be played on dialetheic semantics. The conditional is another key player in this game and many dialetheic and paraconsistent systems work not with the material conditional $P \rightarrow Q$ defined by $\sim P \vee Q$ and for which modus ponens (i.e. disjunctive syllogism) is not sound (in LP and similar logics) but rather with intensional, relevant conditionals. However the prospects for deriving substantial mathematical results from naïve set theory, with the conditionals in the axioms interpreted in this way, also seem bleak (see Priest forthcoming). Overall, then, the programme of developing a reasonable amount of mathematics from naïve set theory together with dialetheic logic seems to be degenerating, at least as evaluated from the perspective of classical logic and set theory. A 'dialetheic recapture' seems unlikely.

It will not do to say, in reply to all this, that the models which provide the counterexample to the entailment of simple mathematical facts from basic axiom systems such as Z are 'pathological' or 'unintended'. All the dialetheist's ZFC models are unintended in the sense that they do not capture anything like the full structure of the naïve universe of sets. This compares unfavourably even with unintended models of first-order number theory: they at least contain the 'real' structure of numbers.

It is true that the dialetheic models of Brady (1989), Restall (1992), and Priest (forthcoming) are much more interesting mathematically than the quantifier-switching semantics for naïve set theory and include much richer models than the degenerate one-element case. For example, there are models of naïve set theory that consist in a segment S of the standard cumulative hierarchy, up to some inaccessible θ plus a 'glutty' set α such that, with a designating $\alpha, x \in a$ takes value B for all assignments to x and $a \in x$ takes value F for all assignments of members of S to x. This classical simulacrum of the naïve universe pictures it as containing the ZF hierarchy as a substructure and of course in this model, even with identity interpreted standardly, it is true that there are at least two individuals, indeed infinity is true in such models.[13] But the existence of some naïve extensions of ZF models in which infinity holds no more proves that ZF dialetheically entails

---

[13] By the extensionality of ZF all the rows in the $\in$ matrix restricted to S are distinct and moreover all are distinct from α's row since they are classical except under the column for α and each contain some Ts whereas the α row is all Fs except under the α column. Hence with identity interpreted

a theorem of infinity than the existence of a model of ZFU (ZF plus urelements) in which Scotland win the World Cup shows that ZFU entails that Scotland will win the World Cup, gratifying though such an entailment would be.

Still the expansions of standard models of ZF to dialetheic ones might seem to justify the following response: there is no problem for the dialetheist in deriving the existence of n things, for any finite n, from ZF: just use classical logic and the classical derivation. Classical semantics can be seen as a special case of dialetheic semantics (the special case in which all sentences take values T or F) and classical logic can then be adjudged legitimate when reasoning from consistent theories such as, we presume, ZF. Compare how the intuitionist accepts classical principles, such as excluded middle and double negation elimination, in restricted domains in which all sentences are decidable.

I think this counter-response is based on a mistaken view of the matter. Certainly the goal of validating classical principles in restricted cases is a legitimate and attractive one for non-classical logicians seeking after classical recapture. In my view, such a recapture, however, ought to respect the universality of logic, the idea that there is no difference in the logic one ought to use in different domains, not one logic for mathematics, another for moral reasoning for instance. We certainly need non-ad-hoc restrictions: it would not do to say *reductio ad absurdum* is licit when applied to assumptions I do not accept but not to ones I do accept. That being said, there is no reason to think there could not be principled, non-ad-hoc, general restrictions, on the structural rules of the logic for instance, which have the effect of rendering classical logic and the favoured non-classical logic equipollent in a particular domain, restrictions that appeal to general properties that happen to be satisfied in that particular domain. Such global restrictions on proof are, after all, present in many formulations of classical logic itself, e.g. in natural deduction quantifier rules such as $\forall$I and $\exists$E.

However a dialetheist theory of classical recapture is a theory of how chunks of classical reasoning can be recaptured in a dialetheic framework. It is entirely irrelevant what the extent of the converse 'dialetheic recapture' is, that is to say how much of dialetheic reasoning can be recaptured classically. We have seen that the prospects for dialetheic recapture are not good but this leaves it open that there can be genuine classical recapture. That is, using naïve set theory as the background semantics rather than ZF (an incorrect theory, according to dialetheists) and using the paraconsistent logic that the dialetheist favours in place of classical logic that the dialetheist rejects, the dialetheist might be able to show that the general principles of logic yield, in a subset of cases, a derivability or entailment relation that matches the classical.

standardly, extensionality is designated. Priest's model is a variant of Restall's (1992: 430–1) but validates extensionality more simply than Restall's.

Why not lay down as a global restriction that when reasoning about 'classical structures', classical logic is licit? The dialetheist may believe as firmly as the classicist that such reasoning is consistent.[14] The obvious way to implement this idea formally is to license classical reasoning when applied to a sub-language in which all sentences take only classical values in all admissible models. For in such a case, LP valuations and classical ones coincide. Perhaps we can give a syntactic sufficiency condition for such classical collapse, e.g. we might suppose that the sub-language in which all quantifiers are restricted to some level of the cumulative hierarchy is classical, each sentence taking only standard non-glutty values. However it is very important to bear in mind, when considering classical recapture, that the classical hierarchy does not exist in the naïve universe. True, there are sets whose formal definition looks identical to the classical one. By naïve comprehension, there is a naïve surrogate ω^N of classical ω^C,[15] defined in terms of the naïve unit set relation and the naïve empty set, $\emptyset^N$. Again, the definition of the latter looks standard. It might be:

$$\emptyset = \iota x(\forall y\, y \notin x)$$

syntactically identical to a classical definition. In the context of the naïve theory, however, $\emptyset$ is defined in terms of the naïve membership relation satisfying naïve comprehension, not the classical one. Thus there is a question whether the naïve surrogates of the classical hierarchy, the entities the dialetheist claims we can reason classically about, even exist.

To see this, imagine that an intuitionist number theorist adds a naïve theory of sets then says, innocent of Russell's paradox, that classical reasoning is legitimate but only with respect to sentences restricted to finite sets. Or a similar claim by someone working with the relevant logic R as her background logic for naïve set theory before Curry came along to show us all that this is trivial. In this pre-Curry theory we can make statements restricted to small sets; our theorist might, for example, consider the sub-language with all quantifiers restricted to ω and plan to use classical logic for inferences among sentences so restricted. If, for any set-theoretic sentence A, A^ω represents such a restriction, what she needs to show is

$$\text{NST} \vdash_R A^\omega \text{ iff ZF} \vdash_C A^\omega$$

where $\vdash_R$ represents derivability in R, $\vdash_C$ is derivability in classical logic, NST is naïve set theory and ZF is, well, ZF. Ideally she should wish to show this using R and NST in the metatheory and show this non-trivially, that is with no reason to believe that the negation of the above biconditional is also provable.

---

[14] Though see Priest (1994).

[15] Using superscripts to indicate metatheoretic terms referring to the elements in the domains of the different semantics, naïve and classical, whereas unsuperscripted 'ω', and so forth, refers to the syntactic terms in the given object language.

What if, *per impossibile*, the above result were demonstrable informally in a classical background theory, i.e. our theorist achieved R-recapture, not classical recapture? Such a result is not totally without value. After all, ZF and classical logic is where we all came from, man: unless we were brought up in a commune and learnt at the knee of radical paraconsistent logicians! We most of us have great confidence in the classical consistency of ZF. So a classical proof of, for example,

$$\text{NST} \vdash_D A^\omega \text{ iff ZF} \vdash_C A^\omega$$

where D is the favoured dialetheic logic, would help boost confidence that the dialetheic theory is non-trivial and that classical reasoning in certain restricted cases is acceptable dialetheically.

But the result would still be far from ideal. Anyway, we know the result for R is not provable classically and the dialetheist must hope it is not provable dialetheically either. This example shows that we cannot conclude from the fact that all the sentences of a given theory, the theory of the natural numbers construed in ZF set theory say, take the value true (only) according to standard theory (i.e. are true in all models of the standard theory) that the same holds in naïve set theory. That is to say, we cannot conclude that those same sentences all take the value true (only) when the membership relation occurring in the sentences is governed axiomatically by naïve set theory, not ZF, and naïve set theory subject in turn to some given non-classical logic. If naïve set theory is trivial in the given logic, as is the case with R, then there are no models of naïve set theory, a fortiori no models that assign true to all the sentences of our theory. We have $\text{NST} \vdash_D A^\omega$ for arbitrary A, including many for which $\text{ZF} \vdash_C A^\omega$ fails. If the theory is not trivial, it may be that many sentences of our favoured theory come out false in some models of the naïve theory and the biconditional above fails in the opposite direction: we have $\text{ZF} \vdash_C A^\omega$ but not $\text{NST} \vdash_D A^\omega$.

All this from the perspective of dialetheic recapture, of course, i.e. as viewed from the vantage point of a classical metatheory. But we have been given no reason to suppose the biconditional can be proven dialetheically (and without a trivializing proof of the negation which all non-dialetheists, at least, would rate as a very Bad contradiction). Moreover, in order to generate enough mathematics for science, the dialetheist needs to recapture more than just number theory.

Could the dialetheist simply pass on attempting to show

$$\text{NST} \vdash_D A^\omega \text{ iff ZF} \vdash_C A^\omega$$

and simply accept the right-hand side? That is, can the dialetheist simply accept ZF as a description of a coherent, determinate structure and reason classically from it? This would involve adopting a highly disjunctive account of derivability, reading it dialetheically from some sets of sentences, and classically from others. But the end result would not, then, be a dialetheic recapture of classical mathematics but a dialetheic capitulation to the classical picture. After all, from the dialetheic perspective, ZF is a false theory (it denies the existence of the universal set and Russell set, for example). Unless the dialetheist adopts a metaphysical picture of a plurality of incommensurable mathematical universes, one naïve, another ZF-ish, with rival logics appropriate for different domains, she has the burden of showing that classical reasoning is dialetheically sound when applied to a sub-category of naïve sets, those that correspond in a certain obvious sense to a segment of the standard cumulative hierarchy. In order to have some reasonable grounds (albeit such grounds, for dialetheists and non-dialetheists alike will always fall short of certainty) for thinking that classical reasoning is safe for the sub-language restricted to naïve sets that correspond to those in ranks of the ZF hierarchy, we need a general soundness proof for the dialetheic system in general. As we have seen, if the whole theory is trivial there are no naïve surrogates of the classical sets. We need a justification on the basis of the theory we accept as true, here naïve set theory, and the logic we accept as sound and ideally want this theory and logic to generate classical recapture, that is, the above biconditionals.

Of course soundness proofs themselves cannot produce certainty, since an unsound system may be able to prove its own soundness, indeed if it is trivial then it is bound to be able to do so. None the less, for a theory to be able to prove its own soundness without there being a known proof also of unsoundness is no mean feat. No classical theory can do this: this is the gist of the Tarskian results on failure of semantic closure. Any such genuinely bootstrapping proof provides a good test of the internal stability of the theory. To prove the soundness of the theory from the background of a *stronger* theory as the classicist does is, by contrast, not a very significant result.

A good comparison here is with naturalized epistemology. Whether or not this can supplant traditional epistemology, it is a good sign of the internal coherence of a total theory of the world if we can explain, from within that theory, how we could reasonably come to believe it. Contrast this with someone who (analogously to classical soundness results) attempts to establish the reliability of perception, for example, by appeal to a 'super-naturalized epistemology' in which one posits a mysterious interaction between brain activity and Cartesian souls mediated by an intermediary link L. If such an epistemologist 'explained' how the link L worked by postulating a link L^{-1} between brain and L and a link L^1 between L and the soul, 'explained' these connections in turn by positing a link L^{-2} between brain and L^{-1} and so forth, no one would think this explanatory regress was virtuously circular. I suggest that proving the soundness of a theory θ by resort to a stronger theory θ^* which one can only show to be sound by appeal to a yet stronger theory θ^{**}, and so on and so on, is as epistemologically empty as the supernaturalized epistemologists explanation of how perception gives us knowledge of the world.

Thus the goal for any proponent of naïve set theory should be to prove the soundness of the system from within the system.[16] If we cannot trust naïve set theory and the logic we use in conjunction with it, why take it seriously? If we have a radical distinction between object language and theory (naïve set theory plus LP) and meta-language and meta-theory (ZF with classical logic) we might as well just stick with the classical picture with its hierarchies and ghostly meta-languages. To have to resort to a meta-language or to a meta-theory that is different from the object theory and language is to acquire all the vices of the classicist without the corresponding virtues of simplicity, familiarity, and utility for current science.

6. SEMANTICS, BELIEF, AND ACCEPTANCE

6.1 Four Assumptions

Perhaps, though, the dialetheist will be able to advance the programme of classical recapture by one of the routes suggested in the previous section or else by working in a more suitable logic than LP.[17] Perhaps the asymmetry between truth and falsity in dialetheism is a bullet that can be bitten without poisoning oneself. I finish, though, with a final difficulty, which I believe is fatal to dialetheism.

Mounting a fatal objection to a substantive and well-defended position cannot be done with making some strong assumptions. Here are what I believe to be the key ones I need for my argument:

1. *In general, belief is involuntary.* This seems plausible, certainly for empirical beliefs. One cannot decide to believe it is sunny and straightaway one will believe this, regardless of such matters as one's current perceptions.

2. *Disbelief is as basic and primitive a notion as belief.* This is more controversial, but making this assumption enables us to give a natural and explanatory account of negation, as I shall argue below.

3. *There is a voluntary attitude closely related to belief.* I will call this attitude 'acceptance'. What I mean by this is perhaps best illustrated, in the limited compass of this chapter, by examples. The defence lawyer believes (though she has no conclusive evidence to this effect) that her client, despite her protestations of innocence, is guilty. None the less she chooses to advocate very strongly in court her client's innocence, attempts to undermine claims to the contrary put forward by the

---

[16] For an attempt to embark on that programme, see Weir (1998*b*, 1999).

[17] Priest (1991) has given consideration to non-monotonic variants of LP. I have misgivings about the very coherence of the notion of a non-monotonic logic, however. If X entails A then in any possible situation in which X is true, A is; but in non-monotonic calculi, $X \models A$ could hold yet A fail to hold in a situation in which X is true together with some other stuff Y. This debars such calculi from being considered as genuine logics, in my view.

prosecution, and so on. The scientist does not believe the fundamental physical theory she has just published in a science journal. Not because she believes an alternative theory but because, unlike most scientists, she has read a little philosophy and has become convinced of the 'pessimistic meta-induction': probably all far-reaching scientific theories humans produce will in fact be false. None the less she defends her theory in print, attempts to rebut her critics, advocates spending large sums of money in testing it, and so forth.

In both those cases, people assert what they do not believe. But that is not the crux of the distinction between 'acceptance' in my sense, and belief, for there can be many reasons for asserting what one does not believe: deception for example. What is happening in the above cases is that the person, though not attempting to deceive anyone, is voluntarily behaving pretty much as you would expect someone to behave who did believe in the client's innocence, or the truth of the theory, at least in those particular contexts, that is of the courtroom or of academic debate, respectively. So a more general account of 'acceptance' should define it relative to a background context and in terms of exhibiting behaviour, verbal and non-verbal, that would be taken, in that limited context, as constitutive of belief. Or something along those lines. For present purposes, I will leave it at this and hope that the basic distinction is fairly obvious and plausible.[18]

I would similarly distinguish between disbelieving a proposition and rejecting it—the lawyer rejects the prosecution claim that her client is guilty, though she does not disbelieve it, the scientist disbelieves her theory but does not reject it. Again the voluntary attitude of rejection is often (but not always) expressed by voluntary actions such as denying a proposition or dissenting from queries regarding it, just as acceptance is often expressed by asserting or assenting to. A third type of example, highly pertinent with respect to our current discussion, is that of a logician drawing conclusions from some overall premisses, or rejecting a premiss because she rejects a conclusion. In this restricted context, the context of the argument as a whole, the logician chooses to accept some premisses or reject some conclusion, independently of belief and disbelief.[19]

The importance of these distinctions lies in their relevance for a fourth and final assumption:

4. *Rationality requires voluntariness—ought implies can (or can and cannot).* This is perhaps the most contentious assumption of all. Graham Priest 1987: 240 ff.;

[18] For an extended treatment, see Cohen (1992). His work in this area has greatly influenced the present treatment, though I would not myself draw the distinction in exactly the same way as he does.

[19] Does making an assumption for later discharge, in a reductio rule for example, count as accepting? I think this is too temporary a phenomenon to be usefully classed as a manifestation of a voluntary attitude closely linked to belief. A better example is affirming and drawing conclusions from some axioms, an attitude one holds constant for the entire argument or discussion. The point of doing this might be to see what follows from, say, the axioms of ZFC, and a mathematician can do this even though she does not believe the axioms.

1993: 38 explicitly rejects (and, I believe, disbelieves) it. Talking of legal cases, he writes:

we can be put in a bind where we are obliged to do the impossible. . . . Maybe rational obligation can produce similar binds too; rationally, we are damned if we do and damned if we don't. λ then, should be both accepted and rejected. This is impossible. *C'est la vie.* (1993: 40–1)

Here λ is a Liar sentence. Or, when considering a version of Littman's Paradox he writes:

Consider the claim β: it is irrational to assert ⟨β⟩. Suppose that someone asserted ⟨β⟩. They would then be asserting something, and at the same time asserting that it is irrational to assert it. This is irrational. Hence asserting ⟨β⟩ is irrational. But this is just ⟨β⟩, and we have established it. Hence it *is* rational to assert ⟨β⟩. (1995: 61)

He later concludes:

That argument [the one immediately above] showed that it is both rational and irrational to assert ⟨β⟩. This is a problem for the gap theorist; but for a glut theorist it is just another contradiction. . . . It does raise a *practical* problem, of course: whether to assert β. One will be (rationally damned) if one does, and damned if one doesn't. Such, unfortunately, may be life. (ibid. 62)[20]

Thus Priest thinks that all we have here are more true contradictions; these can pose a practical problem, one best met by rejecting 'ought implies can'. Here Priest is assuming one cannot both accept and reject a proposition even though one might, in some cases, be rationally obliged to.

Now in the legal case there can certainly be instances of what it is natural to call obligations that one cannot keep. One can have debts one cannot meet because, let us say, one has fallen on hard times through no fault of one's own. Perhaps one has lost one's job; perhaps, to pile misery on misery, the companies one saved and insured with have gone bust and so on. But these legal obligations generate no prescriptions that one cannot keep. In such a case one ought to pay back the debt *when one is able,* but it is not the case that e.g. one ought to starve one's children in order to pay back the debt. What not being able to meet the obligation amounts to, in this sort of case, is that one cannot make true certain clauses in the promise which grounds the debt; but this simply generates a different prescription from that which obtains if one is able to pay back the debt. To go down the road of prescribing actions one cannot perform, thereby cutting the link between norms and voluntariness, is to risk blurring the distinction between culpable actions— voluntarily choosing to kill say—and blameless ones which unintentionally form part of a harmful causal chain—unwittingly triggering a sensor that detonates a bomb, for example.

---

[20] See also his (1998: 426 n. 19).

Moreover the idea that one can have obligations that are incapable of fulfilment is liable to lead to a downplaying of the seriousness of obligations in general. Compare how those who think pacifism is morally obligatory but an unliveable, impractical doctrine tend to disregard moral constraints on the application of war: 'all war is wrong but we are going to engage in it anyway so no big deal if we target non-combatants'. Such 'pacifist warmongers' provide, I think, real-life examples of people with contradictory beliefs. Nor are the contradictions gratuitously arrived at. War is horrendous; but for all but fairly extreme deontologists, it is conceivable that in some cases war can be so much the lesser evil that it is permissible or even obligatory to engage in it. It is even possible that a short ferocious war can be a lesser evil than a longer but much less ferocious one and that this can licence unleashing the ferocity. Thus one can see how someone might hold that all war is impermissible but also permissible and then go on to hold that one will be damned if one does carpet bomb or nuke civilians but also damned (because, it might argued, one lengthens the war) if one does not. From Priest's perspective, it seems there may well be nothing further to say on the matter, no further role for reason to play in deciding whether deliberately targeting civilians is permissible; for what we seem to have here is a contradiction which has intuitive plausibility. Perhaps the dialetheist just tosses a coin to decide what to do in such cases. If one finds this unpalatable, one has strong reasons for holding to a voluntariness condition on rationality, for holding that ought does indeed imply can. For then one knows one may be damned for taking one course, but not the other, hence there is motive to think further on the matter.

6.2 Rational Inference

How do these assumptions make trouble for dialetheism? To see how, we need to return to the semantic point made in the initial, overly quick, response to dialetheism: that espousal of true contradictions involves a trivial adherence to a deviant understanding of conjunction or negation.

Now the fact that we can construct truth tables and models validating classical logic or validating dialetheic logics is not very interesting in itself. We need to know what relevance they have to our actual understanding of conjunction and negation. An obvious place to look here is the Quinean matrices. Quine holds, with a great deal of plausibility, that to understand conjunction one must believe a conjunction iff one believes both conjuncts, disbelieve it, if one disbelieves a conjunct. Similarly, Quine says, one should believe $\sim p$ iff one disbelieves p, disbelieve $\sim p$ iff one believes p. (Here is where a primitive notion of disbelief can help explain the nature of negation.) Hence a dialetheist who believes p & $\sim p$ must, on pain of betraying a misunderstanding of a logical operator, believe p and believe $\sim p$. But the latter, Quine has shown us, requires disbelieving p so the dialetheist would have us both believing and disbelieving p.

Exactly so, says Priest: he believes and disbelieves, he claims, the Liar (and in the same breath, as it were: he can both occurrently believe and occurrently disbelieve it). So that move does not get us very far. None the less there is, I believe, a deeper point in the offing here, one that emerges when one switches from belief and disbelief, attitudes which are rarely under our voluntary control, to the related voluntary attitudes that I am calling 'accepting' and 'rejecting' and which are under our control; better still, we need to attend to the interplay between the voluntary and involuntary attitudes in inference.

For one area where rational norms surely apply is that of reasoning and inference. If there is a voluntariness constraint on rationality, then some aspects of reasoning and inferring must themselves be voluntary (though not necessarily reflectively self-conscious), for instance that of adhering to a given inference rule (or not, as the case may be). First of all, of course, we must settle the question of what is an inference rule. I will be brief and dogmatic here. Inference rules I will take to be schemata with the form:

$$\frac{\varphi_1(p_{\langle 1,1\rangle},\dots p_{\langle 1,f(1)\rangle}),\dots \varphi_n(p_{\langle n,1\rangle},\dots p_{\langle n,f(n)\rangle})}{\Psi_1(q_{\langle 1,1\rangle},\dots q_{\langle 1,g(1)\rangle}),\dots \Psi_m(q_{\langle m,1\rangle},\dots q_{\langle m,g(m)\rangle})}$$

Here the φ_i are the premisses the ψ_j the conclusions and $p_{\langle k,l\rangle}$ is the lth schematic variable of the kth premiss, $q_{\langle k,l\rangle}$ the lth variable of the kth conclusion. These schematic variables are what we substitute for to get instances of the rule schema and may be of any category, though for our purposes here we will consider only propositional variables.

Now consider the simplest class of rules, the 'singular' rules with one premiss and one conclusion, a rule such as &E for example. I propose that one adheres to such a rule if, for every comprehensible instance of the rule, one accepts the conclusion whenever one accepts the premiss and one rejects the premiss whenever one rejects the conclusion. Note the dual emphasis on 'upwards' rejection as well as downwards acceptance. In s. 4 I argued that the dual direction from conclusion to premiss is equally as fundamental to our account of inference (particularly, of course, with regard to such notions as refutation) as the direction from premiss to conclusion.

Granted that, in the context of someone presenting an argument, acceptance is manifested by asserting or assenting to a proposition, rejection by dissenting from or denying it, then the above account will come to this, taking &E as example. If one asserts or assents to a (comprehensible) proposition of the form P&Q and one is prompted on P (or Q) then one will assent to the conjunct. And if one denies or dissents from P (or Q) one will dissent from P&Q, if prompted.

What next of non-singular rules, multiple conclusion rules, or multiple premiss rules such as &I? A first suggestion, bearing in mind this standard classical account of entailment for multiple conclusion systems:

> X $\models_1$ Y iff there is no valuation in which all wffs in X are true and all in Y false

would be that one adheres to a rule iff one never accepts all the premises (of a comprehensible instance) and rejects all the conclusions. But applied to the special case of singular rules this yields the criterion that one adheres to the rule iff one never accepts the premiss and rejects the conclusion. This, however, would allow one to accept the premiss but fail to accept the conclusion so long as one never rejected it or dually reject a conclusion but not a premiss. Suppose, for example, one's attitude to the Liar sentence λ: ∼True⟨λ⟩ is, pace the dialetheist, studied agnosticism. Then on this account one will adopt the inference A ⊢ ∼True⟨λ⟩ and ∼True⟨λ⟩ ⊢ B, for any A, B so that simple transitivity of inference will commit one to triviality. Since it would be very ad hoc to have one criterion for non-singular rules and a different one for singular rules one might then turn to the other standard definition of multiple conclusion entailment (equivalent in classical semantics but not equivalent more generally):

> X $\models_2$ Y iff in every valuation in which all wffs in X are true, one in Y is true

The corresponding criterion here would then be that one adheres to an inference rule only if whenever one accepts all the premises one accepts at least one conclusion. But this means we would never adhere to multiple conclusion ∨E:

$$\frac{A \vee B}{A \quad B}$$

since one may easily accept that the baby will be a boy or a girl but not accept either disjunct (as yet). Moreover, holding to the view that the direction from conclusions to premises is equally important, we should add to the above criterion its dual: one adheres to an inference rule only if whenever one rejects all the conclusions one rejects at least one premiss. But then we do not adhere to &I since one might well reject the conclusion that the baby will be a boy and a girl without rejecting either of the premises, these being both conjuncts.

What criterion, then, can we put in place of these two? I suggest that it is prima facie irrational to reject, to take &I for an example, P & Q, accept P but fail to reject Q. This leads to the following definition: one adheres to inference rule *R* just when, for any comprehensible instance:

> For any conclusion C and premiss P, (a) if one accepts all the premises of *R* and rejects all conclusions but C, one accepts C and (b) if one rejects all conclusions and accepts all premises but P, one rejects P.

If we now apply the above criterion to the standard conjunction rules of &I and &E:

$$\frac{A \,\&\, B}{A} \qquad \frac{A \,\&\, B}{B} \qquad \frac{A \qquad B}{A \,\&\, B}$$

we arrive at the following theory $T_\&$ of what it is to adhere to the conjunction rules. Here '$\rightarrow$' represents the conditional in claims of the form 'if one rejects P&Q then if one accepts P, one rejects Q', though of course there is much dispute about the principles that $\rightarrow$ must satisfy. In the following, the code of a sentence is represented by bracketing, As represents accepting sentence s, similarly Rs represents rejecting it with Is defined by $\sim$As & $\sim$Rs.

$T_\&$:

    (i) $(A\langle P\rangle \,\&\, A\langle Q\rangle) \rightarrow A\langle P \,\&\, Q\rangle$

    (ii) $R\langle P \,\&\, Q\rangle \rightarrow (A\langle P\rangle \rightarrow R\langle Q\rangle)$

    (iii) $R\langle P \,\&\, Q\rangle \rightarrow (A\langle Q\rangle \rightarrow R\langle P\rangle)$

    (all from &I)

    (iv) $A\langle P \,\&\, Q\rangle \rightarrow A\langle P\rangle$

    (v) $A\langle P \,\&\, Q\rangle \rightarrow A\langle Q\rangle$

    (vi) $R\langle P\rangle \rightarrow R\langle P \,\&\, Q\rangle$

    (vii) $R\langle Q\rangle \rightarrow R\langle P \,\&\, Q\rangle$

(all from &E)

This formulation, of course, is a schematic version of $T_\&$. The non-schematic version will take the form of a universal generalization $\forall s \forall t \varphi$ with s and t ranging over sentences, and where φ is a conjunction of the above seven theses with s and t in place of the schematic variables.

Fairly uncontentious logical principles give us, from (i) to (vii)

(a) $A\langle P \,\&\, Q\rangle \leftrightarrow (A\langle P\rangle \,\&\, A\langle Q\rangle)$

and

(b) $(A\langle P\rangle \rightarrow (I\langle Q\rangle \rightarrow I\langle P \,\&\, Q\rangle)) \,\&\, (A\langle Q\rangle \rightarrow (I\langle P\rangle \rightarrow I\langle P \,\&\, Q\rangle))$

We can summarize $T_\&$ as in Fig. 22.3 (though of course this is only a picture; the picture is to be interpreted by the substantive theory given by the seven theses above plus an interpretation of $\rightarrow$).

Here I add the dual diagram for disjunction which encapsulates pictorially the corresponding dual theory $T_\vee$ generated from the multiple conclusion introduction and elimination $\vee$ rules:

$$\frac{A}{A \vee B} \qquad \frac{B}{A \vee B} \qquad \frac{A \vee B}{A \qquad B}$$

The I entries in the conjunction matrix at points $[A\langle P\rangle, I\langle Q\rangle]$, and $[A\langle Q\rangle, I\langle P\rangle]$ are justified by (b) above whilst the exclusion of the accept response from $[I\langle P\rangle, I\langle Q\rangle]$ is justified by (a).

Alan Weir

P&Q	A	I	R
A	A	I	R
P I	I	I/R	R
R	R	R	R

Q

P∨Q	A	I	R
A	A	A	A
P I	A	A/I	R
R	A	I	R

Q

FIG. 22.3.

Are these acceptance and rejection patterns *meaning-constitutive* for the operator &? No, because if that were so then the rules could not be rationally compelling in a non-trivial fashion. Anyone failing to adhere to them would simply mean something non-standard by the ampersand or vel. What we need to do, if we are to explain the rationality of these basic logical rules, is find a separate level of practice with regard to &, one that can in some sense correct or provide an objective ground for the rationality of our voluntary inferential practice. We can do this, I suggest, by focusing on the interplay between acceptance and belief, rejecting and disbelief. Suppose, first, that in these diagrams we replace acceptance (A) with belief (B), rejection (R) with disbelief (D) and indecision (I) with Neither belief nor disbelief (N). The result is shown in Fig. 22.4, and these are just the Quinean verdict matrices for conjunction and disjunction.[21] As to the plausibility of the verdict matrices as an account of the meaning of the constants, all the non-agnostic nodes of the matrix certainly seem right: if one believes a conjunction one believes both conjuncts; if one disbelieves a conjunct one disbelieves the conjunction. Quine thinks the other nodes, particularly the middle N/D and B/N nodes, point to a certain indeterminacy in our notions of conjunction and disjunction, though it is arguable that these are exactly the responses one would expect if the operators were fully determinate but one distinguished, as Quine does not, between agnosticism due to epistemic uncertainty and agnosticism for other reasons—awareness that one is in the presence of a borderline case, for example.

At any rate the key point is this. By making the replacements B for A, D for R, and N for I one can turn $T_\&$ and $T_\lor$ into two semantic theories, $S_\&$ and $S_\lor$, these being two theories of what it is to understand conjunction and disjunction. One reason for thinking that the belief patterns ground meaning and understanding

---

[21] In Quine (1974: 76–8), Quine gives the above tables with ? rather than N/D or B/N as the middle value. However in the prose he allows dissent or indecision in the conjunction table middle value, assent or indecision in the disjunction 'blind quarter'; the fact that he does not expressly allow assent in the first case, dissent in the second, seems to indicate he would agree with the above tables.

```
           Q                              Q

 P & Q │ B   N   D          P ∨ Q │ B   N   D
 ──────┼──────────          ──────┼──────────
     B │ B   N   D              B │ B   B   B

 P   N │ N  N/D  D          P   N │ B  B/N  N

     D │ D   D   D              D │ B   N   D
```

Fig. 22.4.

whereas the acceptance and rejection ones do not is that the meaning of expressions (partially) determines our linguistic behaviour in *all* contexts. By contrast, I have suggested that acceptance and rejection, in my sense, are relativized to and restricted to limited contexts; they are simulations of belief and disbelief, if one likes, as far as that particular context, defending one's client say, goes.[22] So the meaning of logical constants, if given by patterns of linguistic behaviour, must be given by belief/disbelief patterns rather than accept/reject patterns. Furthermore these two sets of patterns are independent of one another, with the possibility of a mismatch. And it is here, I suggest, that the objective grounds of correctness of an inference rule lie. Adhering to an inference rule sets up Accept/Indecision/Reject or **AIR** patterns among complex sentences and their components. My proposal is that a rule is correct just when the patterns it generates match the corresponding **Belief/Neither/Disbelief** or **BND** patterns that constitute grasp of logical constants.

More exactly, take the semantic theory S_O for some operator O specifying belief/disbelief patterns among complex sentences constructed by O and their components. Transform S_O into a theory T_O of accepting and rejecting by the replacement of B with A, D with R, N with I as above. Let R be some inference rule involving O that conforms to our schema for inference rules. From the criterion for adherence to R we will get a theory T_R that entails various conditionals telling us that if we accept P_1 & $\ldots P_n$ but reject $C_1 \ldots C_k$ then we must accept C_i and so on through all the permutations of possible conclusions (with similar clauses for the dual upwards rejection clause). If T_R is inconsistent with T_O (in the background logic we start from) then the inference rule R is incorrect and our belief[23] that its premises directly entail its conclusion is objectively wrong. The proposal then is

[22] But I do not intend ruling out the possibility of both accepting and believing the same proposition, likewise for disbelief and rejection.

[23] Arguably this special type of belief is a voluntary one; so here I depart from Bernard Williams (1973) who holds that all beliefs, not just beliefs representing the external world, for example, are involuntary.

that to be irrational is to be an *AIR*head, one whose AIR patterns do not mirror one's BND patterns.

Why should the BND patterns trump the AIR patterns? Note first that if, when the two patterns mismatch, one alters one's BND patterns to fit one's AIR patterns, there is no way we can construe that as correcting a mistaken belief, for we have seen that in altering one's BND patterns, one alters the meaning of the operator in question. It is a virtue of the above account, then, that it enables us to say when it is that two logicians, disagreeing on the inference rules they accept, are disagreeing substantively, that is with respect to operators that they understand in the same way, namely when their BND patterns are the same though their AIR patterns differ. When their BND patterns differ, they are merely differing terminologically or talking at cross purposes.

But suppose we point out to someone the mismatch between their BND patterns and their AIR patterns and are able to get them to agree that this mismatch exists. They persist in the same belief/disbelief patterns and so do not change the subject but refuse to alter their AIR patterns. Why is this irrational, that is to say why should we think of the BND patterns as *correcting* the AIR patterns so that the entailment belief generated by the inferential behaviour is objectively false? The answer lies in the fact that accepting and rejecting function are part of the *indirect* means by which we control belief and disbelief: with Pascal, one can reasonably expect persistent and stable acceptance of a proposition (affirming and defending it regularly say) to increase significantly one's grade or degree of belief in it. But in the case envisaged, the accepting and rejecting actions cannot possibly achieve this function. In so far as persistence in the AIR patterns succeeds in bringing about a change in the BND patterns to match them, it will also bring about a change in the subject matter, in particular a change in the meaning of the operator or operators in question. It will thus be different propositions that end up being believed. Hence there is an asymmetry between the BND behaviour and the AIR behaviour, an asymmetry in which the former comes out as more fundamental: only changes of the latter behaviour to conform to the former can bring it about that accepting and rejecting can succeed in their function of indirectly controlling belief.

6.3 Negation

I turn now to the notion of negation, crucial in discussions of dialetheism. If one continues to think in terms of BND matrices then three simple forms of negation suggest themselves as underlying a negation BND matrix. 'X', in Fig. 22.5, represents withholding full belief and disbelief for non-epistemic reasons—the presence of a borderline case of a vague concept, for instance. Where N, as before, represents any type of absence of belief and disbelief, including epistemic uncertainty, then

P	~P
B	D
X	X
D	B

P	¬P
B	D
X	D
D	B

P	—P
B	D
X	B
D	B

FIG. 22.5.

P	~P
B	D
N	N
D	B

P	¬P
B	D
N	N/D
D	B

P	—P
B	D
N	N/B
D	B

FIG. 22.6.

the full BND matrices will agree with the above where no epistemic uncertainty is involved (e.g. when only full belief and disbelief are present). But there will also be some constraints on patterning where the general agnostic response N is involved. For looking at the matrices in Fig. 22.5, we can see that some values on a negation determine those for its component: the response D is only given to ~ and—sentences where the components are B; B, for ~ and ¬ sentences, only when the component is given value D. Hence one should not believe a ~ or ¬ sentence unless one disbelieves the component, similarly one should not disbelieve a ~ or— sentence unless one believes the component. This yields, as meaning-constituting matrices for the negations, those shown at Fig. 22.6. (Similar arguments show why the middle values in the & and ∨ tables take the form they do.)

There is not, I think, any very interesting question as to which, if any, of the above negations is the *real* one. The important point is that each of them seems a perfectly coherent operator that might feature in a reasonable language. But we need of course, not the diagrams, but a full semantic theory for the operators.

For $\sim$, the obvious theory is the Quinean $S_\sim$:

(a) $B\langle P \rangle \leftrightarrow D\langle \sim P \rangle$

(b) $N\langle P \rangle \leftrightarrow N\langle \sim P \rangle$

(c) $B\langle \sim P \rangle \leftrightarrow D\langle P \rangle$

corresponding to rows one, two, and three of the matrix respectively. And this BND theory has its AIR mirror $T_\sim$:

(i) $A\langle P \rangle \leftrightarrow R\langle \sim P \rangle$

(ii) $I\langle P \rangle \leftrightarrow I\langle \sim P \rangle$

(iii) $A\langle \sim P \rangle \leftrightarrow R\langle P \rangle$

As before, I claim one lapses into irrationality if one does not match one's BND matrices with one's AIR matrices. But now the dialetheist judges that $p \,\&\, \sim p$, for some p. By the BND matrices, as we have seen, they must both judge that p, that is, have an occurrent belief that p, yet also judge that $\sim p$, that is, disbelieve it. If the dialetheist also accepts $p \,\&\, \sim p$ (p may be a Liar sentence, for instance) then, matching accepting and rejecting to believing and disbelieving, they must therefore simultaneously accept and reject p. But this is impossible, a Bad contradiction. The claim that someone can simultaneously reject and accept the same sentence (with the context fixed) is an absurdity on a par with 'Graham Priest is a fried egg.'

At the time of *In Contradiction*, Priest seems to agree:

Acceptance and rejection are not exhaustive, but they are exclusive. ... One can certainly believe something and believe its negation. One might even argue that one can believe something and not believe it, though this is much more dubious. But it seems difficult to argue that one might both believe something and *refuse* to believe it. Characteristically, the behaviour patterns that go with doing X and refusing to do X cannot be displayed simultaneously.   (Priest 1987: 122–3)[24]

But then he is bound to violate the AIR matrix for $\sim$.[25] Accepting the Liar contradiction $T\langle \lambda \rangle \,\&\, \sim T\langle \lambda \rangle$, he accepts $\sim T\langle \lambda \rangle$ but does not thereby reject $T\langle \lambda \rangle$ since he accepts $T\langle \lambda \rangle$ and it is impossible both to accept and to reject the same proposition.

Priest does argue (ibid. 123) that the AIR patterns are widely violated, in particular that one can reject something without accepting its negation; but his examples seem to me to be poor. A statistician, he says, may reject a statistical hypothesis yet its negation will not normally be a statistical hypothesis. Priest appears to conclude from this, unfathomably to me, that he will therefore not accept the

---

[24] Note also that if simultaneous acceptance and rejection were possible then the Principle R much favoured by dialetheists as a way of capturing something of the power of disjunctive syllogism—R is the principle that if one accepts $p \lor q$ but rejects q then one accepts p—would have to go. For if one accepts and rejects q then (given $\lor$I) one is forced to accept every p.

[25] And indeed the matrices for $\neg$ and—, since they agree with that for $\sim$ on clauses (i) and (iii) of the negation AIR theory, the only clauses that are relevant in the present context.

negation.[26] His other example is that of an intuitionist who, he says, rejects an instance of $p \lor \sim p$ though not accepting $\sim(p \lor \sim p)$. This seems to me to misconstrue intuitionists. They normally reject the general law $\forall p(p \lor \sim p)$ but thereby accept $\sim\forall p(p \lor \sim p)$ as this does not intuitionistically entail $\exists p \sim(p \lor \sim p)$. Where, however, a particular sentence p is currently undecided, intuitionists do not reject the relevant instance $p \lor \sim p$ of the law precisely because that would require them to accept $\sim(p \lor \sim p)$ which intuitionistically leads straight to $(\sim p \,\&\, \sim\sim p)$; in such a case the intuitionists are agnostic on the instance of excluded middle.

Of course there may only be a terminological dispute between myself and Priest here regarding the meanings of 'accept' and 'reject'. My substantive point is that contradictions are unacceptable on my rendering of 'accept' and that this notion and the companion notion of rejection are the ones that connect with normative criteria governing rational inference practices. If the account of logical rationality sketched above is right, this poses a dilemma for the dialetheist. On the one hand, if her actual AIR patternings match her BND patternings then she has a deviant understanding of $\sim$(or $\neg$ or—) and her belief in $p \,\&\, \sim p$ would not be belief in a genuine contradiction, in a conjunction of a sentence with its negation. On the other hand, if the AIR and BND patterns come apart, as seems to be the case, then she is guilty of irrational reasoning with respect to $\sim$(and a similar argument would apply if the AIR pattern for $\&$ is not conjunctive).

Alternatively the dialetheist can bite the bullet and accept that she accepts and rejects propositions such as the Liar; presumably this will lead to the dialetheist holding that among the true contradictions is the contradiction that she both accepts and does not accept (because she also rejects) the Liar. Here, I think, we have reached a point at which the debate between non-dialetheists and dialetheist can proceed no further, as this seems to me to be totally absurd, a Bad, Bad contradiction. Of course dialetheists can simply reject the contentious view of the nature of logical rationality, grasp of the connectives, and so forth that I have proffered, can reject, for example, one of the four basic assumptions with which I started or the argument that I based on them. But in that case, they owe us an alternative account of rationality, one that can also bring out its close links with voluntariness. We have a deep need to see a sharp distinction between behaviour in which someone is an unwitting part of a causal chain—the non-negligent individual who passes on a virus she is unaware of—and, on the other hand, voluntary choices—the malicious individual who infects a city's water supplies; if dialetheism cannot do justice to this distinction, so much the worse for dialetheism.

---

[26] Of course classical statisticians such as Fisher and Pearson have a technical notion of 'rejection' of a hypothesis, linked to rejection rules, that may well not conform very closely to the sense in which I am using the term.

7. CONCLUSION

Dialetheism poses a serious challenge to standard positions because it tries to undermine those positions from within, using the same rational canons as the conventional theorist (classical mathematical logician, for example) applied to paradoxes that the classical position has enormous difficulty in handling adequately. But the dialetheist position fails. It requires, at least as currently developed, an unmotivated, counterintuitive, and harmful asymmetry between the logical roles of truth and falsity. It is unable to secure the recapture of even very basic parts of standard mathematics. Finally, on one explanation of the nature of logical rationality, at least, dialetheic espousal of true contradictions leads to irrationality: to block this the dialetheist owes us an alternative account that does justice to the close links between rationality and free choice and action.

For these reasons, I disbelieve in dialetheism and reject the thesis that there are true contradictions. Dialetheists may agree but not concede because they claim not only to believe and disbelieve the thesis that there are no true contradictions but also to accept as well as reject it. If so, they have chosen to embrace what, for non-dialetheists, is a Very Bad contradiction. At this point, then, fruitful dialogue between dialetheist and non-dialetheist ceases. But I hope this chapter helps make clear that a lot of interesting debate is possible before that stage is reached.[27]

REFERENCES

BRADY, ROSS (1989): 'The Non-Triviality of Dialectical Set Theory', in G. Priest, R. Routley, and J. Norman (eds.), *Paraconsistent Logic: Essays on the Inconsistent* (Munich: Philosophia).

COHEN, L. J. (1992): *An Essay on Belief and Acceptance* (Oxford: Clarendon).

EDGINGTON, DOROTHY (1993): 'Wright and Sainsbury on Higher-Order Vagueness', *Analysis*, 53: 193–200.

PRIEST, GRAHAM (1979): 'The Logic of Paradox', *The Journal of Philosophical Logic*, 8: 219–41.

—— (1987): *In Contradiction* (Dordrecht: Nijhoff).

—— (1991): 'Minimally Inconsistent LP', *Studia Logica*, 50: 321–31.

—— (1993): 'Can Contradictions be True?', *Proceedings of the Aristotelian Society*, Suppl. vol. 67: 35–54.

—— (1994): 'Is Arithmetic Consistent?', *Mind*, 103: 337–49.

—— (1995): 'Gaps and Gluts: Reply to Parsons', *Canadian Journal of Philosophy*, 25: 57–66.

—— (1998): 'What's so Bad about Contradictions?', *The Journal of Philosophy*, 9: 410–26.

---

[27] My thanks to an audience at the University of Leeds, where an early version of this chapter was read, to the referee for Oxford University Press, and especially to the two other referees for extensive comments that have greatly aided me in preparing this chapter. Finally my greatest thanks are to Graham Priest for many extensive discussions as a result of which I hope I have been able to understand dialetheism better, even though unable to embrace it.

—— (forthcoming): 'Paraconsistent Set Theory and Metatheory', in A. Irving (ed.), *Essays in Set Theory* (Oxford: Blackwell.)

QUINE, W. V. (1974): *The Roots of Reference*, (La Salle: Open Court).

RESTALL, GREG (1992): 'A Note on Naïve Set Theory in LP', *Notre Dame Journal of Formal Logic*, 33: 422–32.

SHAPIRO, STEWART (2002): 'Incompleteness and Inconsistency', *Mind*, 111: 817–32.

WEIR, ALAN (1998a): 'Naïve Set Theory is Innocent!', *Mind*, 107: 763–98.

—— (1998b): 'Naïve Set Theory, Paraconsistency and Indeterminacy I', *Logique et Analyse*, 161–3: 219–66.

—— (1999): 'Naïve Set Theory, Paraconsistency and Indeterminacy II', *Logique et Analyse*, 167–8: 283–340.

WILLIAMS, BERNARD (1973): 'Deciding to Believe', in his *Problems of the Self* (Cambridge: Cambridge University Press), 136–51.

23

In Defense of the Law of Non-Contradiction

Edward N. Zalta

An important philosophical puzzle arises whenever we find a group of philosophically interesting sentences that individually appear to be true but jointly imply a contradiction. It is traditional to suppose that since the sentences in the group are jointly inconsistent, we cannot accept them all. This refusal to accept all the sentences in the group is not just grounded in (*a*) the problem of accepting the derivable contradiction, but also in (*b*) the problem that classical logic gives us the means to derive every sentence whatsoever once we have derived a contradiction. But with certain really hard puzzles of this kind, it is difficult to identify even one sentence in the puzzling group to reject. In such cases, there seems to be no good reason or argument for rejecting one of the sentences rather than another. We often find ourselves in the uncomfortable position of having to reject statements that have a strong claim to truth.

Paraconsistent logic and dialetheism constitute a fascinating body of doctrines for critically analyzing this kind of philosophical puzzle. Paraconsistent logic removes problem (*b*), noted above, concerning the presence of contradictions in classical logic. In contrast to classical logic, paraconsistent logic tolerates the derivation of a contradiction without thereby yielding a proof of every sentence. Dialetheism goes one step further, however, and addresses problem (*a*). It is the doctrine that, in some of these really hard cases, there are indeed true contradictions. Dialetheists argue that some sentences are both true *and* false, and that sometimes appearances are not deceiving—there just are special groups of true yet jointly incompatible sentences for which the contradiction they imply is both true and false. We shall suppose, for the purposes of this chapter, that the law of non-contradiction (LNC) is the claim that there are no true contradictions. Thus, dialetheism is the view that the LNC is false. While there are plenty of philosophers who accept, and work within, paraconsistent logic, only a few count themselves as dialetheists.

I take paraconsistent logic and dialetheism seriously, and think that they offer a philosophically worthy approach to these puzzling groups of sentences. The logical investigation of paraconsistent logic is certainly interesting and justified.

I am indebted to Colin Allen, JC Beall, Otávio Bueno, Mark Colyvan, Branden Fitelson, Fred Kroon, and Graham Priest for valuable discussions about the subject matter of this chapter. I also thank the editors for inviting me to contribute to this volume.

We should endeavor to know what are the meta-theoretical features of this logic. Dialetheism also deserves careful study. Truth value gluts may be no worse than truth value gaps,[1] and it is always good to investigate whether, or why, philosophers just take it on faith that no contradictions are true.

But I am not yet convinced that the *arguments* of the dialetheists for rejecting the LNC are conclusive. The arguments that dialetheists have developed against the traditional LNC uniformly fail to consider the logic of encoding. This extension of classical logic, developed in Zalta (1983, 1988) and elsewhere, offers us an analytic tool which, among other things, can resolve apparent contradictions.[2] In this chapter, I shall illustrate this claim by considering many of the apparent contradictions discussed in Priest (1995, 1987). In (1995), Priest examines certain interesting cases in the history of philosophy from the point of view of someone without a prejudice in favor of classical logic. He suggests that each case constitutes an example where there is no other good analysis except that offered by dialetheism. However, in each of these cases, the logic of encoding offers an alternative explanation of the phenomena being discussed while preserving the LNC. But Priest fails to consider this explanation when he describes what options there are in classical logic for analyzing the problem at hand. In what follows, I'll reanalyze these examples from the history of philosophy and then move to the examples that form the heart of the case that Priest develops against the LNC, namely, those embodied by his 'inclosure schema'.

I don't plan to undertake a systematic examination of all the arguments produced against the LNC. Nor do I plan to consider Priest's excellent (1998) piece in which he undermines arguments attempting to establish why contradictions can't be true. Instead, it should suffice if I simply point out certain clear-cut cases where the arguments by the dialetheists against the LNC proceed too quickly. It should be of interest to see just how far the logic of encoding can be used to defend the LNC. It may turn out, in the end, that there are some true (and false) contradictions and that paraconsistent logic is the correct logic. If so, the object theory discussed here could easily be recast in terms of such a logic and remain of interest. But whether or not this latter task is undertaken, our present concern is to discover exactly the point at which the LNC allegedly fails. I think the following shows that more work has to be done to identify that point, should it exist.

Before I begin, let me note that I shall presuppose familiarity with one or another of the canonical presentations of the logic of encoding and the theory of abstract objects that is cast within this logic. My readers should know that the logic of encoding is a classical logic in which two kinds of atomic formulas ($F^n x_1 \ldots x_n$ and xF^1) form the basis of a second-order, quantified modal language and logic (identity is not primitive but is instead defined for both individuals and relations).

---

[1] See Parsons (1990).

[2] In addition to the two books just cited, readers will find applications of the logic of encoding in Zalta (2000*a*, *b*, 1999, and 1993).

The language is extended to include (rigid) definite descriptions and λ-expressions, and the logic is extended with the usual axioms that govern these expressions. A single primitive notion 'x is concrete' (E!x) is used to formulate the definition of 'x is abstract' (A!x) and the axioms for abstract objects are stated within the resulting language and logic. The main axiom of the theory is a comprehension principle that asserts that for any condition ϕ without free xs, there is an abstract object that encodes just the properties satisfying ϕ ($\exists x(A!x \,\&\, \forall F(xF \equiv \phi))$). Readers unfamiliar with this system should consult one of the previously cited works in which the theory has been formally developed.

DISCUSSION OF CUSANUS

In discussing the limits of thought in pre-Kantian philosophy, Priest examines the work of the fifteenth-century German philosopher Nicolas of Cusa. Priest (1995) summarizes Cusanus's argument that God is beyond the limit of that which is expressible. Cusanus, according to Priest, argues that God cannot be (truly) described because God, being infinite, can fall under no finite category. After quoting Cusanus's explanation of this last claim (*Of Learned Ignorance*, I. 3), Priest observes (ibid. 24):

We see that Cusanus is operating with a 'mirror' conception of categorisation. An adequate category must share the relevant properties with the object categorised . . . . But clearly, from a modern perspective, it has no plausibility. Categories hardly ever share crucial properties with the objects categorised. The category of redness is not red; the notion of foreignness is not foreign; the notion of length is not long. And for good measure, the notion of a circle is not circular either.

Of course, Priest is quite right to point out that the property F doesn't share F with the objects categorized as F. However, the logic of encoding offers an analysis that shows that Cusanus wasn't completely off the mark.

In object theory and its logic of encoding, there is an object that is very closely related to the property of F and that does 'share' F with the objects that exemplify F. This analysis was developed in connection with the Self-Predication Principle (i.e. The Form of F is F) in Plato's Theory of Forms. In my (1983), and in Pelletier and Zalta (2000), an analysis of Plato's theory was put forward on which the Form of F is identified not with the property F but with either the abstract object that encodes just F or the abstract object that encodes the properties necessarily implied by F.[3]

---

[3] I proposed the former analysis (i.e. identifying the Form of F with the abstract object that encodes just F), in (1983), and Pelletier and I proposed the latter analysis (i.e. identifying the Form of F with the abstract object that encodes all of the properties necessarily implied by F), in Pelletier and Zalta (2000). But this subtlety will not play a role in what follows. Note also that here I shall assume that 'necessary implication' is defined in the usual way, namely, that F necessarily implies G iff necessarily, everything exemplifying F exemplifies G.

This analysis turned Plato's One Over the Many Principle into a proper thesis of metaphysics instead of a logical truth. Given the ambiguity of the copula 'is', the Self-Predication Principle then received two readings, one of which is *true*. The claim 'The Form of a Circle is circular' comes out true if we analyze 'The Form of a Circle' as denoting the abstract object that encodes circularity and we analyze the copula 'is' as 'encodes'.

So, from the point of view of the logic of encoding, the charitable way to interpret Cusanus is to identify the category of F with the abstract object that encodes F (or, what might be preferable, with the abstract object that encodes every property necessarily implied by F). When the category is understood in that way, it does, in some sense, *share* the property F with the objects that exemplify F. We can predicate redness, foreignness, and length of 'the category of redness', 'the notion of foreignness', and 'the notion of length', respectively, if we understand the predication correctly and analyze the category as an abstract object. So although Cusanus's argument as to why God can't be truly described still fails, his 'mirror' principle (to which Priest alludes) does have one true reading. His intuitions weren't completely off base. However, the exemplification reading of the principle ('the category of F exemplifies F'), which is needed for the argument, is false.

DISCUSSION OF ANSELM

Priest (1995) later goes on to analyze Anselm's *Proslogion*. In his analysis, Priest discusses what Routley (1980) called the Characterization Principle (CP), which states that 'the thing with property ϕ is a ϕ-thing'. The suggestion is that Anselm appeals to this principle when he argues that, that than which nothing greater can be conceived is such that nothing greater can be conceived. In criticizing Anselm, Priest concludes, 'The CP, then, is not a logical truth. I think that it appears so plausible because the claim that a (the) thing that is P is P is easily confused with the claim that everything that is P is P, which is a logical truth' (ibid. 64). Actually, Priest doesn't defend CP by appealing to paraconsistent logic, but rather concludes that 'CP cannot be assumed in general' (ibid. 65).

But with the logic of encoding and the theory of abstract objects, one can defend CP by recognizing that it is subject to an ambiguity connected with the copula 'is'. (This is not to defend Anselm's ontological argument, but only to give an analysis that might explain why Anselm might have been misled into grounding the crucial premise of his argument in something like the Characterization Principle.) Indeed, the Characterization Principle was shown to have one true reading in Zalta (1983: 47–8). I offered a reading of the principle 'The P-thing is P' that is true *in general*. The idea is to interpret 'the P-thing' as denoting the abstract object that encodes just the property P and read the copula as 'encodes'.

The result is a truth, and indeed, one that is provable. We may take the analysis there one step further by instead reading 'the *P*-thing' as 'the abstract object that encodes all and only the properties necessarily implied by *P*'. Then, given that 'is' is ambiguous between exemplification and encoding predication, we have a reading of the Characterization Principle that turns out true, namely, the (abstract object) *x* that encodes all the properties necessarily implied by *P* encodes *P*. This is true in general because the comprehension principle for abstract objects guarantees the existence of a unique object that encodes all the properties necessarily implied by *P*. Moreover, the principle is easily generalized from the single property form 'The *P*-thing is *P*' to the general form 'The so-and-so is so-and-so', where 'the so-and-so' is any definite description of ordinary language. Then the general form of the Characterization Principle can be given the true reading: the abstract object that encodes all and only the properties necessarily implied by being so-and-so encodes being so-and-so. We may represent this formally by representing 'so-and-so' in the usual way as a complex exemplification condition ϕ and by using '$\Rightarrow$' to stand for necessary implication (where $F \Rightarrow G =_{df} \Box\forall x(Fx \rightarrow Gx)$). Then the general Characterization Principle can be formally represented as:

$$\imath x(A!x \,\&\, \forall F(xF \equiv [\lambda y\ \phi] \Rightarrow F))[\lambda y\ \phi]$$

This is an 'atomic' encoding predication with both a complex object term (namely, a description of the form '$\imath x\psi$') and a complex predicate (namely, '$[\lambda y\ \phi]$'). Moreover, it is a *theorem* of the theory of abstract objects.[4]

Now how does this give us a more charitable interpretation of Anselm? Consider a somewhat different example. Suppose someone asks the question, why did Ponce de Leon search for the fountain of youth? It is not too helpful to appeal to CP by answering 'Because the fountain of youth is a fountain of youth.' Instead, we expand upon the truth given by CP and answer by saying 'Because the fountain of youth is a fountain the waters of which confer everlasting life on those who drink from it.' Now here we have what looks like a true statement, namely, the fountain of youth is a fountain the waters of which . . . The encoding logician assumes 'the fountain of youth' refers to a certain intentional object. Depending on the circumstances of utterance, there are two ways to identify this intentional object. In the simplest case, we identify it as the abstract object that encodes just the property of being a fountain of youth (i.e. it encodes just the property of being a fountain the waters of which confer everlasting life upon those who drink from it). In more complex cases, we would identify this object as the abstract object that encodes all and only the properties necessarily implied by being a fountain

---

[4] Note that the reason that it is a truth of metaphysics and not a truth of logic is that its truth depends on the fact that the description has a denotation. This fact is a consequence of a proper axiom of metaphysics, namely, the comprehension principle for abstract objects. See Zalta (1983: 48), for further formal details.

of youth.[5] On either identification, the object indeed does 'have' the property of being a fountain of youth, for it encodes the property of being a fountain of youth. Since encoding is a mode of predication, it is a way of having a property. An appeal to such an object therefore allows us to explain Ponce de Leon's behavior, for why would anyone search for the fountain of youth if there is no sense of 'is' on which it *is* a fountain that confers everlasting life? Although nothing exemplifies the property of being a fountain of youth, there is an intentional object which *is* (in the encoding sense) a fountain of youth.

Similarly, I think it is a more sympathetic analysis of Anselm to suppose that (1) there is an intentional object grounding this thought when he assumes that 'that than which nothing greater can be conceived is such that nothing greater can be conceived', and (2) this intentional object 'is' such that nothing greater can be conceived. You can't identify this intentional object using the standard exemplification reading of the ordinary definite description 'that than which nothing greater can be conceived'. But in the logic of encoding, we can read this description as denoting the abstract object that encodes all and only the properties necessarily implied by the property of being such that nothing greater can be conceived. This abstract object is governed by the general Characterization Principle. Where 'nothing greater (than y) can be conceived' is represented as '$\neg\exists z(Cz \mathbin{\&} Gzy)$', then the following instance of the general Characterization Principle formulated above is derivable in object theory:

$$\imath x(A!x \mathbin{\&} \forall F(xF \equiv [\lambda y \; \neg\exists z(Cz \mathbin{\&} Gzy)] \Rightarrow F))[\lambda y \; \neg\exists z(Cz \mathbin{\&} Gzy)]$$

So the property of being such that nothing greater can be conceived does *characterize* the intentional object, and Anselm was correct to this extent.

Anselm's mistake was to fail to notice the subtle ambiguity in predication when forming descriptions of conceivable objects, namely, that the 'is' of predication for intentional objects is not quite the usual one. He assumed that the property involved in the definite description 'that than which nothing greater can be conceived' would characterize the object of his thought. But there are two modes of predication underlying natural language characterizations and only one of them (encoding) behaves the way that Anselm expected. Unfortunately, it is the other mode of predication (exemplification) that is needed for the ontological argument to succeed. While one can prove in the logic of encoding that there exists an intentional object that encodes the property of being such that nothing greater can be conceived, one cannot prove the existence of an object that *exemplifies* this property.[6]

---

[5] The proper identification depends on the context of utterance and on the way the person uttering the sentence conceives of the fountain of youth.

[6] Some readers may be familiar with the formulation of the ontological argument developed in Oppenheimer and Zalta (1991), in which the distinction between 'being' and 'existence' is regimented by the distinction between '$\exists x\phi$' and '$\exists x(E!x \mathbin{\&} \phi)$'. Oppenheimer and I thought this would give a more accurate representation of the argument. But however one reads the quantifier, the above discussion

BERKELEY'S MASTER ARGUMENT

Priest develops an extremely elegant reconstruction of Berkeley's Master Argument, as presented in *Three Dialogues Between Hylas and Philonous*. The puzzle consists of two premisses and three principles, all of which appear to be true but which jointly appear to yield a contradiction. The first premiss is the claim 'there exists something which is not conceivable' and since a contradiction can be derived from this premiss (together with the second premiss and the three principles), one could take the result to be a *reductio* which yields the negation of the first premiss, namely, that nothing exists which is not conceivable. Priest nicely explains the subtle differences between this conclusion and the conclusion that nothing exists unconceived, but for the present discussion, however, we won't be distracted by this subtlety. The modality in 'conceivable' will not be represented in the argument and so the puzzle will involve no modal inferences.

With this proviso, the two premisses of the argument are formulable with the predicate 'Cx' ('x is conceivable') and a propositional operator '$C\phi$' ('it is conceivable that ϕ'). They are:

> Premiss 1: There exists something which is not conceivable
> $\exists x \neg Cx$
>
> Premiss 2: It is conceivable that there exists something which is not conceivable
> $C\exists x \neg Cx$

Now using ϕ and ψ as metavariables for sentences, $\phi(x)$ as a metavariable for a sentence in which x may or may not be free, and Hilbert epsilon terms of the form '$\epsilon x\phi(x)$', we can state the three principles as follows:

> Conception Scheme: If it is conceivable that ϕ holds of x, then x is conceivable
> $C\phi(x) \rightarrow Cx$
>
> Rule of Conception: If it is provable that ϕ implies ψ, then it is provable that the conceivability of ϕ implies the conceivability of ψ
> If $\vdash \phi \rightarrow \psi$, then $\vdash C\phi \rightarrow C\psi$
>
> Hilbert Scheme: If there exists something such that $\phi(x)$, then $\phi(x)$ holds of an-x-such-that-$\phi(x)$
> $\exists x\phi \rightarrow \phi(\epsilon x\phi(x))$

The reader should consult Priest's (1995: 68–70) justification for these principles. The argument then proceeds as follows:

> 1. $\exists x \neg Cx$ Premiss 1
> 2. $\exists x \neg Cx \rightarrow \neg C(\epsilon x \neg Cx)$ Instance, Hilbert Scheme

should prepare the reader to anticipate my reasons for rejecting Premiss 1 of our formulation of the argument in that paper.

3. $\neg C(\epsilon x \neg Cx)$	Modus Ponens, 1,2
4. $C\exists x \neg Cx$	Premiss 2
5. $C\exists x \neg Cx \rightarrow C\neg C(\epsilon x \neg Cx)$	Rule of Conception, 2
6. $C\neg C(\epsilon x \neg Cx)$	Modus Ponens, 4,5
7. $C\neg C(\epsilon x \neg Cx) \rightarrow C(\epsilon x \neg Cx)$	Conception Scheme Instance
8. $C(\epsilon x \neg Cx)$	Modus Ponens, 6,7
9. $C(\epsilon x \neg Cx) \,\&\, \neg C(\epsilon x \neg Cx)$	&I, 3,8

Of course, before we conclude that Premiss 1 is false (Berkeley) or that we have a true contradiction (Priest), we have to be justified in accepting the various premisses and principles used in the argument. But the justification for the various premisses and principles strikes me as controversial. The Conception Scheme and the Rule of Conception can each be challenged on separate grounds. I won't spend the time here doing so, since I plan to accept them (below) for the sake of argument. Moreover, it seems reasonable to claim that if one accepts the Hilbert Scheme, one shouldn't accept the Conception Scheme. If the Hilbert Scheme legitimizes the inference from an existential claim to a claim involving a defined (but not necessarily well-defined) singular term for an arbitrary object satisfying the existential claim, then why think it *follows* from the *de dicto* conceivability of an existential claim that the thing denoted by the singular term is conceivable *de re*?[7]

But suppose we grant, for the sake of argument, that Premiss 2 and the three principles (Conception Scheme, Rule of Conception, and Hilbert Scheme) are all true. Then it becomes important to point out that one can both accept the ordinary intuition that 'there exists something which is not conceivable' and develop an analysis on which it turns out true, without accepting Premiss 1. Priest takes Premiss 1 to be the only analysis of the intuition 'there exists something that is not conceivable'. But in the logic of encoding, the ordinary claim has additional readings, both of which are true. So one can reject the reading offered by Premiss 1 without rejecting that there exists something that is not conceivable.

The ordinary claim 'there exists something that is not conceivable' has the following two additional readings in the logic of encoding:

$\exists x(x[\lambda y \,\neg Cy])$
(There exists something that encodes being inconceivable.)

$\exists x(\neg xC)$
(There exists something that fails to encode being conceivable.)

---

[7] This question was inspired by Fred Kroon's presentation at the 'author-meets-critics' session on Priest's book, which took place at the July 1998 meetings of the Australasian Association of Philosophy (at Macquarie University) and in which we both participated along with Rod Girle. Kroon's presentation has now been published as Kroon (2001). I'd like to thank the organizers of that conference, and in particular, Peter Menzies, for agreeing to field that session.

Both of these are true. The first one is true because the comprehension principle for abstract objects asserts the existence of abstract objects that encode the property of being inconceivable. The second is true because the comprehension principle asserts the existence of abstract objects that provably fail to encode the property of being conceivable. Using an expression of natural language which is multiply ambiguous to describe these objects, we would say that these abstract objects 'are not conceivable'.[8]

The moral here is that we are not forced to conclude that the ordinary claims underlying the formal Premisses 1 and 2, together with the three principles, jointly yield a true contradiction. When classical logic is extended by the logic of encoding and theory of abstract objects, we have options for analyzing apparent contradictions that the dialetheists have not considered. I am not claiming that the only correct approach to this puzzle is to accept Premiss 2, accept the three principles, reject Premiss 1, and analyze 'there exists something that is not conceivable' in terms of encoding predications. One might wish to reject one of the principles used in the puzzle. Rather, I am claiming only that *if* one accepts Premiss 2 and the three principles involved in the contradiction, then one is not forced either to accept true contradictions or to reject the intuition that 'there exists something that is not conceivable'. An alternative is available.

THE INCLOSURE SCHEMA

Now one of the central parts of Priest's case for dialetheism concerns the so-called inclosure paradoxes. He classifies all of the set theoretic and semantic paradoxes as instances of a general recurring pattern called the 'Inclosure Schema'. This schema, when formulated at the most general level of abstraction, requires notions of set theory. Priest (1995: 147) describes the Inclosure Schema as follows:

We now require two properties, ϕ and ψ, and a function δ satisfying the following conditions:

(1) $\Omega = \{y : \phi(y)\}$ exists and $\psi(\Omega)$ [Existence]
(2) if $x \subseteq \Omega$ such that $\psi(x)$: (a) $\delta(x) \notin x$ [Transcendence]
                                   (b) $\delta(x) \in \Omega$ [Closure]

Given that these conditions are satisfied we still have a contradiction. For since $\psi(\Omega)$, we have $\delta(\Omega) \notin \Omega!$. I will call any Ω that satisfies these conditions (for an appropriate δ) an *inclosure*.[footnote] The conditions themselves, I will call the *Inclosure Schema*, and any paradox of which this is the underlying structure, an *inclosure contradiction*.

---

[8] The ambiguity in the ordinary predicate 'is not conceivable' is twofold. One ambiguity is between reading the negation as either internal to the predicate or external to the sentence. The other is between the exemplification and encoding readings of the copula. In the two new readings cited above, we have focused on the encoding readings, the first of which involves internal negation and the second external.

The exclamation point at the end of the third sentence in this quotation indicates that both the sentence $\delta(\Omega) \notin \Omega$ and its negation are true (ibid. 142). Elsewhere, Priest explains that the δ function can be thought of as the 'diagonalizer' function. He then shows how a wide variety of logical paradoxes, vicious circles, and semantic paradoxes fit into the pattern of this schema, and summarizes his results nicely in (1995: 144, 148, 160 (Tables 7, 8, 9)). In these cases, Priest explains how contradictions stand at the limits of iteration, cognition, conception (definition), or expression.

Priest's book then becomes an extended argument to show that the traditional solutions to the paradoxes are not adequate. He concludes that we must accept dialetheism (and revise classical logic) to accommodate the contradictions at the limits of thought:

In the last two chapters we have, *inter alia*, completed a review of all main contemporary solutions to inclosure contradictions. As we have seen, the solutions are not adequate, even in the limited domains for which they were generally designed. Moreover, not only do they tend to be incompatible, but the piecemeal approach initiated by Ramsey flies in the face of the PUS [Principle of Uniform Solution] and the fact that all such paradoxes instantiate a single underlying structure: the Inclosure Schema. The only satisfactory uniform approach to all these paradoxes is the dialetheic one, which takes the paradoxical contradictions to be exactly what they appear to be. The limits of thought which are the inclosures are truly contradictory objects.   (ibid. 186)

An encoding logician, however, need not accept this. The logic of encoding offers a consistent, non-piecemeal and uniform solution to inclosure contradictions. The solution is to first reject (as false) the formal conditions that assert the existence of, or describe, objects that *exemplify* contradictory properties, and then appeal to objects that *encode* the relevant properties to formally analyze the informal existence claims and descriptions of what appear to be contradictory objects at the limits of thought. On Priest's analysis, either (*a*) informal existence claims for the existence of some object Ω become formalized in inclosure contradictions in the Existence condition for Ω, or (*b*) informal descriptions of contradictory objects become formalized in the well-definedness condition underlying the diagonalizer function δ and presupposed in the Transcendence and Closure conditions. In either case, the only option Priest considers for analyzing the informal existence claims and descriptions is to use the exemplification form of predication in classical logic. The alternative, however, is to (1) analyze Ω as encoding, rather than exemplifying, the contradicting properties embedded in the informal existence condition, or (2) analyze $\delta(x)$ as an object that encodes, rather than exemplifies, the properties defined in the function δ.

Consider, as an example, Priest's analysis of Russell's paradox. Priest analyzes an informal existence claim of naïve set theory ('there exists a unique set of all sets') in terms of an (exemplification-based) Existence condition (this condition is one of the elements of the inclosure contradiction). He alleges that the contradictory object Ω at the limit of thought is the unique object V that exemplifies being a set of all sets.[9] In addition, Priest identifies the informal function 'the set of all elements of the set x which are not members of themselves' as a kind of diagonalizer function δ. (This function plays a role in the Transcendence and Closure conditions that form part of the inclosure contradiction associated with Russell's paradox.) Note that the formally defined function $\rho_x(= \{y \in x | \neg(y \in y)\})$ involves exemplification predications of the form '$y \in x$' and '$y \in y$'. The inclosure contradiction then becomes $\rho_V \in V$ & $\rho_V \notin V$.[10]

The analysis of Russell's paradox from the present theoretical perspective looks very different, however. Assume for the moment that membership ('$\in$') is an ordinary relation that has been added as a primitive to our background metaphysics. Then it follows immediately that nothing exemplifies the property of having as members all and only things that are non-self-membered. That is, the following is a theorem:

$$\neg \exists y([\lambda z \,\forall w(w \in z \equiv w \notin w)]y)$$

However, the comprehension principle for abstract objects gives us an object of thought for our naïve thoughts about 'the object that has as members all and only non-self-membered objects', namely, the abstract object that encodes all and only the properties necessarily implied by $[\lambda z \,\forall w(w \in z \equiv w \notin w)]$. The following instance of comprehension asserts the existence of this abstract object (where $\Rightarrow$ represents necessary implication, as this was defined earlier):

$$\exists x(A!x \,\&\, \forall F(xF \equiv [\lambda z \,\forall w(w \in z \equiv w \notin w)] \Rightarrow F))$$

Readers familiar with the logic of encoding will know that the identity conditions for abstract objects guarantee that there is, in fact, a unique such abstract object. This object *has* (in the encoding sense) the property being-a-member-of-itself-iff-it-is-not, for this latter property is necessarily implied by the property of having as members all and only the non-self-membered objects.[11]But no contradiction is true.

---

[9] See Priest (1995: 144, Table 7).

[10] Clearly, given that V is the set of all sets, $\rho_V \in V$. Now to show that $\rho_V \notin V$, note that if $\rho_V \in \rho_V$, then $\rho_V \notin \rho_V$, by definition of ρ_V. So $\rho_V \notin \rho_V$. But, for reductio, if $\rho_V \in V$, then since $\rho_V \notin \rho_V$, it follows, by definition of ρ_V, that $\rho_V \in \rho_V$, which is a contradiction. So $\rho_V \notin V$.

[11] Here is the proof. Call the abstract object in question 'a'. So we know: $\forall F(aF \equiv [\lambda z \forall w(w \in z \equiv w \notin w)] \Rightarrow F)$. So we want to show that a encodes $[\lambda z\, z \in z \equiv z \notin z)]$. To do this we have to show that: $[\lambda z \forall w(w \in z \equiv w \notin w)] \Rightarrow [\lambda z\, z \in z \equiv z \notin z)]$. That is, we have to show: $\Box \forall x([\lambda z \forall w(w \in z \equiv w \notin w)]x \rightarrow [\lambda z\, z \in z \equiv z \notin z)]x)$. So pick an arbitrary object, say c, and assume that $[\lambda z \forall w(w \in z \equiv w \notin w)]c$. Then, by λ-abstraction, $\forall w(w \in c \equiv w \notin w)$. Instantiating this universal claim to c, it follows that $c \in c \equiv c \notin c$. So, by λ-abstraction, it follows that $[\lambda z\, z \in z \equiv z \notin z)]c$. Since c was arbitrarily chosen, we have proved that: $\forall x([\lambda z \forall w(w \in z \equiv w \notin w)]x \rightarrow [\lambda z\, z \in z \equiv z \notin z)]x)$, and the Rule of Necessitation gets us the modal implication. Thus, a encodes: being a member of itself iff it is not.

Similarly, consider the naïve existence principle for sets, which can be expressed informally as: for any condition expressible in terms of 'membership' and 'set', there is a set whose members are precisely the objects satisfying the condition. Now assume for the moment that the property of being a set (S) is an ordinary property that has been added as a primitive to our background metaphysics. Then the ordinary formalization of the naïve existence principle for sets is provably false. That is, the following is provably *not* an axiom or theorem schema of object theory:

$$\exists y (Sy \,\&\, \forall z (z \in y \equiv \phi)), \quad \text{where } y \text{ is not free in } \phi$$

But comprehension for abstract objects and the logic of encoding offers a general way of preserving the naïve principle. It guarantees, for example, that for any condition expressible in terms of membership and set that is formally representable in the usual way as an exemplification formula ϕ (in terms of $\in$ and S), there is an abstract object that encodes all and only the properties necessarily implied by the property of being a set whose members are precisely the objects satisfying ϕ. The following schema, derivable from the comprehension schema, asserts this:

$$\exists x (A!x \,\&\, \forall F (xF \equiv [\lambda y \; Sy \,\&\, \forall z (z \in y \equiv \phi)] \Rightarrow F)), \quad \text{where } y \text{ is not free in } \phi$$

This constitutes a (true) reading of the naïve existence principle because it yields, for any set-theoretic condition ϕ, an object that has (in the encoding sense) the property of having as members just those objects satisfying ϕ (and any property implied by this). So the informal, naïve existence principle for sets gets both a false and a true reading in the logic of encoding. The true reading doesn't imply a contradiction. In the logic of encoding, the usual moral applies—we can't always assume that 'the set of all x such that $\ldots x \ldots$' is well-defined. But we can prove, for any ordinary sentence '$\ldots x \ldots$' of set theory representable as a (complex) exemplification formula $\phi(x)$, that 'the (abstract) object which has (i.e. encodes) all and only the properties necessarily implied by $[\lambda x \phi]$' is always well-defined. The abstract object in question serves as both the object of thought and the denotation of the ordinary description 'the set of all x such that $\ldots x \ldots$' in those true sentences containing this phrase.

These facts concerning the analysis of Russell's paradox in terms of the logic of encoding stand in contrast to Priest's analysis of the paradox in terms of an inclosure schema leading to a true contradiction. An encoding logician may claim either that the formal assertion for the existence of V is false or that the formal conditions that imply the well-definedness of the function ρ_x are false (or both). He would reject either the idea that something exists which *exemplifies* all the properties described by the Existence condition or the idea that there exists a unique value for ρ_x (interpreted as an exemplification-based function), for each argument x, or both.

There is, of course, no space in the present chapter to take up all the inclosure paradoxes that Priest discusses in his book. But I think that the foregoing discussion gives us a general way of analyzing these inclosure paradoxes without accepting that there are true contradictions. For each inclosure paradox Priest considers, the encoding logician would suggest that one should reject either the formal analysis of the Existence condition for Ω or the principles that guarantee the well-definedness of the formally defined function $\delta(x)$ (i.e. the principle that guarantees that there exists a unique value for $\delta(x)$ for all arguments). Naïve existence assertions of ordinary language can nevertheless be given true readings. If our intuitions, expressed in ordinary natural language, suggest that we should endorse some intuitive but contradictory existence condition, the logic of encoding offers us a reading that asserts the existence of an object that can consistently stand at the limits of thought. An encoding logician holds that the intuitive existence claim is false when analyzed as asserting the existence of an object that *exemplifies* the properties involved in the condition in question, but true when interpreted as asserting the existence of an object that encodes the properties involved. Similarly, an encoding logician holds that the principle that ensures that $\delta(x)$ is always well defined (for each argument x) is false when interpreted as guaranteeing the existence of a value that exemplifies the (properties involved in the) defining condition of δ, but true when interpreted as guaranteeing the existence of a value that encodes the (properties involved in the) condition.

This solution, unlike the other attempts to deny the Existence condition of the Inclosure Schema or the well-definedness of the diagonalizer function δ, always provides us with an appropriate 'object of thought' for the alleged contradictory limit objects. By doing so, the logic of encoding overcomes the problem with classical logic that Priest finds so objectionable (1995: 183). The objects (at the limits) of thought do 'have' the properties attributed to them, but not in quite the way the conditions imply (the conditions are contradictory, after all). The puzzling limit objects such as the set of all sets, the set of all ordinals, the set of all propositions, the set of all truths, etc. can all be analyzed as objects that encode the intuitive but contradictory properties attributed to them by the relevant conditions. Moreover, our analysis is consistent with classical logic, since xF doesn't imply Fx.

Furthermore, on the present view, the very properties and relations themselves involved in the description of these limit objects are by no means guaranteed either to exist or to exemplify the properties they are frequently assumed to have in dialetheism and elsewhere. Take the notion of 'membership', for example. Some notion of membership is essential to the formulation of the Inclosure Schema itself. Earlier, we simply assumed that we could add membership as a primitive, ordinary relation, for the purposes of the subsequent argument. But, strictly speaking, from the present point of view, there is no distinguished 'correct' membership relation, but rather as many abstract membership relations as there are conceptions of membership and theories of sets. Readers familiar with the applications of the typed theory of abstracta described in Zalta (1983: ch. 6; Linsky and Zalta 1995; Zalta 2000b), will recognize that for each theory T in which '$\in$' is primitive or defined, there is an abstract relation (with type $\langle i, i \rangle$) which encodes just the properties of relations attributed to $\in$ in theory T.

To give an example, take Zermelo-Fraenkel (ZF) set theory. In the work cited at the end of the previous paragraph, we identified the membership relation of ZF as that abstract relation that encodes all the properties of relations attributed to $\in$ in ZF. We were able to do this by using the following procedure. We take the axioms of ZF to be 'true in' ZF and represent these facts, for each axiom p, as encoding predications of the form ZF[$\lambda y\ p$] ('ZF encodes being such that p'). Here, we are taking ZF itself to be an abstract object that encodes only properties of the form [$\lambda y\ p$], where p ranges over propositions (i.e. entities of type $\langle \rangle$). Then we assert that 'truth in', as just defined, is closed under logical consequence. That is, if $p_1, \ldots, p_n \vdash q$, and the p_i ($1 \leq i \leq n$) are all true in ZF, then q is true in ZF. This principle allows us to infer, from each theorem of ZF, that it is true in ZF that $\in$ exemplifies a particular property of relations. (For example, from the fact that $\emptyset \in \{\emptyset\}$ is true in ZF, it follows that [$\lambda R\ \emptyset R\{\emptyset\}$]$\in$ is true in ZF.) Now, where 'ZF $\models p$' asserts that p is true in ZF (where this is defined as 'ZF[$\lambda y\ p$]'), we can give a theoretical identification of the membership relation of ZF ('$\in_{ZF}$') as follows:[12]

$$\in_{ZF}\ =\ \iota x^{\langle i,i \rangle}(A!x\ \&\ \forall F(xF \equiv ZF \models F\in))$$

In other words, the membership relation of ZF is that abstract relation (among individuals) which encodes exactly the properties of relations F which $\in$ exemplifies in ZF. This is a rather interesting relation, assuming ZF is consistent.

The above procedure allows us to identify different membership relations for each of the theories Z, ZF, ZFC, the axioms of Aczel's (1988) non-well-founded set theory, etc. Each theory is based on a different conception of the membership relation. For the purposes of this chapter, however, it is interesting to note that our procedure also allows us to identify theoretically the membership relation of naïve set theory. Assume that naïve set theory (NST) is constituted simply by the naïve comprehension principle (as formalized in its inconsistent guise above) and the extensionality principle. By the procedure outlined in the previous paragraph, we may identify the membership relation of NST as follows:

$$\in_{NST}\ =\ \iota x^{\langle i,i \rangle}(A!x\ \&\ \forall F(xF \equiv NST \models F\in))$$

Clearly, this membership relation will encode all of the properties of relations expressible in the language of NST, since every sentence expressible in the language

---

[12] In the following identification, the predicate '$A!$' and the variable 'F' both have type $\langle\ \langle i, i \rangle\ \rangle$. The former denotes a property of relations and the latter is a variable ranging over properties of relations.

of NST is derivable as a truth of NST. As such, it is a rather uninteresting relation. But note that we have identified an object of thought, namely, the membership relation of NSF.

The important point here is that the world itself offers no distinguished, ordinary membership relation. It is only by assuming that there is one distinguished membership relation (governed by distinctively true principles) that a dialetheic logician can formulate the Inclosure Schema as an objective pattern and thereby argue that the law of non-contradiction must be revised. But an encoding logician need not accept this. From the present perspective, predicates such as 'membership', 'set', etc., denote different abstract relations depending on the (formal or informal) principles by which these relations are conceived. This may be the only conception of abstracta that can address the epistemological problems of Platonism, as Linksy and I (1995) argued.

OBSERVATIONS AND REMARKS

I take it that the solution to the inclosure paradoxes offered in this chapter satisfies Priest's Principle of Uniform Solution. Each object at a limit of thought is analyzed as an abstract object that encodes, rather than exemplifies, the contradictory properties. I think the foregoing work shows that the arguments for dialetheism are inconclusive to anyone who adopts the logic of encoding as an analytic method for resolving the inclosure contradictions. This logic offers uniform, classical analyses of those puzzles in which the law of non-contradiction has seemed to fail. The case against this law, therefore, remains unpersuasive to an encoding logician. Whenever a dialetheic logician concludes that some contradiction is true (and false), the data that drives this conclusion can be explained in terms of abstract objects that encode contradictory properties. An encoding logician might therefore conclude that no 'noumenal' object, so to speak, whether ordinary or abstract, exemplifies contradictory properties. However, contradictory properties may characterize both 'phenomenal' objects and our conceptions of objects. Once these phenomenal objects and conceptions are analyzed in terms of abstract individuals or abstract properties, the contradictory behavior can be explained in terms of incompatible encoded properties.

I think the main argument for preserving the classical law of non-contradiction is that it allows us to preserve our pretheoretic understanding of what it is to exemplify or instantiate a property. Since dialetheic logicians conceive (exemplification) predication to be such that there are objects x and properties F such that $Fx \& \neg Fx$, they force us to abandon our pretheoretic understanding of what it is to instantiate or exemplify a property. Our pretheoretic understanding of ordinary predication is grounded in such basic cases as the exemplification of simple and complex properties. Even if we don't have exact analyses for the simple or complex properties in question, we have a pretheoretic understanding of what it is for something to exemplify being red, being round, being straight, being triangular, being a detective, etc. Part of that understanding is that if an object x exemplifies a property P, then it is not the case that x fails to exemplify P. How are we to understand ordinary predication, or understand the idea of an object *exemplifying* such properties as having a color, having a shape, etc. if an object's exemplifying such properties doesn't exclude its failure to exemplify such properties? Of course, a dialetheic logician may counter that they only abandon our ordinary notion of predication in certain special cases. But my claim is that the ordinary cases ground our understanding of *what it is* to exemplify a property—what exemplification is excludes something's both exemplifying and failing to exemplify a property. If the special cases force us to abandon this, then it is unclear whether we really understand what exemplification is.

If logic is the study of the forms and consequences of predication, as I think it is, then it is legitimate to investigate a logical system that preserves this pretheoretic understanding of ordinary predication, especially if that logic has the capability to address the problems posed by impossibilia and contradictory (limit) objects of thought. The logic of encoding is such a logic; it doesn't tamper with our notion of ordinary predication, but rather appeals to a second form of predication to handle the problematic cases.

The technical development of the logic of encoding suggests that there is one constraint that places a limit on thought. This constraint is motivated by the paradoxes of encoding. As discussed in Zalta (1983: appendix), and elsewhere, the paradoxes derive from the interplay of unrestricted comprehension over abstract objects and unrestricted comprehension over relations (the latter includes properties and propositions). A single solution solves *both* paradoxes. The principal paradox is that if the expression $[\lambda x \exists F(xF \ \& \ \neg Fx)]$ were to denote a genuine property, one could produce a contradiction by considering the abstract object that encodes just the property in question and noting that such an object exemplifies that property iff it does not. This is the Clark Paradox.[13] We have formulated our system so as to preclude this result by banishing encoding subformulas from λ-expressions. The formation rules for the expression $[\lambda x_1 \ldots x_n \ \phi]$ require that the formula ϕ not contain encoding subformulas. This constraint also solves the other paradox of encoding, namely, the McMichael Paradox.[14]

---

[13] See Clark (1978) and Rapaport (1978).

[14] See McMichael and Zalta (1980), and Zalta (1983: appendix). A paradox arises if general identity is assumed to be a relation on individuals. On such an assumption, one could assert the existence of the paradoxical abstract object that encodes all and only the properties F such that $\exists y(F = [\lambda z \ z = y] \ \& \ \neg yF)$. But a solution to this paradox falls immediately out of the solution to the Clark paradox if we define '=' for abstract objects in terms of encoding subformulas as we have done (abstract objects x and y are 'identical' whenever they encode the same properties). The condition stating the identity of abstract objects cannot be used in relation comprehension to assert the existence of the relation of identity. Thus, $[\lambda z \ z = y]$ is not well-formed, though the condition $z = y$ is nevertheless well-defined and assertable. Moreover, the existence of a relation of identity on *ordinary* objects is not affected.

The comprehension principle for relations that is derivable from λ-abstraction therefore does not guarantee the existence of relations corresponding to arbitrary formulas ϕ. Instead, it guarantees only that for any formula ϕ free of encoding subformulas (and for which F^n isn't free), there is a relation F^n that objects $x_1, \ldots, x_n$ exemplify iff $x_1, \ldots, x_n$ are such that ϕ.[15] Of course, one may freely add new axioms that assert the existence of properties, relations, and propositions defined in terms of encoding subformulas, but one has to prove that the resulting theory is consistent when one adds such axioms. So the limit on thought is that one may not always assume that arbitrary open (closed) formulas ϕ correspond to relations (propositions).

Now some dialetheists will no doubt charge that the 'no encoding subformulas' restriction on relation comprehension is ad hoc! They might argue that if you take paraconsistent logic as your background logic, no such restrictions are required. I think one can actually meet this charge head on, both by motivating the 'no encoding subformulas' constraint on comprehension for relations and by noting that we are free to formulate our theories in the simplest way that explains the data.[16] But since such a defense probably wouldn't convince a dialetheist, I shall respond (and bring the chapter to a close) simply by pointing out that dialetheism and the theory of abstract objects are on equal footing, as far as this charge goes. While theorists on both sides can justify their approach by saying that by adopting their system they can explain a wide range of data, nevertheless both systems make certain theoretical moves that will seem ad hoc from the point of view of the other. While our constraints on comprehension for relations in the logic of encoding may seem ad hoc from the point of view of dialetheism, the subversion of our pretheoretic understanding of exemplification predication and the LNC by

Ordinary objects x and y are identical whenever they (necessarily) exemplify the same properties, and this identity condition does constitute a relation.

[15] The λ-abstraction principle, which is part of the logic of encoding, asserts: $[\lambda y_1 \ldots y_n \phi] x_1 \ldots x_n \equiv \phi^{x_1, \ldots, x_n}_{y_1, \ldots, y_n}$. This asserts: objects $x_1, \ldots, x_n$ exemplify the relation $[\lambda y_1 \ldots y_n \phi]$ iff $x_1, \ldots, x_n$ are such that ϕ. Since ϕ in $[\lambda y_1 \ldots y_n \phi]$ may not contain encoding formulas, the application of Universal Generalization n times (on the x_i) followed by Existential Generalization on the λ-expression yields the following comprehension principle for relations: $\exists F^n \forall x_1 \ldots \forall x_n (F^n x_1 \ldots x_n \equiv \phi)$, where ϕ has no free F^ns and no encoding subformulas. Note that the comprehension principle for properties falls out as a special case: $\exists F \forall x (Fx \equiv \phi)$, where ϕ has no free Fs and no encoding subformulas. Finally, note that the following is the 0-place instance of λ-abstraction: $[\lambda \phi] \equiv \phi$. This asserts: that-$\phi$ is true iff ϕ. (The notion of truth is what remains of the notion of exemplification in the 0-place, degenerate instance of λ-abstraction.) From this 0-place instance, the following comprehension principle for propositions follows immediately: $\exists p(p \equiv \phi)$, where ϕ has no free ps, and no encoding subformulas. Readers unfamiliar with the logic of encoding should be aware that identity conditions for properties, relations, and propositions have also been formulated, and these are consistent with the idea that necessarily equivalent properties, relations, and propositions may be distinct.

[16] Indeed, the theory in question can be stated informally as follows: hold the domain of properties fixed and suppose that for every condition on properties, there is an abstract object that encodes the properties satisfying the condition. If that is the theory we are trying to formalize, then it is not ad hoc to place restrictions on relation comprehension. The addition of such a restriction is just the way one goes about holding the domain of properties fixed.

dialetheists seems equally ad hoc from the point of view of the logic of encoding. Nor can a dialetheist claim that they are in a superior position, on the grounds that they can 'accept' the theory of abstract objects without having to place any restrictions on comprehension. Abstract object theorists can argue equally well that they can 'accept' (the paraconsistent logic underlying) dialetheism without giving up the LNC. In Zalta (1997), I tried to show that within the logic of encoding, one could develop a *classically based* conception of impossible worlds, i.e. worlds where contradictions are true. I used those worlds to interpret a special consequence relation on propositions $\overset{R}{\Rightarrow}$ that is axiomatized along the lines of a paraconsistent logic.[17]

If there is parity between the logic of encoding and the dialetheist's paraconsistent logic on this charge, then I've established that the arguments of the dialetheists for rejecting the LNC are not yet conclusive. The adequacy, applicability, and fruitfulness of the two systems should be compared along other lines before any decision is to be made as to which offers the deeper insight into the explanation of important philosophical puzzles.

REFERENCES

Aczel, P. (1988), *Non-Well-Founded Sets*, Stanford: CSLI Publications (CSLI Lecture Notes, 14).

Clark, R. (1978), 'Not Every Object of Thought Has Being: A Paradox in Naive Predication Theory', *Noûs*, 12: 181–8.

Kroon, F. (2001), 'Beyond Belief? A Critical Study of Graham Priest's *Beyond the Limits of Thought*', *Theoria*, 67/2: 140–53.

Linsky, B., and Zalta, E. (1995), 'Naturalized Platonism vs. Platonized Naturalism', *The Journal of Philosophy*, 92/10 (October 1995): 525–55.

McMichael, A., and Zalta, E. (1980), 'An Alternative Theory of Nonexistent Objects', *Journal of Philosophical Logic*, 9: 297–313.

Oppenheimer, P., and Zalta, E. (1991), 'On the Logic of the Ontological Argument', *Philosophical Perspectives*, 5: 509–29; republished in *The Philosopher's Annual: 1991*, 14 (1993): 255–75.

Pelletier, F. J., and Zalta, E. (2000), 'How to Say Goodbye to the Third Man', *Noûs*, 34/2 (June): 165–202.

---

[17] Ultimately, the legitimacy of the 'no encoding subformulas' restriction depends on whether the logic of encoding and theory of abstract objects offer a better framework both for analyzing the relevant, pretheoretical data and for asserting (and, sometimes, proving) all of the important philosophical claims we have good reason to assert. I think the present theory will fare well in any comparison and cost-counting with dialetheism, given the variety of other applications described in the works cited in the Bibliography. Even if the two theories were on a par application-wise, it strikes me that the cost of the employing the 'no encoding subformulas' restriction is certainly no more expensive than the cost of accepting certain contradictions as true (and the havoc that plays on the notion of exemplification).

Parsons, T. (1990), 'True Contradictions', *Canadian Journal of Philosophy*, 20/3 (September): 335–53.

Priest, G. (1987), *In Contradiction*, Dordrecht: Nijhoff.

—— (1995), *Beyond the Limits of Thought*, Cambridge: Cambridge University Press.

—— (1998), 'What is So Bad About Contradictions?', *The Journal of Philosophy*, 98: 410–26.

Rapaport, W. (1978), 'Meinongian Theories and a Russellian Paradox', *Noûs*, 12: 153–80.

Routley, R. (1980), *Exploring Meinong's Jungle and Beyond*, Departmental Monograph 3, Philosophy Department, Research School of Social Sciences, Australian National University, Canberra.

Zalta, E. (1983), *Abstract Objects: An Introduction to Axiomatic Metaphysics*, Dordrecht: D. Reidel.

—— (1988), *Intensional Logic and the Metaphysics of Intentionality*, Cambridge, Mass. MIT.

—— (1993), 'Twenty-Five Basic Theorems in Situation and World Theory', *Journal of Philosophical Logic*, 22: 385–428.

—— (1997), 'A Classically-Based Theory of Impossible Worlds', *Notre Dame Journal of Formal Logic*, 38/4 (Fall 1997): 640–60 (Special Issue, with Graham Priest as Guest Editor).

—— (1999), 'Natural Numbers and Natural Cardinals as Abstract Objects: A Partial Reconstruction of Frege's *Grundgesetze* in Object Theory', *Journal of Philosophical Logic*, 28/6: 619–60.

—— (2000a), 'A (Leibnizian) Theory of Concepts', *Philosophiegeschichte und logische Analyse/Logical Analysis and History of Philosophy*, 3: 137–83.

—— (2000b), 'Neo-Logicism? An Ontological Reduction of Mathematics to Metaphysics', *Erkenntnis*, 53/1–2: 219–65.

Index

Abelard, P. 296
abstract objects, theory of 419–20, 426, 429
acceptance 73–4, 78–83, 388–9, 403–5,
    407–12, 414–16
ad hoc hypotheses 32, 33
Adams, E. 276
adaptive (minimally inconsistent)
   logic 199 n. 7, 213, 214
   LP 213–14
   FDE 213–14
adjunction principle 94, 101, 103, 108
admissible 105–6
   interpretations (valuations) 11–14, 198
agency 86, 90 n. 4
Aiehtela 200–12
Aiehtelanu 200–12
Anderson, A. 80, 236
Anselm, St 421–3
AP 198 n. 2
Aristotle 2, 3, 24, 27, 29, 30, 49, 50, 52, 53,
   57, 280–1, 290, 296, 307–8
Armour-Garb, B. 262 n.19, 265 n. 1
Arruda, A. 43
assertion 320
Atlas, J. 311 n. 12
Ayer, A. J. 218 n. 3, 225 n. 12

Bach, K. 310 n.
Balaguer, M. 193 n. 12
Barwise, J. 33, 269 n., 286 n., 314 n. 2
Batens, D. 213, 265 n. 1
bayesianism 273
Beall, J. C. 81, 97 n.7, 114, 123, 124, 157, 165,
   174, 176, 245, 246 n. 1, 252 n. 7,
   262 n.19, 269–70, 274, 318, 320 n. 16
belief 386, 388, 391, 403–4, 406–7, 410–15
   folk theory of 264, 271–2
Bell, J. L. 160
Belnap, N. D. 80, 82, 95, 236, 268, 274, 332 n.
   25
Berkeley, G. 91, 92
Berkeley's master argument 424
biconditional 390, 396, 400–1
Birkhoff, G. 158, 159
bivalence 99
   exact 285
Blackburn, S. 185 n. 5, 193

Boethius 296
Boghosian, P. 182 n. 2, 183 n. 3, 193,
   259 n. 16, 261
Bonevac, D. 51, 53, 54, 56
Boole, G. 25
boolean function 103–4
Brady, R. T. 398
Braithwaite, R. B. 277
Brandom, R. 99 n. 9, 317, 319
Brody, B. 52, 53
Bueno, O. 157, 162, 181 n. 1, 193
Burge, T. 314 n. 2
Burgess, J. 254 n. 9
BX 392

canonical warrant, 231
canonicity requirement 222
Carroll, L. 60, 68, 69, 188, 193
cassatio 304
catch-22 295, 299–301
change, moment of 238
characterization principle 421–3
checking device 95
Cherniak, C. 236
Chihara, C. 122
Chomsky, N. 220 n. 6, 391
Chrisman, M. 193, n. 12
Chrysippus 235
circumstances 99–101, 105
   genuine 96–7
   incomplete 101
   vs. worlds 95
Clark, M. 304
classical 75, 79, 82, 271, 273, 274, 390–2, 395,
   398–403, 406–8, 416
   mathematics 386, 392, 398, 400, 402
   recapture 386, 392–3, 399, 400–2, 403
   semantics 316, 318, 325
Cogburn, J. 221 n. 8
Cohen, L. J. 404 n. 19
coherence, level of 102 n. 15
collective vs. distributive 94–108
Cologne school 25
Colyvan, M. 157, 165, 181 n. 1, 193, 252 n. 7
commitment 77
completion 99–101
comprehension 391–3, 396, 400
conception scheme 424–5

conditional 276, 389–90, 393, 398, 409
conditions 269
conjunction 94, 98–9, 103–8, 385, 391 n.,
        393, 396, 403, 406–10, 415
connective, truth-functional 98, 102–8
consequence relation 73–4
consistency 295, 336–8, 345–54
    default 199 n. 7, 213, 214
consistent restriction (constriction) 101
content 296, 300, 303–5, 307–8, 311
context 314
contradiction 3–5, 246, 248, 252–4, 258–9,
        336–8, 342–5, 345–54
    negated 41–5
    observable 202
    semantic, syntactic, pragmatic and
        ontological accounts 53, 54
    true *see* dialetheism
contraposition 74
Cresswell, M. J. 264 n. 4
Curry, H. B. 400

D4 268–9
Da Costa, N. 6, 43, 158, 159, 174, 266 n., 268,
        273
Daniels, C. B. 267, 274
De Morgan, A. 51, 52, 56
    laws 41–3
    negation *see* negation, De Morgan
decidability 46
definition 298
deflationism 342, 345
    constructive methodological 197
denial 36, 37, 85, 288–90, 320, 339
denotation failure 99, 276, 278
Descartes, R. 402
designated value 11–14
DeVidi, D. 100 n. 12
diagnosis 113
    problem of 116
dialetheia 85, 89, 197, 265, 269, 270, 271, 318
        see also truth value glut
    legal 239
dialetheic 114, 123, 393, 397–9, 401–2, 406
dialetheism 10, 11, 74, 197, 245–6, 252–4,
        260–1, 271, 295, 302, 314–34, 336–54,
        418, 434–5
dieletheist 5–7
disjunction 391 n. 7, 393, 398, 401, 408–10,
        414
disjunction principle 100, 103, 108
disjunctive syllogism 14–15, 35, 81, 214,
        236–7, 239, 316

Dragalin, A., 217 n. 1
dual 279, 284
Dummett, M. A. E. 217, 217 n. 2, 220 n. 7,
        222 n. 9, 223 n. 10, 230–1, 240, 391
Dunn, J. M. 80, 82, 268, 268 n., 274, 277 n.

Edgington, D. 390 n. 5
EFQ, see *ex falso quodlibet*
emotivism 276, 287
empty set 395
entailment 242, 390–1, 395, 397–9, 408, 412
Epimenides, 276
epistemic hostility 236–41, 243
epistemology
    naturalized 402
    normative 184
epsilon terms 424
Epstein, R. L. 245
equality predicate 104–5, 107–8 *see also*
        identity
Etchemendy, J. 282 n., 314 n. 2
Euathlus 301–2
Euclid 281
ex falso (contradictione) quodlibet 103, 108,
        245–6, 265, 296, 302 *see also*
        explosion
exclusion principle 1, 2, 90
explosion (spread law) 5–7, 24, 25, 27, 29,
        31, 44, 47, 176 see also *ex falso*
        quodlibet
explosive sentence 3, 4
extensionality 392, 394–5, 398 n. 14
extensions, naive 9, 10

f (false proposition) 78–84
falsehood, simple 341–2, 344
FDE 11–12, 198
Feferman, S. 277
Felinghetti, L. 235
Feyerabend, P. 387
fiction 96, 101
fictionalism 254–62
Field, H. 157, 158, 162, 165, 174, 182 n. 2,
        193, 276
Fine, K. 99 n. 10, 278
Fisher, J. 193 n. 12
Fisher, R. A. 415
Forbes, G. 51, 53, 54, 56
formal semantics *see* meaning, theory of
forms, theory of 420
foundation 396
Frege, G. 25, 36, 182

Gaifman, H. 314 n. 2
gap *see* truth value gap
Gentzen, G. 283
Gibbard, A. 185 n. 5, 193
glut *see* truth value glut
God 295, 301–2
Gödel, K. 295
Goldstein, L. 295 n., 304 n., 309 n., 311 n. 14,
    334 n. 27
Goodman, N. 181 n. 1, 194
Goodship, L. 229 n. 14
Gorgias 38
graphic *see* truth value, graphic
Grice, P. 210, 339–40, 344
Grim, P. 58, 69, 93, 114
Gupta, A. 33, 332 n. 25

Haack, S. 51, 53, 54, 57
Hallett, M. 160
Hand, M. 193 n. 12
happy-face (solution) 117, 118, 120, 121,
    122, 124
Hardegree, G. M. 277 n.
Harman, G. 236
Hart, H. L. A. 267
Hegel, G. W. F. 29
Heller, J. 299
Heraclitus 29
Herzberger, H. 33
heterological, 298–9
hierarchy 314
Hilbert scheme 424–5
Horn, L. 87 n., 92
Horwich, P. 100 n. 11, 261, 276
Hume, D. 185, 388
Hyde, D. 101 n. 13, 265 n. 2

identity 392–4, 397–8 *see also* equality
    predicate
  folk theory of 264, 272
implicature 102, 339–40, 344
impossible (non-classical) worlds/situations
    27, 29, 94, 98, 176
inclosure 426 ff., 430
inconsistency 76
inconsistent mathematics 1 n. 2, 9 n. 4
indeterminacy
  conceptual *vs.* ontological 99
  of translation 289
indexicals 57
inferential practice 179
inferential role 108
infinity 396–9
interpretation 303–4

intuitionism 240
irrationality 386–9, 405, 408, 412, 414–16

Jackson, F. 252 n. 6
Jennings, R. E. 97 n. 6, 102 n.
Joyce, R. 257 n. 14, 258

K3 12, 14, 277–9
Kahane, H. 52, 53, 54, 93
Kalish, D. 52, 53, 56
Kant, I. 250–1, 258 n. 15
Kitcher, P. 157
Kleene, S. C. 46, 277–9, 315, 390, 391 n.,
    393, 394
knowability requirement 217, 224
Kripke, S. 33, 103, 188, 194, 255 n. 12, 260,
    272–3, 274, 278–80, 303 n., 314 n. 2
Kroon, F. 249 n. 2, 250 n. 3, 251 n. 4
Kyburg, H. E. 103 n.

Lakatos, I. 157
Langholm, T. 268, 274
lattice 75
Laudan, L. 166, 167, 168
law of the excluded middle (LEM) 43–4,
    73–5, 77–9, 81–2, 237, 243 *see also*
    law of non-contradiction
  collective *vs.* distributive reading 99–102
law of non-contradiction (LNC) 41–2, 44–7,
    114, 123, 124, 156, 157, 158, 165, 167,
    169, 170, 171, 172, 173, 174, 189, 191,
    193, 245–6, 254–5, 259, 261, 314, 325,
    334
  collective *vs.* distributive reading 94–108
  and law of excluded middle 98–102, 108
  simple 3, 16
Lawrence, N. 193 n. 12
Leibniz, G. 392 n., 397, 398
Lewis, D. 170, 171, 173, 253, 254 n. 9
liar paradox *see* paradox, liar
liar sentence 314, 317–34
Littmann, G. 314–35
Locke, J. 91, 92
logic 418, 435
  adaptive *see* adaptive logic
  aims of 93, 166, 168, 169, 236
  Brazillian 43, 45
  classical 273, 274
  deontic 239
  discussive 95
  of encoding 419, 423, 425–9, 432–5
  fuzzy 238
  intuitionist 283 n., 399–400, 415
  modal 97

logic (*cont*):
  multiple conclusion 283–6, 390 n. 6,
      407–9
  non-adjunctive 95
  paraconsistent 73, 76, 77, 392, 398–9, 401
  relevance/relevant 73, 77, 236, 239, 242,
      398, 400 f.
  revising 178–94
  Stoic 24
  substructural 77
  theory change in 156, 157, 158, 163, 166,
      167, 169
logical
  apriorism 158, 160, 162, 163
  consequence 11–14, 158, 160, 161, 162,
      164, 167, 168, 169, 172, 198
  intuitions 181
  law 41, 46
  monism 157
  non-apriorism 156, 157, 158, 160, 162,
      165, 166
  pathology 122
  pluralism 97 n. 7, 157
  principles 156, 158, 164, 165, 166, 167,
      168, 169, 170, 172, 173
  theories 180, 192
  truth 11–14, 198, 242, 243
  vs extra-logical 104
LP 11–14, 198, 285 n. 6, 390–3, 395, 397 n.
      13, 398, 400, 403
Łukasiewicz, J. 2, 3, 45, 315

McCullough, C. 232
McGee, V. 33
MacIntyre, A. 233 n. 18
McLaughlin, B. P. 286 n. 9
McLeod (a dog) 240 n. 8
McTaggart, J. M. E. 30
Maddy, P. 168, 174
Mar, G. 52, 53, 56, 93
Marcus, R. 93
Mares, E. D. 168, 268 n., 274
Markman, E. 309
Massey, G. 289
meaning
  rule-following theory of 108
  stipulation of 106
  theory of *vs* formal semantics 103
Mehlberg, H. 99 n. 10
membership relation 430–2
Mendelson, E. 52, 53, 54
meta-completeness 47
metalanguage 317, 318, 319, 334
  vs. object language 97

metalogical principles 167
metaphysical 264, 265, 269–70
meta-theoretic statement 41
methodological
  a priorities 183
  dogmas 183
  principles 166–9, 172
methodology 184
Meyer, R. K. 47
mistake 339–40
model theory 346–54
modus ponens, material 14, 15, 214
monoletheism 332, 334
Montague, R. 52, 53, 56, 93
Moore, A. 193 n. 12
Mortensen, C. 243

Nāgārjuna 235
negation 74, 98, 339, 341–2, 344, 346, 351–4,
      385, 390 n. 4, 391 n. 7, 399–401, 403,
      406, 412–15
  De Morgan 43–4
  and denial 272
  exclusionary 64 ff.
  as failure 271
  mirror-image 42
  option 85–92
Nicholas (of Cusa) 29, 420
Nolan, D. 177
non-cognitivism 185
non-monotonicity 213, 214, 236, 403 n. 18
norms 391, 405, 407, 415

object language 317, 319, 334
omnipotence 302–3
one over many principle 421
ontological
  argument 69, 421, 423
  (non-)contradiction 3, 16
options 86 ff.
Orlandi, N. 194
Osherson, D. 30
ought implies can 97 n. 6
overdefined 267, 271

pair set 396
Papineau, D. 312
paraconsistency 265, 270, *see also* explosion,
      and logic, paraconsistent
  doxastic theory of 265
  epistemic theory of 264
  metaphysical theory of 265
paraconsistent logic *see* logic, paraconsistent
paraconsistentist, strong *vs.* weak 5–7

paradox 114, 116, 123
   assertability/acceptability 320–1
   barber 118, 119, 295–9
   Curry 242
   Grelling's 298–9
   liar 23, 28, 31, 35, 36, 37, 69 n., 115–21,
      171, 172, 303–6, 314–34, 387–8, 405,
      407–8, 414–15
      Epimenidean 297
      Eubulidean 297
      introspective 323–4, 325–6, 333 n. 26
      revenge 314, 322–4, 330–4
   Littman's 405
   lottery 103 n.
   preface 24, 32
   Russell's 9, 10, 297–9, 387, 388–9, 400,
      295, 427–9
   semantic 7–9, 276, 278–9, 285–7, 314,
      317, 328, 333
   surprise examination 297
   warrant 228
partially defined 266–7
Parsons, T. 62, 314 n. 2, 338–9, 341, 342–3
Pascal, B. 412
Pearson, E. 415 n.
penumbral constraint 278
Perry, J. 33, 269 n.
picture 295
Plato 420
Plotinus 91, 92
Popper, K. 390
Port Royale (logic) 36
Poundstone, W. 299 n.
power set 395
pragmatics, mechanisms of 87
Prawitz, D. 108 n. 22
preservationism 102 n.
Price, H. 50, 70, 271, 274
Priest, G. 24, 25, 27, 28, 29, 30, 33, 34, 36, 37,
      38, 50, 61, 62, 82, 90, 91, 92, 94, 103,
      114, 115, 123, 124, 157, 170, 171, 172,
      174, 176, 190 n. 7, 191 n. 8, 194, 237,
      238, 240, 242, 243, 247–54, 257, 261,
      262, 265, 275, 285 n. 6, 297 n.,
      315–20, 333–4, 336–54, 386–8, 390–1,
      393, 397, 398, 399 n., 400 n. 15, 403 n.
      18, 404–7, 414–15
principle R 414 n.
principle of uniform solution 427
Prior, A. N. 50, 51, 52, 56, 69
probability theory 388
proof-theory (of Hilbert) 80
properties, vague 264, 265, 265 n. 2

Protagoras 301–2
Putnam, H. 70, 157, 158, 159, 164, 165

Quine, W. v. O. 28, 52, 53, 97, 182, 183, 184,
      189, 194, 240, 251 n.5, 305–6, 406,
      410, 414

R (the relevant logic) 77–83
Ramsey, F. P. 276–7, 281–4, 287
rationality 236
rationality (non-)contradiction 3, 16
Rawls, J. 181 n. 1, 194
Raz, J. 267
realism 251–3, 261
recognition thesis, 217–19, 226–7, 231
reductio ad absurdum 312
reflective equilibrium 168, 181, 191–2
Reichenbach, H. 52, 53, 54
rejection 44–7, 73–4, 78–83, 404–5, 407–12,
      414–16
Rescher, N. 99 n. 9, 317, 319
Resnik, M. 157, 168, 174, 185, n. 5, 194
Restall, G. 80–1, 97 n. 7, 393 n., 397–8, 399 n.
reticulated model (in logic and science) 166,
      167, 168, 169, 172, 173, 174
Routley (Sylvan), R. 50, 52, 53, 65, 103, 265,
      296
Routley, V. 52, 53, 65
Routley–Meyer semantics 43
RNC 46–7
Rosen, G. 254 n. 9, 257 n. 14, 258
Rosenberg, J. 334 n. 27
rule of conception 424–5
rule following 188
Russell, B. A. W. 323, 307
Russell set 387, 391, 402

S (set theory) 397
Sainsbury, R. M. 51, 56, 121, 124
Saka, P. 50
Sayward, C. 311 n.
Schiffer, S. 116, 117, 118, 122, 124
Schotch, P. K. 97 n. 6, 102 n.
science 386, 390, 392, 401, 403–4
Scotus (Duns) 25
self-predication principle 421 f.
semantic
   closure 114, 115
   consequence 316
   hierarchies 238
   paradox *see* paradox, semantic
   pathology 122
   status 114, 115
   theory 264, 268–9, 265
semantical 8, 8 n. 2., 9, 21, 203, 264–75

set theory 348, 350, 351, 353
  dialectical 42, 44
  naive 391–403, 429, 431–2
  and paradox 258–9
  Z 395, 398, 399
  ZF 392, 398–403
  ZFC 393, 395, 397–8, 404
  ZFU 399
Sextus (Empiricus) 25, 235
shadows 267–8
Shapiro, S. 346, 389
Sher, G. 105n.
Shoesmith, D. J. 284
Simmons, K. 314–35
Slaney, J. K. 47
Slater, B. H. 56
Smiley, T. 60, 284, 346
Soames, S. 256 n. 13, 259 n. 16, 260 n. 18,
    264, 266, 275, 305 n.
Solomon, G. 100 n. 12
Sorensen, R. 249 n. 2, 307
soundness 392, 395, 398, 402–3
Stanley, J. 254 n. 9
statement 295–6, 303, 307–8
stipulation 305–6
Strawson, P. 37, 52–4, 57, 296
Stroud, B. 258
Suber, P. 50, 61
subsets 396
subtraction 80
subvaluation(ism) 101, 103, 107, 284–5,
    289–90
successor concept 273
superassertibility 229
supertruth 99
supervaluation(ism) 99–101, 103, 107,
    277 f., 280 ff., 289–90
syllogistic 24
Sylvan, R. *see* Routley, R.

t (true proposition) 78–83
Tappenden, J. 104, 264, 266, 272, 275
Tarski, A. 33, 105 n., 118, 119, 158, 160, 161,
    162, 163, 164, 171, 172, 173, 270, 280,
    282, 402
tautology 11–14, 73, 77, 198, 295, 307–9, 311
Tennant, N. 217, 217 n. 2, 220, 221 n. 8,
    220 n. 5
theoretical terms 276, 277, 282, 287
theory 75, 80
  full 75
Theseus, ship of 272
TNC 46–7
Todes, S. 267

transcendental arguments 250–1
transition states 28
trivial(-ity) 3, 4, 75, 202 n. 16, 209
trivialism 246–50, 252
true contradiction *see* dialetheia
truth 15, 16, 197
  according to 96
  as if 206, 207, 209
  degree of 295
  condition 303–4
  vs. connectedness or acceptability 95
  and falsehood (exhaustive and mutually
      exclusive) 97 n. 8, 102 n.
  logical *see* logical truth
  and paradox 257–262
  preservation, symmetrical 284–5
  theories of
    contextual 314 nn. 2, 3, 332
    deflationary 207–8, 211–12
    disquotational 276–8
    revision 331–2
    simple 341–2, 344
  as supertruth 99 see also *supervaluation*
  table 309
  value
    gap 74, 80, 89, 97 n. 8, 98, 101, 103,
        240–4, 270, 314, 315
    glut 85, 89, 97 n. 8, 98, 101, 103, 280 *see*
        also dialetheia
    graphic 324–34
T-schema (Tarski biconditional, equivalence
    scheme) 28, 33, 35, 99–100, 167, 171,
    172, 260–1, 316

undecidability 58
unhappy-face (solution) 117, 118, 120, 121,
    122, 124
union 395–6

vacuous 300, 302–5, 307, 312
validity 11–14
Van Fraassen, B. C. 99, 115, 267 n., 269 n.,
    275, 277–8, 280–3
Varzi, A. 97 n., 101 n., 102 n., 105 n., 229 n.
    15, 284
vagueness 99 n. 10, 238, 276, 278, 287
verdict matrices 410
verifiability 215, 218–19, 221, 225–6
verum ex quodlibet (VEQ) 102–8
Voeller, C. 334 n. 27
voluntariness 403–7, 410–11, 415
von Neumann, J. 158, 159

Walton, K. 255 n. 12
war 406

Weir, A. 389, 403 n. 17
Williams, B. 411
Williamson, T. 100 n. 11
Wittgenstein, L. 31, 188, 295, 301–4, 307–9,
    311–12, 391

Wolfram, S. 51, 52, 56
Woodruff, P. 279–80
Wright, C. 182 n. 2, 217, 217 n. 2, 229, 295

Yablo, S. 258–9, 306–7

Lightning Source UK Ltd.
Milton Keynes UK
UKOW031026241011

180844UK00004B/11/P